Penguin Education

Penguin Critical Anthologies
General Editor: Christopher Ricks

Charles Dickens

Edited by Stephen Wall

Charles Dickens
A Critical Anthology

Edited by Stephen Wall
Penguin Books

Penguin Books Ltd, Harmondsworth,
Middlesex, England
Penguin Books Inc., 7110 Ambassador Road,
Baltimore, Md 21207, U.S.A.
Penguin Books Australia Ltd,
Ringwood, Victoria, Australia

First published 1970
This selection copyright © Stephen Wall, 1970
Introductions and notes copyright © Stephen Wall, 1970

Made and printed in Great Britain by
Hazell Watson & Viney Ltd,
Aylesbury, Bucks
Set in Monotype Bembo

Contents

8   Contents

9 Contents

Part Two The Developing Debate

11 Contents

13 Contents

Preface

I am most grateful to Neil McEwan for his invaluable assistance in preparing this anthology. My thanks are also due to my colleagues Richard Green, Denys Potts and Stephen Gill. Christopher Ricks, the general editor of this series, and Martin Lightfoot and Elizabeth Excell of Penguin Education, have been extremely helpful.

Keble College, Oxford   s.w.

Table of Dates

1837   Birth of a son, the first of ten children, the last being born
       in 1852. Dickens and his family move to Doughty Street,
       London. *Oliver Twist: or, the parish boy's progress.*
       Appeared as a monthly serial in *Bentley's Miscellany* (which
       Dickens edited for two years) between February 1837 and
       March 1839; published in three volumes 1838.
       May Death of Mary Hogarth, Dickens's sister-in-law, of
       whom he said 'I solemnly believe so perfect a creature
       never breathed.'

1838   *The Life and Adventures of Nicholas Nickleby: containing a
       faithful account of the fortunes, misfortunes, uprisings,
       downfallings, and complete career of the Nickleby family.* Issued
       in monthly parts between April 1838 and October 1839;
       published in book form 1839. Dickens visited some
       Yorkshire schools of the Dotheboys type before
       beginning the novel.

1839   Dickens and family move to Devonshire Terrace, near
       Regent's Park, London.

1840   *Master Humphrey's Clock* initially a weekly miscellany,
       appears. From the fourth number it contained *The Old
       Curiosity Shop*, which was published in book form in 1841.

1841   *Barnaby Rudge: a tale of the riots of 'eighty.* Appears weekly
       from February in *Master Humphrey's Clock*, which was
       discontinued at the end of the novel. *Barnaby Rudge*
       published in book form in this year. Public banquet in
       Dickens's honour at Edinburgh.

1842   *January–June* First visit to America. Dickens and his wife
       travel to Boston, New York, Washington, St Louis,
       Niagara Falls, Montreal and elsewhere. Dickens
       arouses the hostility of the American press by his
       advocacy of an international copyright agreement.

American Notes: for general circulation. An account of his travels.

1843   *The Life and Adventures of Martin Chuzzlewit: his relatives, friends, and enemies. . . .* Issued in monthly numbers between January 1843 and July 1844; published in book form 1844.
A Christmas Carol: In prose. Being a ghost story of Christmas.

1844   *July* Dickens and family leave England for Italy.
The Chimes: a goblin story of some bells that rang an old year out and a new year in. Dickens returned briefly to England to read this story to a group of friends including Carlyle and, on a second occasion, Macready.

1845   *June* Dickens family return to England.
The Cricket on the Hearth: a fairy tale of home (Christmas book).

1846   Dickens becomes first editor of the *Daily News*, but resigns after seventeen issues.
Pictures from Italy. (First appeared as seven 'Travelling Letters' in the *Daily News*, January–March.)
Dickens and family stay at Lausanne, Switzerland, from June, moving to Paris in November.
Dealings with the Firm of Dombey and Son, Wholesale, Retail, and for Exportation. Issued in monthly parts between October 1846 and April 1848; published in book form 1848.
The Battle of Life: a love story (Christmas book).

1847   Return to London.
Dickens assists Miss Burdett Coutts in the administration of a reform home for prostitutes, and continues to do so until 1858.

1848   Dickens organizes and acts in charity performances of *The Merry Wives of Windsor* and *Every Man in his Humour*, the latter given before Queen Victoria.

The Haunted Man and the ghost's bargain: a fancy for Christmas time.

1849   *The Personal History, Adventures, Experiences, and Observations of David Copperfield the Younger of Blunderstone Rookery (Which he never meant to be published on any account).* Issued in monthly parts between May 1849 and November 1850; published in book form 1850.

1850   *Household Words,* a weekly journal, 'Conducted by Charles Dickens', begins in March. The first number contained a story by Mrs Gaskell; later contributors included Bulwer Lytton, Charles Reade and Wilkie Collins. At its best, *Household Words* sold about forty thousand copies per week.

1851   Further theatrical activities on behalf of the Guild of Literature and Art. Royal performance in May.
Death of Dickens's father (March) and of a baby daughter (April). Moves to Tavistock House, Tavistock Square, London.
A Child's History of England. Appeared in *Household Words* between January 1851 and December 1853; published in three volumes, 1852, 1853, 1854.

1852   *Bleak House.* Issued in monthly parts between March 1852 and September 1853; published in book form 1853.

1853   *December* Readings from the Christmas Books for the benefit of the Birmingham and Midland Institute. These were the first public readings from his own works that Dickens gave.

1854   Visit to Preston, Lancashire, scene of a prolonged strike.
Hard Times: For these times. Appeared in weekly instalments in *Household Words* between April and August; published in book form in this year.

1855   Supports Administrative Reform Association.
       Dickens family in France (from October).
       Little Dorrit. Issued in monthly parts between December
       1855 and June 1857; published in book form 1857.
       (Dickens's original title for *Little Dorrit* was *Nobody's Fault*.)

1856   *March* Dickens buys Gad's Hill Place, near Rochester.
       August Dickens family return to England. Dickens's
       sister-in-law Georgina by now largely in control of his
       household.

1857   *January* Powerful performance by Dickens in Wilkie
       Collins's melodrama *The Frozen Deep*.
       August Charity performances at Manchester given by a
       company including the young actress Ellen Ternan.
       The Lazy Tour of Two Idle Apprentices. Written in
       collaboration with Wilkie Collins, and describing their
       holiday in Cumberland; it appeared in *Household Words* in
       October.

1858   *Reprinted Pieces*. (Articles from *Household Words*.)
       April First public reading by Dickens for his own benefit.
       Legal separation of Dickens and his wife (May), followed
       by personal statement in *Household Words* (June).

1859   *All the Year Round*, a weekly journal, 'conducted by
       Charles Dickens', begins in April, incorporating
       Household Words when the latter ceases publication a month
       later. Within ten years, *All the Year Round* had achieved a
       circulation of three hundred thousand.
       A Tale of Two Cities. Appeared in *All the Year Round* in
       weekly instalments between April and November; also
       issued in monthly parts; published in book form in this
       year.

1860   Dickens sells Tavistock House, and lives at Gad's Hill.
       Great Expectations. Appeared weekly in *All the Year Round*

between December 1860 and August 1861; published in three volumes 1861.

1861   *The Uncommercial Traveller*. Seventeen papers from *All the Year Round*; the next edition (1868) added a further eleven.

1861–3   Second series of public readings.

1863   *January* Dickens's son Walter dies in India, aged twenty-two.
September Dickens's mother dies.
Reconciled with Thackeray (with whom he had quarrelled) shortly before the latter's death.
'Mrs Lirriper's Lodgings' in Christmas number of *All the Year Round*.

1864   *Our Mutual Friend*. Issued in monthly parts between May 1864 and November 1865; published in book form 1865.
'Mrs Lirriper's Legacy' in Christmas number of *All the Year Round*.

1865   *June* Dickens severely shocked after being involved in a train crash while travelling with Ellen Ternan, who by this time was almost certainly his mistress and for whom he provided establishments at Peckham and Slough.
'Dr Marigold's Prescriptions' in Christmas number of *All the Year Round*.

1866–7   Third series of readings.

1867   *November* Second journey to America. Gives readings in Boston, New York, Washington, and elsewhere, despite increasing ill-health.

1868   *April* Returns to England.

1868–9   Third series of public readings, including the sensationally effective murder of Nancy from *Oliver Twist*, which further undermined Dickens's health.

1870   *January–March* Last readings in London.
    The Mystery of Edwin Drood (unfinished). Issued in six
    monthly parts between April and September, and intended
    to be completed in twelve.
    9 June Died, after collapse, aged fifty-eight.
    Buried in Westminster Abbey, London.
    Dickens's estate amounted to £93,000; he had earned
    £45,000 by his readings.
    The following collected editions of Dickens's works
    appeared during his life-time:
    Works, 17 vols. (1847–68) – the 'first cheap edition'.
    Library Edition, 22 vols. (1858–9) – reissued in 30 vols.
    (1861–74).
    Charles Dickens Edition, 21 vols. (1867–74).

Part One Contemporaneous Criticism

Introduction

Dickens became a fact of English life very early in his career, and he has remained one ever since. The usual implications of the adjective 'Dickensian' indicate only a limited part of Dickens's effect on the popular imagination – an effect probably more radical than that made by any other English writer of comparable literary calibre. Some of his characters and some of the situations in his novels soon became and have since remained universally available references, a kind of shorthand of the common imagination. A mention of Scrooge, Pickwick or Micawber, or of the scene in which Oliver asks for more, is immediately intelligible to an extremely wide public. Our conceptions of Christmas, our images of towns and cities (London in particular), our understanding of the way children feel – these are the kinds of area in which Dickens's influence has been so profound that, paradoxically, it has become almost imperceptible, so completely has his way of seeing the world been assimilated into everyday life. This may partly be because, as Humphry House put it at the end of *The Dickens World* (1941), 'He is still the only one of the great English novelists who is read at all widely among simple people.'

However, an awareness of Dickens is not dependent on having read him. Henry Crawford, in chapter 33 of Jane Austen's *Mansfield Park*, says of Shakespeare that

one gets acquainted with [him] without knowing how. It is part of an Englishman's constitution. His thoughts and beauties are so spread abroad that one touches them everywhere, one is intimate with him by instinct.

His words can be applied with even more force and appropriateness to Dickens, whose stories and characters have been the subject of endless dramatization, imitation and adaptation. From the days when crude plagiarisms of *The Pickwick Papers* attempted to cash in on the success of Dickens's first novel and when versions of *Oliver Twist* were playing at three London theatres simultaneously, to the

present period when his books are filmed, televised, made the
subjects of musicals and cannibalized in comic books, the products
of his imagination have been constantly before the public. It is
curious that an author of whom F. R. Leavis has justly said 'in
ease and range there is surely no greater master of English except
Shakespeare' should circulate so persistently in forms which either
select from or even misrepresent what he actually wrote. On the
other hand, there could hardly be a more conclusive demonstration
of the vitality and indestructibility of the world that Dickens
created.

Dickens's first success came with his first book. *Sketches by Boz*,
a collection of descriptive pieces he had written for periodicals,
appeared when he was just twenty-four and attracted some
extremely favourable reviews. The 'sketch' was then a familiar
journalistic convention, but Dickens transformed it by what one
notice called the 'startling fidelity' of his observation. The
Sketches were felt to deal with the world as it recognizably was,
and yet to reveal it in an entirely new way; the Dickensian
balance between reassurance and originality was already forming.
The *Sketches* also manifested the vigour and warmth of their
author's personality, so that when *The Posthumous Papers of the
Pickwick Club* was announced as *Edited by* 'Boz' and began to
appear shortly afterwards, the public already had some idea of
what to expect.

In fact the first instalments seem to have disappointed them, but
after the fourth number the book began to make its way more
forcefully; by the fifteenth number sales exceeded forty thousand;
and by the time the book was completed it was clear that it had
completely outdistanced the previous successes of Scott. *Pickwick*
was to remain the most continuously popular of all Dickens's books
to the readers of his time, and later on there were moments when
its persistent appeal seemed to him something of a liability.

Dickens's life was at all times marked by an extreme

expenditure of energy, and this was particularly true of the years immediately after the success of *Pickwick*. *Oliver Twist* began to appear in February 1837, while the last instalments of *Pickwick* were still being written. Dickens finished writing *Oliver Twist* in September 1838, having already begun to publish *Nicholas Nickleby* the previous April. The first number of *Nickleby* sold fifty thousand copies. The sales of *The Old Curiosity Shop* (1840–41) reached the then astonishing figure of a hundred thousand. With the appearance of *Barnaby Rudge* in 1841, Dickens had completed and published five novels in five years.

Although the writing of his fiction never ceased to be central to Dickens's life, his interests became more diversified, and he never again wrote so much so quickly. Although Dickens was criticized for writing too fast, there is little doubt that these rapidly produced early books, taken together, established a large and loyal public who became committed to 'the Dickens world' and not just to individual novels. Dickens's awareness of the audience that he had thus created remained with him both as a powerful stimulant and as a serious responsibility. The reality and intensity of Dickens's relationship with his audience can be seen at its most extreme (and for many modern readers at its most inexplicable) in the extravagant reception of *The Old Curiosity Shop*. The death of Little Nell, which Landor and Jeffrey thought worthy of Shakespeare, was followed in 1847 by the death of Paul Dombey, which some judges including Thackeray thought unsurpassed. The pathos of these child–deaths, like the warm-heartedness of the early Christmas stories, and the domestic sentiment to be found everywhere in Dickens, may well have been as instrumental as the unequalled humour and high spirits of the earlier novels in creating between Dickens and his public an unprecedented community of feeling.

This bond was created not only by what was in these books, but also by the way in which they appeared. *Pickwick* was published at monthly intervals in 20 parts of 32 pages each (the last two parts being published together in an issue of 48 pages), each part costing a shilling except the last which cost two shillings. All Dickens's novels were subsequently published either in monthly parts on this pattern, or in weekly instalments in periodicals edited by Dickens. Serialization, in fact, was an essential part of his creative method.

Since Dickens never finished a novel before it began to appear serially – indeed, he was sometimes only a few chapters ahead of the printer – the interval between creation and publication was extremely short. Dickens had a real sense of his audience accompanying him as he wrote his weekly or monthly numbers; he was able to gauge the response of the public to a book as it proceeded – partly through the evidence of sales, to which he was very attentive, and partly through the comments and letters he received about the book in progress. The formal dangers of part-issues are obvious – once a section of a novel has appeared it cannot be revised or recast to fit in with later and perhaps unforeseen developments in the story – but from *Dombey and Son* onwards Dickens became extremely skilful at reconciling the balance and distribution of narrative interest within an instalment with the structural demands of the completed work. The advantages of serialization of this kind to so profoundly histrionic an artist as Dickens were great, for, as Kathleen Tillotson has said:

In the serial-writer's relation to his public there is indeed something of the stimulating contact which an actor or a public speaker receives from an audience. Serial publication gave back to story-telling its original context of performance. . . .
(*Novels of the Eighteen-Forties*, 1954, p. 36)

Although Dickens often complained of the compression imposed on him by the shorter instalments of those novels of his which were published in weekly parts, he remained faithful to serial composition and publication throughout his writing life.

The flexibility which serial publication permitted can be seen in the history of *Martin Chuzzlewit*. The sales of the opening numbers of this novel were only in the region of twenty thousand, and it was in an unpremeditated attempt to improve this situation that Dickens sent the hero to North America (where he himself had recently been) in the sixth number. Even so, the circulation of *Chuzzlewit* never rose much above twenty-three thousand. Dickens was worried by this set-back (which, it has been suggested, was really due to the delayed effect of adverse criticisms of *American Notes* and, to a lesser extent, of *Barnaby Rudge*), but not to the extent of doubting his talent. And, whatever its structural weaknesses, Dickens was justified in feeling that there is a sustained comic exuberance in *Chuzzlewit* as great as in *Pickwick* and more original. The presentation of Mrs Gamp, who developed in a way that Dickens had not entirely foreseen, was reasonably claimed by Forster as 'the happiest stroke of humorous art in all the writings of Dickens'. In time, *Chuzzlewit* became one of the most popular of his books.

Dickens clearly realized that he had reached a critical point in his development, and there was an interval of over two years – much of which was spent abroad – between the last instalment of *Chuzzlewit* and the first number of *Dombey and Son*. Dickens was anxious about the reception of *Dombey*, and both its overall design and its local execution show a new degree of care and discipline. He had thought of thirty thousand copies of the first number as the 'limit of the most extreme success', and was deeply relieved when sales exceeded this figure. The confidence of the writing in *Dombey* may reflect this sense of reassurance.

Dickens's position was secured beyond any further question by the success of *David Copperfield*. 'From the first', wrote Forster, 'it had surpassed in popularity, though not in sale, all his previous books excepting *Pickwick*.' *Copperfield* again illustrates the flexibility which serial publication allowed Dickens even when –

as here – he had 'constructed the whole with immense pains'. The person who had unwittingly suggested the character of Miss Mowcher to Dickens remonstrated with him, and in response to her appeal he took away from the fictional personality its intended unpleasantness.

Although there were complaints that Dickens's later novels were forced and sombre compared with the fun of his earlier ones, his public remained loyal to him for the rest of his life. Some of the Christmas stories of his later years (now probably little read) sold in the region of a quarter of a million copies. The circulation of the unfinished *Edwin Drood* was about fifty thousand copies. During Dickens's lifetime there were three separate collected editions of his works; the appearance of the Library Edition in 1858 prompted the long retrospective essay by Walter Bagehot, part of which is reproduced on p. 123.

Dickens's reputation had been established in Europe and America almost as quickly as at home. In the absence of any agreement on copyright, foreign publishers could and did pirate Dickens's works without paying anything at all to their author. Although his advocacy of such an agreement angered many Americans, Dickens refused to avoid it in his speeches during his first visit to the United States; he was supported by a number of American writers, including Washington Irving. 'If there had been international copyright between England and the States', said Dickens, 'I should have been a man of very large fortune, instead of a man of moderate savings. . . .' The extent of Dickens's success in North America is further indicated by the fact that his profits from the readings he gave on his second visit were 'within a hundred or so of £20,000'.

Versions of *Pickwick* began to appear in Germany in 1837, and in Russia and France (one being entitled *Le Club des Pickwistes*) in 1838. The Germans seem to have been particularly eager to read Dickens: during the first eight years of his writing career all his

early works were translated at least three times. The Christmas
books were especially popular in both France and Germany. By
the time of the novelist's death, there were several German
translations of his complete works. Dickens made an agreement
with Bernhard Tauchnitz for his series of English language reprints
in 1843. In 1856 he also agreed with French publishers Hachette
that their translations of his works (1857-74) should state that they
were authorized by the author. 1856 also saw the first appearance
of Hippolyte Taine's highly influential study of Dickens – the first
French critic, according to Floris Delattre, to consider Dickens
as a writer of the first rank and as a representative English
genius.

The outstanding Russian translator of Dickens, Irinarkh
Vvedensky, wrote to him in 1849 that 'for the last eleven years
your name has enjoyed a wide celebrity in Russia, and from the
banks of the Neva to the remotest parts of Siberia you are read
with avidity. Your *Dombey* continues to inspire with enthusiasm the
whole of literary Russia.' It was Vvedensky's versions of
Copperfield and *Pickwick* that Dostoyevsky read in prison in Siberia
in the early 1850s. In a letter of 1880, Dostoyevsky recommended
'all Dickens's works without exception' as suitable educational
reading for his correspondent's daughter.

When Dickens died at the age of fifty-eight, the loss was felt
both nationally and internationally. The London *Times* demanded
that Dickens's special position as the public's 'unassailable and
enduring favourite' should be recognized by his burial in
Westminster Abbey, where thousands paid their respects to his
coffin. The tributes then paid to Dickens (such as those by
Benjamin Jowett and Anthony Trollope, reprinted below on p. 176
and p. 177) are useful indications of the extraordinary reputation
Dickens enjoyed. The words of a letter from Carlyle to Forster
may indicate the extent to which Dickens's death was privately
mourned:

It is an event world-wide, a *unique* of talents suddenly extinct, and has 'eclipsed' (we too may say) 'the harmless gaiety of nations'. No death since 1866 [when Carlyle's wife had died] has fallen on me with such a stroke, no Literary Man's ever did. The good, the gentle, the ever friendly noble Dickens – every inch of him an Honest Man!

This remarkable ascendancy was, of course, the direct result of the popularity of Dickens's novels, but it was not due only to that. Dickens had become something more than an author, partly because of the influence of his books on the tendency and temper of the national life, and partly because of his extra-literary activities.

Early in his career Dickens had perfected the art of speaking at the banquets and institutional dinners of which the Victorians were so fond. Some contemporaries thought Dickens the best speaker of his time for this sort of occasion (some opinions are collected in K. J. Fielding's edition of Dickens's speeches). His manner of speaking – controlled, charming, sincere – was quite different from the histrionic displays he gave when reading from his own works, an occupation Dickens became increasingly addicted to in his later years. There seems little doubt that Dickens was an actor of outstanding talent. As a young man he was to have auditioned before Charles Kemble, but was prevented from doing so by illness. His performance as the rejected lover in Wilkie Collins's melodrama *The Frozen Deep* reduced even his fellow-actors to tears. In his middle years Dickens organized theatrical tours for charity, and the celebrated and, latterly, sensational readings were, from one point of view, a logical development of his gifts. The number of people who had seen as well as read Dickens must have been considerable.

To an even larger public he was familiar as an editor. Although no articles or stories in it were signed, every issue of *Household Words* had 'Conducted by Charles Dickens' prominently printed under the title, and the same words appeared (in small type) at the top of each double page. The magazine everywhere reflected Dickens's interests, causes, ideas and tastes as well as his literary and political independence. Its successor, *All the Year Round,* was also recognizably the product of its creator, and Dickens's constant supervision and meticulous editing of both periodicals kept them firmly under his control. For the last twenty years of his life he had, through them, a weekly means of contact with the public.

Dickens wrote to a correspondent that in *Household Words* he was particularly anxious to deal with 'all social evils, and all home affections and associations'. Dickens's personal contribution to the progress of social reform (he came to despair of political reform) is not easy to estimate, but his magazines reinforced the impression given by his novels of a man energetically devoted to practical improvement, reliably on the side of the people, and democratically against 'Them'. Dickens remained a middle-class writer – whatever their economic reversals, his heroes arrive at the end at a respectable prosperity – and he would not have welcomed the dictatorship of the proletariat; nevertheless, he seemed to many of the more literate working class a trustworthy ally and an accessible friend. A significant number of Dickens's speeches were made to Mechanics' Institutes and similar organizations.

The widespread conviction that Dickens was a powerful force for social progress was not universally accepted and it must remain difficult to say how justified it was. Fitzjames Stephen complained, in his review of *Little Dorrit* (see below, p. 106), that 'he seems ... to get his first notions of an abuse from the discussions which accompany its removal'. In his notice of *A Tale of Two Cities* Stephen censures Dickens for arrogantly distorting the facts of history in the interests of 'working upon the feelings by the coarsest stimulants'. Others looked upon Dickens's attacks on utilitarianism and political economy (especially in *Hard Times*) as simply ignorant and obtuse. Carlyle and Ruskin remained sympathetic, but

Dickens was often under attack in his later years from other
intellectual critics of his day, and he was especially liable to
criticism from those connected with an administrative Establishment
to which Dickens had become increasingly hostile.

Some critics also found his artistic methods unsatisfactory. The
originality of Dickens's language meant that he had always been
criticized for vulgarity and irregularity of style. The episode in Mrs
Gaskell's *Cranford* in which a genteel lady reader, after being made
to listen to some of *Pickwick*, sends for Johnson's *Rasselas* as a
corrective, indicates the 'polite' response to the 'lowness' of early
Dickens. (When *Cranford* was published in *Household Words*, the
reference was changed from *Pickwick* to Thomas Hood's periodical,
Hood's Own.) Later critics continued to regret that Dickens lacked
education and had not formed his style on the best models. G. H.
Lewes deplored Dickens's lack of culture.

The charges of exaggeration of effect and distortion of fact had
been made early on, and Dickens showed some awareness of them
in his Prefaces, which he often revised in the light of such
objections when his novels went through further editions. At first
Dickens was frequently compared with Hogarth; by 1844
Thackeray was complaining that this point had become wearisomely
familiar. (Dickens's own comments on Hogarth can be found in
Forster's *Life*, book 6, Chapter 3). It was not until the success of
Vanity Fair (published at the same time as *Dombey and Son*) that
Thackeray himself emerged as a formidable rival to Dickens. The
habit of contrasting them is reflected in the extract from David
Masson which appears on p. 145. Thackeray's work was preferred
by many genteel and educated readers as being more realistic, more
refined and more correct. Thackeray's feelings about Dickens
wavered, but he left several generous as well as some envious
estimates of Dickens's creative fertility and stamina. Their
relationship was clouded in their later years by their taking opposite
sides in a quarrel, but they were reconciled shortly before

Thackeray's death. Dickens attended Thackeray's funeral with 'a look of bereavement in his face which was indescribable'.

The generous tributes that followed Dickens's own death stressed not so much his literary qualities narrowly considered as the effects of his work on the national life. According to Dean Stanley, he 'made Englishmen feel more as one family than they had ever felt before'. This affirmative view of Dickens's moral influence over his public is worth remembering when, in the modern period, we are asked to see him as alienated and demonic.

Charles Dickens

from the Autobiographical Fragment   1847 (from John Forster, *The Life of Charles Dickens*, book 1, chapters 1, 2, 1872-4; reprinted in Hoppé edition, 1966, vol. 1)

My father had left a small collection of books in a little room upstairs to which I had access (for it adjoined my own), and which nobody else in our house ever troubled. From that blessed little room, *Roderick Random*, *Peregrine Pickle*, *Humphrey Clinker*, *Tom Jones*, *The Vicar of Wakefield*, *Don Quixote*, *Gil Blas* and *Robinson Crusoe* came out, a glorious host, to keep me company. They kept alive my fancy, and my hope of something beyond that place and time – they, and the *Arabian Nights*, and the *Tales of the Genii* – and did me no harm; for, whatever harm was in some of them, was not there for me; *I* knew nothing of it. It is astonishing to me now, how I found time, in the midst of my porings and blunderings over heavier themes, to read those books as I did. It is curious to me how I could ever have consoled myself under my small troubles (which were great troubles to me), by impersonating my favourite characters in them. . . . I have been Tom Jones (a child's Tom Jones, a harmless creature) for a week together. I have sustained my own idea of Roderick Random for a month at a stretch, I verily believe. I had a greedy relish for a few volumes of voyages and travels – I forget what, now – that were on those shelves; and for days and days I can remember to have gone about my region of our house, armed with the centre-piece out of an old set of boot-trees: the perfect realization of Captain Somebody, of the Royal British Navy, in danger of being beset by savages, and resolved to sell his life at a great price. . . . When I think of it, the picture always rises in my mind, of a summer evening, the boys at play in the churchyard, and I sitting on my bed reading as if for life. Every barn in the neighbourhood, every stone in the church, and every foot of the churchyard, had some association of its own, in my mind, connected with these books, and stood for some locality made famous in them. I have seen Tom Pipes go climbing up the church steeple; I have watched Strap, with the knapsack on his back, stopping to rest himself upon the wicket-gate; and I *know* that Com-

modore Trunnion held that club with Mr Pickle in the parlour of our
little village alehouse. . . .
(7–8)

James Lamert, the relative who had lived with us in Bayham Street,
seeing how I was employed from day to day, and knowing what our
domestic circumstances then were, proposed that I should go into the
blacking warehouse, to be as useful as I could, at a salary, I think, of
six shillings a week. I am not clear whether it was six or seven. I am
inclined to believe, from my uncertainty on this head, that it was six at
first, and seven afterwards. At any rate, the offer was accepted very
willingly by my father and mother, and on a Monday morning I went
down to the blacking warehouse to begin my business life.

It is wonderful to me how I could have been so easily cast away at
such an age. It is wonderful to me that, even after my descent into the
poor little drudge I had been since we came to London, no one had
compassion enough on me – a child of singular abilities: quick, eager,
delicate, and soon hurt, bodily or mentally – to suggest that something
might have been spared, as certainly it might have been, to place me
at any common school. Our friends, I take it, were tired out. No one
made any sign. My father and mother were quite satisfied. They
could hardly have been more so, if I had been twenty years of age,
distinguished at a grammar-school and going to Cambridge.

The blacking warehouse was the last house on the left-hand side of
the way, at old Hungerford Stairs. It was a crazy, tumble-down old
house, abutting of course on the river, and literally overrun with rats.
Its wainscotted rooms and its rotten floors and staircase, and the old
grey rats swarming down in the cellars, and the sound of their squeak-
ing and scuffling coming up the stairs at all times, and the dirt and
decay of the place, rise up visibly before me, as if I were there again.
The counting-house was on the first floor, looking over the coal-
barges and the river. There was a recess in it, in which I was to sit and
work. My work was to cover the pots of paste-blacking: first with a
piece of oil-paper and then with a piece of blue paper; to tie them
round with a string; and then to clip the paper close and neat all
round, until it looked as smart as a pot of ointment from an apothecary's shop. When a certain number of grosses of pots had attained this
pitch of perfection, I was to paste on each a printed label; and then
go on again with more pots. Two or three other boys were kept at

similar duty downstairs on similar wages. One of them came up, in a ragged apron and a paper cap, on the first Monday morning, to show me the trick of using the string and tying the knot. His name was Bob Fagin; and I took the liberty of using his name, long afterwards, in *Oliver Twist*.

Our relative had kindly arranged to teach me something in the dinner-hour; from twelve to one, I think it was, every day. But an arrangement so incompatible with counting-house business soon died away, from no fault of his or mine; and for the same reason, my small work-table, and my grosses of pots, my papers, string, scissors, paste-pot and labels, by little and little, vanished out of the recess in the counting-house, and kept company with the other small work-tables, grosses of pots, papers, string, scissors and paste-pots downstairs. It was not long before Bob Fagin and I, and another boy whose name was Paul Green, but who was currently believed to have been christened Poll (a belief which I transferred, long afterwards, again, to Mr Sweedlepipe, in *Martin Chuzzlewit*), worked generally, side by side. Bob Fagin was an orphan, and lived with his brother-in-law, a waterman. Poll Green's father had the additional distinction of being a fireman, and was employed at Drury Lane Theatre; where another relation of Poll's, I think his little sister, did imps in the pantomimes.

No words can express the secret agony of my soul as I sunk into this companionship; compared these everyday associates with those of my happier childhood; and felt my early hopes of growing up to be a learned and distinguished man crushed in my breast. The deep remembrance of the sense I had of being utterly neglected and hopeless; of the shame I felt in my position; of the misery it was to my young heart to believe that, day by day, what I have learned, and thought, and delighted in, and raised my fancy and my emulation up by, was passing away from me, never to be brought back any more, cannot be written. My whole nature was so penetrated with the grief and humiliation of such considerations, that even now, famous and caressed and happy, I often forget in my dreams that I have a dear wife and children; even that I am a man; and wander desolately back to that time of my life.

My mother and my brothers and sisters (excepting Fanny in the royal academy of music) were still encamped, with a young servant-girl from Chatham Workhouse, in the two parlours in the emptied house in Gower Street North. It was a long way to go and return within the dinner-hour, and, usually, I either carried my dinner with me, or went and bought it at some neighbouring shop. In the latter case, it was commonly a saveloy and a penny loaf; sometimes, a four-penny plate of beef from a cook's shop; sometimes, a plate of bread and cheese, and a glass of beer, from a miserable old public-house over the way; the Swan, if I remember right, or the Swan and something else that I have forgotten. Once, I remember tucking my own bread (which I had brought from home in the morning) under my arm, wrapped up in a piece of paper like a book, and going into the best dining-room in Johnson's alamode beef-house in Clare Court, Drury Lane, and magnificently ordering a small plate of alamode beef to eat with it. What the waiter thought of such a strange little appari-tion, coming in all alone, I don't know; but I can see him now, staring at me as I ate my dinner, and bringing up the other waiter to look. I gave him a halfpenny, and I wish, now, that he hadn't taken it. . . .

We had half an hour, I think, for tea. When I had money enough, I used to go to a coffee-shop, and have half a pint of coffee, and a slice of bread and butter. When I had no money, I took a turn in Covent Garden Market, and stared at the pineapples. The coffee-shops to which I most resorted were, one in Maiden Lane; one in a court (non-existent now) close to Hungerford Market; and one in St Martin's Lane, of which I only recollect that it stood near the church, and that in the door there was an oval glass plate, with COFFEE-ROOM painted on it, addressed towards the street. If I ever find myself in a very different kind of coffee-room now, but where there is such an inscription on glass, and read it backward on the wrong side MOOR-EEFFOC (as I often used to do then, in a dismal reverie), a shock goes through my blood.

I know I do not exaggerate, unconsciously and unintentionally, the scantiness of my resources and the difficulties of my life. I know that if a shilling or so were given me by anyone, I spent it in a dinner or a tea. I know that I worked, from morning to night, with common men and boys, a shabby child. I know that I tried, but ineffectually, not to anticipate my money, and to make it last the week through by putting it away in a drawer I had in the counting-house, wrapped into six little parcels, each parcel containing the same amount, and labelled with a different day. I know that I have lounged about the streets, insufficiently and unsatisfactorily fed. I know that, but for the mercy of God, I might easily have been, for any care that was taken of me, a little robber or a little vagabond.

But I held some station at the blacking warehouse too. Besides that my relative at the counting-house did what a man so occupied, and dealing with a thing so anomalous, could, to treat me as one upon a different footing from the rest, I never said, to man or boy, how it was that I came to be there, or gave the least indication of being sorry that I was there. That I suffered in secret, and that I suffered exquisitely, no one ever knew but I. How much I suffered, it is, as I have said already, utterly beyond my power to tell. No man's imagination can overstep the reality. But I kept my own counsel, and I did my work. I knew from the first that, if I could not do my work as well as any of the rest, I could not hold myself above a slight and contempt. I soon became at least as expeditious and as skilful with my hands as either of the other boys. Though perfectly familiar with them, my conduct and manners were different enough from theirs to place a space between us. They, and the men, always spoke of me as 'the young gentleman'. A certain man (a soldier once) named Thomas, who was the foreman, and another named Harry, who was the carman and wore a red jacket, used to call me 'Charles' sometimes, in speaking to me; but I think it was mostly when we were very confidential, and when I had made some efforts to entertain them over our work with the results of some of the old readings, which were fast perishing out of my mind. Poll Green uprose once, and rebelled against the 'young-gentleman' usage; but Bob Fagin settled him speedily. . . .

Bob Fagin was very good to me on the occasion of a bad attack of my old disorder. I suffered such excruciating pain that time, that they made a temporary bed of straw in my old recess in the counting-house, and I rolled about on the floor, and Bob filled empty blacking-bottles with hot water, and applied relays of them to my side, half the day. I got better, and quite easy towards evening; but Bob (who was much bigger and older than I) did not like the idea of my going home alone, and took me under his protection. I was too proud to let him know about the prison; and after making several efforts to get rid of him, to all of which Bob Fagin in his goodness was deaf, shook hands with him on the steps of a house near Southwark Bridge on the Surrey side, making believe that I lived there. As a finishing piece of reality in case of his looking back, I knocked at the door, I recollect, and asked, when the woman opened it, if that was Mr Robert Fagin's house. . . .

At last, one day, my father and the relative so often mentioned quarrelled; quarrelled by letter, for I took the letter from my father to him which caused the explosion, but quarrelled very fiercely. It was about me. It may have had some backward reference, in part, for anything I know, to my employment at the window. All I am certain of is that, soon after I had given him the letter, my cousin (he was a sort of cousin, by marriage) told me he was very much insulted about me; and that it was impossible to keep me, after that. I cried very much, partly because it was so sudden, and partly because in his anger he was violent about my father, though gentle to me. Thomas, the old soldier, comforted me, and said he was sure it was for the best. With a relief so strange that it was like oppression, I went home.

My mother set herself to accommodate the quarrel, and did so next day. She brought home a request for me to return next morning, and a high character of me, which I am very sure I deserved. My father said I should go back no more, and should go to school. I do not write resentfully or angrily: for I know how all these things have worked together to make me what I am: but I never afterwards forgot, I never shall forget, I never can forget, that my mother was warm for my being sent back.

From that hour until this at which I write, no word of that part of my childhood which I have now gladly brought to a close, has passed my lips to any human being. I have no idea how long it lasted; whether for a year, or much more, or less. From that hour, until this, my father and my mother have been stricken dumb upon it. I have never heard the least allusion to it, however far off and remote, from either of them. I have never, until I now impart it to this paper, in any burst of confidence with anyone, my own wife not excepted, raised the curtain I then dropped, thank God.

Until old Hungerford Market was pulled down, until old Hungerford Stairs were destroyed, and the very nature of the ground changed, I never had the courage to go back to the place where my servitude began. I never saw it. I could not endure to go near it. For many years, when I came near to Robert Warrens's in the Strand, I crossed over to the opposite side of the way, to avoid a certain smell of the cement they put upon the blacking-corks, which reminded me of what I was once. It was a very long time before I liked to go up Chandos Street. My old way home by the Borough made me cry, after my eldest child could speak.

In my walks at night I have walked there often, since then, and by degrees I have come to write this. It does not seem a tithe of what I might have written, or of what I meant to write.
(21-33)

Charles Dickens

Preface to the first series of *Sketches by Boz*   1836

In humble imitation of a prudent course, universally adopted by aeronauts, the Author of these volumes throws them up as his pilot balloon, trusting it may catch some favourable current, and devoutly and earnestly hoping it may *go off well* – a sentiment in which his Publisher cordially concurs.

Unlike the generality of pilot balloons which carry no car, in this one it is very possible for a man to embark, not only himself, but all his hopes of future fame, and all his chances of future success. Entertaining no inconsiderable feeling of trepidation, at the idea of making so perilous a voyage in so frail a machine, alone and unaccompanied, the author was naturally desirous to secure the assistance and companionship of some well-known individual, who had frequently contributed to the success, though his well-earned reputation rendered it impossible for him ever to have shared the hazard, of similar undertakings. To whom, as possessing this requisite in an eminent degree, could he apply but to George Cruikshank? The application was readily heard and at once acceded to: this is their first voyage in company, but it may not be the last.

If any further excuse be wanting for adding this book to the hundreds which every season produces, the Author may be permitted to plead the very favourable reception, which several of the following sketches received, on their original appearance in different periodicals. In behalf of the remainder, he can only entreat the kindness and favour of the public: his object has been to present little pictures of life and manners as they really are; and should they be approved of, he hopes to repeat his experiment with increased confidence, and on a more extensive scale.

Charles Dickens

Preface to the first edition of *The Pickwick Papers* 1837

The author's object in this work, was to place before the reader a constant succession of characters and incidents; to paint them in as vivid colours as he could command; and to render them, at the same time, life-like and amusing.

Deferring to the judgement of others in the outset of the undertaking, he adopted the machinery of the club, which was suggested as that best adapted to his purpose: but, finding that it tended rather to his embarrassment than otherwise, he gradually abandoned it, considering it a matter of very little importance to the work whether strictly epic justice were awarded to the club, or not.

The publication of the book in monthly numbers, containing only thirty-two pages in each, rendered it an object of paramount importance that, while the different incidents were linked together by a chain of interest strong enough to prevent their appearing unconnected or impossible, the general design should be so simple as to sustain no injury from this detached and desultory form of publication, extending over no fewer than twenty months. In short, it was necessary – or it appeared so to the author – that every number should be, to a certain extent, complete in itself, and yet that the whole twenty numbers, when collected, should form one tolerably harmonious whole, each leading to the other by a gentle and not unnatural progress of adventure.

It is obvious that in a work published with a view to such considerations, no artfully interwoven or ingeniously complicated plot can with reason be expected. The author ventures to express a hope that he has successfully surmounted the difficulties of his undertaking. And if it be objected to the Pickwick Papers, that they are a mere series of adventures, in which the scenes are ever changing, and the characters come and go like the men and women we encounter in the real world, he can only content himself with the reflection, that they claim to be nothing else, and that the same objection has been made to the works of some of the greatest novelists in the English language.

The following pages have been written from time to time, almost as the periodical occasion arose. Having been written for the most part in the society of a very dear young friend who is now no more, they are connected in the author's mind at once with the happiest period of his life, and with its saddest and most severe affliction.

It is due to the gentleman, whose designs accompany the letter-press, to state that the interval has been so short between the production of each number in manuscript and its appearance in print, that the greater portion of the Illustrations have been executed by the artist from the author's mere verbal description of what he intended to write.

The almost unexampled kindness and favour with which these papers have been received by the public will be a never-failing source of gratifying and pleasant recollection while their author lives. He trusts that, throughout this book, no incident or expression occurs which could call a blush into the most delicate cheek, or wound the feelings of the most sensitive person. If any of his imperfect descriptions, while they afford amusement in the perusal, should induce only one reader to think better of his fellow men, and to look upon the brighter and more kindly side of human nature, he would indeed be proud and happy to have led to such a result.

T. H. Lister (anonymously)

from a review of *Sketches by Boz*, *The Pickwick Papers*, *Nicholas Nickleby* and *Oliver Twist*, *Edinburgh Review*, vol. 68
October 1838

Mr Charles Dickens, the author of the above works, is the most popular writer of his day. Since the publication of the poems and novels of Sir Walter Scott, there has been no work the circulation of which has approached that of *The Pickwick Papers*. Thirty thousand copies of it are said to have been sold. It has been dramatized by several hands, and played in sundry London theatres. A continuation

of it by another writer, has been undertaken as a profitable speculation: and no sooner has its genuine successor, *Nicholas Nickleby*, by
the same author, made its appearance in monthly numbers, than it is
published on the continent, translated into German. Great popularity
is doubtless to be accepted as presumptive evidence of merit – and
should at least induce us to regard with attention the qualities of one
who can exhibit so many suffrages in his favour. But even a cursory
glance over literary history will teach its insufficiency as a *proof* of
merit. We shall, therefore, regard it merely as a claim to notice – and
treat Mr Dickens with no more favour than if he could count only
hundreds instead of myriads, among his readers. His reputation as a
writer of fiction rests at present upon the above four works. The first
consists of detached tales, and descriptive sketches of familiar scenes
and humble life; some of which, before they were collected, had
appeared in the columns of a daily newspaper. The second appeared
in monthly numbers, illustrated with prints. The third, not yet completed, is coming forth in a similar guise; and the fourth is pursuing
its course, still unfinished, through the numbers of a monthly magazine. In all these productions the author has called in the aid of the
pencil, and has been contented to share his success with the caricaturist. He has put them forth in a form attractive, it is true, to that
vast majority, the *idle* readers – but one not indicative of high literary
pretensions, or calculated to inspire a belief of probable permanence
of reputation. They seem, at first sight, to be among the most evanescent of the literary *ephemerae* of their day – mere humorous specimens
of the lightest kind of light reading, expressly calculated to be much
sought and soon forgotten – fit companions for the portfolio of
caricatures – 'good nonsense' – and nothing more. This is the view
which many persons will take of Mr Dickens's writings – but this is
not our deliberate view of them. We think him a very original writer
– well entitled to his popularity – and not likely to lose it – and the
truest and most spirited delineator of English life, amongst the middle
and lower classes, since the days of Smollett and Fielding. He has
remarkable powers of observation, and great skill in communicating
what he has observed – a keen sense of the ludicrous – exuberant
humour – and that mastery in the pathetic which, though it seems
opposed to the gift of humour, is often found in conjunction with it.
Add to these qualities, an unaffected style, fluent, easy, spirited, and

terse – a good deal of dramatic power – and great truthfulness and ability in description. We know no other English writer to whom he bears a marked resemblance. He sometimes imitates other writers, such as Fielding in his introductions, and Washington Irving in his detached tales, and thus exhibits his skill as a parodist. But his own manner is very distinct – and comparison with any other would not serve to illustrate and describe it. We would compare him rather with the painter Hogarth. What Hogarth was in painting, such very nearly is Mr Dickens in prose fiction. The same turn of mind – the same species of power displays itself strongly in each. Like Hogarth he takes a keen and practical view of life – is an able satirist – very successful in depicting the ludicrous side of human nature, and rendering its follies more apparent by humorous exaggeration – peculiarly skilful in his management of details, throwing in circumstances which serve not only to complete the picture before us, but to suggest indirectly antecedent events which cannot be brought before our eyes. Hogarth's cobweb over the poor-box, and the plan for paying off the national debt, hanging from the pocket of a prisoner in the Fleet, are strokes of satire, very similar to some in the writings of Mr Dickens. It is fair, in making this comparison, to add, that it does not hold good throughout; and that Mr Dickens is exempt from two of Hogarth's least agreeable qualities – his cynicism and his coarseness. There is no misanthropy in his satire, and no coarseness in his descriptions – a merit enhanced by the nature of his subjects. His works are chiefly pictures of humble life – frequently of the humblest. The reader is led through scenes of poverty and crime, and all the characters are made to discourse in the appropriate language of their respective classes – and yet we recollect no passage which ought to cause pain to the most sensitive delicacy, if read aloud in female society.

We have said that his satire was not misanthropic. This is eminently true. One of the qualities we most admire in him is his comprehensive spirit of humanity. The tendency of his writings is to make us practically benevolent – to excite our sympathy in behalf of the aggrieved and suffering in all classes; and especially in those who are most removed from observation. He especially directs our attention to the helpless victims of untoward circumstances, or a vicious system – to the imprisoned debtor – the orphan pauper – the parish apprentice – the juvenile criminal – and to the tyranny which, under the combination of parental neglect, with the mercenary brutality of a pedagogue, may be exercised with impunity in schools. His humanity is plain, practical and manly. It is quite untainted with sentimentality. There is no mawkish wailing for ideal distresses – no morbid exaggeration of the evils incident to our lot – no disposition to excite unavailing discontent, or to turn our attention from remediable grievances to those which do not admit a remedy. Though he appeals much to our feelings, we can detect no instance in which he has employed the verbiage of spurious philanthropy.

He is equally exempt from the meretricious cant of spurious philosophy. He never endeavours to mislead our sympathies – to pervert plain notions of right and wrong – to make vice interesting in our eyes – and shake our confidence in those whose conduct is irreproachable, by dwelling on the hollowness of seeming virtue. His vicious characters are just what experience shows the average to be; and what the natural operation of those circumstances to which they have been exposed would lead us to expect. We are made to feel both what they are, and *why* they are what we find them. We find no monsters of unmitigated and unredeemable villainy; no creatures blending with their crimes the most incongruous and romantic virtues; but very natural and unattractive combinations of human qualities, in which the bad is found to predominate in such a proportion as the position of the party would render probable. In short, he has eschewed that vulgar and theatrical device for producing effect – the representation of human beings as they are likely *not* to be.

Good feeling and sound sense are shown in his application of ridicule. It is never levelled at poverty or misfortune; or at circumstances which can be rendered ludicrous only by their deviation from artificial forms; or by regarding them through the medium of a conventional standard. Residence in the regions of Bloomsbury, ill-dressed dinners and ill-made liveries, are crimes which he suffers to go unlashed; but follies or abuses, such as would be admitted alike in every sphere of society to be fit objects for his satire, are hit with remarkable vigour and precision. Nor does he confine himself to such as are obvious; but elicits and illustrates absurdities which, though at once acknowledged when displayed, are plausible and comparatively unobserved.

(75–8)

Charles Dickens

Preface to the first edition of *Nicholas Nickleby*   1839

It has afforded the Author great amusement and satisfaction, during the progress of this work, to learn from country friends and from a variety of ludicrous statements concerning himself in provincial newspapers, that more than one Yorkshire schoolmaster lays claim to being the original of Mr Squeers. One worthy, he has reason to believe, has actually consulted authorities learned in the law, as to his having good grounds on which to rest an action for libel; another has meditated a journey to London, for the express purpose of committing an assault and battery upon his traducer; a third perfectly remembers being waited on last January twelvemonth by two gentlemen, one of whom held him in conversation while the other took his likeness; and, although Mr Squeers has but one eye, and he has two, and the published sketch does not resemble him (whoever he may be) in any other respect, still he and all his friends and neighbours know at once for whom it is meant, because – the character is *so* like him.

While the Author cannot but feel the full force of the compliment thus conveyed to him, he ventures to suggest that these contentions may arise from the fact that Mr Squeers is the representative of a class, and not of an individual. Where imposture, ignorance and brutal cupidity, are the stock in trade of a small body of men, and one is described by these characteristics, all his fellows will recognize something belonging to themselves, and each will have a misgiving that the portrait is his own.

To this general description, as to most others, there may be some exceptions; and although the Author neither saw nor heard of any in the course of an excursion which he made into Yorkshire, before he commenced these adventures, or before or since, it affords him much more pleasure to assume their existence than to doubt it. He has dwelt thus long upon this point, because his object in calling public attention to the system would be very imperfectly fulfilled, if he did not state now in his own person, emphatically and earnestly, that Mr Squeers and his school are faint and feeble pictures of an existing reality, purposely subdued and kept down lest they should be deemed impossible – that there are upon record trials at law in which damages have been sought as a poor recompense for lasting agonies and dis-figurements inflicted upon children by the treatment of the master in these places, involving such offensive and foul details of neglect, cruelty and disease, as no writer of fiction would have the boldness to imagine – and that, since he has been engaged upon these Adventures, he has received from private quarters far beyond the reach of suspicion or distrust, accounts of atrocities, in the perpetration of which upon neglected or repudiated children these schools have been the main instruments, very far exceeding any that appear in these pages.

To turn to a more pleasant subject, it may be right to say, that there *are* two characters in this book which are drawn from life. It is remarkable that what we call the world, which is so very credulous in what professes to be true, is most incredulous in what professes to be imaginary; and that while every day in real life it will allow in one man no blemishes, and in another no virtues, it will seldom admit a very strongly-marked character, either good or bad, in a fictitious narrative, to be within the limits of probability. For this reason, they have been very slightly and imperfectly sketched. Those who take an interest in this tale will be glad to learn that the Brothers Cheeryble live; that their liberal charity, their singleness of heart, their noble nature and their unbounded benevolence, are no creations of the Author's brain; but are prompting every day (and oftenest by stealth) some munificent and generous deed in that town of which they are the pride and honour.

It only now remains for the writer of these passages, with that feeling of regret with which we leave almost any pursuit that has for a long time occupied us and engaged our thoughts, and which is naturally augmented in such a case as this, when that pursuit has been surrounded by all that could animate and cheer him on – it only now remains for him, before abandoning his task, to bid his readers fare-well.

The author of a periodical performance (says Mackenzie)
has indeed a claim to the attention and regard of his readers,
more interesting than that of any other writer. Other writers
submit their sentiments to their readers, with the reserve and
circumspection of him who has had time to prepare for a

public appearance. He who has followed Horace's rule, of keeping his book nine years in this study, must have withdrawn many an idea which in the warmth of composition he had conceived, and altered many an expression which in the hurry of writing he had set down. But the periodical essayist commits to his readers the feelings of the day, in the language which those feelings have prompted. As he has delivered himself with the freedom of intimacy and the cordiality of friendship, he will naturally look for the indulgence which those relations may claim; and when he bids his readers adieu, will hope, as well as feel, the regrets of an acquaintance and the tenderness of a friend.

With such feelings and such hopes the periodical essayist, the Author of these pages, now lays them before his readers in a completed form, flattering himself, like the writer just quoted, that on the first of next month they may miss his company at the accustomed time as something which used to be expected with pleasure; and think of the papers which on that day of so many past months they have read, as the correspondence of one who wished their happiness, and contributed to their amusement.

Thomas Hood (anonymously)

from a review of *Master Humphrey's Clock*, vol. I, *Athenaeum*
7 November 1840

... we do not know where we have met, in fiction, with a more striking and picturesque combination of images than is presented by the simple childish figure of Little Nelly, amidst a chaos of such obsolete, old world commodities as form the stock in trade of the Old Curiosity Shop. Look at the Artist's picture of the Child, asleep in her little bed, surrounded, or rather mobbed, by ancient armour and arms, antique furniture, and relics sacred or profane, hideous and grotesque: it is like an Allegory of the peace and innocence of childhood in the midst of Violence, Superstition and all the hateful or hurtful Passions of the world. How sweet and fresh the youthful figure! How much sweeter and fresher for the misty, musty, fusty atmosphere of such accessories and their associations! How soothing the moral, that Gentleness, Purity and Truth, sometimes dormant but never dead, have survived and will outlive Fraud and Force, though backed by gold and encased in steel! As a companion picture, we would select the Mending of the Puppets in the Churchyard, with the mocking figure of Punch perched on a grave-stone – a touch quite Hogarthian in its satirical significance.

As for Little Nelly herself, we should say that she thinks, speaks and acts in a style beyond her years, if we did not know how poverty and misfortune are apt to make advances of wordly knowledge to the young at a most ruinous discount – a painful sacrifice of the very capital of childhood. Like some of the patent sharpeners that give a hasty edge to the knife, at the expense of a rapid waste of metal, so does care act on the juvenile spirit; and the observer may daily see but too many of such young blades precociously worn thin, and so unnaturally keen, that like our over-sharpened knives they could almost cut with their backs.

(887–8)

William Makepeace Thackeray

from 'Catherine', *Fraser's Magazine*, vol. 21 February 1840

To begin with Mr Dickens. No one has read that remarkable tale of *Oliver Twist* without being interested in poor Nancy and her murderer; and especially amused and tickled by the gambols of the Artful Dodger and his companions. The power of the writer is so amazing, that the reader at once becomes his captive, and must follow him whithersoever he leads; and to what are we led? Breathless to watch all the crimes of Fagin, tenderly to deplore the errors of Nancy, to have for Bill Sikes a kind of pity and admiration, and an absolute love for the society of the Dodger. All these heroes stepped from the novel on to the stage; and the whole London public, from peers to chimney-sweeps, were interested about a set of ruffians whose occupations are thievery, murder and prostitution. A most agreeable set of rascals, indeed, who have their virtues, too, but not good company for any man. We had better pass them by in decent silence; for, as no writer can or dare tell the *whole* truth concerning them, and faithfully explain their vices, there is no need to give *ex-parte* statements of their virtues.

And what came of *Oliver Twist*? The public wanted something more extravagant still, more sympathy for thieves, and so *Jack Sheppard* makes his appearance. Jack and his two wives, and his faithful Blueskin, and his gin-drinking mother, that sweet Magdalen! – with what a wonderful gravity are all their adventures related, with what an honest simplicity and vigour does Jack's biographer record his actions and virtues! ... But in the sorrows of Nancy and the exploits of Sheppard, there is no such lurking moral, as far as we have been able to discover; we are asked for downright sympathy in the one case, and are called on in the second to admire the gallantry of a thief. The street-walker may be a very virtuous person, and the robber as brave as Wellington; but it is better to leave them alone, and their qualities, good and bad. The pathos of the workhouse scenes in *Oliver Twist*, of the Fleet Prison descriptions in *Pickwick*, *is* genuine and pure – as much of this as you please; as tender a hand to the poor, as kindly a word to the unhappy, as you will; but, in the name of commonsense, let us not expend our sympathies on cut-throats, and other such prodigies of evil!

(211)

Charles Dickens

from a letter to John Forster ?8 January 1841

...this part of the story [chapters 71 and 72 of *The Old Curiosity Shop*] is not to be galloped over, I can tell you. I think it will come famously – but I am the wretchedest of the wretched. It casts the most horrible shadow upon me, and it is as much as I can do to keep moving at all. I tremble to approach the place a great deal more than Kit; a great deal more than Mr Garland; a great deal more than the Single Gentleman. I shan't recover it for a long time. Nobody will miss her like I shall. It is such a very painful thing to me, that I really cannot express my sorrow. Old wounds bleed afresh when I only think of the way of doing it: what the actual doing it will be,

God knows. I can't preach to myself the school-master's consolation, though I try. Dear Mary[1] died yesterday, when I think of this sad story.

Charles Dickens

from a letter to John Forster   ?17 January 1841

When I first began (on your valued suggestion), to keep my thoughts upon this ending of the tale, I resolved to try and do something which might be read by people about whom Death had been, with a softened feeling, and with consolation. ... After you left last night, I took my desk upstairs; and writing until four o'Clock this morning, finished the old story. It makes me very melancholy to think that all these people are lost to me for ever, and I feel as if I never could become attached to any new set of characters.[2]

Charles Dickens

Preface to the third edition of *Oliver Twist*   1841 (first edition, 1838)

Some of the author's friends cried, 'Lookee, gentlemen, the man is a villain; but it is Nature for all that'; and the young critics of the age, the clerks, apprentices, &c., called it low, and fell a groaning. – Fielding

The greater part of this Tale was originally published in a magazine. When I completed it, and put it forth in its present form three years ago, I fully expected it would be objected to on some very high moral grounds in some very high moral quarters. The result did not fail to prove the justice of my anticipations.

I embrace the present opportunity of saying a few words in

1 The 'Mary' referred to is Dickens's sister-in-law, Mary Hogarth. [Ed.]
2 According to Forster, the tragic ending of *The Old Curiosity Shop* was the result of a suggestion made by him to Dickens when the novel was about half-written or earlier. [Ed.]

explanation of my aim and object in its production. It is in some sort a duty with me to do so, in gratitude to those who sympathized with me and divined my purpose at the time, and who, perhaps, will not be sorry to have their impression confirmed under my own hand.

It is, it seems, a very coarse and shocking circumstance, that some of the characters in these pages are chosen from the most criminal and degraded of London's population; that Sikes is a thief, and Fagin a receiver of stolen goods; that the boys are pickpockets, and the girl is a prostitute.

I confess I have yet to learn that a lesson of the purest good may not be drawn from the vilest evil. I have always believed this to be a recognized and established truth, laid down by the greatest men the world has ever seen, constantly acted upon by the best and wisest natures, and confirmed by the reason and experience of every thinking mind. I saw no reason, when I wrote this book, why the very dregs of life, so long as their speech did not offend the ear, should not serve the purpose of a moral, at least as well as its froth and cream. Nor did I doubt that there lay festering in Saint Giles's as good materials towards the truth as any flaunting in Saint James's.

In this spirit, when I wished to show, in little Oliver, the principle of Good surviving through every adverse circumstance, and triumphing at last; and when I considered among what companions I could try him best, having regard to that kind of men into whose hands he would most naturally fall; I bethought myself of those who figure in these volumes. When I came to discuss the subject more maturely with myself, I saw many strong reasons for pursuing the course to which I was inclined. I had read of thieves by scores – seductive fellows (amiable for the most part), faultless in dress, plump in pocket, choice in horseflesh, bold in bearing, fortunate in gallantry, great at a song, a bottle, pack of cards or dice-box, and fit companions for the bravest. But I had never met (except in Hogarth) with the miserable reality. It appeared to me that to draw a knot of such associates in crime as really do exist; to paint them in all their deformity, in all their wretchedness, in all the squalid poverty of their lives; to show them as they really are, for ever skulking uneasily through the dirtiest paths of life, with the great, black, ghastly gallows closing up their prospect, turn them where they may; it appeared to me that to do this, would be to attempt a something which was greatly needed, and which would be a service to society. And therefore I did it as I best could.

In every book I know, where such characters are treated of at all, certain allurements and fascinations are thrown around them. Even in the Beggar's Opera, the thieves are represented as leading a life which is rather to be envied than otherwise; while Macheath, with all the captivations of command, and the devotion of the most beautiful girl and only pure character in the piece, is as much to be admired and emulated by weak beholders, as any fine gentleman in a red coat who has purchased, as Voltaire says, the right to command a couple of thousand men, or so, and to affront death at their head. Johnson's question, whether any man will turn thief because Macheath is reprieved, seems to me beside the matter. I ask myself, whether any man will be deterred from turning thief because of his being sentenced to death, and because of the existence of Peachum and Lockit; and remembering the captain's roaring life, great appearance, vast success and strong advantages, I feel assured that nobody having a bent that way will take any warning from him, or will see anything in the play but a very flowery and pleasant road, conducting an honourable ambition in course of time, to Tyburn Tree.

In fact, Gay's witty satire on society had a general object, which made him careless of example in this respect, and gave him other, wider and higher aims. The same may be said of Sir Edward Bulwer's admirable and most powerful novel of Paul Clifford, which cannot be fairly considered as having, or being intended to have, any bearing on this part of the subject, one way or other.

What manner of life is that which is described in these pages, as the everyday existence of a Thief? What charms has it for the young and ill-disposed, what allurements for the most jolter-headed of juveniles? Here are no canterings upon moonlit heaths, no merry-makings in the snuggest of all possible caverns, none of the attractions of dress, no embroidery, no lace, no jack-boots, no crimson coats and ruffles, none of the dash and freedom with which 'the road' has been, time out of mind, invested. The cold, wet, shelterless midnight streets of London; the foul and frowsy dens, where vice is closely packed and lacks the room to turn; the haunts of hunger and disease, the shabby rags that scarcely hold together: where are the attractions of these things? Have they no lesson, and do they not whisper something beyond the little-regarded warning of a moral precept?

But there are people of so refined and delicate a nature, that they cannot bear the contemplation of these horrors. Not that they turn instinctively from crime; but that criminal characters, to suit them, must be, like their meat, in delicate disguise. A Massaroni in green velvet is quite an enchanting creature; but a Sikes in fustian is insupportable. A Mrs Massaroni, being a lady in short petticoats and a fancy dress, is a thing to imitate in tableaux and have in lithograph on pretty songs; but a Nancy, being a creature in a cotton gown and cheap shawl, is not to be thought of. It is wonderful how Virtue turns from dirty stockings; and how Vice, married to ribbons and a little gay attire, changes her name, as wedded ladies do, and becomes Romance.

Now, as the stern and plain truth, even in the dress of this (in novels) much exalted race, was a part of the purpose of this book, I will not, for these readers, abate one hole in the Dodger's coat, or one scrap of curl-paper in the girl's dishevelled hair. I have no faith in the delicacy which cannot bear to look upon them. I have no desire to make proselytes among such people. I have no respect for their opinion, good or bad; do not covet their approval; and do not write for their amusement. I venture to say this without reserve; for I am not aware of any writer in our language having a respect for himself, or held in any respect by his posterity, who ever has descended to the taste of this fastidious class.

On the other hand, if I look for examples, and for precedents, I find them in the noblest range of English literature. Fielding, Defoe, Goldsmith, Smollett, Richardson, Mackenzie – all these for wise purposes, and especially the two first, brought upon the scene the very scum and refuse of the land. Hogarth, the moralist, and censor of his age – in whose great works the times in which he lived, and the characters of every time, will never cease to be reflected – did the like, without the compromise of a hair's breadth; with a power and depth of thought which belonged to few men before him, and will probably appertain to fewer still in time to come. Where does this giant stand now in the estimation of his countrymen? And yet, if I turn back to the days in which he or any of these men flourished, I find the same reproach levelled against them every one, each in his turn, by the insects of the hour, who raised their little hum, and died, and were forgotten.

Cervantes laughed Spain's chivalry away, by showing Spain its impossible and wild absurdity. It was my attempt, in my humble and far-distant sphere, to dim the false glitter surrounding something which really did exist, by showing it in its unattractive and repulsive truth. No less consulting my own taste, than the manners of the age, I endeavoured, while I painted it in all its fallen and degraded aspect, to banish from the lips of the lowest character I introduced, any expression that could by possibility offend; and rather to lead to the unavoidable inference that its existence was of the most debased and vicious kind, than to prove it elaborately by words and deeds. In the case of the girl, in particular, I kept this intention constantly in view. Whether it is apparent in the narrative, and how it is executed, I leave my readers to determine.

It has been observed of this girl, that her devotion to the brutal housebreaker does not seem natural, and it has been objected to Sikes in the same breath – with some inconsistency, as I venture to think – that he is surely overdrawn, because in him there would appear to be none of those redeeming traits which are objected to as unnatural in his mistress. Of the latter objection I will merely say, that I fear there are in the world some insensible and callous natures that do become, at last, utterly and irredeemably bad. But whether this be so or not, of one thing I am certain: that there are such men as Sikes, who, being closely followed through the same space of time, and through the same current of circumstances, would not give, by one look or action of a moment, the faintest indication of a better nature. Whether every gentler human feeling is dead within such bosoms, or the proper chord to strike has rusted and is hard to find, I do not know; but that the fact is so, I am sure.

It is useless to discuss whether the conduct and character of the girl seems natural or unnatural, probable or improbable, right or wrong. IT IS TRUE. Every man who has watched these melancholy shades of life knows it to be so. Suggested to my mind long ago – long before I dealt in fiction – by what I often saw and read of, in actual life around me, I have, for years, tracked it through many profligate and noisome ways, and found it still the same. From the first introduction of that poor wretch, to her laying her bloody head upon the robber's breast, there is not one word exaggerated or over-wrought. It is emphatically God's truth for it is the truth He leaves in such depraved and miserable breasts; the hope yet lingering behind; the last fair drop of water at the bottom of the dried-up weed-choked well. It involves the best and worst shades of our common nature; much of its ugliest hues, and something of its most beautiful; it is a contradiction, an anomaly, an apparent impossibility, but it is a truth. I am glad to have had it doubted, for in that circumstance I find a sufficient assurance that it needed to be told.

Charles Dickens

from a speech at Edinburgh   25 June 1841

The way to your good opinion, favour and support, has been to me very pleasant – a path strewn with flowers and cheered with sunshine. I feel as if I stood amongst old friends, whom I have intimately known and highly valued. I feel as if the deaths of the fictitious creatures, in which you have been kind enough to express an interest, had endeared us to each other as real afflictions deepen friendships in actual life; I feel as if they had been real persons, whose fortunes we had pursued together in inseparable connexion, and that I had never known them apart from you.

It is a difficult thing for a man to speak of himself or of his works. But perhaps on this occasion I may, without impropriety, venture to say a word on the spirit in which mine were conceived. I felt an earnest and humble desire, and shall do till I die, to increase the stock of harmless cheerfulness. I felt that the world was not utterly to be despised; that it was worthy of living in for many reasons. I was anxious to find, as the Professor has said, if I could, in evil things, that soul of goodness which the Creator has put in them. I was anxious to show that virtue may be found on the by-ways of the world, that it was not incompatible with poverty and even with rags, and to keep steadily through life the motto, expressed in the burning words of your Northern poet[1]

1 Robert Burns. [Ed.]

The rank is but the guinea's stamp
  The Man's the gowd for a' that.

[*Loud cheers.*] And in following this track, where could I have better assurance that I was right, or where could I have stronger assurance to cheer me on than in your kindness on this, to me, memorable night? [*Loud cheers.*]

I am anxious and glad to have an opportunity of saying a word in reference to one incident in which I am happy to know you were interested and still more happy to know, though it may sound paradoxical, that you were disappointed: I mean the death of the little heroine. When I first conceived the idea of conducting that simple story to its termination, I determined rigidly to adhere to it, and never forsake the end I had in view. Not untried in the school of affliction, in the death of those we love, I thought what a good thing it would be if in my little work of pleasant amusement I could substitute a garland of fresh flowers for the sculptured horrors which disgrace the tomb. If I have put into my book anything which can fill the young mind with better thoughts of death, or soften the grief of older hearts; if I have written one word which can afford pleasure or consolation to old or young in time of trial, I shall consider it as something achieved – something which I shall be glad to look back upon in after life. Therefore I kept to my purpose, notwithstanding that towards the conclusion of the story, I daily received letters of remonstrance, especially from the ladies.

Charles Dickens

from the preface to the first edition of *Barnaby Rudge* 1841

No account of the Gordon Riots having been to my knowledge introduced into any Work of Fiction, and the subject presenting very extraordinary and remarkable features, I was led to project this Tale.

It is unnecessary to say, that those shameful tumults, while they reflect indelible disgrace upon the time in which they occurred, and all who had act or part in them, teach a good lesson. That what we falsely call a religious cry is easily raised by men who have no religion, and who in their daily practice set at nought the commonest principles of right and wrong; that it is begotten of intolerance and persecution; that it is senseless, besotted, inveterate, and unmerciful; all History teaches us. But perhaps we do not know it in our hearts too well, to profit by even so humble an example as the 'No Popery' riots of 1780.

However imperfectly those disturbances are set forth in the following pages, they are impartially painted by one who has no sympathy with the Romish Church, although he acknowledges, as most men do, some esteemed friends among the followers of its creed.

It may be observed that, in the description of the principal outrages, reference has been had to the best authorities of that time, such as they are; the account given in this Tale, of all the main features of the Riots, is substantially correct.

It may be further remarked, that Mr Dennis's allusion to the flourishing condition of his trade in those days, have their foundation in Truth, not in the Author's fancy. Any file of old Newspapers, or odd volume of the Annual Register, will prove this with terrible ease.

Even the case of Mary Jones, dwelt upon with so much pleasure by the same character, is no effort of invention. The facts were stated exactly as they are stated here, in the House of Commons. Whether they afforded as much entertainment to the merry gentlemen assembled there, as some other most affecting circumstances of a similar nature mentioned by Sir Samuel Romilly, is not recorded.

William Wordsworth

from a letter to Edward Moxon   ?1 April 1842

Pray tell me what you think is the main cause of the great falling off in the sale of books. The young men in the Universities cannot be supposed to be straitened much in their allowance, yet I find that scarcely any books are sold them. Dr Arnold told me that his lads seemed to care for nothing but Bozzy's next No., and the Classics suffered accordingly. Can that Man's public and others of the like kind materially affect the question? I am quite in the dark.

Ralph Waldo Emerson

from his journal   25 November 1842

Yesterday I read Dickens's *American Notes*. It answers its end very well, which plainly was to make a readable book, nothing more. Truth is not his object for a single instant, but merely to make good points in a lively sequence, and he proceeds very well. As an account of America it is not to be considered for a moment: it is too short, and too narrow, too superficial, and too ignorant, too slight, and too fabulous, and the man totally unequal to the work. A very lively rattle on that nuisance, a sea voyage, is the first chapter; and a pretty fair example of the historical truth of the whole book. We can hear throughout every page the dialogue between the author and his publisher – 'Mr Dickens, the book must be entertaining – that is the essential point. Truth? Damn truth! I tell you, it must be entertaining.' As a picture of American manners nothing can be falser. No such conversations ever occur in this country in real life, as he relates. He has picked up and noted with eagerness each odd local phrase that he met with, and, when he had a story to relate, has joined them together, so that the result is the broadest caricature; and the scene might as truly have been laid in Wales or in England as in the States. Monstrous exaggeration is an easy secret of romance. But Americans who, like some of us Massachusetts people, are not fond of spitting, will go from Maine to New Orleans, and meet no more annoyance than we should in Britain or France. So with 'yes', so with 'fixings', so with soap and towels; and all the other trivialities which this trifler detected in travelling over half the world. The book makes but a poor apology for its author, who certainly appears in no dignified or enviable position.

Charles Dickens

from a letter to John Forster   2 November 1843

You know, as well as I, that I think *Chuzzlewit* in a hundred points immeasurably the best of my stories. That I feel my power now, more than I ever did. That I have a greater confidence in myself than I ever had. That I *know*, if I have health, I could sustain my place in the minds of thinking men, though fifty writers started up to-morrow. But how many readers do *not* think! How many take it upon trust from knaves and idiots, that one writes too fast, or runs a thing to death! How coldly did this very book go on for months, until it forced itself up in people's opinion, without forcing itself up in sale! If I wrote for forty thousand Forsters, or for forty thousand people who know I write because I can't help it, I should have no need to leave the scene. But this very book warns me that if I *can* leave it for a time, I had better do so, and must do so. Apart from that again, I feel that longer rest after this story would do me good. You say two or three months, because you have been used to see me for eight years never leaving off. But it is not rest enough. It is impossible to go on working the brain to that extent for ever. The very spirit of the thing, in doing it, leaves a horrible despondency behind, when it is done; which must be prejudicial to the mind, so soon renewed and so seldom let alone. What would poor Scott have given to have gone abroad, of his own free will, a young man, instead of creeping there, a driveller, in his miserable decay!

Charles Dickens

from a letter to C. G. Felton   2 January 1844

Now, if instantly on the receipt of this you will send a free and independent citizen down to the Cunard wharf at Boston, you will find that Captain Hewett, of the Britannia steamship (my ship), has a small parcel for Professor Felton of Cambridge: and in that parcel you will find a Christmas Carol in prose; being a short story of Christmas by Charles Dickens. Over which Christmas Carol Charles Dickens wept and laughed and wept again, and excited himself in a most extraordinary manner in the composition; and thinking whereof he walked about the black streets of London, fifteen and twenty miles many a night when all the sober folks had gone to bed. . . . Its success is most prodigious. And by every post all manner of strangers write all manner of letters to him about their homes and hearths, and how this same Carol is read aloud there, and kept on a little shelf by itself. Indeed, it is the greatest success, as I am told, that this ruffian and rascal has ever achieved.

William Makepeace Thackeray

from 'A Box of Novels', *Fraser's Magazine*, vol. 29 February 1844

And now there is but one book left in the box, the smallest one, but oh! how much the best of all. It is the work of the master of all the English humourists now alive; the young man who came and took his place calmly at the head of the whole tribe, and who has kept it. Think of all we owe Mr Dickens since those half-dozen years, the store of happy hours that he has made us pass, the kindly and pleasant companions whom he has introduced to us; the harmless laughter, the generous wit, the frank, manly, human love which he has taught us to feel! Every month of those years has brought us some kind token from this delightful genius. His books may have lost in art, perhaps, but could we afford to wait? Since the days when the *Spectator* was produced by a man of kindred mind and temper, what books have appeared that have taken so affectionate a hold of the English public as these? They have made millions of rich and poor happy; they might have been locked up for nine years, doubtless, and pruned here and there and improved (which I doubt), but where would have been the reader's benefit all this time, while the author was elaborating his performance? Would the communion between the writer and the public have been what it is now – something continual, confidential, something like personal affection? . . .

As for the *Christmas Carol*, or any other book of a like nature which the public takes upon itself to criticize, the individual critic had quite best hold his peace. One remembers what Bonaparte replied to some Austrian critics, of much correctness and acumen, who doubted about acknowledging the French republic. I do not mean that the *Christmas Carol* is quite as brilliant or self-evident as the sun at noonday; but it is so spread over England by this time that no sceptic, no *Fraser's Magazine*, no, not even the godlike and ancient *Quarterly* itself (venerable, Saturnian, big-wigged dynasty!), could review it down. 'Unhappy people! deluded race!' one hears the cauliflowered god exclaim, mournfully shaking the powder out of his ambrosial curls, 'what strange new folly is this? What new deity do ye worship? Know ye what ye do? Know ye that your new idol hath little Latin and less Greek? Know ye that he has never tasted the birch of Eton, nor trodden the flags of Carfax, nor paced the academic flats of Trumpington? Know ye that in mathematics, or logics, this wretched ignoramus is not fit to hold a candle to a wooden spoon? See ye not how, from describing low humours, he now, forsooth, will attempt the sublime? Discern ye not his faults of taste, his deplorable propensity to write blank verse? Come back to your ancient, venerable, and natural instructors. Leave this new, low and intoxicating draught at which ye rush, and let us lead you back to the old wells of classic lore. Come and repose with us there. We are your gods; we are the ancient oracles, and no mistake. Come listen to us once more, and we will sing to you the mystic numbers of *as in praesenti* under the arches of the Pons Asinorum.' But the children of the present generation hear not; for they reply, 'Rush to the Strand! and purchase five thousand more copies of the *Christmas Carol*.'

In fact, one might as well detail the plot of the *Merry Wives of Windsor*, or *Robinson Crusoe*, as recapitulate here the adventures of Scrooge the miser, and his Christmas conversion. I am not sure that the allegory is a very complete one, and protest, with the classics, against the use of blank verse in prose; but here all objections stop. Who can listen to objections regarding such a book as this? It seems to me a national benefit, and to every man or woman who reads it a personal kindness. The last two people I heard speak of it were women; neither knew the other, or the author, and both said, by way of criticism, 'God bless him!' A Scotch philosopher, who nationally does not keep Christmas Day, on reading the book, sent out for a turkey, and asked two friends to dine – this is a fact! Many men were known to sit down after perusing it, and write off letters to their friends, not about business, but out of their fullness of heart, and to wish old acquaintances a happy Christmas. Had the book appeared a fortnight earlier, all the prize cattle would have been gobbled up in pure love and friendship, Epping denuded of sausages, and not a turkey left in Norfolk. His Royal Highness's fat stock would have fetched unheard-of prices, and Alderman Bannister would have been tired of slaying. But there is a Christmas for 1844, too; the book will be as early then as now, and so let speculators look out.

As for Tiny Tim, there is a certain passage in the book regarding that young gentleman, about which a man should hardly venture to speak in print or in public, any more than he would of any other affections of his private heart. There is not a reader in England but that little creature will be a bond of union between the author and him; and he will say of Charles Dickens, as the woman just now, 'God bless him!' What a feeling is this for a writer to be able to inspire, and what a reward to reap!

(167–9)

Charles Dickens

from a letter to J. V. Staples   3 April 1844

I have been very much gratified by the receipt of your interesting letter, and I assure you that it would have given me heartfelt satisfaction to have been in your place when you read my little *Carol* to the Poor in your neighbourhood. I have great faith in the poor; to the best of my ability I always endeavour to present them in a favourable light to the rich; and I shall never cease, I hope, until I die, to advocate their being made as happy and as wise as the circumstances of their condition, in its utmost improvement, will admit of their becoming. I mention this to assure you of two things. Firstly, that I try to deserve their attention; and secondly, that any such marks of their approval and confidence as you relate to me are most acceptable to my feelings, and go at once to my heart.

R. H. Horne

from 'Charles Dickens', *A New Spirit of the Age*, vol. 1   1844

Mr Dickens is one of those happily constituted individuals who can 'touch pitch without soiling his fingers'; the peculiar rarity, in his case, being that he can do so without gloves; and, grasping its clinging blackness with both hands, shall yet retain no soil, nor ugly memory. That he is at home in a wood – in green lanes and all sweet pastoral scenes – who can doubt it that has ever dwelt among them? But he has also been through the back slums of many a St Giles's. He never 'picks his way', but goes splashing on through mud and mire. The mud and mire fly up, and lose themselves like ether – he bears away no stain – nobody has one splash. Nor is the squalid place so bad as it was before he entered it, for some 'touch of nature' – of unadulterated pathos – of a crushed human heart uttering a sound from out the darkness and the slough, has left its echo in the air, and half purified it from its malaria of depravity. . . .

The methods by which such characters and scenes as have been alluded to, are conveyed to the reader with all the force of verisimilitude, yet without offence, are various, though it would perhaps be hardly fair to lift the curtain, and show the busy-browed artist 'as he appeared' with his hands full. One means only, as adopted by Mr Dickens, shall be mentioned, and chiefly as it tends to bring out a trait of his genius as well as art. When he has introduced a girl – her cheeks blotched with rouge, her frock bright red, her boots green, her hair stuck over with yellow hair-papers, and a glass of 'ruin' in her hand – the very next time he alludes to her, he calls her 'this young lady'! Now, if he had called this girl by her actual designation, as awarded to her by indignant, moral man – who has nothing whatever to do with such degradation – the book would have been destroyed; whereas, the reader perfectly well knows what class the poor gaudy outcast belongs to, and the author gains a humorous effect by the evasive appellation. In like manner he deals with a dirty young thief, as 'the first-named young gentleman'; while the old Jew Fagin – a horrible compound of all sorts of villainy, who teaches 'the young idea' the handicraft of picking pockets, under pretence of having an amusing game of play with the boys – the author designates as 'the merry old gentleman'! Everybody knows what this grisly old hyena-bearded wretch really is, and everybody is struck with a sense of the ludicrous at the preposterous nature of the compliment. In this way the author avoids disgust – loses no point of his true meaning – and gains in the humour of his scene. . . .

It is observable that neither Hogarth nor Dickens ever portray a mere sentimental character, nor a morbid one. Perhaps the only exception in all Mr Dickens's works is his character of Monks which is a failure – a weak villain, whose pretended power is badly suggested by black scowlings and melodramatic night-wanderings in a dark cloak, and mouths-full of extravagant curses of devils, and pale-faced frothings at the mouth, and fits of convulsion. That the subtle old Fagin should have stood in any awe of him is incredible: even the worthy old gentleman, Mr Brownlow, is too many for him, and the stronger character of the two. In fact, this Monks is a pretender, and genuine characters only suit the hand of our author. A merely respectable and amiable common-place character is also pretty certain to present rather a wearisome, prosy appearance in the scenes of Hogarth and of Dickens. They are only admirable, and in their true element, when dealing with characters full of unscrupulous life, of genial humour, or of depravities and follies; or with characters of tragic force and heart-felt pathos.

Both have been accused of a predilection for the lower classes of society, from inability to portray those of the upper classes. Now, the predilection being admitted, the reason of this is chiefly attributable to the fact that there is little, if any, humour or genuine wit in the upper classes, where all *gusto* of that kind is polished away; and also to the fact that both of them have a direct moral purpose in view, viz., a desire to ameliorate the condition of the poorer classes by showing what society has made of them, or allowed them to become – and to continue.

Neither of these great artists ever concentrates the interest upon any one great character, nor even upon two or three, but while their principals are always highly finished, and sufficiently prominent on important occasions, they are nevertheless often used as centres of attraction, or as a means for progressively introducing numerous other characters which cross them at every turn, and circle them continually with a buzzing world of outward vitality.

There is a profusion and prodigality of character in the works of these two artists. A man, woman or child, cannot buy a morsel of pickled salmon, look at his shoe, or bring in a mug of ale; a solitary object cannot pass on the other side of the way; a boy cannot take a bite at a turnip or hold a horse; a by-stander cannot answer the simplest question; a dog cannot fall into a doze; a bird cannot whet his bill; a pony cannot have a peculiar nose, nor a pig one ear, but out peeps the first germ of 'a character'. Nor does the ruling tendency and seed-filled hand stop with such as these; for inanimate objects become endowed with consciousness and purpose, and mingle appropriately in the background of the scene. Sometimes they even act as principals, and efficient ones too, either for merriment and light comedy, genial beauty and sweetness, or the most squalid panto-mimists of the 'heavy line of business'. Lamb particularly notices what he terms 'the dumb rhetoric of the scenery – for tables, and chairs, and joint-stools in Hogarth are living and significant things', and Hazlitt very finely remarks on the drunken appearance of the houses in 'Gin Lane', which 'seem reeling and tumbling about in all directions, as if possessed with the frenzy of the scene'. All this is equally apparent in the works of Dickens. He not only animates furniture, and stocks and stones, or even the wind, with human purposes, but often gives them an individual rather than a merely generalized character. To his perceptions, old deserted broken-windowed houses grow crazed with 'staring each other out of countenance', and crook-backed chimney-pots in cowls turn slowly round with witch-like mutter and sad whispering moan, to cast a hollow spell upon the scene. The interior of the house of the miser Gride, where there stands an 'old grim clock, whose iron heart beats heavily within his dusty case', and where the tottering old clothes-presses 'slink away from the sight' into their melancholy murky corners – is a good instance of this; and yet equally so is the description of the house in which the Kenwigses, Newman Noggs and Crowl, have their abode, where the parlour of one of them is, perhaps, 'a thought dirtier' (no substantial difference being possible to the eye, the room is left to its own self-consciousness) than any of its neighbours, and in front of which 'the fowls who peck about the kennels, jerk their bodies hither and thither with a gait which none but town fowls are ever seen to adopt'. Nor can we forget the neighbourhood of 'Todgers's', where 'strange, solitary pumps were found hiding themselves, for the most part, in blind alleys, and keeping company with fire-ladders'. All these things are thoroughly characteristic of the condition and eccentricity of the inmates, and of the whole street, even as the beadle's pocket-book 'which, like himself, was corpulent'. A gloomy building, with chambers in it, up a yard, where it had so

little business to be, 'that one could scarcely help fancying it must have
run there when it was a young house, playing at hide-and-seek with
other houses, and have forgotten the way out again'; and the potatoes,
which, after Cratchit had blown the fire, 'bubbled up, and knocked
loudly at the saucepan lid, to be let out, and peeled' – these are among
the innumerable instances to which we have alluded. These descriptions and characteristics are always appropriate; and are not thrown
in for the mere sake of fun and farcicality. That they have, at the same
time, a marvellous tendency to be very amusing, may cause the
sceptic to shake his head at some of these opinions; the pleasurable
fact, nevertheless, is in any case quite as well for the author and his
readers.

Mr Dickens's characters, numerous as they are, have each the
roundness of individual reality combined with generalization – most
of them representing a class. The method by which he accomplishes
this is worth observing, and easily observed, as the process is always
the same. He never develops a character from within, but commences
by showing how the nature of the individual has *been* developed
externally by his whole life in the world. To this effect, he first paints
his portrait at full length; sometimes his dress before his face, and
most commonly his dress and demeanour. When he has done this to
his satisfaction, he *feels in* the man, and the first words that man utters
are the key-note of the character, and of all that he subsequently says
and does. The author's hand never wavers, never becomes untrue to
his creations. What they promise to be at first (except in the case of
Mr Pickwick, about whom the author evidently half-changed his
mind as he proceeded) they continue to the end.

That Mr Dickens often caricatures, has been said by many people;
but if they examined their own minds they would be very likely to
find that this opinion chiefly originated, and was supported by certain undoubted caricatures among the illustrations. . . .

Yet again, an objection of another kind – for Mr Dickens has quite
enough strength to be dealt with unsparingly. It has been previously
said, and the reasons for the opinion have been stated, that *Oliver
Twist*, the work which is open to most animadversion, has a beneficial
moral tendency, and is full of touches of tenderness, and pathos,
and of generous actions and emotions. The objection about to be
offered, is on the ground of justice being made vindictive and

ferocious, which, be it ever so just, has not a good moral tendency. This is said with reference to the death of a most detestable ruffian – Sikes – and it was important that no sympathy should, by any possibility, be induced towards so brutalized a villain. Such, however, is the case; for the author having taken over-elaborate and extreme pains to prevent it, the 'extremes meet'. After the brutal murder of the poor girl Nancy, the perpetrator hurries away, he knows not whither, and for days and nights wanders and lurks about fields and lanes, pursued by the most horrible phantoms and imaginings, amidst exhaustion from hunger and fatigue and a constant terror of discovery. Far from making a morbid hero of him, in any degree, or being guilty of the frequent error of late years, that of endeavouring to surround an atrocious villain with various romantic associations, Mr Dickens has shown the murderer in all his wretchedness, horror and utter bewilderment consequent on his crime. So far, the moral tendency is perfect. A climax is required; and here the author overshoots his aim. Perhaps, in reality, no retribution, on earth, could very well be too heavy for such a detestable wretch as Sikes to suffer; but we cannot bear to see so much. The author hunts down the victim, like a wild beast, through mud and mire, and darkness, and squalid ways, with crowds upon crowds, like hell-hounds gnashing and baying at his heels. Round the grim and desolate old edifice, the haunt of crime and desperation, rising out of a deep corrosion of filth, as if it had actually grown up, like a loathsome thing out of the huge ditch, round this darksome and hideous abode, in which the murderer has taken his last refuge with thrice-barred doors, the infuriate masses of human beings accumulate, throng upon throng, like surge after surge, all clamouring for his life. Hunted with tenfold more ferocity than ever was fox, or boar or midnight wolf – having scarce a chance of escape – certain to be torn and trampled amidst his mad, delirious struggles, into a miry death, when caught – our sympathies go with the hunted victim in this his last extremity. It is not 'Sikes, the murderer', of whom we think – it is no longer the 'criminal' in whose fate we are interested – it is for that one worn and haggard man with all the world against him – that one hunted human creature, with an infuriate host pursuing him, howling beneath for his blood, and striving to get at him, and tear him limb from limb. All his old friends turn away from him – look mutely at him, and aghast – and down below, all round the hideous house, in hideous torch-light boils up the surging sea of a maddened multitude. His throwing up the window, and menacing the crowd below, had a grandeur in it – it rouses the blood – we menace with him – we would cast off from his plunging horse, that man who 'showed such fury', and offered money for his blood – from the bridge, that man who incessantly called out that the hunted victim would escape from the back – and we would have silenced the voice from the broken wall, that screamed away the last chance of a desperate man for his life. In truth, we would fairly have had him escape – whether to die in the black moat below, or alone in some dark and far-off field. We are with this hunted-down human being, brought home to our sympathies by the extremity of his distress; and we are *not* with the howling mass of demons outside. The only human beings we recognize are the victim – and his dog.

If the above feeling be at all shared by general readers, it will then appear that Mr Dickens has defeated his own aim, and made the criminal an object of sympathy, owing to the vindictive fury with which he is pursued to his destruction, because the author was so anxious to cut him off from *all* sympathy. The over-strained terror of the intended moral, has thus an immoral tendency. It may, perhaps, be argued that as the sympathy only commences at that very point, where the detestable individual is lost sight of, and verges into the generalized impression of a human being in the last degree of distress – there is no sympathy *given* to the *criminal*? The moment he is again thought of as the murderer Sikes, the sympathy vanishes; and therefore no harm is done. This would present very fair grounds for a tough metaphysical contest, but it is never good to throw the feelings into a puzzle, and we prefer to enter a direct protest against the accumulation of vindictive ferocity with which this criminal is pursued, as tending to defeat the unquestionable moral aim of the author.

Certainly not the highest, but certainly the most prominent characteristic of Mr Dickens's mind, is his humour. His works furnish a constant commentary on the distinction between wit and humour; for of sheer wit, either in remark or repartee, there is scarcely an instance in any of his volumes, while of humour there is a fullness and *gusto* in every page, which would be searched for in vain to such an extent, among all other authors. It is not meant that there are not several authors, and of the present time, who might equal the best points of humour in any of Mr Dickens's works, but there is no author who can 'keep it up' as he does; no author who can fill page after page with unfailing and irresistible humour, the only 'relief' to which, if any, shall be fun, and the exuberance of animal spirits – a surplus vitality like that which makes him, after signing his name to a letter or note, give such a whirl of flourishing, which resembles an immense capering over a thing done, before he is 'off' to something else. . . .

So far as a single epithet can convey an impression of the operation of his genius, it may be said that Mr Dickens is an *instinctive* writer. His best things are suddenly revealed to him; he does not search for them in his mind; they come to him; they break suddenly upon him, or drop out of his pen. He does not tax his brain, he transcribes what he finds writing itself there. This is the peculiar prerogative of a true creative genius. His instincts manifest themselves in many subtle ways, both seriously and humorously. Thus: when Lord Verisopht, the foolish young nobleman who has wasted his life in all sorts of utter folly, is on his way to fight a duel which is fated to close his career, it is said that 'the fields, trees, gardens, hedges, everything looked very beautiful; the young man scarcely seemed to have noticed them before, though he had passed the same objects a thousand times'. The whole of the passage should be carefully read: it is deeply pathetic. It is as though Nature, whom the foolish young lord had forgotten during his whole life, had gently touched his heart, reminding him that he should take one look at her, thus to refine and sweeten with her balmy tenderness and truth the last brief interval of his existence. It should also be remarked that the author calls him 'the young man' this once only – previously he was always a scion of nobility – now he is simplified for the grave. No hard study and head-work, no skill in art and writing, can produce such things as these. They are the result of a fine instinct identifying itself with given characters, circumstances, and elementary principles. When Sikes hurries homeward with the determination of destroying the girl, it is said that he 'never once turned his head to the right or left, or raised his eyes to the sky, or lowered them to the ground, but *looked straight before him*', and this will be found to be the invariable characteristic of every fierce physical resolution in advancing towards its object. Before he commits the murder he extinguishes the candle though it is scarce daybreak, but says that 'there is light enough for what he has *got to do*' – the tone of expression suggesting a vague notion of some excuse to himself for his contemplated ferocity, as if it were a sort of duty. Allusion may also be made to his not daring to turn his back towards the dead body all the time he remained in the room; to the circumstances attending his flight, and to the conduct of his dog. . . .

Of a humorous kind the instances are too abundant even to be referred to; one or two only shall be noticed. After Mr Mould, the undertaker, has discoursed about certain prospective funerals, and looked out of his window into a churchyard 'with an artist's eye to the graves', while sipping a tumbler of punch, he covers his head with a silk handkerchief, and takes *a little nap* – an expressive comment upon an undertaker's composed and pleasant idea of death. When 'poor Tom Pinch' has lighted old Martin Chuzzlewit with a lanthorn across the fields at night, he immediately blows out the candle for his own return – prompted, as it seems, by a sensation of no sort of consequence being attached to himself, and unconsciously influenced by the strictly frugal habits of his employer. In speaking to Jonas of a little surprise he contemplated for his daughters (who evidently knew all about it,) Mr Pecksniff lowers his voice, and treads on tip-toe, though his daughters are two miles off; his sensation actually coinciding with an imaginative impulse derived from his own lie. . . .

The death of Nelly, and her burial, are well-known scenes, of deep pathetic beauty.

A curious circumstance is observable in a great portion of the scenes last mentioned, which it *is* possible may have been the result of harmonious accident, and the author not even subsequently fully conscious of it. It is that they are written in blank verse, of irregular metre and rhythms, which Southey and Shelley, and some other poets have occasionally adopted. The passage properly divided into lines, will stand thus:

Nelly's Funeral

And now the bell – the bell
She had so often heard by night and day,
  And listened to with solemn pleasure,
    E'en as a living voice –
Rung its remorseless toll for her,
So young, so beautiful, so good.

Decrepit age, and vigorous life,
And blooming youth, and helpless infancy,
Poured forth – on crutches, in the pride of strength
    And health, in the full blush
  Of promise, the mere dawn of life –
To gather round her tomb. Old men were there,
      Whose eyes were dim
      And senses failing –
Grandames, who might have died ten years ago,
And still been old – the deaf, the blind, the lame,
    The palsied,
The living dead in many shapes and forms,
To see the closing of this early grave.
    What was the death it would shut in,
To that which still could crawl and creep above it!
Along the crowded path they bore her now;
    Pure as the new-fallen snow
  That covered it; whose day on earth
    Had been as fleeting.
Under that porch, where she had sat when Heaven
In mercy brought her to that peaceful spot,
  She passed again, and the old church
  Received her in its quiet shade.

Throughout the whole of the above only two unimportant words
have been omitted – *in* and *its*; 'grandames' has been substituted for
'grandmothers', and 'e'en' for 'almost'. All that remains is exactly
as in the original, not a single word transposed, and the punctuation
the same to a comma. The brief homily that concludes the funeral is
profoundly beautiful.

Oh! it is hard to take to heart
The lesson that such deaths will teach,
    But let no man reject it,
  For it is one that all must learn,
And is a mighty, universal Truth.
When Death strikes down the innocent and young,
For every fragile form from which he lets

> The parting spirit free,
>   A hundred virtues rise,
> In shapes of mercy, charity, and love,
>   To walk the world and bless it.
>   Of every tear
> That sorrowing mortals shed on such green graves,
> Some good is born, some gentler nature comes.

Not a word of the original is changed in the above quotation, which is worthy of the best passages in Wordsworth, and thus, meeting on the common ground of a deeply truthful sentiment, the two most unlike men in the literature of the country are brought into the closest approximation.

(13–68)

Charles Dickens

Preface to the first edition of *Martin Chuzzlewit*   1844

I attach a few preliminary words to *The Life and Adventures of Martin Chuzzlewit*: more because I am unwilling to depart from any custom which has become endeared to me by having prevailed between myself and my readers on former occasions of the same kind, than because I have anything particular to say.

Like a troublesome guest who lingers in the Hall after he has taken leave, I cannot help loitering on the threshold of my book, though those two words, THE END: anticipated through twenty months, yet sorrowfully penned at last: stare at me, in capitals, from the printed page.

I set out, on this journey which is now concluded; with the design of exhibiting, in various aspects, the commonest of all the vices. It is almost needless to add, that the commoner the folly or the crime which an author endeavours to illustrate, the greater is the risk he runs of being charged with exaggeration; for, as no man ever yet recognized an imitation of himself, no man will admit the correctness of a sketch in which his own character is delineated, however faithfully.

But, although Mr Pecksniff will by no means concede to me, that Mr Pecksniff is natural; I am consoled by finding him keenly susceptible of the truthfulness of Mrs Gamp. And though Mrs Gamp considers her own portrait to be quite unlike, and altogether out of drawing, she recompenses me for the severity of her criticism on that failure, by awarding unbounded praise to the picture of Mrs Prig.

I have endeavoured in the progress of this Tale, to resist the temptation of the current Monthly Number, and to keep a steadier eye upon the general purpose and design. With this object in view, I have put a strong constraint upon myself from time to time, in many places; and I hope the story is the better for it, now.

At any rate, if my readers have derived but half the pleasure and interest from its perusal, which its composition has afforded me, I have ample reason to be gratified. And if they part from any of my visionary friends, with the least tinge of that reluctance and regret which I feel in dismissing them; my success has been complete, indeed.

Charles Dickens

from a letter to Mrs Dickens   2 December 1844

The little book [*The Chimes*] is now, as far as I am concerned, all ready. One cut of Doyle's and one of Leech's I found so unlike my ideas, that I had them both to breakfast with me this morning, and with that winning manner which you know of, got them with the highest good humour to do both afresh. They are now hard at it. Stanfield's readiness, delight, wonder at my being pleased with what he has done is delicious. Mac's frontispiece is charming. The book is quite splendid; the expenses will be very great, I have no doubt.

Anybody who has heard it has been moved in the most extraordinary manner. Forster read it (for dramatic purposes) to A'Beckett. He cried so much and so painfully, that Forster didn't know whether to go on or stop; and he called next day to say that any expression of his feeling was beyond his power. But that he believed it, and felt it to be – I won't say what. . . .

P.S.   If you had seen Macready last night, undisguisedly sobbing and crying on the sofa as I read, you would have felt, as I did, what a thing it is to have power.

Charles Dickens

from a letter to John Forster 25 July 1846

I will now go on to give you an outline of my immediate intentions in reference to *Dombey*. I design to show Mr D. with that one idea of the Son taking firmer and firmer possession of him, and swelling and bloating his pride to a prodigious extent. As the boy begins to grow up, I shall show him quite impatient for his getting on, and urging his masters to set him great tasks, and the like. But the natural affection of the boy will turn towards the despised sister; and I purpose showing her learning all sorts of things, of her own application and determination, to assist him in his lessons: and helping him always. When the boy is about ten years old (in the fourth number), he will be taken ill, and will die; and when he is ill, and when he is dying, I mean to make him turn always for refuge to the sister still, and keep the stern affection of the father at a distance. So Mr Dombey – for all his greatness, and for all his devotion to the child – will find himself at arms' length from him even then; and will see that his love and confidence are all bestowed upon his sister, whom Mr Dombey has used – and so has the boy himself too, for that matter – as a mere convenience and handle to him. The death of the boy is a death-blow, of course, to all the father's schemes and cherished hopes; and 'Dombey and Son', as Miss Tox will say at the end of the number, 'is a Daughter after all.' . . . From that time, I purpose changing his feeling of indifference and uneasiness towards his daughter into a positive hatred. For he will always remember how the boy had his arm round her neck when he was dying, and whispered to her, and would take things only from her hand, and never thought of him. . . . At the same time I shall, change *her* feeling towards *him* for one of a greater desire to love him and to be loved by him; engendered in her compassion for his loss, and her love for the dead boy whom, in his way, he loved so well too. So I mean to carry the story on, through all the branches and off-shoots and meanderings that come up; and through the decay and downfall of the house, and the bankruptcy of Dombey, and all the rest of it; when his only staff and treasure, and his unknown Good Genius always, will be this rejected daughter, who will come out better than any son at last, and whose love for him, when discovered and understood, will be his bitterest reproach. For the struggle with himself, which goes on in all such obstinate natures, will have ended then; and the sense of his injustice, which you may be sure has never quitted him, will have at last a gentler office than that of only making him more harshly unjust. ... I rely very much on Susan Nipper grown up, and acting partly as Florence's maid, and partly as a kind of companion to her, for a strong character throughout the book. I also rely on the Toodles, and on Polly, who, like everybody else, will be found by Mr Dombey to have gone over to his daughter and become attached to her. This is what cooks call 'the stock of the soup'. All kinds of things will be added to it, of course.

Charles Dickens

from a letter to John Forster   30 August 1846

Invention, thank God, seems the easiest thing in the world; and I seem to have such a preposterous sense of the ridiculous, after this long rest [it was now over two years since the close of *Chuzzlewit*], as to be constantly requiring to restrain myself from launching into extravagances in the height of my enjoyment. But the difficulty of going at what I call a rapid pace, is prodigious: it is almost an impossibility. I suppose this is partly the effect of two years' ease, and partly of the absence of streets and numbers of figures. I can't express how much I want these. It seems as if they supplied something to my brain, which it cannot bear, when busy, to lose. For a week or a fortnight I can write prodigiously in a retired place (as at Broadstairs), and a day in London sets me up again and starts me. But the toil and labour of writing, day after day, without that magic lantern, is *immense*!! I don't say this at all in low spirits, for we are perfectly comfortable here, and I like the place very much indeed, and the people are even more friendly and fond of me than they were in Genoa. I only mention it as a curious fact, which I have never had an opportunity of finding out before. *My* figures seem disposed to stagnate without crowds about them.

Francis, Lord Jeffrey

from a letter to Dickens   January 1847

Oh, my dear, dear Dickens! what a No. 5 you have now given us! I
have so cried and sobbed over it last night, and again this morning;
and felt my heart purified by those tears, and blessed and loved you
for making me shed them; and I never can bless and love you enough.
Since the divine Nelly was found dead on her humble couch, beneath
the snow and the ivy, there has been nothing like the actual dying of
that sweet Paul, in the summer sunshine of that lofty room. And the
long vista that leads us so gently and sadly, and yet so gracefully and
winningly, to the plain consummation! Every trait so true, and so
touching – and yet lightened by the fearless innocence which goes
playfully to the brink of the grave, and that pure affection which bears
the unstained spirit, on its soft and lambent flash, at once to its source
in eternity.

Charles Dickens

Preface to the cheap edition of *The Pickwick Papers*   1847

An author who has much to communicate under his head, and expects
to have it attended to, may be compared to a man who takes his
friend by the button at a Theatre Door, and seeks to entertain him
with a personal gossip before he goes in to the play.

Nevertheless, as Prefaces, though seldom read, are continually
written, no doubt for the behoof of that so richly and so disinterestedly
endowed personage, Posterity (who will come into an immense fortune), I add my legacy to the general remembrance; the rather as ten
years have elapsed since *The Pickwick Papers* appeared in a completed
form, and nearly twelve since the first monthly part was published.

It was observed, in the Preface to the original Edition, that they were
designed for the introduction of diverting characters and incidents;
that no ingenuity of plot was attempted, or even at that time considered very feasible by the author in connexion with the desultory

mode of publication adopted; and that the machinery of the Club, proving cumbrous in the management, was gradually abandoned as the work progressed. Although, on one of these points, experience and study have since taught me something, and I could perhaps wish now that these chapters were strung together on a stronger thread of general interest, still, what they are they were designed to be.

In the course of the last dozen years, I have seen various accounts of the origin of these Pickwick Papers; which have, at all events, possessed – for me – the charm of perfect novelty. As I may infer, from the occasional appearance of such histories, that my readers have an interest in the matter, I will relate how they came into existence.

I was a young man of three-and-twenty, when the present publishers, attracted by some pieces I was as that time writing in the *Morning Chronicle* newspaper (of which one series had lately been collected and published in two volumes, illustrated by my esteemed friend Mr George Cruikshank), waited upon me to propose a something that should be published in shilling numbers – then only known to me, or I believe, to anybody else, by a dim recollection of certain interminable novels in that form, which used, some five-and-twenty years ago, to be carried about the country by pedlars, and over some of which I remember to have shed innumerable tears, before I served my apprenticeship to Life.

When I opened my door in Furnival's Inn to the managing partner who represented the firm, I recognized in him the person from whose hand I had bought, two or three years previously, and whom I had never seen before or since, my first copy of the Magazine in which my first effusion – dropped stealthily one evening at twilight, with fear and trembling, into a dark letter-box, in a dark office, up a dark court in Fleet Street – appeared in all the glory of print; on which occasion by-the-by – how well I recollect it! – I walked down to Westminster Hall, and turned into it for half-an-hour, because my eyes were so dimmed with joy and pride, that they could not bear the street, and were not fit to be seen there. I told my visitor of the coincidence, which we both hailed as a good omen; and so fell to business.

The idea propounded to me was that the monthly something should be a vehicle for certain plates to be executed by Mr Seymour, and there was a notion, either on the part of that admirable humourous artist, or of my visitor (I forget which), that a 'Nimrod Club', the members of which were to go out shooting, fishing, and so forth, and getting themselves into difficulties through their want of dexterity, would be the best means of introducing these. I objected, on consideration, that although born and partly bred in the country I was no great sportsman, except in regard of all kinds of locomotion; that the idea was not novel, and had been already much used; that it would be infinitely better for the plates to arise naturally out of the text; and that I should like to take my own way, with a freer range of English scenes and people, and was afraid I should ultimately do so in any case, whatever course I might prescribe to myself at starting. My views being deferred to, I thought of Mr Pickwick, and wrote the first number; from the proof sheets of which, Mr Seymour made his drawing of the Club, and that happy portrait of its founder, by which he is always recognized, and which may be said to have made him a reality. I connected Mr Pickwick with a club, because of the original suggestion, and I put in Mr Winkle expressly for the use of Mr Seymour. We started with a number of twenty-four pages instead of thirty-two, and four illustrations in lieu of a couple. Mr Seymour's sudden and lamented death before the second number was published, brought about a quick decision upon a point already in agitation; the number became one of thirty-two pages with two illustrations, and remained so to the end. My friends told me it was a low, cheap form of publication, by which I should ruin all my rising hopes; and how right my friends turned out to be, everybody now knows.

'Boz', my signature in the *Morning Chronicle*, appended to the monthly cover of this book, and retained long afterwards, was the nickname of a pet child, a younger brother, whom I had dubbed Moses, in honour of the Vicar of Wakefield; which being facetiously pronounced through the nose, became Boses, and being shortened, became Boz. 'Boz' was a very familiar household word to me, long before I was an author, and so I came to adopt it.

It has been observed of Mr Pickwick, that there is a decided change in his character, as these pages proceed, and that he becomes more good and more sensible. I do not think this change will appear forced or unnatural to my readers, if they will reflect that in real life the peculiarities and oddities of a man who has anything whimsical about him, generally impress us first, and that it is not until we are better acquainted with him that we usually begin to look below these super-ficial traits, and to know the better part of him.

Lest there should be any well-intentioned persons who do not perceive the difference (as some such could not, when *Old Mortality* was newly published) between religion and the cant of religion, piety and the pretence of piety, a humble reverence for the great truths of scripture and an audacious and offensive obtrusion of its letter and not its spirit in the commonest dissensions and meanest affairs of life, to the extraordinary confusion of ignorant minds, let them understand that it is always the latter, and never the former, which is satirized here. Further, that the latter is here satirized as being, according to all experience, inconsistent with the former, impossible of union with it, and one of the most evil and mischievous falsehoods existent in society – whether it establish its headquarters, for the time being, in Exeter Hall, or Ebenezer Chapel, or both. It may appear unnecessary to offer a word of observation on so plain a head. But it is never out of season to protest against that coarse familiarity with sacred things which is busy on the lip, and idle in the heart; or against the confounding of Christianity with any class of persons who, in the words of Swift, have just enough religion to make them hate, and not enough to make them love, one another.

I have found it curious and interesting, looking over the sheets of this reprint, to mark what important social improvements have taken place about us, almost imperceptibly, even since they were originally written. The license of Counsel, and the degree to which Juries are ingeniously bewildered, are yet susceptible of moderation; while an improvement in the mode of conducting Parliamentary Elections (especially for counties) is still within the bounds of possibility. But legal reforms have pared the claws of Messrs Dodson and Fogg; a spirit of self-respect, mutual forbearance, education and co-operation, for such good ends, has diffused itself among their clerks; places far apart are brought together, to the present convenience and advan-tage of the Public, and to the certain destruction, in time, of a host of petty jealousies, blindnesses and prejudices, by which the Public alone have always been the sufferers; the laws relating to imprison-ment for debt are altered; and the Fleet Prison is pulled down!

With such a retrospect, extending through so short a period, I shall cherish the hope that every volume of this Edition will afford me an opportunity of recording the extermination of some wrong or abuse set forth in it. Who knows, but by the time the series reaches its conclusion, it may be discovered that there are even magistrates in town and country, who should be taught to shake hands every day with Commonsense and Justice; that even Poor Laws may have mercy on the weak, the aged and unfortunate; that Schools, on the broad principles of Christianity are the best adornment for the length and breadth of this civilized land; that Prison doors should be barred on the outside, no less heavily and carefully than they are barred within; that the universal diffusion of common means of decency and health is as much the right of the poorest of the poor, as it is indispensable to the safety of the rich, and of the State; that a few petty boards and bodies – less than drops in the great ocean of humanity, which roars around them – are not to let loose Fever and Consumption on God's creatures at their will, or always to keep their little fiddles going, for a Dance of Death!

And that Cheap Literature is not behind-hand with the Age, but holds its place, and strives to do its duty, I trust the series in itself may help much worthy company to show.

Charles Dickens

from a letter to John Forster   21 December 1847

Note from Jeffrey this morning, who won't believe (positively refuses) that Edith is Carker's mistress. What do you think of a kind of inverted Maid's Tragedy, and a tremendous scene of her undeceiving Carker, and giving him to know that she never meant that?

Charles Dickens

from the Preface to the cheap edition of *Nicholas Nickleby*   1848

This story was begun, within a few months after the publication of the completed *Pickwick Papers*. There were, then, a good many cheap Yorkshire schools in existence. There are very few now.

Of the monstrous neglect of education in England, and the disregard of it by the State as a means of forming good or bad citizens, and miserable or happy men, private schools long afforded a notable example. Although any man who had proved his unfitness for any other occupation in life, was free, without examination or qualification, to open a school anywhere; although preparation for the functions he undertook, was required in the surgeon who assisted to bring a boy into the world, or might one day assist, perhaps, to send him out of it; in the chemist, the attorney, the butcher, the baker, the candlestick maker; the whole round of crafts and trades, the schoolmaster excepted; and although schoolmasters, as a race, were the blockheads and imposters who might naturally be expected to spring from such a state of things, and to flourish in it; these Yorkshire schoolmasters were the lowest and most rotten round in the whole ladder. Traders in the avarice, indifference or imbecility of parents, and the helplessness of children; ignorant, sordid, brutal men, to whom few considerate persons would have entrusted the board and lodging of a horse or a dog; they formed the worthy cornerstone of a structure which, for absurdity and a magnificent high-minded *laissez-aller* neglect, has rarely been exceeded in the world.

We hear sometimes of an action for damages against the unqualified medical practitioner, who has deformed a broken limb in pretending to heal it. But, what of the hundreds of thousands of minds that have been deformed for ever by the incapable pettifoggers who have pretended to form them!

I make mention of the race, as of the Yorkshire schoolmasters, in the past tense. Though it has not yet finally disappeared, it is dwindling daily. A long day's work remains to be done about us in the way of education, Heaven knows; but great improvements and facilities towards the attainment of a good one, have been furnished, of late years.

I cannot call to mind, now, how I came to hear about Yorkshire schools when I was a not very robust child, sitting in bye-places near Rochester Castle, with a head full of Partridge, Strap, Tom Pipes and Sancho Panza; but I know that my first impressions of them were picked up at that time, and that they were somehow or other connected with a suppurated abscess that some boy had come home with, in consequence of his Yorkshire guide, philosopher, and friend, having ripped it open with an inky pen knife. The impression made upon me, however made, never left me. I was always curious about Yorkshire schools – fell, long afterwards and at sundry times, into the way of hearing more about them – at last, having an audience, resolved to write about them.

With that intent I went down into Yorkshire before I began this book, in very severe winter time which is pretty faithfully described herein. As I wanted to see a schoolmaster or two, and was fore-warned that those gentlemen might, in their modesty, be shy of receiving a visit from the author of the *Pickwick Papers*, I consulted with a professional friend who had a Yorkshire connexion, and with whom I concerted a pious fraud. He gave me some letters of intro-duction, in the name, I think, of my travelling companion; they bore reference to a supposititious little boy who had been left with a widowed mother who didn't know what to do with him; the poor lady had thought, as a means of thawing the tardy compassion of her relations in his behalf, of sending him to a Yorkshire school; I was the poor lady's friend, travelling that way; and if the recipient of the letter could inform me of a school in his neighbourhood, the writer would be very much obliged.

I went to several places in that part of the country where I under-stood the schools to be most plentifully sprinkled, and had no occa-sion to deliver a letter until I came to a certain town which shall be nameless. The person to whom it was addressed, was not at home; but he came down at night, through the snow, to the inn where I was staying. It was after dinner; and he needed little persuasion to sit down by the fire in a warm corner, and take his share of the wine that was on the table.

I am afraid he is dead now. I recollect he was a jovial, ruddy, broad-faced man; that we got acquainted directly; and that we talked on all kinds of subjects, except the school, which he showed a great anxiety to avoid. 'Was there any large school near?' I asked him, in reference to the letter. 'Oh yes,' he said; 'there was a pratty big 'un.' 'Was it a good one?' I asked. 'Ey!' he said, 'it was as good as anoother; that was a' a matther of opinion'; and fell to looking at the fire, staring round the room, and whistling a little. On my reverting to some other topic that we had been discussing, he recovered immediately; but, though I tried him again and again, I never approached the question of the school, even if he were in the middle of a laugh, without observing that his countenance fell, and that he became uncomfortable. At last, when we had passed a couple of hours or so, very agreeably, he suddenly took up his hat, and leaning over the table and looking me full in the face, said, in a low voice: 'Weel Misther, we've been vara pleasant toogather, and ar'll spak' my moind tiv'ee. Dinnot let the weedur send her lattle boy to yan o' our school-measthers, while there's a harse to hoold in a' Lunnun, or a gootther to lie asleep in. Ar wouldn't mak' ill words amang my neeburs, and ar speak tiv'ee quiet loike. But I'm dom'd if ar can gang to bed and not tellee, for weedur's sak', to keep the lattle boy from a' sike scoondrels while there's a harse to hoold in a' Lunnun, or a gootther to lie asleep in!' Repeating these words with great heartiness, and with a solemnity on his jolly face that made it look twice as large as before, he shook hands and went away. I never saw him afterwards, but I sometimes imagine that I descry a faint reflection of him in John Browdie.

Charles Dickens

Preface to the cheap edition of *The Old Curiosity Shop*　1848

In April 1840, I issued the first number of a new weekly publication, price threepence, called *Master Humphrey's Clock*. It was intended to consist, for the most part, of detached papers, but was to include one continuous story, to be resumed, from time to time, with such indefinite intervals between each period of resumption as might best accord with the exigencies and capabilities of the proposed Miscellany.

The first chapter of this tale appeared in the fourth number of *Master Humphrey's Clock*, when I had already been made uneasy by the desultory character of that work, and when, I believe, my readers had thoroughly participated in the feeling. The commencement of a story was a great satisfaction to me, and I had reason to believe that my readers participated in this feeling too. Hence, being pledged to some interruptions and some pursuit of the original design, I set cheerfully about disentangling myself from those impediments as fast as I could; and, that done, from that time until its completion *The Old Curiosity Shop* was written and published from week to week, in weekly parts.

When the story was finished, that it might be freed from the incumbrance of associations and interruptions with which it had no kind of concern, I caused the few sheets of *Master Humphrey's Clock*, which had been printed in connexion with it, to be cancelled; and, like the unfinished tale of the windy night and the notary in The Sentimental Journey, they became the property of the trunkmaker and the butterman. I was especially unwilling, I confess, to enrich those respectable trades with the opening paper of the abandoned design, in which Master Humphrey described himself and his manner of life. Though I now affect to make the confession philosophically, as referring to a by-gone emotion, I am conscious that my pen winces a little even while I write these words. But it was done, and wisely done, and *Master Humphrey's Clock*, as originally constructed, became one of the lost books of the earth – which, we all know, are far more precious than any that can be read for love or money.

In reference to the tale itself, I desire to say very little here. The many friends it won me, and the many hearts it turned to me when they were full of private sorrow, invest it with an interest, in my mind, which is not a public one, and the rightful place of which appears to be 'a more removed ground'.

I will merely observe, therefore, that, in writing the book, I had it always in my fancy to surround the lonely figure of the child with grotesque and wild, but not impossible, companions, and to gather about her innocent face and pure intentions, associates as strange and uncongenial as the grim objects that are about her bed when her history is first foreshadowed.

Master Humphrey (before his devotion to the trunk and butter business) was originally supposed to be the narrator of the story. As it was constructed from the beginning, however, with a view to separate publication when completed, his demise has not involved the necessity of any alteration.

I have a mournful pride in one recollection associated with 'little Nell'. While she was yet upon her wanderings, not then concluded, there appeared in a literary journal, an essay of which she was the principal theme, so earnestly, so eloquently and tenderly appreciative

of her, and of all her shadowy kith and kin, that it would have been
insensibility in me, if I could have read it without an unusual glow of
pleasure and encouragement. Long afterwards, and when I had come
to know him well, and to see him, stout of heart, going slowly down
into his grave, I knew the writer of that essay to be Thomas Hood.

Charles Dickens

Preface to the first edition of *Dombey and Son*   1848

I cannot forgo my usual opportunity of saying farewell to my
readers in this greeting-place, though I have only to acknowledge the
unbounded warmth and earnestness of their sympathy in every stage
of the journey we have just concluded.

  If any of them have felt a sorrow in one of the principal incidents
on which this fiction turns, I hope it may be a sorrow of that sort
which endears the sharers in it, one to another. This is not unselfish
in me. I may claim to have felt it, at least as much as anybody else;
and I would fain be remembered kindly for my part in the experience.

Charles Dickens

from a letter to John Forster   10 July 1849

I really think I have done it [the introduction of the autobiographical
fragment into *David Copperfield*] ingeniously, and with a very complicated interweaving of truth and fiction.

Charles Dickens

from a letter to M. de Cerjat   29 December 1849

I had previously observed much of what you say about the poor girls.
In all you suggest with so much feeling about their return to virtue
being cruelly cut off, I concur with a sore heart. I have been turning

it over in my mind for some time, and hope, in the history of Little Em'ly (who *must* fall – there is no hope for her), to put it before the thoughts of people in a new and pathetic way, and perhaps to do some good.

Charles Dickens

from 'A Preliminary Word', *Household Words*, no. 1   30 March 1850

The name that we have chosen for this publication expresses, generally, the desire we have at heart in originating it.

We aspire to live in the Household affections, and to be numbered among the Household thoughts, of our readers. We hope to be the comrade and friend of many thousands of people, of both sexes, and of all ages and conditions, on whose faces we may never look. We seek to bring into innumerable homes, from the stirring world around us, the knowledge of many social wonders, good and evil, that are not calculated to render any of us less ardently perservering in ourselves, less tolerant of one another, less faithful in the progress of mankind, less thankful for the privilege of living in this summer-dawn of time.

No mere utilitarian spirit, no iron binding of the mind to grim realities, will give a harsh tone to our Household Words. In the bosoms of the young and old, of the well-to-do and of the poor, we would tenderly cherish that light of Fancy which is inherent in the human breast; which, according to its nurture, burns with an inspiring flame, or sinks into a sullen glare, but which (or woe betide that day!) can never be extinguished. To show to all, that in all familiar things, even in those which are repellant on the surface, there is Romance enough, if we will find it out: – to teach the hardest workers at this whirling wheel of toil, that their lot is not necessarily a moody, brutal fact, excluded from the sympathies and graces of imagination; to bring the greater and the lesser in degree, together, upon that wide field, and mutually dispose them to a better acquaintance and a kinder understanding – is one main object of our Household Words.

The mightier inventions of this age are not, to our thinking, all material, but have a kind of soul in their stupendous bodies which may find expression in Household Words. The traveller whom we accompany on his railroad or his steamboat journey, may gain, we hope, some compensation for incidents which these later generations have outlived, in new associations with the Power that bears him onward; with the habitations and the ways of life of crowds of his fellow creatures among whom he passes like the wind; even with the towering chimneys he may see, spurting out fire and smoke upon the prospect. The swart giants, Slaves of the Lamp of Knowledge, have their thousand and one tales, no less than the Genii of the East; and these, in all their wild, grotesque and fanciful aspects, in all their many phases of endurance, in all their many moving lessons of compassion and consideration, we design to tell.

Charles Dickens

from a speech to the Metropolitan Sanitary Association   10 May 1851

And I can honestly declare tonight, that all the use I have since made of my eyes – or nose (*laughter*) – that all the information I have since been able to acquire through any of my senses, has strengthened me in the conviction that Searching Sanitary Reform must precede all other social remedies (*cheers*), and that even Education and Religion can do nothing where they are most needed, until the way is paved for their ministrations by Cleanliness and Decency. (*Hear.*) Am I singular in this opinion? You will remember the speech made this night by the Right Reverend Prelate, which no true Sanitary Reformer can have heard without emotion. (*Hear, hear.*) What avails it to send a Missionary to me, a miserable man or woman living in a foetid Court where every sense bestowed upon me for my delight becomes a torment, and every minute of my life is new mire added to the heap under which I lie degraded? To what natural feeling within me is he to address himself? What ancient chord within me can he hope to touch? Is it my remembrance of my children? It is a remembrance of distortion and decay, scrofula and fever? Would he address himself to my hopes of immortality? I am so surrounded by material filth that my Soul cannot rise to the contemplation of an immaterial existence? Or, if I be a miserable child, born and nurtured in the same wretched place, and tempted, in these better times, to the Ragged School, what can the few hours' teaching that I get there do for me, against the noxious, constant, ever-renewed lesson of my whole existence. (*Hear, hear.*) But, give me my first glimpse of Heaven through a little of its light and air – give me water – help me to be clean – lighten this heavy atmosphere in which my spirit droops and I become the indifferent and callous creature that you see me – gently and kindly take the body of my dead relation out of the small room where I grow to be so familiar with the awful change that even *its* sanctity is lost to me – and, Teacher, then I'll hear, you know how willingly, of Him whose thoughts were so much with the Poor, and who had compassion for all human sorrow! (*Applause.*)

Charles Dickens

from a speech at Birmingham   6 January 1853

To the great compact phalanx of the people, by whose industry, perserverance and intelligence, and their result in money-wealth such places as Birmingham, and many others like it, have arisen – to that great centre of support, that comprehensive experience and that beating heart – Literature has turned happily from individual patrons, sometimes munificent, often sordid, always few, and has found there at once its highest purpose, its natural range of action and its best reward. (*Loud cheers.*) Therefore it is right also, as it seems to me, not only that Literature should receive honour here, but that it should render honour too, remembering that if it has undoubtedly done good to Birmingham, Birmingham has undoubtedly done good to it. (*Cheers.*) From the shame of the purchased dedication, from the scurrilous and dirty work of Grub Street, from the dependent seat on sufference at my Lord Duke's table today, and from the sponging-house and Marshalsea tomorrow, from that venality which, by a fine moral retribution, has degraded statesmen even to a greater extent than authors, because the statesman entertained a low belief in the universality of corruption, while the author yielded only to the dire necessity of his calling – from all such evils the people have set Literature free.

And my creed in the exercise of that profession is, that Literature cannot be too faithful to the people in return – cannot too ardently advocate the cause of their advancement, happiness and prosperity. (*Loud applause.*) Gentlemen, I have heard it sometimes said – and what is worse, as expressing something more cold-blooded, I have sometimes seen it written – that Literature has suffered by this change, that it has degenerated by being made cheaper. I have not found that to be the case. (*Cries of 'Hear, hear.'*) Nor do I believe that you have made that discovery either. But let a good book in these 'bad times' be made accessible – even upon an abstruse and difficult subject – and my life upon it, it shall be extensively bought, read and well considered. (*Cheers.*)

Charles Dickens

Preface to the first edition of *Bleak House* 1853

A few months ago, on a public occasion, a Chancery Judge had the kindness to inform me, as one of a company of some hundred and fifty men and women not labouring under any suspicions of lunacy, that the Court of Chancery, though the shining subject of much popular prejudice (at which point I thought the Judge's eye had a cast in my direction), was almost immaculate. There had been, he admitted, a trivial blemish or so in its rate of progress, but this was exaggerated, and had been entirely owing to the 'parsimony of the public'; which guilty public, it appeared, had been until lately bent in the most determined manner on by no means enlarging the number of Chancery Judges appointed – I believe by Richard the Second, but any other King will do as well.

This seemed to me too profound a joke to be inserted in the body of this book, or I should have restored it to Conversation Kenge or to Mr Vholes, with one or other of whom I think it must have originated. In such mouths I might have coupled it with an apt quotation from one of Shakespeare's Sonnets:

> My nature is subdued
> To what it works in, like the dyer's hand:
> Pity me then, and wish I were renew'd!

But as it is wholesome that the parsimonious public should know what has been doing, and still is doing, in this connexion, I mention here that everything set forth in these pages concerning the Court of Chancery is substantially true, and within the truth. The case of Gridley is in no essential altered from one of actual occurrence, made public by a disinterested person who was professionally acquainted with the whole of the monstrous wrong from beginning to end. At the present moment there is a suit before the Court which was commenced nearly twenty years ago; in which from thirty to forty counsel have been known to appear at one time; in which costs have been incurred to the amount of seventy thousand pounds; which is *a friendly suit*; and which is (I am assured) no nearer to its termination now than when it was begun. There is another well-known suit in Chancery, not yet decided, which was commenced before the close of the last century, and in which more than double the amount of seventy thousand pounds has been swallowed up in costs. If I wanted other authorities for Jarndyce and Jarndyce, I could rain them on these pages, to the shame of – a parsimonious public.

There is only one other point on which I offer a word of remark. The possibility of what is called Spontaneous Combustion has been denied since the death of Mr Krook; and my good friend Mr Lewes (quite mistaken, as he soon found, in supposing the thing to have been abandoned by all authorities) published some ingenious letters to me at the time when that event was chronicled, arguing that Spontaneous Combustion could not possibly be. I have no need to observe that I do not wilfully or negligently mislead my readers, and that before I wrote that description I took pains to investigate the subject. There are about thirty cases on record, of which the most famous, that of the Countess Cornelia de Bandi Cesenate was minutely investigated and described by Giuseppe Bianchini, prebendary of Verona, otherwise distinguished in letters, who published an account of it at Verona, in 1731, which he afterwards republished at Rome. The appearances beyond all rational doubt observed in that case, are the appearances observed in Mr Krook's case. The next most famous instance happened at Rheims, six years earlier; and the historian in that case is Le Cat, one of the most renowned surgeons produced by France. The subject was a woman, whose husband was ignorantly convicted of having murdered her; but, on solemn appeal to a higher court, he was acquitted, because it was shown upon the evidence that she had died the death to which this name of Spontaneous Combustion is given. I do not think it necessary to add to these notable facts, and that general reference to the authorities which will be found at page 329, the recorded opinions and experiences of distinguished medical professors, French, English and Scotch, in more modern days; contenting myself with observing, that I shall not abandon the facts until there shall have been a considerable Spontaneous Combustion of the testimony on which human occurrences are usually received.

In *Bleak House*, I have purposely dwelt upon the romantic side of familiar things. I believe I have never had so many readers as in this book. May we meet again!

John Stuart Mill

from a letter to his wife   March 1854

That creature Dickens, whose last story, *Bleak House*, I found accidentally at the London Library the other day and took home and read, much the worst of his things, and the only one of them I altogether dislike, has the vulgar impudence in this thing to ridicule rights of women. It is done too in the very vulgarest way, just the style in which vulgar men used to ridicule 'learned ladies' as neglecting their children and household.

Charles Dickens

from a letter to the Hon. Mrs Richard Watson   1 November 1854

Why I found myself so 'used up' after *Hard Times* I scarcely know, perhaps because I intended to do nothing in that way for a year, when the idea laid hold of me by the throat in a very violent manner, and because the compression and close condensation necessary for that disjointed form of publication gave me perpetual trouble.

Charles Dickens

from a letter to Charles Knight   30 January 1855

My satire [in *Hard Times*] is against those who see figures and averages and nothing else – the representatives of the wickedest and most enormous vice of this time – the men who, through long years to come, will do more to damage the real useful truths of political economy than I could do (if I tried) in my whole life; the addled heads who would take the average of cold in the Crimea during twelve months as a reason for clothing a soldier in nankeens on a night when he would be frozen to death in fur, and who would comfort the labourer in travelling twelve miles a day to and from his work, by telling him that the average distance of one inhabited place from another in the whole area of England, is not more than four miles.

Charles Dickens

from a letter to Mrs Maria Winter   3 April 1855

I hold my inventive capacity on the stern condition that it must master my whole life, often have complete possession of me, make its own demands upon me, and sometimes for months together put everything else away from me. If I had not known long ago that my place could never be held unless I were at any moment ready to devote myself to it entirely, I should have dropped out of it very soon. All this I can hardly expect you to understand – or the restlessness or waywardness of an author's mind. You have never seen it before you, or lived with it or had occasion to think or care about it, and you cannot have the necessary consideration for it. 'It is only half an hour' – 'it is only an afternoon' – 'it is only an evening' – people say to me over and over again – but they don't know that it is impossible to command one's self sometimes to any stipulated and set disposal of five minutes – or that the mere consciousness of an engagement will sometimes worry a whole day. These are the penalties paid for writing books. Whoever is devoted to an Art must be content to deliver himself wholly up to it, and to find his recompense in it.

Charles Dickens

from a letter to W. C. Macready   4 October 1855

As to the suffrage, I have lost hope even in the ballot. We appear to me to have proved the failure of representative institutions without an educated and advanced people to support them. What with teaching people to 'keep in their stations', what with bringing up the soul and body of the land to be a good child, or to go to the beershop, to go a-poaching and go to the devil; what with having no such thing as a middle class (for though we are perpetually bragging of it as our safety, it is nothing but a poor fringe on the mantle of the upper); what with flunkyism, toadyism, letting the most contemptible lords come in for all manner of places, reading *The Court Circular* for the New Testament, I do reluctantly believe that the English people are habitually consenting parties to the miserable imbecility into which we have fallen, *and never will help themselves out of it*. Who is to do it, if anybody is, God knows. But at present we are on the downhill road to being conquered, and the people WILL be content to bear it, sing 'Rule Britannia', and WILL NOT be saved.

In No. 3 of my new book [*Little Dorrit*] I have been blowing off a little of indignant steam which would otherwise blow me up, and with God's leave I shall walk in the same all the days of my life; but I have no present political faith or hope – not a grain.

Charles Dickens

from a letter to John Forster ?December 1855

I don't quite apprehend what you mean by my overrating the strength of the feeling of five-and-twenty years ago. If you mean of my own feeling, and will only think what the desperate intensity of my nature is, and that this began when I was Charley's age; that it excluded every other idea from my mind for four years, at a time of life when four years are equal to four times four; and that I went at it with a determination to overcome all the difficulties, which fairly lifted me up into that newspaper life, and floated me away over a hundred men's heads: then you are wrong, because nothing can exaggerate that. I have positively stood amazed at myself ever since! – And so I suffered, and so worked, and so beat and hammered away at the maddest romances that ever got into any boy's head and stayed there, that to see the mere cause of it all, now, loosens my hold upon myself. Without for a moment sincerely believing that it would have been better if we had never got separated, I cannot see the occasion of so much emotion as I should see anyone else. No one can imagine in the most distant degree what pain the recollection gave me in *Copperfield*. And, just as I can never open that book as I open any other book, I cannot see the face (even at four-and-forty), or hear the voice, without going wandering away over the ashes of all that youth and hope in the wildest manner.

George Eliot (anonymously)

from 'The Natural History of German Life', *Westminster Review*, vol. 66 July 1856

The thing for mankind to know is, not what are the motives and influences which the moralist thinks *ought* to act on the labourer or the artisan, but what are the motives and influences which *do* act on him. We want to be taught to feel, not for the heroic artisan or the sentimental peasant, but for the peasant in all his coarse apathy, and the artisan in all his suspicious selfishness.

We have one great novelist who is gifted with the utmost power of rendering the external traits of our town population; and if he could give us their psychological character – their conceptions of life, and their emotions – with the same truth as their idiom and manners, his books would be the greatest contribution Art has ever made to the awakening of social sympathies. But while he can copy Mrs Plornish's colloquial style with the delicate accuracy of a sun-picture, while there is the same startling inspiration in his description of the gestures and phrases of 'Boots', as in the speeches of Shakespeare's mobs or numbskulls, he scarcely ever passes from the humorous and external to the emotional and tragic, without becoming as transcendent in his unreality as he was a moment before in his artistic truth-

fulness. But for the precious salt of his humour, which compels him
to reproduce external traits that serve, in some degree, as a corrective
to his frequently false psychology, his preternaturally virtuous poor
children and artisans, his melodramatic boatmen and courtesans,
would be as noxious as Eugène Sue's idealized proletaires in encouraging the miserable fallacy that high morality and refined sentiment can
grow out of harsh social relations, ignorance and want; or that the
working classes are in a condition to enter at once into a millennial
state of *altruism*, wherein everyone is caring for everyone else, and
no one for himself.
(54–5)

Hippolyte Taine

from 'Charles Dickens, son talent et ses oeuvres', *Revue des Deux
Mondes* February 1856 (later incorporated into his *History of
English Literature*, book 5, chapter 1, 1871, translated by
H. Van Laun)

The difference between a madman and a man of genius is not very
great. Napoleon, who knew men, said so to Esquirol. The same faculty
leads us to glory or throws us into a cell in a lunatic asylum. It is
visionary imagination which forges the phantoms of the madman and
creates the personages of an artist, and the classifications serving for the
first may serve for the second. The imagination of Dickens is like that
of monomaniacs. To plunge oneself into an idea, to be absorbed by it,
to see nothing else, to repeat it under a hundred forms, to enlarge it, to
carry it, thus enlarged, to the eye of the spectator, to dazzle and over-
whelm him with it, to stamp it upon him so firmly and deeply that he
can never again tear it from his memory – these are the great features
of this imagination and style. In this, *David Copperfield* is a masterpiece. Never did objects remain more visible and present to the memory of a reader than those which he describes. The old house, the
parlour, the kitchen, Peggotty's boat, and above all the school play-
ground, are interiors whose relief, energy and precision are unequalled.
Dickens has the passion and patience of the painters of his nation; he
reckons his details one by one, notes the various hues of the old tree-

trunks; sees the dilapidated cask, the greenish and broken flagstones, the chinks of the damp walls; he distinguishes the strange smells which rise from them; marks the size of the mildewed spots, reads the names of the scholars carved on the door, and dwells on the form of the letters. And this minute description has nothing cold about it: if it is thus detailed, it is because the contemplation was intense; it proves its passion by its exactness. We felt this passion without accounting for it; suddenly we find it at the end of a page; the boldness of the style renders it visible, and the violence of the phrase attests the violence of the impression. Excessive metaphors bring before the mind grotesque fancies. We feel ourselves beset by extravagant visions. Mr Mell takes his flute, and blows on it, says Copperfield, 'until I almost thought he would gradually blow his whole being into the large hole at the top, and ooze away at the keys' (chapter 5). Tom Pinch, disabused at last, discovers that his master Pecksniff is a hypocritical rogue. He 'had so long been used to steep the Pecksniff of his fancy in his tea, and spread him out upon his toast, and take him as a relish with his beer, that he made but a poor breakfast on the first morning after his expulsion' (*Martin Chuzzlewit*, chapter 36). We think of Hoffmann's fanastic tales; we are arrested by a fixed idea, and our head begins to ache. These eccentricities are in the style of sickness rather than of health.

Therefore Dickens is admirable in depicting hallucinations. We see that he feels himself those of his characters, that he is engrossed by their ideas, that he enters into their madness. As an Englishman and a moralist, he has described remorse frequently. Perhaps it may be said that he makes a scarecrow of it, and that an artist is wrong to transform himself into an assistant of the policeman and the preacher. What of that? The portrait of Jonas Chuzzlewit is so terrible, that we may pardon it for being useful. Jonas, leaving his chamber secretly, has treacherously murdered his enemy, and thinks henceforth to breathe in peace; but the recollection of the murder gradually disorganizes his mind, like poison. He is no longer able to control his ideas; they bear him on with the fury of a terrified horse. He is for ever thinking, and shuddering as he thinks, of the room where people believed he slept. He sees this room, counts the tiles of the floor, pictures the long folds of the dark curtains, the tumbled bed, the door at which someone might have knocked. The more he wants

to escape from this vision, the more he is immersed in it; it is a burning abyss in which he rolls, struggling, with cries and sweats of
agony. He fancies himself lying in his bed, as he ought to be, and an
instant after he sees himself there. He fears this other self. The dream
is so vivid, that he is not sure that he is not in London. 'He became in
a manner his own ghost and phantom.' And this imaginary being,
like a mirror, only redoubles before his conscience the image of
assassination and punishment. He returns, and shuffles, with pale face,
to the door of his chamber. He, a man of business, a man of figures,
a coarse machine of positive reasoning, has become as fanciful as a
nervous woman. 'He stole on, to the door, on tiptoe, as if he dreaded
to disturb his own imaginary rest.' At the moment when he turns the
key in the lock, 'a monstrous fear beset his mind. What if the murdered
man were there before him.' At last he enters, and tumbles into bed,
burnt up with fever. 'He buried himself beneath the blankets', so as
to try not to see 'that infernal room'; he sees it more clearly still. The
rustling of the clothes, the buzz of an insect, the beatings of his heart,
all cry to him Murderer! His mind fixed with 'an agony of listening'
on the door, he ends by thinking that people open it; he hears it
creak. His senses are distorted; he dares not mistrust them, he dares no
longer believe in them; and in this nightmare, in which drowned
reason leaves nothing but a chaos of hideous forms, he finds no reality
but the incessant burden of his convulsive despair. Thenceforth all his
thoughts, dangers, the whole world disappears for him in 'the one
dread question only', 'When would they find the body in the wood?'
He forces himself to distract his thoughts from this; they remain
stamped and glued to it; they hold him to it as by a chain of iron. He
continually figures himself going into the wood, 'going softly about
it and about it among the leaves, approaching it nearer and nearer
through a gap in the boughs, and startling the very flies, that were
thickly sprinkled all over it, like heaps of dried currants'. His mind
was fixed and fastened on the discovery, for intelligence of which he
listened intently to every cry and shout; listened when anyone came
in, or went out; watched from the window the people who passed
up and down the street.' At the same time, he has ever before his eyes
that corpse 'lying alone in the wood'; 'he was for ever showing and
presenting it, as it were, to every creature whom he saw. 'Look here!
do you know of this? Is it found? Do you suspect *me*?' If he had been

condemned to bear the body in his arms, and lay it down for recognition at the feet of every one he met, it could not have been more constantly with him, or a cause of more monotonous and dismal occupation than it was in this state of his mind' (chapter 47).

Jonas is on the verge of madness. There are other characters quite mad. Dickens has drawn three or four portraits of madmen, very funny at first sight, but so true that they are in reality horrible. It needed an imagination like his, irregular, excessive, capable of fixed ideas, to exhibit the derangements of reason. Two especially there are, which make us laugh, and which make us shudder. Augustus, a gloomy maniac, who is on the point of marrying Miss Pecksniff; and poor Mr Dick, partly an idiot, partly a monomaniac, who lives with Miss Trotwood. To understand these sudden exaltations, these unforeseen gloominesses, these incredible summersaults of perverted sensitiveness; to reproduce these hiatuses of thought, these interruptions of reasoning, this recurrence of a word, always the same, which breaks in upon a phrase attempted and overturns renascent reason; to see the stupid smile, the vacant look, the foolish and uneasy physiognomy of these haggard old children who painfully grope about from one idea to another, and stumble at every step on the threshold of the truth which they cannot attain, is a faculty which Hoffmann alone has possessed in an equal degree with Dickens. The play of these shattered reasons is like the creaking of a door on its rusty hinges; it makes one sick to hear it. We find in it, if we like, a discordant burst of laughter, but we discover still more easily a groan and a lamentation, and we are terrified to gauge the lucidity, strangeness, exaltation, violence of imagination which has produced such creations, which has carried them on and sustained them unbendingly to the end, and which found itself in its proper sphere in imitating and producing their irrationality. . . .

Take away the grotesque characters, who are only introduced to fill up and to excite laughter, and you will find that all Dickens's characters belong to two classes – people who have feelings and emotions, and people who have none. He contrasts the souls which nature creates with those which society deforms. One of his last novels, *Hard Times*, is an abstract of all the rest. He there exalts instinct above reason, intuition of heart above positive knowledge; he attacks education built on statistics, figures and facts; overwhelms the positive and mercantile spirit with misfortune and ridicule; and the aristocrat; falls foul of manufacturing towns, combats the pride, harshness, selfishness of the merchant towns of smoke and mud, which fetter the body in an artificial atmosphere, and the mind in a factitious existence. He seeks out poor artisans, mountebanks, a foundling, and crushes beneath their common sense, generosity, delicacy, courage and gentleness, the false science, false happiness and false virtue of the rich and powerful who despise them. He satirizes oppressive society; mourns over oppressed nature; and his elegiac genius, like his satirical genius, finds ready to his hand in the English world around him, the sphere which it needs for its development. . . .

In reality, the novels of Dickens can all be reduced to one phrase, to wit: Be good, and love; there is genuine joy only in the emotions of the heart; sensibility is the whole man. Leave science to the wise, pride to the nobles, luxury to the rich; have compassion on humble wretchedness; the smallest and most despised being may in himself be worth as much as thousands of the powerful and the proud. Take care not to bruise the delicate souls which flourish in all conditions, under all costumes, in all ages. Believe that humanity, pity, forgiveness, are the finest things in man; believe that intimacy, expansion, tenderness, tears, are the sweetest things in the world. To live is nothing; to be powerful, learned, illustrious, is little; to be useful is not enough. He alone has lived and is a man who has wept at the remembrance of a kind action which he himself has performed or received.

Charles Dickens

from a letter to John Forster   ?1856

I don't see the practicability of making the History of a Self-Tormentor, with which I took great pains, a written narrative. But I do see the possibility of making it a chapter by itself, which might enable me to dispense with the necessity of the turned commas. Do you think that would be better? I have no doubt that a great part of Fielding's reason for the introduced story, and Smollett's, also, was, that it is sometimes really impossible to present, in a full book, the idea it contains (which yet it may be on all accounts desirable to present), without supposing the reader to be possessed of almost as much romantic allowance as would put him on a level with the writer. In Miss Wade I had an idea, which I thought a new one, of making the introduced story so fit into surroundings impossible of separation from the main story, as to make the blood of the book circulate through both. But I can only suppose, from what you say, that I have not exactly succeeded in this.

Charles Dickens

Preface to the first edition of *Little Dorrit*　1857

I have been occupied with this story, during many working hours of two years. I must have been very ill employed, if I could not leave its merits and demerits as a whole, to express themselves on its being read as a whole. But, as it is not unreasonable to suppose that I may have held its various threads with a more continuous attention than anyone else can have given to them during its desultory publication, it is not unreasonable to ask that the weaving may be looked at in its completed state, and with the pattern finished.

If I might offer any apology for so exaggerated a fiction as the Barnacles and the Circumlocution Office, I would seek it in the common experience of an Englishman, without presuming to mention the unimportant fact of my having done that violence to good manners, in the days of a Russian war, and of a Court of Inquiry at Chelsea. If I might make so bold as to defend that extravagant conception, Mr Merdle, I would hint that it originated after the Railroad-share epoch, in the times of a certain Irish bank, and of one or two other equally laudable enterprises. If I were to plead anything in mitigation of the preposterous fancy that a bad design will sometimes claim to be a good and an expressly religious design, it would be the curious coincidence that it has been brought to its climax in these pages, in the days of the public examination of late Directors of a Royal British Bank. But, I submit myself to suffer judgement to go by default on all these counts, if need be, and to accept the assurance (on good authority) that nothing like them was ever known in this land.

Some of my readers may have an interest in being informed whether or no any portions of the Marshalsea Prison are yet standing. I did not know, myself, until the sixth of this present month, when I went to look. I found the outer front courtyard, often mentioned in this story, metamorphosed into a butter-shop; and I then almost gave up every brick of the jail for lost. Wandering, however, down a certain adjacent 'Angel Court, leading to Bermondsey', I came to 'Marshalsea Place': the houses in which I recognized, not only as the great block of the former prison, but as preserving the rooms that arose in my mind's-eye when I became Little Dorrit's biographer. The smallest boy I ever conversed with, carrying the largest baby I ever saw, offered a supernaturally intelligent explanation of the locality in its old uses, and was very nearly correct. How this young Newton (for such I judge him to be) came by his information, I don't know; he was a quarter of a century too young to know anything about it of himself. I pointed to the window of the room where Little Dorrit was born, and where her father lived so long, and asked him what was the name of the lodger who tenanted that apartment at present? He said 'Tom Pythick'. I asked him who was Tom Pythick? and he said, 'Joe Pythick's uncle.'

A little further on, I found the older and smaller wall, which used to enclose the pent-up inner prison where nobody was put, except for ceremony. But, whosoever goes in Marshalsea Place, turning out of Angel Court, leading to Bermondsey, will find his feet on the very paving-stones of the extinct Marshalsea Jail; will see its narrow yard to the right and to the left, very little altered if at all, except that the walls were lowered when the place got free; will look upon the rooms in which the debtors lived; and will stand among the crowding ghosts of many miserable years.

In the Preface to *Bleak House* I remarked that I had never had so many readers. In the Preface to its next successor, *Little Dorrit*, I have still to repeat the same words. Deeply sensible of the affection and confidence that have grown up between us, I add to this Preface, as I added to that, May we meet again!

Sir James Fitzjames Stephen (anonymously)

from 'The License of Modern Novelists', *Edinburgh Review*, vol. 106
July 1857

Little Dorrit is not one of the most pleasing or interesting of Mr
Dickens's novels. The plot is singularly cumbrous and confused –
the characters rather uninteresting – and the style often strained to
excess. We are not however tempted, by the comparative inferiority
of this production of a great novelist, to forget the indisputable
merits of Mr Dickens. Even those who dislike a good deal of the
society to which he introduces his readers, and who are not accustomed to the language of his personages, must readily acknowledge
that he has described modern English low life with infinite humour
and fidelity, but without coarseness. He has caught and reproduced
that native wit which is heard to perfection in the repartees of an
English crowd: and though his path has often lain through scenes of
gloom, and poverty, and wretchedness, and guilt, he leaves behind
him a spirit of tenderness and humanity which does honour to his
heart. We wish he had dealt as fairly and kindly with the upper classes
of society as he has with the lower; and that he had more liberally
portrayed those manly, disinterested and energetic qualities which
make up the character of an English gentleman. Acute observer as he
is, it is to be regretted that he should have mistaken a Lord Decimus
for the type of an English statesman, or Mr Tite Barnacle for a fair
specimen of a public servant. But in truth we cannot recall any single
character in his novels, intended to belong to the higher ranks of
English life, who is drawn with the slightest approach to truth or
probability. His injustice to the institutions of English society is,
however, even more flagrant than his animosity to particular classes
in that society. The rich and the great are commonly held up to
ridicule for their folly, or to hatred for their selfishness. But the
institutions of the country, the laws, the administration, in a word the
government under which we live, are regarded and described by Mr
Dickens as all that is most odious and absurd in despotism or in
oligarchy. In every new novel he selects one or two of the popular
cries of the day, to serve as seasoning to the dish which he sets before
his readers. It may be the Poor Laws, or Imprisonment for Debt, or

the Court of Chancery, or the harshness of Mill-owners, or the stupidity of Parliament, or the inefficiency of the Government, or the insolence of District Visitors, or the observance of Sunday, or Mammon-worship, or whatever else you please. He is equally familiar with all these subjects. If there was a popular cry against the management of a hospital, he would no doubt write a novel on a month's warning about the ignorance and temerity with which surgical operations are performed; and if his lot had been cast in the days when it was fashionable to call the English law the perfection of reason, he would probably have published monthly denunciations of Lord Mansfield's Judgement in *Perrin* v. *Blake*, in blue covers adorned with curious hieroglyphics, intended to represent springing uses, executory devises, and contingent remainders. We recommend him to draw the materials of his next work from Dr Hassall on the Adulteration of Food, or the Report on Scotch Lunatics. Even the catastrophe in *Little Dorrit* is evidently borrowed from the recent fall of houses in Tottenham Court Road, which happens to have appeared in the newspapers at a convenient moment. . . .

It is not a little curious to consider what qualifications a man ought to possess before he could, with any kind of propriety, hold the language Mr Dickens sometimes holds about the various departments of social life. Scott, we all know, was a lawyer and an antiquarian. Sir Edward Lytton has distinguished himself in political life, and his books contain unquestionable evidence of a considerable amount of classical and historical reading. Mr Thackeray hardly ever steps beyond those regions of society and literature which he has carefully explored. But in Mr Dickens's voluminous works, we do not remember to have found many traces of these solid acquirements; and we must be permitted to say, for it is no reflection on any man out of the legal profession, that his notions of law, which occupy so large a space in his books, are precisely those of an attorney's clerk. He knows what arrest for debt is, he knows how affidavits are sworn. He knows the physiognomy of courts of justice, and he has heard that Chancery suits sometimes last forty years; though he seems not to have the remotest notion that there is any difference between suits for the administration of estates and suits for the settlement of disputed rights, and that the delay which is an abuse in the one case, is inevitable in the other. The greatest of our statesmen, lawyers and philosophers would shrink from delivering any trenchant and unqualified opinion upon so complicated and obscure a subject as the merits of the whole administrative Government of the empire. To Mr Dickens the question presents no such difficulty. He stumbles upon the happy phrase of 'the Circumlocution Office' as an impersonation of the Government; strikes out the brilliant thought, repeated just ten times in twenty-three lines, that whereas ordinary people want to know how to do their business, the whole art of Government lies in discovering 'how not to do it'; and with these somewhat unmeaning phrases he proceeds to describe, in a light and playful tone, the government of his country.

Everybody has read chapter 10 of *Little Dorrit*; but we are not equally sure that everybody has asked himself what it really means. It means, if it means anything, that the result of the British constitution, of our boasted freedom, of parliamentary representation, and of all we possess, is to give us the worst government on the face of the earth – the clatter of a mill grinding no corn, the stroke of an engine drawing no water. . . .

The Circumlocution Office forms one of the standing decorations of the work in which it is depicted. The cover of the book is adorned by a picture, representing, amongst other things, Britannia in a bath-chair, drawn by a set of effete idiots, an old woman, a worn-out cripple in a military uniform, and a supercilious young dandy, who buries the head of his cane in his moustaches. The chair is pushed on behind by six men in foolscaps, who are followed by a crowd of all ages and both sexes, intended, we presume, to represent that universal system of jobbing and favouritism, which was introduced into the public service by Sir Charles Trevelyan and Sir Stafford Northcote, shortly before the time when Mr Dickens began his novel. The spirit of the whole book is the same. The Circumlocution Office is constantly introduced as a splendid example of all that is base and stupid. Messrs Tite Barnacle and Stiltstalking are uniformly put forward as the representatives of the twenty or thirty permanent under-secretaries and heads of departments, by whom so large a portion of the public affairs is conducted, and every species of meanness, folly and vulgarity is laid to their charge.

It is difficult to extract the specific accusations which Mr Dickens means to bring against the Government; but we take the principal counts in his indictment to be, that the business of the country is done very slowly and very ill; that inventors and projectors of improvements are treated with insolent neglect; and that the Government is conducted by, and for the interest of, a few aristocratic families, whose whole public life is a constant career of personal jobs. Most men will consider these rather serious charges.

But the burlesque manner and extravagant language in which they are made are at once Mr Dickens's shield and his sword. 'How can you suppose', he might say, 'that I mean any harm by such representations as these? I am neither a lawyer nor a politician; but I take a fling at the subjects of the day, just in order to give my writings a little local colour, and a little temporary piquancy.' Probably enough this is the true account of the matter, and it forms the very gravamen of our complaint. Men of the world may laugh at books which represent all who govern as fools, knaves, hypocrites and dawdling tyrants. They know very well that such language is meant to be understood subject to modifications; but the poor and uneducated take such words in their natural and undiluted strength, and draw from them practical conclusions of corresponding importance; whilst the young and inexperienced are led to think far too meanly of the various careers which the organization of society places before them, and to waste in premature cynicism and self-satisfied indolence some of the most precious opportunities which life affords.

It is not necessary to discuss the justice of Mr Dickens's charges, but it is so much the fashion of the day to speak with unmeasured contempt both of the honesty and ability of the executive government, that we will lay before our readers a few considerations upon the general character of the public service, and upon the principles which ought to govern discussions as to its merits.

The first question which presents itself is: What is the standard of comparison? It would require a knowledge of the details of the administrative system of other countries, which we do not pretend to possess, to institute a detailed comparison between their governments and our own. But without entering on so vast a subject, we think that any person of ordinary fairness and information may easily satisfy himself that the British Government need not shrink from a comparison, either with the transactions of mercantile men, or with those of great public companies. Mr Dickens, and many other denouncers of the incapacity of the Government, have long indulged in the pleasant habit of looking only at one side of the subject. They read in the newspapers of the failures, the prejudices and the stupidity of the executive; and it never occurs to them that they do not hear of the cases in which the official mechanism works well. We must have some notion of the magnitude of the operations which the Government has to conduct, before we can duly estimate the immense weight of the testimony in its favour, which is conveyed by the absence of complaint on so many subjects. But the testimony so conveyed is positive as well as negative. Here, as in the other affairs of life, we must look at broad general results; and from them we may readily gather abundant confirmation of our position, that whatever defects may exist in the administration of public affairs, their general condition proves that much capacity and honesty is employed upon them.

If we turn, for example, to the management of the Revenue, is Mr Dickens aware of the complexity and extent of the operations which are involved in collecting, disbursing and accounting for something like sixty million pounds, and of making such arrangements with respect to it, that there shall always be enough in hand to make every payment at its appointed period, whatever irregularities may occur in the receipt of the income? Has he any notion of the variety and intricacy of the system of accounts which such transactions render necessary? If any mercantile firm had establishments at every seaport and in every considerable inland town; if they employed several thousand servants of different grades, in order to collect an income of the amount which we have mentioned; if they had to adjust their receipts and expenditure with such scrupulous exactness as to be able to pay away about half of their gross income to an immense body of mortgagees by quarterly instalments; and if all the business which these operations implied were conducted with the regularity of clockwork, without gross fraud, with little, if any, peculation, and with such method that the shareholders were annually furnished with accounts embracing the very minutest details of so enormous an outlay, how Mr Dickens would triumph in contrasting the businesslike habits of the middle classes with the blundering stupidity of the Circumlocution Office. Yet this is a literal and most scanty account of the occupations of one single department of that Circumlocution Office which is the subject of Mr Dickens's extreme contempt.

The administration of the British Empire has no doubt many shortcomings and imperfections, but are we seeking to perpetuate them or to remove them? If a man's house is not to his mind, he either builds a new one or repairs the old one; and whichever of the two operations may be the wisest, there can be no doubt that the English nation have in all constitutional reforms adopted the latter. There has never been at any period of our history a *tabula rasa*, like that which at the end of the last century existed for a time in France, on which homogeneous and consistent structures, either of law or government, could be raised. The consequence is, that our law is full of fictions, and our public offices full of intricacy. This is, no doubt, an evil to be remedied, but it is one which the present generation inherited, and which earlier generations considered a cheap price for the acquisition of political liberty.

Inefficiency, however, is only one of Mr Dickens's charges against the Government. Neglect of useful inventions and gross corruption are thrown in by way of makeweight. Thus in the following oracular conversation in *Little Dorrit*:

'What I mean to say is, that however this comes to be the
regular way of our government, it is its regular way. Have
you ever heard of any proprietor or inventor who failed to
find it all but inaccessible, and whom it did not discourage
and ill-treat?'
    'I cannot say I ever have.'
    'Have you ever known it to be beforehand in the adoption
of any useful thing? Ever known it to set an example of any
useful kind?'
    'I am a good deal older than my friend here,' said Mr
Meagles, and I'll answer that. *Never*.'
(chapter 10)

With respect to the first of these charges, we may mention one or two specific instances of the application of inventive power to the regular objects of administration. What does Mr Dickens think of the whole organization of the Post Office, and of the system of cheap postage, which was invented in this country, and has been adopted by almost every State on the Continent? Every branch of this establishment shows the greatest power of arrangement and contrivance – even mechanical contrivance. Mr Dickens can never tear a penny stamp from its fellows without having before his eyes an illustration of the watchful ingenuity of this branch of the Circumlocution Office. To take another special illustration: what does Mr Dickens say to the London Police? What he has said on the subject, anyone may see, by referring to *Household Words*, in which he will find the organization of the force praised in almost hyperbolical language. It is not a little characteristic that Mr Dickens should praise one branch of the Circumlocution Office in one of his organs, and shortly afterwards denounce the whole institution as a mass of clumsy stupidity in another. There can hardly be a more delicate administrative problem than that of protecting the persons and property without endangering the liberties of the public; and we should feel some curiosity to see a statement by Mr Dickens of the comparative value of the solutions arrived at by the French, the Russian and the English Governments.

As to the personal corruption, and the neglect of talent, which Mr Dickens charges against the Government of the country, we can only say that any careful observer of his method might have predicted with confidence that he would begin a novel on that subject within a very few months after the establishment of a system of competitive examinations for admission into the Civil Service. He seems, as a general rule, to get his first notions of an abuse from the discussions which accompany its removal, and begins to open his trenches and mount his batteries as soon as the place to be attacked has surrendered. This was his course with respect both to imprisonment for debt and to Chancery reform; but in the present instance, he has attacked an abuse which never existed to anything like the extent which he describes. A large proportion of the higher permanent offices of state have always been filled by men of great talent, whose promotion was owing to their talent. Did Mr Dickens ever hear that Mr Hallam, Mr William Hamilton, Mr Phillips, Sir George Barrow, Sir A. Spearman, Sir James Stephen, Sir C. Trevelyan, Mr Merivale, Mr Henry Taylor or Mr Greg are, or have been, members of the permanent Civil Service? Will he assert that these gentlemen were promoted simply from family motives, or that they are fairly represented by such a lump of folly and conceit as the Mr Stiltstalking of his story? Or, to take a single and well-known example, how does he account for the career of Mr Rowland Hill? A gentleman in a private and not very conspicuous position, writes a pamphlet recommending what amounted to a revolution in a most important department of the Government. Did the Circumlocution Office neglect him, traduce him, break his heart and ruin his fortune? They adopted his scheme, and gave him the leading share in carrying it out, and yet this is the Government which Mr Dickens declares to be a sworn foe to talent, and a systematic enemy to ingenuity.

(126–34)

Charles Dickens

'Curious Misprint in the *Edinburgh Review*', *Household Words*, vol. 16   1 August 1857

The *Edinburgh Review*, in an article in its last number, on 'The License of Modern Novelists', is angry with Mr Dickens and other modern novelists, for not confining themselves to the mere amusement of their readers, and for testifying in their works that they seriously feel the interest of true Englishmen in the welfare and honour of their country. To them should be left the making of easy occasional books for idle young gentlemen and ladies to take up and lay down on sofas, drawing-room tables and window-seats; to the *Edinburgh Review* should be reserved the settlement of all social and political questions, and the strangulation of all complainers. Mr Thackeray may write upon Snobs, but there must be none in the superior government departments. There is no positive objection to Mr Reade having to do, in a Platonic way, with a Scottish fishwoman or so; but he must by no means connect himself with Prison Discipline. That is the in-alienable property of official personages; and, until Mr Reade can show that he has so much a year, paid quarterly, for understanding (or not understanding) the subject, it is none of his, and it is impossible that he can be allowed to deal with it.

The name of Mr Dickens is at the head of this page, and the hand of Mr Dickens writes this paper. He will shelter himself under no affectation of being anyone else, in having a few words of earnest but temperate remonstrance with the *Edinburgh Review*, before pointing out its curious misprint. Temperate, for the honour of Literature; temperate, because of the great services which the *Edinburgh Review* has rendered in its time to good literature, and good government; temperate, in remembrance of the loving affection of Jeffrey, the friendship of Sidney Smith, and the faithful sympathy of both.

'The License of Modern Novelists' is a taking title. But it suggests another – 'The License of Modern Reviewers.' Mr Dickens's libel on the wonderfully exact and vigorous English government, which is always ready for any emergency, and which, as everybody knows, has never shown itself to be at all feeble at a pinch within the memory of men, is License in a novelist. Will the *Edinburgh Review* forgive Mr Dickens for taking the liberty to point out what is License in a Reviewer?

Even the catastrophe in *Little Dorrit*, is evidently borrowed from the recent fall of houses in Tottenham Court Road, which happens to have appeared in the newspapers at a convenient period.

Thus, the Reviewer. The Novelist begs to ask him whether there is no License in his writing those words and stating that assumption as a truth, when any man accustomed to the critical examination of a book cannot fail, attentively turning over the pages of *Little Dorrit*, to observe that that catastrophe is carefully prepared for from the very first presentation of the old house in the story; that when Rigaud, the man who is crushed by the fall of the house, first enters it (hundreds of pages before the end), he is beset by a mysterious fear and shuddering; that the rotten and crazy state of the house is laboriously kept before the reader, whenever the house is shown; that the way to the demolition of the man and the house together, is paved all through the book with a painful minuteness and reiterated care of preparation, the necessity of which (in order that the thread may be kept in the reader's mind through nearly two years), is one of the adverse incidents of that social form of publication? It may be nothing to the question that Mr Dickens now publicly declares, on his word and honour, that that catastrophe was written, was engraven on steel, was printed, had passed through the hands of compositors, readers for the press and pressmen, and was in type and in proof in the Printing House of Messrs Bradbury and Evans, before the accident in Tottenham Court Road occurred. But, it is much to the question that an honourable reviewer might have easily traced this out in the internal evidence of the book itself, before he stated, for a fact, what is utterly and entirely, in every particular and respect, untrue. More; if the Editor of the *Edinburgh Review* (unbending from the severe official duties of a blameless branch of the Circumlocution Office) had happened to condescend to cast his eye on the passage, and had referred even its mechanical probabilities and improbabilities to his publishers, those experienced gentlemen must have warned him that he was getting into danger; must have told him that on a comparison of dates, and with a reference to the number printed of *Little Dorrit*, with that very incident illustrated, and to the date of the publication of the completed book in a volume, they hardly perceived how Mr Dickens *could* have waited, with such a desperate Micawberism, for a fall of houses in Tottenham Court Road, to get him out of his difficulties, and yet could have come up to time with the needful punctuality. Does the *Edinburgh Review* make no charges at random? Does it live in a blue and yellow glass house, and yet throw such big stones over the roof? Will the licensed Reviewer apologize to the licensed Novelist, for *his* little Circumlocution Office? Will he 'examine the justice' of his own 'general charges', as well as Mr Dickens's? Will he apply his own words to himself, and come to the conclusion that it really is 'a little curious to consider what qualifications a man ought to possess, before he could with any kind of propriety hold this language'?

The Novelist now proceeds to the Reviewer's curious misprint. The Reviewer, in his laudation of the great official departments, and in his indignant denial of there being any trace of a Circumlocution Office to be detected among them all, begs to know, 'what does Mr Dickens think of the whole organization of the Post Office, and of the system of cheap Postage?' Taking St Martins-le-grand in tow, the wrathful Circumlocution steamer, puffing at Mr Dickens to crush him with all the weight of that first-rate vessel, demands, 'to take a single and well-known example, how does he account for the career of Mr Rowland Hill? A gentleman in a private and not very conspicuous position, writes a pamphlet recommending what amounted to a revolution in a most important department of the Government. Did the Circumlocution Office neglect him, traduce him, break his heart and ruin his fortune? They adopted his scheme, and gave him the leading share in carrying it out, and yet this is the government which Mr Dickens declares to be a sworn foe to talent, and a systematic enemy to ingenuity.'

The curious misprint, here, is the name of Mr Rowland Hill. Some other and perfectly different name must have been sent to the printer. Mr Rowland Hill!! Why, if Mr Rowland Hill were not, in toughness, a man of a hundred thousand; if he had not had in the struggles of his career a steadfastness of purpose overriding all sensitiveness, and steadily staring grim despair out of countenance, the Circumlocution Office would have made a dead man of him long and long ago. Mr Dickens among his other darings, dares to state, that the Circumlocution Office most heartily hated Mr Rowland Hill; that the Circumlocution Office most characteristically opposed him as long as opposition was in any way possible; that the Circumlocution Office would have been most devoutly glad if it could have harried Mr Rowland Hill's soul out of his body, and consigned him and his troublesome penny project to the grave together.

Mr Rowland Hill!! Now, see the impossibility of Mr Rowland Hill being the name which the *Edinburgh Review* sent to the printer. It may have relied on the forbearance of Mr Dickens towards living gentlemen, for his being mute on a mighty job that was jobbed in that very Post-Office when Mr Rowland Hill was *taboo* there, and it shall not rely upon his courtesy in vain: though there be breezes on the southern side of mid-Strand, London, in which the scent of it is yet strong on quarter-days. But, the *Edinburgh Review* never can have put up Mr Rowland Hill for the putting down of Mr Dickens's idle fiction of a Circumlocution Office. The 'license' would have been too great, the absurdity would have been too transparent, the Circumlocution Office dictation and partisanship would have been much too manifest.

'The Circumlocution Office adopted his scheme, and gave him the leading share in carrying it out.' The words are clearly not applicable to Mr Rowland Hill. Does the Reviewer remember the history of Mr Rowland Hill's scheme? The Novelist does, and will state it here, exactly; in spite of its being one of the eternal decrees that the Reviewer, in virtue of his license, shall know everything, and that the Novelist in virtue of *his* license, shall know nothing.

Mr Rowland Hill published his pamphlet on the establishment of one uniform penny postage, in the beginning of the year eighteen hundred and thirty-seven. Mr Wallace, member for Greenock, who had long been opposed to the then existing Post-Office system, moved for a Committee on the subject. Its appointment was opposed by the Government – or, let us say, the Circumlocution Office – but was afterwards conceded. Before that Committee, the Circumlocution Office and Mr Rowland Hill were perpetually in conflict on questions of fact; and it invariably turned out that Mr Rowland Hill was always right in his facts, and that the Circumlocution Office was always wrong. Even on so plain a point as the average number of letters at that very time passing through the Post Office, Mr Rowland Hill was right, and the Circumlocution Office was wrong.

Says the *Edinburgh Review*, in what it calls a 'general' way: 'The Circumlocution Office adopted his scheme.' Did it? Not just then, certainly; for, nothing whatever was done, arising out of the in-quiries of that Committee. But, it happened that the Whig Govern-ment afterwards came to be beaten on the Jamaica question, by reason of the Radicals voting against them. Sir Robert Peel was commanded to form a Government, but failed, in consequence of the difficulties that arose (our readers will remember them) about the Ladies of the Bedchamber. The Ladies of the Bedchamber brought the Whigs in again, and then the Radicals (being always for the destruction of everything) made it one of the conditions of their rendering their support to the new Whig Government that the penny-postage system should be adopted. This was two years after the appointment of the Committee: that is to say, in eighteen hundred and thirty-nine. The Circumlocution Office had, to that time, done nothing towards the penny postage, but oppose, delay, contradict and show itself uniformly wrong.

'They adopted his scheme, and gave him the leading share in carry-ing it out.' Of course they gave him the leading share in carrying it out, then, at the time when they adopted it, and took the credit and popularity of it? Not so. In eighteen hundred and thirty-nine, Mr Rowland Hill was appointed – not to the Post Office, but to the Treasury. Was he appointed to the Treasury to carry out his own scheme? No. He was appointed 'to advise'. In other words, to instruct the ignorant Circumlocution Office how to do without him, if it by any means could. On the tenth of January, eighteen hundred and forty, the penny-postage system was adopted. Then, of course, the

Circumlocution Òffice gave Mr Rowland Hill 'the leading share in carrying it out'? Not exactly, but it gave him the leading share in carrying himself out: for, in eighteen hundred and forty-two, it summarily dismissed Mr Rowland Hill altogether!

When the Circumlocution Office had come to that pass in its patriotic course, so much admired by the *Edinburgh Review*, of protecting and patronizing Mr Rowland Hill, whom any child who is not a Novelist can perceive to have been in its peculiar *protégé*; the public mind (always perverse) became much excited on the subject. Sir Thomas Wilde moved for another Committee. Circumlocution Office interposed. Nothing was done. The public subscribed and presented to Mr Rowland Hill, sixteen thousand pounds. Circumlocution Office remained true to itself and its functions. Did nothing; would do nothing. It was not until 1846, four years afterwards, that Mr Rowland Hill was appointed to a place in the Post Office. Was he appointed, even then, to the 'leading share in carrying out' his scheme? He was permitted to creep into the Post Office up the back stairs, through having a place created for him. This post of dignity and honour, this Circumlocution Office crown, was called 'Secretary to the Post-Master General'; there being already a Secretary to the Post Office, of whom the Circumlocution Office had declared, as its reason for dismissing Mr Rowland Hill, that his functions and Mr Rowland Hill's could not be made to harmonize.

They did not harmonize. They were in perpetual discord. Penny postage is but one reform of a number of Post Office reforms effected by Mr Rowland Hill; and these, for eight years longer, were thwarted and opposed by the Circumlocution Office, tooth and nail. It was not until eighteen hundred and fifty-four, fourteen years after the appointment of Mr Wallace's Committee, that Mr Rowland Hill (having, as was openly stated at the time, threatened to resign and to give his reasons for doing so), was at last made sole Secretary at the Post Office, and the inharmonious secretary (of whom no more shall be said) was otherwise disposed of. It is only since that date of eighteen hundred and fifty-four, that such reforms as the amalgamation of the general and district posts, the division of London into ten towns, the earlier delivery of letters all over the country, the book and parcels post, the increase of letter-receiving houses everywhere, and the management of the Post Office with a great increased efficiency, have been brought about by Mr Rowland Hill for the public benefit and the public convenience.

If the *Edinburgh Review* could seriously want to know 'how Mr Dickens accounts for the career of Mr Rowland Hill', Mr Dickens would account for it by his being a Birmingham man of such imperturbable steadiness and strength of purpose, that the Circulocution Office, by its utmost endeavours, very freely tried, could not weaken his determination, sharpen his razor or break his heart. By his being a man in whose behalf the public gallantry was roused, and the public spirit awakened. By his having a project, in its nature so plainly and directly tending to the immediate benefit of every man, woman and child in the State, that the Circumlocution Office could not blind them, though it could for a time cripple it. By his having thus, from the first to the last, made his way in spite of the Circumlocution Office, and dead against it as his natural enemy.

But, the name is evidently a curious misprint and an unfortunate mistake. The Novelist will await the Reviewer's correction of the press, and substitution of the right name.

Will the *Edinburgh Review* also take its next opportunity of manfully expressing its regret that in too distempered a zeal for the Circumlocution Office, it has been betrayed, as to that Tottenham Court Road assertion, into a hasty substitution of untruth for truth; the discredit of which, it might have saved itself, if it had been sufficiently cool and considerate to be simply just? It will, too possibly, have much to do by that time in championing its Circumlocution Office in new triumphs on the voyage out to India (God knows that the Novelist has his private as well as his public reasons for writing the foreboding with no triumphant heart!); but even party occupation, the Reviewer's license, or the editorial plural, does not absolve a gentleman from a gentleman's duty, a gentleman's restraint and a gentleman's generosity.

Mr Dickens will willingly do his best to 'account for' any new case of Circumlocution Office protection that the Review may make a gauntlet of. He may be trusted to do so, he hopes, with a just respect for the Review, for himself, and for his calling; beyond the sound, healthy, legitimate uses and influences of which, he has no purpose to serve, and no ambition in life to gratify.

(97–100)

Charles Dickens

from a speech to the Royal General Theatrical Fund[1]   29 March 1858

Gentlemen, it is not for me at this time and place to take upon myself to flutter before you the well-thumbed pages of Mr Thackeray's books, and to take upon myself to call upon you to observe how full of wit they are, how full of wisdom they are, how full of outspoken meaning – and yet, though out-speaking, how devoid of fear and how devoid of favour. (*Hear, hear.*) But I may take leave to remark, in paying my little due of homage and respect to them, what I think it is a most appropriate and fit thing to have such a writer as my friend, and such an art as the dramatic brought face to face, as we see them here tonight. (*Cheers.*) Every good actor plays direct to every good author, and every writer of fiction, though he may not adopt the dramatic form, writes in effect for the stage. He may write novels always, and plays never, but the truth and wisdom that are in him must permeate the art of which truth and passion are the life, and must be more or less reflected in that great mirror which he holds up to nature. (*Cheers.*) Now, gentlemen, actors and managers and authors are all represented in this present company. We may, without any great effort of imagination, suppose that all of them have studied the mighty deep secrets of the human heart in many theatres of many kinds, great and small, but I am sure that none of them can have studied those mysterious workings in any theatre from the stage wagon of Thespis downwards, to greater advantage, to greater profit, and to greater contentment than in the airy booths of *Vanity Fair*.

Anonymous

from a review of the Library Edition of Dickens's works, *Saturday Review*, vol. 5   8 May 1858

Mr Dickens is the very Avatar of chaff, and bigwigs of every description are his game. The joviality, the animal spirits, and the

1 Dickens proposed the toast to Thackeray, who was in the chair. [Ed.]

freshness with which he acted this part in his earliest books are wonderful. We cannot mention any caricature so perfect and so ludicrous as the description of Messrs Dodson and Fogg, and that of the trial of *Bardell* v. *Pickwick*. The mere skill of his workmanship would have unquestionably secured the success of such a writer; but the harmony between his own temper and that of his audience must be appreciated before we can understand the way in which approbation grew into enthusiasm.

It would, however, be a big mistake to suppose that it was merely to banter that Mr Dickens owed his marvellous success. Mere banter soon grows wearisome; and Mr Dickens was led by nature as much as by art to mix up a very strong dose of sentiment with his caricature. From first to last, he has tried about as much to make his readers cry as to make them laugh; and there is a very large section of the British public – and especially of the younger, weaker and more ignorant part of it – which considers these two functions as comprising the whole duty of novelists. The outrageous rants, surgical operations and *post mortem* examinations which afford such lively pleasure to Parisian readers, would be out of place here; but if anyone can get a pretty little girl to go to heaven prattling about her dolls, and her little brothers and sisters, and quoting texts of Scripture with appropriate gasps, dashes and broken sentences, he may send half the women in London, with tears in their eyes, to Mr Mudie's or Mr Booth's. This kind of taste has not only been flattered, but prodigiously developed, by Mr Dickens. He is the intellectual parent of a whole class of fictions, of which *The Heir of Redclyffe* was perhaps the most successful. No man can offer to the public so large a stock of death-beds adapted for either sex and for any age from five-and-twenty downwards. There are idiot death-beds, where the patient cries ha! ha! and points wildly at vacancy – pauper death-beds, with unfeeling nurses to match – male and female children's death-beds, where the young ladies or gentlemen sit up in bed, pray to the angels and see golden water on the walls. In short, there never was a man to whom the King of Terrors was so useful a lay figure.

This union of banter and sentiment appears to us to form the essence of Mr Dickens's view of life. In the main, it is a very lovely world, a very good and a very happy world, in which we live. We ought all to be particularly fond of each other and infinitely pleased with our position. The only drawback to this charming state of things is that a great number of people have got up a silly set of conventional rules, which the rest of us are foolish enough to submit to. The proper course with them is good-natured ridicule and caricature, which cannot fail to make them conscious of the absurdity of their position. Here and there, no doubt, is to be found a villain who has laid the dagger, the bowl and the Spanish cloak, which by rights he ought to carry, for some of the many costumes worn by English men in the nineteenth century; and there are plenty of erring brothers and sisters who have lost all but their picturesqueness, which is in itself enough to constitute the highest claim to our sympathy. It would be no uninteresting task to trace the stream downwards from the fountain head and to show how this view pervades the long series of works to which we have referred, though the exigencies of fecundity and an enlarged acquaintance with the world have modified it very considerably, especially by way of acidulation. We are all dear brothers and sisters in *Bleak House* and *Little Dorrit*, just as we were in *Pickwick Papers* and *Nicholas Nickleby*; but we have reached a time of life in which family quarrels must be expected, and we have learned that good-natured banter, when kept up for a quarter of a century, is apt, with the kindest intentions in the world, to degenerate into serious and angry discussion. . . .

Mr Dickens's writings are the apotheosis of what has been called newspaper English. He makes points everywhere, gives unfamiliar names to the commonest objects, and lavishes a marvellous quantity of language on the most ordinary incidents . . . there can be no doubt that the triumphs which this style has attained in Mr Dickens's hands have exercised and will continue to exercise very considerable influence on the mould into which people will continue to cast their thoughts, and indirectly upon their thoughts themselves. We cannot affect to say that we look upon the growth of this habit with much satisfaction.

(474–5)

Walter Bagehot

from 'Charles Dickens', a review of the Library Edition of
Dickens's Works, *National Review*, vol. 7   October 1858
(reprinted in *Literary Studies*, vol. 2, 1911)

After such a beginning, there must be great enjoyment in looking at
the long series of closely printed green volumes, in remembering
their marvellous popularity, in knowing that they are a familiar
literature wherever the English language is spoken – that they are
read with admiring appreciation by persons of the highest culture at
the centre of civilization – that they amuse, and are fit to amuse, the
roughest settler in Vancouver's Island.

The penetrating power of this remarkable genius among all classes
at home is not inferior to its diffusive energy abroad. The phrase
'Household book' has, when applied to the works of Mr Dickens, a
peculiar propriety. There is no contemporary English writer, whose
works are read so generally through the whole house, who can give
pleasure to the servants as well as to the mistress, to the children as well
as to the master. Mr Thackeray without doubt exercises a more potent
and plastic fascination within his sphere, but that sphere is limited. It
is restricted to that part of the middle class which gazes inquisitively
at the *Vanity Fair* world. The delicate touches of our great satirist
have, for such readers, not only the charm of wit, but likewise the
interest of valuable information; he tells them of the topics which they
want to know. But below this class there is another and far larger,
which is incapable of comprehending the idling world, or of appre-
ciating the accuracy of delineations drawn from it – which would not
know the difference between a picture of Grosvenor Square by Mr
Thackeray and the picture of it in a Minerva-Press novel – which
only cares for or knows of its own multifarious, industrial, fig-selling
world – and over these also Mr Dickens has power.

It cannot be amiss to take this opportunity of investigating, even
slightly, the causes of so great a popularity. And if, in the course of
our article, we may seem to be ready with over-refining criticism, or
to be unduly captious with theoretical objection, we hope not to
forget that so great and so diffused an influence is a *datum* for literary
investigation – that books which have been thus *tried* upon mankind

and have thus succeeded, must be books of immense genius – and that it is our duty as critics to explain, as far as we can, the nature and the limits of that genius, but never for one moment to deny or question its existence. . . .

His range is very varied. He has attempted to describe every kind of scene in English life, from quite the lowest to almost the highest. He has not endeavoured to secure success by confining himself to a single path, nor wearied the public with repetitions of the subjects by the delineation of which he originally obtained fame. In his earlier works he never writes long without saying something well; something which no other man would have said; but even in them it is the characteristic of his power that it is apt to fail him at once; from masterly strength we pass without interval to almost infantine weakness, – something like disgust succeeds in a moment to an extreme admiration. Such is the natural fate of an unequal mind employing itself on a vast and various subject. On a recent occasion we ventured to make a division of novels into the ubiquitous – it would have been perhaps better to say the miscellaneous – and the sentimental; the first, as its name implies, busying itself with the whole of human life, the second restricting itself within a peculiar and limited theme. Mr Dickens's novels are all of the former class. They aim to delineate nearly all that part of our national life which can be delineated – at least, within the limits which social morality prescribes to social art; but you cannot read his delineation of any part without being struck with its singular incompleteness. An artist once said of the best work of another artist, 'Yes, it is a pretty patch.' If we might venture on the phrase, we should say that Mr Dickens's pictures are graphic scraps; his best books are compilations of them.

The truth is, that Mr Dickens wholly wants the two elements which we have spoken of as one or other requisite for a symmetrical genius. He is utterly deficient in the faculty of reasoning, 'Mamma, what shall I think about?' said the small girl. 'My dear, don't think,' was the old-fashioned reply. We do not allege that in the strict theory of education this was a correct reply; modern writers think otherwise; but we wish someone would say it to Mr Dickens. He is often troubled with the idea that he must reflect, and his reflections are perhaps the worst reading in the world. There is a sentimental confusion about them; we never find the consecutive precision of mature theory, or the cold distinctness of clear thought. Vivid facts stand out in his imagination; and a fresh illustrative style brings them home to the imagination of his readers; but his continuous philosophy utterly fails in the attempt to harmonize them, – to educe a theory or elaborate a precept from them. Of his social thinking we shall have a few words to say in detail; his didactic humour is very unfortunate: no writer is less fitted for an excursion to the imperative mood. At present, we only say, what is so obvious as scarcely to need saying, that his abstract understanding is so far inferior to his picturesque imagination as to give even to his best works the sense of jar and incompleteness, and to deprive them altogether of the crystalline finish which is characteristic of the clear and cultured understanding.

Nor has Mr Dickens the easy and various sagacity which, as has been said, gives a unity to all which it touches. He has, indeed, a quality which is near allied to it in appearance. His shrewdness in some things, especially in traits and small things, is wonderful. His works are full of acute remarks on petty doings, and well exemplify the telling power of minute circumstantiality. But the minor species of perceptive sharpness is so different from diffused sagacity, that the two scarcely ever are to be found in the same mind. There is nothing less like the great lawyer, acquainted with broad principles and applying them with distinct deduction, than the attorney's clerk who catches at small points like a dog biting at flies. 'Over-sharpness' in the student is the most unpromising symptom of the logical jurist. You must not ask a horse in blinkers for a large view of a landscape. In the same way, a detective ingenuity in microscopic detail is of all mental qualities most unlike the broad sagacity by which the great painters of human affairs have unintentionally stamped the mark of unity on their productions. They show by their treatment of each case that they understand the whole of life; the special delineator of fragments and points shows that he understands them only. In one respect the defect is more striking in Mr Dickens than in any other novelist of the present day. The most remarkable deficiency in modern fiction is its omission of the business of life, of all those countless occupations, pursuits and callings in which most men live and move, and by which they have their being. In most novels money *grows*. You have no idea of the toil, the patience and the wearing anxiety by which men of action provide for the day, and lay up for the future, and support those that are given into their care. Mr Dickens is not chargeable with this omission. He perpetually deals with the pecuniary part of life. Almost all his characters have determined occupations, of which he is apt to talk even at too much length. When he rises from the toiling to the luxurious classes, his genius in most cases deserts him. The delicate refinement and discriminating taste of the idling orders are not in his way; he knows the dry arches of London Bridge better than Belgravia. He excels in inventories of poor furniture, and is learned in pawnbrokers' tickets. But, although his creative power lives and works among the middle class and industrial section of English society, he has never painted the highest part of their daily intellectual life. He made, indeed, an attempt to paint specimens of the apt and able man of business in *Nicholas Nickleby*; but the Messrs Cheeryble are among the stupidest of his characters. He forgot that breadth of platitude is rather different from breadth of sagacity. His delineations of middle-class life have in consequence a harshness and meanness which do not belong to that life in reality. He omits the relieving element. He describes the figs which are sold, but not the talent which sells figs well. And it is the same want of the diffused sagacity in his own nature which has made his pictures of life so odd and disjointed, and which has deprived them of symmetry and unity.

The *bizarrerie* of Mr Dickens's genius is rendered more remarkable by the inordinate measure of his special excellences. The first of these is his power of observation in detail. We have heard – we do not know whether correctly or incorrectly – that he can go down a crowded street, and tell you all that is in it, what each shop was, what the grocer's name was, how many scraps of orange-peel there were on the pavement. His works give you exactly the same idea. The amount of detail which there is in them is something amazing – to an ordinary writer something incredible. There are single pages containing telling minutiae which other people would have thought enough for a volume. Nor is his sensibility to external objects, though omnivorous, insensible to the artistic effect of each. There are scarcely anywhere such pictures of London as he draws. No writer has equally comprehended the artistic material which is given by its extent, its congregation of different elements, its mouldiness, its brilliancy.

Nor does his genius, though, from some idiosyncrasy of mind or accident of external situation, it is more especially directed to city life – at all stop at the city wall. He is especially at home in the picturesque and obvious parts of country life, particularly in the comfortable and (so to say) mouldering portion of it. . . .

Mr Dickens has, however, no feeling analogous to the nature-worship of some other recent writers. There is nothing Wordsworthian in his bent; the interpreting inspiration (as that school speak) is not his. Nor has he the erudition in difficult names which has filled some pages in late novelists with mineralogy and botany. His descriptions of nature are fresh and superficial; they are not sermonic or scientific.

Nevertheless, it may be said that Mr Dickens's genius is especially suited to the delineation of city life. London is like a newspaper. Everything is there, and everything is disconnected. There is every kind of person in some houses; but there is no more connexion between the houses than between the neighbours in the lists of 'births, marriages and deaths'. As we change from the broad leader to the squalid police-report, we pass a corner and we are in a changed world. This is advantageous to Mr Dickens's genius. His memory is full of instances of old buildings and curious people, and he does not care to piece them together. On the contrary, each scene, to his mind, is a separate scene, each street a separate street. He has, too, the peculiar alertness of observation that is observable in those who live by it. He describes London like a special correspondent for posterity.

A second most wonderful special faculty which Mr Dickens possesses in what we may call his *vivification* of character, or rather of characteristics. His marvellous power of observation has been exercised upon men and women even more than upon town or country; and the store of human detail, so to speak, in his books is endless and enormous. The boots at the inn, the pickpocket in the street, the undertaker, the Mrs Gamp, are all of them at his disposal; he knows each trait and incident, and he invests them with a kind of perfection in detail which in reality they do not possess. He has a very peculiar power of taking hold of some particular traits, and making a character out of them. He is especially apt to incarnate particular professions in this way. Many of his people never speak without some allusion to their occupation. You cannot separate them from it. Nor does the writer ever separate them. What would Mr Mould be if not an undertaker? or Mrs Gamp if not a nurse? or Charley Bates if not a pickpocket? Not only is human nature in them subdued to what it works in, but there seems to be no nature to subdue; the whole character is the idealization of a trade, and is not in fancy or thought distinguishable from it. Accordingly, of necessity, such delineations become caricatures. We do not in general contrast them with reality; but as soon as we do, we are struck with the monstrous exaggerations which they present. You could no more fancy Sam Weller, or Mark Tapley or the Artful Dodger really existing, walking about among common ordinary men and women, than you can fancy a talking duck or a writing bear. They are utterly beyond the pale of ordinary social intercourse. We suspect, indeed, that Mr Dickens does not conceive his characters to himself as mixing in the society he mixes in. He sees people in the street, doing certain things, talking in a certain way, and his fancy petrifies them in the act. He goes on fancying hundreds of reduplications of that act and that speech; he frames an existence in which there is nothing else but that aspect which attracted his attention. Sam Weller is an example. He is a man-servant, who makes a peculiar kind of jokes, and is wonderfully felicitous in certain similes. . . .

Sam Weller's father is even a stronger and simpler instance. He is simply nothing but an old coachman of the stout and extinct sort: you cannot separate him from the idea of that occupation. But how amusing he is! We dare not quote a single word of his talk; because we should go on quoting so long, and every one knows it so well. Some persons may think that this is not a very high species of delineative art. The idea of personifying traits and trades may seem to them poor and meagre. Anybody, they may fancy, can do that. But how would they do it? Whose fancy would not break down in a page, – in five lines? Who could carry on the vivification with zest and energy and humour for volume after volume? Endless fertility in laughter-causing detail is Mr Dickens's most astonishing peculiarity. It requires a continuous and careful reading of his works to be aware of his enormous wealth. Writers have attained the greatest reputation for wit and humour, whose whole works do not contain so much of either as are to be found in a very few pages of his.

Mr Dickens's humour is indeed very much a result of the two peculiarities of which we have been speaking: His power of detailed

observation and his power of idealizing individual traits of character –
sometimes of one or other of them, sometimes of both of them
together. His similes on matters of external observation are so
admirable that everybody appreciates them, and it would be absurd
to quote specimens of them; nor is it the sort of excellence which best
bears to be paraded for the purposes of critical example. Its off-hand
air and natural connexion with the adjacent circumstances are
inherent parts of its peculiar merit. Every reader of Mr Dickens's
works knows well what we mean. And who is not a reader of them?

But his peculiar humour is even more indebted to his habit of
vivifying external traits, than to his power of external observation.
He, as we have explained, expands traits into people; and it is a source
of true humour to place these, when so expanded, in circumstances
in which only people – that is complete human beings – can appropriately act. The humour of Mr Pickwick's character is entirely of
this kind. He is a kind of incarnation of simple-mindedness and what
we may call obvious-mindedness. The conclusion which each occurrence or position in life most immediately presents to the unsophis-
ticated mind is that which Mr Pickwick is sure to accept. The proper
accompaniments are given to him. He is a stout gentleman in easy
circumstances, who is irritated into originality by no impulse from
within, and by no stimulus from without. He is stated to have 'retired
from business'. But no one can fancy what he was in business. Such
guileless simplicity of heart and easy impressibility of disposition would
soon have induced a painful failure amid the harsh struggles and the
tempting speculations of pecuniary life. As he is represented in the
narrative, however, nobody dreams of such antecedents. Mr Pickwick moves easily over all the surface of English life from Goswell
Street to Dingley Dell, from Dingley Dell to the Ipswich elections,
from drinking milk-punch in a wheelbarrow to sleeping in the
approximate pound, and no one ever thinks of applying to him the
ordinary maxims which we should apply to any common person in
life, or to any common personage in a fiction. Nobody thinks it is
wrong in Mr Pickwick to drink too much milk-punch in a wheelbarrow, to introduce worthless people of whom he knows nothing
to the families of people for whom he really cares; nobody holds him
responsible for the consequences; nobody thinks there is anything
wrong in his taking Mr Bob Sawyer and Mr Benjamin Allen to visit

Mr Winkle senior, and thereby almost irretrievably offending him with his son's marriage. We do not reject moral remarks such as these, but they never occur to us. Indeed the indistinct consciousness that such observations are possible, and that they are hovering about our minds, enhances the humour of the narrative. We are in a conventional world, where the mere maxims of common life do not apply, and yet which has all the amusing detail, and picturesque elements, and singular eccentricities of common life. Mr Pickwick is a personified ideal; a kind of amateur in life, whose course we watch through all the circumstances of ordinary existence, and at whose follies we are amused just as really skilled people are at the mistakes of an amateur in their art. His being in the pound is not wrong; his being the victim of Messrs Dodson is not foolish. 'Always shout with the mob,' said Mr Pickwick. 'But suppose there are two mobs,' said Mr Snodgrass. 'Then shout with the loudest,' said Mr Pickwick. This is not in him weakness or time-serving, or want of principle, as in most even of fictitious people it would be. It is his way. Mr Pickwick was expected to say something, so he said 'Ah' in a grave voice. This is not pompous as we might fancy, or clever as it might be if intentionally devised; it is simply his way. Mr Pickwick gets late at night over the wall behind the back-door of a young ladies' school, is found in that sequestered place by the schoolmistress and the boarders and the cook, and there is a dialogue between them. There is nothing out of possibility in this; it is his way. The humour essentially consists in treating as a moral agent a being who really is not a moral agent. We treat a vivified accident as a man, and we are surprised at the absurd results. We are reading about an acting thing, and we wonder at its scrapes, and laugh at them as if they were those of the man. There is something of this humour in every sort of farce. Everybody knows these are not real beings acting in real life, though they talk as if they were, and want us to believe that they are. Here, as in Mr Dickens's books, we have exaggerations pretending to comport themselves as ordinary beings, caricatures acting as if they were characters. . . .

There is one class of Mr Dickens's pictures which may seem to form an exception to this criticism. It is the delineation of the outlaw, we might say the anti-law, world in *Oliver Twist*. In one or two instances Mr Dickens has been so fortunate as to hit on characteristics which, by his system of idealization and continual repetition, might really be brought to look like a character. A man's trade or profession in regular life can only exhaust a very small portion of his nature; no approach is made to the essence of humanity by the exaggeration of the traits which typify a beadle or an undertaker. With the outlaw world it is somewhat different. The bare fact of a man belonging to that world is so important to his nature, that if it is artistically developed with coherent accessories, some approximation to a distinctly natural character will be almost inevitably made. In the characters of Bill Sikes and Nancy this is so. The former is the skulking ruffian who may be seen any day at the police-courts, and whom anyone may fancy he sees by walking through St Giles's. You cannot attempt to figure to your imagination the existence of such a person without being thrown into the region of the passions, the will and the conscience; the mere fact of his maintaining, as a condition of life and by settled profession, a struggle with regular society necessarily brings these deep parts of his nature into prominence; great crime usually proceeds from abnormal impulses or strange effort. Accordingly Mr Sikes is the character most approaching to a coherent man who is to be found in Mr Dickens's works. We do not say that even here there is not some undue heightening admixture of caricature, but this defect is scarcely thought of amid the general coherence of the picture, the painful subject and the wonderful command of strange accessories. Miss Nancy is a still more delicate artistic effort. She is an idealization of the girl who may also be seen at the police-courts and St Giles's; as bad, according to occupation and common character, as a woman can be, yet retaining a tinge of womanhood, and a certain compassion for interesting suffering, which under favouring circumstances might be the germ of a regenerating influence. We need not stay to prove how much the imaginative development of such a personage must concern itself with our deeper humanity; how strongly, if excellent, it must be contrasted with everything conventional or casual or superficial. Mr Dickens's delineation is in the highest degree excellent. It possesses not only the more obvious merits belonging to the subject, but also that of a singular delicacy of expression and idea. Nobody fancies for a moment that they are reading about anything beyond the pale of ordinary propriety. We read the account of the life which Miss Nancy leads with Bill Sikes, without such an idea occurring to us: yet when we reflect upon it, few things in literary painting are more wonderful than the depiction of a professional life of sin and sorrow, so as not even to startle those to whom the deeper forms of either are but names and shadows. Other writers would have given as vivid a picture: Defoe would have poured out even a more copious measure of telling circumstantiality, but he would have narrated his story with an inhuman distinctness, which if not impure is *un*pure; French writers, whom we need not name, would have enhanced the interest of their narrative by trading on the excitement of stimulating scenes. It would be injustice to Mr Dickens to say that he has surmounted these temptations; the unconscious evidence of innumerable details proves that, from a certain delicacy of imagination and purity of spirit, he has not even experienced them. Criticism is the more bound to dwell at length on the merits of these delineations, because no artistic merit can make *Oliver Twist* a pleasing work. The squalid detail of crime and misery oppresses us too much. If it is to be read at all, it should be read in the first hardness of the youthful imagination, which no touch can move too deeply, and which is never stirred with tremulous suffering at the 'still sad music of humanity'. The coldest critic in later life may never hope to have again the apathy of his boyhood.

It perhaps follows from what has been said of the characteristics of Mr Dickens's genius, that he would be little skilled in planning plots for his novels. He certainly is not so skilled. He says in his preface to the *Pickwick Papers* 'that they were designed for the introduction of diverting characters and incidents; that no ingenuity of plot was attempted, or even at that time considered feasible by the author in connexion with the desultory plan of publication adopted'; and he adds an expression of regret that 'these chapters had not been strung together on a thread of more general interest'. It is extremely fortunate that no such attempt was made. In the cases in which Mr Dickens has attempted to make a long connected story, or to develop into scenes or incidents a plan in any degree elaborate, the result has been a complete failure. A certain consistency of genius seems necessary for the construction of a consecutive plot. An irregular mind naturally shows itself in incoherency of incident and aberration of character. The method in which Mr Dickens's mind works, if we are correct in our criticism upon it, tends naturally to these blemishes.

Caricatures are necessarily isolated; they are produced by the exaggeration of certain conspicuous traits and features; each being is enlarged on its greatest side; and we laugh at the grotesque grouping and the startling contrast. But the connexion between human beings on which a plot depends is rather severed than elucidated by the enhancement of their diversities. Interesting stories are founded on the intimate relations of men and women. These intimate relations are based not on their superficial traits, or common occupations, or most visible externalities, but on the inner life of heart and feeling. You simply divert attention from that secret life by enhancing the perceptible diversities of common human nature, and the strange anomalies into which it may be distorted. The original germ of *Pickwick* was a 'Club of Oddities'. The idea was professedly abandoned; but traces of it are to be found in all Mr Dickens's books. It illustrates the professed grotesqueness of the characters as well as their slender connexion.

The defect of plot is heightened by Mr Dickens's great, we might say complete, inability to make a love-story. A pair of lovers is by custom a necessity of narrative fiction, and writers who possess a great general range of mundane knowledge, and but little knowledge of the special sentimental subject, are often in amusing difficulties. The watchful reader observes the transition from the hearty description of well-known scenes, of prosaic streets, or journeys by wood and river, to the pale colours of ill-attempted poetry, to such sights as the novelist wishes he need not try to see. But few writers exhibit the difficulty in so aggravated a form as Mr Dickens. Most men by taking thought can make a lay figure to look not so very unlike a young gentleman, and can compose a telling schedule of ladylike charms. Mr Dickens has no power of doing either. The heroic character – we do not mean the form of character so called in life and action, but that which is hereditary in the heroes of novels – is not suited to his style of art. Hazlitt wrote an essay to inquire 'Why the heroes of romances are insipid'; and without going that length it may safely be said that the character of the agreeable young gentleman who loves and is loved should not be of the most marked sort. Flirtation ought not to be an exaggerated pursuit. Young ladies and their admirers should not express themselves in the heightened and imaginative phraseology suited to Charley Bates and the Dodger. Humour is of no use, for no one makes love in jokes: a tinge of insidious satire may perhaps be permitted as a rare and occasional relief, but it will not be thought 'a pretty book', if so malicious an element be at all habitually perceptible. The broad farce in which Mr Dickens indulges is thoroughly out of place. If you caricature a pair of lovers ever so little, by the necessity of their calling you make them ridiculous. One of Sheridan's best comedies is remarkable for having no scene in which the hero and heroine are on the stage together; and Mr Moore suggests that the shrewd wit distrusted his skill in the light dropping love-talk which would have been necessary. Mr Dickens would have done well to imitate so astute a policy; but he has none of the managing shrewdness which those who look at Sheridan's career attentively will probably think not the least remarkable feature in his singular character. Mr Dickens, on the contrary, pours out painful sentiments as if he wished the abundance should make up for the inferior quality. The excruciating writing which is expended on Miss Ruth Pinch passes belief. Mr Dickens is not only unable to make lovers talk, but to describe heroines in mere narrative. As has been said, most men can make a tumble of blue eyes and fair hair and pearly teeth, that does very well for a young lady, at least for a good while; but Mr Dickens will not, probably cannot, attain even to this humble measure of descriptive art. He vitiates the repose by broad humour, or disenchants the delicacy by an unctuous admiration.

This deficiency is probably nearly connected with one of Mr Dickens's most remarkable excellences. No one can read Mr Thackeray's writings without feeling that he is perpetually treading as close as he dare to the border-line that separates the world which may be described in books from the world which it is prohibited so to describe. No one knows better than this accomplished artist where that line is, and how curious are its windings and turns. The charge against him is that he knows it but too well; that with an anxious care and a wistful eye he is ever approximating to its edge, and hinting with subtle art how thoroughly he is familiar with, and how interesting he could make the interdicted region on the other side. He never violates a single conventional rule; but at the same time the shadow of the immorality that is not seen is scarcely ever wanting to his delineation of the society that is seen. Everyone may perceive what is passing in his fancy. Mr Dickens is chargeable with no such defect:

he does not seem to feel the temptation. By what we may fairly call an instinctive purity of genius, he not only observes the conventional rules, but makes excursions into topics which no other novelist could safely handle and, by a felicitous instinct, deprives them of all impropriety. No other writer could have managed the humour of Mrs Gamp without becoming unendurable. At the same time it is difficult not to believe that this singular insensibility to the temptations to which many of the greatest novelists have succumbed is in some measure connected with his utter inaptitude for delineating the portion of life to which their art is specially inclined. He delineates neither the love-affairs which ought to be nor those which ought not to be.

Mr Dickens's indisposition to 'make capital' out of the most commonly tempting part of human sentiment is the more remarkable because he certainly does not show the same indisposition in other cases. He has naturally great powers of pathos; his imagination is familiar with the common sorts of human suffering; and his marvellous conversancy with the detail of existence enables him to describe sick-beds and death-beds with an excellence very rarely seen in literature. A nature far more sympathetic than that of most authors has familiarized him with such subjects. In general, a certain apathy is characteristic of book-writers, and dulls the efficacy of their pathos. Mr Dickens is quite exempt from this defect; but, on the other hand, is exceedingly prone to a very ostentatious exhibition of the opposite excellence. He dwells on dismal scenes with a kind of fawning fondness; and he seems unwilling to leave them, long after his readers have had more than enough of them. He describes Mr Dennis the hangman as having a professional fondness for his occupation: he has the same sort of fondness apparently for the profession of death-painter. The painful details he accumulates are a very serious drawback from the agreeableness of his writings. Dismal 'light literature' is the dismallest of reading. The reality of the police-reports is sufficiently bad, but a fictitious police-report would be the most disagreeable of conceivable compositions. Some portions of Mr Dickens's books are liable to a good many of the same objections. They are squalid from noisome trivialities, and horrid with terrifying crime. In his earlier books this is commonly relieved at frequent intervals by a graphic and original mirth. As we will not say age, but maturity, has passed over his powers, this counteractive element has been lessened; the humour is not so happy as it was, but the wonderful fertility in painful minutiae still remains.

Mr Dickens's political opinions have subjected him to a good deal of criticism, and to some ridicule. He has shown, on many occasions, the desire – which we see so frequent among able and influential men – to start as a political reformer. Mr Spurgeon said, with an application to himself, 'If you've got the ear of the public, *of course* you must begin to tell it its faults.' Mr Dickens has been quite disposed to make this use of his popular influence. Even in *Pickwick* there are many traces of this tendency; and the way in which it shows itself in that book and in others is very characteristic of the time at which they appeared. The most instructive political characteristic of the years from 1823 to 1845 is the growth and influence of the scheme of opinion which we call Radicalism. There are several species of creeds which are comprehended under this generic name, but they all evince a marked reaction against the worship of the English constitution and the affection for the English *status quo*, which were then the established creed and sentiment. All Radicals are anti-Eldonites. This is equally true of the Benthamite or philosophical radicalism of the early period, and the Manchester, or 'definite-grievance radicalism', among the last vestiges of which we are now living. Mr Dickens represents a species different from either. His is what we may call the 'sentimental radicalism'; and if we recur to the history of the time, we shall find that there would not originally have been any opprobrium attaching to such a name. The whole course of the legislation, and still more of the administration, of the first twenty years of the nineteenth century was marked by a harsh unfeelingness which is of all faults the most contrary to any with which we are chargeable now. The world of the 'Six Acts', of the frequent executions for death, of the Draconic criminal law, is so far removed from us that we cannot comprehend its having ever existed. It is more easy to understand the recoil which has followed. All the social speculation, and much of the social action of the few years succeeding the Reform Bill bear the most marked traces of the reaction. The spirit which animates Mr Dickens's political reasonings and observations expresses it exactly. The vice of the then existing social authorities and of the then existing public had been the forgetfulness of the pain which their own acts evidently produced – an unrealizing habit which adhered to official rules and established maxims, and which would not be shocked by the evident consequences, by proximate human suffering. The sure result of this habit was the excitement of the habit precisely opposed to it. Mr Carlyle, in his *Chartism*, we think, observes of the poor-law reform: 'It was then, above all things, necessary that outdoor relief should cease. But how? What means did great Nature take for accomplishing that most desirable end? She created a race of men who believed the cessation of outdoor relief to be the one thing needful.' In the same way, and by the same propensity to exaggerated opposition which is inherent in human nature, the unfeeling obtuseness of the early part of this century was to be corrected by an extreme, perhaps an excessive, sensibility to human suffering in the years which have followed. There was most adequate reason for the sentiment in its origin, and it had a great task to perform in ameliorating harsh customs and repealing dreadful penalties; but it has continued to repine at such evils long after they ceased to exist, and when the only facts that at all resemble them are the necessary painfulness of due punishment and the necessary rigidity of established law. Mr Dickens is an example both of the proper use and of the abuse of the sentiment. His earlier works have many excellent descriptions of the abuses which had descended to the present generation from others whose sympathy with pain was less tender. Nothing can be better than the description of the poor debtors' gaols in *Pickwick*, or of the old parochial authorities in *Oliver Twist*. No doubt these descriptions are caricatures, all his delineations are so; but the beneficial use of such art can hardly be better exemplified. Human nature endures the aggravation of vices and foibles in written description better than that of excellencies. We cannot bear to hear even the hero of a book for ever called 'just'; we detest the recurring praise even of beauty, much more of virtue. The moment you begin to exaggerate a character of true excellence, you spoil it; the traits are too delicate not to be injured by heightening or marred by over-emphasis. But a beadle is made for caricature. The slight measure of pomposity that humanizes his unfeelingness introduces the requisite comic element; even the turnkeys of a debtors' prison may by skilful hands be similarly used. The contrast between the destitute condition of Job Trotter and Mr Jingle and their former swindling triumph, is made comic by a rarer touch of unconscious art. Mr Pickwick's warm heart takes so eager an interest in the misery of his old enemies, that our colder nature is tempted to smile. We endure the over-intensity, at any rate the unnecessary aggravation, of the surrounding misery; and we endure it willingly, because it brings out better than anything else could have done the half-comic intensity of a sympathetic nature.

It is painful to pass from these happy instances of well-used power to the glaring abuses of the same faculty in Mr Dickens's later books. He began by describing really removable evils in a style which would induce all persons, however insensible, to remove them if they could; he has ended by describing the natural evils and inevitable pains of the present state of being in such a manner as must tend to excite discontent and repining. The result is aggravated, because Mr Dickens never ceases to hint that these evils are removable, though he does not say by what means. Nothing is easier than to show the evils of anything. Mr Dickens has not unfrequently spoken, and what is worse, he has taught a great number of parrot-like imitators to speak, in what really is, if they knew it, a tone of objection to the necessary constitution of human society. If you will only write a description of it, any form of government will seem ridiculous. What is more absurd than a despotism, even at its best? A king of ability or an able minister sits in an orderly room filled with memorials, and returns, and documents and memoranda. These are his world; among these he of necessity lives and moves. Yet how little of the real life of the nation he governs can be represented in an official form! How much of real suffering is there that statistics can never tell! How much of obvious good is there that no memorandum to a minister will ever mention! How much deception is there in what such documents contain! How monstrous must be the ignorance of the closet statesman, after all his life of labour, of much that a ploughman could tell him of! A free government is almost worse, as it must read in a written delineation. Instead of the real attention of a laborious and anxious statesman, we have now the shifting caprices of a popular assembly – elected for one object, deciding on another; changing with the turn of debate; shifting in its very composition; one set of men coming down to vote today, tomorrow another and often unlike set, most of them eager for the dinner-hour, actuated by unseen influences – by a respect for their constituents, by the dread of an attorney in a far-off borough. What people are these to control a nation's destinies, and wield the power of an empire, and regulate the happiness of millions! Either way we are at fault. Free government seems an absurdity, and despotism is so too. Again, every form of law has a distinct expression, a rigid procedure, customary rules and forms. It is administered by human beings liable to mistake, confusion and forgetfulness, and in the long run, and on the average, is sure to be tainted with vice and fraud. Nothing can be easier than to make a case, as we may say, against any particular system, by pointing out with emphatic caricature its inevitable miscarriages and by pointing out nothing else. Those who so address us may assume a tone of philanthropy, and for ever exult that they are not so unfeeling as other men are; but the real tendency of their exhortations is to make men dissatisfied with their inevitable condition, and what is worse, to make them fancy that its irremediable evils can be remedied, and indulge in a succession of vague strivings and restless changes. Such, however, though in a style of expression somewhat different, is very much the tone with which Mr Dickens and his followers have in later years made us familiar. To the second-hand repeaters of a cry so feeble, we can have nothing to say; if silly people cry because they think the world is silly, let them cry; but the founder of the school cannot, we are persuaded, peruse without mirth the lachrymose eloquence which his disciples have perpetrated. The soft moisture of irrelevant sentiment cannot have entirely entered into his soul. A truthful genius must have forbidden it. Let us hope that his pernicious example may incite someone of equal genius to preach with equal efficiency a sterner and a wiser gospel; but there is no need just now for us to preach it without genius.

There has been much controversy about Mr Dickens's taste. A great many cultivated people will scarcely concede that he has any taste at all; a still larger number of fervent admirers point, on the other hand, to a hundred felicitous descriptions and delineations which abound in apt expressions and skilful turns and happy images, in which it would be impossible to alter a single word without altering for the worse; and naturally inquire whether such excellences in what is written do not indicate good taste in the writer. The truth is, that Mr Dickens has what we may call creative taste; that is to say, the habit or faculty, whichever we may choose to call it, which at the critical instant of artistic production offers to the mind the right word, and the right word only. If he is engaged on a good subject for caricature, there will be no defect of taste to preclude the caricature from being excellent. But it is only in moments of imaginative production that he has any taste at all. His works nowhere indicate that he possesses in any degree the passive taste which decides what is good in the writings of other people and what is not, and which performs the same critical duty upon a writer's own efforts when the confusing mists of productive imagination have passed away. Nor has Mr Dickens the gentlemanly instinct which in many minds supplies the place of purely critical discernment, and which, by constant association with those who know what is best, acquires a second-hand perception of that which is best. He has no tendency to conventionalism for good or for evil; his merits are far removed from the ordinary path of writers, and it was not probably so much effort to him as to other men to step so far out of that path: he scarcely knew how far it was. For the same reason he cannot tell how faulty his writing will often be thought, for he cannot tell what people will think.

A few pedantic critics have regretted that Mr Dickens had not received what they call a regular education. And if we understand their meaning, we believe they mean to regret that he had not received a course of discipline which would probably have impaired his powers. A regular education should mean that ordinary system of regulation and instruction which experience has shown to fit men best for the ordinary pursuits of life. It applies the requisite discipline to each faculty in the exact proportion in which that faculty is wanted in the pursuits of life; it develops understanding and memory, and imagination, each in accordance with the scale prescribed. To men of ordinary faculties this is nearly essential; it is the only mode in which they can be fitted for the inevitable competition of existence. To men of regular and symmetrical genius also, such a training will often be beneficial. The world knows pretty well what are the great tasks of the human mind, and has learnt in the course of ages with some accuracy what is the kind of culture likely to promote their exact performance. A man of abilities extraordinary in degree but harmonious in proportion, will be the better for having submitted to the kind of discipline which has been ascertained to fit a man for the work to which powers in that proportion are best fitted; he will do what he has to do better and more gracefully; culture will add a touch to the finish of nature. But the case is very different with men of irregular and anomalous genius, whose excellences consist in the *aggravation* of some special faculty, or at the most of one or two. The discipline which will fit him for the production of great literary works is that which will most develop the peculiar powers in which he excels; the rest of the mind will be far less important, it will not be likely that the culture which is adapted to promote this special development will also be that which is most fitted for expanding the powers of common men in common directions. The precise problem is to develop the powers of a strange man in a strange direction. In the case of Mr Dickens, it would have been absurd to have shut up his observant youth within the walls of a college. They would have taught him nothing about Mrs Gamp there; Sam Weller took no degree. The kind of early life fitted to develop the power of apprehensive observation is a brooding life in stirring scenes; the idler in the streets of life knows the streets; the bystander knows the picturesque effect of life better than the player, and the meditative idler amid the hum of existence is much more likely to know its sound and to take in and comprehend its depths and meanings than the scholastic student intent on books, which, if they represent any world, represent one which has long passed away – which commonly try rather to develop the reasoning understanding than the seeing observation – which are written in languages that have long been dead. You will not train by such discipline a caricaturist of obvious manners.

Perhaps, too, a regular instruction and daily experience of the searching ridicule of critical associates would have detracted from the *pluck* which Mr Dickens shows in all his writings. It requires a great deal of courage to be a humorous writer; you are always afraid that people will laugh at you instead of with you: undoubtedly there is a certain eccentricity about it. You take up the esteemed writers, Thucydides and the *Saturday Review*; after all, they do not make you laugh. It is not the function of really artistic productions to contribute to the mirth of human beings. All sensible men are afraid of it, and it is only with an extreme effort that a printed joke attains to the perusal of the public; the chances are many to one that the anxious producer loses heart in the correction of the press, and that the world never laughs at all. Mr Dickens is quite exempt from this weakness. He has what a Frenchman might call the courage of his faculty. The real daring which is shown in *Pickwick Papers* in the whole character of Mr Weller senior, as well as in that of his son, is immense, far surpassing any which has been shown by any other contemporary writer. The brooding irregular mind is in its first stage prone to this sort of courage. It perhaps knows that its ideas are 'out of the way'; but with the infantine simplicity of youth, it supposes that originality is an advantage. Persons more familiar with the ridicule of their equals in station (and this is to most men the great instructress of the college time) well know that of all qualities this one most requires to be clipped and pared and measured. Posterity we doubt not will be entirely perfect in every conceivable element of judgement; but the existing generation like what they have heard before – it is much easier. It required great courage in Mr Dickens to write what his genius has compelled them to appreciate.

We have throughout spoken of Mr Dickens as he was, rather than as he is; or, to use a less discourteous phrase, and we hope a truer, of his early works rather than of those which are more recent. We could not do otherwise consistently with the true code of criticism. A man of great genius, who has written great and enduring works, must be judged mainly by them; and not by the inferior productions which, from the necessities of personal position, a fatal facility of composition or other cause, he may pour forth at moments less favourable to his powers. Those who are called on to review these inferior productions themselves, must speak of them in the terms they may deserve; but those who have the more pleasant task of estimating as a whole the genius of the writer, may confine their attention almost wholly to those happier efforts which illustrate that genius. We should not like to have to speak in detail of Mr Dickens's later works, and we have not done so. There are, indeed, peculiar reasons why a genius constituted as his is (at least if we are correct in the view which we have taken of it) would not endure without injury during a long life the applause of the many, the temptations of composition, and the general excitement of existence. Even in his earlier works it was impossible not to fancy that there was a weakness of fibre unfavourable to the longevity of excellence. This was the effect of his deficiency in those masculine faculties of which we have said so much – the reasoning understanding and firm far-seeing sagacity. It is these two component elements which stiffen the mind, and give a consistency to the creed and a coherence to its effects, which enable it to protect itself from the rush of circumstances. If to a deficiency in these we add an extreme sensibility to circumstances – a mobility, as Lord Byron used to call it, of emotion, which is easily impressed, and still more easily carried away by impression – we have the idea of a character peculiarly unfitted to bear the flux of time and chance. A man of very great determination could hardly bear up against them with such slight aids from within and with such peculiar sensibility to temptation. A man of merely ordinary determination would succumb to it; and Mr Dickens has succumbed. His position was certainly unfavourable. He has told us that the works of his later years, inferior as all good critics have deemed them, have yet been more read than those of his earlier and healthier years. The most characteristic part of his audience, the lower middle-class, were ready to receive with delight the least favourable productions of his genius. Human nature cannot endure this; it is too much to have to endure a coincident temptation both from within and from without. Mr Dickens was too much inclined by natural disposition to lachrymose eloquence and exaggerated caricature. Such was the kind of writing which he wrote most easily. He found likewise that such was the kind of writing that was read most readily; and of course he wrote that kind. Who would have done otherwise? No critic is entitled to speak very harshly of such degeneracy, if he is not sure that he could have coped with difficulties so peculiar. If that rule is to be observed, who is there that will not be silent? No other Englishman has attained such a hold on the vast populace; it is little, therefore, to say that no other has surmounted its attendant tempations.

(459–86)

Charles Dickens

from a letter to John Forster 10 October 1858

As to the truth of the readings, I cannot tell you what the demonstrations of personal regard and respect are. How the densest and most uncomfortably packed crowd will be hushed in an instant when

I show my face. How the youth of colleges, and the old men of business in the town, seem equally unable to get near enough to me when they cheer me away at night. How common people and gentle-folks will stop me in the streets and say: 'Mr Dickens, will you let me touch the hand that has filled my home with so many friends?' And if you saw the mothers, and fathers, and sisters, and brothers in mourning, who invariably come to 'Little Dombey', and if you studied the wonderful expression of comfort and reliance with which they hang about me, as if I had been with them, all kindness and delicacy, at their own little death-bed, you would think it one of the strangest things in the world.

As to the mere effect, of course I don't go on doing the thing so often without carefully observing myself and the people too in every little thing, and without (in consequence) greatly improving in it.

At Aberdeen, we were crammed to the street twice in one day. At Perth (where I thought when I arrived there literally could be nobody to come), the nobility came posting in from thirty miles round, and the whole town came and filled an immense hall. As to the effect, if you had seen them after Lilian died, in *The Chimes*, or when Scrooge woke and talked to the boy outside the window, I doubt if you would ever have forgotten it. And at the end of *Dombey* yesterday afternoon, in the cold light of day, they all got up, after a short pause, gentle and simple, and thundered and waved their hats with that astonishing heartiness and fondness for me, that for the first time in all my public career they took me completely off my legs, and I saw the whole eighteen hundred of them reel on one side as if a shock from without had shaken the hall.

Charles Dickens

from a letter to John Forster   25 August 1859

Nothing but the interest of the subject [of *A Tale of Two Cities*], and the pleasure of striving with the difficulty of the form of treatment – nothing in the way of mere money, I mean – could else repay the time and trouble of the incessant condensation. But I set myself the little task of making *a picturesque story*, rising in every chapter, with characters true to nature, but whom the story should express more than they should express themselves by dialogue. I mean in other words, that I fancied a story of incident might be written (in place of the odious stuff that *is* written under that pretence), pounding the characters in its own mortar, and beating their interest out of them. If you could have read the story all at once, I hope you wouldn't have stopped halfway.

Charles Dickens

Preface to the first edition of *A Tale of Two Cities*   1859

When I was acting, with my children and friends, in Mr Wilkie Collins's drama of *The Frozen Deep*, I first conceived the main idea of this story. A strong desire was upon me then, to embody it in my own person; and I traced out in my fancy, the state of mind of which it would necessitate the presentation to an observant spectator, with particular care and interest.

As the idea became familiar to me, it gradually shaped itself into its present form. Throughout its execution, it has had complete possession of me; I have so far verified what is done and suffered in these pages, as that I have certainly done and suffered it all myself.

Whenever any reference (however slight) is made here to the condition of the French people before or during the Revolution, it is truly made, on the faith of trustworthy witnesses. It has been one of my hopes to add something to the popular and picturesque means of understanding that terrible time, though no one can hope to add anything to the philosophy of Mr Carlyle's wonderful book.

David Masson

from *British Novelists and their Styles*   1859

Prose Fiction in Britain – nay, in the rest of Europe and in America too – has received a fresh impulse and has taken on a new set of characteristics since Dickens and Thackeray became, for us, its chief representatives. These two writers belong to the classic roll; they are now in their living activity, and the buzz of critics is about them; but a time will come when they shall have their settled places, and, the buzz having transferred itself to others whose turn of penance it will then be, they shall be seen in their full proportions relatively to the Fieldings and Smolletts and Sternes that went before them, and men, noting their differences in comparison with these, may assert also, more boldly than we, what shall seem their superiorities. Dickens, as you are aware, was the first in the field. His *Sketches by Boz* appeared in 1836 followed, within the next ten years, by his *Pickwick*, his *Nicholas Nickleby*, his *Oliver Twist* (previously published in magazine parts), his *Humphrey's Clock* (including *The Old Curiosity Shop* and *Barnaby Rudge*), his *Martin Chuzzlewit*, and several of his Christmas Stories. It was not till after these ten years of Dickens's established popularity, or till about the year 1847, that Mr Thackeray – whose extraordinary powers had already, however, been long recognized within a limited circle of intellectual men, in virtue of his numerous scattered publications and papers – stepped forth into equally extensive celebrity. His *Vanity Fair* was the first efficient proclamation to the public at large of the existence of this signal British talent, increasingly known since by the republication of those *Miscellanies* which had been buried in magazines and other periodicals, and by the successive triumphs of the *Snob Papers*, *Pendennis*, *Esmond*, the *Newcomes* and various Christmas Books. Parallel with these had been running later fictions from Mr Dickens's pen – *Dombey and Son*, *David Copperfield* and *Bleak House*. Mr Dickens also had the last word in his *Little Dorrit*, until the other day, when Mr Thackeray recommenced in his *Virginians*. For, with the two writers, according to the serial system, it seems to be, whether by arrangement or by necessity, as with Castor and Pollux; both cannot be above the horizon of the publishing world at once, and, when the one is there, the other takes his turn in Tartarus. But whether simultaneously visible or alternate, the two are now so closely associated in the public mind that whenever the one is mentioned the other is thought of. It is now Dickens and Thackeray, Thackeray and Dickens, all the world over. Nay, not content with associating them, people have got into the habit of contrasting them and naming them in opposition to each other. There is a Dickens faction, and there is a Thackeray faction; and there is no debate more common, wherever literary talk goes on, than the debate as to the respective merits of Dickens and Thackeray.

Perhaps there is a certain ungraciousness in our thus always comparing and contrasting the two writers. We ought to be but too glad that we have such a pair of contemporaries, yet living and in their prime, to cheer on against each other. . . .

And yet, in instituting such comparisons, the public are guided by a right critical instinct. There can be no doubt that the two writers bring out and throw into relief each other's peculiarities – that they are, in some respects, the opposites of each other; and that each is most accurately studied when his differences from the other are noted and scrutinized.

But, first, as to their general resemblances. Both novelists belong, in the main, though by no means exclusively, to the order of Humorists, or writers of Comic Fiction. Moreover, under this distinction, both stand very much in the same relation to their predecessors in respect of the kind or kinds of fiction, previously in use, to which they have attached themselves, and in respect of the extension of range which that kind or those kinds of fiction have received at their hands. The connexions of both at first were chiefly with that which we have distinguished as the Novel of English Life and Manners; and both, in working this kind of Novel, have added immensely to its achievements and capabilities in one particular field – that of the Metropolis. The Novels of Dickens and Thackeray are, most of them, novels of London; it is in the multifarious circumstance of London life and its peculiar humours that they move most frequently and have their most characteristic being. A fact not unimportant in the appreciation of both! As the greatest aggregate of human beings on the face of the earth, as a population of several millions crushed together in one dense mass on a space of a few square miles – this mass consisting, for the most part, of Englishmen, but containing also as many Scotchmen as there are in Edinburgh, as many Irishmen as there are in Dublin, and a perfect Polyglott of other nations in addition – London is as good an epitome of the world as anywhere exists, presenting all those phenomena of interest, whether serious or humorous, which result from great numbers, heterogeneousness of composition, and close social packing; besides which, as the metropolis of the British Empire, it is the centre whither all the sensations of the Empire tend, and whence the motive currents issue that thrill to the extremities. If any city could generate and sustain a species of Novel entirely out of its own resources, it might surely be London; nor would ten thousand novels exhaust it. After all the mining efforts of previous novelists in so rich a field, Dickens and Thackeray have certainly sunk new shafts in it, and have come upon valuable veins not previously disturbed. So much is this the case that, without injustice to Fielding and others, Dickens and Thackeray might well be considered as the founders of a peculiar sub-variety of the Novel of English Life and Manners, to be called 'The British Metropolitan Novel'. As Londoners, however, do not always stay in London, or, while in London, are not always engrossed by what is passing there, so our two novelists both range, and range about equally, beyond the bounds of the kind of fiction thus designated. They do give us English life and manners out of London; nay, they have both, as we have seen, given us specimens also of their ability in at least two varieties of the Novel distinct from that of English life and manners – the Traveller's Novel, and the Historical Novel. If, in this respect of external range, either has the advantage, it is perhaps Dickens – who, in his Christmas Stories, and in stories interspersed through his larger fictions, has given us specimens of his skill in a kind of prose phantasy which Thackeray has not attempted.

In addition to the difference just indicated, critics have pointed out, or readers have discovered for themselves, not a few other differences between Dickens and Thackeray.

In the mere matter of literary style, there is a very obvious difference. Mr Thackeray, according to the general opinion, is the more terse and idiomatic, and Mr Dickens the more diffuse and luxuriant writer. There is an Horatian strictness and strength in Thackeray which satisfies the most cultivated taste and wins the respect of the severest critic; but Dickens, if he is the more rapid and careless on the whole, seems more susceptible to passion, and rises to a keener and wilder song. . . . Referring the difference of style to its origin in difference of intellectual constitution, critics are accustomed to say that Thackeray's is the mind of closer and harder, and Dickens's the mind of looser and richer texture – that the intellect of the one is the more penetrating and reflective, and that of the other the more excursive and intuitive. . . .

As to the difference of ethical spirit, or of general philosophy, between the two writers, the public have come to a very definite conclusion. Dickens, it is said, is the more genial, kindly, cheerful and sentimental; Thackeray, the more harsh, caustic, cynical, and satirical writer. And, proceeding on this distinction, the two factions argue, consistently with it, in behalf of their respective favourites – the adherents of Dickens objecting to what they call Thackeray's merciless views of human life, and his perception of the mean at the roots of everything; and the adherents of Thackeray, on the other hand, maintaining the wholesome effect of his bracing sense in comparison with what they call Dickens's sickly sentimentalism. For us, joining neither of the factions, it is enough to recognize the fact of the difference on which they argue so constantly. The philosophy of Dickens certainly *is* the professed philosophy of kindliness, of a genial interest in all things great and small, of a light English joyousness, and a sunny universal benevolence; whereas, though I do not agree with those that represent Thackeray's writings as mainly cynical, but think that, in such characters as his Warrington, he has shown his belief in manly nobleness, and his power of representing it – yet it seems clear that the pervading philosophy of his writings, far more than those of Dickens, is that of a profoundly reasoned pococurantism, of a sceptical acquiescence in the world as it is; or, to use his own words in describing the state of mind of his hero Pendennis, 'of a belief, qualified with scorn, in all things extant'. The difference is perhaps best seen, and with most advantage to Thackeray, when it is expressed negatively – that is, with reference not to what the two writers respectively inculcate, but to what they respectively attack and oppose. Stated so (but such a method of statement, it should be remembered, is not the fairest for all purposes), the philosophy of Dickens may be defined as Anti-Puritanism, whereas that of Thackeray may be defined as Anti-Snobbism. Whatever practice, institution or mode of thinking is adverse, in Mr Dickens's view, to natural enjoyment and festivity, against that he makes war; whereas that which Mr Thackeray hunts out and hunts down everywhere is Snobbism. Although, in their positive forms, both philosophies are good, perhaps in their negative applications Mr Thackeray's is the least liable to exception. Anti-Snobbism, it may indeed be admitted, is not a perfect summary of the whole decalogue; but, in the present day, and especially in and about London, it is that which most nearly passes for such a summary; and, seeing that there is no question anywhere but that Snob-bism is a bad thing, and little difficulty anywhere in knowing what it is, Mr Thackeray's doctrine is one to which there needs to be less hesitation in wishing universal good speed than to the corresponding doctrine of his rival – a doctrine which would too hastily extinguish that, about the nature of which, and its proper varieties, there may well be much controversy. Further, it is to Mr Thackeray's advantage, in the opinion of many, that in his satires in behalf of Anti-Snobbism, or of any other doctrine that he may hold, it is men and their modes of thinking and acting that he attacks, and not social institutions. To do battle with the vanity, the affectation, the insincerity, the Snob-bism, that lies under each man's own hat, and actuates each man's own gestures and conduct, is Mr Thackeray's way; and rarely or never does he concern himself with social anomalies or abuses. In this respect he is singularly acquiescent and conservative for a man of such general strength of intellect. Mr Dickens, on the other hand, is singularly aggressive and opinionative. There is scarcely a social ques-tion on which he has not touched; and there are few of his novels in which he has not blended the functions of a social and political critic with those of the artist, to a degree detrimental, as many think, to his genius in the latter capacity. For Mr Dickens's wonderful powers of description are no guarantee for the correctness of his critical judge-ments in those particulars to which he may apply them.

We may owe one degree of respect [I have said] to Dickens, as the describer of Squeers and Creakle, and quite another degree of respect when he tells us how he would have boys educated. Mr Spenlow may be a capital likeness of a Doctors' Commons lawyer; and yet this would not be the proper ground for concluding Mr Dickens's view of a reform in the Ecclesiastical Courts to be right. No man has given more picturesque illustrations of London criminal life; yet he might not be equally trustworthy in his notions of prison-discipline. His Dennis, the hangman, is a powerfully conceived character; yet this is no reason for accepting his opinion on capital punishments.

And yet how much we owe to Mr Dickens for this very opinionative-ness! With his real shrewdness, his thoughtfulness, his courage, what

noble hits he has made! The Administrative Reform Association
might have worked for ten years without producing half of the effect
which Mr Dickens has produced in the same direction, by flinging
out the phrase, 'The Circumlocution Office'. He has thrown out a
score of such phrases, equally efficacious for social reform; and it
matters little that some of them might turn out on inquiry to be
ludicrous exaggerations.

All these differences, however, between Dickens and Thackeray,
and still others that might be pointed out, resolve themselves into the
one fundamental difference, that they are artists of opposite schools.
Thackeray is a novelist of what is called the Real school; Dickens is a
novelist of the Ideal or Romantic school. (The terms Real and Ideal
have been so run upon of late, that their repetition begins to nauseate;
but they must be kept, for all that, till better equivalents are provided.) It is Thackeray's aim to represent life as it is actually and historically – men and women, as they are, in those situations in which
they are usually placed, with that mixture of good and evil and of
strength and foible which is to be found in their characters, and liable
only to those incidents which are of ordinary occurrence. He will have
no faultless characters, no demigods – nothing but men and brethren.
And from this it results that, when once he has conceived a character,
he works downwards and inwards in his treatment of it, making it firm
and clear at all points in its relations to hard fact, and cutting down,
where necessary, to the very foundations. Dickens, on the other hand,
with all his keenness of observation, is more light and poetic in his
method. Having once caught a hint from actual fact, he generalizes it,
runs away with this generalization into a corner, and develops it there
into a character to match; which character he then transports, along
with others similarly suggested, into a world of semi-fantastic conditions, where the laws need not be those of ordinary probability. He
has characters of ideal perfection and beauty, as well as of ideal ugli-
ness and brutality – characters of a human kind verging on the supernatural, as well as characters actually belonging to the supernatural.
Even his situations and scenery often lie in a region beyond the margin
of everyday life. Now both kinds of art are legitimate; and each
writer is to be tried within his own kind by the success he has attained
in it. . . .

All honour to Thackeray and the prose-fiction of social reality; but

much honour, too, to Dickens, for maintaining among us, even in the
realm of the light and the amusing, some representation in prose of
that art of ideal phantasy, the total absence of which in the literature
of any age would be a sign nothing short of hideous. The true objection to Dickens is, that his idealism tends too much to extravagance
and caricature. It would be possible for an ill-natured critic to go
through all his works, and to draw out in one long column a list of
their chief characters, annexing in a parallel column the phrases or
labels by which these characters are distinguished, and of which they
are generalizations – the 'There's some credit in being jolly here' of
Mark Tapley; the 'It isn't of the slightest consequence' of Toots;
the 'Something will turn up' of Mr Micawber, &c., &c. Even this,
however, is a mode of art legitimate, I believe, in principle, as it is
certainly most effective in fact. There never was a Mr Micawber in
nature, exactly as he appears in the pages of Dickens; but Micawberism pervades nature through and through; and to have extracted
this quality from nature, embodying the full essence of a thousand
instances of it in one ideal monstrosity, is a feat of invention. From the
incessant repetition by Mr Dickens of this inventive process openly
and without variation, except in the results, the public have caught
what is called his mannerism or trick; and hence a certain recoil from
his later writings among the cultivated and fastidious. But let anyone
observe our current table-talk or our current literature and, despite
this profession of dissatisfaction, and in the very circles where it most
abounds, let him note how gladly Dickens is used, and how frequently his phrases, his fancies and the names of his characters come
in, as illustration, embellishment, proverb and seasoning. Take any
periodical in which there is a severe criticism of Dickens's last publication; and, ten to one, in the same periodical, and perhaps by the same
hand, there will be a leading article, setting out with a quotation from
Dickens that flashes on the mind of the reader the thought which the
whole article is meant to convey, or containing some allusion to one
of Dickens's characters which enriches the text in the middle and
floods it an inch round with colour and humour.

(233–52)

Otto Ludwig

from a note on *Hard Times* ?1860 (published posthumously in
Epische Studien, vol. 6 of his *Complete Works*, 1891, translated by
R. F. Green)

Dickens is truly a poet, and a great one. Always action and feeling,
never abstract reflection, Fantasy is the basis of his poetry as of all true
poetry, the other faculties that serve fantasy are completely transformed into it.

His figures are abstractions; but the manner in which he is able to
vary their often slender content arouses our admiration. Most of them
actually have nothing inside them, they are poetic automata which
perform a certain number of motions by clockwork.

One of his principal arts is that of dialogue. It is marvellous how he
is able to spin the slightest content out into long conversations which
do not weary the reader, rather the reverse. It must be said of Boz as
of Shakespeare that he entertains the reader not merely *by* his works,
but also *in* them. He knows how to seize on the entertaining side of
every figure. There is one thing about him which might be found
displeasing. His works are in the true sense of the word tendentious:
this certainly makes them all the more interesting, but the evident
intention leaves one cold. He demonstrates the injustice of a law, the
perverseness of a custom etc., practically, by giving an example of its
evil effects. However, the figures and the events are deliberately contrived in such a way as to bring such effects about.

(344-5)

Otto Ludwig

from a note on *Little Dorrit* ?1860 (published posthumously in
Epische Studien, vol. 6 of his *Complete Works*, 1891, translated by
R. F. Green)

Like many of Dickens's other novels, *Little Dorrit* is a comic-horrific
fairytale, in the manner of the *Thousand and One Nights* – the strangest

coupling of the weirdest exertions of liberated fantasy with the most commonplace reality, only without the involvement of admitted fairies and ghosts. The characters are in part no more than a nose, a mouth, or some other characteristic individual feature, monstrously magnified, and consequently less real people than a strange race of changeling children, of addled eggs of fancy, not fertilized with life; as a result the process itself is a weird dream through which we follow or accompany the author now with anxiously bated breath, now laughing, now awakened by our own moaning or laughter. Boz's poetry is popular romanticism, a synthesis of Tieck, Jean Paul, Hoffmann, Arnim, Shakespeare's grimacing mask returned to the land of its fair original, but remaining a grimacing mask, or rather having only now truly become one. Those German poets do after all still have the poetic truth which is still possible in the realm of the fantastic. I must admit, however much I was gripped at many points in this novel, I am glad now that I have it behind me; I feel roughly as if I had been visiting a lunatic asylum and was now outside again. What air, what a sky out here! In there even air and sky were like madmen. Table, chair, walls, houses, river, bridge, coalfire etc., everything alive, but – mad.

(352–3)

Charles Dickens

Letter to Sir Edward Bulwer Lytton   5 June 1860

I am very much interested and gratified by your letter concerning *A Tale of Two Cities*. I do not quite agree with you on two points, but that is no deduction from my pleasure.

In the first place, although the surrender of the feudal privileges (on a motion seconded by a nobleman of great rank) was the occasion of a sentimental scene, I see no reason to doubt, but on the contrary, many reasons to believe, that some of these privileges had been used to the frightful oppression of the peasant, quite as near to the time of the Revolution as the doctor's narrative, which, you will remember, dates long before the Terror. And surely when the new philosophy was the talk of the salons and the slang of the hour, it is not unreasonable or unallowable to suppose a nobleman wedded to the old cruel ideas, and representing the time going out, as his nephew represents the time coming in; as to the condition of the peasant in France generally at that day, I take it that if anything be certain on earth it is certain that it was intolerable. No *ex post facto* inquiries and provings by figures will hold water, surely, against the tremendous testimony of men living at the time.

There is a curious book printed at Amsterdam, written to make out no case whatever, and tiresome enough in its literal dictionary-like minuteness, scattered up and down the pages of which is full authority for my marquis. This is 'Mercier's Tableau de Paris'. Rousseau is the authority for the peasant's shutting up his house when he had a bit of meat. The tax-taker was the authority for the wretched creature's impoverishment.

I am not clear, and I never have been clear, respecting that canon of fiction which forbids the interposition of accident in such a case as Madame Defarge's death. Where the accident is inseparable from the passion and emotion of the character, where it is strictly consistent with the whole design, and arises out of some culminating proceeding on the part of the character which the whole story has led up to, it seems to me to become, as it were, an act of divine justice. And when I use Miss Pross (though this is quite another question) to bring about that catastrophe, I have the positive intention of making that half-comic intervention a part of the desperate woman's failure, and of opposing that mean death – instead of a desperate one in the streets, which she wouldn't have minded – to the dignity of Carton's wrong or right; this *was* the design, and seemed to be in the fitness of things.

Charles Dickens

from a letter to John Forster   ? October 1860

The book [*Great Expectations*] will be written in the first person throughout, and during these first three weekly numbers you will find the hero to be a boy-child, like David. Then he will be an apprentice. You will not have to complain of the want of humour as in the *Tale of Two Cities*. I have made the opening, I hope, in its general effect exceedingly droll. I have put a child and a good-natured foolish man, in relations that seem to me very funny. Of course I have got in the pivot on which the story will turn too – and which indeed, as you remember, was the grotesque tragi-comic conception that first encouraged me. To be quite sure I had fallen into no unconscious repetitions, I read *David Copperfield* again the other day, and was affected by it to a degree you would hardly believe.

Charles Dickens

from a letter to Sir Edward Bulwer Lytton 24 June 1861

I send you the enclosed, the whole of the concluding weekly No. of *Great Expectations*, in order that you may the more readily understand where I have made the change.

My difficulty was to avoid doing too much. My tendency, when I began to unwind the thread that I thought I had wound for ever, was to labour it and get out of proportion.

So I have done it in as few words as possible: and I hope you will like the alteration that is entirely due to you.

Charles Dickens

from a letter to John Forster 1 July 1861

You will be surprised to hear that I have changed the end of *Great Expectations* from and after Pip's return to Joe's, and finding his little likeness there.

Bulwer (who has been, as I think I told you, extraordinarily taken by the book) so strongly urged it upon me, after reading the proofs, and supported his views with such good reasons, that I resolved to make the change. You shall have it when you come back to town. I have put in a very pretty piece of writing, and I have no doubt the story will be more acceptable through the alteration.

Charles Dickens

The original ending to *Great Expectations* 1861
(from John Forster, *The Life of Charles Dickens*, book 9, chapter 3,
1872-4; reprinted in Hoppé edition, 1966, vol. 1)

There was no chapter 20 as now; but the sentence which opens it
('For eleven years' in the original, altered to 'eight years') followed
the paragraph about his business partnership with Herbert, and led to
Biddy's question whether he is sure he does not fret for Estella ('I am
sure and certain, Biddy' as originally written, altered to 'O no – I
think not, Biddy'): from which point here was the close. 'It was two
years more, before I saw herself. I had heard of her as leading a most
unhappy life, and as being separated from her husband who had used
her with great cruelty, and who had become quite renowned as a
compound of pride, brutality and meanness. I had heard of the death
of her husband (from an accident consequent on ill-treating a horse),
and of her being married again to a Shropshire doctor, who, against
his interest, had once very manfully interposed, on an occasion when
he was in professional attendance on Mr Drummle, and had witnessed
some outrageous treatment of her. I had heard that the Shropshire
doctor was not rich, and that they lived on her own personal fortune.
I was in England again – in London, and walking along Piccadilly with
little Pip – when a servant came running after me to ask would I step
back to a lady in a carriage who wished to speak to me. It was a little
pony carriage, which the lady was driving; and the lady and I looked
sadly enough on one another. 'I am greatly changed, I know; but I
thought you would like to shake hands with Estella too, Pip. Lift up
that pretty child and let me kiss it!' (She supposed the child, I think,
to be my child.) I was very glad afterwards to have had the interview;
for in her face and in her voice, and in her touch, she gave me the
assurance, that suffering had been stronger than Miss Havisham's
teaching, and had given her a heart to understand what my heart used
to be.'
(441 n)

Margaret Oliphant (anonymously)

from 'Sensation Novels', *Blackwood's Magazine*, vol. 91   May 1862

There can scarcely be a greater contrast between two works which aim in their different individualities at something of a similar effect, than there exists between Mr Wilkie Collins's powerful story [*The Woman in White*] and the last work of his Master in Art. Mr Dickens's successes in sensation are great. Even in *Great Expectations*, which is far from being one of his best works, he manages to impress distinct images of horror, surprise and pain upon the mind of his reader with vivid power and distinctness; but his performances go on an entirely different principle, and use other agencies than those which, in the hands of his disciple, heighten the effect by the evident simplicity of the means. Mr Dickens was one of the first popular writers who brought pictures of what is called common life into fashion. It is he who has been mainly instrumental in leading the present generation of authors to disregard to a great extent the pictorial advantages of life on the upper levels of society, and to find a counter-picturesqueness in the experiences of the poor. But while this is the case, it is equally certain that Mr Dickens, for his own part, has never ventured to depend for his special effects upon the common incidents of life. He has shifted the fashionable ground, and sought his heroes among penniless clerks and adventurers, as little beholden to their ancestors as to fortune. He has made washerwomen as interesting as duchesses, and found domestic angels among the vagabonds of a circus, on the very edge between lawlessness and crime; but whenever he has aimed at a scene, he has hurried aside into regions of exaggeration, and shown his own distrust of the common and usual by fantastic eccentricities, and accumulations of every description of high-strained oddity. The characters upon which he depends are not individual only, with a due recognizable difference to distinguish them from their fellows, but always peculiar, and set forth with a quaintly exaggerated distortion, by which we identify in a moment, not the character described, but the author who has made it, and of whom these oddities are characteristic. If it were possible to quicken these curious originals into life, what an odd crowd of ragamuffins and monsters would that be which should pursue this Frankenstein through the world! In the flush of fresh life and invention, when Sam Wellers and Mark Tapleys led the throng, we all awaited with impatience and received with delight the new oddities with which the great novelist filled his pages; but it is impossible to deny that nowadays that fertile fullness has failed, and that the persistent devotion to the eccentric which has distinguished Mr Dickens through all his literary life, does now no longer produce fruits such as earn him our forgiveness for all the daring steps he takes beyond the modesty of nature. In his last work, symptoms of a dangerous adherence to, and departure from, his old habitudes, will strike most of his faithful readers. The oddity remains, but much of the character has evaporated. The personages in *Great Expectations* are less out of the way, and the circumstances more so. Strange situations and fantastic predicaments have very much taken the place of those quaint and overstrained but still lifelike phases of humanity in which the author used to delight. He now carves his furniture grotesquely, and makes quaint masks upon his friezes; but he has no longer patience to keep up the strain so long as is necessary for the perfection of a character. After an indication of what he means this and that figure to be, he goes on with his story, too indifferent about it, one could suppose, to enter into the old elaboration. The book reminds us of a painter's rapid memoranda of some picture, in which he uses his pencil to help his memory. After he has dashed in the outline and composition, he scribbles a hasty 'carmine' or 'ultramarine' where those colours come. So the reds and blues of Mr Dickens's picture are only written in. He means us to fill in the glow of the natural hue from the feeble symbol of the word which represents it, or perhaps to go back in our own memory to those forcible and abundant days when he wrought out his own odd conceptions minutely as if he loved them. Perhaps it was not at any time the wholesomest kind of art, but it was certainly much more satisfactory and piquant than now.

So far as *Great Expectations* is a sensation novel, it occupies itself with incidents all but impossible, and in themselves strange, dangerous and exciting; but so far as it is one of the series of Mr Dickens's works, it is feeble, fatigued and colourless. One feels that he must have got tired of it as the work went on, and that the creatures he had called into being, but who are no longer the lively men and women they used to be, must have bored him unspeakably before it was time to cut short their career, and throw a hasty and impatient hint of their

future to stop the tiresome public appetite. Joe Gargery the blacksmith alone represents the ancient mood of the author. He is as good,
as true, patient and affectionate, as ungrammatical and confused in his
faculty of speech, as could be desired; and shields the poor little Pip
when he is a child on his hands, and forgives him when he is a man
too grand for the blacksmith, with all that affecting tenderness and
refinement of affection with which Mr Dickens has the faculty of
making his poor blacksmiths and fishermen much more interesting
than anything he has ever produced in the condition of gentleman.
(574–5)

John Ruskin

from *Unto This Last* 1862 (reprinted in E. T. Cook and
A. Wedderburn (eds.), *The Works of John Ruskin*, vol. 17, 1912)

The essential value and truth of Dickens's writings have been unwisely
lost sight of by many thoughtful persons, merely because he presents
his truth with some colour of caricature. Unwisely, because Dickens's
caricature, though often gross, is never mistaken. Allowing for his
manner of telling them, the things he tells us are always true. I wish
that he could think it right to limit his brilliant exaggeration to works
written only for public amusement; and when he takes up a subject
of high national importance, such as that which he handled in *Hard
Times*, that he would use severer and more accurate analysis. The use-
fulness of that work (to my mind, in several respects the greatest he
has written) is with many persons seriously diminished because Mr
Bounderby is a dramatic monster, instead of a characteristic example
of a worldly master; and Stephen Blackpool a dramatic perfection,
instead of a characteristic example of an honest workman. But let us
not lose the use of Dickens's wit and insight, because he chooses to
speak in a circle of stage fire. He is entirely right in his main drift and
purpose in every book he has written; and all of them, but especially
Hard Times, should be studied with close and earnest care by persons
interested in social questions. They will find much that is partial,
and, because partial, apparently unjust; but if they examine all the

evidence on the other side, which Dickens seems to overlook, it will appear, after all their trouble, that his view was the finally right one, grossly and sharply told.

(31)

Charles Dickens

from a letter to Mrs Eliza Davis   10 July 1863

I must take leave to say, that if there be any general feeling on the part of the intelligent Jewish people, that I have done them what you describe as 'a great wrong', they are a far less sensible, a far less just, and a far less good-tempered people than I have always supposed them to be. Fagin, in *Oliver Twist*, is a Jew, because it unfortunately was true of the time to which that story refers, that that class of criminal almost invariably was a Jew. But surely no sensible man or woman of your persuasion can fail to observe – firstly, that all the rest of the wicked *dramatis personae* are Christians; and secondly, that he is called the 'Jew', not because of his religion, but because of his race.[1]

Charles Dickens

Letter to Marcus Stone   23 February 1864

I think the design for the cover *excellent*, and do not doubt its coming out to perfection. The slight alteration I am going to suggest originates in a business consideration not to be overlooked.

The word 'Our' in the title must be out in the open like 'Mutual Friend,' making the title three distinct large lines – 'Our' as big as 'Mutual Friend.' This would give you too much design at the bottom. I would therefore take out the dustman, and put the Wegg and Boffin composition (which is capital) in its place. I don't want Mr

1 Dickens's further reply to Mrs Davis's reproach was the benevolent Jew Riah, in *Our Mutual Friend*. [Ed.]

Inspector or the murder reward bill, because these points are sufficiently indicated in the river at the top. Therefore you can have an
indication of the dustman in Mr Inspector's place. Note, that the dustman's face should be droll, and not horrible. Twemlow's elbow will
still go out of the frame as it does now, and the same with Lizzie's
skirts on the opposite side. With these changes, work away!

Mrs Boffin, as I judge of her from the sketch, 'very good, indeed'.
I want Boffin's oddity, without being at all blinked, to be an oddity
of a very honest kind, that people will like.

The doll's dressmaker is immensely better than she was. I think she
should now come extremely well. A weird sharpness not without
beauty is the thing I want.

Charles Dickens

Postscript to the first edition of *Our Mutual Friend*   1865

When I devised this story, I foresaw the likelihood that a class of
readers and commentators would suppose that I was at great pains to
conceal exactly what I was at great pains to suggest: namely, that Mr
John Harmon was not slain, and that Mr John Rokesmith was he.
Pleasing myself with the idea that the supposition might in part arise
out of some ingenuity in the story, and thinking it worthwhile, in
the interests of art, to hint to an audience that an artist (of whatever
denomination) may perhaps be trusted to know what he is about in
his vocation, if they will concede him a little patience, I was not
alarmed by the anticipation.

To keep for a long time unsuspected, yet always working itself out,
another purpose originating in that leading incident, and turning it to
a pleasant and useful account at last, was at once the most interesting
and the most difficult part of my design. Its difficulty was much
enhanced by the mode of publication; for, it would be very unreasonable to expect that many readers, pursuing a story in portions from
month to month through nineteen months, will, until they have it
before them complete, perceive the relations of its finer threads to the
whole pattern which is always before the eyes of the story weaver at
his loom. Yet, that I hold the advantages of the mode of publication

to outweigh its disadvantages, may be easily believed of one who revived it in the Pickwick Papers after long disuse, and has pursued it ever since.

There is sometimes an odd disposition in this country to dispute as improbable in fiction, what are the commonest experiences in fact. Therefore, I note here, though it may not be at all necessary, that there are hundreds of Will Cases (as they are called), far more remarkable than that fancied in this book; and that the stores of the Prerogative Office teem with instances of testators who have made, changed, contradicted, hidden, forgotten, left cancelled, and left uncancelled, each many more wills than were ever made by the elder Mr Harmon of Harmony Jail.

In my social experiences since Mrs Betty Higden came upon the scene and left it, I have found Circumlocutional champions disposed to be warm with me on the subject of my view of the Poor Law. My friend Mr Bounderby could never see any difference between leaving the Coketown 'hands' exactly as they were, and requiring them to be fed with turtle soup and venison out of gold spoons. Idiotic propositions of a parallel nature have been freely offered for my acceptance, and I have been called upon to admit that I would give Poor Law relief to anybody, anywhere, anyhow. Putting this nonsense aside, I have observed a suspicious tendency in the champions to divide into two parties; the one, contending that there are no deserving Poor who prefer death by slow starvation and bitter weather, to the mercies of some Relieving Officers and some Union Houses; the other, admitting that there are such Poor, but denying that they have any cause or reason for what they do. The records in our newspapers, the late exposure by the *Lancet*, and the common sense and senses of common people, furnish too abundant evidence against both defences. But, that my view of the Poor Law may not be mistaken or misrepresented, I will state it. I believe there has been in England, since the days of the Stuarts, no law so often infamously administered, no law so often openly violated, no law habitually so ill-supervised. In the majority of the shameful cases of disease and death from destitution, that shock the Public and disgrace the country, the illegality is quite equal to the inhumanity – and known language could say no more of their lawlessness.

On Friday the Ninth of June in the present year, Mr and Mrs

Boffin (in their manuscript dress of receiving Mr and Mrs Lammle at breakfast) were on the South-Eastern Railway with me, in a terribly destructive accident. When I had done what I could to help others, I climbed back into my carriage – nearly turned over a viaduct, and caught aslant upon the turn – to extricate the worthy couple. They were much soiled, but otherwise unhurt. The same happy result attended Miss Bella Wilfer on her wedding day, and Mr Riderhood inspecting Bradley Headstone's red neckerchief as he lay asleep. I remember with devout thankfulness that I can never be much nearer parting company with my readers for ever than I was then, until there shall be written against my life, the two words with which I have this day closed this book – THE END.

Henry James (anonymously)

Review of *Our Mutual Friend*, *Nation*, vol. 1   21 December 1865

Our Mutual Friend is, to our perception, the poorest of Mr Dickens's works. And it is poor with the poverty not of momentary embarrassment, but of permanent exhaustion. It is wanting in inspiration. For the last ten years it has seemed to us that Mr Dickens has been unmistakably forcing himself. *Bleak House* was forced; *Little Dorrit* was laboured; the present work is dug out, as with a spade and pickaxe. Of course – to anticipate the usual argument – who but Dickens could have written it? Who, indeed? Who else would have established a lady in business in a novel on the admirably solid basis of her always putting on gloves and tying a handkerchief round her head in moments of grief, and of her habitually addressing her family with 'Peace! Hold!' It is needless to say that Mrs Reginald Wilfer is first and last the occasion of considerable true humour. When, after conducting her daughter to Mrs Boffin's carriage, in sight of all the envious neighbours, she is described as enjoying her triumph during the next quarter of an hour by airing herself on the doorstep 'in a kind of splendidly serene trance', we laugh with as uncritical a laugh as could be desired of us. We pay the same tribute to her assertions, as she narrates the glories of the society she enjoyed at her father's table, that she has known as many as three copperplate engravers exchanging the most exquisite sallies and retorts there at one time. But when to these we have added a dozen more happy examples of the humour which was exhaled from every line of Mr Dickens's earlier writings, we shall have closed the list of the merits of the work before us. To say that the conduct of the story, with all its complications, betrays a long-practised hand, is to pay no compliment worthy the author. If this were, indeed, a compliment, we should be inclined to carry it further, and congratulate him on his success in what we should call the manufacture of fiction; for in so doing we should express a feeling that has attended us throughout the book. Seldom, we reflected, had we read a book so intensely *written*, so little seen, known or felt.

In all Mr Dickens's works the fantastic has been his great resource; and while his fancy was lively and vigorous it accomplished great things. But the fantastic, when the fancy is dead, is a very poor business. The movement of Mr Dickens's fancy in Mrs Wilfer and Mr Boffin and Lady Tippins, and the Lammles and Miss Wren, and even in Eugene Wrayburn, is, to our mind, a movement lifeless, forced, mechanical. It is the letter of his old humour without the spirit. It is hardly too much to say that every character here put before us is a mere bundle of eccentricities, animated by no principle of nature whatever. In former days there reigned in Mr Dickens's extravagances a comparative consistency; they were exaggerated statements of types that really existed. We had, perhaps, never known a Newman Noggs, nor a Pecksniff, nor a Micawber; but we had known persons of whom these figures were but the strictly logical consummation. But among the grotesque creatures who occupy the pages before us, there is not one whom we can refer to as an existing type. In all Mr Dickens's stories, indeed, the reader has been called upon, and has willingly consented, to accept a certain number of figures or creatures of pure fancy, for this was the author's poetry. He was, moreover, always repaid for his concession by a peculiar beauty or power in these exceptional characters. But he is now expected to make the same concession with a very inadequate reward. What do we get in return for accepting Miss Jenny Wren as a possible person? This young lady is the type of a certain class of characters of which Mr Dickens has made a specialty, and with which he has been accustomed to draw alternate smiles and tears, according as he pressed one spring or another. But this is very cheap merriment and very cheap pathos. Miss

Jenny Wren is a poor little dwarf, afflicted, as she constantly reiterates, with a 'bad back' and 'queer legs', who makes doll's dresses, and is forever pricking at those with whom she converses, in the air, with her needle, and assuring them that she knows their 'tricks and their manners'. Like all Mr Dickens's pathetic characters, she is a little monster; she is deformed, unhealthy, unnatural; she belongs to the troop of hunchbacks, imbeciles and precocious children who have carried on the sentimental business in all Mr Dickens's novels; the little Nells, the Smikes, the Paul Dombeys.

Mr Dickens goes as far out of the way for his wicked people as he does for his good ones. Rogue Riderhood, indeed, in the present story, is villainous with a sufficiently natural villainy; he belongs to that quarter of society in which the author is most at his ease. But was there ever such wickedness as that of the Lammles and Mr Fledgeby? Not that people have not been as mischievous as they; but was anyone ever mischievous in that singular fashion? Did a couple of elegant swindlers ever take such particular pains to be aggressively inhuman? – for we can find no other word for the gratuitous distortions to which they are subjected. The word *humanity* strikes us as strangely discordant, in the midst of these pages; for, let us boldly declare it, there is no humanity here. Humanity is nearer home than the Boffins, and the Lammles, and the Wilfers, and the Veneerings. It is in what men have in common with each other, and not in what they have in distinction. The people just named have nothing in common with each other, except the fact that they have nothing in common with mankind at large. What a world were this world if the world of *Our Mutual Friend* were an honest reflection of it! But a community of eccentrics is impossible. Rules alone are consistent with each other; exceptions are inconsistent. Society is maintained by natural sense and natural feeling. We cannot conceive a society in which these principles are not in some manner represented. Where in these pages are the depositaries of that intelligence without which the movement of life would cease? Who represents nature? Accepting half of Mr Dickens's persons as intentionally grotesque, where are those exemplars of sound humanity who should afford us the proper measure of their companion's variations? We ought not, in justice to the author, to seek them among his weaker – that is, his mere conventional – characters; in John Harmon, Lizzie Hexam or Mortimer Lightwood;

but we assuredly cannot find them among his stronger – that is, his artificial creations. Suppose we take Eugene Wrayburn and Bradley Headstone. They occupy a half-way position between the habitual probable of nature and the habitual impossible of Mr Dickens. A large portion of the story rests upon the enmity borne by Headstone to Wrayburn, both being in love with the same woman. Wrayburn is a gentleman, and Headstone is one of the people. Wrayburn is well-bred, careless, elegant, sceptical and idle: Headstone is a high-tempered, hard-working, ambitious young schoolmaster. There lay in the opposition of these two characters a very good story. But the prime requisite was that they should *be* characters: Mr Dickens, according to his usual plan, has made them simply figures, and between them the story that was to be, the story that should have been, has evaporated. Wrayburn lounges about with his hands in his pockets, smoking a cigar and talking nonsense. Headstone strides about, clenching his fists and biting his lips and grasping his stick. There is one scene in which Wrayburn chaffs the schoolmaster with easy insolence, while the latter writhes impotently under his well-bred sarcasm. This scene is very clever, but it is very insufficient. If the majority of readers were not so very timid in the use of words we should call it vulgar. By this we do not mean to indicate the conventional impropriety of two gentlemen exchanging lively personalities; we mean to emphasize the essentially small character of these personalities. In other words, the moment, dramatically, is great, while the author's conception is weak. The friction of two *men*, of two characters, of two passions, produces stronger sparks than Wrayburn's boyish repartees and Headstone's melodramatic commonplaces. Such scenes as this are useful in fixing the limits of Mr Dickens's insight. Insight is, perhaps, too strong a word; for we are convinced that it is one of the chief conditions of his genius not to see beneath the surface of things. If we might hazard a definition of his literary character, we should, accordingly, call him the greatest of superficial novelists. We are aware that this definition confines him to an inferior rank in the department of letters which he adorns; but we accept this consequence of our proposition. It were, in our opinion, an offence against humanity to place Mr Dickens among the greatest novelists. For, to repeat what we have already intimated, he has created nothing but figures. He has added nothing to our understanding of human character. He is master of but two alternatives; he reconciles us to what is commonplace, and he reconciles us to what is odd. The value of the former service is questionable; and the manner in which Mr Dickens performs it sometimes conveys a certain impression of charlatanism. The value of the latter service is incontestable, and here Mr Dickens is an honest, an admirable artist. But what is the condition of the truly great novelist? For him there are no alternatives, for him there are no oddities, for him there is nothing outside of humanity. He cannot shirk it; it imposes itself upon him. For him alone, therefore, there is a true and a false; for him alone it is possible to be right, because it is possible to be wrong. Mr Dickens is a great observer and a great humorist, but he is nothing of a philosopher. Some people may hereupon say, so much the better; we say, so much the worse. For a novelist very soon has need of a little philosophy. In treating of Micawber, and Boffin, and Pickwick, *et hoc genus omne*, he can, indeed, dispense with it, for this – we say it with all deference – is not serious writing. But when he comes to tell the story of a passion, a story like that of Headstone and Wrayburn, he becomes a moralist as well as an artist. He must know *man* as well as *men*, and to know man is to be a philosopher. The writer who knows men alone, if he have Mr Dickens's humour and fancy, will give us figures and pictures for which we cannot be too grateful, for he will enlarge our knowledge of the world. But when he introduces men and women whose interest is preconceived to lie not in the poverty, the weakness, the drollery of their natures, but in their complete and unconscious subjection to ordinary and healthy human emotions, all his humour, all his fancy, will avail him nothing if, out of the fullness of his sympathy, he is unable to prosecute those generalizations in which alone consists the real greatness of a work of art. This may sound like very subtle talk about a very simple matter; it is rather very simple talk about a very subtle matter. A story based upon those elementary passions in which alone we seek the true and final manifestation of character must be told in a spirit of intellectual superiority to those passions. That is, the author must understand what he is talking about. The perusal of a story so told is one of the most elevating experiences within the reach of the human mind. The perusal of a story which is not so told is infinitely depressing and unprofitable.

(786–7)

Charles Dickens

Preface to the Charles Dickens Edition of *Martin Chuzzlewit* 1867

What is exaggeration to one class of minds and perceptions, is plain truth to another. That which is commonly called a long-sight, perceives in a prospect innumerable features and bearings non-existent to a short-sighted person. I sometimes ask myself whether there may occasionally be a difference of this kind between some writers and some readers; whether it is *always* the writer who colours highly, or whether it is now and then the reader whose eye for colour is a little dull?

On this head of exaggeration I have a positive experience, more curious than the speculation I have just set down. It is this: – I have never touched a character precisely from the life, but some counterpart of that character has incredulously asked me: 'Now really, did I ever really see one like it?'

All the Pecksniff family upon earth are quite agreed, I believe, that Mr Pecksniff is an exaggeration, and that no such character ever existed. I will not offer any plea on his behalf to so powerful and genteel a body, but will make a remark on the character of Jonas Chuzzlewit.

I conceive that the sordid coarseness and brutality of Jonas would be unnatural, if there had been nothing in his early education, and in the precept and example always before him, to engender and develop the vices that make him odious. But, so born and so bred; admired for that which made him hateful, and justified from his cradle in cunning, treachery and avarice; I claim him as the legitimate issue of the father upon whom those vices are seen to recoil. And I submit that their recoil upon that old man, in his unhonoured age, is not a mere piece of poetical justice, but is the extreme exposition of a direct truth.

I make this comment and solicit the reader's attention to it in his or her consideration of this tale, because nothing is more common in real life than a want of profitable reflection on the causes of many vices and crimes that awaken general horror. What is substantially true of families in this respect, is true of a whole commonwealth. As we sow, we reap. Let the reader go into the children's side of any prison in England, or I grieve to add, of many workhouses, and judge whether those are monsters who disgrace our streets, people our hulks and penitentiaries, and overcrowd our penal colonies, or are creatures whom we have deliberately suffered to be bred for misery and ruin.

The American portion of this story is in no other respect a caricature, than as it is an exhibition, for the most part (Mr Bevan excepted) of a ludicrous side, *only*, of the American character – of that side which was, four-and-twenty years ago, from its nature, the most obtrusive, and the most likely to be seen by such travellers as Young Martin and Mark Tapley. As I had never, in writing fiction, had any disposition to soften what is ridiculous or wrong at home, so I then hoped that the good-humoured people of the United States would not be generally disposed to quarrel with me for carrying the same usage abroad. I am happy to believe that my confidence in that great nation was not misplaced.

When this book was first published, I was given to understand, by some authorities, that the Watertoast Association and eloquence were beyond all bounds of belief. Therefore, I record the fact that all that portion of Martin Chuzzlewit's experiences is a literal paraphrase of some reports of public proceedings in the United States (especially of the proceedings of a certain Brandywine Association), which were printed in *The Times* Newspaper in June and July 1843, at about the time when I was engaged in writing those parts of the book; and which remain on the file of *The Times* Newspaper, of course.

In all my writings, I hope I have taken every available opportunity of showing the want of sanitary improvements in the neglected dwellings of the poor. Mrs Sarah Gamp was, four-and-twenty years ago, a fair representation of the hired attendant on the poor in sickness. The Hospitals of London were, in many respects, noble Institutions; in others, very defective. I think it not the least among the instances of their mismanagement, that Mrs Betsey Prig was a fair specimen of a Hospital Nurse; and that the Hospitals, with their means and funds, should have left it to private humanity and enterprise to enter on an attempt to improve that class of persons – since, greatly improved through the agency of good women.

Charles Dickens

Preface to the Charles Dickens Edition of *Dombey and Son*   1867

I make so bold as to believe that the faculty (or the habit) of correctly observing the characters of men, is a rare one. I have not even found, within my experience, that the faculty (or the habit) of correctly observing so much as the faces of men, is a general one by any means. The two commonest mistakes in judgement that I suppose to arise from the former default, are, the confounding of shyness with arrogance – a very common mistake indeed – and the not understanding that an obstinate nature exists in a perpetual struggle with itself.

Mr Dombey undergoes no violent change, either in this book, or in real life. A sense of his injustice is within him, all along. The more he represses it, the more unjust he necessarily is. Internal shame and external circumstances may bring the contest to a close in a week, or a day; but, it has been a contest for years, and is only fought out after a long balance of victory.

I began this book by the Lake of Geneva, and went on with it for some months in France, before pursuing it in England. The association between the writing and the place of writing is so curiously strong in my mind, that at this day, although I know, in my fancy, every stair in the little midshipman's house, and could swear to every pew in the church in which Florence was married, or to every young gentleman's bedstead in Doctor Blimber's establishment, I yet confusedly imagine Captain Cuttle as secluding himself from Mrs Mac-Stinger among the mountains of Switzerland. Similarly, when I am reminded by any chance of what it was that the waves were always saying, my remembrance wanders for a whole winter night about the streets of Paris – as I restlessly did with a heavy heart, on the night when I had written the chapter in which my little friend and I parted company.

Charles Dickens

Preface to the Charles Dickens Edition of *David Copperfield* 1867

I remarked in the original Preface to this Book, that I did not find it easy to get sufficiently far away from it, in the first sensations of having finished it, to refer to it with the composure which this formal heading would seem to require. My interest in it was so recent and strong, and my mind was so divided between pleasure and regret – pleasure in the achievement of a long design, regret in the separation from many companions – that I was in danger of wearying the reader with personal confidences and private emotions.

Besides which, all that I could have said of the Story to any purpose, I had endeavoured to say in it.

It would concern the reader little, perhaps, to know how sorrowfully the pen is laid down at the close of a two-years' imaginative task; or how an Author feels as if he were dismissing some portion of himself into the shadowy world, when a crowd of the creatures of his brain are going from him for ever. Yet, I had nothing else to tell; unless, indeed, I were to confess (which might be of less moment still), that no one can ever believe this Narrative in the reading more than I believed it in the writing.

So true are these avowals at the present day, that I can now only take the reader into one confidence more. Of all my books, I like this the best. It will be easily believed that I am a fond parent to every child of my fancy, and that no one can ever love that family as dearly as I love them. But, like many fond parents, I have in my heart of hearts a favourite child. And his name is DAVID COPPERFIELD.

Fyodor Dostoyevsky

from a letter to his niece, Sofia Alexandrovna 1 January 1868
(translated by E. C. Mayne, *Letters of Dostoyevsky*, 1914)

The idea of the book [*The Idiot*] is the old one which I always have so greatly liked; but it is so difficult that hitherto I never have had the courage to carry it out; and if I'm setting to work to it now, it's only because I'm in such a desperate plight. The basic idea is the representation of a truly perfect and noble man. And this is more difficult than anything else in the world, particularly nowadays. All writers, not ours alone but foreigners also, who have sought to represent Absolute Beauty, were unequal to the task, for it is an infinitely difficult one. The beautiful is the ideal; but ideals, with us as in civilized Europe, have long been wavering. There is in the world only one figure of absolute beauty: Christ. That infinitely lovely figure is, as a matter of course, an infinite marvel. . . . I will only say further that of all the noble figures in Christian literature, I reckon Don Quixote as the most perfect. But Don Quixote is noble only by being at the same time comic. And Dickens's Pickwickians (they were certainly much weaker than Don Quixote, but still it's a powerful work) are comic, and this it is which gives them their great value. The reader feels sympathy and compassion with the Beautiful, derided and unconscious of its own worth. The secret of humour consists precisely in this art of wakening the reader's sympathy.

Charles Dickens

from a letter to John Forster   6 August 1869 (quoted by John Forster, *The Life of Charles Dickens*, book 11, chapter 2; reprinted in Hoppé edition, 1966, vol. 2)

I laid aside the fancy I told you of, and have a very curious and new idea for my new story. Not a communicable idea (or the interest of the book would be gone), but a very strong one, though difficult to work.

[Forster added to this the following information about *Edwin Drood*.]

The story, I learnt immediately afterward, was to be that of the murder of a nephew by his uncle; the originality of which was to consist in the review of the murderer's career by himself at the close, when its temptations were to be dwelt upon as if, not he the culprit, but some other man, were the tempted. The last chapters were to be written in the condemned cell, to which his wickedness, all elaborately elicited from him as if told of another, had brought him. Discovery by the murderer of the utter needlessness of the murder for its object, was to follow hard upon commission of the deed; but all discovery of the murderer was to be baffled till towards the close, when, by means of a gold ring which had resisted the corrosive effects of the lime into which he had thrown the body, not only the person murdered was to be identified but the locality of the crime and the man who committed it. So much was told to me before any of the book was written; and it will be recollected that the ring, taken by Drood to be given to his betrothed only if their engagement went on, was brought away with him from their last interview. Rosa was to marry Tartar, and Crisparkle the sister of Landless, who was himself, I think, to have perished in assisting Tartar finally to unmask and seize the murderer.

(366)

Charles Dickens

from a speech at Birmingham   6 January 1870

When I was here last autumn I made, in reference to some remarks of your respected member, Mr Dixon, a short confession of my political faith (*applause*), or perhaps I should better say, want of faith. (*Laughter*.) It imported that I have very little faith in the people who govern us – please to observe 'people' there will be with a small 'p' (*laughter*), but that I have great confidence in the People whom they govern: please to observe 'People' there with a large 'P'. (*Renewed laughter*.) This was shortly and elliptically stated; and was, with no evil intention I am absolutely sure, in some quarters inversely explained. Perhaps as the inventor of a certain extravagant fiction, but one which I do see rather frequently quoted as if there were grains of truth at the bottom of it, a fiction called 'The Circumlocution Office' (*laughter*), and perhaps also as the writer of an idle book or two, whose public opinions are not obscurely stated – perhaps in these respects I do not sufficiently bear in mind Hamlet's caution to speak by the card lest equivocation should undo me. (*Laughter and applause*.)

Anyhow I complain of nobody, but simply in order that there may be no mistake as to what I did mean, and as to what I do mean, I will restate my meaning, and I will do so in the words of a great thinker, a great writer and a great scholar – whose life, unfortunately for mankind, was cut short – in his *History of Civilization in England*:

They ... may talk as they will about the reforms which government has introduced, and the improvements to be expected from legislation. But whoever will take a wider and more commanding view of affairs, will soon discover that such hopes are chimerical. They will learn that lawgivers are nearly always the obstructors of society, instead of its helpers; and that in the extremely few cases in which their measures have turned out well, their success has been owing to the fact that, contrary to their usual custom, they have implicitly obeyed the spirit of their time, and have been, as they always should be, the mere servants of the people, to whose wishes they are bound to give a public and legal sanction.[1] (*Loud applause.*)

Charles Dickens

from a letter (?)   n.d. (quoted by John Forster, *The Life of Charles Dickens*, 1872–4, book 9, chapter 1; reprinted in Hoppé edition, 1966, vol. 2)

It does not seem to me to be enough to say of any description that it is the exact truth. The exact truth must be there; but the merit or art in the narrator, is the manner of stating the truth. As to which thing in literature, it always seems to me that there is a world to be done. And in these times, when the tendency is to be frightfully literal and catalogue-like – to make the thing, in short, a sort of sum in reduction that any miserable creature can do in the way – I have an idea (really founded on the love of what I profess), that the very holding of popular literature through a kind of popular dark age, may depend on such fanciful treatment.
(279)

1 H. T. Buckle, *History of Civilization in England*, Longmans, 1902, vol. 3, p. 170.

Benjamin Jowett

Sermon at Dickens's funeral service, *The Times* 20 June 1870

He whom we now mourn was the friend of mankind, a philanthropist in the true sense, the friend of youth, the friend of the poor, the enemy of every form of meanness and oppression. I am not going to attempt to draw a portrait of him. Men of genius are different from what we suppose them to be; they have greater pleasures and greater pains, and greater temptations than the generality of mankind, and they can never be altogether understood by their fellow-men. We do not wish to intrude upon them, or analyse their lives and characters. They are extraordinary persons, and we cannot prescribe to them what they should be. But we feel that a light has gone out, the world is darker to us when they depart. There are so very few of them that we cannot afford to lose them one by one and we look vainly round for others who may supply their places.

And he whose loss we now mourn occupied a greater space than any other writer in the minds of Englishmen during the last thirty-five years. We read him, talked about him, acted him; we laughed with him, we were roused by him to a consciousness of the misery of others, and to a pathetic interest in human life. The workhouse child, the cripple, and half-clothed and half-starved inhabitant of a debtors' prison found a way to his heart, and, through the exertions of his genius, touch to our hearts also. Works of fiction would be intolerable if they attempted to be sermons directly to instruct us; but indirectly they are great instructors of this world, and we can hardly exaggerate the debt of gratitude which is due to a writer who has led us to sympathize with these good, true, sincere, honest English characters of ordinary life, and to laugh at the egotism, the hypocrisy, the false respectability of religious professors and others.

To another great humorist who lies in this church the words have been applied that the gaiety of nations was eclipsed by his death. But of him who has been recently taken I would rather say, in humbler language, that no one was ever so much beloved or so much mourned. Men seem to have lost, not a great writer only, but one whom they had personally known. And so we bid him farewell.

Anthony Trollope

'Charles Dickens', *St Paul's Mazagine*, vol. 6   July 1870

It seems to have been but the other day that, sitting where I now sit, in the same chair, at the same table, with the same familiar things around me, I wrote for the *Cornhill Magazine* a few lines in remembrance of Thackeray, who had then been taken from us; and, when those lines appeared, they were preceded by others, very full of feeling, from his much older friend, Charles Dickens. Now I take up my pen again, because Charles Dickens has also gone, and because it is not fit that this publication should go forth without a word spoken to his honour.

It is singular that two men in age so nearly equal, in career so nearly allied, friends so old, and rivals so close, should each have left us so suddenly, without any of that notice, first doubting and then assured, which illness gives; so that in the case of the one as of the other, the tidings of death's dealings have struck us a hard and startling blow, inflicting, not only sorrow, but for a while that positive, physical pain which comes from evil tidings which are totally unexpected. It was but a week or two since that I was discussing at the club that vexed question of American copyright with Mr Dickens, and, while differing from him somewhat, was wondering at the youthful vitality of the man who seemed to have done his forty years of work without having a trace of it left upon him to lessen his energy, or rob his feelings of their freshness. It was but the other day that he spoke at the Academy dinner, and those who heard him then heard him at his best; and those who did not hear him, but only read his words, felt how fortunate it was that there should be such a man to speak for literature on such an occasion. When he took farewell of the public as a public reader, a few months since, the public wondered that a man in the very prime of his capacity should retire from such a career. But though there was to be an end of his readings, there was not, therefore, to be an end of his labours. He was to resume, and did resume, his old work, and when the first number of Edwin Drood's Mystery was bought up with unprecedented avidity by the lovers of Dickens's stories, it was feared, probably, by none but one that he might not live to finish his chronicle. He was a man, as we all thought, to live to be a hundred. He looked to be full of health, he walked vigorously, he stood, and spoke, and, above all, he laughed like a man in the full vigour of his life. He had never become impassive as men do who have grown old beneath burdens too heavy for their shoulders. Whatever he did seemed to come from him easily, as though he delighted in the doing of it. To hear him speak was to long to be a speaker oneself; because the thing, when properly managed, could evidently be done so easily, so pleasantly, with such gratification not only to all hearers but to oneself! We were, indeed, told some time since that he was ill, and must seek rest for a while; but anyone may be ill for a period. What working man does not suffer occasionally? But he never looked ill when he was seen at his work. As I am now writing, it is just two years and two months since I entered the harbour of New York as he was leaving it, and I then called on him on board the 'Russia'. I found him with one of his feet bound up, and he told me, with that pleasant smile that was so common to him, that he had lectured himself off his legs; otherwise he was quite well. When I heard afterwards of his labours in the States, and of the condition in which those labours had been continued, it seemed to be marvellous that any constitution should have stood it. He himself knew, no doubt, where the shoe pinched him, where the burden was too heavy, where the strain told, – that strain, without which such work as his could not adequately be done; but there was a vitality in the man, and a certain manliness of demeanour, which made those who looked upon him believe that nothing that he had yet done had acted injuriously upon the machine of his body. But that it had so acted there can now be but little doubt. We have been told that he complained in his own home that his present work was burdensome to him, and that the task of composition was difficult. When making pecuniary arrangements for the publication of *Edwin Drood*, he especially stipulated by deed that the publishers should be reimbursed for any possible loss that might accrue to them should he be prevented by death or sickness from completing his work – a stipulation which can hardly have been necessary, but which, as it betrays his own nervousness, so also gives evidence of his high honour and thoughtful integrity.

The event, which he alone thought probable enough to require prevision, has taken place; and *Edwin Drood*, like *Denis Duval* and

Wives and Daughters – the novel on which Mrs Gaskell was engaged when she died – will be left unfinished. To speak here of the circumstances of his life – or of the manner of the sad catastrophe which has taken him from us, would be unnecessary. The daily and weekly newspapers have already told the public all that can be told at once; and that which will require later and careful telling, will we hope be told with care. Of the man's public work and public character it may perhaps not be amiss for one who remembers well the *Sketches by Boz* when they first came out, to say a few words. Of his novels, the first striking circumstance is their unprecedented popularity. This is not the time for exact criticism; but, even were it so, no critic is justified in putting aside the consideration of that circumstance. When the masses of English readers, in all English-reading countries, have agreed to love the writings of any writer, their verdict will be stronger than that of any one judge, let that judge be ever so learned and ever so thoughtful. However the writer may have achieved his object, he has accomplished that which must be the desire of every author, he has spoken to men and women who have opened their ears to his words, and have listened to them. He has reached the goal which all authors seek. In this respect Dickens was, probably, more fortunate during his own life than any writer that ever lived. The English-speaking public may be counted, perhaps, as a hundred millions, and wherever English is read these books are popular from the highest to the lowest, among all classes that read. In England his novels are found in every house in which books are kept; but in America his circulation is much more extended than it is in England, because the houses in which books exist are much more numerous. I remember another novelist saying to me of Dickens – my friend and his friend, Charles Lever – that Dickens knew exactly how to tap the ever newly growing mass of readers as it sprang up among the lower classes. He could measure the reading public – probably taking his measure of it unconsciously – and knew what the public wanted of him. Consequently the sale of his books has been hitherto so far from ephemeral – their circulation has been so different from that which is expected for ordinary novels – that it has resembled in its nature the sales of legs of mutton or of loaves of bread. The butcher or baker will know how many of this or of that article he will 'do' in a summer or in a winter quarter, and so does the bookseller know how many

'Pickwicks' and how many 'Nicklebys' he will 'do'. That there should be an average and continued demand for books as for other commodities, is not astonishing. That readers should require an increasing number of Shakespeares, or of Euclids, or of 'Robinson Crusoes', is not strange. But it is very strange that such a demand of an author's works should have grown up during his own life, that the demand should be made in regard to novels, that it should have continued with unabated force – and that it should exceed, as I believe it does exceed, the demand for the works of any other one writer in the language.

And no other writer of English language except Shakespeare has left so many types of character as Dickens has done, characters which are known by their names familiarly as household words, and which bring to our minds vividly and at once, a certain well-understood set of ideas, habits, phrases and costumes, making together a man, or woman, or child, whom we know at a glance and recognize at a sound, as we do our own intimate friends. And it may be doubted whether even Shakespeare has done this for so wide a circle of acquaintances. To constant readers of Shakespeare, Iago and Shylock, Rosalind and Juliet, Falstaff and Sir Toby, Lear and Lady Macbeth, have their characters so clearly discernible as to have become a part and parcel of their lives: but such readers are as yet comparatively few in numbers. And other great authors have achieved the same thing with, perhaps, one or two characters. Bobadil, Squire Western, the Vicar of Wakefield and Colonel Newcomb, are among our very intimate friends, and have become types. With Scott's characters, glorious as they are, this is hardly the case. We know well the characters, as Scott has drawn them, of Ivanhoe, Meg Merrilies, Mr Oldbuck, Balfour of Burley, and the Master of Ravenswood; but we know them as creations of Scott, and not as people in our own everyday world. We never meet with Meg Merrilies, or have any among our acquaintance whom we rank as being of the order of Ivanhoe. If we saw them in the flesh we should not recognize them at a glance. But Pickwick and Sam Weller, Mrs Nickleby and Wackford Squeers, Fagin and Bill Sikes, Micawber, Mrs Gamp, Pecksniff and Bucket the Detective, are persons so well known to us that we think that they, who are in any way of the professions of these worthies, are untrue to themselves if they depart in aught from their recognized and understood portraits. Pickwick can never be repeated; *nulli similis aut secundus*, he is among our dearest and nearest, and we expect no one to be like him. But a 'boots' at an hotel is more of a boots the closer he resembles Sam Weller. Many ladies talk like Mrs Nickleby, and are perfect or imperfect in our estimation as they adhere or depart from their great prototype. With murderous Jews and their murdering agents we have probably but a distant acquaintance, but we fancy that they should be as are Fagin and Sikes. A schoolmaster who lives by starving his boys will certainly have but one eye, as was the case with Mr Squeers. The man with whom something is ever about to turn up, is well known to us, and is always considered by us to be going under an alias when he is not called Micawber. The lady who follows a certain profession that has ever been open to ladies is no longer called by the old name, but is Mrs Gamp. Every hypocrite who knows his part, wears the Pecksniff shirt-collar. Every detective is to us a Bucket. And Dickens has given us conventional phrases of which everybody knows the meaning, though many are ignorant whence they come. To have 'one's greens on one's mind' is as good English as 'to be at sea' or 'to be down in the mouth'; but many who can do nothing while their greens are on their mind, who are always talking of their greens, forget that the phrase began with that old warrior Mrs Bagnet.

Most of us have probably heard Dickens's works often criticized, want of art in the choice of words and want of nature in the creation of character, having been the faults most frequently attributed to him. But his words have been so potent, whether they may be right or wrong according to any fixed rule, that they have justified themselves by making themselves into a language which is in itself popular; and his characters, if unnatural, have made a second nature by their own force. It is fatuous to condemn that as deficient in art which has been so full of art as to captivate all men. If the thing be done which was the aim of the artist – fully done – done beyond the power of other artists to accomplish – the time for criticizing the mode of doing it is gone by. Rules are needed in order that a certain effect may be obtained; but if the effect has certainly been obtained, what need to seek whether or no the rule has been obeyed? The example, indeed may be dangerous to others; as they have found who have imitated Dickens, and others will find who may imitate him in future.

It always seemed to me that no man ever devoted himself so entirely as Charles Dickens to things which he understood, and in which he could work with effect. Of other matters he seemed to have a disregard, and for many things almost a contempt which was marvellous. To literature in all its branches his attachment was deep, and his belief in it was a thorough conviction. He could speak about it as no other man spoke. He was always enthusiastic in its interests, ready to push on beginners, quick to encourage those who were winning their way to success, sympathetic with his contemporaries, and greatly generous to aid those who were failing. He thoroughly believed in literature; but in politics he seemed to have no belief at all. Men in so-called public life were to him, I will not say insincere men, but so placed as to be by their calling almost beyond the pale of sincerity. To his feeling, all departmental work was the bungled, muddled routine of a Circumlocution Office. Statecraft was odious to him; and though he would probably never have asserted that a country could be maintained without legislative or executive, he seemed to regard such devices as things so prone to evil, that the less of them the better it would be for the country, and the farther a man kept himself from their immediate influence the better it would be for him. I never heard any man call Dickens a radical; but if any man ever was so, he was a radical at heart, believing entirely in the people, writing for them, speaking for them, and always desirous to take their part as against some undescribed and indiscernible tyrant, who to his mind loomed large as an official rather than as an aristocratic despot. He hardly thought that our parliamentary rulers could be trusted to accomplish aught that was good for us. Good would come gradually, but it would come by the strength of the people and in opposition to the blundering of our rulers.

No man ever kept himself more aloof than Dickens from the ordinary honours of life. No titles were written after his name. He was not CB, or DCL, or FRS; nor did he ever attempt to become MP. What titles of honour may ever have been offered to him, I cannot say; but that titles were offered I do not doubt. Lord Russell, a year or two ago, proposed a measure by which, if carried, certain men of high character and great capacity would have been selected as peers for life; but Charles Dickens would never have been made a lord. He probably fully appreciated his own position; and had a noble confidence in himself, which made him feel that nothing Queen, Parliament or Minister, could do for him would make him greater than he was. No title to his ear could have been higher than that name which he made familiar to the ears of all reading men and women.

He would attempt nothing – show no interest in anything – which he could not do, and which he did not understand. But he was not on that account forced to confine himself to literature. Everyone knows how he read. Most readers of these lines, though they may never have seen him act, as I never did, still know that his acting was excellent. As an actor he would have been at the top of his profession. And he had another gift, had it so wonderfully, that it may almost be said that he has left no equal behind him. He spoke so well, that a public dinner became a blessing instead of a curse, if he was in the chair, had its compensating twenty minutes of pleasure, even if he were called upon to propose a toast, or to thank the company for drinking his health. For myself, I never could tell how far his speeches were ordinarily prepared; but I can declare that I have heard him speak admirably when he has had to do so with no moment of preparation.

A great man has gone from us; such a one that we may surely say of him that we shall not look upon his like again. As years roll on, we shall learn to appreciate his loss. He now rests in the spot consecrated to the memory of our greatest and noblest; and Englishmen would certainly not have been contented had he been laid elsewhere.

(370–75)

Part Two The Developing Debate

Introduction

Two years after Dickens's death Forster's biography began to appear; its three volumes were completed in 1874. There is no doubt that Forster was uniquely qualified to write Dickens's life: his association with the novelist spanned virtually the whole of Dickens's writing career; Dickens had often asked his advice and used his services; he was in possession of a large number of relevant documents, including the fragment of autobiography. The account of the blacking warehouse episode contained in the latter was a revelation not only to the public at large, but also to Dickens's children – so powerful had been Dickens's reserve over this traumatic experience. The significance of these early ordeals was immediately perceived by at least one reviewer of Forster's *Life*:

Charles Dickens, having crushed into his childish experience a whole world of sorrow and humorous insight, so loaded his soul that he never grew any older. He was a great, grown-up, dreamy, impulsive child, just as much a child as little Paul Dombey or little David Copperfield. He saw all from a child's point of view – strange, odd, queer, puzzling .... Never, perhaps, has a fragment of biography wakened more interest or amazement than the first chapters of Mr Forster's biography....
(*St Paul's Magazine*, vol. 10, 1872)

Forster was criticized for obtruding himself too much into his account, and it is clear that he does not give a full picture of some aspects of Dickens's life. Given the period in which he wrote, he can hardly be blamed for his reticence over Dickens's marriage and separation from his wife; he might, however, have given more prominence to the position of Wilkie Collins as one of Dickens's closest friends in his later years – a time when Forster and Dickens were less close than they had been. (Collins's surviving comments on Dickens are disappointingly scrappy). Forster's narrative of such episodes as the American journeys, on the other hand, is disproportionately detailed – no doubt because he had an abundance of material in Dickens's letters. In his use of letters Forster was not more scrupulous than many others of his age: he did not hesitate to alter, rearrange and reassign them for his own purposes. Since the original MSS. from which he quotes have mostly been destroyed, there now seems to be no way of knowing the degree of his interference in many cases. But the damage done may not be great; in the opinion of the editors of the Pilgrim edition of the letters, Forster committed 'numerous small distortions of fact, but paradoxically these distortions were in the interest of a larger, or ideal, truth'. His *Life* is bound to remain of the greatest importance to all students of Dickens.

As a critic Forster is often disappointing. In the chapter on 'Dickens as a Novelist' his attempts to refute the arguments of Taine and Lewes are undistinguished and even querulous, although his insistence that Dickens's 'leading quality was Humour' was an important corrective emphasis. Forster was probably too close to Dickens to prove a persuasive critic on his behalf; moreover, the *Life* was the work of an ageing man in poor health (Forster died in 1876).

During the latter part of the nineteenth century there naturally remained many people who had known Dickens, and evidence from memoirs and reminiscences accumulated. George Dolby's book on the reading tours he managed suggests something of the spell Dickens exerted on these occasions (Dolby's account of the last reading is given on p. 218). The memories of the elderly Henry James (p. 253) present an attitude to Dickens very different from the caustic review of *Our Mutual Friend* which he wrote as a young man (reprinted in the previous section of this book). In *A Personal Record* (1912) Joseph Conrad recalled that his first introduction to English imaginative literature was *Nicholas Nickleby*, in a Polish translation. As for *Bleak House*, it was 'a work of the master for which I have such an admiration, or rather such an intense and unreasoning affection, dating from the days of my childhood, that its very weaknesses are more precious to me than the strength of other men's work. I have read it innumerable times, both in Polish and in English'.

Dickens retained his capacity to command the loyalty of his readers. There must have been many families in which Dickens was still read aloud. Apart from the tenacious devotion of admirers like Swinburne (who re-read his work through every three years), this feeling found institutional expression in the founding of the Dickens Fellowship in 1902; the periodical *The Dickensian* began in 1905, and still continues. One of the most striking features of Dickens's reputation as it now began to develop was his ability to satisfy critics of divergent tastes and using entirely different criteria. The books by Gissing (1898) and Chesterton (1906) were probably the most valuable full-length studies to appear during this period. Gissing's stress on the realism of Dickens, and his argument that what appears as exaggeration was in fact a faithful representation of life as it really was in Dickens's day, is hardly compatible with Chesterton's celebration of the novelist as a buoyant and festive mythologist. Equally at odds with Chesterton's view (which favoured the earlier novels at the expense of the later) was that of Bernard Shaw. His introductions to two of Dickens's novels (significantly, *Hard Times* and *Great Expectations*) were written at different times in his long life, but he had always insisted on the subversive nature of Dickens's view of society, and had acknowledged Dickens's influence on his own work. At the end of this period Orwell again took a different view: Dickens was not a revolutionary, but a moralist. These discrepant assessments present an apparently confused situation in which the character of the author that each critic produces is so different from previous portraits as to seem the likeness of another person – even though their common subject recognizably remains Dickens. Saintsbury's

observation that no English author has been admired for such
different reasons has continued to remain true.

Dickens's works did not undergo the kind of slump in sales that
overtook his contemporaries, but his critical reputation did suffer
from the reaction against Victorianism reflected in the derisive
work of Lytton Strachey. When the previously suppressed
information, such as it was, about Dickens's liaison with Ellen
Ternan finally emerged in the 1930s, it seemed to many to confirm
their suspicions that all eminent Victorians had discreditable
skeletons locked away in hypocritically concealed cupboards. The
allegations about Ellen were vigorously resisted by some loyal
Dickensians.

To the cultivated taste of the inter-war period Dickens's work
often seemed juvenile and his sentimentality intolerable – Aldous
Huxley's strictures (see p. 280) develop Oscar Wilde's remark that
one would need a heart of stone not to laugh at the death of Little
Nell. Leslie Stephen's estimate of Dickens in the *Dictionary of
National Biography* had been cool, and his daughter, Virginia
Woolf, wrote on Dickens rarely and with strong reservations. The
immense prestige of the great Russian novelists among such readers
also worked to Dickens's disadvantage, since his forced effects were
contrasted unfavourably with the psychological penetration of
Tolstoy and Dostoyevsky. Edmund Wilson was to complain (in
'Dickens: The Two Scrooges') that 'the Bloomsbury that talked
about Dostoyevsky ignored Dostoyevsky's master, Dickens'. In his
critical study of 1898, Gissing had made the case for a 'spiritual
kindred' between the English and the Russian novelist. Gissing
concedes that Raskolnikoff's confession to Sonia in *Crime and
Punishment* was beyond Dickens, but felt that even so with a
'change of birth and breeding, Dickens might well have written
the whole book'.

Sustained and serious study of Dickens in relation to his time
cannot really be said to begin until Humphrey House's *The Dickens*

World (1941), but as early as 1904 Louis Cazamian had considered Dickens and others in *Le Roman Social en Angleterre* – a pioneering work of historical criticism which has never appeared in a complete English translation (an extract appears on p. 240 of this book). The monumental work on Dickens by the German scholar Wilhelm Dibelius, which first appeared in 1916, has also lacked a translator. Orwell's long and vigorous essay on Dickens, which concludes this section, (p. 297) is – for all the modernity of its tone and insights – still critically in the tradition of Gissing.

John Ruskin

from a letter to Charles Eliot Norton   19 June 1870

I knew you would deeply feel the death of Dickens. It is very frightful to me – among the blows struck by the fates at worthy men, while all mischievous ones have ceaseless strength. The literary loss is infinite – the political one I care less for than you do. Dickens was a pure modernist – a leader of the steam-whistle party *par excellence* – and he had no understanding of any power of antiquity except a sort of jackdaw sentiment for cathedral towers. He knew nothing of the nobler power of superstition – was essentially a stage manager, and used everything for effect on the pit. His Christmas meant mistletoe and pudding – neither resurrection from dead, nor rising of new stars, nor teaching of wise men, nor shepherds. His hero is essentially the ironmaster; in spite of *Hard Times*, he has advanced by his influence every principle that makes them harder – the love of excitement, in all classes, and the fury of business competition, and the distrust both of nobility and clergy which, wide enough and fatal enough, and too justly founded, needed no apostle to the mob, but a grave teacher of priests and nobles themselves, for whom Dickens had essentially no word.

George Henry Lewes

from 'Dickens in Relation to Criticism', *Fortnightly Review*, vol. 17 February 1872

And this brings me to the noticeable fact that there probably never was a writer of so vast a popularity whose genius was so little *appreciated* by the critics. The very splendour of his successes so deepened the shadow of his failures that to many eyes the shadows supplanted the splendour. Fastidious readers were loath to admit that a writer could be justly called great whose defects were so glaring. They admitted, because it was indisputable, that Dickens delighted thousands, that his admirers were found in all classes, and in all countries;

that he stirred the sympathy of masses not easily reached through Literature, and always stirred healthy, generous emotions; that he impressed a new direction on popular writing, and modified the Literature of his age, in its spirit no less than in its form; but they nevertheless insisted on his defects as if these outweighed all positive qualities; and spoke of him either with condescending patronage, or with sneering irritation. Surely this is a fact worthy of investigation? Were the critics wrong, and if so, in what consisted their error? How are we to reconcile this immense popularity with this critical contempt? The private readers and the public critics who were eager to take up each successive number of his works as it appeared, whose very talk was seasoned with quotations from and allusions to these works, who, to my knowledge, were wont to lay aside books of which they could only speak in terms of eulogy, in order to bury themselves in the 'new number' when the well-known green cover made its appearance – were nevertheless at this very time niggard in their praise, and lavish in their scorn of the popular humorist. It is not long since I heard a very distinguished man express measureless contempt for Dickens, and a few minutes afterwards, in reply to some representations on the other side, admit that Dickens had 'entered into his life'.

Dickens has proved his power by a popularity almost unexampled, embracing all classes. Surely it is a task for criticism to exhibit the sources of that power? If everything that has ever been alleged against the works be admitted, there still remains an immense success to be accounted for. It was not by their defects that these works were carried over Europe and America. It was not their defects which made them the delight of grey heads on the bench, and the study of youngsters in the counting-house and school-room. Other writers have been exaggerated, untrue, fantastic and melodramatic; but they have gained so little notice that no one thinks of pointing out their defects. It is clear, therefore, that Dickens had powers which enabled him to triumph in spite of the weaknesses which clogged them; and it is worth inquiring what those powers were, and their relation to his undeniable defects.

I am not about to attempt such an inquiry, but simply to indicate two or three general points of view. It will be enough merely to mention in passing the primary cause of his success, his overflowing fun, because even uncompromising opponents admit it. They may be ashamed of their laughter, but they laugh. A revulsion of feeling at the preposterousness or extravagance of the image may follow the burst of laughter, but the laughter is irresistible, whether rational or not, and there is no arguing away such a fact.

Great as Dickens is in fun, so great that Fielding and Smollett are small in comparison, he would have been only a passing amusement for the world had he not been gifted with an imagination of marvellous vividness, and an emotional, sympathetic nature capable of furnishing that imagination with elements of universal power. Of him it may be said with less exaggeration than of most poets, that he was of 'imagination all compact'; if the other higher faculties were singularly deficient in him, this faculty was imperial. He was a seer of visions; and his visions were of objects at once familiar and potent. Psychologists will understand both the extent and the limitation of the remark, when I say that in no other perfectly sane mind (Blake, I believe, was not perfectly sane) have I observed vividness of imagination approaching so closely to hallucination. Many who are not psychologists may have had some experience in themselves, or in others, of that abnormal condition in which a man hears voices, and sees objects, with the distinctness of direct perception, although silence and darkness are without him; these *revived* impressions, revived by an internal cause, have precisely the same force and clearness which the impressions originally had when produced by an external cause. In the same degree of vividness are the images *constructed* by his mind in explanation of the voices heard or objects seen: when he imagines that the voice proceeds from a personal friend or from Satan tempting him, the friend or Satan stands before him with the distinctness of objective reality; when he imagines that he himself has been transformed into a bear, his hands are seen by him as paws. In vain you represent to him that the voices he hears have no external existence; he will answer, as a patient pertinently answered Lélut: 'You believe that I am speaking to you because you hear me, is it not so? Very well, I believe that voices are speaking to me because I hear them.' There is no power of effacing such conviction by argument. You may get the patient to assent to any premises you please, he will not swerve from his conclusions. I once argued with a patient who believed he had been transformed into a bear; he was quite willing to admit that the idea of such a transformation was utterly at variance with all experience; but he always returned to his position that God being omnipotent there was no reason to doubt his power of transforming men into bears: what remained fixed in his mind was the image of himself under a bear's form.

The characteristic point in the hallucinations of the insane, that which distinguishes them from hallucinations equally vivid in the sane, is the coercion of the image in *suppressing comparison* and all control of experience. Belief always accompanies a vivid image, for a time; but in the sane this belief will not persist against rational control. If I see a stick partly under water, it is impossible for me not to have the same feeling which would be produced by a bent stick out of the water – if I see two plane images in the stereoscope, it is impossible not to have the feeling of seeing one solid object. But these beliefs are rapidly displaced by reference to experience. I know the stick is not bent, and that it will not appear bent when removed from the water. I know the seeming solid is not an object in relief, but two plane pictures. It is by similar focal adjustment of the mind that sane people know that their hallucinations are unreal. The images may have the vividness of real objects, but they have not the properties of real objects, they do not preserve consistent relations with other facts, they appear in contradiction to other beliefs. Thus if I see a black cat on the chair opposite, yet on my approaching the chair feel no soft object, and if my terrier on the hearthrug looking in the direction of the chair shows none of the well-known agitation which the sight of a cat produces, I conclude, in spite of its distinctness, that the image is an hallucination.

Returning from this digression, let me say that I am very far indeed from wishing to imply any agreement in the common notion that 'great wits to madness nearly are allied'; on the contrary, my studies have led to the conviction that nothing is less like genius than insanity, although some men of genius have had occasional attacks; and further, that I have never observed any trace of the insane temperament in Dickens's works, or life, they being indeed singularly free even from eccentricities which often accompany exceptional powers; nevertheless, with all due limitations, it is true that there is considerable light shed upon his works by the action of the imagination in hallucination. To him also *revived* images have the vividness of sensations; to him also *created* images have the coercive force of realities, excluding all control, all contradiction. What seems preposterously impossible to us, seemed to him simple fact of observation. When he imagined a street, a house, a room, a figure, he saw it not in the vague schematic way of ordinary imagination, but in the sharp definition of actual perception, all the salient details obtruding themselves on his attention. He, seeing it thus vividly, made us also see it; and believing in its reality, however fantastic, he communicated something of his belief to us. He presented it in such relief that we ceased to think of it as a picture. So definite and insistent was the image, that even while knowing it was false we could not help, for a moment, being affected, as it were, by his hallucination.

This glorious energy of imagination is that which Dickens had in common with all great writers. It was this which made him a creator, and made his creations universally intelligible, no matter how fantastic and unreal. His types established themselves in the public mind like personal experiences. Their falsity was unnoticed in the blaze of their illumination. Every humbug seemed a Pecksniff, every nurse a Gamp, every jovial improvident a Micawber, every stinted serving-wench a Marchioness. Universal experiences became individualized in these types; an image and a name were given, and the image was so suggestive that it seemed to *express* all that it was found to *recall*, and Dickens was held to have depicted what his readers supplied. Against such power criticism was almost idle. In vain critical reflection showed these figures to be merely masks – not characters, but personified characteristics, caricatures and distortions of human nature – the vividness of their presentation triumphed over reflection: their creator managed to communicate to the public his own unhesitating belief. Unreal and impossible as these types were, speaking a language never heard in life, moving like pieces of simple mechanism always in one way (instead of moving with the infinite fluctuations of organisms, incalculable yet intelligible, surprising yet familiar), these unreal figures affected the uncritical reader with the force of reality; and they did so in virtue of their embodiment of some real characteristic vividly presented. The imagination of the author laid hold of some well-marked physical trait, some peculiarity of aspect, speech or manner which everyone recognized at once; and the force with which this was presented made it occupy the mind to the exclusion of all critical doubts: only reflection could detect the incongruity. Think of what this implies! Think how little the mass of men are given to reflect on their impressions, and how their minds are for the most part occupied with sensations rather than ideas, and you will see why Dickens held an undisputed sway. Give a child a wooden horse, with hair for mane and tail, and wafer-spots for colouring, he will never be disturbed by the fact that this horse does not move its legs, but runs on wheels – the general suggestion suffices for his belief; and this wooden horse, which he can handle and draw, is believed in more than a pictured horse by a Wouvermanns or an Ansdell. It may be said of Dickens's human figures that they too are wooden, and run on wheels; but these are details which scarcely disturb the belief of admirers. Just as the wooden horse is brought within the range of the child's emotions, and dramatizing tendencies, when he can handle and draw it, so Dickens's figures are brought within the range of the reader's interests, and receive from these interests a sudden illumination, when they are the puppets of a drama every incident of which appeals to the sympathies. With a fine felicity of instinct he seized upon situations having an irresistible hold over the domestic affections and ordinary sympathies. He spoke in the mother-tongue of the heart, and was always sure of ready listeners. He painted the life he knew, the life everyone knew; for if the scenes and manners were unlike those we were familiar with, the feelings and motives, the joys and griefs, the mistakes and efforts of the actors were universal, and therefore universally intelligible; so that even critical spectators who complained that these broadly painted pictures were artistic daubs, could not wholly resist their effective suggestiveness. He set in motion the secret springs of sympathy by touching the domestic affections. He painted nothing ideal, heroic; but all the resources of the bourgeois epic were in his grasp. The world of thought and passion lay beyond his horizon. But the joys and pains of childhood, the petty tyrannies of ignoble natures, the genial pleasantries of happy natures, the life of the poor, the struggles of the street and back parlour, the insolence of office, the sharp social contrasts, east wind and Christmas jollity, hunger, misery, and hot punch – these he could deal with, so that we laughed and cried, were startled at the revelation of familiar facts hitherto unnoted, and felt our pulses quicken as we were hurried along with him in his fanciful flight.

Such were the sources of his power. To understand how it is that critics quite competent to recognize such power, and even so far amenable to it as to be moved and interested by the works in spite of all their drawbacks, should have forgotten this undenied power, and written or spoken of Dickens with mingled irritation and contempt, we must take into account two natural tendencies – the bias of opposition, and the bias of technical estimate.

The bias of opposition may be illustrated in a parallel case. Let us suppose a scientific book to be attracting the attention of Europe by the boldness, suggestiveness and theoretic plausibility of its hypotheses; this work falls into the hands of a critic sufficiently grounded in the science treated to be aware that its writer, although gifted with great theoretic power and occasional insight into unexplored relations, is nevertheless pitiably ignorant of the elementary facts and principles of the science; the critic noticing the power, and the talent of lucid exposition, is yet perplexed and irritated at ignorance which is inexcusable, and a reckless twisting of known facts into impossible relations, which seems wilful; will he not pass from marvelling at this inextricable web of sense and nonsense, suggestive insight and mischievous error, so jumbled together that the combination of this sagacity with this glaring inefficiency is a paradox, and be driven by the anger of opposition into an emphatic assertion that the belauded philosopher is a charlatan and an ignoramus? A chorus of admirers proclaims the author to be a great teacher, before whom all contemporaries must bow; and the critic observes this teacher on one page throwing out a striking hypothesis of some geometric relations in the planetary movements, and on another assuming that the hypothenuse is equal to its perpendicular and base, because the square of the hypothenuse is equal to the squares of its sides – in one chapter ridiculing the atomic theory, and in another arguing that carbonic acid is obtained from carbon and nitrogen – can this critic be expected to join in the chorus of admirers? and will he not rather be exasperated into an opposition which will lead him to undervalue the undeniable qualities in his insistence on the undeniable defects?

Something like this is the feeling produced by Dickens's works in many cultivated and critical readers. They see there human character and ordinary events portrayed with a mingled verisimilitude and falsity altogether unexampled. The drawing is so vivid yet so incorrect, or else is so blurred and formless, with such excess of *effort* (as of a showman beating on the drum) that the doubt arises how an observer so remarkably keen could make observations so remarkably false, and miss such very obvious facts; how the rapid glance which could swoop down on a peculiarity with hawk-like precision, could overlook all that accompanied and was organically related to that peculiarity; how the eye for characteristics could be so blind to character, and the ear for dramatic idiom be so deaf to dramatic language; finally, how the writer's exquisite susceptibility to the grotesque could be insensible to the occasional grotesqueness of his own attitude. Michelangelo is intelligible, and Giotto is intelligible; but a critic is nonplussed at finding the invention of Angelo with the drawing of Giotto. It is indeed surprising that Dickens should have observed man, and not been impressed with the fact that man is, in the words of Montaigne, *un être ondoyant et divers*. And the critic is distressed to observe the substitution of mechanisms for minds, puppets for characters. It is needless to dwell on such monstrous failures as Mantalini, Rosa Dartle, Lady Dedlock, Esther Summerson, Mr Dick, Arthur Gride, Edith Dombey, Mr Carker – needless, because if one studies the successful figures one finds even in them only touches of verisimilitude. When one thinks of Micawber always presenting himself in the same situation, moved with the same springs, and uttering the same sounds, always confident of something turning up, always crushed and rebounding, always making punch – and his wife always declaring she will never part from him, always referring to his talents and her family – when one thinks of the 'catchwords' personified as characters, one is reminded of the frogs whose brains have been taken out for physiological purposes, and whose actions henceforth want the distinctive peculiarity of organic action, that of fluctuating spontaneity. Place one of these brainless frogs on his back and he will at once recover the sitting posture; draw a leg from under him, and he will draw it back again; tickle or prick him and he will push away the object, or take *one* hop out of the way; stroke his back, and he will utter *one* croak. All these things resemble the actions of the unmutilated frog, but they differ in being *isolated* actions, and *always the same*: they are as uniform and calculable as the movements of a machine. The uninjured frog may or may not croak, may or may not hop away; the result is never calculable, and is rarely a single croak or a single hop. It is this complexity of the organism which Dickens wholly fails to conceive; his characters have nothing fluctuating and incalculable in them, even when they embody true observations; and very often they are creations so fantastic that one is at a loss to understand how he could, without hallucination, believe them to be like reality. There are dialogues bearing the traces of straining effort at effect, which in their incongruity painfully resemble the absurd and eager expositions which insane patients pour into the listener's ear when detailing their wrongs, or their schemes. Dickens once declared to me that every word said by his characters was distinctly *heard* by him; I was at first not a little puzzled to account for the fact that he could hear language so utterly unlike the language of real feeling, and not be aware of its preposterousness; but the surprise vanished when I thought of the phenomena of hallucination. And here it may be needful to remark in passing that it is not because the characters are badly drawn and their language unreal, that they are to be classed among the excesses of imagination; otherwise all the bad novelists and dramatists would be credited with that which they especially want – powerful imagination. His peculiarity is not the incorrectness of the drawing, but the vividness of the imagination which while rendering that incorrectness insensible to him, also renders it potent with multitudes of his fellowmen. For although his weakness comes from excess in one direction, the force which is in excess must not be overlooked; and it is overlooked or undervalued by critics who, with what I have called the bias of opposition, insist only on the weakness.

This leads me to the second point, the bias of technical estimate. The main purpose of Art is delight. Whatever influences may radiate from that centre – and however it may elevate or modify – the one primary condition of influence is stirred emotion. No Art can teach which does not move; no Art can move without teaching. Criticism has to consider Art under two aspects, that of emotional pleasure, and that of technical pleasure. We all – public and critics – are susceptible of the former, are capable of being moved and are delighted with what stirs the emotions, filling the mind with images having emotional influence; but only the critics are much affected by technical skill, and the pleasure it creates. *What* is done, what is suggested, constitutes the first aspect; *how* it is done the second. We all delight in imitation, and in the skill which represents one object in another medium; but the refinements of skill can only be appreciated by study. To a savage there is so little suggestion of a human face and form in a painted portrait that it is not even recognized as the representation of a man; whereas the same savage would delight in a waxwork figure, or a wooden Scotchman at the door of a tobacconist. The educated eye sees exquisite skill in the portrait, a skill which gives exquisite delight; but this eye which traces and estimates the subtle effects of colour and distribution of light and shade in the portrait, turns with disgust from the wax figure, or the wooden Highlander. In the course of time the pleasure derived from the perception of difficulty overcome, leads to such a preponderance of the technical estimate, that the sweep of the brush, or the composition of lines, becomes of supreme importance, and the connoisseur no longer asks, What is painted? but How is it painted? The *what* may be a patch of meadow, the bend of a river or a street boy munching bread and cheese, and yet give greater delight by its *how*, than another picture which represented the Andes, Niagara or a Madonna and Child. When the critic observes technical skill in a picture, he pronounces the painter to be admirable, and is quite unmoved by any great subject badly painted. In like manner a great poet is estimated by the greatness of his execution of great conceptions, not by the greatness of his intention.

How easily the critic falls into the mistake of overvaluing technical skill, and not allowing for the primary condition, how easily he misjudges works by applying to them technical rules derived from the works of others, need not here be dwelt on. What I wish to indicate is the bias of technical estimate which, acting with that bias of opposition just noted, has caused the critics to overlook in Dickens the great artistic powers which are proved by his immense success; and to dwell only on those great artistic deficiencies which exclude him from the class of exquisite writers. He worked in delf, not in porcelain. But his prodigal imagination created in delf forms which delighted thousands. He only touched common life, but he touched it to 'fine issues'; and since we are all susceptible of being moved by pictures of children in droll and pathetic situations, and by pictures of common suffering and common joy, any writer who can paint such pictures with sufficient skill to awaken these emotions is powerful in proportion to the emotion stirred. That Dickens had this skill is undisputed; and if critical reflection shows that the means he employs are not such as will satisfy the technical estimate, and consequently that the pictures will not move the cultivated mind, nor give it the deep content which perfect Art continues to create, making the work a 'joy for ever', we must still remember that in the present state of Literature, with hundreds daily exerting their utmost efforts to paint such pictures, it requires prodigious force and rare skill to impress images that will stir the universal heart. Murders are perpetrated without stint, but the murder of Nancy is unforgettable. Children figure in numberless plays and novels, but the deaths of little Nell and little Paul were national griefs. Seduction is one of the commonest of tragedies, but the scene in Peggotty's boat-house burns itself into the memory. Captain Cuttle and Richard Swiveller, the Marchioness and Tilly Slowboy, Pecksniff and Micawber, Tiny Tim and Mrs Gamp, may be imperfect presentations of human character, but they are types which no one can forget. Dr Johnson explained the popularity of some writer by saying, 'Sir, *his* nonsense suited *their* nonsense'; let us add, 'and his sense suited their sense', and it will explain the popularity of Dickens. Readers to whom all the refinements of Art and Literature are as meaningless hieroglyphs, were at once laid hold of by the reproduction of their own feelings, their own experiences, their own prejudices, in the irradiating splendour of his imagination; while readers whose cultivated sensibilities were alive to the most delicate and evanescent touches were, by virtue of their common nature, ready to be moved and delighted at his pictures and suggestions. The cultivated and uncultivated were affected by his admirable *mise en scène*, his fertile invention, his striking selection of incident, his intense vision of physical details. Only the cultivated who are made fastidious by cultivation paused to consider the pervading commonness of the works, and remarked that they are wholly without glimpses of a nobler life; and that the writer presents an almost unique example of a mind of singular force in which, so to speak, sensations never passed into ideas. Dickens sees and feels, but the logic of feeling seems the only logic he can manage. Thought is strangely absent from his works. I do not suppose a single thoughtful remark on life or character could be found throughout the twenty volumes. Not only is there a marked absence of the reflective tendency, but one sees no indication of the past life of humanity having ever occupied him; keenly as he observes the objects before him, he never connects his observations into a general expression, never seems interested in general relations of things. Compared with that of Fielding or Thackeray, his was merely an *animal* intelligence, i.e. restricted to perceptions. On this ground his early education was more fruitful and less injurious than it would have been to a nature constructed on a more reflective and intellectual type. It furnished him with rare and valuable experience, early developed his sympathies with the lowly and struggling, and did not starve any intellectual ambition. He never was and never would have been a student.

(143-51)

John Forster

from *The Life of Charles Dickens*, book 8, chapter 2   1872-4
(reprinted in Hoppé edition, 1966, vol, 2)

Not his genius only, but his whole nature, was too exclusively made up of sympathy for, and with, the real in its most intense form, to be sufficiently provided against failure in the realities around him. There was for him no 'city of the mind' against outward ills, for inner consolation and shelter. It was in and from the actual he still stretched forward to find the freedom and satisfactions of an ideal, and by his very attempts to escape the world he was driven back into the thick of it.

(200)

John Forster

from *The Life of Charles Dickens*, book 9, chapter 1   1872-4
(reprinted in Hoppé edition, 1966, vol. 2)

His leading quality was Humour. It has no mention in either of the criticisms cited, but it was his highest faculty; and it accounts for his magnificent successes, as well as for his not infrequent failures, in

characteristic delineation. He was conscious of this himself. Five years
before he died, a great and generous brother-artist, Lord Lytton, amid
much ungrudging praise of a work he was then publishing, asked him
to consider, as to one part of it, if the modesties of art were not a little
overpassed.

'I cannot tell you,' he replied, 'how highly I prize your
letter, or with what pride and pleasure it inspires me. Not do
I for a moment question its criticism (if objection so generous
and easy may be called by that hard name) otherwise than
on this ground – that I work slowly and with great care, and
never give way to my invention recklessly, but constantly
restrain it; and that I think it is my infirmity to fancy or
perceive relations in things which are not apparent generally.
Also, I have such an inexpressible enjoyment of what I see
in a droll light, that I dare say I pet it as if it were a spoilt
child. This is all I have to offer in arrest of judgement.'

To perceive relations in things which are not apparent generally, is
one of those exquisite properties of humour by which are discovered
the affinities between the high and the low, the attractive and the
repulsive, the rarest things and things of every day, which bring us
all upon the level of a common humanity. It is this which gives
humour an immortal touch that does not belong of necessity to
pictures, even the most exquisite, of mere character or manners; the
property which in its highest aspects Carlyle so subtly described as a
sort of inverse sublimity, exalting into our affections what is below us
as the other draws down into our affections what is above us. But it
has a danger which Dickens also hints at, and into which he often fell.
All humour has in it, is indeed identical with, what ordinary people
are apt to call exaggeration; but there is an excess beyond the allow-
able even here, and to 'pet' or magnify out of proper bounds its
sense of what is droll, is to put the merely grotesque in its place. What
might have been overlooked in a writer with no uncommon faculty
of invention, was thrown into overpowering prominence by Dickens's
wealth of fancy; and a splendid excess of his genius came to be
objected to as its integral and essential quality.
(272–3)

John Ruskin

from *Fors Clavigera: Letters to the Workmen and Labourers of Great
Britain*, Letter 28 April 1873 (reprinted in E. T. Cook and
A. Wedderburn (eds.), *The Works of John Ruskin*, vol. 27, 1908)

And yet, have you ever taken a wise man's real opinion on this
matter? You are not fond of hearing opinions of wise men; you like
your anonymous penny-a-liners' opinions better. But do you think
you could tolerantly receive that of a moderately and popularly wise
man – such a one as Charles Dickens, for example? Have you ever
considered seriously what *his* opinion was, about 'Dependants' and
'Menials'? He did not perhaps quite know what it was himself; it
needs wisdom of stronger make than his to be sure of what it *does*
think. He would talk, in his moral passages, about Independence, and
Self-dependence, and making one's way in the world, just like any
hack of the 'Eatanswill Independent'. But which of the people of his
imagination, of his own true children, did he love and honour most?
Who are your favourites in his books – as they have been his? Menials,
it strikes me, many of them. Sam, Mark, Kit, Peggotty, Mary-my-
dear – even the poor little Marchioness! I don't think Dickens intended you to look upon any of them disrespectfully. Or going one
grade higher in his society, Tom Pinch, Newman Noggs, Tim
Linkinwater, Oliver Twist – how independent, all of them! Very
nearly menial, in soul, if they chance on a good master; none of them
brilliant in fortune, nor vigorous in action. Is not the entire testimony
of Dickens, traced in its true force, that no position is so *good* for men
and women, none so likely to bring out their best human character,
as that of a dependent, or menial? And yet with your supreme modern
logic, instead of enthusiastically concluding from his works 'let us all
be servants', one would think the notion he put in your heads was
quite the other, 'let us all be masters', and that you understood his
ideal of heroic English character to be given in Mr Pecksniff or Sir
Mulberry Hawk!
(519–20)

R. H. Hutton

'The Genius of Dickens', *Spectator*   7 February 1874

Lord Derby not long ago recalled to one of his audiences at Liverpool
the old definition of Genius, that it is only a power of taking much
greater pains about a certain class of subjects than it is in other people
to take. In other words, genius, so defined, flows from the labour and
concentration of attention, though the taste or predisposition which
renders that labour and concentration possible because delightful, may
fairly be regarded as the ultimate root of it. That is a very good definition of a good deal of what the world calls genius. But it would be
difficult to imagine any definition which would be further from the
mark of the kind of genius which must be ascribed to Dickens. At
least, if the great humorist's genius is to be brought within this definition at all, we must describe all the brightness and truth of momentary
flashes of perception, and equally momentary humorous combinations, to a power of *taking pains*, which would certainly be a very
eccentric and forced construction of the term. Indeed, it can hardly be
said that in any intellectual way Dickens *had* much power of taking
pains in the common sense of that term. It has been observed that if he
went down a street, he had more power of telling you what he had
seen in that street than all the rest of the passers-by in the whole day
would have made out amongst them. He caught character, so far as it
could be caught in a glance of the eye, as no other Englishman probably ever yet caught it. Mr Forster, who in his new volume resents
warmly a criticism of Mr Lewes's on the want of true individual
characteristics in Dickens's set of types character – such as Pecksniff,
who is pure humbug; Micawber, who is 'always confident of something turning up, always crushed and rebounding, and always making
punch'; Mrs Gamp, who is always referring to 'sicking', and 'month-
lying', and so forth – Mr Forster, we say, rashly maintains that there
is nothing of this sort in the earlier tales, especially *Pickwick* and its
immediate followers. Surely Mr Wardle's fat boy, Sawyer late
Knockemorf, Mr Jingle, Mr Tupman, Mr Winkle, Mr Pickwick himself, Mr Weller, senior, nay, we will say even the great Sam Weller
himself, are all types made in keeping with one ruling feature, though
Dickens's wonderful fancy and curious store of miscellaneous obser-

vations enabled him so to vary the appropriate illustrations of that ruling feature, that something which looked like the variety and ease of life resulted from the variation. It seems to us almost absurd to deny that the power of kaleidoscopic variation and multiplication of the same general characteristic, is the main key to Dickens's humour and power. Even in *Oliver Twist*, where Nancy and Sikes at least seem to reach a stage of individualization beyond anything that can be thus accounted for, by far the greater part of the book is occupied with sketches which fall under the same general rule, such as those of Noah Claypole, of the Dodger, and Flash Toby Crackit. But not the less do I quite agree with Mr Forster that Mr Lewes's mode of explaining Dickens's popularity as the result of a kind of glamour of enthusiasm which he threw over his figures, like that which the child throws over a wooden horse, till it really represents to him an actual horse, is a mere blunder. I should say, on the contrary, that that popularity is due to the wonderful breadth of real life which Dickens was able to lay under contribution for the illustration of his various types, and that he had little or no power of throwing a deceptive glamour of enthusiasm over inadequate descriptions. All that could be known by the help of astounding capacity for swift, sudden and keen vision, and through that large sense of humour which brings an indefinite range of analogy and contrast within the field of view at any one moment, Dickens knew and painted. The result was that he easily divined the secret of almost every crotchety and superficial vein of character that came within his view. Everyone tells you that they have met with a real Mrs Nickleby and with a real Mr Micawber, and I could quote sayings of a person known to me, far more Micawberish than Micawber's own. So all the secrets of any professional life with which he was familiar, were made by Dickens completely his own. Nothing so perfect as his pawnbrokers and his undertakers, his beadles and his matrons, his boarding-housekeepers and his bone-articulators, his dolls' dressmakers, his Yorkshire schoolmasters, his travelling players, and his waxwork men, his fire-eating editors and his Yankee rogues, were ever produced for us before. But then all these characters are photographs from a superficial stratum of real life, which he hardly ever goes beneath and where, if he does go beneath it, he is apt to fail. While he sticks to his local colour, only varying it as his extraordinary experience in the varieties of local colour taught him to do, he is a wonder and a delight to his readers. Directly he tries to create anything in which his swift decisive knowledge of detail does not help him, anything in which a general knowledge of the passions and heart and intellect of man is more needed than a special knowledge of the dialect of a profession or the habits of a class, he too often loses all his certainty of touch and becomes a painful mannerist. Compare Nicholas and Kate Nickleby with their mother and little Miss La Creevy. The former are nobodies, the latter great successes. Compare Mr Brownlow, or Rose Maylie, or any of the ordinary human beings in *Oliver Twist* or even Oliver himself when he has ceased to be the terrified little boy, with any of the thieves or scoundrels in that delightful book. Compare the merely human beings in *Martin Chuzzlewit* with the typical beings, and it is always the same. Directly the shaft is sunk beneath the characterizing stratum of some particular type of manners, the fountain no longer seems bubbling-up with life. It does not follow that Dickens did not produce a vast number of really life-like figures. It rather follows that he did. Not only do eccentricities, who really are moulded on the type of a few remarkable traits, actually exist, but characters so much moulded by class as to breathe, at first at least, all the class-flavour, all the professional bouquet which Dickens attributes to them, actually exist. Sam Weller is hardly more than the distilled life of a sharp, cockney servant, a wit of the lower class, who knows London trickery well, and never loses his temper; but then such characters, no doubt, have existed; and the only defect about Sam Weller is one which no one would feel who had not known such a person intimately enough to find out that he had passions and superstitions and affections of his own which would not completely fit into the typical framework, which were apt sometimes to break through it. Dickens seems to me never to fail in this kind of typical sketch, unless he prolongs his story so as to exhaust his stock of illustrations for it, and then he often does fail by harping monotonously on the fundamental string. Everyone is sick of Carker's teeth and Susan Nipper's pertness long before the end of *Dombey*. Even Toots's pack of cards, 'for Mr Dombey, for Mrs Dombey, for Miss Dombey', pall upon us. Honest John Browdie's loud Yorkshire jollity grows tiresome before *Nicholas Nickleby* is at an end, and Lord Frederick Verisopht only regains a gleam of individual character at the moment of his death. John Willett's stupid study of the

Boiler in *Barnaby Rudge* is exhausted almost before it is begun, and even Miss Miggs's malice and hypocrisy are worked a little too hard before the tale is out. As for the good characters – the young lady who 'points upwards', for instance, in *Copperfield* – they are hardly ever tolerable after their first appearance. Dickens had no special store of experience from which to paint them, and his general knowledge of the human heart and mind was by no means profound.

Indeed this is a natural result of his biographer's admission that Dickens had no refuge within himself, no 'city of the mind' for inward consolation. Without that it would have been hardly possible for him to gain the command of the deeper secrets of human emotion and passion. No author indeed could draw more powerfully than he the mood of a man haunted by a fixed idea, a shadowy apprehension, a fear, a dream, a remorse. If Dickens had to describe the restlessness of a murderer, or the panic of a man apprehending murder, he did it with a vigour and force that make the blood curdle. But there, again, he was studying in a world of most specific experience. He was a vivid dreamer, and no one knew better the sort of supremacy which a given idea gets over the mind in a dream, and in those waking states of nervous apprehension akin to dreams. Where he utterly fails is in giving the breadth of ordinary life to ordinary characters. He never drew a *mere* artisan, or a mere labourer or labourer's wife, or a mere shopkeeper, or a mere gentleman or lady, or a mere man or woman of rank. Without something to render such characters peculiar and special, he made the most wooden work of them, simply because he had no field of special experience upon which to draw for their delineation.

But after all, wonderful as are the riches of the various specific worlds which Dickens ransacked for his creations, there is nothing in him, as the most realistic and picturesque of describers, to equal his humour. The wealth and subtlety of his contrasts, the fine aim of his exaggerations, the presence of mind (which is the soul of wit) displayed in his satire, the exquisitely professional character of the sentiments and metaphors which fall from his characters, the combined audacity and microscopic delicacy of his shading in caricature, the quaint flights of his fancy in illustrating a monstrous absurdity, the suddenness of his strokes at one moment, the cumulative perseverance of his touches at another, all make him such a humorist as many centuries are not likely to reproduce. But then humour of this kind is

not necessarily connected with any deep knowledge of the heart and mind of man, and of such a knowledge I can see little trace in Dickens. He had a memory which could retain, and an imagination which could sublimate, and a fancy which could indefinitely vary almost any trait which had once fixed itself in his mind; but the traits which did so fix themselves, were almost always peculiarities, and his human figures are only real so far as they reproduce the real oddities of life, or what to a man in Dickens's rank and class seemed real oddities; and of course, while there are many real oddities in the world, these are not the staple of our average life – with which indeed Dickens's genius never dealt either willingly or successfully.
(169–70)

Harriet Martineau

from *Autobiography*, vol. 2 1877

Of Mr Dickens I have seen but little in face-to-face intercourse; but I am glad to have enjoyed that little. There may be, and I believe there are, many who go beyond me in admiration of his works – high and strong as is my delight in some of them. Many can more keenly enjoy his peculiar humour – delightful as it is to me; and few seem to miss as I do the pure plain daylight in the atmosphere of his scenery. So many fine painters have been mannerists as to atmosphere and colour that it may be unreasonable to object to one more: but the very excellence and diversity of Mr Dickens's powers makes one long that they should exercise their full force under the broad open sky of nature, instead of in the most brilliant palace of art. While he tells us a world of things that are natural and even true, his personages are generally, as I suppose is undeniable, profoundly unreal. It is a curious speculation what effects his universally read works will have on the foreign conception of English character. Washington Irving came here expecting to find the English life of Queen Anne's days, as his *Sketchbook* shows; and very unlike his preconception was the England he found. And thus it must be with Germans, Americans and French who take Mr Dickens's books to be pictures of our real life – another vexation in his vigorous erroneousness about matters of science as shown in *Oliver Twist* about the new poor-law (which he confounds with the abrogated old one) and in *Hard Times*, about the controversies of employers. Nobody wants to make Mr Dickens a political economist; but there are many who wish that he would abstain from a set of difficult subjects, on which all true sentiment must be underlain by a sort of knowledge which he has not. The more fervent and inexhaustible his kindliness (and it is fervent and inexhaustible), the more important it is that it should be well-informed and well-directed, that no errors of his may mislead his readers on the one hand, nor lessen his own genial influence on the other.

The finest thing in Mr Dickens's case is that he, from time to time, proves himself capable of progress – however vast his preceding achievements had been. In humour, he will hardly surpass *Pickwick*, simply because *Pickwick* is scarcely surpassable in humour: but in several crises, as it were, of his fame, when everybody was disappointed, and his faults seemed running his graces down, there has appeared something so prodigiously fine as to make us all joyfully exclaim that Dickens can never permanently fail.

(377–9)

Edward FitzGerald

from a letter to Fanny Kemble   25 April 1879

What a touch when Peggotty – the man – at last finds the lost Girl, and – throws a handkerchief over her face when he takes her to his arms – never to leave her! I maintain it – a little Shakespeare – a Cockney Shakespeare, if you will: but as distinct, if not so great, a piece of pure Genius as was born in Stratford. Oh, I am quite sure of that, had I to choose but one of them, I would choose Dickens's hundred delightful Caricatures rather than Thackeray's half-dozen terrible Photographs.

Edward FitzGerald

from a letter to Fanny Kemble   3 February 1880

The intended Pathos is, as usual, missed: but just turn to little Dombey's Funeral, where the Acrobat in the Street suspends his performance till the Funeral has passed, and his wife wonders if the little Acrobat in her Arms will so far outlive the little Boy in the Hearse as to wear a Ribbon through his hair, following his Father's Calling. It is in such Side-touches, you know, that Dickens is inspired to Create like a little God Almighty.

John Ruskin

'Fiction, Fair and Foul', *Nineteenth Century*   June 1880 (reprinted in E. T. Cook and A. Wedderburn (eds.), *The Works of John Ruskin*, vol. 34, 1908)

The monotony of life in the central streets of any great modern city, but especially in those of London, where every emotion intended to be derived by men from the sight of nature, or the sense of art, is forbidden for ever, leaves the craving of the heart for a sincere, yet changeful, interest, to be fed from one source only. Under natural conditions the degree of mental excitement necessary to bodily health is provided by the course of the seasons, and the various skill and fortune of agriculture. In the country every morning of the year brings with it a new aspect of springing or fading nature; a new duty to be fulfilled upon earth, and a new promise or warning in heaven. No day is without its innocent hope, its special prudence, its kindly gift and its sublime danger; and in every process of wise husbandry, and every effort of contending or remedial courage, the wholesome passions, pride and bodily power of the labourer are excited and exerted in happiest unison. The companionship of domestic, the care of serviceable, animals, soften and enlarge his life with lowly charities, and discipline him in familiar wisdoms and unboastful fortitudes; while the divine laws of seed-time which cannot be recalled, harvest which cannot be hastened, and winter in which no man can work, compel the impatiences and coveting of his heart into labour too submissive to be anxious, and rest too sweet to be wanton. What thought can enough comprehend the contrast between such life, and that in streets where summer and winter are only alternations of heat and cold; where snow never fell white, nor sunshine clear; where the ground is only a pavement, and the sky no more than the glass roof of an arcade; where the utmost power of a storm is to choke the gutters, and the finest magic of spring, to change mud into dust: where – chief and most fatal difference in state – there is no interest of occupation for any of the inhabitants but the routine of counter or desk within doors, and the effort to pass each other without collision outside; so that from morning to evening the only possible variation of the monotony of the hours, and lightening of the penalty of existence, must be some kind of mischief, limited, unless by more than ordinary godsend of fatality, to the fall of a horse, or the slitting of a pocket?

I said that under these laws of inanition, the craving of the human heart for some kind of excitement could be supplied from *one* source only. It might have been thought by any other than a sternly tentative philosopher, that the denial of their natural food to human feelings would have provoked a reactionary desire for it; and that the dreariness of the street would have been gilded by dreams of pastoral felicity. Experience has shown the fact to be otherwise; the thoroughly trained Londoner can enjoy no more excitement than that to which he has been accustomed, but asks for *that* in continually more ardent or more virulent concentration; and the ultimate power of fiction to entertain him is by varying to his fancy the modes, and defining for his dullness the horrors, of Death. In the single novel of *Bleak House* there are nine deaths (or left for deaths, in the drop scene) carefully wrought out or led up to, either by way of pleasing surprise, as the baby's at the brickmaker's, or finished in their threatenings and sufferings, with as much enjoyment as can be contrived in the anticipation, and as much pathology as can be concentrated in the description. Under the following varieties of method:

One by assassination   Mr Tulkinghorn
One by starvation, with phthisis Joe
One by chagrin   Richard

One by spontaneous combustion	Mr Krook
One by sorrow	Lady Dedlock's lover
One by remorse	Lady Dedlock
One by insanity	Miss Flite
One by paralysis	Sir Leicester

Besides the baby, by fever, and a lively young French woman left to be hanged.

And all this, observe, not in a tragic, adventurous or military story, but merely as the further enlivenment of a narrative intended to be amusing; and as a properly representative average of the statistics of civilian mortality in the centre of London.

Observe further, and chiefly. It is not the mere number of deaths (which, if we count the odd troopers in the last scene, is exceeded in *Old Mortality*, and reached within one or two, both in *Waverley* and *Guy Mannering*) that marks the peculiar tone of the modern novel. It is the fact that all these deaths, but one, are of inoffensive, or at least in the world's estimate, respectable persons; and that they are all grotesquely either violent or miserable, purporting thus to illustrate the modern theology that the appointed destiny of a large average of our population is to die like rats in a drain, either by trap or poison. Not, indeed, that a lawyer in full practice can be usually supposed as faultless in the eye of Heaven as a dove or a woodcock; but it is not, in former divinities, thought the will of Providence that he should be dropped by a shot from a client behind his fire-screen, and retrieved in the morning by his housemaid under the chandelier. Neither is Lady Dedlock less reprehensible in her conduct than many women of fashion have been and will be: but it would not therefore have been thought poetically just, in old-fashioned morality, that she should be found by her daughter lying dead with her face in the mud of a St Giles's churchyard.

In the work of the great masters death is always either heroic, deserved, or quiet and natural (unless their purpose be totally and deeply tragic, when collateral meaner death is permitted, like that of Polonius or Roderigo). In *Old Mortality*, four of the deaths, Bothwell's, Ensign Grahame's, Macbriar's and Evandale's, are magnificently heroic; Burley's and Olifant's long deserved, and swift; the troopers', met in the discharge of their military duty; and the old miser's, as

gentle as the passing of a cloud, and almost beautiful in its last words
of – now unselfish – care: –

' "Ailie" (he aye ca'd me Ailie, we were auld acquaintance),
"Ailie, take ye care and haud the gear weel thegither; for the
name of Morton of Milnwood's gane out like the last sough
of an auld sang." And sae he fell out o' ae dwam into
another, and ne'er spak a word mair, unless it were
something we cou'dna mak out, about a dipped candle being
gude eneugh to see to dee wi'. He cou'd ne'er bide to see a
moulded ane, and there was ane, by ill luck, on the table.'

In *Guy Mannering*, the murder, though unpremeditated, of a single
person (himself not entirely innocent, but at least by heartlessness in
a cruel function earning his fate,), is avenged to the uttermost on all
the men conscious of the crime; Mr Bertram's death, like that of his
wife, brief in pain, and each told in the space of half-a-dozen lines;
and that of the heroine of the tale, self-devoted heroic in the highest,
and happy.

Nor is it ever to be forgotten, in the comparison of Scott's with
inferior work, that his own splendid powers were, even in early life,
tainted, and in his latter years destroyed, by modern conditions of
commercial excitement, then first, but rapidly, developing themselves. There are parts even in his best novels coloured to meet tastes
which he despised; and many pages written in his later ones to
lengthen his article for the indiscriminate market.

But there was one weakness of which his healthy mind remained
incapable to the last. In modern stories prepared for more refined or
fastidious audiences than those of Dickens, the funereal excitement is
obtained, for the most part, not by the infliction of violent or disgusting death; but in the suspense, the pathos, and the more or less by
all felt, and recognized, mortal phenomena of the sick-room. The
temptation, to weak writers, of this order of subject is especially
great, because the study of it from the living – or dying – model is so
easy, and to many has been the most impressive part of their own
personal experience; while, if the description be given even with
mediocre accuracy, a very large section of readers will admire its
truth, and cherish its melancholy. Few authors of second or third rate
genius can either record or invent a probable conversation in ordinary

life; but few, on the other hand, are so destitute of observant faculty as to be unable to chronicle the broken syllables and languid movements of an invalid. The easily rendered, and too surely recognized, image of familiar suffering is felt at once to be real where all else had been false; and the historian of the gestures of fever and words of delirium can count on the applause of a gratified audience as surely as the dramatist who introduces on the stage of his flagging action a carriage that can be driven or a fountain that will flow. But the masters of strong imagination disdain such work, and those of deep sensibility shrink from it.[1] Only under conditions of personal weakness, presently to be noted, would Scott comply with the cravings of his lower audience in scenes of terror like the death of Front-de-Boeuf. But he never once withdrew the sacred curtain of the sick-chamber, nor permitted the disgrace of wanton tears round the humiliation of strength, or the wreck of beauty.
(270–75)

Matthew Arnold

from 'The Incompatibles', *Nineteenth Century*, vol. 9   April 1881
(collected in *Irish Essays*, 1882)

There is a book familiar to us all, and the more familiar now, probably, to many of us because Mr Gladstone solaced himself with it after his illness, and so set all good Liberals (of whom I wish to be considered one) upon reading it over again. I mean *David Copperfield*. Much as I have published, I do not think it has ever yet happened to me to comment in print upon any production of Charles Dickens. What a pleasure to have the opportunity of praising a work so sound, a work so rich in merit, as *David Copperfield*! 'Man lese nicht die mit-strebende, mit-wirkende!' says Goethe: 'do not read your fellow-strivers, your fellow-workers!' Of the contemporary rubbish which is shot so plentifully all around us, we can, indeed, hardly read

---

1 Nell, in *The Old Curiosity Shop*, was simply killed for the market, as a butcher kills a lamb (see Forster's *Life*), and Paul was written under the same conditions of illness which affected Scott – a part of the ominous palsies grasping alike author and subject both in *Dombey* and *Little Dorrit*.

too little. But to contemporary work so good as *David Copperfield*, we are in danger of perhaps not paying respect enough, of reading it (for who could help reading it?) too hastily, and then putting it aside for something else and forgetting it. What treasures of gaiety, invention, life, are in that book! what alertness and resource! what a soul of good nature and kindness governing the whole! Such is the admirable work which I am now going to call in evidence.

Intimately, indeed, did Dickens know the middle class; he was bone of its bone and flesh of its flesh. Intimately he knew its bringing up. With the hand of a master he has drawn for us a type of the teachers and trainers of its youth, a type of its places of education. Mr Creakle and Salem House are immortal. The type itself, it is to be hoped, will perish; but the drawing of it which Dickens has given cannot die. Mr Creakle, the stout gentleman with a bunch of watch-chain and seals, in an arm-chair, with the fiery face and the thick veins in his forehead; Mr Creakle sitting at his breakfast with the cane, and a newspaper, and the buttered toast before him, will sit on, like Theseus, for ever. For ever will last the recollection of Salem House, and of 'the daily strife and struggle' there; the recollection

of the frosty mornings when we were rung out of bed, and
the cold, cold smell of the dark nights when we were rung
into bed again; of the evening schoolroom dimly lighted and
indifferently warmed, and the morning schoolroom which
was nothing but a great shivering machine; of the alternation
of boiled beef with roast beef, and boiled mutton with roast
mutton; of clods of bread and butter, dog's-eared
lesson-books, cracked slates, tear-blotted copy-books, canings,
rulerings, hair-cuttings, rainy Sundays, suet-puddings, and a
dirty atmosphere of ink surrounding all.

A man of much knowledge and much intelligence, Mr Baring Gould, published not long ago a book about Germany, in which he adduced testimony which, in a curious manner, proves how true and to the life this picture of Salem House and of Mr Creakle is. The public schools of Germany come to be spoken of in that book, and the training which the whole middle class of German gets in them; and Mr Gould mentions what is reported by young Germans trained in their own German schools, who have afterwards served as teachers

of foreign languages and ushers in the ordinary private schools for the
middle class in England. With one voice they tell us of establishments
like Salem House and principals like Mr Creakle. They are astonished, disgusted. They cannot understand how such things can be, and
how a great and well-to-do class can be content with such an ignoble
bringing-up. But so things are, and they report their experience of
them, and their experience brings before us, over and over again, Mr
Creakle and Salem House. . . .

We may even go further still in our use of that charming and
instructive book, the *History of David Copperfield*. We may lay our
finger there on the very types in adult life which are the natural
product of Salem House and of Mr Creakle; the very types of our
middle class, nay of Englishmen and the English nature in general, as
to the Irish imagination they appear. We have only to recall, on the
one hand, Mr Murdstone. Mr Murdstone may be called the natural
product of a course of Salem House and of Mr Creakle, acting upon
hard, stern and narrow natures. Let us recall, then, Mr Murdstone;
Mr Murdstone with his firmness and severity, with his austere religion
and his tremendous visage in church; with his view of the world as
'a place for action, and not for moping and droning in'; his view of
young Copperfield's disposition as 'requiring a great deal of correct-
ing, and to which no greater service can be done than to force it to
conform to the ways of the working world, and to bend it and break
it'. We may recall, too, Miss Murdstone, his sister, with the same
religion, the same tremendous visage in church, the same firmness;
Miss Murdstone with her 'hard steel purse', and her 'uncompromising hard black boxes with her initials on the lids in hard black nails';
severe and formidable like her brother, 'whom she greatly resembled
in face and voice'. These two people, with their hardness, their narrowness, their want of consideration for other people's feelings, their
inability to enter into them, are just the type of the Englishman and
his civilization as he presents himself to the Irish mind by his serious
side. His energy, firmness, industry, religion, exhibit themselves with
these unpleasant features; his bad qualities exhibit themselves without
mitigation or relief.

(709-26)

George Dolby

from *Charles Dickens As I Knew Him* 1885

The final farewell Reading of Tuesday, 15 March 1870, was one of the hardest struggles he had to face, but he went through it with a manliness and good temper which eclipsed all his previous efforts. The previous Readings of this series had far surpassed, in the matter of receipts, any that had gone before them in England; but this one was the crowning triumph.

The largest audience that had ever assembled in the great St James's Hall for a Reading was present for this 'Farewell'. It was a representative gathering, not only in an artistic point of view, but a far wider sense, for all sorts and conditions of men came to bid a public farewell to their great favourite, to the man who, more than any other writer of his generation, had addressed himself to 'the people'. . . .

Long before the doors were opened, an immense crowd had assembled at the Regent Street and Piccadilly entrances, and it was but the work of a few moments to sell sufficient tickets to fill the 'shilling' seats. The numbers turned away were far greater than those that were able to be admitted. Had the hall been twice or three times the size, we should have filled it easily. The fact that the highest-priced seat was five shillings and the lowest a shilling makes the receipts all the more astonishing.

The Readings on this memorable occasion were, the *Christmas Carol* and the 'Trial from *Pickwick*', and as eight o'clock, the time for commencing, drew near, the excitement of the people increased. Punctually to the moment, Mr Dickens walked on to the platform, book in hand, but evidently much agitated. He was thinking, I dare say, that this was to be the very last time he would address an audience in his capacity of reader.

He had taken scarcely less pleasure and delight in his public Readings than in the pursuit of his legitimate calling, and at the thought that he was about to abandon them, there was a struggle in his mind which his fine features reflected. But no feeling of sadness could have been retained in face of the unanimity and splendour of the reception that was accorded him. The immense audience rose to their feet and cheered him to the echo. This lasted some minutes. In spontaneity and warmth it was a provincial rather than a metropolitan reception. It had the instant effect of nerving him up to his work, and he never read the *Carol* more earnestly, more fervently or more effectively than on this occasion. The audience, needless to say, were in supreme sympathy with the reader. Not a word was lost. They seemed to feel that they were hearing him for the last time.

The same may be said of the 'Trial from *Pickwick*', which concluded the evening's entertainment. All the old familiar characters seemed to stand out more deliciously clear than ever; and each was cheered as the reader presented him to the mind's eye of the listener. Sergeant Buzfuz, Mrs Cluppins, Nathaniel Winkle, Sam Weller and the little puisne judge ('puny') Mr Dickens used to say with action, pointing to the late Lord Chief Justice Cockburn when he was present, as he was on this occasion – all of these had their own particular reception.

After this came the saddest, and (so far as Mr Dickens was concerned) the most dreaded part of all. He had responded several times to the calls for his reappearance, but seemed anxious to defer as long as possible the few words of farewell he had mentally prepared. But it had to be done, and, nerving himself up for this crowning effort, he returned once more to the little table (for the last time and for ever), and, with a voice full of emotion, and amid breathless silence, he spoke as follows:

'Ladies and Gentlemen – It would be worse than idle, for it would be hypocritical and unfeeling, if I were to disguise that I close this episode of my life with feelings of very considerable pain. For some fifteen years in this hall, and in many kindred places, I have had the honour of presenting my own cherished ideas before you for your recognition, and in closely observing your reception of them, I have enjoyed an amount of artistic delight and instruction which perhaps it is given to few men to know.

'In this task, and in every other I have ever undertaken as a faithful servant of the public, always imbued with the sense of duty to them, and always striving to do his best, I have been uniformly cheered by the readiest response, the most generous sympathy and the most stimulating support.

'Nevertheless, I have thought it well in the full flood tide of your favour to retire upon those older associations between us which date much farther back than these, and thenceforth to devote myself exclusively to the art that first brought us together.

'Ladies and Gentlemen – In two short weeks from this time I hope that you may enter in your own homes on a new series of readings at which my assistance will be indispensable; but from these garish lights I vanish now for evermore, with a heartfelt, grateful, respectful and affectionate farewell.'

During the delivery of this short and impressive speech, notwithstanding his visible emotion, he never paused or made an instant's hesitation, and the strength of his feelings was only slightly observable in the words (and the accent accompanying them), 'from these garish lights I vanish now for evermore'. These carry with them to this day a sad significance in the remembrance of those still living who, in return for the love and affection he bestowed on them, felt they could never do enough to relieve him, if it were possible, of the sufferings which were only too apparent in their almost daily intercourse with him.

Leaving the platform, amidst acclamations of the most tumultuous kind, he proceeded to his retiring-room with quite a mournful gait, and tears rolling down his cheeks. But he had to go forward yet once again, to be stunned by a more surprising outburst than before, and dazzled by the waving of handkerchiefs. Respectfully kissing his hand, Mr Dickens retired for the last time.

(445–50)

George Lear

from a letter   December 1886

Going back for a moment to the old chambers in Holborn Court, I have the most perfect recollection of the laundress as she was called – the old woman who used to sweep out the offices, light the fires in winter, etc. – though why she was thus called I never could make out, for she never washed anything that I could see, certainly not herself; I suppose it was *lucus a non lucendo*. Dickens took great interest in her, and would mimic her manner of speech, her ways, her excuses, etc., to the very life. He could imitate, in a manner that I have never heard equalled, the low population of the streets of London in all their varieties, whether mere loafers or sellers of fruit, vegetables or anything else. He could also excel in mimicking the popular singers of that day, whether comic or patriotic; as to his acting, he could give us Shakespeare by the ten minutes, and imitate all the leading actors of that time. His father, he said, was intimate with many of them, among whom I particularly recollect Young, Macready, J. P. Harley, etc. He told me he had often taken parts in amateur theatricals before he came to us.

Having been in London two years, I thought I knew something of town, but after a little talk with Dickens I found that I knew nothing. He knew it all from Bow to Brentford.

Sir Leslie Stephen

from 'Dickens', entry in the *Dictionary of National Biography*, vol. 15   1888

His weaknesses are sufficiently obvious, and are reflected in his writings. If literary fame could be safely measured by popularity with the half-educated, Dickens must claim the highest position among English novelists. It is said, apparently on authority (Mr Mowbray Morris in *Fortnightly Review* for December 1882) that 4,239,000 volumes of his works had been sold in England in the twelve years after his death. The criticism of more severe critics chiefly consists in the assertion that his merits are such as suit the half-educated. They admit his fun to be irresistible; his pathos, they say, though it shows boundless vivacity, implies little real depth or tenderness of feeling; and his amazing powers of observation were out of proportion to his powers of reflection. The social and political views, which he constantly inculcates, imply a deliberate preference of spontaneous instinct to genuine reasoned conviction; his style is clear, vigorous, and often felicitous, but mannered and more forcible than delicate; he writes too clearly for readers who cannot take a joke till it has been well hammered into their heads; his vivid perception of external oddities passes into something like hallucination; and in his later books the constant strain to produce effects only legitimate when spontaneous becomes painful. His books are therefore inimitable caricatures of contemporary 'humours' rather than the masterpieces of a great observer of human nature. The decision between these and more eulogistic opinions must be left to a future edition of this dictionary.

Wilkie Collins

A note on *Oliver Twist*, in his copy of Forster's *Life*, reported in *Pall Mall Gazette*   20 January 1890

The one defect in that wonderful book is the helplessly bad construction of the story. The character of 'Nancy' is the finest thing he ever did. He never afterwards saw all sides of a woman's character – saw all round her. That the same man who could create 'Nancy' created the second Mrs Dombey is the most incomprehensible anomaly that I know of in literature.

George Gissing

'Characterization', *Charles Dickens*, chapter 5   1898

The familiar objection to Dickens's characters that they are 'so unreal' (a criticism common in the mouths of persons who would be the last to tolerate downright veracity in fiction), is in part explained – in part justified – by the dramatic conduct of his stories. What unreality there is, arises for the most part from necessities of 'plot'. This may be illustrated by a comparison between two figures wherein the master has embodied so much homely sweetness and rectitude that both are popular favourites. The boatman Peggotty and Joe Gargery the blacksmith are drawn on similar lines; in both the gentlest nature is manifest beneath a ruggedness proper to their callings. There is a certain resemblance, too, between the stories in which each plays his part; childlike in their simple virtues, both become strongly attached to a child – not their own – living under the same roof, and both suffer a grave disappointment in this affection; the boatman's niece is beguiled from him to her ruin, the blacksmith's little relative grows into a conceited youth ashamed of the old companion and the old home. To readers in general I presume that Peggotty is better known than Joe; *David Copperfield* being more frequently read than *Great Expectations*; but if we compare the two figures as to their 'reality', we must decide in favour of Gargery. I think him a better piece of workmanship all round; the prime reason, however, for his standing out so much more solidly in one's mind than Little Emily's uncle is that he lives in a world, not of melodrama, but of everyday cause and effect. The convict Magwitch and his strange doings make no such demand upon one's credulity as the story of Emily and Steerforth, told as it is, with its extravagant situations and flagrantly artificial development. Pip is so thoroughly alive that we can forget his dim relations with Satis House. But who can put faith in Mr Peggotty, when he sets forth to search for his niece over the highways and by-ways of Europe? Who can for a moment put faith in Emily herself after she has ceased to be the betrothed of Ham? As easily could one believe that David Copperfield actually overheard that wildly fantastic dialogue in the lodging-house between the lost girl and Rosa Dartle.

Many such examples might be adduced of excellent, or masterly, characterization spoilt by the demand for effective intrigue. We call to mind this or that person in circumstances impossible of credit; and hastily declare that character and situation are alike unreal. And hereby hangs another point worth touching upon. I have heard it very truly remarked that, in our day, people for the most part criticize Dickens from a recollection of their reading in childhood; they do not come fresh to him with mature minds; in general, they never read him at all after childish years. This is an obvious source of much injustice. Dickens is good reading for all times of life, as are all the great imaginative writers. Let him be read by children together with Don Quixote. But who can speak with authority of Cervantes who knows him only from an acquaintance made at ten years old? To the mind of a child Dickens is, or ought to be, fascinating – (alas for the whole subject of children's reading nowadays!) – and most of the fascination is due to that romantic treatment of common life which is part, indeed, of Dickens's merit, but has smaller value and interest to the older mind. Much of his finest humour is lost upon children; much of his perfect description; and all his highest achievement in characterization. Taking Dickens 'as read', people inflict a loss upon themselves and do a wrong to the author. Who, in childhood, ever cared much for *Little Dorrit*? The reason is plain; in this book Dickens has comparatively little of his wonted buoyancy; throughout, it is in a graver key. True, a house falls down in a most exciting way, and this the reader will remember; all else is to him a waste. We hear, accordingly, that nothing good can be said for *Little Dorrit*. Whereas, a competent judge, taking up the book as he would any other, will find in it some of the best work Dickens ever did; and especially in this matter of characterization; pictures so wholly admirable, so marvellously observed and so exquisitely presented, that he is tempted to call *Little Dorrit* the best book of all.

Again, it is not unusual to seek in Dickens's characters for something he never intended to be there; in other words, his figures are often slighted because they represent a class in society which lacks many qualities desired by cultivated readers, and possesses very prominently the distasteful features such a critic could well dispense with. You lay down, for instance, Thackeray's *Pendennis*, and soon after you happen to take up *Dombey and Son*. Comparisons arise. Whilst reading of Major Bagstock, you find your thoughts wandering to Major Pendennis; when occupied (rather disdainfully) with Mr Toots, you suddenly recall Foker. What can be the immediate outcome of such contrast? It seems impossible to deny to Thackeray a great superiority in the drawing of character; his aristocratic Major and his wealthy young jackass are so much more 'real', that is to say, so much more familiar, than the promoted vulgarian Bagstock and the enriched whipper-snapper Toots. A hasty person would be capable of exclaiming that Dickens had plainly taken suggestions from Thackeray, and made but poor use of them. Observe, however, that *Dombey and Son* appeared, complete, in 1848; *Pendennis* in 1849. Observe, too, the explanation of the whole matter; that Bagstock and Toots represent quite as truthfully figures possible in a certain class, as do Thackeray's characters those to be found in a rank distinctly higher. If Thackeray (who needed no suggestions from others' books) was indeed conscious of his whimsical parallel, we can only admire the skill and finish with which he worked it out. But assuredly he dreamt of no slight to Dickens's performance. They had wrought in different material. Social distinctions are sufficiently pronounced even in our time of revolution; fifty years ago they were much more so. And precisely what estranges the cultivated reader in Bagstock and Toots, is nothing more nor less than evidence of their creator's truthfulness.

A wider question confronts one in looking steadfastly at the masterpieces of a novelist concerned with the lower, sometimes the lowest, modes of life in a great city. Among all the names immortalized by Dickens none is more widely familiar than that of Mrs Gamp. It is universally admitted that in Mrs Gamp we have a creation such as can be met with only in the greatest writers; a figure at once individual and typical; a marvel of humorous presentment; vital in the highest degree attainable by this art of fiction. From the day of her first appearance on the stage, Mrs Gamp has been a delight, a wonder, a byword. She stands unique, no other novelist can show a piece of work, in the same kind, worthy of a place beside her; he must go to the very heights of world literature, to him who bodied forth Dame Quickly, and Juliet's nurse, for the suggestion of equivalent power. Granted, then, that Mrs Gamp has indubitable existence; who and what is she? Well, a sick nurse, living in Kingsgate Street, Holborn, in a filthy room somewhere upstairs, and summoned for nursing of all kinds by persons more or less well-to-do, who are so unfortunate as to know of no less offensive substitute. We are told, and can believe, that in the year 1844 (the date of *Martin Chuzzlewit*) few people did know of any substitute for Mrs Gamp; that she was an institution; that she carried her odious vices and her criminal incompetence from house to house in decent parts of London. Dickens knew her only too well; had observed her at moments of domestic crisis; had learnt her language and could reproduce it (or most of it) with surprising accuracy. In plain words, then, we are speaking of a very loathsome creature; a sluttish, drunken, avaricious, dishonest woman. Meeting her in the flesh, we should shrink disgusted, so well does the foulness of her person correspond with the baseness of her mind. Hearing her speak, we should turn away in half-amused contempt. Yet, when we encounter her in the pages of Dickens, we cannot have too much of Mrs Gamp's company; her talk is an occasion of uproarious mirth, we never dream of calling her to moral judgement, but laugh the more, the more infamously she sees fit to behave. Now, in what sense can this figure in literature be called a copy of the human original?

I am perfectly aware that this inquiry goes to the roots of the theory of Art. Here I have no space (nor would it be the proper moment) to discuss all the issues that are involved in a question so direct and natural; but if we are to talk at all about the people in Dickens, we must needs start with some understanding of what is implied when we call them true, life-like, finely presented. Is not the fact in itself very remarkable, that by dint (it seems) of *omitting* those very features which in life most strongly impress us, an artist in fiction can produce something which we applaud as an inimitable portrait? That for disgust he can give us delight, and yet leave us glorying in his verisimilitude?

Turn to another art. Open the great volume of Hogarth, and look at the several figures of women which present a fair correspondence with that of Mrs Gamp. We admire the artist's observation, his great skill, his moral significance, even his grim humour; then – we close the book with a feeling of relief. With these faces who would spend hours of leisure? The thing has been supremely well done, and we are glad of it, and will praise the artist unreservedly; but his basely grinning and leering women must not hang upon the wall, to be looked at and talked of with all and sundry. Hogarth has copied – in the strict sense of the word. He gives us life – and we cannot bear it.

The Mrs Gamp of our novel is a piece of the most delicate idealism. It is a sublimation of the essence of Gamp. No novelist (say what he will) ever gave us a picture of life which was not idealized; but there are degrees; degrees of purpose and of power. Juliet's nurse is an idealized portrait, but it comes much nearer to the real thing than Mrs Gamp; in our middle-class England we cannot altogether away with the free-spoken dame of Verona; we Bowdlerize her – of course damaging her in the process. Mrs Berry, in *Richard Feverel*, is idealized, but she smacks too strongly of the truth for boudoir readers. Why, Moll Flanders herself is touched and softened, for all the authors illusive directness. In Mrs Gamp, Dickens has done his own Bowdlerizing, but with a dexterity which serves only to heighten his figure's effectiveness. Vulgarity he leaves; that is of the essence of the matter; vulgarity unsurpassable is the note of Mrs Gamp. Vileness, on the other hand, becomes grotesquerie, wonderfully converted into a subject of laughter. Her speech, the basest ever heard from human tongue, by a process of infinite subtlety, which leaves it the same yet not the same, is made an endless amusement, a source of quotation for laughing lips incapable of unclean utterance.

Idealism, then: confessed idealism. But let us take another character from another book, also a woman supposed to represent a phase of low life in London. Do you recall 'good Mrs Brown', the hag who strips little Florence Dombey of her clothes? And do you remember that this creature has a daughter, her name Alice Marlow, who – presumably having been a domestic servant, or a shopgirl, or something of the kind – was led astray by Mr Carker of the shining teeth, and has become a wandering nondescript? Now in Alice Marlow we again have idealism; but of a different kind. This child of good Mrs Brown, tramping into London on a bitter night, is found on the roadside and taken home for tendance by Mr Carker's sister, neither being aware of the other's identity; and having submitted to this kindness, and having accepted money, the girl goes her way. That same night she learns who has befriended her, and forthwith rushes back a few miles, through storm and darkness, to fling the alms at the giver. Outlines of a story sufficiently theatrical; but the dialogue! One fails to understand how Dickens brought himself to pen the language – at great length – he puts into this puppet's mouth. It is doubtful whether one could pick out a single sentence, a single phrase, such as the real Alice Marlow could conceivably have used. Her passion is vehement; no impossible thing. The words in which she utters it would be appropriate to the most stagey of wronged heroines – be that who it may. A figure less life-like will not be found in any novel ever written. Yet Dickens doubtless intended it as legitimate idealization; a sort of type of the doleful multitude of betrayed women. He meant it for imagination exalting common fact. But the fact is not exalted; it has simply vanished. And the imagination is of a kind that avails nothing on any theme. In Mrs Gamp a portion of truth is omitted; in Alice Marlow there is substitution of falsity. By the former process, true idealism *may* be reached; by the latter, one arrives at nothing but attitude and sham.

Of course omission and veiling do not suffice to create Mrs Gamp. In his alchemy, Dickens had command of the *menstruum* which alone is powerful enough to effect such transmutation as this; it is called humour. Humour, be it remembered, is inseparable from charity. Not only did it enable him to see this coarse creature as an amusing person; it inspired him with that large tolerance which looks through things external, gives its full weight to circumstance, and preserves a modesty, a humility, in human judgement. We can form some notion of what Mrs Gamp would have become in the hands of a rigorous realist, with scorn and disgust (implied inevitably) taking the place of humour. We reject the photograph; it avails us nothing in art or life. Humour deals gently with fact and fate; in its smile there is forbearance, in its laugh there is kindliness. With falsehood – however well meant – it is incompatible; when it has done its work as solvent, the gross adherents are dissipated, the essential truth remains. Do you ask for the Platonic *idea* of London's monthly nurse early in Queen Victoria's reign? Dickens shows it you embodied. At such a thing as this, crawling between earth and heaven, what can one do but laugh? Its existence is a puzzle, a wonder. The class it represents shall be got rid of as speedily as possible; well and good; we cannot tolerate such a public nuisance. But the individual – so perfect a specimen – shall be preserved for all time by the magic of a great writer's deep-seeing humour, and shall be known as Mrs Gamp.

For a moment, contrast with this masterpiece a picture in which Dickens has used his idealism on material more promising, though sought amid surroundings sufficiently like those which formed the portrait of Kingsgate Street. The most successful character in his stories written to be read at Christmas is Mrs Lirriper. She belongs to a class distinguished then, as now, by its uncleanness, its rapacity, its knavery, its ignorance. Mrs Lirriper keeps a London lodging-house. Here, in depicting an individual, Dickens has not typified a class. He idealizes this woman, but finds in her, ready to his hand, the qualities of goodness and tenderness and cheery honesty, so that there is no question of transmuting a subject repulsive to the senses. Mrs Lirriper is quite possible, even in a London lodging-house; in the flesh, however, we should not exactly seek her society. Her talk (idealized with excellent adroitness) would too often jar upon the ear; her person would be, to say the least, unattractive. In the book, she has lost these accidents of position: we are first amused, then drawn on to like, to admire, to love her. An unfortunate blemish – the ever-recurring artificiality of story – threatens to make her dim; but Mrs Lirriper triumphs over this. We bear her in memory as a person known – a person most unhappily circumstanced, set in a gloomy sphere; but of such sweet nature that we forget her inevitable defects, even as we should those of an actual acquaintance of like character.

In looking back on the events of life, do we not see them otherwise than, at the time, they appeared to us? The harsh is smoothed; the worst of everything is forgotten; things pleasant come into relief. This (a great argument for optimism) is a similitude of Dickens's art. Like Time, he obscures the unpleasing, emphasizes all we are glad to remember. Time does not falsify; neither does Dickens, whenever his art is unalloyed.

Let us turn to his literary method. It is that of all the great novelists. To set before his reader the image so vivid in his own mind, he simply describes and reports. We have, in general, a very precise and complete picture of externals – the face, the gesture, the habit. In this Dickens excels; he proves to us by sheer force of visible detail, how actual was the mental form from which he drew. We learn the tone of voice, the trick of utterance; he declared that every word spoken by his characters was audible to him. Then does the man reveal himself in colloquy; sometimes once for all, sometimes by degrees, in chapter after chapter – though this is seldom the case. We know these people because we see and hear them.

In a few instances he added deliberate analysis; it was never well done – always superfluous. Very rarely has analysis of character justified itself in fiction. To Dickens the method was alien: he could make no use whatever of it. In the early book which illustrates all his defects, *Nicholas Nickleby*, we have some dreary pages concerned with the inner man of Ralph Nickleby; seeing that the outer is but shadowy, these details cannot interest; they show, moreover, much crudity and conventionality of thought. Later, an analysis is attempted of Mr Dombey – very laborious, very long. It does not help us in the least to understand Paul's father, himself one of the least satisfactory of Dickens's leading persons. One may surmise that the author felt something of this, and went out of his wonted way in an endeavour to give the image more life.

It results from Dickens's weakness in the devising of incidents, in the planning of story, that he seldom develops character through circumstance. There are conversions, but we do not much believe in them; they smack of the stage. Possibly young Martin Chuzzlewit may be counted an exception; but there is never much life in him.

From this point of view Dickens's best bit of work is Pip, in *Great Expectations*; Pip, the narrator of his own story, who exhibits very well indeed the growth of a personality, the interaction of character and event. One is not permitted to lose sight of the actual author; though so much more living than Esther Summerson, Pip is yet embarrassed, like her, with the gift of humour. We know very well whose voice comes from behind the scenes when Pip is describing Mr Wopsle's dramatic venture. Save for this, we acknowledge a true self-revelation. What could be better than the lad's picture of his state of mind, when, after learning that he has 'great expectations', he quits the country home of his childhood and goes to London? 'I formed a plan in outline for bestowing a dinner of roast beef and plum-pudding, a pint of ale, and a gallon of condescension upon everybody in the village' (chapter 19). It is one of many touches which give high value to this book.

As a rule, the more elaborate Dickens's conception of character, the smaller his success in working it out. Again and again he endeavoured to present men and women of exceptionally strong passions: the kind of persons who make such a figure on the boards, where they frown and clench their fists, and utter terrible phrases. It began in *Oliver Twist* with the man called Monks; in *Barnaby* came the murderer; in *Chuzzlewit* appears the mask known as old Martin, a thing of saw-dust. Later, the efforts in this direction are more conscientious, more laboured, but rarely more successful. An exception, perhaps, may be noted in Bradley Headstone, the lover of Lizzie Hexam, whose consuming passion here and there convinces, all the more for its well-contrived contrast with the character of the man whom Lizzie prefers. Charley Hexam, too, is life-like, on a lower plane. The popular voice pleads for Sidney Carton; yes, he is well presented – but so easy to forget. Think, on the other hand, of the long list of women meant to be tragic, who, one and all, must be judged failures. Edith Dombey, with her silent wrath and ludicrous behaviour, who, intended for a strong, scornful nature, dumbly goes to the sacrifice when bidden by her foolish mother, and then rails at the old wordling for the miseries needlessly brought upon herself. Rosa Dartle, at first a promising suggestion, but falling away into exaggerations of limelight frenzy. Lady Dedlock and her maid Hortense – which is the more obvious waxwork? Mrs Clennam, in *Little Dorrit*, is wrought so patiently and placed in so picturesque a scene that one laments over her impossibility; her so-called talk is, perhaps, less readable than anything in Dickens. The same book shows us, or aims at showing us, Miss Wade and Tattycoram, from both of whom we turn incredulous. Of Miss Havisham one grudges to speak; her ghostly presence does its best to spoil an admirable novel. Women all these, only in name; a cause of grief to the lovers of the master, a matter of scoffing to his idler critics. When we come to women of everyday stature, then indeed it is a different thing. So numerous are these, and so important in an estimate of Dickens's power of characterization, that I must give them a chapter to themselves.

Neither at a black-hearted villain was he really good, though he prided himself on his achievements in this kind. Jonas Chuzzlewit is the earliest worth mention; and what can be said of Jonas, save that he is a surly ruffian of whom one knows very little? The 'setting' of his part is very strong; much powerful writing goes to narrate his history; but the man remains mechanical. Mr Carker hardly aims at such completeness of scoundreldom, but he would be a fierce rascal – if not so bent on exhibiting his teeth, which remind one of the working wires. Other shapes hover in lurid vagueness. Whether, last of all, John Jasper would have shown a great advance, must remain doubtful. The first half of *Edwin Drood* shows him picturesquely, and little more. We discover no hint of real tragedy. The man seems to us a very vulgar assassin, and we care not at all what becomes of him.

Against these set the gallery of portraits in which Dickens had displayed to us the legal world of his day. Here he painted from nature, and with an artist's love of his subject. From the attorneys and barristers of *Pickwick*, sportive themselves and a cause of infinite mirth in others, to the Old Bailey practitioners so admirably grim in *Great Expectations*, one's eye passes along a row of masterpieces. Nay, it is idle to use the pictorial simile; here are men with blood in their veins – some of them with a good deal of it on their hands. They will not be forgotten; whether we watch the light comedy of Jorkins and Spenlow, or observe the grim gravity of Mr Jaggers, it is with the same entire conviction. In this department of his work Dickens can be said to idealize only in the sense of the finest art; no praise can exaggerate his dexterity in setting forth these examples of supreme realism. As a picture of actual life in a certain small world, *Bleak House* is his greatest book; from office-boy to judge, here are all who walk in 'the valley of the Shadow of the Law'. Impossible to run through the list, much as one would enjoy it. Think only of Mr Vholes. In the whole range of fiction there is no character more vivid than this; exhibited so briefly yet so completely, with such rightness in every touch, such impressiveness of total effect, that the thing becomes a miracle. No strain of improbable intrigue can threaten the vitality of these dusty figures. The clerks are as much alive as their employers; the law-stationer stands for ever face to face with Mr Tulkinghorn; Inspector Buckett has warmer flesh than that of any other detective in the library of detective literature. As for Jaggers and Wemmick, we should presume them unsurpassable had we not known their predecessors. They would make a novelist's reputation.

Among the finest examples of characterization (I postpone a review of the figures which belong more distinctly to satire) must be mentioned the Father of the Marshalsea. Should ever proof be demanded – as often it has been – that Dickens is capable of high comedy, let it be sought in the thirty-first chapter of book I of Little Dorrit. There will be seen the old Marshalsea prisoner, the bankrupt of half a lifetime, entertaining and patronizing his workhouse pensioner, old Mr Nandy. For delicacy of treatment, for fineness of observation, this scene, I am inclined to think, is unequalled in all the novels. Of exaggeration there is no trace; nothing raises a laugh; at most one smiles, and may very likely be kept grave by profound interest and a certain emotion of wonder. We are in a debtors' prison, among vulgar folk; yet the exquisite finish of this study of human nature forbids one to judge it by any but the highest standards. The Dorrit brothers are both well drawn; they are characterizations in the best sense of the word; and in this scene we have the culmination of the author's genius. That it reveals itself so quietly is but the final assurance of consummate power.

With the normal in character, with what (all things considered) we may call wholesome normality, Dickens does not often concern himself. Of course there are his homely-minded 'little women', of whom more in another place. And there are his benevolent old boys (I call them so advisedly) whom one would like to be able to class with everyday people, but who cannot in strictness be considered here. Walking-gentlemen appear often enough; amiable shadows, such as

Tom Pinch's friend Westlock; figures meant to be prominent, such as Arthur Clennam. There remain a few instances of genuine characterization within ordinary limits. I cannot fall in with the common judgement that Dickens never shows us a gentleman. Twice, certainly, he has done so, with the interesting distinction that in one case he depicts a gentleman of the old school; in the other, a representative of the refined manhood which came into existence (or became commonly observable) in his latter years. In John Jarndyce I can detect no vulgarity; he appears to me compact of good sense, honour and gentle feeling. His eccentricity does not pass bounds; the better we know him the less observable it grows. Though we are told nothing expressly of his intellectual acquirements, it is plain that he had a liberal education, and that his tastes are studious. Impossible not to like and to respect Mr Jarndyce. Compare him with Mr Pickwick, or with the Cheerybles, and we see at once the author's intention of social superiority, no less than his increased skill in portraiture. The second figure, belonging to a changed time, is Mr Crisparkle, for whose sake especially one regrets the unfinished state of *Edwin Drood*. His breezy manner, his athletic habits, his pleasant speech, give no bad idea of the classical tutor who is neither an upstart nor a pedant. Dickens was careful in his choice of names; we see how he formed that of Crisparkle, and recognize its fitness.

Two other names occur to me, which carry with them a suggestion of true gentility – if the word is permitted; but their bearers can hardly rank with normal personages. Sir Leicester Dedlock, though by no means unsympathetically presented, belongs rather to the region of satire; he is a gentleman, indeed, and meant to be representative of a class, but his special characteristic overcharges the portrait. Incomparably more of a human being than his wife, he might, with less satirical emphasis, have been a very true gentleman indeed. Then, in *Dombey and Son*, does one not remember Cousin Feenix? The name this time, is unfortunate; this weak-legged scion of aristocracy deserved better treatment. For he is no phantasm; has no part with the puppets of supposed high-birth whom Dickens occasionally set up only for the pleasure of knocking them down again. However incapable of walking straight across a room, however restricted in his views of life, Cousin Feenix has the instincts of birth and breeding. I think one may say that he is Dickens's least disputable success in a sketch (it is only a sketch) from the aristocratic world. His talk does not seem to me exaggerated, and it is unusually interesting; his heart is right, his apprehensions are delicate. That he should be shown as feeble in mind, no less than at the knees, is merely part of the author's scheme; and, after all, the feebleness is more apparent than real. Dickens, moreover, very often associates kindness of disposition with lack of brains; it connects itself, I fancy, with his attitude towards liberal education, which has already been discussed, as well as with his Radicalism, still to be spoken of. No distinctly intellectual person figures in his books; David Copperfield is only a seeming exception, for who really thinks of David as a literary man? To his autobiography let all praise be given – with the reserve that we see the man himself less clearly than any other person of whom he speaks. Decidedly he is *not* 'the hero of his own story'. Had Dickens intended to show us a man of letters, he would here have failed most grievously; of course he aimed at no such thing; the attempt would have cost him half his public. And so it is that one never thinks of the good David as a character at all, never for a moment credits *him*, the long-suffering youth for whom Dora 'held the pens', with that glorious endowment of genius which went to the writing of his life.

Of an average middle-class family in Dickens's earlier time – decent, kindly, not unintelligent folk – we have the best example in the Meagles group, from *Little Dorrit*. This household may be contrasted with, say, that of the Maylies in *Oliver Twist*, which is merely immature work, and with the more familiar family circles on which Dickens lavishes his mirth and his benevolence. The Meagles do not much interest us, which is quite right; they are thoroughly realized, and take their place in social history. Well done, too, is the Pocket family in *Great Expectations*, an interesting pendant to that of the Jellybys in *Bleak House*; showing how well, when he chose, Dickens could satirize without extravagance. Mrs Pocket is decidedly more credible than Mrs Jellyby; it might be urged, perhaps, that she belongs to the Sixties instead of to the Fifties, a point of some importance. The likeness in dissimilitiude between these ladies' husbands is very instructive. As for the son, Herbert Pocket, he is a capital specimen of the healthy, right-minded, and fairly educated middle-class youth. Very skilfully indeed is he placed side by side with Pip; each throwing into relief the other's natural and acquired characteristics.

We see how long it will take the blacksmith's foster-child (he telling the tale himself) to reach the point of mental and moral refinement to which Herbert Pocket has been bred.

One more illustration of the ordinary in life and character. Evidently Dickens took much pains with Walter Gay, in *Dombey and Son*, meaning to represent an average middle-class boy, high-spirited, frank, affectionate and full of cheerful ambition. I have already mentioned the darker design, so quickly abandoned; we feel sure its working out would not have carried conviction, for Walter Gay, from the first, does not ring quite true. The note seems forced; we are not stirred by his exuberance of jollity, and he never for a moment awakens strong interest. Is it any better with Richard Carstone – in whom the tragic idea was, with modification, carried through? Yes, Richard is more interesting; by necessity of his fortunes, and by virtue of artistic effort. He has his place in a book pervaded with the atmosphere of doom. Vivid he never becomes; we see him as a passive victim of fate, rather than as a struggling man; if he made a better fight, or if we were allowed to see more of his human weakness (partly forbidden by our proprieties), his destiny would affect us more than it does. In truth, this kind of thing cannot be done under Dickens's restrictions. Thackeray *could* have done it magnificently; but there was 'the great, big, stupid public'.

The 'gentleman' Dickens loved to contemplate was – in echo of Burns's phrase – he who derives his patent of gentility straight from Almighty God. These he found abundantly among the humble of estate, the poor in spirit; or indulged his fine humanity in the belief that they abounded. A broken squire, reduced to miserly service, but keeping through all faults and misfortunes the better part of his honest and kindly nature; grotesque in person, of fantastic demeanour, but always lovable; of this dream comes Newman Noggs. A city clerk, grey in conscientious labour for one house, glorying in the perfection of his ledger, taking it ill if his employers insist on raising his salary; the vision is christened Tim Linkinwater. A young man of bumpkinish appearance, shy, ungainly, who has somehow drifted into the household of a country architect; who nourishes his soul at the church organ; who is so good and simple and reverential that years of experience cannot teach him what everyone else sees at a glance – the hypocritical rascality of his master; he takes shape, and is known to us as Tom Pinch. A village blacksmith, with heart as tender as his thews are tough; delighting above all things in the society of a little child; so dull of brain that he gives up in despair the effort to learn his alphabet; so sweet of temper that he endures in silence the nagging of an outrageous wife; so delicate of sensibility that he perspires at the thought of seeming to intrude upon an old friend risen in life; – what name can be his but Joe Gargery? These, and many another like unto them, did the master lovingly create, and there would be something of sacrilege in a cold scrutiny of his work. Whether or no their prototypes existed in the hurrying crowd of English life, which obscures so much good as well as evil, these figures have fixed themselves in the English imagination, and their names are part of our language. Dickens saw them, and heard them speak; to us, when we choose to enjoy without criticizing, they seem no less present. Every such creation was a good deed; the results for good have been incalculable. Would he have been better occupied, had he pried into each character, revealed its vices, insisted on its sordid weaknesses, thrown bare its frequent hypocrisy, and emphasized its dreary unintelligence? Indeed, I think not. I will only permit myself the regret that he who could come so near to truth, and yet so move the affections, as in Joe Gargery, was at other times content with that inferior idealism which addresses itself only to unripe minds or to transitory moods.

The point to be kept in view regarding these ideal figures is that, however little their speech or conduct may smack of earth, their worldly surroundings are shown with marvellous fidelity. Tom Pinch worshipping at the shrine of Pecksniff may not hold our attention; but Tom Pinch walking towards Salisbury on the frosty road, or going to market in London with his sister, is unforgettable. This is what makes the difference between an impossible person in Dickens and the same kind of vision in the work of smaller writers. One cannot repeat too often that, in our literary slang, he 'visualized' every character – Little Nell no less than Mr Jaggers. Seeing *them*, he saw the house in which they lived, the table at which they ate, and all the little habits of their day-to-day life. Here is an invaluable method of illusion, if an author can adopt it. Thus fortified, Dickens's least substantial imaginings have a durability not to be hoped for the laborious accuracies of an artist uninspired.

Pass to another group in this scarcely exhaustible world – the confessed eccentrics. Here Dickens revels. An English novelist must needs be occupied to some extent with grotesque abnormalities of thought and demeanour. Dickens saw them about him even more commonly than we of today, and delighted in noting, selecting, combining. The result is seen in those persons of his drama who are frankly given up by many who will defend his verisimilitude in other directions. Mantalini, for example; Quilp, Captain Cuttle, Silas Wegg, and many another. For Silas Wegg, I fear, nothing can be urged, save the trifle that we know him; he becomes a bore, one of the worst instances of this form of humour weakened by extenuation. Even Dickens occasionally suffered from the necessity of filling a certain space. Think how long his novels are, and marvel that the difficulty does not more often declare itself. Of Mr Boythorn we are accustomed to think as drawn from Landor, but then it is Landor with all the intellect left out; his roaring as gently as any sucking-dove does not greatly charm us, but his talk has good qualities. More of a character, in the proper sense of the word, is Harold Skimpole, whose portrait gave such offence to Leigh Hunt. Now Skimpole is one of the few people in Dickens whom we dislike, and so, *a priori*, demands attention. If we incline to think his eccentricity overdone, be it remembered that the man was in part an actor, and a very clever actor too. Skimpole is excellent work, and stands with fine individuality among the representatives of true unworldliness.

To which category belongs Mr Micawber? The art of living without an income may be successfully cultivated in very different moods. It is possible for a man of the most generous instincts to achieve great things in this line of endeavour; but the fact remains that, sooner or later, somebody has the honour of discharging his liabilities. To speak severely of Mr Micawber is beyond the power of the most conscientious critic, whether in life or art; the most rigid economist would be glad to grasp him by the hand and to pay for the bowl of punch over which this type of genial impecuniosity would dilate upon his embarrassments and his hopes; the least compromising realist has but to open at a dialogue or a letter in which Mr Micawber's name is seen, and straightway he forgets his theories. No selfish intention can be attributed to him. His bill might *not* be provided for when he declared it *was*, and, in consequence, poor Traddles may lose the table he has

purchased for 'the dearest girl in the world', but Mr Micawber had
all the time been firmly assured that something would turn up; he
will sympathize profoundly with Traddles, and write him an epistle
which makes amends for the loss of many tables. No man ever lived
who was so consistently delightful – certainly Dickens's father cannot
have been so – but in this idealized portraiture we have essential
truth. Men of this stamp do not abound, but they are met with, even
today. As a rule, he who waits for something to turn up, mixing
punch the while, does so with a very keen eye on his neighbour's
pocket, and is recommended to us neither by Skimpole's fantastic
gaiety nor by Micawber's eloquence and warmth of heart; nevertheless, one knows the irrepressibly hopeful man, full of kindliness, often
distinguished by unconscious affectations of speech, who goes through
life an unreluctant pensioner on the friends won by his many good
and genial qualities. The one point on which experience gives no support to the imaginative figure is his conversion to practical activity.
Mr Micawber in Australia does the heart good; but he is a pious
vision. We refuse to think of a wife worn out by anxieties, of children
growing up in squalor; we gladly accept the flourishing colonist; but
this is tribute to the author whom we love. Dickens never wrought
more successfully for our pleasure and for his own fame. He is ever at
his best when dealing with an amiable weakness. And in Micawber he
gives us no purely national type – such men are peculiar to no
country; all the characteristics of this wonderful picture can be appreciated by civilized readers throughout the world. It is not so in regard
to many of his creations, though all the finest have traits of universal
humanity. Should time deal hardly with him; should his emphasis of
time and place begin to weigh against his wide acceptance; it is difficult to believe that the beaming visage of Wilkins Micawber will not
continue to be recognized wherever men care for literary art.

This chapter must conclude with a glance at a class of human beings
prominent in Dickens's earlier books, but of small artistic interest
when treated in the manner peculiar to him. He was fond of characters hovering between eccentricity and madness, and in one case he
depicted what he himself calls an idiot, though idiocy is not strictly
speaking the form of disease exhibited. Lunatics were more often
found at large in his day than in ours; perhaps that accounts for our
introduction to such persons as Mrs Nickleby's wooer and Mr Dick;

Miss Flite of course, had another significance. The crazy gentleman on the garden walk, who at once flatters and terrifies Mrs Nickleby, can hardly be regarded as anything but an actor in broad farce; his talk, indeed, is midsummer madness, but is meant only to raise a laugh. At the end of the century, one does not laugh with such agreeable facility. Mrs Nickleby commands our attention – at a respectful distance; and here, as always, behaves after her kind, illustrating the eternal feminine; but the madman we cannot accept. Betsy Trotwood's *protégé* comes nearer to the recognizable; nevertheless Mr Dick's presence in such a book as *David Copperfield* would seem waste of space, but for certain considerations. He illustrates the formidable lady's goodness and common sense; he served a very practical purpose, and that of recommending rational treatment of the insane; and he had his place in the pages of an author whose humanity includes all that are in any way afflicted, in mind, body or estate. Moreover, the craze about King Charles's head has been, and is likely to be, a great resource to literary persons in search of a familiar allusion. In passing to *Barnaby Rudge*, we are on different ground. Whatever else, Barnaby is a very picturesque figure, and I presume it was merely on this account that Dickens selected such a hero. In an earlier chapter, I said that this story seemed to me to bear traces of the influence of Scott; its narrative style and certain dialogues in the historical part are suggestive of this. May not the crazy Barnaby have originated in a recollection of Madge Wildfire? Crazy, I call him; an idiot he certainly is not. An idiot does not live a life of exalted imagination. But certain lunatics are of imagination all compact, and Barnaby, poetically speaking, makes a good representative of the class. Of psychology – a word unknown to Dickens – we, of course, have nothing; to ask for it is out of place. The idea, all things considered, cannot be judged a happy one. Whilst writing the latter part of the book Dickens thought for a moment of showing the rioters as led by a commanding figure, who, in the end, should prove to have escaped from Bedlam. We see his motive for this, but are not sorry he abandoned the idea. Probably *Barnaby Rudge*, good as it is, would have been still better had the suggestion of an insane central figure been also discarded.

(96–127)

A. C. Swinburne

from a letter to Sydney C. Cockerell   5 August 1903

I am equally interested and delighted to hear what you tell me.[1] I trust you will make it public. The appreciation of so great a man as Tolstoy – so glorious a genius and so glorious a personality – does what no other living man's could do: it adds a crowning ray of glory to the fame of Dickens. Above all, what a superb and crushing reply to the vulgar insults of such malignant boobies and criticasters as G. H. Lewes and Co. (too numerous a Co.!) is the witness of such a man as this – such a man of men – to the lifelike reality of his characters and their capacity to make themselves our 'personal friends'!

I thank you for having given me a very keen pleasure and a very deep satisfaction. After all, like will to like – genius will find out genius, and goodness will recognize goodness.

Louis Cazamian

from 'Dickens: Christmas Philosophy', *Le Roman Social en Angleterre*   1904 (translated by Stephen Wall)

What emerges if this tale [*The Chimes*] is put together with the other Christmas Stories, and with scattered passages in his work where Dickens defined his thought distinctly, is 'Christmas Philosophy'. It is a vague and sentimental form of Christian socialism. Bolder in making criticisms than in offering positive policies, it extols intervention in the name of religious idealism. Considered historically, it answers the needs of a society which had by then half-disappeared. It

1 Cockerell had visited Tolstoy in July 1903, who had said of Dickens, 'All his characters are my personal friends – I am constantly comparing them with living persons, and living persons with them, and what a spirit there was in all he wrote.'

Tolstoy wrote in his Notebook: 'The first condition of an author's popularity, the prime means to make people like him, is the love with which he treats his characters. That is why Dickens's characters are the friends of all mankind; they are a bond of union between man in America and man in Petersburg' (Aylmer Maude, *The Life of Tolstoy*, 1929). [Ed.]

suits the personal relationships of the family business and the small workshop. In this sense it could be called reactionary, but from all other points of view, it is progressive. Dickens unreservedly disapproves of explicit manifestations of reactionary social attitudes. He refuses to let the need for benevolent authority tempt him into a desire for the political tutelage of the people.

Here the Christian element, indirectly apparent everywhere in Dickens's work, crystallizes round the Christmas festival. In the first story [*The Christmas Carol*] the birth of Christ itself becomes the symbol of a moral and social renewal. In *The Chimes* it is the church bells, the religious voices of the season, which preach to the poor their duties and their hopes; Christmas time merges with the turn of the year, the end of an unhappy past, the beginning of a better future. In both cases Dickens wanted to suggest a natural affinity between his gospel and this renewal of spirit and season. He felt and loved both the hushed contemplation and the overflowing joy of Christmas week deeply. No one has known better how to express the traditional feelings of a whole people. Strengthened by his sense of harmony with the national instinct, Dickens made a noble effort to expand it, and to employ it towards the peaceful solution of social problems. Christmas was already the supreme religious and family festival; on that day hearts opened, dead and withered feelings revived, souls were touched by pity, and separated, divided families came together round the parental hearth. Why not similarly unite, in heart and soul, the hostile brothers of the great national family? If this day has a magic which prompts goodness, why not let it shine beyond the confines of the house on everyone, the suffering, the defeated, the poor and the humble? If physical intoxication itself, groaning boards, roaring fires, trees hung with toys, the innocent happiness of children, and the fluttering of young girls kissed under the mistletoe, are healthy and good because they rekindle a joy in living, why not give a thought to those who on that day suffer more than ever from hunger and cold? In this way the Christian festival, a time of moral transformation, becomes the centre of a spreading and widening charity; the Christmas Stories make the connexion in Dickens between Christianity and social doctrine clearly discernible.

On the constructive side this doctrine is extremely simple. Between men there exists a natural fellowship established by moral duties inseparable from religious feeling. This ought to reveal itself by the active concern which members of society show for each other; rich and poor have their duties. The latter already possess unsuspected virtues; among them devotion and self-sacrifice prosper; they are better, when they could so naturally be worse. But it is still necessary for them to make the most difficult effort of all: to maintain, along with charity, faith and hope; to resist despair and social hatred. Dickens condemns, even if he understands, revolutionary violence. William Fern comes from Dorset, like the six Tolpuddle martyrs; through him the author both accounts for and disapproves of agrarian riots. Nowhere is there any question of Chartism. Toby Veck is severely punished for having mistrusted human nature, and for being involuntarily the sport of oppressors of the people and of agitators. Courageous energy and steady hope ought to allow the poor to look forward to the just rewards that the future holds for them. Such rewards will not come of themselves; the rich, the fortunate, and the powerful should do their utmost to correct social injustices. How will they act? Dickens has no thought of doing away with inequalities of wealth; he seems to have had only a vague conception of the socialist ideal, as if it was one of the fanciful dreams of revolution. But the appeal which the poor make to the rich has the strength of a legitimate demand. Dickens, like the leaders of the new philanthropy, acknowledged the right to relief. The governing classes are responsible for social evils; over the ignorant and the weak they have the natural authority of a father over his children. It is necessary for the individual and the State to intervene in the life of the lower classes; private or public charity, devoted, sincere and patient action, must assuage and cure without respite. The first Christmas Story especially instructs the rich in their duties. No deed is without value, no goodwill useless. From the highest to the lowest, all those in authority have the cure of souls. If Scrooge, the businessman, increases the salary of Bob Cratchit, his clerk, he will have made a contribution to social peace; if all employers were like old Fezziwig, and treated their workers in a friendly way, there would be less bitter hatred. Within the limits of things as they are and the system as it is, society's physical and spiritual scars must fade away. Otherwise, the abyss between the classes will deepen every day, and the already impending revolution will sweep away both rich and poor. And Dickens had a clear picture of this social catastrophe taken from Carlyle's epic *The French Revolution*. One of his novels [*A Tale of Two Cities*] plainly reflects this influence.

The negative aspect of this doctrine is even clearer. It grapples with two enemies. One is 'stupid' Conservatism, the party of sheer habit, instinctively and selfishly reactionary. Here Dickens's radicalism is apparent in his revolt against a proud and overbearing philanthropy. He includes aristocratic socialism among the vain and hypocritical forms of charity. Sir Joseph Bowley obviously belongs to the Young England movement. But Dickens's main effort was not at all in this direction. He was displeased by the insulting manner of feudal benevolence, but at bottom he did not think it essential that the people should emancipate themselves: for him, as for Carlyle, salvation must come from above. One ought to remember his friendship with Lord Ashley; and it should be noted that the campaign of the 'Corn-Law League' – pre-eminently a radical, middle-class movement – nowhere figures in his novels. The fact is that it was the work of radical individualists, and individualism was the enemy against which Dickens swore the most inveterate hostility. He invariably exposed it and fought against it in all its forms: economic dogmatism, utilitarian theory, middle-class custom. He loathed it on instinct, since it was the social manifestation of an inner coldness poles apart from his own emotional temperament; through feeling, since it was contrary to morality and Christian charity; through reason, in so far as he did reason, since it was the theory of selfishness. In the uncompromising and premature application of mathematics to life represented by the Malthusian Filer, he sensed rather than understood an exaggerated and dangerous theory; and the practical 'common sense' of the alderman, the cold and pitiless vision of material interest, seemed to him a moral impoverishment of a similar kind and effect. His intuition made him sense the link between the emotional aridity of the businessman and the tyranny of narrow abstractions among economists. Unable to refute the latter, he attacked the former. Dickens's whole work is a huge attempt to destroy the psychological effects on the public of an apathy based on reason, and to substitute a willingness to intervene based on emotion.

(243–8)

G. K. Chesterton

from *Charles Dickens*   1906

In *The Pickwick Papers* Dickens sprang suddenly from a comparatively low level to a very high one. To the level of *Sketches by Boz* he never afterwards descended. To the level of *The Pickwick Papers* it is doubtful if he ever afterwards rose. *Pickwick*, indeed, is not a good novel; but it is not a bad novel, for it is not a novel at all. In one sense, indeed, it is something nobler than a novel, for no novel with a plot and a proper termination could emit that sense of everlasting youth – a sense as of the gods gone wandering in England. This is not a novel, for all novels have an end; and *Pickwick*, properly speaking, has no end – he is equal unto the angels. The point at which, as a fact, we find the printed matter terminates is not an end in any artistic sense of the word. Even as a boy I believed there were some more pages that were torn out of my copy, and I am looking for them still. The book might have been cut short anywhere else. It might have been cut short after Mr Pickwick was released by Mr Nupkins, or after Mr Pickwick was fished out of the water, or at a hundred other places. And we should still have known that this was not really the story's end. We should have known that Mr Pickwick was still having the same high adventures on the same high roads. As it happens the book ends after Mr Pickwick has taken a house in the neighbourhood of Dulwich. But we know he did not stop there. We know he broke out, that he took again the road of the high adventures; we know that if we take it ourselves in any acre of England, we may come suddenly upon him in a lane.

But this relation of *Pickwick* to the strict form of fiction demands a further word, which should indeed be said in any case before the consideration of any or all of the Dickens tales. Dickens's work is not to be reckoned in novels at all. Dickens's work is to be reckoned always by characters, sometimes by groups, oftener by episodes, but never by novels. You cannot discuss whether *Nicholas Nickleby* is a good novel, or whether *Our Mutual Friend* is a bad novel. Strictly, there is no such novel as *Nicholas Nickleby*. There is no such novel as *Our Mutual Friend*. They are simply lengths cut from the flowing and mixed substance called Dickens – a substance of which any given length will be certain to contain a given proportion of brilliant and of bad stuff. You can say, according to your opinions, 'the Crummles part is perfect', or 'the Boffins are a mistake', just as a man watching a river go by him could count here a floating flower, and there a streak of scum. But you cannot artistically divide the output into books. The best of his work can be found in the worst of his works. *The Tale of Two Cities* is a good novel; *Little Dorrit* is not a good novel. But the description of The Circumlocution Office in *Little Dorrit* is quite as good as the description of Tellson's Bank in *The Tale of Two Cities*. *The Old Curiosity Shop* is not so good as *David Copperfield*, but Swiveller is quite as good as Micawber. Nor is there any reason why these superb creatures, as a general rule, should be in one novel any more than another. There is no reason why Sam Weller, in the course of his wanderings, should not wander into *Nicholas Nickleby*. There is no reason why Major Bagstock, in his brisk way, should not walk straight out of *Dombey and Son* and straight into *Martin Chuzzlewit*. To this generalization some modification should be added. *Pickwick* stands by itself, and has even a sort of unity in not pretending to unity. *David Copperfield*, in a less degree, stands by itself, as being the only book in which Dickens wrote of himself; and *The Tale of Two Cities* stands by itself as being the only book in which Dickens slightly altered himself. But as a whole, this should be firmly grasped, that the units of Dickens, the primary elements, are not the stories, but the characters who affect the stories – or, more often still, the characters who do not affect the stories.

This is a plain matter; but, unless it be stated and felt, Dickens may be greatly misunderstood and greatly underrated. For not only is his whole machinery directed to facilitating the self-display of certain characters, but something more deep and more unmodern still is also true of him. It is also true that all the *moving* machinery exists only to display entirely *static* character. Things in the Dickens story shift and change only in order to give us glimpses of great characters that do not change at all. If we had a sequel of Pickwick ten years afterwards, Pickwick would be exactly the same age. We know he would not have fallen into that strange and beautiful second childhood which soothed and simplified the end of Colonel Newcome. Newcome, throughout the book, is in an atmosphere of time: Pickwick, throughout the book, is not. This will probably be taken by most modern people as praise of Thackeray and dispraise of Dickens. But this only shows how few modern people understand Dickens. It also shows how few understand the faiths and the fables of mankind. The matter can only be roughly stated in one way. Dickens did not strictly make a literature; he made a mythology. . . .

Dickens was a mythologist rather than a novelist; he was the last of the mythologists, and perhaps the greatest. He did not always manage to make his characters men, but he always managed, at the least, to make them gods. They are creatures like Punch or Father Christmas. They live statically, in a perpetual summer of being themselves. It was not the aim of Dickens to show the effect of time and circumstance upon a character; it was not even his aim to show the effect of a character on time and circumstance. It is worth remark, in passing, that whenever he tried to describe change in a character, he made a mess of it, as in the repentance of Dombey or the apparent deterioration of Boffin. It was his aim to show character hung in a kind of happy void, in a world apart from time – yes, and essentially apart from circumstance, though the phrase may seem odd in connexion with the godlike horse-play of *Pickwick*. But all the Pickwickian events, wild as they often are, were only designed to display the greater wildness of souls, or sometimes merely to bring the reader within touch, so to speak, of that wildness. The author would have fired Mr Pickwick out of a cannon to get him to Wardle's by Christmas; he would have taken the roof off to drop him into Bob Sawyer's party. But once put Pickwick at Wardle's, with his punch and a group of gorgeous personalities, and nothing will move him from his chair. Once he is at Sawyer's party, he forgets how he got there; he forgets Mrs Bardell and all his story. For the story was but an incantation to call up a god, and the god (Mr Jack Hopkins) is present in divine power. Once the great characters are face to face, the ladder by which they climbed is forgotten and falls down, the structure of the story drops to pieces, the plot is abandoned; the other characters deserted at every kind of crisis; the whole crowded thoroughfare of the tale is blocked by two or three talkers, who take their immortal ease as if they were already in Paradise. For they do not exist for the story; the story exists for them; and they know it.

To every man alive, one must hope, it has in some manner happened that he has talked with his more fascinating friends round a table on some night when all the numerous personalities unfolded themselves like great tropical flowers. All fell into their parts as in some delightful impromptu play. Every man was more himself than he had ever been in this vale of tears. Every man was a beautiful caricature of himself. The man who has known such nights will understand the exaggerations of *Pickwick*. The man who has not known such nights will not enjoy *Pickwick* nor (I imagine) heaven. For, as I have said, Dickens is, in this matter, close to popular religion, which is the ultimate and reliable religion. He conceives an endless joy; he conceives creatures as permanent as Puck or Pan – creatures whose will to live aeons upon aeons cannot satisfy. He is not come, as a writer, that his creatures may copy life and copy its narrowness; he is come that they may have life, and that they may have it more abundantly. It is absurd indeed that Christians should be called the enemies of life because they wish life to last for ever; it is more absurd still to call the old comic writers dull because they wished their unchanging characters to last for ever. Both popular religion, with its endless joys, and the old comic story, with its endless jokes, have in our time faded together. We are too weak to desire that undying vigour. We believe that you can have too much of a good thing – a blasphemous belief, which at one blow wrecks all the heavens that men have hoped for. The grand old defiers of God were not afraid of an eternity of torment. We have come to be afraid of an eternity of joy. It is not my business here to take sides in this division between those who like life and long novels and those who like death and short stories; my only business is to point out that those who see in Dickens's unchanging characters and recurring catch-words a mere stiffness and lack of living movement miss the point and nature of his work. His tradition is another tradition altogether; his aim is another aim altogether to those of the modern novelists who trace the alchemy of experience and the autumn tints of character. He is there, like the common people of all ages, to make deities; he is there, as I have said, to exaggerate life in the direction of life. The spirit he at bottom celebrates is that of two friends drinking wine together and talking through the night. But for him they are two deathless friends talking through an endless night and pouring wine from an inexhaustible bottle.

This, then, is the first firm fact to grasp about *Pickwick* – about

Pickwick more than about any of the other stories. It is, first and foremost, a supernatural story. Mr Pickwick was a fairy. So was old Mr
Weller. This does not imply that they were suited to swing in a
trapeze of gossamer; it merely implies that if they had fallen out of it
on their heads they would not have died. But, to speak more strictly,
Mr Samuel Pickwick is not the fairy; he is the fairy prince; that is to
say, he is the abstract wanderer and wonderer, the Ulysses of comedy;
the half-human and half-elfin creature – human enough to wander,
human enough to wonder, but still sustained with that merry
fatalism that is natural to immortal beings – sustained by that hint of
divinity which tells him in the darkest hour that he is doomed to live
happily ever afterwards. He has set out walking to the end of the
world, but he knows he will find an inn there. . . .
(79–91)

It is characteristic of Dickens that his atmospheres are more
important than his stories. The Christmas atmosphere is more important than Scrooge, or the ghosts either; in a sense, the background is
more important than the figures. The same thing may be noticed in
his dealings with that other atmosphere (besides that of good humour)
which he excelled in creating, an atmosphere of mystery and wrong,
such as that which gathers round Mrs Clennam, rigid in her chair, or
old Miss Havisham, ironically robed as a bride. Here again the atmosphere altogether eclipses the story, which often seems disappointing
in comparison. The secrecy is sensational; the secret is tame. The surface of the thing seems more awful than the core of it. It seems
almost as if these grisly figures, Mrs Chadband and Mrs Clennam,
Miss Havisham, and Miss Flite, Nemo and Sally Brass, were keeping
something back from the author as well as from the reader. When
the book closes we do not know their real secret. They soothed the
optimistic Dickens with something less terrible than the truth. The
dark house of Arthur Clennam's childhood really depresses us; it is a
true glimpse into that quiet street in hell, where live the children of
that unique dispensation which theologians call Calvinism and Christians devil-worship. But some stranger crime had really been done
there, some more monstrous blasphemy or human sacrifice than the
suppression of some silly document advantageous to the silly Dorrits.
Something worse than a common tale of jilting lay behind the mas-

querade and madness of the awful Miss Havisham. Something worse was whispered by the mis-shapen Quilp to the sinister Sally in that wild, wet summer-house by the river, something worse than the clumsy plot against the clumsy Kit. These dark pictures seem almost as if they were literally visions: things, that is, that Dickens saw but did not understand.

And as with his backgrounds of gloom, so with his backgrounds of goodwill, in such tales as *The Christmas Carol*. The tone of the tale is kept throughout in a happy monotony, though the tale is everywhere irregular and in some places weak. It has the same kind of artistic unity that belongs to a dream. A dream may begin with the end of the world and end with a tea-party; but either the end of the world will seem as trivial as a tea-party or that tea-party will be as terrible as the day of doom. The incidents change wildly; the story scarcely changes at all. *The Christmas Carol* is a kind of philanthropic dream, an enjoyable nightmare, in which the scenes shift bewilderingly and seem as miscellaneous as the pictures in a scrap-book, but in which there is one constant state of the soul, a state of rowdy benediction and a hunger for human faces. The beginning is about a winter day and a miser; yet the beginning is in no way bleak. The author starts with a kind of happy howl; he bangs on our door like a drunken carol singer; his style is festive and popular; he compares the snow and hail to philanthropists who 'come down handsomely'; he compares the fog to unlimited beer. Scrooge is not really inhuman at the beginning any more than he is at the end. There is a heartiness in his inhospitable sentiments that is akin to humour and therefore to humanity; he is only a crusty old bachelor, and had (I strongly suspect) given away turkeys secretly all his life. The beauty and the real blessing of the story do not lie in the mechanical plot if it, the repentance of Scrooge, probable or improbable; they lie in the great furnace of real happiness that glows through Scrooge and everything around him; that great furnace, the heart of Dickens. Whether the Christmas visions would or would not convert Scrooge, they convert us. Whether or no the visions were evoked by real Spirits of the Past, Present and Future, they were evoked by that truly exalted order of angels who are correctly called High Spirits. They are impelled and sustained by a quality which our contemporary artists ignore or almost deny, but which in a life decently lived is as normal and attainable as sleep, positive, passionate, conscious joy. The story sings from end to end like a happy man going home; and, like a happy and good man, when it cannot sing it yells. It is lyric and exclamatory, from the first exclamatory words of it. It is strictly a Christmas carol. (168–75)

Franz Kafka

from his diary   20 August 1911 (translated by Max Brod)

I have been reading about Dickens. It is so difficult and can an outsider understand that you experience a story within yourself from its beginning, from the distant point up to the approaching locomotives of steel, coal and steam, and you don't abandon it even now, but want to be pursued by it and have time for it, therefore are pursued by it and of your own volition run before it wherever it may thrust and wherever you may lure it.

A. C. Swinburne

from *Charles Dickens*   1913

The conception of *Little Dorrit* was far happier and more promising than that of *Dombey and Son*; which indeed is not much to say for it. Mr Dombey is a doll; Mr Dorrit is an everlasting figure of comedy in its most tragic aspect and tragedy in its most comic phase. Little Dorrit herself might be less untruly than unkindly described as Little Nell grown big, or, in Milton's phrase, 'writ large'. But on that very account she is a more credible and therefore a more really and rationally pathetic figure. The incomparable incoherence of the parts which pretend in vain to compose the incomposite story may be gauged by the collapse of some of them and the vehement hurry of cramped and halting invention which huddles up the close of it without an attempt at the rational and natural evolution of others. It is like a child's dissected map with some of the counties or kingdoms missing. Much, though certainly not all, of the humour is of the poorest kind possible to Dickens; and the reiterated repetition of comic catchwords and tragic illustrations of character is such as to affect the nerves no less than the intelligence of the reader with irrepressible irritation. But this, if he be wise, will be got over and kept under by his sense of admiration and of gratitude for the unsurpassable excellence of the finest passages and chapters. The day after the death of Mr Merdle is one of the most memorable dates in all the record of creative history – or, to use one word in place of two, in all the record of fiction. The fusion of humour and horror in the marvellous chapter which describes it is comparable only with the kinddred work of such creators as the authors of *Les Misérables* and *King Lear*. And nothing in the work of Balzac is newer and truer and more terrible than the relentless yet not unmerciful evolution of the central figure in the story. The Father of the Marshalsea is so pitiably worthy of pity as well as of scorn that it would have seemed impossible to heighten or to deepen the contempt or the compassion of the reader; but when he falls from adversity to prosperity he succeeds in soaring down and sinking up to a more tragicomic ignominy of more aspiring degradation. And his end is magnificent.

And how much more might be said – would the gods annihilate but time and space for a worthier purpose than that of making two lovers happy – of the splendid successes to be noted in the least successful book or books of this great and inexhaustible writer! And if the figure or development of the story in *Little Dorrit*, the shapeliness in parts or the proportions of the whole, may seem to have suffered from tight-lacing in this part and from padding in that, the harmony and unity of the masterpiece which followed it made ample and magnificent amends. In *A Tale of Two Cities* Dickens, for the second and last time, did history the honour to enrol it in the service of fiction. This faultless work of tragic and creative art has nothing of the rich and various exuberance which makes of *Barnaby Rudge* so marvellous an example of youthful genius in all the glowing growth of its bright and fiery April; but it has the classic and poetic symmetry of perfect execution and of perfect design. One or two of the figures in the story which immediately preceded it are unusually liable to the usually fatuous objection which dullness has not yet grown decently ashamed of bringing against the characters of Dickens: to the charge of exaggeration and unreality in the posture or the mechanism of puppets and of daubs, which found its final and supremely offensive expression in the chattering duncery and the impudent malignity of so consummate and pseudosophical a quack as George Henry Lewes. Not even such a past-master in the noble science of defamation could plausibly have dared to cite in support of his insolent and idiotic impeachment either the leading or the supplementary characters in *A Tale of Two Cities*. The pathetic and heroic figure of Sydney Carton seems rather to have cast into the shade of comparative neglect the no less living and admirable figures among and over which it stands and towers in our memory. Miss Pross and Mr Lorry, Madame Defarge and her husband, are equally and indisputably to be recognized by the sign of eternal life.

Among the highest landmarks of success ever reared for immortality by the triumphant genius of Dickens, the story of *Great Expectations* must for ever stand eminent beside that of *David Copperfield*. These are his great twin masterpieces. Great as they are, there is nothing in them greater than the very best things in some of his other books: there is certainly no person preferable and there is possibly no person comparable to Samuel Weller or to Sarah Gamp. Of the two childish and boyish autobiographers, David is the better little fellow though not the more lifelike little friend; but of all first chapters is there any comparable for impression and for fusion of humour and terror and pity and fancy and truth to that which confronts the child with the convict on the marshes in the twilight? And the story is incomparably the finer story of the two; there can be none superior, if there be any equal to it, in the whole range of English fiction. And except in *Vanity Fair* and *The Newcomes*, if even they may claim exception, there can surely be found no equal or nearly equal number of living and everliving figures. The tragedy and the comedy, the realism and the dreamery of life, are fused or mingled together with little less than Shakespearean strength and skill of hand. To have created Abel Magwitch is to be a god indeed among the creators of deathless men. Pumblechook is actually better and droller and truer to imaginative life than Pecksniff: Joe Gargery is worthy to have been praised and loved at once by Fielding and by Sterne: Mr Jaggers and his clients, Mr Wemmick and his parent and his bride, are such figures as Shakespeare, when dropping out of poetry, might have created, if his lot had been cast in a later century. Can as much be said for the creatures of any other man or god? The ghastly tragedy of Miss Havisham could only have been made at once credible and endurable by Dickens; he alone could have reconciled the strange and sordid horror with the noble and pathetic survival of possible emotion and repentance.

(44–54)

Henry James

from *A Small Boy and Others* 1913

Such at least was to be the force of the Dickens imprint, however applied, in the soft clay of our generation; it was to resist so serenely the wash of the waves of time. To be brought up thus against the author of it, or to speak at all of the dawn of one's early consciousness of it and of his presence and power, is to begin to tread ground at once sacred and boundless, the associations of which, looming large, warn us off even while they hold. He did too much for us surely ever to leave us free – free of judgement, free of reaction, even should we care to be, which heaven forbid: he laid his hand on us in a way to undermine as in no other case the power of detached appraisement. We react against other productions of the general kind without 'liking' them the less, but we somehow liked Dickens the more for having forfeited half the claim to appreciation. That process belongs to the fact that criticism, round about him, is somehow futile and tasteless. His own taste is easily impugned, but he entered so early into the blood and bone of our intelligence that it always remained better than the taste of overhauling him. When I take him up to-day and find myself holding off, I simply stop: not holding off, that is, but holding on, and from the very fear to do so; which sounds, I recognize, like perusal, like renewal, of the scantest. I don't renew, I wouldn't renew for the world; wouldn't, that is, with one's treasure so hoarded in the dusty chamber of youth, let in the intellectual air. Happy the house of life in which such chambers still hold out, even with the draught of the intellect whistling through the passages. We were practically contemporary, contemporary with the issues, the fluttering monthly numbers – that was the point; it made for us a good fortune, constituted for us in itself romance, on which nothing, to the end, succeeds in laying its hands.

The whole question dwells for me in a single small reminiscence, though there are others still: that of my having been sent to bed one evening, in Fourteenth Street, as a very small boy, at an hour when, in the library and under the lamp, one of the elder cousins from Albany, the youngest of an orphaned brood of four, of my grandmother's most extravagant adoption, had begun to read aloud to my mother the new, which must have been the first, instalment of *David Copperfield*. I had feigned to withdraw, but had only retreated to cover close at hand, the friendly shade of some screen or drooping table-cloth, folded up behind which and glued to the carpet, I held my breath and listened. I listened long and drank deep while the wondrous picture grew, but the tense cord at last snapped under the strain of the Murdstones and I broke into the sobs of sympathy that disclosed my subterfuge. I was this time effectively banished, but the ply then taken was ineffaceable. I remember indeed just afterwards finding the sequel, in especial the vast extrusion of the Micawbers, beyond my actual capacity; which took a few years to grow adequate – years in which the general contagious consciousness, and our own household response not least, breathed heavily through *Hard Times*, *Bleak House* and *Little Dorrit*; the seeds of acquaintance with *Chuzzlewit* and *Dombey and Son*, these coming thickly on, I had found already sown. I was to feel that I had been born, born to a rich awareness, under the very meridian; there sprouted in those years no such other crop of ready references as the golden harvest of *Copperfield*. Yet if I was to wait to achieve the happier of these recognitions I had already pored over *Oliver Twist* – albeit now uncertain of the relation borne by that experience to the incident just recalled. When Oliver was new to me, at any rate, he was already old to my betters; whose view of his particular adventures and exposures must have been concerned, I think, moreover, in the fact of my public and lively wonder about them. It was an exhibition deprecated – to infant innocence I judge; unless indeed my remembrance of enjoying it only on the terms of fitful snatches in another, though a kindred, house is due mainly to the existence there of George Cruikshank's splendid form of the work, of which our own foreground was clear. It perhaps even seemed to me more Cruikshank's than Dickens's; it was a thing of such

vividly terrible images, and all marked with that peculiarity of Cruikshank that the offered flowers or goodnesses, the scenes and figures
intended to comfort and cheer, present themselves under his hand as
but more subtly sinister, or more suggestively queer, than the frank
badnesses and horrors. The nice people and the happy moments, in
the plates, frightened me almost as much as the low and the awkward;
which didn't however make the volumes a source of attraction the less
toward that high and square old back-parlour just westward of Sixth
Avenue (as we in the same street were related to it) that formed
romantically, half our alternative domestic field and offered to our
small inquiring steps a larger range and privilege. If the Dickens of
those years was, as I have just called him, the great actuality of the
current imagination, so I at once meet him in force as a feature even
of conditions in which he was but indirectly involved.
(122–6)

George Saintsbury

from 'Dickens', *The Cambridge History of English Literature*, vol. 13,
no. 2, chapter 10   1916

There is a point in the consideration of the subject of the present
chapter which, though of the most obvious to uncritical, as well as to
critical, appreciation, is, perhaps, worthy of more attention in respect
of criticism proper than has usually been given to it. This point is
the immense popularity of Dickens, as it is vulgarly called, or (as it
may be put in a form more critically useful) the immense amount of
pleasure which he has given to a number of people who, from the
very vastness of that number, must, necessarily, have included
individuals and whole sections of readers of the most various tastes,
powers and qualifications. Except Shakespeare and Scott, there is,
probably, no other English writer who can match him in this respect.
Now, mere popularity, especially of an ephemeral kind, of course,
proves nothing as to merit; and, though it is never exactly negligible
to the critic (for he must satisfy himself as to its causes), he can scarcely
allow it to affect his judgement. But very long-continued popularity
is in a different case; and popularity which has been attained in the

case of very dissimilar classes and individuals, and, therefore, by very dissimilar appeals, is in a different case again. These latter kinds of popularity not only cannot be neglected, but they cannot, without danger, be slightly recognized by the critic, and, especially, by the historical critic.

It may be said, perhaps, that Dickens's popularity has not yet had time, as Shakespeare's has, to vindicate itself by the test of long continuance and some vicissitudes. More than a century has, indeed, elapsed since his birth and nearly half a century since his death: but instances could be produced of reputations which, after towering for at least as long, have dropped to a much lower level, if they have not fallen altogether. Complaints, undoubtedly, are, sometimes, made that his atmosphere is becoming difficult to breathe; and, though the lungs which feel this difficulty are probably rather weak, their complaint must be registered. But, in regard to the other point, there is no possibility of rational and well informed doubt. It is probably safe to say (here making no exception at all and giving him no companions) that no author in our literary history has been both admired and enjoyed for such different reasons; by such different tastes and intellects; by whole classes of readers unlike each other. He is 'made one with Nature', not, indeed, by a Shakespearean universality – for there are wide, numerous and, sometimes, unfortunate gaps in his appeal – but by the great range and diversity of that appeal. The uncritical lover of the sentimental and the melodramatic; the frank devotee of mere 'fun'; the people who simply desire to pass their time by witnessing a lively and interesting set of scenes and figures; the respectable yearners for social and political reform; the not quite so respectable seekers after scandal and satire on the upper and wealthier and more accomplished classes: these and a dozen or a hundred other types all fly to Dickens as to a magnet. And – what is most remarkable of all and most unparalleled in other cases – the very critics who find it their duty to object to his faults most strongly, who think his sentiment too often worse than mawkish, and his melodrama not seldom more than ridiculous; who rank his characters too close to 'character *parts*', in the lower theatrical sense; who consider his style too often tawdry; his satire strained, yet falling short or wide of its object; his politics unpractical and, sometimes, positively mischievous; his plots either non-existent or tediously complicated for no real purpose; who fully admit the quaint unreality of his realism and the strange 'some-other-worldliness' of much of his atmosphere – these very persons, not unfrequently, read him for choice again and again. In fact, neither the uncritical nor the critical lover of Dickens ever tires of him, as both often do of some writers whom they have admired. Some of his books will, of course, in different cases, be read oftener than others; but, generally, the Dickens quality, mixed and diverse as it is, never loses its attraction for anyone who has once felt it. The road to Eatanswill is never hard or hackneyed; the company of Mrs Gamp never ceases to be as delightful in fiction as it would be disgusting (especially supposing her to be on duty) in real life.

It results infallibly from these facts that the quality in question must, as it has been called, be extraordinarily 'mixed'. The simpler kinds of genius never attain to this result. They being of a 'higher' (to use the question-begging but unavoidable word) strain, may create a higher satisfaction, and, as we flatter ourselves, appeal to a higher order of mind; but this, of itself, means limitation. And it follows that mixed genius of the Dickens kind requires a corresponding variety of analysis to understand itself, its causes and its manifestations.

(303–5)

Franz Kafka

from his diary 8 October 1917 (translated by Max Brod)

Dickens's *Copperfield*. 'The Stoker'[1] a sheer imitation of Dickens, the projected novel even more so. The story of the trunk, the boy who delights and charms everyone, the menial labor, his sweetheart in the country house, the dirty houses, *et al.*, but above all the method. It was my intention, as I now see, to write a Dickens novel, but enhanced by the sharper lights I should have taken from the times and the duller ones I should have got from myself. Dickens's opulence and

1 'The Stoker' became the first chapter of the 'projected novel', published posthumously in 1927 under the title *Amerika*. [Ed.]

great, careless prodigality, but in consequence passages of awful insipidity in which he wearily works over effects he has already achieved. Gives one a barbaric impression because the whole does not make sense, a barbarism that I, it is true, thanks to my weakness and wiser for my epigonism, have been able to avoid. There is a heartlessness behind his sentimentally overflowing style. These rude characterizations which are artificially stamped on everyone and without which Dickens would not be able to get on with his story even for a moment.

George Santayana

from 'Dickens', *Dial*, vol. 71 1921 (reprinted in *Soliloquies in England*, 1922)

If Christendom should lose everything that is now in the melting pot, human life would still remain amiable and quite adequately human. I draw this comforting assurance from the pages of Dickens. Who could not be happy in his world? Yet there is nothing essential to it which the most destructive revolution would be able to destroy. People would still be as different, as absurd, and as charming as are his characters; the springs of kindness and folly in their lives would not be dried up. Indeed, there is much in Dickens which communism, if it came, would only emphasize and render universal. Those schools, those poor-houses, those prisons, with those surviving shreds of family life in them, show us what in the coming age (with some sanitary improvements) would be the nursery and home of everybody. Everybody would be a waif, like Oliver Twist, like Smike, like Pip, and like David Copperfield; and amongst the agents and underlings of social government, to whom all these waifs would be entrusted, there would surely be a goodly sprinkling of Pecksniffs, Squeerses, and Fangs; whilst the Fagins would be everywhere commissioners of the people. Nor would there fail to be, in high places and in low, the occasional sparkle of some Pickwick or Cheeryble Brothers or Sam Weller or Mark Tapley; and the voluble Flora Finchings would be everywhere in evidence, and the strong-minded

Betsey Trotwoods in office. There would also be, among the inefficient, many a Dora and Agnes and Little Emily – with her charm but
without her tragedy, since this is one of the things which the promised
social reform would happily render impossible; I mean, by removing
all the disgrace of it. The only element in the world of Dickens which
would become obsolete would be the setting, the atmosphere of
material instrumentalities and arrangements, as travelling by coach is
obsolete; but travelling by rail, by motor, or by airship will emotionally be much the same thing. It is worth noting how such instrumentalities, which absorb modern life, are admired and enjoyed by
Dickens, as they were by Homer. The poets ought not to be afraid of
them; they exercise the mind congenially, and can be played with
joyfully. Consider the black ships and the chariots of Homer, the
coaches and river-boats of Dickens, and the aeroplanes of today; to
what would an unspoiled young mind turn with more interest?
Dickens tells us little of English sports, but he shares the sporting
nature of the Englishman, to whom the whole material world is a
playing-field, the scene giving ample scope to his love of action,
legality and pleasant achievement. His art is to sport according to the
rules of the game, and to do things for the sake of doing them, rather
than for any ulterior motive.

It is remarkable, in spite of his ardent simplicity and openness of
heart, how insensible Dickens was to the greater themes of the
human imagination – religion, science, politics, art. He was a waif
himself, and utterly disinherited. For example, the terrible heritage of
contentious religions which fills the world seems not to exist for him.
In this matter he was like a sensitive child, with a most religious disposition, but no religious ideas. Perhaps, properly speaking, he had no
ideas on any subject; what he had was a vast sympathetic participation
in the daily life of mankind; and what he saw of ancient institutions
made him hate them, as needless sources of oppression, misery, selfishness, and rancour. His one political passion was philanthropy,
genuine but felt only on its negative, reforming side; of positive
utopias, or enthusiasms, we hear nothing. The political background
of Christendom is only, so to speak, an old faded back-drop for his
stage; a castle, a frigate, a gallows and a large female angel with white
wings standing above an orphan by an open grave – a decoration
which has to serve for all the melodramas in his theatre, intellectually

so provincial and poor. Common life as it is lived was varied and lovable enough for Dickens, if only the pests and cruelties could be removed from it. Suffering wounded him, but not vulgarity; whatever pleased his senses and whatever shocked them filled his mind alike with romantic wonder, with the endless delight of observation. Vulgarity – and what can we relish, if we recoil at vulgarity? – was innocent and amusing; in fact, for the humorist, it was the spice of life. There was more piety in being human than in being pious. In reviving Christmas, Dickens transformed it from the celebration of a metaphysical mystery into a feast of overflowing simple kindness and good cheer; the church bells were still there – in the orchestra; and the angels of Bethlehem were still there – painted on the back-curtain. Churches, in his novels, are vague, desolate places where one has ghastly experiences, and where only the pew-opener is human; and such religious and political conflicts as he depicts in *Barnaby Rudge* and in *A Tale of Two Cities* are street brawls and prison scenes and conspiracies in taverns, without any indication of the contrasts in mind or interests between the opposed parties. Nor had Dickens any lively sense for fine art, classical tradition, science, or even the manners and feelings of the upper classes in his own time and country; in his novels we may almost say there is no army, no navy, no church, no sport, no distant travel, no daring adventure, no feelings for the watery wastes and the motley nations of the planet, and – luckily, with his notion of them – no lords and ladies. Even love of the traditional sort is hardly in Dickens's sphere – I mean the soldierly passion in which a rather rakish gallantry was sobered by devotion, and loyalty rested on pride. In Dickens love is sentimental or benevolent or merry or sneaking or canine; in his last book he was going to describe a love that was passionate and criminal; but love for him was never chivalrous, never poetical. What he paints most tragically is a quasi-paternal devotion in the old to the young, the love of Mr Peggotty for Little Emily, or of Solomon Gills for Walter Gay. A series of shabby little adventures, such as might absorb the interest of an average youth, were romantic enough for Dickens.

I say he was disinherited, but he inherited the most terrible negations. Religion lay on him like the weight of the atmosphere, sixteen pounds to the square inch, yet never noticed nor mentioned. He lived and wrote in the shadow of the most awful prohibitions. Hearts petrified by legality and falsified by worldliness offered, indeed, a good subject for a novelist, and Dickens availed himself of it to the extent of always contrasting natural goodness and happiness with whatever is morose; but his morose people were wicked, not virtuous in their own way; so that the protest of his temperament against his environment never took a radical form nor went back to first principles. He needed to feel, in his writing, that he was carrying the sympathies of every man with him. In him conscience was single, and he could not conceive how it could ever be divided in other men. He denounced scandals without exposing shams, and conformed willingly and scrupulously to the proprieties. Lady Dedlock's secret, for instance, he treats as if it were the sin of Adam, remote, mysterious, inexpiable. Mrs Dombey is not allowed to deceive her husband except by pretending to deceive him. The seduction of Little Emily is left out altogether, with the whole character of Steerforth, the development of which would have been so important in the moral experience of David Copperfield himself. But it is not public prejudice alone that plays the censor over Dickens's art; his own kindness and even weakness of heart act sometimes as marplots. The character of Miss Mowcher, for example, so brilliantly introduced, was evidently intended to be shady, and to play a very important part in the story; but its original in real life, which was recognized, had to be conciliated, and the sequel was omitted and patched up with an apology – itself admirable – for the poor dwarf. Such a sacrifice does honour to Dickens's heart; but artists should meditate on their works in time, and it is easy to remove any too great likeness in a portrait by a few touches making it more consistent than real people are apt to be; and in this case, if the little creature had been really guilty, how much more subtle and tragic her apology for herself might have been, like that of the bastard Edmund in *King Lear*! So, too, in *Dombey and Son*, Dickens could not bear to let Walter Gay turn out badly, as he had been meant to do, and to break his uncle's heart as well as the heroine's; he was accordingly transformed into a stage hero miraculously saved from shipwreck, and Florence was not allowed to reward the admirable Toots as she should have done, with her trembling hand. But Dickens was no free artist; he had more genius than taste, a warm fancy not aided by a thorough understanding of complex characters. He worked under pressure, for money and applause, and often had to cheapen in execution what his inspiration had so vividly conceived.

What, then, is there left, if Dickens has all these limitations? In our romantic disgust we might be tempted to say, Nothing. But in fact almost everything is left, almost everything that counts in the daily life of mankind, or that by its presence or absence can determine whether life shall be worth living or not; because a simple good life is worth living, and an elaborate bad life is not. There remain in the first place eating and drinking; relished not bestially, but humanly, jovially, as the sane and exhilarating basis for everything else. This is a sound English beginning; but the immediate sequel, as the England of that day presented it to Dickens, is no less delightful. There is the ruddy glow of the hearth; the sparkle of glasses and brasses and well-scrubbed pewter; the savoury fumes of the hot punch, after the tingle of the wintry air; the coaching-scenes, the motley figures and absurd incidents of travel; the changing sights and joys of the road. And then, to balance this, the traffic of ports and cities, the hubbub of crowded streets, the luxury of shop-windows and of palaces not to be entered; the procession of the passers-by, shabby or ludicrously genteel; the dingy look and musty smell of their lodgings; the labyrinth of back-alleys, courts and mews, with their crying children, and scolding old women and listless, half-drunken loiterers. These sights, like fables, have a sort of moral in them to which Dickens was very sensitive; the important airs of nobodies on great occasions, the sadness and preoccupation of the great as they hasten by in their mourning or on their pressing affairs; the sadly comic characters of the tavern; the diligence of shop-keepers, like squirrels turning in their cages; the children peeping out everywhere like grass in an untrodden street; the charm of humble things, the nobleness of humble people, the horror of crime, the ghastliness of vice, the deft hand and shining face of virtue passing through the midst of it all; and finally a fresh wind of indifference and change blowing across our troubles and clearing the most lurid sky.

I do not know whether it was Christian charity or naturalistic insight, or a mixture of both (for they are closely akin) that attracted Dickens particularly to the deformed, the half-witted, the abandoned, or those impeded or misunderstood by virtue of some singular inner consecration. The visible moral of these things, when brutal prejudice does not blind us to it, comes very near to true philosophy; one turn of the screw, one flash or reflection, and we have understood nature and human morality and the relation between them.

In his love of roads and wayfarers, of river-ports and wharves and the idle or sinister figures that lounge about them, Dickens was like Walt Whitman; and I think a second Dickens may any day appear in America, when it is possible in that land of hurry to reach the same degree of saturation, the same unquestioning pleasure in the familiar facts. The spirit of Dickens would be better able to do justice to America than was that of Walt Whitman; because America, although it may seem nothing but a noisy nebula to the impressionist, is not a nebula but a concourse of very distinct individual bodies, natural and social, each with its definite interest and story. Walt Whitman had a sort of transcendental philosophy which swallowed the universe whole, supposing there was a universal spirit in things identical with the absolute spirit that observed them; but Dickens was innocent of any such clap-trap, and remained a true spirit in his own person. Kindly and clear-sighted, but self-identical and unequivocally human, he glided through the slums like one of his own little heroes, uncontaminated by their squalor and confusion, courageous and firm in his clear allegiances amid the flux of things, a pale angel at the Carnival, his heart aflame, his voice always flutelike in its tenderness and warning. This is the true relation of spirit to existence, not the other which confuses them; for this earth (I cannot speak for the universe at large) has no spirit of its own, but brings forth spirits only at certain points, in the hearts and brains of frail living creatures, who like insects flit through it, buzzing and gathering what sweets they can; and it is the spaces they traverse in this career, charged with their own moral burden, that they can report on or describe, not things rolling on to infinity in their vain tides. To be hypnotized by that flood would be a heathen idolatry. Accordingly Walt Whitman, in his comprehensive democratic vistas, could never see the trees for the wood, and remained incapable, for all his diffuse love of the human herd, of ever painting a character or telling a story: the very things in which Dickens was a master. It is this life of the individual, as it may be lived in a given nation, that determines the whole value of that nation to the poet, to the moralist and to the judicious historian. But for the excellence of the typical single life, no nation deserves to be remembered more than the sands of the sea; and America will not be a success, if every American is a failure

Dickens entered the theatre of this world by the stage door; the shabby little adventures of the actors in their private capacity replace for him the mock tragedies which they enact before a dreaming public. Mediocrity of circumstances and mediocrity of soul forever return to the centre of his stage; a more wretched or a grander existence is sometimes broached, but the pendulum soon swings back, and we return, with the relief with which we put on our slippers after the most romantic excursion, to a golden mediocrity – to mutton and beer, and to love and babies in a suburban villa with one frowsy maid. Dickens is the poet of those acres of yellow brick streets which the traveller sees from the railway viaducts as he approaches London; they need a poet, and they deserve one, since a complete human life may very well be lived there. Their little excitements and sorrows, their hopes and humours are like those of the Wooden Midshipman in *Dombey and Son*; but the sea is not far off, and sky – Dickens never forgets it – is above all those brief troubles. He had a sentiment in the presence of this vast flatness of human fates, in spite of their individual pungency, which I think might well be the dominant sentiment of mankind in the future; a sense of happy freedom in littleness, an open-eyed reverence and religion without words. This universal human anonymity is like a sea, an infinite democratic desert, chock-full and yet the very image of emptiness, with nothing in it for the mind, except, as the Moslems say, the presence of Allah. Awe is the counterpart of humility – and this is perhaps religion enough. The atom in the universal vortex ought to be humble; he ought to see that, materially, he doesn't much matter, and that morally his loves are merely his own, without authority over the universe. He can admit without obloquy that he is what he is; and he can rejoice in his own being, and in that of all other things in so far as he can share it sympathetically. The apportionment of existence and of fortune is in Other Hands; his own portion is contentment, vision, love and laughter.

Having humility, that most liberating of sentiments, having a true vision of human existence and joy in that vision, Dickens had in a superlative degree the gift of humour, of mimicry, of unrestrained farce. He was the perfect comedian. When people say Dickens exaggerates, it seems to me they can have no eyes and no ears. They probably have only *notions* of what things and people are; they accept them conventionally, at their diplomatic value. Their minds run on in the region of discourse, where there are masks only and no faces, ideas and no facts; they have little sense for those living grimaces that play from moment to moment upon the countenance of the world. The world is a perpetual caricature of itself; at every moment it is the mockery and the contradiction of what it is pretending to be. But as it nevertheless intends all the time to be something different and highly dignified, at the next moment it corrects and checks and tries to cover up the absurd thing it was; so that a conventional world, a world of masks, is superimposed on the reality, and passes in every sphere of human interest for the reality itself. Humour is the perception of this illusion, the fact allowed to pierce here and there through the convention, whilst the convention continues to be maintained, as if we had not observed its absurdity. Pure comedy is more radical, cruder, in a certain sense less human; because comedy throws the convention over altogether, revels for a moment in the fact, and brutally says to the notions of mankind, as if it slapped them in the face, There, take that! That's what you really are! At this the polite world pretends to laugh, not tolerantly as it does at humour, but a little angrily. It does not like to see itself by chance in the glass, without having had time to compose its features for demure self-contemplation. 'What a bad mirror,' it exclaims; 'it must be concave or convex; for surely I never looked like that. Mere caricature, farce and horse play. Dickens exaggerates; *I* never was so sentimental as that; *I* never saw anything so dreadful; *I* don't believe there were ever any people like Quilp, or Squeers, or Serjeant Buzfuz.' But the polite world is lying; there *are* such people; we are such people ourselves in our true moments, in our veritable impulses; but we are careful to stifle and to hide those moments from ourselves and from the world; to purse and pucker ourselves into the mask of our conventional personality; and so simpering, we profess that it is very coarse and inartistic of Dickens to undo our life's work for us in an instant, and remind us of what we are. And as to other people, though we may allow that considered superficially they are often absurd, we do not wish to dwell on their eccentricities, nor to mimic them. On the contrary, it is good manners to look away quickly, to suppress a smile, and to say to ourselves that the ludicrous figure in the street is not at all comic, but a dull ordinary Christian, and that it is foolish to give any importance to the fact that its hat has blown off, that it has slipped on an orange-peel and unintentionally sat on the pavement, that it has a pimple on its nose, that its one tooth projects over its lower lip, that it is angry with things in general, and that it is looking everywhere for the penny which it holds tightly in its hand. That may fairly represent the moral condition of most of us at most times; but we do not want to think of it; we do not want to see; we gloss the fact over; we console ourselves before we are grieved, and reassert our composure before we have laughed. We are afraid, ashamed, anxious to be spared. What displeases us in Dickens is that he does not spare us; he mimics things to the full; he dilates and exhausts and repeats; he wallows. He is too intent on the passing experience to look over his shoulder, and consider whether we have not already understood, and had enough. He is not thinking of us; he is obeying the impulse of the passion, the person, or the story he is enacting. This faculty, which renders him a consummate comedian, is just what alienated from him a later generation in which people of taste were aesthetes and virtuous people were higher snobs; they wanted a mincing art, and he gave them copious improvisation, they wanted analysis and development, and he gave them absolute comedy. I must confess, though the fault is mine and not his, that sometimes his absoluteness is too much for me. When I come to the death of Little Nell, or to What the Waves were always Saying, or even to the incorrigible perversities of the pretty Dora, I skip. I can't take my liquor neat in such draughts, and my inner man says to Dickens, Please don't. But then I am a coward in so many ways! There are so many things in this world that I skip, as I skip the undiluted Dickens! When I reach Dover on a rough day, I wait there until the Channel is smoother; am I not travelling for pleasure? But my prudence does not blind me to the admirable virtue of the sailors that cross in all weathers, nor even to the automatic determination of the seasick ladies, who might so easily have followed my example, if they were not the slaves of their railway tickets and of their labelled luggage. They are loyal to their tour, and I to my philosophy. Yet as wrapped in my great-coat and sure of a good dinner, I pace the windy pier and soliloquize, I feel the superiority of the bluff tar, glad of breeze, stretching a firm arm to the unsteady passenger, and watching with a masterful thrill of emotion the home cliffs receding and the foreign coasts ahead. It is only courage (which Dickens had without knowing it) and universal kindness (which he knew he had) that are requisite to nerve us for a true vision of this world. And as some of us are cowards about crossing the Channel, and others about 'crossing the bar', so almost everybody is a coward about his own humanity. We do not consent to be absurd, though absurd we are. We have no fundamental humility. We do not wish the moments of our lives to be caught by a quick eye in their grotesque initiative, and to be pilloried in this way before our own eyes. For that reason we don't like Dickens, and don't like comedy, and don't like the truth. Dickens could don the comic mask with innocent courage; he could wear it with a grace, ease, and irresistible vivacity seldom given to men. We must go back for anything like it to the very greatest comic poets, to Shakespeare or to Aristophanes. Who else, for instance, could have penned this:

'It was all Mrs Bumble. She *would* do it,' urged Mr Bumble; first looking round to ascertain that his partner had left the room.

'That is no excuse,' replied Mr Brownlow. 'You were present on the occasion of the destruction of these trinkets, and indeed are the more guilty of the two, in the eye of the law; for the law supposes that your wife acts under your direction.'

'If the law supposes that,' said Mr Bumble, squeezing his hat emphatically in both hands, 'The law is a ass, a idiot. If that's the eye of the law, the law is a bachelor; and the worse I wish the law is, that his eye may be opened by experience – by experience.'

Laying great stress on the repetition of these two words, Mr Bumble fixed his hat on very tight, and putting his hands in his pockets, followed his helpmate downstairs.
(*Oliver Twist*, chapter 51)

This is high comedy; the irresistible, absurd, intense dream of the old fool, personifying the law in order to convince and to punish it. I can understand that this sort of thing should not be common in English literature, nor much relished; because pure comedy is scornful, merciless, devastating, holding no door open to anything beyond. Cultivated English feeling winces at this brutality, although the com-

mon people love it in clowns and in puppet shows; and I think they
are right. Dickens, who surely was tender enough, had so irresistible
a comic genius that it carried him beyond the gentle humour which
most Englishmen possess to the absolute grotesque reality. Squeers,
for instance, when he sips the wretched dilution which he has prepared
for his starved and shivering little pupils, smacks his lips and cries:
'Here's richness!' It is savage comedy; humour would come in if we
understood (what Dickens does not tell us) that the little creatures
were duly impressed and thought the thin liquid truly delicious. I
suspect that English sensibility prefers the humour and wit of Hamlet
to the pure comedy of Falstaff; and that even in Aristophanes it seeks
consolation in the lyrical poetry for the flaying of human life in the
comedy itself. Tastes are free; but we should not deny that in merciless and rollicking comedy life is caught in the act. The most grotesque
creatures of Dickens are not exaggerations or mockeries of something
other than themselves; they arise because nature generates them, like
toadstools; they exist because they can't help it, as we all do. The fact
that these perfectly self-justified beings are absurd appears only by
comparison, and from outside; circumstances, or the expectations of
other people, make them ridiculous and force them to contradict
themselves; but in nature it is no crime to be exceptional. Often, but
for the savagery of the average man, it would not even be a misfortune. The sleepy fat boy in *Pickwick* looks foolish; but in himself
he is no more foolish, nor less solidly self-justified, than a pumpkin
lying on the ground. Toots seems ridiculous; and we laugh heartily
at his incoherence, his beautiful waistcoats, and his extreme modesty;
but when did anybody more obviously grow into what he is because
he couldn't grow otherwise? So with Mr Pickwick, and Sam Weller,
and Mrs Gamp, and Micawber, and all the rest of this wonderful
gallery; they are ridiculous only by accident, and in a context in
which they never intended to appear. If Oedipus and Lear and
Cleopatra do not seem ridiculous, it is only because tragic reflection
has taken them out of the context in which, in real life, they would
have figured. If we saw them as facts, and not as emanations of a
poet's dream, we should laugh at them till doomsday; what grotesque
presumption, what silly whims, what mad contradiction of the
simplest realities! Yet we should not laugh at them without feeling
how real their griefs were; as real and terrible as the griefs of children

and of dreams. But facts, however serious inwardly, are always absurd outwardly; and the just critic of life sees both truths at once, as Cervantes did in *Don Quixote*. A pompous idealist who does not see the ridiculous in *all* things is the dupe of his sympathy and abstraction; and a clown, who does not see that these ridiculous creatures are living quite in earnest, is the dupe of his egotism. Dickens saw the absurdity, and understood the life; I think he was a good philosopher.

(537–47)

Percy Lubbock

from *The Craft of Fiction* 1921

Stevenson noted how Dickens's way of dealing with his romantic intrigues was to lead gradually into them, through well-populated scenes of character and humour; so that his world is actual, its air familiar, by the time that his plot begins to thicken. He gives himself an ample margin in which to make the impression of the kind of truth he needs, before beginning to concentrate upon the fabulous action of the climax. *Bleak House* is a very good case; the highly coloured climax in that book is approached with great skill and caution, all in his most masterly style. A broad stream of diversified life moves slowly in a certain direction, so deliberately at first that its scope, its spread, is much more evident than its movement. The book is a big survey of a quantity of odd and amusing people, and it is only by degrees that the discursive method is abandoned and the narrative brought to a point. Presently we are in the thick of the story, hurrying to the catastrophe, without having noticed at all, it may be, that our novel of manners has turned into a romantic drama, with a mysterious crime to crown it. Dickens manages it far more artfully than Balzac, because his imagination is not, like Balzac's, divided against itself. The world which he peopled with Skimpole and Guppy and the Bayham Badgers was a world that could easily include Lady Dedlock, for though she is perhaps of the theatre, they are certainly not of the common earth. They and she alike are at the same angle to literal fact, they diverging one way, she another; they accordingly make a kind of reality which can assimilate her romance. Dickens was saved from trying to write two books at once by the fact that one completely satisfied him. It expressed the exciting, amazing, exhilarating world he lived in himself, with its consistent transmutation of all values, and he knew no other.

The method which he finally worked out for himself was exactly what he required. There might be much to say of it, for it is by no means simple, but I am only concerned with one or two points in it. The chief characteristic I take to be this careful introduction of violent drama into a scene already prepared to vouch for it – a scene so alive that it compels belief, so queer that almost anything might happen there naturally. The effect which Dickens gets from the picture in his novels, as opposed to the action, is used as a sort of attestation of the action; and it surely fulfils its mission very strikingly in the best of his work – the best from this point of view – *Bleak House*, *Dombey and Son*, *Our Mutual Friend*. His incurable love of labyrinthine mystification, when it really ran away with him, certainly defeated all precautions; not even old Dorrit's Marshalsea, not even Flora and Mr F.'s Aunt, can do anything to carry off the story of the Clennams. But so long as he was content with a fairly straightforward romance, all went well; the magnificent life that he projected was prepared to receive and to speed it. Blimber and Mrs Pipchin and Miss Tox, the Podsnaps and Twemlow and the Veneerings, all contribute out of their overflow of energy to the force of a drama – a drama in which they may take no specific part, but which depends on them for the furnishing of an appropriate scene, a favouring background, a world attuned. This and so much more they do that it may seem like insulting them even to think for a moment of their subordination to the general design, which is indeed a great deal less interesting than they. But Dickens's method is sound and good, and not the less so because he used it for comparatively trivial purposes. It is strange that he should have known how to invent such a scene, and then have found no better drama to enact on it – strange and always stranger, with every re-reading. That does not affect his handling of a subject, which is all that I deal with here.

The life which he creates and distributes right and left, in such a book as Bleak House, before bending to his story – this I call his picture, for picture it is in effect, not dramatic action. It exhibits the world in which Lady Dedlock is to meditate murder, the fog of the suit in Chancery out of which the intrigue of the book is to emerge. It is the summary of a situation, with its elements spreading widely and touching many lives; it gathers them in and gives an impression of them all. It is pictorial as a whole, and quite as much so as any of Thackeray's broad visions. But I have noted before how inevitably Dickens's picture, unlike Thackeray's, is presented in the *form* of scenic action, and here is a case in point. All this impression of life, stretching from the fog-bound law courts to the marshes of Chesney Wold, from Krook and Miss Flite to Sir Leicester and Volumnia, is rendered as incident, as a succession of particular occasions – never, or very seldom, as general and far-seeing narrative, after Thackeray's manner. Dickens continually holds to the immediate scene, even when his object is undramatic; he is always readier to work in action and dialogue than to describe at large; he is happier in placing a character there before us, as the man or woman talked and behaved in a certain hour, on a certain spot, than in reflecting a long impression of their manner of living. In Thackeray's hands the life of Miss Flite, for instance, would have become a legend, recalled and lingered over, illustrated by passing glimpses of her ways and oddities. With Dickens she is always a little human being who figures upon a scene, in a group, a visible creature acting her small part; she is always dramatic.

And Dickens, using this method everywhere, even in such a case as hers – even where his purpose, that is to say, is pictorial, to give the sense of a various and vivacious background – is forced to crystallize and formulate his characters very sharply, if they are to make their effect; it is why he is so often reduced to the expedient of labelling his people with a trick or a phrase, which they have to bring with them every time they appear. Their opportunities are strictly limited; the author does not help them out by glancing freely into their lives and sketching them broadly. Flite, Snagsby, Chadband and the rest of them – whatever they are, they must be all of it within narrow bounds within the few scenes that can be allotted to them; and if one of them fails now and then it is not surprising, the wonder is that most of them succeed so brilliantly. In thus translating his picture into action Dickens chose the most exigent way, but it was always the right way for him. He was curiously incapable in the other; when occasionally he tries his hand at picture-making in Thackeray's manner – attempting to summarize an impression of social life among the Veneerings, of official life among the Barnacles – his touch is wild indeed. Away from a definite episode in an hour prescribed he is seldom at ease.

But though the actual presentation is thus dramatic, his books are in fact examples of the pictured scene that opens and spreads very gradually, in order to make a valid world for a drama that could not be precipitated forthwith, a drama that would be naked romance if it stood by itself.

(213–17)

André Gide

from *Dostoyevsky* 1923 (English translation, 1925)

Despite the extraordinarily rich diversity of his *Comédie Humaine*, Dostoyevsky's characters group and arrange themselves always on one plane only, that of humility and pride. This system of grouping discomfits us; indeed, at first, it appears far from clear, for the very simple reason that we do not usually approach the problem of making a diversion at such an angle and that we distribute mankind in hierarchies. Let me explain my idea: in Dickens's wonderful novels, for instance, I am often uneasy at the conventionality, childishness even, of his *hierarchy*, or to use Nietzsche's phrase, *scale of values*. While reading him I have the impression that I am contemplating one of Fra Angelico's *Last Judgements* where you have the redeemed, the damned and the indeterminate (not too numerous!) over whom angel and demon struggle. The balance that weighs them all, as in an Egyptian bas-relief, reckons only the positive or negative quality of their virtue. Heaven for the just: for the wicked, Hell. Herein Dickens is true to the opinion of his countrymen and of his time. It does happen that the evil prosper, while the just are sacrificed – to the great shame of this earthly existence and of society as we have organized it. All his novels endeavour to show us and make us realize the shining superiority of qualities of heart over qualities of head. I have selected Dickens as a type because of all the great novelists we know he uses this classification in its simplest form : which – if I may say in conclusion – is the secret of his popularity.

(86)

Virginia Woolf

'*David Copperfield*', *Nation*   22 August 1925 (collected in *The Moment and Other Essays*, 1947)

Like the ripening of strawberries, the swelling of apples and all other natural processes, new editions of Dickens – cheap, pleasant-looking, well printed – are born into the world and call for no more notice than the season's plums and strawberries, save when by some chance the emergence of one of these masterpieces in its fresh green binding suggests an odd and overwhelming enterprise – that one should read *David Copperfield* for the second time. There is perhaps no person living who can remember reading *David Copperfield* for the first time. Like *Robinson Crusoe* and *Grimm's Fairy Tales* and the Waverley Novels, *Pickwick* and *David Copperfield* are not books, but stories communicated by word of mouth in those tender years when fact and fiction merge, and thus belong to the memories and myths of life, and not to its aesthetic experience. When we lift it from this hazy atmosphere, when we consider it as a book, bound and printed and ordered by the rules of art, what impression does *David Copperfield* make upon us? As Peggotty and Barkis, the rooks and the workbox with the picture of St Paul's, Traddles who drew skeletons, the donkeys who would cross the green, Mr Dick and the Memorial, Betsey Trotwood and Jip and Dora and Agnes and the Heeps and the Micawbers once more come to life with all their appurtenances and peculiarities, are they still possessed of the old fascination or have they in the interval been attacked by that parching wind which blows about books and, without our reading them, remodels them and changes their features while we sleep? The rumour about Dickens is to the effect that his sentiment is disgusting and his style commonplace; that in reading him every refinement must be hidden and every sensibility kept under glass; but that with these precautions and reservations he is of course Shakespearian; like Scott, a born creator; like Balzac, prodigious in his fecundity; but, rumour adds, it is strange that while one reads Shakespeare and one reads Scott, the precise moment for reading Dickens seldom comes our way.

This last charge may be resolved into this – that he lacks charm and idiosyncrasy, is everybody's writer and no one's in particular, is an institution, a monument, a public thoroughfare trodden dusty by a million feet. It is based largely upon the fact that of all great writers Dickens is both the least personally charming and the least personally present in his books. No one has ever loved Dickens as he loves Shakespeare and Scott. Both in his life and in his work the impression that he makes is the same. He has to perfection the virtues conventionally ascribed to the male; he is self-assertive, self-reliant, self-assured; energetic in the extreme. His message, when he parts the veil of the story and steps forward in person, is plain and forcible; he preaches the value of 'plain hardworking qualities', of punctuality, order, diligence, of doing what lies before one with all one's might. Agitated as he was by the most violent passions, ablaze with indignation, teeming with queer characters, unable to keep the dreams out of his head at night, nobody appears, as we read him, more free from the foibles and eccentricities and charms of genius. He comes before us, as one of his biographers described him, 'like a prosperous sea captain', stalwart, weather-beaten, self-reliant, with a great contempt for the finicky, the inefficient, or the effeminate. His sympathies indeed have strict limitations. Speaking roughly, they fail him whenever a man or woman has more than two thousand a year, has been to the university, or can count his ancestors back to the third generation. They fail him when he has to treat of the mature emotions – the seduction of Emily, for example, or the death of Dora; whenever it is no longer possible to keep moving and creating, but it is necessary to stand still and search into things and penetrate to the depths of what is there. Then, indeed, he fails grotesquely, and the pages in which he describes what in our convention are the peaks and pinnacles of human life, the explanation of Mrs Strong, the despair of Mrs Steerforth, or the anguish of Ham, are of an indescribable unreality – of that uncomfortable complexion which, if we heard Dickens talking so in real life, would either make us blush to the roots of our hair or dash out of the room to conceal our laughter. '. . . Tell him then,' says Emily, 'that when I hear the wind blowing at night I feel as if it was passing angrily from seeing him and uncle, and was going up to God against me.' Miss Dartle raves – about carrion and pollution and earthworms, and worthless spangles and broken toys, and how she will have Emily 'proclaimed on the common stair'. The failure is akin to that other failure to think deeply, to describe beautifully. Of the men who go to make up the perfect novelist and should live in amity under his hat, two – the poet and the philosopher – failed to come when Dickens called them.

But the greater the creator the more derelict the regions where his powers fail him; all about their fertile lands are deserts where not a blade of grass grows, swamps where the foot sinks deep in mud. Nevertheless, while we are under their spell these great geniuses make us see the world any shape they choose. We remodel our psychological geography when we read Dickens; we forget that we have ever felt the delights of solitude or observed with wonder the intricate emotions of our friends, or luxuriated in the beauty of nature. What we remember is the ardour, the excitement, the humour, the oddity of people's characters; the smell and savour and soot of London; the incredible coincidences which hook the most remote lives together; the city, the law courts; this man's nose, that man's limp; some scene under an archway or on the high road; and above all some gigantic and dominating figure, so stuffed and swollen with life that he does not exist singly and solitarily, but seems to need for his own realization a host of others, to call into existence the severed parts that complete him, so that wherever he goes he is the centre of conviviality and merriment and punch-making; the room is full, the lights are bright; there are Mrs Micawber, the twins, Traddles, Betsey Trotwood – all in full swing.

This is the power which cannot fade or fail in its effect – the power not to analyse or to interpret, but to produce, apparently without thought or effort or calculation of the effect upon the story, characters who exist not in detail, not accurately or exactly, but abundantly in a cluster of wild and yet extraordinarily revealing remarks, bubble climbing on the top of bubble as the breath of the creator fills them. And the fecundity and apparent irreflectiveness have a strange effect. They make creators of us, and not merely readers and spectators. As we listen to Micawber pouring himself forth and venturing perpetually some new flight of astonishing imagination, we see, unknown to Mr Micawber, into the depths of his soul. We say, as Dickens himself says while Micawber holds forth: 'How wonderfully like Mr Micawber that is!' Why trouble, then, if the scenes where emotion and psychology are to be expected fail us completely? Subtlety and complexity are all there if we know where to look for them, if we can get over the surprise of finding them – as it seems to us, who have another convention in these matters – in the wrong places. As a creator of character his peculiarity is that he creates wherever his eyes rest – he has the visualizing power in the extreme. His people are branded upon our eyeballs before we hear them speak, by what he sees them doing, and it seems as if it were the sight that sets his thought in action. He saw Uriah Heep 'breathing into the pony's nostrils and immediately covering them with his hand'; he saw David Copperfield looking in the glass to see how red his eyes were after his mother's death; he saw oddities and blemishes, gestures and incidents, scars, eyebrows, everything that was in the room, in a second. His eye brings in almost too rich a harvest for him to deal with, and gives him an aloofness and a hardness which freeze his sentimentalism and make it seem a concession to the public, a veil thrown over the penetrating glance which left to itself pierced to the bone. With such a power at his command Dickens made his books blaze up, not by tightening the plot or sharpening the wit, but by throwing another handful of people upon the fire. The interest flags and he creates Miss Mowcher, completely alive, equipped in every detail as if she were to play a great part in the story, whereas once the dull stretch of road is passed by her help, she disappears; she is needed no longer. Hence a Dickens novel is apt to become a bunch of separate characters loosely held together, often by the most arbitrary conventions, who tend to fly asunder and split our attention into so many different parts that we drop the book in despair. But that danger is surmounted in *David Copperfield*. There, though characters swarm and life flows into every creek and cranny, some common feeling – youth, gaiety, hope – envelops the tumult, brings the scattered parts together, and invests the most perfect of all the Dickens novels with an atmosphere of beauty.[1]

(65–9)

1 The following letter by Virginia Woolf appears in the *Nation* of 12 September 1925.
Sir,
  Fear of a sudden death very naturally distracted Kappa's mind from my article on *David Copperfield* or he would, I think, have taken my meaning. That nobody can remember reading *David Copperfield* for the first time is a proof not, as he infers, that the reading makes so little impression that it slips off the mind unremembered, but that *David Copperfield* takes such rank among our classics

E. M. Forster

from *Aspects of the Novel*, chapter 4   1927

We may divide characters into flat and round.

Flat characters were called 'humours' in the seventeenth century, and are sometimes called types, and sometimes caricatures. In their purest form, they are constructed round a single idea or quality: when there is more than one factor in them, we get the beginning of the curve towards the round. The really flat character can be expressed in one sentence such as 'I never will desert Mr Micawber.' There is Mrs Micawber – she says she won't desert Mr Micawber; she doesn't, and there she is. . . .

Dickens's people are nearly all flat (Pip and David Copperfield attempt roundness, but so diffidently that they seem more like bubbles than solids). Nearly every one can be summed up in a sentence, and yet there is this wonderful feeling of human depth. Probably the immense vitality of Dickens causes his characters to vibrate a little, so that they borrow his life and appear to lead one of their own. It is a conjuring trick; at any moment we may look at Mr Pickwick edgeways and find him no thicker than a gramophone record. But we never get the sideways view. Mr Pickwick is far too adroit and well trained. He always has the air of weighing something, and when he is put into the cupboard of the young ladies' school at Windsor he

---

and is a book of such astonishing vividness that parents will read it aloud to their children before they can quite distinguish fact from fiction, and they will never in later life be able to recall the first time they read it. *Grimm's Fairy Tales* and *Robinson Crusoe* are for many people in the same case.

Questions of affection are of course always disputable. I can only reiterate that while I would cheerfully become Shakespeare's cat, Scott's pig, or Keats's canary, if by so doing I could share the society of these great men, I would not cross the road (reasons of curiosity apart) to dine with Wordsworth, Byron or Dickens. Yet I venerate their genius; and my tears would certainly help to swell the 'unparalleled flow of popular grief' at their deaths. It only means that writers have characters apart from their books, which are sympathetic to some, antipathetic to others. And I maintain that if it could be put to the vote, Which do you prefer as man, Shakespeare, Scott, or Dickens? Shakespeare would be first, Scott second and Dickens nowhere at all.

Yours, etc.,

Virginia Woolf

278 T. S. Eliot

seems as heavy as Falstaff in the buck-basket at Windsor. Part of the genius of Dickens is that he does use types and caricatures, people whom we recognize the instant they re-enter, and yet achieves effects that are not mechanical and a vision of humanity that is not shallow. Those who dislike Dickens have an excellent case. He ought to be bad. He is actually one of our big writers, and his immense success with types suggests that there may be more in flatness than the severer critics admit.

(93–9)

T. S. Eliot

'Wilkie Collins and Dickens', *The Times Literary Supplement*
4 August 1927 (collected in *Selected Essays*, 1932)

It is to be hoped that some scholarly and philosophic critic of the present generation may be inspired to write a book on the history and aesthetic of melodrama. The golden age of melodrama passed, it is true, before any person living was aware of its existence: in the very middle of the last century. But there are many living who are not too young to remember the melodramatic stage before the cinema replaced it; who have sat entranced, in the front stalls of local or provincial theatres, before some representation of *East Lynne*, or *The White Slave*, or *No Mother to Guide Her*; and who are not too old to have observed with curious interest the replacement of dramatic melodrama by cinematographic melodrama, and the dissociation of the elements of the old three-volume melodramatic novel into the various types of the modern 300-page novel. Those who have lived before such terms as 'high-brow fiction', 'thrillers' and 'detective fiction' were invented realize that melodrama is perennial and that the craving for it is perennial and must be satisfied. If we cannot get this satisfaction out of what the publishers present as 'literature', then we will read – with less and less pretence of concealment – what we call 'thrillers'. But in the golden age of melodramatic fiction there was no such distinction. The best novels *were* thrilling; the distinction of genre between such-and-such a profound 'psychological' novel of today and such-and-such a masterly 'detective' novel of today is

279 T. S. Eliot

greater than the distinction of genre between *Wuthering Heights*, or even *The Mill on the Floss* and *East Lynne*, the last of which 'achieved an enormous and instantaneous success, and was translated into every known language, including Parsee and Hindustani'. We believe that several contemporary novels have been 'translated into every known language'; but we are sure that they have less in common with *The Golden Bowl*, or *Ulysses*, or even *Beauchamp's Career*, than *East Lynne* has in common with *Bleak House*.

In order to enjoy and to appreciate the work of Wilkie Collins, we ought to be able to reassemble the elements which have been dissociated in the modern novel. Collins is the contemporary of Dickens, Thackeray, George Eliot; of Charles Reade and almost of Captain Marryat. He has something in common with all of these novelists; but particularly and significantly with Dickens. Collins was the friend and sometimes the collaborator of Dickens; and the work of the two men ought to be studied side by side. There is, unhappily for the literary critic, no full biography of Wilkie Collins; and Forster's *Life of Dickens* is, from this point of view, most unsatisfactory. Forster was a notable biographer; but as a critic of the work of Dickens his view was a very narrow view. To anyone who knows the bare facts of Dickens's acquaintance with Collins, and who has studied the work of the two men, their relationship and their influence upon one another is an important subject of study. And a comparative study of their novels can do much to illuminate the question of the difference between the dramatic and the melodramatic in fiction.

Dickens's 'best novel' is probably *Bleak House*; that is Mr Chesterton's opinion, and there is no better critic of Dickens living than Mr Chesterton. Collins's best novel – or, at any rate, the only one of Collins's novels which everyone knows – is *The Woman in White*. Now *Bleak House* is the novel in which Dickens most closely approaches Collins (and after *Bleak House*, *Little Dorrit* and parts of *Martin Chuzzlewit*); and *The Woman in White* is the novel in which Collins most closely approaches Dickens. Dickens excelled in character; in the creation of characters of greater intensity than human beings. Collins was not usually strong in the creation of character; but he was a master of plot and situation, of those elements of drama which are most essential to melodrama. *Bleak House* is Dickens's finest piece of construction; and *The Woman in White* contains Collins's most real characterization. Everyone knows Count Fosco and Marion Halcombe intimately; only the most perfect Collins reader can remember even half a dozen of his other characters by name.

Count Fosco and Marion are indeed real personages to us; as 'real' as much greater characters are, as real as Becky Sharp or Emma Bovary. In comparison with the characters of Dickens they lack only that kind of reality which is almost supernatural, which hardly seems to belong to the character by natural right, but seems rather to descend upon him by a kind of inspiration or grace. Collins's best characters are fabricated, with consummate skill, before our eyes; in Dickens's greatest figures we see no process or calculation. Dickens's figures belong to poetry, like figures of Dante or Shakespeare, in that a single phrase, either by them or about them, may be enough to set them wholly before us. Collins has no phrases. Dickens can with a phrase make a character as real as flesh and blood – '*What a life young Bailey's was!*' – like Farinata,

Chi fur gli maggior tui?

or like Cleopatra,

> *I saw her once*
> *Hop forty paces through the public street.*

Dickens's characters are real because there is no one like them; Collins's because they are so painstakingly coherent and lifelike. Whereas Dickens often introduces a great character carelessly, so that we do not realize, until the story is far advanced, with what a powerful personage we have to do, Collins, at least in these two figures in *The Woman in White*, employs every advantage of dramatic effect. (408–10)

Aldous Huxley

from *Vulgarity in Literature* 1930

The case of Dickens is a strange one. The really monstrous emotional vulgarity, of which he is guilty now and then in all his books and almost continuously in *The Old Curiosity Shop*, is not the emotional vulgarity of one who simulates feelings which he does not have. It is evident, on the contrary, that Dickens felt most poignantly for and with his Little Nell; that he wept over her sufferings, piously revered her goodness and exulted in her joys. He had an overflowing heart; but the trouble was that it overflowed with such curious and even rather repellant secretions. The creator of the later Pickwick and the Cheeryble Brothers, of Tim Linkinwater the bachelor and Mr Garland and so many other gruesome old Peter Pans was obviously a little abnormal in his emotional reactions. There was something rather wrong with a man who could take this lachrymose and tremulous pleasure in adult infantility. He would doubtless have justified his rather frightful emotional taste by a reference to the New Testament. But the child-like qualities of character commended by Jesus are certainly not the same as those which distinguish the old infants in Dickens's novels. There is all the difference in the world between infants and children. Infants are stupid and unaware and sub-human. Children are remarkable for their intelligence and ardour, for their curiosity, their intolerance of shams, the clarity and ruthlessness of their vision. From all accounts Jesus must have been child-like, not at all infantile. A child-like man is not a man whose development has been arrested; on the contrary, he is a man who has given himself a chance of continuing to develop long after most adults have muffled themselves in the cocoon of middle-aged habit and convention. An infantile man is one who has not developed at all, or who has regressed towards the womb, into a comfortable unawareness. So far from being attractive and commendable, an infantile man is really a most repulsive, because a truly monstrous and misshapen, being. A writer who can tearfully adore these stout or cadaverous old babies, snugly ensconced in their mental and economic womb-substitutes and sucking, between false teeth, their thumbs, must have something seriously amiss with his emotional constitution.

One of Dickens's most striking peculiarities is that, whenever in his writing he becomes emotional, he ceases instantly to use his intelligence. The overflowing of his heart drowns his head and even dims his eyes; for, whenever he is in the melting mood, Dickens ceases to be able and probably ceases even to wish to see reality. His one and only desire on these occasions is just to overflow, nothing else. Which he does, with a vengeance and in an atrocious blank verse that is meant to be poetical prose and succeeds only in being the worst kind of fustian. 'When Death strikes down the innocent and young, from every fragile form from which he lets the panting spirit free, a hundred virtues rise, in shapes of mercy, charity and love, to walk the world and bless it. Of every tear that sorrowing mortals shed on such green graves, some good is born, some gentler nature comes. In the Destroyer's steps there spring up bright creations that defy his power, and his dark path becomes a way of light to Heaven.' And so on, a staunchless flux.

Mentally drowned and blinded by the sticky overflowings of his heart, Dickens was incapable, when moved, of re-creating, in terms of art, the reality which had moved him, was even, it would seem, unable to perceive that reality. Little Nelly's sufferings and death distressed him as, in real life, they would distress any normally constituted man; for the suffering and death of children raise the problem of evil in its most unanswerable form. It was Dickens's business as a writer to re-create in terms of his art this distressing reality. He failed. The history of Little Nell is distressing indeed, but not as Dickens presumably meant it to be distressing; it is distressing in its ineptitude and vulgar sentimentality.

A child, Ilusha, suffers and dies in Dostoyevsky's *Brothers Karamazov*. Why is this history so agonizingly moving, when the tale of Little Nell leaves us not merely cold, but derisive? Comparing the two stories, we are instantly struck by the incomparably greater richness in factual detail of Dostoyevsky's creation. Feeling did not prevent him from seeing and recording, or rather re-creating. All that happened round Ilusha's deathbed he saw, unerringly. The emotion-blinded Dickens noticed practically nothing of what went on in Little Nelly's neighbourhood during the child's last days. We are almost forced, indeed, to believe that he didn't want to see anything. He wanted to be unaware himself and he wanted his readers to be unaware of everything except Little Nell's sufferings on the one hand and her goodness and innocence on the other. But goodness and innocence and the undeservedness of suffering and even, to some extent, suffering itself are only significant in relation to the actual realities of human life. Isolated, they cease to mean anything, perhaps to exist. Even the classical writers surrounded their abstract and algebraical personages with at least the abstract and algebraical implication of the human realities, in relation to which virtues and vices are significant. Thanks to Dickens's pathologically deliberate unawareness, Nell's virtues are marooned, as it were, in the midst of a boundless waste of unreality; isolated, they fade and die. Even her sufferings and death lack significance because of this isolation. Dickens's unawareness was the death of death itself.

(54–8)

G. M. Young

from *Victorian England: Portrait of an Age*   1936

All through the thirties we are aware of a growing disaffection, of which Carlyle and Dickens are the mouthpieces, with the delays and irrelevancies of parliamentary government, which, as the years went on, seemed to be degenerating more and more into an unseemly scuffle between In and Outs. The political satire of Dickens is tedious and ignorant. But it registers, what *Past and Present* conveys more passionately, the disillusionment which followed on the hopes of 1830. . . .

(29)

The failure of the New Poor Law to fulfil its promise, the inevitable harshness of a new administration suddenly applied to a people with no idea of administration at all, the brutality that went on in some workhouses and the gorging in others, the petty tyranny of officials and the petty corruption of Guardians, discredited the scientific Radicals and brought the sentimental Radicals to the front. *The Pickwick Papers* is not a Victorian document: it belongs to a sunnier time, which perhaps had never existed. The group of novels that follow, *Oliver Twist, Nicholas Nickleby, The Old Curiosity Shop*, is charged with the atmosphere of the thirties. They have the Radical faith in progress, the Radical dislike of obstruction and privilege, the Radical indifference to the historic appeal. But they part from the Radicalism of the Benthamites in their equal indifference to the scientific appeal. Dickens's ideal England was not very far from Robert Owen's. But it was to be built by some magic of goodwill

overriding the egoism of progress; not by law, and most emphatically not by logic.
(49–50)

George Bernard Shaw

Foreword to the Edinburgh limited edition of *Great Expectations*
1937 (reprinted in 'The Novel Library' edition, 1947)

Great Expectations is the last of the three full-length stories written by
Dickens in the form of an autobiography. Of the three, *Bleak House*,
as the autobiography of Miss Esther Summerson, is naturally the least
personal, as Esther is not only a woman but a maddening prig, though
we are forced to admit that such paragons exist and are perhaps
worthy of the reverent admiration with which Dickens regarded
them. Ruling her out, we have *David Copperfield* and *Great Expectations*. David was, for a time at least, Dickens's favourite child, perhaps
because he had used him to express the bitterness of that episode in his
own experience which had wounded his boyish self-respect most
deeply. For Dickens, in spite of exuberance, was a deeply reserved
man: the exuberance was imagination and acting (his imagination
was ceaseless, and his outward life a feat of acting from beginning to
end); and we shall never know whether in that immensely broadened
outlook and knowledge of the world which began with *Hard Times*
and *Little Dorrit*, and left all his earlier works behind, he may not have
come to see that making his living by sticking labels on blacking
bottles and rubbing shoulders with boys who were not gentlemen,
was as little shameful as being the genteel apprentice in the office of
Mr Spenlow, or the shorthand writer recording the unending twaddle
of the House of Commons and electioneering bunk on the hustings
of all the Eatanswills in the country.

That there was a tragic change in his valuations can be shown by
contrasting Micawber with William Dorrit, in which light Micawber
suddenly becomes a mere marionette pantaloon with a funny bag of
tricks which he repeats until we can bear no more of him, and Dorrit
a portrait of the deadliest and deepest truth to nature. Now contrast
David with Pip; and believe, if you can, that there was no revision of

his estimate of the favorite child David as a work of art and even as a vehicle of experience. The adult David fades into what stage managers call a walking gentleman. The reappearance of Mr Dickens in the character of a blacksmith's boy may be regarded as an apology to Mealy Potatoes.

Dickens did in fact know that *Great Expectations* was his most compactly perfect book. In all the other books, there are episodes of wild extravagance, extraordinary funny if they catch you at the right age, but recklessly grotesque as nature studies. Even in *Little Dorrit*, Dickens's masterpiece among many masterpieces, it is impossible to believe that the perfectly authentic Mr Pancks really stopped the equally authentic Mr Casby in a crowded street in London and cut his hair; and though Mr F.'s aunt is a first-rate clinical study of senile deficiency in a shrewd old woman, her collisions with Arthur Clennam are too funny to be taken seriously. We cannot say of Casby, Pancks and the aunt, as we can say of Sam Weller, that such people never existed; for most of us have met their counterparts in real life; but we can say that Dickens's sense of fun ran away with him over them. If we have absolutely no fun in us we may even state gravely that there has been a lapse from the artistic integrity of the tragic picture of English society which is the subject of the book.

In *Great Expectations* we have Wopsle and Trabbs's boy; but they have their part and purpose in the story and do not overstep the immodesty of nature. It is hardly decent to compare Mr F.'s aunt with Miss Havisham; but as contrasted studies of madwomen they make you shudder at the thought of what Dickens might have made of Miss Havisham if he had seen her as a comic personage. For life is no laughing matter in *Great Expectations*; the book is all-of-one piece and consistently truthful as none of the other books are, not even the compact *Tale of Two Cities*, which is pure sentimental melodrama from beginning to end, and shockingly wanting in any philosophy of history in its view of the French Revolution.

Dickens never regarded himself as a revolutionist, though he certainly was one. His implacable contempt for the House of Commons, founded on his experience as a parliamentary reporter, never wavered from the account of the Eatanswill election and of Nicholas Nickleby's interview with Pugstyles to the Veneering election in *Our Mutual Friend*, his last book (*Edwin Drood* is only a gesture by a man three-quarters dead). And this was not mere satire, of which there had been plenty. Dickens was the first writer to perceive and state definitely that the House of Commons, working on the Party system, is an extraordinarily efficient device for dissipating all our reforming energy and ability in Party debate and when anything urgently needs to be done, finding out 'how not to do it'. It took very little time to get an ineffective Factory Act. It took fifty years to make it effective, though the labour conditions in the factories and mines were horrible. After Dickens's death, it took thirty years to pass an Irish Home Rule Bill, which was promptly repudiated by the military plutocracy, leaving the question to be settled by a competition in slaughter and house burning, just as it would have been between two tribes of savages. Liberty under the British parliamentary system means slavery for nine-tenths of the people, and slave exploitation or parasitic idolatry and snobbery for the rest. Parliament men – one cannot call them statesmen – and even historians, keep declaring that the British parliamentary system is one of the greatest blessings British political genius has given to the world; and the world has taken it at its self-valuation and set up imitations of it all over Europe and America, always with the same result: political students outside Parliament exposing the most frightful social evils and prescribing their remedies, and Parliament ignoring them as long as possible and then engulfing their disciples and changing them from reformers into partisans with time for nothing but keeping their party in power or opposing the Government, rightly or wrongly ('it is the duty of the Opposition to oppose') as the case might be. In the middle of the nineteenth century Dickens saw this and said it. He had to be ignored, as he would not stand for Parliament and be paralysed.

Europe has had to learn from experience what it would not learn from Dickens. The Fascist and Communist revolutions which swept the great parliamentary sham into the dustbin after it had produced a colossal Anarchist war, made no mention of Dickens; but on the parliamentary point he was as much their prophet as Marx was the economic prophet of the Soviets. Yet a recent reactionist against Dickens worship declares that he 'never went ahead of his public'.

Marx and Dickens were contemporaries living in the same city and pursuing the same profession of literature; yet they seem to us like creatures of a different species living in different worlds. Dickens, if he had ever become conscious of Karl Marx, would have been classed with him as a revolutionist. The difference between a revolutionist and what Marx called a bourgeois is that the bourgeois regards the existing social order as the permanent and natural order of human society, needing reforms now and then and here and there, but essentially good and sane and right and respectable and proper and everlasting. To the revolutionist it is transitory, mistaken, objectionable and pathological: a social disease to be cured, not to be endured. We have only to compare Thackeray and Trollope with Dickens to perceive this contrast. Thackeray reviled the dominant classes with a savagery which would have been unchivalrous in Dickens: he denied to his governing class characters even the common good qualities and accomplishments of ladies and gentlemen, making them mean, illiterate, dishonest, ignorant, sycophantic to an inhuman degree, whilst Dickens, even when making his aristocrats ridiculous and futile, at least made gentlemen of them. Trollope, who regarded Thackeray as his master and exemplar, had none of his venom, and has left us a far better balanced and more truthful picture of Victorian well-off society, never consciously whitewashing it, though allowing it its full complement of black sheep of both sexes. But Trollope's politics were those of the country house and the hunting field just as were Thackeray's. Accordingly, Thackeray and Trollope were received and approved by fashionable society with complete confidence. Dickens, though able to fascinate all classes, was never so received or approved except by quite goodnatured or stupid ladies and gentlemen who were incapable of criticizing anyone who could make them laugh and cry. He was told that he could not describe a gentleman and that *Little Dorrit* is twaddle. And the reason was that in his books the west-end heaven appears as a fool's paradise that must pass away instead of being an indispensable preparatory school for the New Jerusalem of Revelation. A leading encyclopedia tells us that Dickens had 'no knowledge of country gentlemen'. It would have been nearer the mark to say that Dickens knew all that really mattered about Sir Leicester Dedlock and that Trollope knew nothing that really mattered about him. Trollope and Thackeray could see Chesney Wold; but Dickens could see through it. And this was no joke to Dickens. He was deeply concerned about it, and understood how revolutions begin with burning the chateaux.

The difference between Marx and Dickens was that Marx knew that he was a revolutionist whilst Dickens had not the faintest suspicion of that part of his calling. Compare the young Dickens looking for a job in a lawyer's office and teaching himself shorthand to escape from his office stool to the reporters' gallery, with the young Trotsky, the young Lenin, quite deliberately facing disreputable poverty and adopting revolution as their profession with every alternative of bourgeois security and respectability much more fully open to them than to Dickens.

And this bring us to Dickens's position as a member of the educated and cultured classes who had neither education nor culture. This was fortunate for him and for the world in one way, as he escaped the school and university routine which complicates cultural Philistinism with the mentality of a Red Indian brave. Better no schooling at all than the schooling of Rudyard Kipling and Winston Churchill. But there are homes in which a mentally acquisitive boy can make contact with the fine arts. I myself learnt nothing at school, but gained in my home an extensive and highly educational knowledge of music. I had access to illustrated books on painting which sent me to the National Gallery; so that I was able to support myself as a critic of music and painting as Dickens supported himself by shorthand. I devoured books on science and on the religious controversies of the day. It is in this way, and not in our public schools and universities that such culture as there is in England is kept alive.

Now the Dickenses seem to have been complete barbarians. Dickens mentions the delight with which he discovered in an attic a heap of eighteenth-century novels. But Smollett was a grosser barbarian than Dickens himself; and *Don Quixote* and *The Arabian Nights*, though they gave the cue to his eager imagination, left him quite in the dark as to the philosophy and art of his day. To him a philosopher, an intellectual, was a figure of fun. Count Smorltork is the creation by a street Arab: Dickens did not even know that the Count's method of studying Chinese metaphysics by studying metaphysics and China and 'combining the information' was not only sensible and correct, but the only possible method. To Dickens as to most Victorian Englishmen metaphysics were ridiculous, useless, unpractical and the mark of a fool. He was musical enough to have a repertory of popular ballads which he sang all over the house to keep his voice in order; and he made Tom Pinch play the organ in church as an amiable accomplishment; but I cannot remember hearing that he ever went to a classical concert, or even knew of the existence of such entertainments. The articles on the National Gallery in *All the Year Round*, though extremely funny in their descriptions of 'The Apotheosis' of 'William the Silent' (the title alone would make a cat laugh), and on some profane points sensible enough, are those of a complete Philistine. One cannot say that he disliked all painters in the face of his friendship with Maclise and Clarkson Stanfield; but it was not a cultural friendship: Stanfield was a scene painter who appealed to that English love of landscape which is so often confused with a love of art; and Maclise was a pictorial anecdotist who presented scenes from Shakespear's plays exactly as they were presented on the stage. When Dickens introduced in his stories a character whom he intensely disliked he chose an artistic profession for him. Henry Gowan in *Little Dorrit* is a painter. Pecksniff is an architect. Harold Skimpole is a musician. There is real hatred in his treatment of them.

Now far be it from me to imply that they are false to nature. Artists are often detestable human beings; and the famous Anti-Scrape, officially The Society for the Protection of Ancient Buildings, was founded by William Morris and his friends to protect ancient buildings from architects. What is more, the ultra-artistic sets, the Pre-Raphaelites and the aesthetes grouped round Rossetti and Morris and Ruskin, were all Dickens worshippers who made a sort of cult of Trabbs's boy and would have regarded me as a traitor if they had read what I am now writing. They knew better than anyone else that Leigh Hunt deserved all he got as Harold Skimpole, that Gowan's shallow sort of painting was a nuisance, and that architecture was just the right profession for a parasite on Salisbury Cathedral like Pecksniff. But all their Dickensian enthusiasm, and all the truth to life of Dickens's portraiture cannot extenuate the fact that the cultural side of art was as little known to Dickens as it is possible for a thing so public to remain to a man so apprehensive. You may read the stories of Dickens from beginning to end without ever learning that he lived through a period of fierce revivals and revolutionary movements in art, in philosophy, in sociology, in religion: in short, in culture. Dean Inge's remark that 'the number of great subjects in which Dickens took no interest whatever is amazing' hits the nail exactly on the head. As to finding such as person as Karl Marx among his characters, one would as soon look for a nautilus in a nursery.

Yet *Little Dorrit* is a more seditious book than *Das Kapital*. All over Europe men and women are in prison for pamphlets and speeches which are to *Little Dorrit* as red pepper to dynamite. Fortunately for social evolution Governments never know where to strike. Barnacle and Stiltstalking were far too conceited to recognize their own portraits. Parliament, wearying its leaders out in a few years in the ceaseless drudgery of finding out how not to do it, and smothering it in talk, could not conceive that its heartbreaking industry could have any relation to the ridiculous fiction of the Coodle–Doodle discussions in Sir Leicester Dedlock's drawing-room. As to the Circumlocution Office, well, perhaps the staffs, owing their posts to patronage and regarding them as sinecures, were a bit too insolent to the public, and would be none the worse for a little chaff from a funny fellow like Dickens; but their inefficiency as a public service was actually a good thing, as it provided a standing object lesson in the superiority of private enterprise. Mr Sparkler was not offended: he stuck to his job and never read anything. *Little Dorrit* and *Das Kapital* were all the same to him: they never entered his world; and to him that world was the whole world.

The mass of Dickens readers, finding all these people too funny to be credible, continued to idolize Coodle and Doodle as great statesmen, and made no distinction between John Stuart Mill at the India Office and Mr Sparkler. In fact the picture was not only too funny to be credible: it was too truthful to be credible. But the fun was no fun to Dickens: the truth was too bitter. When you laugh at Jack Bunsby, or at The Orfling when the handle of her corkscrew came off and smote her on the chin, you have no doubt that Dickens is laughing with you like a street boy, despite Bunsby's tragic end. But whilst you laugh at Sparkler or young Barnacle, Dickens is in deadly earnest: he means that both of them must go into the dustbin if England is to survive.

And yet Dickens never saw himself as a revolutionist. It never occurred to him to found a Red International, as Marx did, not even to join one out of the dozens of political reform societies that were about him. He was an English gentleman of the professional class, who would not allow his daughter to go on the stage because it was not respectable. He knew so little about revolutionists that when Mazzini called on him and sent in his card, Dickens, much puzzled, concluded that the unknown foreign gentleman wanted money, and very kindly sent him down a sovereign to get rid of him. He discovered for himself all the grievances he exposed, and had no sense of belonging to a movement, nor any desire to combine with others who shared his subversive views. To educate his children religiously and historically he wrote *A Child's History of England* which had not even the excuse of being childish, and a paraphrase of the gospel biography which is only a belittling of it for little children. He had much better have left the history to Little Arthur and Mrs Markham and Goldsmith, and taken into account the extraordinary educational value of the Authorized Version as a work of literary art. He probably thought as seldom of himself as a literary artist as of himself as a revolutionist; and he had his share in the revolt against the supernatural pretension of the Bible which was to end in the vogue of Agnosticism and the pontificate of Darwin. It blinded that generation to the artistic importance of the fact that at a moment when all the literary energy in England was in full eruption, when Shakespear was just dead and Milton just born, a picked body of scholars undertook the task of translating into English what they believed to be the words of God himself. Under the strain of that conviction they surpassed all their normal powers, transfiguring the original texts into literary masterpieces of a splendor that no merely mortal writers can ever again hope to achieve. But the nineteenth century either did not dare think of the Bible in that way, it being fetish, or else it was in such furious reaction against the fetishism that it would not allow the so-called Holy Scriptures even an artistic merit. At all events Dickens thought his Little Nell style better for his children than the English of King James's inspired scribes. He took them (for a time at least) to churches of the Unitarian persuasion, where they could be both sceptical and respectable; but it is hard to say what Dickens believed or did not believe metaphysically or metapolitically, though he left us in no doubt as to his opinion of the Lords, the Commons and the ante-Crimean Civil Service.

On the positive side he had nothing to say. Marxism and Darwinism came too late for him. He might have been a Comtist – perhaps ought to have been a Comtist, but was not. He was an independent Dickensian, a sort of unphilosophic Radical, with a complete disbelief in government by the people and an equally complete hostility to government in any other interest than theirs. He exposed many abuses and called passionately on the rulers of the people to remedy them; but he never called on the people themselves. He would as soon have thought of calling on them to write their own novels.

Meanwhile he overloaded himself and his unfortunate wife with such a host of children that he was forced to work himself to death prematurely to provide for them and for the well-to-do life he led. The reading public cannot bear to think of its pet authors as struggling with the economic pressures that often conflict so cruelly with the urge of genius. This pressure was harder on Dickens than on many poorer men. He had a solid bourgeois conscience which made it impossible for him to let wife and children starve whilst he followed the path of destiny. Marx let his wife go crazy with prolonged poverty whilst he wrote a book which changed the mind of the world. But then Marx had been comfortably brought up and thoroughly educated in the German manner. Dickens knew far too much of the horrors of impecuniosity to put his wife through what his mother had gone through, or have his children pasting labels on blacking bottles. He had to please his public or lapse into that sort of poverty. Under such circumstances the domestic conscience inevitably pushes the artistic conscience into the second place. We shall never know how much of Dickens's cheery optimism belied his real outlook on life. He went his own way far enough to make it clear that when he was not infectiously laughing he was a melancholy fellow. Arthur Clennam is one of the Dismal Jemmies of literature. For any gaiety of heart we have to turn to the impossible Dick Swiveller, who by the way, was designed as a revoltingly coarse fortune hunter, and still appears in that character in the single scene which precedes his sudden appeal to Dickens's sense of fun, and consequent transformation into a highly entertaining and entirely fantastic clown. This was a genuine conversion and not a concession to public taste; but the case of Walter Gay in *Dombey and Son*, whose high spirits were planned as a prelude to his degeneration and ruin, is a flagrant case of a manufactured happy ending to save a painful one. Martin Chuzzlewit begins as a study in selfishness and ends nowhere. Mr Boffin, corrupted by riches, gets discharged without a stain on his character by explaining that he was only pretending for benevolent purposes, but leaves us with a feeling that some of his pretences were highly suspicious. Jarndyce, a violently good man, keeps on doing generous things, yet ends by practising a heartlessly cruel and indelicate deception on Esther Summerson for the sake of giving her a pleasant melodramatic surprise. I will not go so far as to say that Dickens's novels are full of melancholy intentions which he dares not carry through to their unhappy conclusions; but he gave us no vitally happy heroes and heroines after Pickwick (begun, like Don Quixote, as a contemptible butt). Their happy endings are manufactured to make the books pleasant. Nobody who has endured the novels of our twentieth-century emancipated women, enormously cleverer and better informed than the novels of Dickens, and ruthlessly calculated to leave their readers hopelessly discouraged and miserable, will feel anything but gratitude to Dickens for his humanity in speeding his parting guests with happy faces by turning from the world of destiny to the world of accidental good luck; but as our minds grow stronger some of his consolations become unnecessary and even irritating. And it happens that it is just such a consolation that *Great Expectations* ends.

It did not always end so. Dickens wrote two endings, and made a mess of both. In the first ending, which Bulwer Lytton persuaded him to discard, Pip takes little Pip for a walk in Piccadilly and is stopped by Estella, who is passing in her carriage. She is comfortably married to a Shropshire doctor, and just says how d'y'do to Pip and kisses the little boy before they both pass on out of one another's lives. This, though it is marred by Pip's pious hope that her husband may have thrashed into her some understanding of how much she has made him suffer, is true to nature. But it is much too matter-of-fact to be the right ending to a tragedy. Piccadilly was impossible in such a context; and the passing carriage was unconsciously borrowed from *A Day's Ride: A Life's Romance*, the novel by Lever which was so unpopular that *Great Expectations* had to be written to replace it in *All The Year Round*. But in Lever's story it is the man who stops the carriage, only to be cut dead by the lady. Dickens must have felt that there was something wrong with this ending; and Bulwer's objection confirmed his doubt. Accordingly, he wrote a new ending in which he got rid of Piccadilly and substituted a perfectly congruous and beautifully touching scene and hour and atmosphere for the meeting. He abolished the Shropshire doctor and left out the little boy. So far the new ending was in every way better than the first one.

Unfortunately, what Bulwer wanted was what is called a happy ending, presenting Pip and Estella as reunited lovers who were going to marry and live happily ever after; and Dickens, though he could not bring himself to be quite so explicit in sentimental falsehood, did, at the end of the very last line, allow himself to say that there was 'no shadow of parting' between them. If Pip had said 'Since that parting I have been able to think of her without the old unhappiness; but I have never tried to see her again, and I know I never shall' he would have been left with at least the prospect of a bearable life. But the notion that he could ever have been happy with Estella: indeed that anyone could ever have been happy with Estella, is positively unpleasant. I can remember when the Cowden Clarks ventured to hint a doubt whether Benedick and Beatrice had a very delightful union to look forward to; but that did not greatly matter, as Benedick and Beatrice have none of the reality of Pip and Estella. Shakespear could afford to trifle with *Much Ado About Nothing*, which is avowedly a potboiler; but *Great Expectations* is a different matter. Dickens put nearly all his thought into it. It is too serious a book to be a trivially happy one. Its beginning is unhappy; its middle is unhappy; and the conventional happy ending is an outrage on it.

Estella is a curious addition to the gallery of unamiable women painted by Dickens. In my youth it was commonly said that Dickens could not draw women. The people who said this were thinking of Agnes Wickfield and Esther Summerson, of Little Dorrit and Florence Dombey, and thinking of them as ridiculous idealizations of their sex. Gissing put a stop to that by asking whether shrews like Mrs Raddle, Mrs Macstinger, Mrs Gargery, fools like Mrs Nickleby and Flora Finching, warped spinsters like Rosa Dartle and Miss Wade, were not masterpieces of woman drawing. And they are all unamiable. But for Betsey Trotwood, who is a very lovable fairy godmother and yet a genuine nature study, and an old dear like Mrs Boffin, one would be tempted to ask whether Dickens had ever in his life met an amiable female. The transformation of Dora into Flora is diabolical, but frightfully true to nature. Of course Dickens with his imagination could invent amiable women by the dozen; but somehow he could not or would not bring them to life as he brought the others. We doubt whether he ever knew a little Dorrit; but Fanny Dorrit is from the life unmistakably. So is Estella. She is a much more elaborate study than Fanny, and, I should guess, a recent one.

Dickens, when he let himself go in *Great Expectations*, was separated from his wife and free to make more intimate acquaintances with women than a domesticated man can. I know nothing of his adventures in this phase of his career, though I daresay a good deal of it will be dug out by the little sect of anti-Dickensites whose fanaticism has been provoked by the Dickens Fellowships. It is not necessary to suggest a love affair; for Dickens could get from a passing glance a hint which he could expand into a full-grown character. The point concerns us here only because it is the point on which the ending of *Great Expectations* turns: namely, that Estella is a born tormentor. She deliberately torments Pip all through for the fun of it; and in the little we hear of her intercourse with others there is no suggestion of a moment of kindness: in fact her tormenting of Pip is almost affectionate in contrast to the cold disdain of her attitude towards the people who were not worth tormenting. It is not surprising that the unfortunate Bentley Drummle, whom she marries in the stupidity of sheer perversity, is obliged to defend himself from her clever malice with his fists: a consolation to us for Pip's broken heart, but not altogether a credible one; for the real Estellas can usually intimidate the real Bentley Drummles. At all events the final sugary suggestion of Estella redeemed by Bentley's thrashings and waste of her money, and living happily with Pip for ever after, provoked even Dickens's eldest son to rebel against it, most justly.

Apart from this the story is the most perfect of Dickens's works. In it he does not muddle himself with the ridiculous plots that appear like vestiges of the stone age in many of his books, from *Oliver Twist* to the end. The story is built round a single and simple catastrophe: the revelation to Pip of the source of his great expectations. There is, it is true, a trace of the old plot superstition in Estella turning out to be Magwitch's daughter; but it provides a touchingly happy ending for that heroic Warmint. Who could have the heart to grudge it to him?

As our social conscience expands and makes the intense class snobbery of the nineteenth century seem less natural to us, the tragedy of *Great Expectations* will lose some of its appeal. I have already wondered whether Dickens himself ever came to see that his agonizing sensitiveness about the blacking bottles and his resentment of his mother's opposition to his escape from them was not too snobbish to deserve all the sympathy he claimed for it. Compare the case of H. G. Wells, our nearest to a twentieth-century Dickens. Wells hated being a draper's assistant as much as Dickens hated being a warehouse boy; but he was not in the least ashamed of it, and did not blame his mother for regarding it as the summit of her ambition for him. Fate having imposed on that engaging cricketer, Mr Wells's father, an incongruous means of livelihood in the shape of a small shop, shopkeeping did not present itself to the young Wells as beneath him, whereas to the genteel Dickens being a warehouse boy was an unbearable comedown. Still, I cannot help speculating on whether if Dickens had not killed himself prematurely to pile up money for that excessive family of his, he might not have reached a stage at which he could have got as much fun out of the blacking bottles as Mr Wells got out of his abhorred draper's counter.

Dickens never reached that stage; and there is no provision of it in *Great Expectations*; for in it he never raises the question why Pip should refuse Magwitch's endowment and shrink from him with such inhuman loathing. Magwith no doubt was a Warmint from the point of view of the genteel Dickens family and even from his own; but Victor Hugo would have made him a magnificent hero, another Valjean. Inspired by an altogether noble fixed idea, he had lifted himself out of his rut of crime and honestly made a fortune for the child who had fed him when he was starving. If Pip had no objection to be a parasite instead of an honest blacksmith, at least he had a better claim to be a parasite on Magwitch's earnings than, as he imagined, on Miss Havisham's property. It is curious that this should not have occurred to Dickens; for nothing could exceed the bitterness of his exposure of the futility of Pip's parasitism. If all that came of sponging on Miss Havisham (as he thought) was the privilege of being one of the Finches of the Grove, he need not have felt his dependence on Magwitch to be incompatible with his entirely baseless self-respect. But Pip – and I am afraid Pip must be to this extent identified with Dickens – could not see Magwitch as an animal of the same species as himself or Miss Havisham. His feeling is true to the nature of snobbery; but his creator says no word in criticism of that ephemeral limitation.

The basic truth of the situation is that Pip, like his creator, has no culture and no religion. Joe Gargary, when Pip tells a monstrous string of lies about Miss Havisham, advises him to say a repentant word about it in his prayers; but Pip never prays; and church means nothing to him but Mr Wopsle's orotundity. In this he resembles David Copperfield, who has gentility but neither culture nor religion. Pip's world is therefore a very melancholy place, and his conduct, good or bad, always helpless. This is why Dickens worked against so black a background after he was roused from his ignorant middle-class cheery optimism by Carlyle. When he lost his belief in bourgeois society and with it his lightness of heart he had neither an economic Utopia nor a credible religion to hitch on to. His world becomes a world of great expectations cruelly disappointed. The Wells world is a world of greater and greater expectations continually being fulfilled. This is a huge improvement. Dickens never had time to form a philosophy or define a faith; and his later and greater books are saddened by the evil that is done under the sun; but at least he preserved his intellectual innocence sufficiently to escape the dismal pseudo-scientific fatalism that was descending on the world in his later days, founded on the preposterous error as to causation in which the future is determined by the present, which has been determined by the past. The true causation, of course, is always the incessant irresistible activity of the evolutionary appetite.
(v-xx)

George Orwell

'Charles Dickens', *Inside the Whale*   1940

The truth is that Dickens's criticism of society is almost exclusively moral. Hence the utter lack of any constructive suggestion anywhere in his work. He attacks the law, parliamentary government, the educational system and so forth, without ever clearly suggesting what he would put in their places. Of course it is not necessarily the business of a novelist, or a satirist, to make constructive suggestions, but the point is that Dickens's attitude is at bottom not even destructive. There is no clear sign that he wants the existing order to be overthrown, or that he believes it would make very much difference if it *were* overthrown. For in reality his target is not so much society as 'human nature'. It would be difficult to point anywhere in his books to a passage suggesting that the economic system is wrong *as a system*. Nowhere, for instance, does he make any attack on private enterprise or private property. Even in a book like *Our Mutual Friend*, which turns on the power of corpses to interfere with living people by means of idiotic wills, it does not occur to him to suggest that individuals ought not to have this irresponsible power. Of course one can draw this inference for oneself, and one can draw it again from the remarks about Bounderby's will at the end of *Hard Times*, and indeed from the whole of Dickens's work one can infer the evil of *laissez-faire* capitalism; but Dickens makes no such inference himself. It is said that Macaulay refused to review *Hard Times* because he disapproved of its 'sullen Socialism'. Obviously Macaulay is here using the word 'Socialism' in the same sense in which, twenty years ago, a vegetarian meal or a Cubist picture used to be referred to as 'Bolshevism'. There is not a line in the book that can properly be called Socialistic; indeed, its tendency if anything is pro-capitalist, because its whole moral is that capitalists ought to be kind, not that workers ought to be rebellious. Bounderby is a bullying windbag and Gradgrind has been morally blinded, but if they were better men, the system would work well enough – that, all through, is the implication. And so far as social criticism goes, one can never extract much more from Dickens than this, unless one deliberately reads meanings into him. His whole 'message' is one that at first glance looks like an enormous platitude: If men would behave decently the world would be decent.

Naturally this calls for a few characters who are in positions of authority and who *do* behave decently. Hence that recurrent Dickens figure, the Good Rich Man. This character belongs especially to Dickens's early optimistic period. He is usually a 'merchant' (we are not necessarily told what merchandise he deals in) and he is always a superhumanly kind-hearted old gentleman who 'trots' to and fro, raising his employees' wages, patting children on the head, getting debtors out of jail and, in general, acting the fairy godmother. Of course he is a pure dream figure, much further from real life than, say, Squeers or Micawber. Even Dickens must have reflected occasionally that anyone who was so anxious to give his money away would never have acquired it in the first place. Mr Pickwick, for instance, had 'been in the city', but it is difficult to imagine him making a fortune there. Nevertheless this character runs like a connecting thread through most of the earlier books. Pickwick, the Cheerybles, old Chuzzlewit, Scrooge – it is the same figure over and over again, the good rich man, handing out guineas. Dickens does however show signs of development here. In the books of the middle period the good rich man fades out to some extent. There is no one who plays this part in *A Tale of Two Cities*, nor in *Great Expectations – Great Expectations* is, in fact, definitely an attack on patronage – and in *Hard Times* it is only very doubtfully played by Gradgrind after his reformation. The character reappears in a rather different form as Meagles in *Little Dorrit* and John Jarndyce in *Bleak House* – one night perhaps add Betsy Trotwood in *David Copperfield*. But in these books the good rich man has dwindled from a 'merchant' to a rentier. This is significant. A rentier is part of the possessing class, he can and, almost without knowing it, does make other people work for him, but he has very little direct power. Unlike Scrooge or the Cheerybles, he cannot put everything right by raising everybody's wages. The seeming inference from the rather despondent books that Dickens wrote in the fifties is that by that time he had grasped the helplessness of well-meaning individuals in a corrupt society. Nevertheless in the last completed novel, *Our Mutual Friend* (published 1864–5), the good rich man comes back in full glory in the person of Boffin. Boffin is a proletarian by origin and only rich by inheritance, but he is the usual *deus ex machina*, solving everybody's problems by showering money in all directions. He even 'trots', like the Cheerybles. In several ways *Our Mutual Friend* is a return to the earlier manner, and not an unsuccessful return either. Dickens's thoughts seem to have come full circle. Once again, individual kindliness is the remedy for everything. . . .

It seems that in every attack Dickens makes upon society he is always pointing to a change of spirit rather than a change of structure. It is hopeless to try and pin him down to any definite remedy, still more to any political doctrine. His approach is always along the moral plane, and his attitude is sufficiently summed up in that remark about Strong's school being as different from Creakle's 'as good is from evil'. Two things can be very much alike and yet abysmally different.

Heaven and Hell are in the same place. Useless to change institutions without a 'change of heart' – that, essentially, is what he is always saying.

If that were all, he might be no more than a cheer-up writer, a reactionary humbug. A 'change of heart' is in fact *the* alibi of people who do not wish to endanger the *status quo*. But Dickens is not a humbug, except in minor matters, and the strongest single impression one carries away from his books is that of a hatred of tyranny. I said earlier that Dickens is not *in the accepted sense* a revolutionary writer. But it is not at all certain that a merely moral criticism of society may not be just as 'revolutionary' – and revolution, after all, means turning things upside down – as the politico-economic criticism which is fashionable at this moment. Blake was not a politician, but there is more understanding of the nature of capitalist society in a poem like 'I wander through each charter'd street' than in three-quarters of Socialist literature. Progress is not an illusion, it happens, but it is slow and invariably disappointing. There is always a new tyrant waiting to take over from the old – generally not quite so bad, but still a tyrant. Consequently two viewpoints are always tenable. The one, how can you improve human nature until you have changed the system? The other, what is the use of changing the system before you have improved human nature? They appeal to different individuals, and they probably show a tendency to alternate in point of time. The moralist and the revolutionary are constantly undermining one another. Marx exploded a hundred tons of dynamite beneath the moralist position, and we are still living in the echo of that tremendous crash. But already, somewhere or other, the sappers are at work and fresh dynamite is being tamped in place to blow Marx at the moon. Then Marx, or somebody like him, will come back with yet more dynamite, and so the process continues, to an end we cannot yet foresee. The central problem – how to prevent power from being abused – remains unsolved. Dickens, who had not the vision to see that private property is an obstructive nuisance, had the vision to see that. 'If men would behave decently the world would be decent' is not such a platitude as it sounds. . . .

It is not merely a coincidence that Dickens never writes about agriculture and writes endlessly about food. He was a Cockney, and London is the centre of the earth in rather the same sense that the belly is the centre of the body. It is a city of consumers, of people who are deeply civilized but not primarily useful. A thing that strikes one when one looks below the surface of Dickens's books is that, as nineteenth-century novelists go, he is rather ignorant. He knows very little about the way things really happen. At first sight this statement looks flatly untrue and it needs some qualification.

Dickens had had vivid glimpses of 'low life' – life in a debtor's prison, for example – and he was also a popular novelist and able to write about ordinary people. So were all the characteristic English novelists of the nineteenth century. They felt at home in the world they lived in, whereas a writer nowadays is so hopelessly isolated that the typical modern novel is a novel about a novelist. Even when Joyce, for instance, spends a decade or so in patient efforts to make contact with the 'common man', his 'common man' finally turns out to be a Jew, and a bit of a highbrow at that. Dickens at least does not suffer from this kind of thing. He has no difficulty in introducing the common motives, love, ambition, avarice, vengeance and so forth. What he does not noticeably write about, however, is *work*.

In Dickens's novels anything in the nature of work happens offstage. The only one of his heroes who has a plausible profession is David Copperfield, who is first a shorthand writer and then a novelist, like Dickens himself. With most of the others, the way they earn their living is very much in the background. Pip, for instance, 'goes into business' in Egypt; we are not told what business, and Pip's working life occupies about half a page of the book. Clennam has been in some unspecified business in China, and later goes into another barely specified business with Doyce, Martin Chuzzlewit is an architect, but does not seem to get much time for practising. In no case do their adventures spring directly out of their work. Here the contrast between Dickens and, say, Trollope is startling. And one reason for this is undoubtedly that Dickens knows very little about the professions his characters are supposed to follow. What exactly went on in Gradgrind's factories? How did Podsnap make his money? How did Merdle work his swindles? One knows that Dickens could never follow up the details of Parliamentary elections and Stock Exchange rackets as Trollope could. As soon as he has to deal with trade, finance, industry or politics he takes refuge in vagueness, or in satire. This is the case even with legal processes, about which actually he must have known a good deal. Compare any lawsuit in Dickens with the lawsuit in *Orley Farm*, for instance.

And this partly accounts for the needless ramifications of Dickens's novels, the awful Victorian 'plot'. It is true that not all his novels are alike in this. *A Tale of Two Cities* is a very good and fairly simple story, and so in its different ways is *Hard Times*; but these are just the two which are always rejected as 'not like Dickens' – and incidentally they were not published in monthly numbers.[1] The two first-person novels are also good stories, apart from their sub-plots. But the typical Dickens novel, *Nicholas Nickleby*, *Oliver Twist*, *Martin Chuzzlewit*, *Our Mutual Friend*, always exists round a framework of melodrama. The last thing anyone ever remembers about these books is their central story. On the other hand, I suppose no one has ever read them without carrying the memory of individual pages to the day of his death. Dickens sees human beings with the most intense vividness, but he sees them always in private life, as 'characters', not as functional members of society; that is to say, he sees them statically. Consequently his greatest success is *The Pickwick Papers*, which is not a story at all, merely a series of sketches; there is little attempt at development – the characters simply go on and on, behaving like idiots, in a kind of eternity. As soon as he tries to bring his characters into action, the melodrama begins. He cannot make the action revolve round their ordinary occupations; hence the crossword puzzle of co-incidences, intrigues, murders, disguises, buried wills, long-lost brothers, etc. etc. In the end even people like Squeers and Micawber get sucked into the machinery.

Of course it would be absurd to say that Dickens is a vague or merely melodramatic writer. Much that he wrote is extremely factual, and in the power of evoking visual images he has probably never been equalled. When Dickens has once described something you see it for the rest of your life. But in a way the concreteness of his vision is a sign of what he is missing. For, after all, that is what the merely casual onlooker always sees – the outward appearance, the non-

1 *Hard Times* was published as a serial in *Household Words* and *Great Expectations* and *A Tale of Two Cities* in *All the Year Round*. Forster says that the shortness of the weekly instalments made it 'much more difficult to get sufficient interest into each'. Dickens himself complained of the lack of 'elbow-room'. In other words, he had to stick more closely to the story.

functional, the surfaces of things. No one who is really involved in the landscape ever sees the landscape. Wonderfully as he can describe an *appearance* Dickens does not often describe a *process*. The vivid pictures that he succeeds in leaving in one's memory are nearly always the pictures of things seen in leisure moments, in the coffee-rooms of country inns or through the windows of a stage-coach; the kind of things he notices are inn-signs, brass door-knockers, painted jugs, the interiors of shops and private houses, clothes, faces and, above all, food. Everything is seen from the consumer angle. When he writes about Coketown he manages to evoke, in just a few paragraphs, the atmosphere of a Lancashire town as a slightly disgusted southern visitor would see it. 'It had a black canal in it, and a river that ran purple with evil-smelling dye, and vast piles of buildings full of windows where there was a-rattling and a-trembling all day long, where the piston of the steam-engine worked monotonously up and down, like the head of an elephant in a state of melancholy madness.'

That is as near as Dickens ever gets to the machinery of the mills. An engineer or a cotton-broker would see it differently; but then neither of them would be capable of that impressionistic touch about the heads of the elephants. . . .

With the doubtful exception of David Copperfield (merely Dickens himself) one cannot point to a single one of his central characters who is primarily interested in his job. His heroes work in order to make a living and to marry the heroine, not because they feel a passionate interest in one particular subject. Martin Chuzzlewit, for instance, is not burning with zeal to be an architect; he might just as well be a doctor or a barrister. In any case, in the typical Dickens novel, the *deus ex machina* enters with a bag of gold in the last chapter and the hero is absolved from further struggle. The feeling, 'This is what I came into the world to do. Everything else is uninteresting. I will do this even if it means starvation', which turns men of differing temperaments into scientists, inventors, artists, priests, explorers and revolutionaries – this motif is almost entirely absent from Dickens's books. He himself, as is well known, worked like a slave and believed in his work as few novelists have ever done. But there seems to be no calling except novel-writing (and perhaps acting) towards which he can imagine this kind of devotion. And, after all, it is natural enough, considering his rather negative attitude towards society. In the last resort there is nothing he admires except common decency. Science is uninteresting and machinery is cruel and ugly (the heads of the elephants). Business is only for ruffians like Bounderby. As for politics – leave that to the Tite Barnacles. Really there is no objective except to marry the heroine, settle down, live solvently and be kind. And you can do that much better in private life.

Here, perhaps, one gets a glimpse of Dickens's secret imaginative background. What did he think of as the most desirable way to live? When Martin Chuzzlewit had made it up with his uncle, when Nicholas Nickleby had married money, when John Harman had been enriched by Boffin – what did they *do*?

The answer evidently is that they did nothing. Nicholas Nickleby invested his wife's money with the Cheerybles and 'became a rich and prosperous merchant', but as he immediately retired to Devonshire, we can assume that he did not work very hard. Mr and Mrs Snodgrass 'purchased and cultivated a small farm, more for occupation than profit'. That is the spirit in which most of Dickens's books end – a sort of radiant idleness. Where he appears to disapprove of young men who do not work (Harthouse, Harry Gowan, Richard Carstone, Wrayburn before his reformation), it is because they are cynical and immoral or because they are a burden on somebody else; if you are 'good', and also self-supporting, there is no reason why you should not spend fifty years in simply drawing your dividends. Home life is always enough. And, after all, it was the general assumption of his age. The 'genteel sufficiency', the 'competence', the 'gentleman of independent means' (or 'in easy circumstances') – the very phrases tell one all about the strange, empty dream of the eighteenth- and nineteenth-century middle bourgeoisie. It was a dream of *complete idleness*. Charles Reade conveys its spirit perfectly in the ending of *Hard Cash*. Alfred Hardie, hero of *Hard Cash*, is the typical nineteenth-century novel-hero (public-school style), with gifts which Reade describes as amounting to 'genius'. He is an old Etonian and a scholar of Oxford, he knows most of the Greek and Latin classics by heart, he can box with prize-fighters and win the Diamond Sculls at Henley. He goes through incredible adventures in which, of course, he behaves with faultless heroism, and then, at the age of twenty-five, he inherits a fortune, marries his Julia Dodd and settles down in the suburbs of Liverpool, in the same house as his parents-in-law:

They all lived together at Albion Villa, thanks to Alfred. . . .
Oh, you happy little villa! You were as like Paradise as any
mortal dwelling can be. A day came, however, when your
walls could no longer hold all the happy inmates. Julia
presented Alfred with a lovely boy; enter two nurses and the
villa showed symptoms of bursting. Two months more, and
Alfred and his wife overflowed into the next villa. It was but
twenty yards off; and there was a double reason for the
migration. As often happens after a long separation, Heaven
bestowed on Captain and Mrs Dodd another infant to play
about their knees, etc. etc. etc.

This is the type of the Victorian happy ending – a vision of a huge,
loving family of three or four generations, all crammed together in
the same house and constantly multiplying, like a bed of oysters.
What is striking about it is the utterly soft, sheltered, effortless life that
it implies. It is not even a violent idleness, like Squire Western's. That
is the signficance of Dickens's urban background and his non-
interest in the blackguardly-sporting-military side of life. His
heroes, once they had come into money and 'settled down', would
not only do no work; they would not even ride, hunt, shoot, fight
duels, elope with actresses or lose money at the races. They would
simply live at home in feather-bed respectability, and preferably next
door to a blood-relation living exactly the same life:

The first act of Nicholas, when he became a rich and
prosperous merchant, was to buy his father's old house. As
time crept on, and there came gradually about him a group
of lovely children, it was altered and enlarged; but none of
the old rooms were ever pulled down, no old tree was ever
rooted up, nothing with which there was any association of
bygone times was ever removed or changed.
    Within a stone's-throw was another retreat enlivened by
children's pleasant voices too; and here was Kate . . . the
same true, gentle creature, the same fond sister, the same in
the love of all about her, as in her girlish days.

It is the same incestuous atmosphere as in the passage quoted from
Reade. And evidently this is Dickens's ideal ending. It is perfectly

attained in *Nicholas Nickleby*, *Martin Chuzzlewit* and *Pickwick*, and it is approximated to in varying degrees in almost all the others. The exceptions are *Hard Times* and *Great Expectations* – the latter actually has a 'happy ending', but it contradicts the general tendency of the book, and it was put in at the request of Bulwer Lytton.

The ideal to be striven after, then, appears to be something like this: a hundred thousand pounds, a quaint old house with plenty of ivy on it, a sweetly womanly wife, a horde of children, and no work. Everything is safe, soft, peaceful and, above all, domestic. In the moss-grown churchyard down the road are the graves of the loved ones who passed away before the happy ending happened. The servants are comic and feudal, the children prattle round your feet, the old friends sit at your fireside, talking of past days, there is the endless succession of enormous meals, the cold punch and sherry negus, the feather beds and warming-pans, the Christmas parties with charades and blind man's buff; but nothing ever happens, except the yearly childbirth. The curious thing is that it is a genuinely happy picture, or so Dickens is able to make it appear. The thought of that kind of existence is satisfying to him. This alone would be enough to tell one that more than a hundred years have passed since Dickens's first book was written. No modern man could combine such purposelessness with so much vitality.

By this time anyone who is a lover of Dickens, and who has read as far as this, will probably be angry with me.

I have been discussing Dickens simply in terms of his 'message', and almost ignoring his literary qualities. But every writer, especially every novelist, *has* a 'message', whether he admits it or not, and the minutest details of his work are influenced by it. All art is propaganda. Neither Dickens himself nor the majority of Victorian novelists would have thought of denying this. On the other hand, not all propaganda is art. As I said earlier, Dickens is one of those writers who are felt to be worth stealing. He has been stolen by Marxists, by Catholics and, above all, by Conservatives. The question is, What is there to steal? Why does anyone care about Dickens? Why do *I* care about Dickens?

That kind of question is never easy to answer. As a rule, an aesthetic preference is either something inexplicable or it is so corrupted by non-aesthetic motives as to make one wonder whether the whole of literary criticism is not a huge network of humbug. In Dickens's case the complicating factor is his familiarity. He happens to be one of those 'great authors' who are ladled down everyone's throat in childhood. At the time this causes rebellion and vomiting, but it may have different after-effects in later life. For instance, nearly everyone feels a sneaking affection for the patriotic poems that he learned by heart as a child, *Ye Mariners of England*, the *Charge of the Light Brigade* and so forth. What one enjoys is not much the poems themselves as the memories they call up. And with Dickens the same forces of association are at work. Probably there are copies of one or two of his books laying about in an actual majority of English homes. Many children begin to know his characters by sight before they can even read, for on the whole Dickens was lucky in his illustrators. A thing that is absorbed as early as that does not come up against any critical judgement. And when one thinks of this, one thinks of all that is bad and silly in Dickens – the cast-iron 'plots', the characters who don't come off, the *longueurs*, the paragraphs in blank verse, the awful pages of 'pathos'. And then the thought arises, when I say I like Dickens, do I simply mean that I like thinking about my childhood? Is Dickens merely an institution?

If so, he is an institution that there is no getting away from. How often one really thinks about any writer, even a writer one cares for, is a difficult thing to decide; but I should doubt whether anyone who has actually read Dickens can go a week without remembering him in one context or another. Whether you approve of him or not, he is *there*, like the Nelson Column. At any moment some scene or character, which may come from some book you cannot even remember the name of, is liable to drop into your mind. Micawber's letters! Winkle in the witness-box! Mrs Gamp! Mrs Wititterly and Sir Tumley Snuffim! Todgers's! (George Gissing said that when he passed the Monument it was never of the Fire of London that he thought, always of Todgers's.) Mrs Leo Hunter! Squeers! Silas Wegg and the Decline and Fall-off of the Russian Empire! Miss Mills and the Desert of Sahara! Wopsle acting Hamlet! Mrs Jellyby! Mantalini, Jerry Cruncher, Barkis, Pumblechook, Tracy Tupman, Skimpole, Joe Gargery, Pecksniff – and so it goes on and on. It is not so much a series of books, it is more like a world. And not a purely comic world either, for part of what one remembers in Dickens is his Victorian morbidness and necrophilia and the blood-and-thunder scenes – the death of Sikes, Krook's spontaneous combustion, Fagin in the condemned cell, the women knitting round the guillotine. To a surprising extent all this has entered even into the minds of people who do not care about it. A music-hall comedian can (or at any rate could quite recently) go on the stage and impersonate Micawber or Mrs Gamp with a fair certainty of being understood, although not one in twenty of the audience had ever read a book of Dickens's right through. Even people who affect to despise him quote him unconsciously.

Dickens is a writer who can be imitated, up to a certain point. In genuinely popular literature – for instance, the Elephant and Castle version of *Sweeney Todd* – he has been plagiarized quite shamelessly. What has been imitated, however, is simply a tradition that Dickens himself took from earlier novelists and developed, the cult of 'character', i.e. eccentricity. The thing that cannot be imitated is his fertility of invention not so much of characters, still less of 'situations', as of turns of phrase and concrete details. The outstanding, unmistakable mark of Dickens's writing is the *unnecessary detail*. ... And in all of Dickens's most characteristic passages it is the same. His imagination overwhelms everything, like a kind of weed. Squeers stands up to address his boys, and immediately we are hearing about Bolder's father who was two pounds ten short, and Mobbs's stepmother who took to her bed on hearing that Mobbs wouldn't eat fat and hoped Mr Squeers would flog him into a happier state of mind. Mrs Leo Hunter writes a poem, 'Expiring Frog'; two full stanzas are given. Boffin takes a fancy to pose as a miser, and instantly we are down among the squalid biographies of eighteenth-century misers, with names like Vulture Hopkins and the Rev. Blewberry Jones and chapter headings like 'The Story of the Mutton Pies' and 'The Treasures of a Dunghill'. Mrs Harris, who does not even exist, has more detail piled on her than any three characters in an ordinary novel. Merely in the middle of a sentence we learn, for instance, that her infant nephew has been seen in a bottle at Greenwich Fair, along with the pink-eyed lady, the Prussian dwarf and the living skeleton. Joe Gargery describes how the robbers broke into the house of Pumblechook, the corn and seed merchant – 'and they took his till, and they took his cashbox, and they drinked his wine, and they partook of his wittles, and they slapped his face, and they pulled his nose, and they tied him up to his bedpust, and they give him a dozen, and they stuffed his mouth full of flowering annuals to perwent his crying out'. Once again the unmistakable Dickens touch, the flowering annuals; but any other novelist would only have mentioned about half of these outrages. Everything is piled up and up, detail on detail, embroidery on embroidery. It is futile to object that this kind of thing is rococo – one might as well make the same objection to a wedding-cake. Either you like it or you do not like it. Other nineteenth-century writers, Surtees, Barham, Thackeray, even Marryat, have something of Dickens's profuse, overflowing quality, but none of them on anything like the same scale. The appeal of all these writers now depends partly on period-flavour and though Marryat is still officially a 'boy's writer' and Surtees has a sort of legendary fame among hunting men, it is probable that they are read mostly by bookish people.

Significantly, Dickens's most successful books (not his *best* books) are *The Pickwick Papers*, which is not a novel, and *Hard Times* and *A Tale of Two Cities*, which are not funny. As a novelist his natural fertility greatly hampers him, because the burlesque which he is never able to resist, is constantly breaking into what ought to be serious situations. There is a good example of this in the opening chapter of *Great Expectations*. The escaped convict, Magwitch, has just captured the six-year-old Pip in the churchyard. The scene starts terrifyingly enough, from Pip's point of view. The convict, smothered in mud and with chain trailing from his leg, suddenly starts up among the tombs, grabs the child, turns him upside down and robs his pockets. Then he begins terrorizing him into bringing food and a file:

He held me by the arms in an upright position on the top of the stone, and went on in these fearful terms:

'You bring me, to-morrow morning early, that file and them wittles. You bring the lot to me, at that old Battery over yonder. You do it and you never dare to say a word or dare to make a sign concerning your having seen such a person as me, or any person sumever, and you shall be let to live. You fail, or you go from my words in any partickler, no matter how small it is, and your heart and liver shall be

tore out, roasted and ate. Now, I ain't alone, as you may
think I am. There's a young man hid with me, in comparison
with which young man I am a Angel. That young man
hears the words I speak. That young man has a secret way
pecooliar to himself, of getting at a boy, and at his heart, and
at his liver. It is in wain for a boy to attempt to hide himself
from that young man. A boy may lock his doors, may be
warm in bed, may tuck himself up, may draw the clothes
over his head, may think himself comfortable and safe, but
that young man will softly creep his way to him and tear
him open. I am keeping that young man from harming you
at the present moment, but with great difficulty. I find it
wery hard to hold that young man off of your inside. Now,
what do you say?'

Here Dickens has simply yielded to temptation. To begin with, no
starving and hunted man would speak in the least like that. Moreover,
although the speech shows a remarkable knowledge of the way in
which a child's mind works, its actual words are quite out of tune
with what is to follow. It turns Magwitch into a sort of pantomime
wicked uncle, or, if one sees him through the child's eyes, into an
appalling monster. Later in the book he is to be represented as neither,
and his exaggerated gratitude, on which the plot turns, is to be incredible because of just this speech. As usual, Dickens's imagination
has overwhelmed him. The picturesque details were too good to be
left out. Even with characters who are more of a piece than Magwitch
he is liable to be tripped up by some seductive phrase. Mr Murdstone,
for instance, is in the habit of ending David Copperfield's lessons
every morning with a dreadful sum in arithmetic. 'If I go into a
cheesemonger's shop, and buy four thousand Double Gloucester
cheeses at fourpence halfpenny each, present payment,' it always begins. Once again the typical Dickens detail, the double-Gloucester
cheeses. But it is far too human a touch for Murdstone; he would
have made it five thousand cashboxes. Every time this note is struck,
the unity of the novel suffers. Not that it matters very much, because
Dickens is obviously a writer whose parts are greater than his wholes.
Hs is all fragments, all details – rotten architecture, but wonderful
gargoyles – and never better than when he is building up some charac-

ter who will later on be forced to act inconsistently.

Of course it is not usual to urge against Dickens that he makes his characters behave inconsistently. Generally he is accused of doing just the opposite. His characters are supposed to be mere 'types', each crudely representing some single trait and fitted with a kind of label by which you recognize him. Dickens is 'only a caricaturist' – that is the usual accusation, and it does him both more and less than justice. To begin with, he did not think of himself as a caricaturist, and was constantly setting into action characters who ought to have been purely static. Squeers, Micawber, Miss Mowcher,[1] Wegg, Skimpole, Pecksniff and many others are finally involved in 'plots' where they are out of place and where they behave quite incredibly. They start off as magic-lantern slides and they end by getting mixed up in a third-rate movie. Sometimes one can put one's finger on a single sentence in which the original illusion is destroyed. There is such a sentence in *David Copperfield*. After the famous dinner-party (the one where the leg of mutton was underdone), David is showing his guests out. He stops Traddles at the top of the stairs:

'Traddles,' said I, 'Mr Micawber don't mean any harm, poor fellow: but if I were you I wouldn't lend him anything.'
'My dear Copperfield,' returned Traddles smiling, 'I haven't got anything to lend.'
'You have got a name, you know,' I said.
(chapter 28)

At the place where one reads it this remark jars a little though something of the kind was inevitable sooner or later. The story is a fairly realistic one, and David is growing up; ultimately he is bound to see Mr Micawber for what he is, a cadging scoundrel. Afterwards, of course, Dickens's sentimentality overcomes him and Micawber is made to turn over a new leaf. But from then on, the original Micawber is never quite recaptured, in spite of desperate efforts. As a rule, the 'plot' in which Dickens's characters get entangled is not particu-

---

1 Dickens turned Miss Mowcher into a sort of heroine because the real woman whom he had caricatured had read the earlier chapters and was bitterly hurt. He had previously meant her to play a villainous part. But *any* action by such a character would seem incongruous.

larly credible, but at least it makes some pretence at reality, whereas the world to which they belong is a never-never land, a kind of eternity. But just here one sees that 'only a caricaturist' is not really a condemnation. The fact that Dickens is always thought of as a caricaturist, although he was constantly trying to be something else, is perhaps the surest mark of his genius. The monstrosities that he created are still remembered as monstrosities, in spite of getting mixed up in would-be probable melodramas. Their first impact is so vivid that nothing that comes afterwards effaces it. As with the people one knew in childhood, one seems always to remember them in one particular attitude, doing one particular thing. Mrs Squeers is always ladling out brimstone and treacle, Mrs Gummidge is always weeping, Mrs Gargery is always banging her husband's head against the wall, Mrs Jellyby is always scribbling tracts while her children fall into the area – and there they all are, fixed up for ever like little twinkling miniatures painted on snuffbox lids, completely fantastic and incredible, and yet somehow more solid and infinitely more memorable than the efforts of serious novelists. Even by the standards of his time Dickens was an exceptionally artificial writer. As Ruskin said, he 'chose to work in a circle of stage fire'. His characters are even more distorted and simplified than Smollett's. But there are no rules in novel-writing, and for any work of art there is only one test worth bothering about – survival. By this test Dickens's characters have succeeded, even if the people who remember them hardly think of them as human beings. They are monsters, but at any rate they *exist*.

But all the same there is a disadvantage in writing about monsters. It amounts to this, that it is only certain moods that Dickens can speak to. There are large areas of the human mind that he never touches. There is no poetic feeling anywhere in his books, and no genuine tragedy, and even sexual love is almost outside his scope. Actually his books are not so sexless as they are sometimes declared to be, and considering the time in which he was writing, he is reasonably frank. But there is not a trace in him of the feeling that one finds in *Manon Lescaut, Salammbô, Carmen, Wuthering Heights*. According to Aldous Huxley, D. H. Lawrence once said that Balzac was 'a gigantic dwarf', and in a sense the same is true of Dickens. There are whole worlds which he either knows nothing about or does not wish to mention. Except in a rather roundabout way, one cannot *learn* very much from Dickens. And to say this is to think almost immediately of the great Russian novelists of the nineteenth century. Why is it that Tolstoy's grasp seems to be so much larger than Dickens's – why is it that he seems able to tell you so much more *about yourself*? It is not that he is more gifted, or even, in the last analysis, more intelligent. It is because he is writing about people who are growing. His characters are struggling to make their souls, whereas Dickens's are already finished and perfect. In my own mind Dickens's people are present far more often and far more vividly than Tolstoy's, but always in a single unchangeable attitude, like pictures or pieces of furniture. You cannot hold an imaginary conversation with a Dickens character as you can with, say, Peter Bezoukhov. And this is not merely because of Tolstoy's greater seriousness, for there are also comic characters that you can imagine yourself talking to – Bloom, for instance, or Pécuchet, or even Wells's Mr Polly. It is because Dickens's characters have no mental life. They say perfectly the thing that they have to say, but they cannot be conceived as talking about anything else. They never learn, never speculate. Perhaps the most meditative of his characters is Paul Dombey, and his thoughts are mush. Does this mean that Tolstoy's novels are 'better' than Dickens's? The truth is that it is absurd to make such comparisons in terms of 'better' and 'worse'. If I were forced to compare Tolstoy with Dickens, I should say that Tolstoy's appeal will probably be wider in the long run, because Dickens is scarcely intelligible outside the English-speaking culture; on the other hand, Dickens is able to reach simple people, which Tolstoy is not. Tolstoy's characters can cross a frontier, Dickens's can be portrayed on a cigarette-card. But one is no more obliged to choose between them than between a sausage and a rose. Their purposes barely intersect.

(13–80)

Part Three **Modern Views**

Introduction

The decline in reputation that the novelists of the mid-nineteenth century suffered in the early decades of the twentieth may have affected Dickens less than most, but he was bound to benefit from the revival of interest in the Victorian period and the rehabilitation of its literature which have been so marked in the post-war period. In any reconsideration of Victorianism, Dickens must be taken as one of its dominant and representative figures. The modern reassessment of so variously approachable a writer as Dickens has inevitably been complex in its development, but many of the ways in which we now think about Dickens can be traced back to the publication, in 1941, of two highly influential works: Humphry House's book, *The Dickens World*, and Edmund Wilson's essay, 'Dickens: The Two Scrooges' (collected in the volume *The Wound and the Bow*).

House's book laid the foundations of modern Dickens scholarship. He explicitly dissociated himself from the traditional Dickensianism of enthusiasts preoccupied with identifying the originals of persons and places in the novels and habituated to a selective and essentially nostalgic view of Dickens's fiction. He also aimed to correct the interpretations of Dickens's social thinking by critics like those Marxists of the 1930s who, in his view, had been misleadingly ready to claim Dickens as a kindred spirit. The aim of *The Dickens World* was

to show in a broad and simple way the connexion between what Dickens wrote and the times in which he wrote it, between his reformism and some of the things he wanted reformed, between the attitude to life shown in his books and the society in which he lived.

House took as evidence not only the novels themselves but also Dickens's periodicals, whose value as indications of Dickens's attitudes was thus decisively made clear. House also correlated the fiction with historical fact – demonstrating the topicality of Oliver

Twist's asking for more, for instance, by quoting a dietary approved by the Poor Law Commissioners in 1836 which included (with not very much else) a ration of one and a half pints of gruel a day. Among the many important features of *The Dickens World* (from which an extended extract is given on p. 323) are House's discussion of the often confusing internal chronology of the novels; his assertion that in many things Dickens 'was following rather than leading public opinion'; and, generally, his substitution of sometimes disconcerting conclusions about Dickens's attitudes based on evidence, for the comforting and received distortions of popular misconception and myth.

House would never have claimed that *The Dickens World* offered a complete account of the relations between Dickens's creative life and the society in which he lived, and since its appearance many studies have helped to fill out its picture – most notably, perhaps, the two books by Philip Collins, *Dickens and Crime* (1962) and *Dickens and Education* (1963). What has emerged from inquiries of this kind is the nature and degree of Dickens's involvement in certain aspects of social policy. His interest in penal conditions and reform, for instance, doubtless owes much to his early experiences, but his visiting of prisons and his admiring accompanying of the police on their rounds were not simply the actions of a man at the mercy of his private obsessions: they were an expression of the intense practicality of his nature, always attracted by those areas of social work where there was something immediate and positive to be *done*. Dickens's letters to Miss Burdett Coutts (which were published by Edgar Johnson in 1952) about the home for prostitutes which she financed are concerned with administrative detail and human problems, and are remarkably free from the moralizing that might have been expected from a Victorian (as conventionally understood) on such a subject.

As a result of such work, we now have a fuller and more

accurate picture of the multifarious ways in which Dickens
impinged on the life of his period, and if much more remains to
be done, it is partly because Dickens was a man of such prodigious
energies that it needs a great deal of effort to catch up with him.
The astonishing amount of sheer activity in Dickens's life is
reflected in his letters. Of these no satisfactory or widely available
edition existed until the Pilgrim Edition was begun in 1949 under
the direction of Humphry House (who died in 1955); the first
volume, covering the years from 1820 to 1839, appeared in 1965,
the second, for 1840-41, followed in 1969. The completed edition will
include about twelve thousand letters, and these represent only a
proportion of those Dickens is known to have written, since many
were destroyed by Dickens himself and by others. The style of the
letters themselves is often marked by the intense linguistic vitality
natural to their author.

The beginning of the Pilgrim Edition of the letters is one aspect
of the necessarily gradual provision of the essential materials for
the academic study of Dickens. For such a study, reliable texts of
the novels are needed. John Butt and Kathleen Tillotson complained
in 1957, in the Preface to their *Dickens at Work*, that at that time
'Dickens studies have hardly passed beyond the early
nineteenth-century phase of Shakespeare studies; while the study of
his text seems arrested in the early eighteenth century'. *Dickens at
Work* gave for the first time a detailed analysis of how Dickens
combined the exigencies of serial publication with the disciplines
of art. Using the evidence of manuscripts, proofs and memoranda
(mostly in the Forster collection at the Victoria and Albert Museum,
London), and taking into account such factors as the cover designs
of the serial part-issues, this book demonstrated how much could
be learned about Dickens's intentions and his creative processes by
scholarly investigation. The chapter on *David Copperfield*, in
Dickens at Work, uses the number-plans which Dickens made for
his own convenience in order to provide a month by month

account of the development of the novel's composition.

John Butt and Kathleen Tillotson were also responsible for the inception of the Clarendon Dickens, the first edition of the novels to offer a critical text established by collating all the editions published during Dickens's lifetime. Professor Tillotson's edition of *Oliver Twist*, which appeared in 1966, gives not only a full apparatus of textual variants, but much additional material from prefaces, descriptive headlines, illustrations, and so on. Although the Clarendon Dickens will clearly become, as it proceeds, the authoritative edition of his works, there will still be a need (which it does not attempt to meet) for texts which have comprehensively explanatory notes.

The need for a biography of Dickens that incorporated all that had been established since the discreet revelations of Forster's *Life* was finally met by an American scholar, Edgar Johnson. His *Charles Dickens, His Tragedy and Triumph* (New York, 1952; London, 1953) made extensive use of Dickens's letters and of the periodicals he edited, and drew on much unpublished material. It presents an absorbing and enthusiastically written narrative of Dickens's life in all its ascertainable aspects, in which his association with Ellen Ternan is seen in tolerant perspective. Johnson's criticism of the novels, which is hived off into separate chapters, emphasizes Dickens's force as a critic of his society.

The personal significance of Dickens's attitude to society had been one of the themes of Edmund Wilson's essay. His 'Dickens: The Two Scrooges'[1] has been extremely influential (especially perhaps on subsequent American criticism) partly because it presents a brief biographical account of Dickens in terms of an easily grasped psychological pattern. Wilson began by stating his conviction that the estimate of Dickens held by Chesterton and Shaw was correct: Dickens was 'the greatest dramatic writer that

1 The essay is too long to reprint here in full, and Mr Wilson does not allow its reproduction in part.

the English had had since Shakespeare, and he created the largest and most varied world'. This refusal to discuss Dickens in the accents of apology or concession was in itself a significant factor in his critical rehabilitation. After stressing the persistance of the trauma created by the blacking warehouse episode, Wilson drew attention to the interpolated tales in *The Pickwick Papers* – not because of their literary value, which is negligible, but because their interest in murder, madness and the Marshalsea indicate in an unguarded way the ruling obsessions of Dickens's life. The alternation of the comic and the macabre suggests a dualism which, in Wilson's view, runs through Dickens's whole career, and which was finally to be allegorized in the character of John Jasper, in the unfinished *Edwin Drood*. (Wilson's account of the way this novel was to develop and conclude is speculative, as all accounts must be.) Jasper is outwardly respected and respectable; secretly, he is an opium smoker and a murderer. Wilson maintained that this dual personality was the logical expression of Dickens's own divided nature; apparently accepted and unquestionably successful, he whose childhood had been 'crushed by the cruelty of organized society' was thereby made a rebel against it.

The man of powerful will who finds himself opposed to society must, if he cannot upset it or if his impulse to do so is blocked, feel a compulsion to commit what society regards as one of the capital crimes against itself. With the anti-social heroes of Dostoyevsky, this crime is usually murder or rape; with Dickens it is usually murder.

Wilson thus connected Dickens's feeling of isolated hostility to the prevailing social order with his obsessive interest in those criminals (Bill Sikes, Jonas Chuzzlewit, Bradley Headstone) who transgress the moral order.

Wilson's essay touched many other aspects of Dickens's life and work by the way, and nearly always suggestively. He speaks respectfully of Dickens's symbolism because 'people who like to talk about the symbols of Kafka and Mann and Joyce have been discouraged from looking for anything of the kind in Dickens, and usually have not read him, at least with mature minds'. He credits Dickens with the invention of 'a new literary *genre*. . .: the novel of the social group', which enabled him to convert his melodramatic intrigues into 'devices of artistic dignity'. He stresses the truculence of Dickens's manner towards the Establishment of his day: 'Dickens is one of the very small group of British intellectuals to whom the opportunity has been offered to be taken up by the governing class and who actually declined that honour'. Dickens's case against the governing class, in Wilson's view, was that the people it governed were not real to them; 'none has surpassed Dickens' in showing us those 'human actualities' which figure in politics and economics as mere data and statistics.

A substantial amount of modern criticism of Dickens has consisted of filling in Wilson's outlines and developing his implications. There has, too, been a reaction against Wilson, which claims that his portrait of the artist as a manic-depressive is a serious distortion, or, at the least, a misleading exaggeration. In the modern period, in fact, the range of adopted critical attitudes to Dickens widens spectacularly. This must partly be attributed, of course, to the unprecedented expansion of English studies in the 1950s and 1960s, but it is also due to the exceptionally hospitable nature of Dickens's writing. His fiction has been plausibly discussed in more of the currently available critical dialects than are usually applied to novels. One result of this pluralism of approach has been that the same novel has been made to yield quite different, and indeed incompatible, meanings. Consider, for instance, the following suggestions about the essential significance of *Oliver Twist*. For Arnold Kettle, '. . . the living pattern and conflict of the book. . . is the struggle of the poor against the bourgeois state'; to Graham Greene, 'This world of Dickens is a world without God. . . . In this Manichean world we can believe in evil-doing, but goodness wilts into philanthropy, kindness . . .'; for Steven Marcus, on the other hand, *Oliver Twist* is 'a secular drama of salvation'; A. O. J. Cockshut feels that 'The book is like a continuous and unsuccessful attempt to pin down, externalize and face the overwhelming nightmares of childhood'; J. Hillis Miller suggests that 'The main axis of the nuclear structure of *Oliver Twist* is a fear of exclusion which alternates with a fear of enclosure.' Clearly, Dickens has become a mine with many levels. What these extracts (which have been taken violently and unfairly out of their contexts) tend to have in common with much modern criticism of Dickens is a seriousness, even a solemnity of manner that contrasts strikingly with the more sprightly tone of earlier discussions. But although, in the new climate of academic professionalism, natural successors of Shaw and Orwell have been rare, Dickens has retained his capacity to stimulate good critics to write at their best.

It was partly because 'the adult mind doesn't as a rule find in Dickens a challenge to an unusual and sustained seriousness' that F. R. Leavis felt unable to include most of Dickens in what he defined as the Great Tradition of the English novel. His selection and analysis of *Hard Times* as the one novel which did satisfy the terms of this tradition had the effect of giving it an unaccustomed celebrity. In fact, Dr Leavis's attitude to Dickens has often been misunderstood: *The Great Tradition* itself had no doubt that 'Dickens was a great genius and is permanently among the classics', and an article on *Dombey and Son* (which first appeared in the *Sewanee Review* in 1962) indicates a more open sympathy with Dickens than this critic has often been credited with.

Even so, *Dombey and Son* is a book with a manifest seriousness of intention, and it is to the mature, responsible and prophetic Dickens that the majority of recent critics have felt most drawn.

The orthodox view has become the opposite of the traditional Dickensian's: it is now in the late works that Dickens is felt both to be most relevant to our own age and most truly himself. John Bayley's critical aside about 'the overbearing pretension of the later novels' implies a judgement that has become – at least among professional commentators – a minority opinion. Recent critics have had relatively little to say about Dickens as a celebratory writer; discussions of *The Christmas Carol* and its successors have become almost as infrequent as the festival itself; and Scrooge has done poorly compared with Gradgrind. The earlier novels have often been accommodated by neglecting their comic qualities and by disinterring the buried layers of darker meaning, and have sometimes been treated as if their main interest was to be found in the ways in which they anticipate later works. It has become possible to read entire volumes on Dickens without ever being made aware that he has traditionally been regarded as one of the greatest humorists in English. But, as Lionel Trilling, in a well-known essay on *Little Dorrit*, has philosophically put it:

With a body of works as large and as enduring as that of Dickens, taste and opinion will never be done. They will shift and veer as they have shifted and veered with the canon of Shakespeare, and each generation will have its favourites and make its surprised discoveries.

Humphry House

from 'The Changing Scene', *The Dickens World*   1941 (second edition, 1942)

Dickens lived through the years which saw the making of modern England, and of the middle-class oligarchy which is its government. His boyhood ended with the struggles for Catholic Emancipation and the Reform Bill: his writing life coincided almost exactly with the rule of the Ten-Pound Householders. Middle-class government then meant midde-class reform – the assault on obsolete privileges and procedure, the abolition of restraints on trade, industry and acquisitiveness, and the painful construction of a legal and administrative system adapted to the conditions which gave the middle classes their power.

The technical achievements of the years between 1812 and 1870 had a far greater effect on those who saw them than any such achievements since: railways altered the whole pattern of the country's life more deeply than cars or aeroplanes. For us, accustomed to ever-accelerating change, it is difficult to recover the mood of mixed utilitarian satisfaction and emotional excitement with which railway, telegraph and submarine cable were greeted. Our grandfathers were enthralled by such books as Lardner's on the steam-engine and his *Museum of Science and Art* 'illustrated by engravings on wood'. The cuts of cranks and valves provoked them to something like aesthetic enthusiasm; the titbits of astronomy[1] and geology made them think seriously, and often with disastrous results, about the Creation of the World; the chapters on cables and telegraphs urged them irresistibly to quote the boast of Puck. The more thoughtful perhaps shared something of Carlyle's apprehension, first voiced in 1829,[2] that mechanization of external life might mean a baleful mechanization of

1 See letter of Dickens to Mrs Watson, 1 November 1854: 'I think you will be interested with a controversy between Whewell and Brewster, on the question of the shining orbs about us being inhabited or no. Whewell's book is called, *On the Plurality of Worlds*; Brewster's, *More Worlds than One.* . . . They bring together a vast number of points of great interest in natural philosophy, and some very curious reasoning on both sides, and leave the matter pretty much where it was.' Cf. Charlotte's question to Eleanor in *Barchester Towers*, chapter 19.
2 'Signs of the Times', *Edinburgh Review*, no. 98.

the mind. But all alike, after a first hesitation or resistance, were compelled to accept the new world and the social changes that it brought: all were part of it, and there was no more escape for Dickens than for anybody else.

Some measure of the changes can be made if we compare *Pickwick* with *Our Mutual Friend*. The books are plainly by the same author; but when all allowances have been made for the obvious differences of form, theme, mood and setting, for the influence of Dickens's private life upon his art, for developments in his art itself, it still remains clear that the two books are the produce of different climates. It is sometimes said in discussions of Dickens's technique as novelist that any of his great characters could step out of one book into another without materially disturbing the arrangement of either. But if we try to imagine Sam Weller in *Our Mutual Friend* the limitations of this formal criticism are at once plain. The physique, features and complexion of the characters have changed between the two books almost as much as their clothes: the grimaces of villains have conformed to a new fashion; manners are so altered that one would as little expect that Boffin should get drunk as that John Harmon should fight a duel. We feel that people use knives and forks in a different style. Everybody is more restrained. The eccentrics and monsters in the earlier books walk through a crowd without exciting particular attention: in the latter they are likely to be pointed at in the streets, and are forced into bitter seclusion; social conformity has taken on a new meaning. Silas Wegg and Mr Venus are at odds and ends with their world as Daniel Quilp was not. The middle classes are more self-important, the lower less self-assured. London, though vastly bigger in extent, is smaller in mystery: it has been opened up by the police. The whole scene seems narrower, more crowded, and, in a peculiar way, more stuffy. The very air seems to have changed in quality, and to tax the powers of Sanitary Reform to the uttermost.[1] In *Pickwick* a bad smell was a bad smell; in *Our Mutual Friend* it is a problem.

These changes cannot be attributed to machinery only, nor to any one cause: but the cumulative effect of difference is so striking that it is impossible to understand Dickens without following in some detail the impact of external changes on his work. Chesterton loved to push

1 This was partly caused by the enormous increase in the use of coal; the London fog in *Our Mutual Friend* is thicker and dirtier even than that in *Bleak House*.

him back into the world of Gillray, Rowlandson and Cobbett, to stress that he 'carries on a rank, rowdy, jolly tradition, of men falling off coaches, before the sons of Science and the Great Exhibition began to travel primly on rails – or grooves'. We have already considered some of the reasons why Dickens wrote so much about the Cobbett world; and one or two quotations showing his early conformity to it may perhaps be the best way of pointing his important later changes. Here is an extract from the *Memoirs* of Henry Hunt, written in 1820 or 1821:

I could not avoid observing to myself the contrast between the elegant apartment I was now in and that which I had just quitted in Graystock-place; the name Thistlewood was still tinkling upon the drum of my ear, I having quite forgotten where I had heard it before.

   In a few minutes two gentlemen walked in; the one dressed in a handsome dressing-gown and morocco slippers, the other in a shabby-genteel black. The former addressed me very familiarly by name, saying, that he was Mr Thistlewood, and he begged to introduce his friend Dr Watson.

The Watson family seem to have been generally accepted as shabby-genteel people; and the Doctor's son, when wanted in 1817 by the Home Office for his glorious attempt to capture the Tower of London, appeared in the official description as a full-dress Dickens figure, improved by Cruikshank:

... has a mark or mole with a few hairs on it on his Left Cheek Bone near the Eye, the left Eyelid rather dropping over the Eye, very faint remains of Smallpox in his Face, has a rather wide Mouth, and shows his Teeth (which are very black) when he laughs; he sometimes wore a Brown Great Coat, Black Under Coat, Black Waistcoat, Blue Pantaloons, and Hessian Boots; his Appearance shabby genteel: He formerly lodged in *Hyde Street, Bloomsbury*.[1]

These people obviously have a close likeness in appearance, dress and social position to characters in *Pickwick*, *Oliver Twist*, *Nicholas Nickleby*

1 Home Office Papers, 42, 164.

and *The Old Curiosity Shop*: the language of the descriptions is, abating genius, the language of those books. There is, in fact, a closer likeness between the Watsons and the early Dickens characters in all externals than between the early Dickens characters and the later. It is dangerous to be too exact, but it is clear that in the Forties a different style of person comes on the Dickens scene, and that the scene itself changes. There is a difference of atmosphere between *A Christmas Carol* (1843), which is a story of vague undated benevolence, and *The Chimes* (1844), which is a topical satire. *Martin Chuzzlewit* is uncertain ground; but it is safe to say that in *Dombey and Son* the new style is so far developed as to be unmistakable. The people, places and things become 'modern'.

The general chronology of *Dombey* works out quite well if we assume that the book's plot ended with the writing of it in 1848. Florence was then the mother of a son old enough to talk intelligently about his 'poor little uncle': supposing she was then twenty-one or two, Paul would have been born about 1833[1] and died 1840–41. This fits some of the main episodes that can be dated by historical events. The journey of Dombey and the Major to Leamington happened soon after Paul's death: the London and Birmingham Railway, by which they travelled, was fully opened in September 1838, and the Royal Hotel Leamington, at which they stayed, was pulled down about 1841–2.[2] In describing the Leamington scenes Dickens was obviously drawing on memories of a holiday he had there with Hablôt Browne in the autumn of 1838; and Browne was their illustrator. Mr Carker's death at Paddock Wood station was only possible after 1844, when the branch line was opened from there to Maidstone. The book and the period thus hang together without any serious problems of anachronism. In it there is still a lot from the 1820s. Sol Gills with his decaying, out-of-date business, and even the Dombey firm itself, living on the worn maxim, ill-observed, of a pushing eighteenth-century merchant, are intended to appear as survivals from another age. As a whole the book shows an emotional as well as a practical 'consciousness of living in a world of change', an apprehension of what the changes meant in detail every day, the new

1 He was not weaned when work began at the London end of the Birmingham Railway – April 1834.

2 B. W. Matz, *Dickensian Inns and Taverns*, pp. 134 ff.

quality of life they brought. *Dombey*, more than any of his major works, shows how quickly and surely Dickens could sense the mood of his time, and incorporate new sensations in imaginative literature.

The new mood and atmosphere are very largely caused by the railways: the publication of the book coincided with the railway mania of the middle Forties.[1] It would be hard to exaggerate the effect of those years on English social life. Practically the whole country was money-mad; the public attitude to investment was quite altered, and it then first became clear that Joint Stock companies, however imperfectly managed, were certain to become a permanent and influential feature of finance. Railway works helped to absorb the unemployed and so to remove the fear of revolution. The growth of home consumption was enormously accelerated by improved transport: diet, furniture, fireplaces and all the physical appurtenances of life changed character more rapidly; the very landscape was given a new aesthetic character – even perhaps a new standard[2] – by embankments, cuttings and viaducts. But, above all, the scope and tempo of individual living were revolutionized, even for a workman and his family, on a Parliamentary train.

These vast and various changes were, of course, spread over a considerable period: but the years between 1844 and 1848 brought them dramatically into public notice, and saw the climax of a process begun in the later twenties. Dickens had been prompt to record in unobtrusive ways the earlier impact of railways on his world. One characteristic attitude found expression in Mr Weller's well-known outburst in *Master Humphrey's Clock* against the 'unconstitootional inwaser o' privileges... a nasty, wheezin', creakin', gaspin', puffin', bustin'

1 The peak year for the authorization of new lines by Parliament was 1846, with 4538 miles; and for the opening of new lines for traffic 1848, with 1182 miles, of which 604 had been authorized in 1845 and 403 in 1946. These figures are for the whole of the United Kingdom. *Punch's Almanack* for 1846 is the only one based entirely on a railway motif.
2 It is hardly fanciful to associate the neater hedging and ditching of the middle and later Victorian age with the necessary primness of railway works. More scientific farming played its part; but there was also a new pride in neatness for its own sake, which abolished the tangled hedgerows of Constable.

... only ten or twelve
Strokes of havoc unselve
    The sweet especial scene.

monster, always out o' breath, with a shiny green-and-gold back, like a unpleasant beetle in that 'ere gas magnifier'. Dickens also used the contrast between coach and train in the essay he wrote when giving up the editorship of *Bentley's Miscellany* in 1839, and was

led insensibly into an anticipation of those days to-come when mail-coach guards shall no longer be judges of horse-flesh – when a mail-coach guard shall never even have seen a horse – when stations shall have superseded stables, and corn shall have given place to coke. 'In those dawning times,' thought I, 'exhibition rooms shall teem with portraits of Her Majesty's favourite engine, with boilers after Nature by future Landseers. . . .'[1]

It is interesting to find him so early (and in an essay mainly implying regret) taking it for granted even in a joke that railways would be everywhere victorious. Yet their comparatively small development combined with his own retrospective habit prevented mention of them in his major works. There is little railway in *Martin Chuzzlewit* (1843–5)[2] – there is a lot of comic and melodramatic business with coaches and chaises in the Pickwick style – but *Dombey*, written in the mania years, is full of it. It is first the ambition and then the life of fireman Toodle; it is the Car of Juggernaut as seen by *Punch*, with red eyes, bleared and dim, in the daylight, which licked up Carker's 'stream of life with its fiery heat, and cast his mutilated fragments in the air'. 'Express comes through at four, sir. – It don't stop.'

The first railway journey fully described in Dickens is that of Dombey and the Major on their way to Leamington. They started from Euston, where Hardwick's gateway 'exhibiting the Grecian Doric upon a scale hitherto unattempted in modern times', not yet obscured by buildings round about it nor centralized by miles of solid building to the North, seemed indeed a monumental boundary to the town and an invitation to adventure beyond. To contemporaries the station was a matter for pride and curiosity:

1 In fact the railways caused a great increase in the number of horses, and a considerable increase, too, in horse-snobbery.
2 It would be interesting to know how much truth there was in Mrs Gamp's account of the many miscarriages caused by railway-travelling. It was believed that trains induced 'suicidal delirium' in nervous people.

On passing within this gateway, we feel at once that as the the
the mode of conveyance is different, so is the place. We are
not within the narrow precincts of an inn-yard, jostled by
porters and ostlers, and incommoded by luggage; everything
is on a large scale. Yet one's old associations are disturbed by
the sight of men in uniform keeping strict 'watch and ward',
and by the necessary yet rigid exactness of all the
arrangements. . . . 'First' and 'second' class passengers have
their different entrances, and their separate booking desks;
and on passing through the building have to produce their
tickets as passports into the covered yard where the trains
lie.[1]

Dombey travelled, as was then common, in his own carriage fastened
to a flat truck. This comfortable independence of the gentry had its
dangers no less than the inconveniences which Bagstock found; but it
persisted for many years, and well on in the Fifties Dr Dionysius
Lardner had to include among his rules for travellers: 'If you travel
with your private carriage, do not sit in it on the railway. Take your
place by preference in one of the regular railway carriages.'

Dombey and Bagstock apparently went right through to Birmingham (instead of leaving the train, as they might have done, at Rugby
or Coventry), and drove down to Leamington from there. This made
it possible for Dickens to extend his description of the travelling itself;
and in doing so he established a standard, almost a formula, for such
writing, which he followed several times later. The amount of observation he compresses into a few paragraphs is amazing. Some is of
what we have all wondered at from childhood – the 'objects close at
hand and almost in the grasp, ever flying from the traveller' contrasted with the slow movement of 'the deceitful distance'; the
sensation of whirling backwards in a tunnel; the indifference of the
train to weather; the drippings from a hydrant spout. The rhythm of
the wheels he tried to catch in a rather blatant theme: 'Away, with a
shriek, and a roar, and a rattle', too often repeated; but in fact he
catches it far more subtly and with brilliant success in the lists of
things and scenes which the train passes; building on a fairly regular
anapaestic base, he manages by many variations to convey those

shifts and suspensions of beat caused in fact on a railway by passing points and crossings, by shorter lengths of rail and by a slight difference, perhaps, in the fixing of the chairs. The thing must be read aloud. Some of the description belongs to an early astonishment which we can never recapture; such, for instance, is the engineering-geological interest in cuttings – 'through the chalk, through the mould, through the clay, through the rock' – which has so large a place in the popular railway literature of the time,[1] and focused in particular upon the works at Tring and Blisworth on the Birmingham line.

The method of the description as a whole is to combine the more immediate effects of speed upon the sight and hearing – 'massive bridges crossing up above, fall like a beam of shadow an inch broad, upon the eye' – with a quick kaleidoscopic view of passing scenes,[2] which compel in their succession a number of social contrasts. Things seen from a carriage window enforced once more the gravity of the 'condition of England question'. The homes of the Two Nations might be seen as if from a single viewpoint, yet in their own settings. And on such a journey as this, which passed at least through the fringes of the Black Country, the southerner looked out with new surprise upon the industrial landscape. . . .

The scenery and mood of *Dombey* belong to the Railway Age and the London townscape, too, is transformed: it is in London that Dickens's pulse must be taken. The very office of 'The firm of Dombey and Son, Wholesale, Retail and for Exportation' has failed to keep his attention; many details in it are certainly described, but they are dead – hardly a reader would remember them. All his passionate interest in office furniture and routine, ledgers and rulers and ink, which leaves a trail of immortal offices through others of his books, has here declined into perfunctory humdrum. The focus of his attention has shifted from the well-known scenes of his youth to the new

1 e.g. Lardner's books, George Measom's illustrated Guides, Smiles's *Life of George Stephenson*, and *Our Iron Roads*, by Frederick S. Williams.
2 This is the method used also in *A Flight* (*Household Words*, vol. 3, 30 August 1851), which describes a journey by SER from London to Folkestone. The route was then: London Bridge, New Cross, Croydon, Reigate, Tunbridge, Ashford. The line: hrough Sevenoaks was not built. And see *Our Mutual Friend*, book 4, chapter 11.

London of his manhood. The focus is on Stuccovia, the suburbs and the terminus districts. The Dombey house 'between Portland Place and Bryanston Square' is the first of a series of dreary mansions continued in the houses of Merdle and Boffin. The relevant businessmen no longer lived over their offices; and Dickens, moving west, through Regency Bloomsbury towards Belgravia, was moving in his art towards the problem of boredom. How was dullness to be enforced without being dull? One of his answers is the beginning of chapter 21 of *Little Dorrit*.

It has often been debated by Dickensians whether Dickens 'loved' London or not. An anonymous writer some years ago tried to answer part of this curious and complex question as follows:[1]

If we are thinking of the real London, it is plain that such a thoroughly Philistine Radical as Dickens, who cared not twopence for history, who perceived chiefly the Tite Barnacles at St Stephen's, 'wiglomeration' at Westminster and the stench of rotting corpses in the City churches, was deprived of the most obvious reasons for loving it. No ancient city is a particularly lovable place to a keen reformer with a strong taste for police work. But the truth is probably that London got less and less lovable to him as he grew older, for it was continually losing the features he cared for most. Nooks of tranquillity; such naïve pleasures as circuses, cheap waxworks and melodramas; tavern life and the leisure to enjoy it; racy and contrasting types; queer trades, quaint shops and the suggestive melancholy of decay – these things were being pulverized by machinery. The London of *Our Mutual Friend* is grimmer and drabber than the London of *Pickwick*, and Dickens clearly enjoys it less.

But the effects of machinery were very various. The Thames steamboats, for instance, started in 1814, were intensely popular with the public of the thirties, and definitely belonged to the London of Dickens's youth. In the *Sketches* they are a normal instrument of pleasure, opening up a London which neither the travellers nor

1 *The Times Literary Supplement*, 5 June 1924, reviewing *The London of Charles Dickens*, by E. Beresford Chancellor.

Dickens thought of as grim, drab, tranquil, or decaying. It is not impossible that but for the steamboats Dickens himself might never have begun to be interested in the waterside; and it is certain that their coming on the Thames was regarded by lower- and middle-class Londoners as an extension of their resources in leisure. Even Ruth Pinch, who haunts most memories in Fountain Court, had 'never half so good a stroll as down among the steam-boats on a bright morning'; and Tom himself, straight from the peace of Wiltshire, found new delights for his wondering eyes in the turmoil at the starting of the 'Ankwerks package'. The London even of Dickens's retrospection was partly mechanized; and he enjoyed it.

Nor is regret the prominent tone of his many descriptions of changing London in *Dombey* and afterwards. The London of *Dombey* is being altered chiefly by the railways. It is the London of the forties, where Tennyson and Carlyle used to walk together at night, and Carlyle raved against the suburbs as a 'black jumble of black cottages where there used to be pleasant fields', and they would both agree that it was growing into 'a strange chaos of odds and ends, this London'.[1] Dickens did not rave; he observed the chaos in ways that implied his comment: here is his description of the ambiguous belt on the northern side, where he put the house of John and Harriet Carker:

The second home is on the other side of London, near to where the busy great north road of bygone days is silent and almost deserted, except by wayfarers who toil along on foot. ... The neighbourhood in which it stands has as little of the country to recommend it, as it has of the town. It is neither of the town nor country. The former, like the giant in his travelling boots, has made a stride and passed it, and has set his brick-and-mortar heel a long way in advance; but the intermediate space between the giant's feet, as yet, is only blighted country, and not town; and, here, among a few tall chimneys belching smoke all day and night, and among the brick-fields and the lanes where turf is cut, and where the fences tumble down, and where the dusty nettles grow, and where a scrap or two of hedge may yet be seen, and where

1 *Tennyson: A Memoir*, by Hallam, Lord Tennyson, vol. 1, p. 267.

the bird-catcher still comes occasionally, though he swears
every time to come no more – this second home is to be
found.
(chapter 33)

And he notes the jerrybuilders' work as 'a disorderly crop of beginnings of mean houses, rising out of the rubbish, as if they had been
unskilfully sown there'. A similar tract of muddled territory in the
fifties or early sixties on the south side is described in *Our Mutual
Friend*, book 2, chapter 1:

The schools ... were down in that district of the flat
country tending to the Thames, where Kent and Surrey
meet, and where the railways still bestride the market-
gardens that will soon die under them. ... They were in a
neighbourhood which looked like a toy neighbourhood taken
in blocks out of a box by a child of particularly incoherent
mind, and set up anyhow; here, one side of a new street;
there, a large solitary public-house facing nowhere; here,
another unfinished street already in ruins; there, a church;
here, an immense new warehouse; there, a dilapidated old
country villa; then, a medley of black ditch, sparkling
cucumber-frame, rank field, richly cultivated kitchen-garden,
brick viaduct, arch-spanned canal, and disorder of frowsiness
and fog. As if the child had given the table a kick and gone
to sleep.

The counterparts of this creeping expansion across the fields are the
sudden changes closer in, which are directly the railway's doing:
within the short life of little Paul the whole Camden Town district
was transformed:

There was no such place as Stagg's Gardens. It had vanished
from the earth. Where the old rotten summerhouses once
had stood, palaces now reared their heads, and granite
columns of gigantic girth opened a vista to the railway world
beyond. The miserable waste ground, where the refuse
matter had been heaped of yore, was swallowed up and
gone; and in its frowsy stead were tiers of warehouses,
crammed with rich goods and costly merchandise. The old

by-streets now swarmed with passengers and vehicles of
every kind; the new streets that had stopped disheartened in
the mud and waggon-ruts, formed towns within themselves,
originating wholesome comforts and conveniences belonging
to themselves, and never tried nor thought of until they
sprung into existence. Bridges that had led to nothing, led to
villas, gardens, churches, healthy public walks. The carcasses
of houses, and beginnings of new thoroughfares, had started
off upon the line at steam's own speed, and shot away into
the country in a monster train.
(chapter 15)

It is interesting to compare this reformer's admiration for what had
been done with the plain delight of the earlier description of Camden
Town in chapter 6; the district had then just been rent by the first
shock of the railway earthquake which produced 'a hundred thousand
shapes and substances of incompleteness, wildly mingled out of their
places'. The contrast is not between anything old and interesting and
beautiful with the prosaic new which has replaced it, but between the
process of change and the achievement. The process truly fascinated
Dickens, the achievement merely wins sober moral approval; his
love of everything strange and confused had splendid scope in the odd
lines and shapes and disorders, the disruption of the normal visual
pattern, caused by large public works; even when 'Our School' had
gone, fascination came before regret:

We went to look at it, only this last Midsummer, and found
that the Railway had cut it up root and branch. A great
trunk-line had swallowed the play-ground, sliced away the
schoolroom, and pared off the corner of the house; which,
thus curtailed of its proportions, presented itself, in a green
stage of stucco, profilewise towards the road, like a forlorn
flat-iron without a handle, standing on end.[1]

To the railways also must partly be attributed the greater uniformity of manners which becomes apparent in Dickens's later books. It
was said as early as 1844:

1 *Household Words*, Saturday, 11 October 1851.

We cannot help noticing the visible, and in general beneficial, influence of railroad travelling upon public manners. . . . The bringing various ranks and classes of mankind into more familiar intercourse and better humour with each other – the emancipation of the fair sex, and particularly of the middle and higher classes, from the prohibition from travelling in public carriages, which with the majority was a prohibition from travelling at all – the opportunities, so frequently improved, of making agreeable acquaintances – the circulation, as it were, of the current coin of the intellect – and the general tone of mutual frankness and civility so observable in railroad travellers, and *so new in the English character*, are producing rapid and important effects – and it seems as if we might say of this new *art* – as of the old – 'Emollit mores, nec sinit esse feros'.[1]

Dr Arnold remarked, as he watched a train on the Rugby line: 'I rejoice to see it, and think that feudality is gone for ever.'[2] But the mixing of the classes hardly extended to the poor: the third-class accommodation was scandalous, and the introduction of Parliamentary trains, intended to give the poor greater facilities, in fact gave statutory sanction to a social distinction which the companies had already established. It was regarded as a startling innovation when, as late as 1872, the Midland began to run third-class carriages on all trains. There is no description of a third-class journey in all Dickens: when his poor people travel by train, they do so generally in the company of 'their betters', who apparently pay the fares. The mixing of the classes was of the upper with the middle, and of the various sections of the middle class with each other: and this reflected the general process of readjustment that was taking place between *Pickwick* and *Our Mutual Friend*.[3]

A great deal has been written and said about Dickens as a writer for 'the people'. Yet his chief public was among the middle and lower-middle classes, rather than among the proletarian mass. His mood and

1 *Quarterly Review*, vol. 74, pp. 250–51, footnote.
2 Quoted by Mona Wilson, *Early Victorian England*, vol. 2, p. 291.
3 'The peer face to face with the farmer and the merchant,' said Harriet Martineau, 'and the mechanic face to face with mountain and forest and sea': *History*, book 6, chapter 17.

idiom were those of the class from which he came, and his morality throve upon class distinctions even when it claimed to supersede them. He belonged to the generation which first used the phrase 'the great unwashed' and provided a Chadwick to scrub the people clean. His 'class' character was well described by *Blackwood's* in June 1855:

We cannot but express out conviction that it is to the fact that he represents a class that he owes his speedy elevation to the top of the wave of popular favour. He is a man of very liberal sentiments – an assailer of constituted wrongs and authorities – one of the advocates in the plea of Poor versus Rich, to the progress of which he has lent no small aid in his day. But he is, notwithstanding, perhaps more distinctly than any other author of the time, a *class* writer, the historian and representative of one circle in the many ranks of our social scale. Despite their descents into the lowest class, and their occasional flights into the less familiar ground of fashion, it is the air and breath of middle-class respectability which fills the books of Mr Dickens.

It should hardly be necessary to stress the substantial truth of this judgement; but Dickens has so often been claimed as popular in other senses – by Chesterton as if he were the leader of a kind of peasants' revolt in Bloomsbury; by Mr Jackson as if his heart were really devoted to the uniting of the workers of the world – that some insistence on it here, in addition to what has already been implied in other chapters, must be forgiven.

   Many misunderstandings have been caused by the fact that Dickens himself so often and in so many voices proclaimed the gospel that class distinctions do not matter so much as common humanity, nor rank so much as virtue. In his speeches he loved to quote:

The rank is but the guinea stamp,
The man's the gowd for a' that.
(Robert Burns, *For a' that and a' that*)

In one speech (1844) he quoted 'the words of a great living poet, who is one of us, and who uses his great gifts, as he holds them in trust, for the general welfare –

Howe'er it be, it seems to me,
    'Tis only noble to be good.
True hearts are more than coronets,
    And simple faith than Norman blood.'
(Alfred, Lord Tennyson, *Lady Clara Vere de Vere*, vi)

But that he *could* make such quotations, as he did, to audiences of working men, without the slightest trace of self-consciousness or condescension, only shows the confidence he had in his own class position. In the same speech in which he made the Tennyson quotation he also said: 'Differences of wealth, of rank, of intellect, we know there must be, and we respect them.' Sentiments like that of Tennyson so frequent in Victorian literature, have their origin more in the assertion by the bourgeois of his essential similarity to the aristocrat than in any levelling denial of all differences everywhere. The English aristocracy, for centuries recruited from the middle classes, was forced into still closer cultural and social contact with them in the generation after 1832: only then began those interminable controversies about what a gentleman is, and the countless jokes about snobs. Compared with Thackeray and most of the *Punch* circle, for instance, Dickens steered through these dangers handsomely.

The snob problem was not acute before the Forties. In Dickens's earlier books the strata of class are different from those of the later. Even those *Sketches* which turn on counter-jumping treat it rather as a legitimate and intelligible sport than as a social menace. Mr Pickwick thought of himself as a gentleman, but he slides quite easily up and down a considerable distance on the social scale: he would gladly have met the Cheerybles, who did not think of themselves as gentlemen, on equal terms, without needing to exploit his benevolence. The important thing is that people like Pickwick, Mr Garland and the Cheerybles in the positively good camp, others like Nupkins, Slammer and Benjamin Allen among the neutrals, though not without class-consciousness, are quite without class pedantry. The same is true of nearly all the characters in *Martin Chuzzlewit*, though they are mostly bourgeois.[1] The predominant class theme in these novels is benevolence towards the poor and the satirization, as in Miss Mon-

1 An exception must be made of the incidental account of the 'lofty family' of the brass and copper founder in chapter 9, which foreshadows later developments.

flathers, of its opposite: class is treated more as a problem in morals than in manners. Only in *Nicholas Nickleby* among the early novels is the question of manners and style of life at all prominent: the heavy attack on the more bounderish symptoms of aristocracy is perhaps of less importance than the unfortunate-gentlewoman tone of Mrs Nickleby and the acute sensibility of such people as Miss Knag and the Kenwigses to the trials and ambiguities of their social position: but even in these there is nothing that might not have been described in the eighteenth century.

The general vagueness about class distinctions in these books has sometimes been attributed to a supposed deficiency in young Dickens's knowledge of the world; but Dickens's 18 was most men's 25, and in his work in Doctors' Commons and Parliament and in miscellaneous reporting all over the country he must have had unusually good opportunities of observing all the details of social difference; and *David Copperfield* is reason enough for supposing that he did observe them. But why were they not used till 1849–50? The answer seems to be that the social atmosphere of the forties led him to revise his pattern of interpretation; and that as the shifting and mingling of classes became more *apparent* in the habits of London society he was better able to understand the implications of what he had observed in earlier years. In his own work this shifting is first plain in *Dombey and Son*.

Dombey himself is the first full-length Dickens businessman to be solemnly self-conscious about his 'station and its duties', and a good deal of his pride is class-pride. 'I beg,' he says to Edith, 'that Mrs Granger's very different experiences may now come to the instruction of Mrs Dombey.' He plays his wealth against Granger's family and speaks of Edith's 'worldly advancement' in her second marriage. He differs from businessmen like Pickwick, Brownlow, the Cheerybles, and the Chuzzlewits not only in living far more expensively, but in the importance he attaches to doing so. His father had probably been the first to break away from the Chuzzlewit set, and he is the first to aim at the Skewtons's: but the only kind of conquest he recognizes is assimilation. Historically, he represents the process of taming the aristocrats till they are fit for bourgeois society: he is successful only through his daughter, which is as it should be. Dickens originally set himself in Dombey a problem in personal psychology: he did not make it very interesting; but in proportion as he failed to make convincing the workings of Dombey's mind he gave more attention to the money-class context in which they were expressed. The effectiveness of his later portraits of middle-class snobs – Merdles, Podsnaps, Veneerings, and the rest – is largely achieved by the deliberate identification of the whole personality with the context.

Dickens was attempting to define within the middle classes some such boundary as he had already accepted in the lower between the respectable and the low. In the last resort he shared Magwitch's belief that money and education can make a 'gentleman', that birth and tradition count for little or nothing in the formation of style. The final wonder of *Great Expectations* is that in spite of all Pip's neglect of Joe and coldness towards Biddy and all the remorse and self-recrimination that they caused him, he is made to appear at the end of it all a really better person than he was at the beginning. It is a remarkable achievement to have kept the reader's sympathy throughout a snob's progress. The book is the clearest artistic triumph of the Victorian bourgeoisie on its own special ground. The expectations lose their greatness, and Pip is saved from the grosser dangers of wealth; but by the end he has gained a wider and deeper knowledge of life, he is less rough, better spoken, better read, better mannered; he has friends as various as Herbert Pocket, Jaggers and Wemmick; he has earned in his business abroad enough to pay his debts, he has become third partner in a firm that 'had a good name, and worked for its profits, and did very well'. Who is to say that these are not advantages? Certainly not Dickens. But he shirks the implications of the reconciliation with Joe and Biddy: there is one emotional scene with friendliness all round, which shows that in spite of his new accent and new manners Pip is the same decent little fellow after all: but what if he had had no Herbert to fall back on, and had been forced to build his fortunes again from scratch in the old village with Gargerys and Wopsles? Dickens does not face this: he takes Pip's new class position as established, and whisks him off to the East, where gentlemen grow like mushrooms. Yet we do not feel that this is artistically wrong, as the final marriage to Estella is wrong:[1] for the book is the sincere, uncritical expression of a time when the whole class-drift was upward

1 The ending was altered to suit Bulwer Lytton, but only 'from and after Pip's return to Joe's, and finding his little likeness there'. Pip's success abroad was thus in the original scheme (Forster, book 9, ch. 3).

and there was no reason to suppose that it would ever stop being so. The social ideals of Pip and Magwitch differ only in taste. Though Pip has shuddered at the convict for being coarse and low, he consoles him on his death-bed with the very thought that first fired and then kept alive his own love for Estella: 'You had a child. . . . She is a lady and very beautiful.' . . . As things were he was a good pin to prick Pip's conceit, but if he himself had come into a fortune, he would have been just as nasty about it as Pip in his own way; and his way might have been worse.

Great Expectations is the perfect expression of a phase of English society: it is a statement, to be taken as it stands, of what money can do, good and bad; of how it can change and make distinctions of class; how it can pervert virtue, sweeten manners, open up new fields of enjoyment and suspicion. The mood of the book belongs not to the imaginary date of its plot, but to the time in which it was written; for the unquestioned assumptions that Pip can be transformed by money and the minor graces it can buy, and that the loss of one fortune can be repaired on the strength of incidental gains in voice and friends, were only possible in a country secure in its internal economy, with expanding markets abroad: this could hardly be said of England in the twenties and thirties.

Pip's acquired 'culture' was an entirely bourgeois thing: it came to little more than accent, table manners and clothes. In these respects a country gentleman with an estate in a remoter part of England would probably have been, even at Queen Victoria's accession, more like the neighbouring farmers than like Mr Dombey. The process of diffusing standard 'educated', London and Home Counties, speech as the norm expected of a gentleman was by no means complete: its rapid continuance through the Dickens period was an essential part of the increasing social uniformity between the middle and upper classes, helped on by the development of the 'public' schools.[1]

We are told that Pip 'read' a great deal, and that he enjoyed it; but

---

1 It is interesting that there is no description of such a school anywhere in Dickens, though he describes so many different kinds of private school, and sent his own sons to Eton. The extension of the term 'public school' to an increasing number of boarding schools was a process of the forties. (See, for instance, McCulloch's *Account of the British Empire*, 3rd edn, 1847, vol. 2, p. 329.) It was, of course, the most influential expression of the 'gentleman' idea.

we do not know what he read, or how it affected his mind, or what kind of pleasures he got from it. He knew enough about Shakespeare and acting to realize that Mr Wopsle turned Waldengarver was ridiculous; but what other delights he found in theatre-going in his prosperous days we are left to judge for ourselves; painting and music certainly had no large part in his life. People like Pip, Herbert Pocket and Traddles have no culture but domestic comfort and moral decency. They are sensitive, lovable and intelligent, but their normal activities are entirely limited to a profession and a fireside. When one of their kind extends his activities beyond this range it is in the direction of 'social work', and even that is likely to be governed by his profession, as Allan Woodcourt is a good doctor, and Mr Milvey a good parson. David Copperfield's other activity is to write novels like *Great Expectations* and *David Copperfield*: so we come full circle.

David, of course, gives the clearest view of Dickens's social position, and it is very clear indeed. The shame and horror of manual work which runs through chapter 11 was even something less than Dickens confessed to Forster he had felt himself:

I became, at ten years old, a little labouring hind in the
service of Murdstone and Grinby. . . . There were three or
four of us, counting me. . . . No words can express the secret
agony of my soul as I sunk into this companionship. . . . I
worked from morning until night, with common men and
boys, a shabby child. . . . I might easily have been, for any
care that was taken of me, a little robber or a little vagabond.
. . . That I suffered in secret and that I suffered exquisitely,
no one ever knew but I. . . . But I kept my own counsel,
and I did my work. I knew from the first, that, if I could not
do my work as well as any of the rest, I could not hold
myself above slight and contempt. I soon became at least as
expeditious and as skilful as either of the other boys. Though
perfectly familiar with them, my conduct and manner were
different enough from theirs to place a space between us.
They and the men generally spoke of me as 'the little gent',
or 'the young Suffolker'. . . . Mealy Potatoes uprose once,
and rebelled against my being so distinguished; but Mick
Walker settled him in no time.

These sentences are scattered over ten pages or so; but bringing them together in this way causes no distortion of emphasis. The emphasis is equally clear in David's relations with the Peggottys: for all his friendliness he is never anything but 'Mas'r Davy'. The friendliness exists not so much in spite of class barriers as because it derives its peculiar quality from crossing, without ignoring them.

The class problem obviously becomes most acute when sexual love attempts to cross the boundaries. The calf-love of Kit for Miss Nell, resolved by death, is nothing beside the love of Gill Davis, in *The Perils of Certain English Prisoners*[1] for Miss Maryon:

I well knew what an immense and hopeless distance there
was between me and Miss Maryon; I well knew that I was no
fitter company for her than I was for the angels; I well
knew that she was as high above my reach as the sky over
my head; and yet I loved her. What put it in my low heart
to be so daring ... I am unable to say; still, the suffering to
me was just as great as if I had been a gentleman. I suffered
agony – agony. I suffered hard, and I suffered long.

'Her poor, old, faithful, humble soldier' ends, unmarried, as a kind of domestic pensioner to the lady when she has long been the wife of Admiral Sir George Carton, Baronet.

But the typical situation is when the social position of the sexes is reversed. Dickens twice treated at length the theme of the gentleman falling for the common girl, in *David Copperfield* and *Our Mutual Friend*; he skirmished round it a third time in *Little Dorrit*. Steerforth's seduction of Emily is prepared for by his slick dictum about the lower classes:

They are not to be expected to be as sensitive as we are.
Their delicacy is not to be shocked, or hurt very easily. They
are wonderfully virtuous, I dare say. Some people contend
for that, at least; and I am sure I don't want to contradict
them. But they have not very fine natures, and they may be
thankful that, like their coarse, rough skins, they are not
easily wounded.
(chapter 20)

1 Christmas Story, *Household Words*, vol. 16, 1857. The first chapter and the third, from which this extract comes, were by Dickens.

The contempt of the Steerforth group for the Peggotty group is thrown into melodramatic relief in chapter 32 when David takes Mr Peggotty to the Steerforth house. The lower classes are there plainly shown to be emotionally sensitive as well as virtuous; but Peggotty's first and sincere intention is to get Emily married to a man he thinks a scoundrel; his prepared answers to Mrs Steerforth's objections are 'Raise her up' and 'Teach her better'. Emily is meanwhile justifying his faith in her by chatting colloquially to boatmen's children on the Italian shore. 'The young woman,' said Littimer, 'was very improvable, and spoke the languages; and wouldn't have been known for the same country person.' Everything, in fact, shows Emily worthy to become the lady she hoped to be. Even Pamela only did better in being more cunning.

The likeness to Pamela is closer in Lizzie Hexham, who enhances her attractiveness and her virtue by running away; but Eugene Wrayburn is more interesting and complex than Steerforth. In place of the glamour of school heroics there is the glamour of parasitic culture. It needs assault, battery and all but drowning to bring him to the point of proposing marriage: Lizzie only gets a rather damaged gentleman, but even he is a prize. It is impossible not to take the voice of Twemlow, in the last chapter of *Our Mutual Friend*, as the voice of Dickens:

> If this gentleman's feelings of gratitude, of respect, of
> admiration, induced him (as I presume they did) to marry
> this lady ... I think he is the greater gentleman for the
> action, and makes her the greater lady. I beg to say that
> when I use the word gentleman, I use it in the sense in
> which the degree may be attained by any man.

But the application is solely to Eugene: and how can any action of his make a 'greater lady' of a girl whose moral superiority to him has been hammered in with such unremitting emphasis, except on the assumption that she gains in status by becoming his wife?

Two things are interesting in this speech: its obvious sincerity and its obvious sophistry. Twemlow's ingenious phrasing very imperfectly conceals a sort of satisfaction in the fact that Eugene is really doing a very generous thing in marrying Lizzie, and that she is doing very well for herself by marrying him. This satisfaction is based on the acceptance of existing class distinctions in general, while allowing that in particular cases the right thing is to cross them: they are not ignored as irrelevant, otherwise all the relish in the crossing would be lost. It was essential to the strength of a large bourgeoisie like the English to admit the principle of recruitment from below as a counterpart to the claim to provide recruits for the aristocracy; but such recruitment had to be controlled by a certain standard of taste and morals: money alone was not enough.

A great part of Dickens's later social satire is directed against people who believe that genteel territory can be entered with no passport but wealth; it is a common enough theme, but it was of peculiar importance in the mid-Victorian Age, and Dickens's attitude to it can only be understood by looking at economic developments from the forties to the seventies. In a previous chapter we saw the immense importance he attached to money in everything he wrote, and noted then that in the earlier novels finance is very individualistic, and that the typical bad rich man is the usurer. Beneath his hatred of people like Ralph Nickleby, Gride and Quilp is the ancient moral feeling that usury is wrong because it enables people to make money without having to work for it, and that the power conferred by money earned in this way is the more hateful for its illegitimacy. Dickens was very careful, even when he was detaching his benevolent rich men from the immediate economic struggle, to insist that they *had*, at least in the past, worked for what they spent so generously. It is immaterial that he did so in an unconvincing way: the important thing is that people like the Cheerybles and Pickwick represent a stage of capitalist development in which the capitalist is normally an active member of a fairly small firm – that is also what Nicholas, Pip and Arthur Clennam become – a man whose work bears a relation to his income similar to that of professional people to theirs. Such people as this (together with the professionals) were the basis of the 'respectable' middle class that Dickens represented.

The speculating manias of 1825–6 and 1837 on the whole endorsed the morality behind this view of society, because they were followed by economic collapse, meaning loss and ruin for people like Mr Nickleby. The railway boom of 1845–6 meant ruin, too, for many, but it meant success for others, and by establishing the joint-stock company in a number of enormous undertakings pointed the way to the later developments of investing. By an Act of 1844 all joint-stock companies had to be registered with an official registrar, and this helped to restrain the activities of such people as Montague Tigg: and the principle of limited liability was first recognized in the legislation of 1855–6. The years between 1850 and 1866 were marked by a great increase in the number of small investors, and the later part of the period saw the growth of the system of finance companies, of which the most famous was the firm of Overend and Gurney.

These changes are clearly reflected in Dickens's work. With *Dombey and Son* the perpetual interest in money enters on a new phase. The famous dialogue between Paul and his father beginning 'Papa! what's money?' has often been quoted to show how Dickens rose above sordid and worldly things: but there is a special interest in the answer Mr Dombey might have given, but did not:

Mr Dombey was in a difficulty. He would have liked to
give him some explanation involving the terms circulating-
medium, currency, depreciation of currency, paper, bullion,
rates of exchange, value of precious metals in the market,
and so forth; but looking down at the little chair, and seeing
what a long way down it was, he answered: 'Gold, and
silver, and copper. Guineas, shillings, half-pence. You know
what they are?'
(chapter 8)

In the earlier novels finance is very individualistic; from *Dombey* onwards, though the interest in money's personal power still continues, and is indeed a main theme of *Great Expectations*, money as a system is even more important. The fortunes of nearly everybody in *Little Dorrit* and *Our Mutual Friend* hang on the big capitalists. Dickens does not make the mysteries of their finance clear, and does not mean to.

Mr Merdle was immensely rich; a man of prodigious
enterprise; a Midas without the ears, who turned all he
touched to gold. He was in everything good, from banking
to building. He was in Parliament, of course. He was in the
City, necessarily. He was Chairman of this, Trustee of that,
President of the other. The weightiest of men had said to

projectors, 'Now, what name have you got? Have you got
Merdle?' And, the reply being in the negative, had said,
'Then I won't look at you.'
(*Little Dorrit*, chapter 21)

His power over people is greater in the long run because it is indirect;
but it is not a terrifying power like Quilp's – he does not bully people
with investments – for the success of Merdle is the success of all; so
far his dupes, and the system they all belong to, are to blame. The
villain is 'the City'. Dickens cannot build up Merdle as a villain; in
fact he makes him rather attractive, shuffling and slinking through the
pointless grandeur, frightened of the butler he has hired and the
bosom he has bought. His imitation of a Roman death brings ruin to
thousands whose names he never even knew; but their anger turns as
much against those who, by their trust and avarice, established his
credit, as against him. According to the imaginary date of the book the
Merdle crash is part of the financial collapse of 1825–6; but the extent
of Merdle's operations, the number of small investors involved in
them, and the position they give him in society belong entirely to the
fifties. It is noticeable too that the part played by Mr Meagles in this
financial atmosphere is muted and cautious; he still represents the old
idea of generous benevolence, but he has no longer the same freedom,
scope and innocence of the Christmassy people. He is relatively
powerless in circumstances which can lure even the staid Arthur
Clennam into speculation.

The treatment of money and investment is even broader and more
scathing in *Our Mutual Friend*. To begin with, the great Harmon fortune, on which everything turns, has not been made from banking or
building, nor from railways even, but from dust. Dickens had evidently had these great suburban dust-heaps in mind for at least fourteen years: a sort of story-article on them had appeared in *Household
Words* on 13 July 1850. Their chief value was then said to be in the
ashes which were used for brickmaking, while the soot section of the
heap was good for manure.

Their worth, however, varies not only with their
magnitude . . . but with the demand. About the year 1820,
the Marylebone Dust-heap produced between four thousand
and five thousand pounds. In 1832, St George's paid Mr

Stapleton five hundred pounds a year, not to leave the Heap
standing, but to carry it away. Of course he was only too
glad to be paid highly for selling his dust.

They also had other more accidental sources of value; gold and silver
articles were sometimes found in them, and in one heap in 1847 a
banker's cheque for a considerable amount turned up. But this
article does not deal with the really sinister question that must be
asked about the Harmon mounds. One of the main jobs of a dust-
contractor in Early Victorian London was to collect the contents of
the privies and the piles of mixed dung and ashes which were made in
the poorer streets; and the term 'dust' was often used as a euphemism
for decaying human excrement, which was exceedingly valuable as a
fertilizer. Some contemporary readers at least must have thought of
the mounds as being partly composed of such stuff; and then the idea
of Silas Wegg prodding them with his wooden leg becomes almost
intolerable.

By choosing such a source for the money on which his whole story
was to depend and adding a jumble of intricate wills (though he protested that such things were quite true to life), Dickens makes plain
enough that the whole business of earning money or inheriting it can
be detached altogether from any reasonable scheme of life. Collecting
dirt is not a kind of work that deserves munificent rewards. Apart
from the Harmon fortune the financial system is more explicitly
condemned: the Podsnaps, Veneerings and Lammles live in a world
in which investment has taken the place of work:

As is well known to the wise in their generation, traffic in
Shares is the one thing to have to do with in this world.
Have no antecedents, no established character, no cultivation,
no ideas, no manners; have Shares. Have Shares enough
to be on Boards of Direction in capital letters, oscillate on
mysterious business between London and Paris, and be
great. Where does he come from? Shares. Where is he going
to? Shares. What are his tastes? Shares. Has he any principles?
Shares. What squeezes him into Parliament? Shares. Perhaps
he never of himself achieved success in anything, never
originated anything, never produced anything! Sufficient
answer to all; Shares. O mighty Shares! To set those

blaring images so high, and to cause us smaller vermin, as
under the influence of henbane or opium, to cry out night
and day, 'Relieve us of our money, scatter it for us, buy us
and sell us, ruin us, only we beseech ye take rank among
the powers of the earth, and fatten on us!'
(*Our Mutual Friend*, book 1, chapter 10)

This paragraph would have had special force in the years just before
the crisis of 1866, which saw the failure of Overend and Gurney and
the collapse of many companies that had come into existence in the
past ten years.

The increase of the rentier class and of entirely 'new' people like
the Veneerings seriously disturbed Dickens's idea of the extent to
which good individuals could redress the evils of social inequality. It
is often said that because Boffin appears in *Our Mutual Friend* Dickens
never really abandoned the optimistic view that if you had enough
Cheerybles all would be well; but Boffin's whole behaviour is so
wildly different from that of the earlier benevolent people that he
seems almost to be a critical caricature of them. To begin with (for his
wife's sake, so he says), he makes concessions to fashion the Cheerybles never dreamed of making, and goes in for all the business of
carriages and parties as strong as the Veneerings themselves. Even
apart from his pretended miserhood he behaves to Silas Wegg rather
like mistresses who leave half-crowns in corners hoping the servants
will steal them; and the episode of the miserhood is so convincingly
done that one is tempted to wonder whether Dickens did not mean it
to be genuine and only changed his mind towards the end. But even
if he meant it to be a deception all along, it shows the need he felt for
some very elaborate artifice to get the mercenary ideas out of Bella's
head in the kind of society she was living in; everything is corrupted
and distorted by money, and even some of Boffin's benevolent
schemes are thwarted. Roughly one may say that he belongs to the
Cheeryble group; Sloppy is his Smike, the Rev. Frank his Trimmers:
but he is operating against greater obstacles, with less confidence and
less success. For Dickens felt that his old solution did not so surely
apply in high mid-Victorian prosperity, when the simpler social cate-
gories within which he had worked had broken down.
(133–69)

V. S. Pritchett

from 'Edwin Drood', The Living Novel   1946

The shocks in Edwin Drood come not from the sudden levelling of his fantasy and the appearance of realism. They occur when Dickens acts his realism – see the showdown between Jasper and Rosa – and we realize that it is really alien to Dickens's gift that his people should be made to talk to each other. When he attempts this he merely succeeds in making them talk at each other, like actors. His natural genius is for human soliloquy not human intercourse.

In criticism of the English novel and in appeals to what is called 'the English tradition', there has been a misunderstanding, I think, about this intrinsic quality of Dickens. One hears the word Dickensian on all sides. One hears of Dickens's influence on the English novel on the one hand, and of the failure of the English novel to produce a comparable genius. While the word Dickensian lasts, the English novel will be suffocated. For the convivial and gregarious extravagance and the picaresque disorder which are supposedly Dickensian are not Dickens's especial contribution to the English novel. They are his inheritance from Sterne, Smollett and, on the sentimental side, from Richardson, an inheritance which may be traced back to the comedy of Jonson. What Dickens really contributed may be seen by a glance at the only novelists who have seriously developed his contribution – in Dostoyevsky above all and, to a lesser degree, in Gogol. (There is more of Dickens, to my mind, in James Joyce's Ulysses than in books like Kipps or Tono Bungay.) For the distinguishing quality of Dickens's people is that they are solitaries. They are people caught living in a world of their own. They soliloquize in it. They do not talk to one another; they talk to themselves. The pressure of society has created fits of twitching in mind and speech, and fantasies in the soul. It has been said that Dickens creates merely external caricatures, but Mr Sapsea's musings on his 'somewhat extensive knowledge' and Mr Crisparkle's sparrings in front of his mirror are fragments of inner life. In how many of that famous congress of 'characters' – Micawber, Barkis, Traddles, Jingle, Mrs Gamp or Miss Twitteron: take them at random – and in how many of the straight personages, like Jasper and Neville Landless in Edwin Drood, are we chiefly made aware of the

individual's obliviousness of any existence but his own? The whole of
Dickens's emotional radicalism, his hatred of the utilitarians and
philanthropists and all his attacks on institutions, are based on his
strongest and fiercest sense: isolation. In every kind of way Dickens
was isolated. Isolation was the foundation not only of his fantasy and
his hysteria, but also – I am sure Mr Edmund Wilson is correct here –
of the twin strains of rebel and criminal in his nature. The solitariness
of people is paralleled by the solitariness of things. Fog operates as a
separate presence, houses quietly rot or boisterously prosper on their
own. The veneer of the Veneerings becomes almost tangible, whipped
up by the repetitions. Cloisterham believes itself more important than
the world at large, the Law sports like some stale and dilapidated
circus across human lives. Philanthropy attacks people like a humour
or an observable germ. The people and the things of Dickens are all
out of touch and out of hearing of each other, each conducting its own
inner monologue, grandiloquent or dismaying. By this dissociation
Dickens brings to us something of the fright of childhood, and the
kind of realism employed in *Edwin Drood* reads like an attempt to re-
construct and co-ordinate his world, like a preparation for a final confession of guilt.
(77–9)

Robert Liddell

from *A Treatise on the Novel* 1947

Of the symbolists, Dickens is supreme: he provides vast, Wagnerian
settings for his dramas. The Thames in *Our Mutual Friend*, the marshes
in *Great Expectations* are symbolic and exciting. They prepare us to see
extraordinary things and people – and Dickens's people are big
enough to set against their background, while Hardy's are apt to get
lost on Egdon Heath. Dickens does not forget that it is for the sake of
the human drama that the background is provided. If, in *Bleak House*,
it rains in Lincolnshire, it is because it rains in the heart of Lady
Dedlock.

The waters are out in Lincolnshire. An arch of the bridge
in the park has been sapped and sopped away. The adjacent

low-lying ground, for half a mile in breadth, is a stagnant river, with melancholy trees for islands in it, and a surface punctured all over, all day long, with falling rain. . . . The weather, for many a day and night, has been so wet that the trees seem wet through, and the soft loppings and prunings of the workman's axe can make no crash or crackle as they fall. The deer, looking soaked, leave quagmires, where they pass. The shot of a rifle loses its sharpness in the moist air, and its smoke moves in a tardy little cloud towards the green rise, coppice-topped, that makes a background for the falling rain.
(chapter 2)

The feeling of damp chill is the physical counterpart to Lady Dedlock's fears, and the remorseless rain a fit background to her approaching ruin. Unfortunately the actual drama in this case, as so often in Dickens, is strained and impossible. A truer pity and terror at Lady Dedlock's plight is produced by the echoing terrace at Chesney Wold and the Lincolnshire floods, than by the preposterous schemes of Mr Tulkinghorn. Dickens is a great artist, nevertheless it must be said that it is more creditable to cause pity and terror by the happenings in a story, rather than by the atmosphere.
(115–16)

Humphry House

'The Macabre Dickens' 1947[1] (published in *All in Due Time*, 1955)

The present lively interest in Dickens has in it an element never before prominent in all his hundred years of popularity – an interest in his mastery of the macabre and terrible in scene and character. His understanding of and power of describing evil and cruelty, fear and mania and guilt; his overburdening sense, in the crises, of the ultimate loneliness of human life – things like these are now seen to be among the causes of his enigmatic hold on people's hearts. He has worked as

1. This was a talk on the BBC Third Programme, 3 June 1947. [Ed.]

much beneath the surface as above it; and he was possibly not himself fully conscious of what he was putting into his books. The floor of consciousness has been lowered. The awful area of human experience in which small cruelty and meanness and stupidity may swell and topple over into murder, insane revenge, sadistic, bloody violence and riot; the area where dream and reality are confused or swiftly alternating – these are now seen to be closer to ourselves and to common life than our grandfathers suspected. They thought that Dickens on his violent and evil side – when he wrote about Sikes and Jonas Chuzzlewit and Bradley Headstone – was writing about a special, separate class called criminals; that Miss Havisham, Mr Dick and Miss Flite belonged to another separate class called lunatics – at most social problems; at least, wild exaggerated flights of fancy. We now see more plainly that John Jasper may be any one of us; that the murderer is not far beneath the skin; that the thickness of a sheet of paper may divide the proud successful man of the world from the suicide or the lunatic. We have also lived again into what used to be dismissed as melodrama.

Lord Acton once wrote in a letter that Dickens 'knows nothing of sin when it is not crime'. Within the narrow limits of theological pigeon-holes this is true; the word 'sin' hardly occurs in the novels; wickedness is not regarded as an offence against a personal God. But if the judgement is that Dickens knows nothing of evil unless it is recognized and punishable by the law, it is quite false. The great black, ghastly gallows, hanging over all, of which Dickens writes in the Preface to *Oliver Twist*, is not just the official retribution of society against those who break its rules; it is a symbol of the internal knowledge of guilt, the knowledge that makes Sikes wander back and forth in the country north of London, dogged not by fear of the police but by the phantom of Nancy, the knowledge that produces the last vision of her eyes which is the immediate cause of his death. Acton, with the logic of Catholicism, thought it a fault in Dickens that he 'loved his neighbour for his neighbour's sake'; but, within the range of moral action that this allows, Dickens is continually dealing with the forms of evil which the absence or failure of love may breed, and with the more terrible effects of emotional greed, the exploitation of one person by another, which often overflows into cruelty and violence. His methods of dealing with these moral problems and the conflicts they involve are various, but they are always peculiar and oblique; they are rarely brought out openly on the main surface of the story; they are never analysed as the story goes along. They are sometimes displayed through a grotesque character in such a way that they become so sharp and hideous that it is hard to recognize their seriousness and truth. Such, for example, is Quilp's cruelty towards his wife, which seems a fantastic travesty of human action if one overlooks Mrs Quilp's one phrase:

Quilp has such a way with him when he likes, that the best-looking woman here couldn't refuse him if I was dead.

That one sentence goes to the core of Quilp: for all his grotesque exterior he has in him a secret and serious human *power*: he is no figure of fun.

Except in such sudden phrases as these, Dickens's imagination usually concentrates through all the greater part of a story now on the black, now on the white, exclusively: the two don't interpenetrate. It is only in the portraits of boyhood and adolescence, such as those of Pip and the early Copperfield, that the medley of moral direction is really convincing. The adult characters for most of their course drive headstrong forward, virtuously or villainously or in some grotesque neutral zone where moral decisions do not have to be made. It is as if Dickens was afraid of attempting to portray the full complexity of an adult. Then, quite suddenly, a portentous thing happens. It is worth noticing first what does *not* happen. I cannot think of a single instance in which one of the good characters suddenly reveals a streak of evil: the Jarndyces and Cheerybles and Brownlows persevere infallible and unsullied to the end. The startling thing that *does* happen is that the villains suddenly reveal, if not a streak of good, a streak of vivid power, and then an immense depth of intricate, confused and pitiable humanity. Suddenly their awakened sense of guilt, their fears, remorse, regrets, and above all their terrible loneliness strike out like lightning from the complex plot. As death comes upon them they are transformed, not by any crude magic of reformation such as works wonders with Scrooge, but by an understanding and sympathy, a knowledge of their fears and weakness, far more heart-rending than the moral judgements which convention and the plot pass against them. Examples of this are Fagin, Sikes, Jonas Chuzzlewit, even

Quilp: but for the moment let us look closely at Mr Carker in *Dombey and Son*.

Carker has most often been regarded as a typical villain out of melodrama. One critic at least has called his drive across France from Dijon to the coast a 'masterpiece of melodrama'. So persistent has this way of regarding it been that this same critic himself heightens the scene by speaking of Carker's 'last journey through the *stormy* night'. But Dickens makes no mention of any storm whatever; in fact he writes in quite a different mood of 'a sigh of mountain air from the distant Jura, fading along the plain'. It is nearer the truth to say that in this scene Carker shakes off the last suggestion of melodrama and becomes a figure of immense significance. I will quote a few paragraphs – not continuous – from the description of the later part of this drive:

Gathered up moodily in a corner of the carriage, and only intent on going fast – except when he stood up, for a mile together, and looked back; which he would do whenever there was a piece of open country – he went on, still postponing thought indefinitely, and still always tormented with thinking to no purpose.

Shame, disappointment and discomfiture gnawed at his heart; a constant apprehension of being overtaken, or met – for he was groundlessly afraid even of travellers, who came towards him by the way he was going – oppressed him heavily. The same intolerable awe and dread that had come upon him in the night, returned unweakened in the day. The monotonous ringing of the bells and tramping of the horses; the monotony of his anxiety, and useless rage; the monotonous wheel of fear, regret and passion, he kept turning round and round; made the journey like a vision, in which nothing was quite real but his own torment. . . .

It was a fevered vision of things past and present all confounded together; of his life and journey blended into one. Of being madly hurried somewhere, whither he must go. Of old scenes starting up among the novelties through which he travelled. Of musing and brooding over what was past and distant, and seeming to take no notice of the actual

objects he encountered, but with a wearisome exhausting
consciousness of being bewildered by them, and having their
images all crowded in his hot brain after they were gone.
(chapter 55)

Whatever language this is, it is not the language of melodrama; it is
a tremendous analysis of the psychological effects of guilt, shame and
thwarted vanity. It is only in the light of these great final scenes that
Carker's character as shown earlier in the book becomes intelligible;
it is then seen that he is not the motivelessly malignant villain of melodrama: he is a man of intellect, of great ambition and great sexual
vitality; his worse flaws are self-centredness and vanity. It is exactly
this sort of man who would be afflicted with a total blindness about
what Edith Dombey, in a position, as he thinks, to satisfy both his
ambition and his sexual desires, was really thinking and feeling. The
final disclosure would have been bitter to Carker for many reasons, but
bitterest perhaps because it showed him that he had been abysmally
blind and *stupid*; yet he was too self-centred, intricate and cunning to
allow reflection on his own stupidity to come uppermost in his tortured thoughts. There is much of Dickens himself in Mr Carker: and
it is startling to see the hopelessness of his wheels within wheels of
thought: there is no solution but death.

One of the problems that face the critic of Dickens is to explain how
this intimate understanding of morbid and near-morbid psychology
links on to his apparent optimism, and above all to his humour. I
think we can safely say that the countless scenes of gregarious and
hearty happiness, which seem to us so unconvincing, seem so because
they represent a revulsion from the abysses of evil, a strenuous and
ardent *wish* to achieve happiness, rather than the realization of it. But
what of the great grotesque and humorous characters – Mrs Gamp,
Pecksniff, Mr Turveydrop and the rest? One very fruitful suggestion
was made by George Henry Lewes, only two years after Dickens's
death:

In no other perfectly sane mind (Blake I believe was not
perfectly sane) have I observed vividness of imagination
approaching so closely to hallucination. . . . Dickens once
declared to me that every word said by his characters was
distinctly *heard* by him; I was at first not a little puzzled to

account for the fact that he could hear language so utterly
unlike the language of real feeling; but the surprise vanished
when I thought of the phenomena of hallucination.

Lewes applied this idea both to the speaking of certain characters and
also to the visual descriptions of persons and scenes. In each case it was
the definiteness and insistence of the image or the sound which were
abnormal. This idea is, I think, extremely useful in helping to explain
the impression one gets from the books of isolated spells of intense
imagination which then stop; it also helps to explain the feeling of
isolation about the characters: one almost hallucinatory experience
succeeded by another, the two being mutually exclusive. There was
no comprehensive, constructive, master imagination which held the
diverse experiences together, except in very rare instances, mostly to
do with memories of childhood. The great grotesque comic characters – Mrs Gamp is the purest of the type – are the best examples of
this exclusive, one-track intense development and could not have
their unique stature without it. In other instances the form of hallucination was not that of something seen or heard externally, but an
internal illusion by which Dickens himself virtually assumed the
character of which he was writing. His daughter Mamie described
how she saw him grimacing in a glass, talking aloud the speeches of
a character, completely unaware of his actual surroundings, not even
noticing that she was in the room.

If one starts by thinking of Dickens as a man with an imagination
of this quality and intensity and exclusiveness, it helps to explain not
only the recurrent treatment in the novels of various forms of mania
and illusion, but also the preoccupation with evil. Similar processes of
concentration, exclusion and distortion must have occurred in the
mental part of his own life, as distinct from his written work. Edmund
Wilson, in his essay *The Two Scrooges*, argued that Dickens was 'the
victim of a manic-depressive cycle, and a very uncomfortable person'.
His own life was, in a sense far beyond what could be said of most
men, acting out, or attempting to act out, his own imaginings. His
passion for theatricals was only a symptom of the trouble, or an effort
to work it off without serious consequences. In real living the con-
comitant of blindness, especially to the thoughts and feelings of other
people, may be resentment and hatred, even to the point of imagining

murder, against those who fail to conform to the policy or come up to the idea of themselves that it entails. But there will also be moments of terrible awakening when the illusion and the self-deceit it involved are ended, and there will be a great wave of remorse and guilt and shame for the evils imagined or other evils actually done. There is evidence enough to show that Dickens's personality was strong enough, especially over women, to project his own imagined policies upon others so that in general they conformed; at certain crises the attempt failed and a hideous major conflict came out into the open. Lewes said he saw no traces of insanity in Dickens's life; nor would he; for Dickens normally had a very strong conscious control, and was able to work out many of his conflicts through his novels. But his daughter Kate, Mrs Perugini, did significantly say to a friend that after his wife left their home Dickens behaved towards the children 'like a madman', that all the worst in him came out; and she added that her father was 'a very wicked man'.

This is a very different matter from saying that he was a commonplace bounder; there is no need for Dickens's descendants to defend him against charges of being a dishonest drunken libertine: neither the charges nor the defence are relevant to a man of his size and complexity and importance. It is clear from the evidence of the novels alone that Dickens's acquaintance with evil was not just acquired *ab extra*, by reading the police-court reports (much as he loved them) and wandering about Seven Dials and the Waterside by night; it was acquired also by introspection. His own temptations and imaginings, isolated and heightened by the peculiar, narrowing, intense quality of his imagination, fed daily by the immense power which he felt himself to possess over others' personalities – these were the authentic sources of his great criminal characters. Their ultimate trembling loneliness, or hunted wanderings, or self-haunted hallucinations, or endless, destroying self-analysis, came also from himself. Our generation has come to recognize this by introspection, too.

(183–9)

Arnold Kettle

from 'Oliver Twist', An Introduction to the English Novel,
vol. 1 1951

What is the secret of the [novel's] power? Is it merely the objective
existence of the horrors, the fact that such things were, that strikes at
our minds? Fairly obviously not or we should be moved in just the
same way by a social history. There is a particularity about this world
which is not the effect of even a well-documented history. It is not just
any evocation of the life of the poor after the Industrial Revolution;
when we read the Hammonds' *Town Labourer* or Engels's *Condition
of the Working Class in England in 1844* our reaction may not be less
profound than our reaction to *Oliver Twist*, but it is different, more
generalized, less vivid, less intense.

The most obvious difference between *Oliver Twist* and a social history is, of course, that it deals with actual characters whose personalities we envisage, whose careers we follow, and whose feelings we
share. But this difference is not, I think, quite so important as we
might assume. For in fact we do not become involved in the world of
Oliver Twist in the way we become involved in the world of *Emma*.
We do not really know very much about any of these characters, even
Oliver himself, or participate very closely in their motives and reactions. We are sorry for Oliver; we are on his side; but our feeling for
him is not very different from our feeling for any child we see ill-
treated in the street. We are outraged and our sense of outrage no
doubt comes, ultimately, from a feeling of common humanity, a kind
of identification of ourselves with the child in his misery and struggles
but our entanglement in his situation is not really very deep.

In the famous scene when Oliver asks for more it is not the precise
sense of Oliver's feelings and reactions that grips us; we do not feel
what he is feeling in the way we share Miss Bates's emotion on Box
Hill, and in this sense Oliver is less close to us and matters to us less
than Miss Bates and Emma. But in another way Oliver matters to us a
great deal more. For when he walks up to the master of the workhouse and asks for more gruel, issues are at stake which make the
whole world of Jane Austen tremble. We care, we are involved, not

because it is Oliver and we are close to Oliver (though that of course enters into it), but because every starved orphan in the world, and indeed everyone who is poor and oppressed and hungry is involved, and the master of the workhouse (his name has not been revealed) is not anyone in particular but every agent of an oppressive system everywhere. And that, incidentally, is why millions of people all over the world (including many who have never read a page of Dickens) can tell you what happened in Oliver Twist's workhouse, while comparatively few can tell you what happened on Box Hill.

That this episode from *Oliver Twist* should have become a myth, a part of the cultural consciousness of the people, is due not merely to its subject-matter but to the kind of novel Dickens wrote. He is dealing not, like Jane Austen, with personal relationships, not with the quality of feeling involved in detailed living, but with something which can without fatuity be called Life. What we get from *Oliver Twist* is not a greater precision of sensitiveness about the day-to-day problems of human behaviour but a sharpened sense of the large movement of life within which particular problems arise. It is pointless to argue whether the way Dickens tackles life is better or worse than the way Jane Austen tackles it. One might just as well argue whether it is better to earn one's living or to get married. Not merely are the two issues not exclusive, they are indissolubly bound up. In a sense they are the same problem – how best to live in society – but, for all their interdependence, one does not tackle them in precisely the same way.
(124–6)

Graham Greene

from 'The Young Dickens', *The Lost Childhood and Other Essays* 1951

What strikes the attention most in this closed Fagin universe are the different levels of unreality. If, as one is inclined to believe, the creative writer perceives his world once and for all in childhood and adolescence, and his whole career is an effort to illustrate his private world in terms of the great public world we all share, we can understand why Fagin and Sikes in their most extreme exaggerations move us more than the benevolence of Mr Brownlow or the sweetness of Mrs Maylie – they touch with fear as the others never really touch with love. It was not that the unhappy child, with his hurt pride and his sense of hopeless insecurity, had not encountered human goodness – he had simply failed to recognize it in those streets between Gadshill and Hungerford Market which had been as narrowly enclosed as Oliver Twist's. When Dickens at this early period tried to describe goodness he seems to have remembered the small stationers' shops on the way to the blacking factory with their coloured paper scraps of angels and virgins, or perhaps the face of some old gentleman who had spoken kindly to him outside Warren's factory. He has swum up towards goodness from the deepest world of his experience, and on this shallow level the conscious brain has taken a hand, trying to construct characters to represent virtue and, because his age demanded it, triumphant virtue, but all he can produce are powdered wigs and gleaming spectacles and a lot of bustle with bowls of broth and a pale angelic face. Compare the way in which we first meet evil with his introduction of goodness.

The walls and ceiling of the room were perfectly black with age and dirt. There was a deal table before the fire: upon which were a candle, stuck in a ginger-beer bottle, two or three pewter pots, a loaf and butter, and a plate. In a frying-pan, which was on the fire, and which was secured to the mantelshelf by a string, some sausages were cooking; and standing over them, with a toasting-fork in his hand, was a very old shrivelled Jew, whose villainous-looking and repulsive face was obscured by a quantity of matted red hair. He was dressed in a greasy flannel gown, with his throat bare. . . .

'This is him, Fagin,' said Jack Dawkins: 'my friend Oliver Twist.'

The Jew grinned; and, making a low obeisance to Oliver, took him by the hand, and hoped he should have the honour of his intimate acquaintance.

(chapter 8)

Fagin has always about him this quality of darkness and nightmare. He never appears on the daylight streets. Even when we see him last in the condemned cell, it is in the hours before the dawn. In the Fagin darkness Dickens's hand seldom fumbles. Hear him turning the screw of horror when Nancy speaks of the thoughts of death that have haunted her:

'Imagination,' said the gentleman, soothing her.
'No imagination,' replied the girl in a hoarse voice. 'I'll swear I saw "coffin" written in every page of the book in large black letters – aye, and they carried one close to me, in the streets tonight.'
'There is nothing unusual in that,' said the gentleman. 'They have passed me often.'
'*Real* ones,' rejoined the girl. 'This was not.'
(chapter 46)

Now turn to the daylight world and our first sight of Rose:

The younger lady was in the lovely bloom and springtime of womanhood; at that age, when, if ever angels be for God's good purposes enthroned in mortal forms, they may be, without impiety, supposed to abide in such as hers.
She was not past seventeen. Cast in so slight and exquisite a mould; so mild and gentle; so pure and beautiful; that earth seemed not her element, nor its rough creatures her fit companions.
(chapter 29)

Or Mr Brownlow as he first appeared to Oliver:

Now, the old gentleman came in as brisk as need be; but he had no sooner raised his spectacles on his forehead, and thrust his hands behind the skirts of his dressing-gown to take a good long look at Oliver, than his countenance underwent a very great variety of odd contortions. . . . The fact is, if the truth must be told, that Mr Brownlow's heart, being large enough for any six ordinary old gentlemen of humane disposition, forced a supply of tears into his eyes, by some hydraulic process which we are not sufficiently philosophical to be in a condition to explain.
(chapter 12)

How can we really believe that these inadequate ghosts of goodness can triumph over Fagin, Monks and Sikes? And the answer, of course, is that they never could have triumphed without the elaborate machinery of the plot disclosed in the last pages. This world of Dickens is a world without God; and as a substitute for the power and the glory of the omnipotent and omniscient are a few sentimental references to heaven, angels, the sweet faces of the dead, and Oliver saying, 'Heaven is a long way off, and they are too happy there to come down to the bedside of a poor boy.' In this Manichean world we can believe in evil-doing, but goodness wilts into philanthropy, kindness, and those strange vague sicknesses into which Dickens's young women so frequently fall and which seem in his eyes a kind of badge of virtue, as though there were a merit in death.

But how instinctively Dickens's genius recognized the flaw and made a virtue out of it. We cannot believe in the power of Mr Brownlow, but nor did Dickens, and from his inability to believe in his own good characters springs the real tension of his novel. The boy Oliver may not lodge in our brain like David Copperfield, and though many of Mr Bumble's phrases have become and deserve to have become familiar quotations we can feel he was manufactured: he never breathes like Mr Dorrit; yet Oliver's predicament, the nightmare fight between the darkness where the demons walk and the sunlight where ineffective goodness makes its last stand in a condemned world, will remain part of our imaginations forever. We read of the defeat of Monks, and of Fagin screaming in the condemned cell, and of Sikes dangling from his self-made noose, but we don't believe. We have witnessed Oliver's temporary escapes too often and his inevitable recapture: *there* is the truth and the creative experience. We know that when Oliver leaves Mr Brownlow's house to walk a few hundred yards to the bookseller, his friends will wait in vain for his return. All London outside the quiet, shady street in Pentonville belongs to his pursuers; and when he escapes again into the house of Mrs Maylie in the fields beyond Shepperton, we know his security is false. The seasons may pass, but safety depends not on time but on daylight. As children we all knew that: how all day we could forget the dark and the journey to bed. It is with a sense of relief that at last in twilight we see the faces of the Jew and Monks peer into the cottage window between the sprays of jessamine. At that moment we realize how the whole world, and not London only, belongs to these two after dark. Dickens, dealing out his happy endings and his unreal retributions, can never ruin the validity and dignity of that moment. 'They had recognized him, and he them; and their look was as firmly impressed upon his memory, as if it had been deeply carved in stone, and set before him from his birth.'

'From his birth' – Dickens may have intended that phrase to refer to the complicated imbroglios of the plot that lie outside the novel, 'something less terrible than the truth'. As for the truth, is it too fantastic to imagine that in his novel, as in many of his later books, creeps in, unrecognized by the author, the eternal and alluring taint of the Manichee, with its simple and terrible explanation of our plight, how the world was made by Satan and not by God, lulling us with the music of despair?

(54–7)

Lionel Trilling

'Little Dorrit', Introduction to New Oxford Illustrated Dickens 1953 (reprinted in *The Opposing Self*, 1955)

Little Dorrit is one of the three great novels of Dickens's great last period, but of the three it is perhaps the least established with modern readers. When it first appeared – in monthly parts from December 1855 to June 1857 – its success was even more decisive than that of *Bleak House*, but the suffrage of later audiences has gone the other way, and of all Dickens's later works it is *Bleak House* that has come to be the best known. As for *Our Mutual Friend*, after having for some time met with adverse critical opinion among the enlightened – one recalls that the youthful Henry James attacked it for standing in the way of art and truth – it has of recent years been regarded with ever-growing admiration. But *Little Dorrit* seems to have retired to the background and shadow of our consciousness of Dickens.

This does not make an occasion for concern or indignation. With a body of works as large and as enduring as that of Dickens, taste and opinion will never be done. They will shift and veer as they have shifted and veered with the canon of Shakespeare, and each generation will have its special favourites and make its surprised discoveries. *Little Dorrit*, one of the most profound of Dickens's novels and one of the most significant works of the nineteenth century, will not fail to be thought of as speaking with a peculiar and passionate intimacy to our own time.

Little Dorrit is about society, which certainly does not distinguish it from the rest of Dickens's novels unless we go on to say, as we must, that it is *more* about society than any other of the novels, that it is about society in its very essence. This essential quality of the book has become apparent as many of the particular social conditions to which it refers have passed into history. Some of these conditions were already of the past when Dickens wrote, for although imprisonment for debt was indeed not wholly given up until 1869, yet imprisonment for small debts had been done away with in 1844, the prison of the Marshalsea had been abolished in 1842 and the Court of the Marshalsea in 1849. Bernard Shaw said of *Little Dorrit* that it converted him to socialism; it is not likely that any contemporary English reader would feel it appropriate to respond to its social message in the same way. The dead hand of outworn tradition no longer supports special privilege in England. For good or bad, in scarcely any country in the world can the whole art of government be said to be How Not To Do It. Mrs General cannot impose the genteel discipline of Prunes and Prisms, and no prestige whatever attaches to 'the truly refined mind' of her definition – 'one that will seem to be ignorant of the existence of anything that is not perfectly proper, placid and pleasant'. At no point, perhaps, do the particular abuses and absurdities upon which Dickens directed his terrible cold anger represent the problems of social life as we now conceive them.

Yet this makes *Little Dorrit* not less but more relevant to our sense of things. As the particulars seem less immediate to our case, the general force of the novel becomes greater, and *Little Dorrit* is seen to be about a problem which does not yield easily to time. It is about society in relation to the individual human will. This is certainly a matter general enough – general to the point of tautology, were it not for the bitterness with which the tautology is articulated, were it not for the specificity and the subtlety and the boldness with which the human will is anatomized.

The subject of *Little Dorrit* is borne in upon us by the symbol, or emblem, of the book, which is the prison. The story opens in a prison in Marseilles. It goes on to the Marshalsea, which in effect it never leaves. The second of the two parts of the novel begins in what we are urged to think of as a sort of prison, the monastery of the Great St Bernard. The Circumlocution Office is the prison of the creative mind of England. Mr Merdle is shown habitually holding himself by the wrist, taking himself into custody, and in a score of ways the theme of incarceration is carried out, persons and classes being imprisoned by their notions of their predestined fate or their religious duty, or by their occupations, their life schemes, their ideas of themselves, their very habits of language.

Symbolic or emblematic devices are used by Dickens to one degree or another in several of the novels of his late period, but nowhere to such good effects as in *Little Dorrit*. The fog of *Bleak House*, the dust heap and the river of *Our Mutual Friend* are very striking, but they scarcely equal in force the prison image which dominates *Little Dorrit*. This is because the prison is an actuality before it is ever a symbol:[1] its connexion with the will is real, it is the practical instrument for the negation of man's will which the will of society has contrived. As such, the prison haunted the mind of the nineteenth century, which may be said to have had its birth at the fall of the Bastille. The genius of the age, conceiving itself as creative will, naturally thought of the prisons from which it must be freed, and the trumpet call of the 'Leonore' overture sounds through the century, the signal for the opening of the gates, for a general deliverance, although it grows fainter as men come to think of the prison not as a political instrument but merely as the ineluctable condition of life in society. 'Most men in a brazen prison live' – the line in which

1 Since writing this, I have had to revise my idea of the actuality of the symbol of *Our Mutual Friend*. Professor Johnson's biography of Dickens has taught me much about the nature of dust heaps, including their monetary value, which was very large, quite large enough to represent a considerable fortune: I had never quite believed that Dickens was telling the literal truth about this. From Professor Dodd's *The Age of Paradox* I have learned to what an extent the Thames was visibly the sewer of London, of how pressing was the problem of the sewage in the city as Dickens knew it, of how present to the mind was the sensible and even the tangible evidence that the problem was not being solved. The moral *disgust* of the book is thus seen to be quite adequately comprehended by the symbols which are used to represent it.

Matthew Arnold echoes Wordsworth's 'shades of the prison-house begin to close | Upon the growing boy,' might have served as the epigraph of *Little Dorrit*. In the mind of Dickens himself the idea of the prison was obsessive, not merely because of his own boyhood experience of prison life through his father's three months in the Marshalsea (although this must be given great weight in our understanding of his intense preoccupation with the theme), but because of his own consciousness of the force and scope of his will.

If we speak of the place which the image of the prison occupied in the mind of the nineteenth century, we ought to recollect a certain German picture of the time, inconsiderable in itself but made significant by its use in a famous work of the early twentieth century. It represents a man lying in a medieval dungeon; he is asleep, his head pillowed on straw, and we know that he dreams of freedom because the bars on his window are shown being sawed by gnomes. This picture serves as the frontispiece of Freud's *Introductory Lectures on Psychoanalysis* – Freud uses it to make plain one of the more elementary ideas of his psychology, the idea of the fulfilment in dream or fantasy of impulses of the will that cannot be fulfilled in actuality. His choice of this particular picture is not fortuitous; other graphic representations of wish-fulfilment exist which might have served equally well his immediate didactic purpose, but Freud's general conception of the mind does indeed make the prison image peculiarly appropriate. And Freud is in point here because in a passage of *Little Dorrit* Dickens anticipates one of Freud 's ideas, and not one of the simplest but nothing less bold and inclusive than the essential theory of the neurosis.

The brief passage to which I make reference occurs in the course of Arthur Clennam's pursuit of the obsessive notion that his family is in some way guilty, that its fortune, although now greatly diminished, has been built on injury done to someone. And he conjectures that the injured person is William Dorrit, who has been confined for debt in the Marshalsea for twenty years. Clennam is not wholly wrong in his supposition – there is indeed guilt in the family, incurred by Arthur's mother, and it consists in part of an injury done to a member of the Dorrit family. But he is not wholly right, for Mr Dorrit has not been imprisoned through the wish or agency of Mrs Clennam. The reasoning by which Arthur reaches his partly mistaken conclusion is of the greatest interest. It is based upon the fact that his mother, although mentally very vigorous, has lived as an invalid for many years. She has been imprisoned in a single room of her house, confined to her chair, which she leaves only for her bed. And her son conjectures that her imprisoning illness is the price she pays for the guilty gratification of keeping William Dorrit in *his* prison – that is, in order to have the right to injure another, she must unconsciously injure herself in an equivalent way:

A swift thought shot into [Arthur Clennam's] mind. In that long imprisonment here [i.e. Mr Dorrit's] and in her long confinement to her room, did his mother find a balance to be struck? I admit that I was accessory to that man's captivity. I have suffered it in kind. He has decayed in his prison; I in mine. I have paid the penalty.
(chapter 8)

I have dwelt on this detail because it suggests, even more than the naked fact of the prison itself, the nature of the vision of society of *Little Dorrit*. One way of describing Freud's conception of the mind is to say that it is based upon the primacy of the will, and that the organization of the internal life is in the form, often fantastically parodic, of a criminal process in which the mind is at once the criminal, the victim, the police, the judge and the executioner. And this is a fair description of Dickens's own view of the mind, as, having received the social impress, it becomes in turn the matrix of society.

In emphasizing the psychological aspects of the representation of society of *Little Dorrit* I do not wish to slight those more immediate institutional aspects of which earlier readers of the novel were chiefly aware. These are of as great importance now as they ever were in Dickens's career. Dickens is far from having lost his sense of the cruelty and stupidity of institutions and functionaries, his sense of the general rightness of the people as a whole and of the general wrongness of those who are put in authority over them. He certainly has not moved to that specious position in which all injustice is laid at the door of the original Old Adam in each of us, not to be done away with until we shall all, at the same moment, become the new Adam. The Circumlocution Office is a constraint upon the life of England which nothing can justify. Mr Dorrit's sufferings and the injustice done to him are not denied or mitigated by his passionate commitment to some of the worst aspects of the society which deals with him so badly.

Yet the emphasis on the internal life and on personal responsibility is very strong in *Little Dorrit*. Thus, to take but one example, in the matter of the Circumlocution Office Dickens is at pains to remind us that the responsibility for its existence lies even with so good a man as Mr Meagles. In the alliance against the torpor of the Office which he has made with Daniel Doyce, the engineer and inventor, Mr Meagles has been undeviatingly faithful. Yet Clennam finds occasion to wonder whether there might not be 'in the breast of this honest, affectionate and cordial Mr Meagles, any microscopic portion of the mustard-seed that had sprung up into the great tree of the Circumlocution Office'. He is led to this speculation by his awareness that Mr Meagles feels 'a general superiority to Daniel Doyce, which seemed to be founded, not so much on anything in Doyce's personal character, as on the mere fact of [Doyce's] being an originator and a man out of the beaten track of other men'.

Perhaps the single best index of the degree of complexity with which Dickens views society in *Little Dorrit* is afforded by the character of Blandois and his place in the novel. Blandois is wholly wicked, the embodiment of evil; he is, indeed, a devil. One of the effects of his presence in *Little Dorrit* is to complicate our response to the theme of the prison, to deprive us of the comfortable, philanthropic thought that prisons are nothing but instruments of injustice. Because Blandois exists, prisons are necessary. The generation of readers that preceded our own was inclined, I think, to withhold credence from Blandois – they did not believe in his aesthetic actuality because they did not believe in his moral actuality, the less so because they could not account for his existence in specific terms of social causation. But events have required us to believe that there really are people who seem entirely wicked, and almost unaccountably so; the social causes of their badness lie so far back that they can scarcely be reached, and in any case causation pales into irrelevance before the effects of their actions; our effort to 'understand' them becomes a mere form of thought.

In this novel about the will and society, the devilish nature of Blandois is confirmed by his maniac insistence upon his gentility, his mad reiteration that it is the right and necessity of his existence to be served by others. He is the exemplification of the line in *Lear*: 'The prince of darkness is a gentleman.' The influence of Dickens upon Dostoyevsky is perhaps nowhere exhibited in a more detailed way than in the similarities between Blandois and the shabby-genteel devil of *The Brothers Karamazov*, and also between him and Smerdyakov of the same novel. It is of consequence to Dickens as to Dostoyevsky that the evil of the unmitigated social will should own no country, yet that the flavor of its cosmopolitanism should be 'French' – that is, rationalistic and subversive of the very assumption of society. Blandois enfolds himself in the soiled tatters of the revolutionary pathos. So long as he can play the game in his chosen style, he is nature's gentleman dispossessed of his rightful place, he is the natural genius against whom the philistine world closes its dull ranks. And when the disguise, which deceives no one, is off, he makes use of the classic social rationalization: Society has made him what he is; he does in his own person only what society does in its corporate form and with its corporate self-justification. 'Society sells itself and sells me: and I sell society.'[1]

Around Blandois are grouped certain characters of the novel of whose manner of life he is the pure principle. In these people the social will, the will to status, is the ruling faculty. To be recognized, deferred to and served – this is their master passion. Money is of course of great consequence in the exercise of this passion, yet in *Little Dorrit* the desire for money is subordinated to the desire for deference. The Midas figure of Mr Merdle must not mislead us on this point – should, indeed, guide us aright, for Mr Merdle, despite his destructive power, is an innocent and passive man among those who live by the social will. It is to be noted of all these people that they justify their insensate demand for status by some version of Blandois's pathos; they are confirmed in their lives by self-pity, they rely on the

1 This is in effect the doctrine of Balzac's philosophical-anarchist criminal, Vautrin. But in all other respects the difference between Blandois and Vautrin is extreme. Vautrin is a 'noble' and justified character; for all his cynicism, he is on the side of virtue and innocence. He is not corrupted by the social injustices he has suffered and perceived, by the self-pity to which they might have given rise; his wholesomeness may be said to be the result of his preference for power as against the status which Blandois desires. The development of Blandois from Vautrin - I do not know whether Dickens's creation was actually influenced by Balzac's - is a literary fact which has considerable social import.

great modern strategy of being the insulted and injured. Mr Dorrit is too soft a man for his gentility mania ever to be quite diabolical, but his younger daughter Fanny sells herself to the devil, damns herself entirely, in order to torture the woman who once questioned her social position. Henry Gowan, the cynical, incompetent gentleman-artist who associates himself with Blandois in order to *épater* society, is very nearly as diabolical as his companion. From his mother – who must dismiss once and for all any lingering doubt of Dickens's ability to portray what Chesterton calls the delicate or deadly in human character – he has learned to base his attack on society upon the unquestionable rightness of wronged gentility. Miss Wade lives a life of tortured self-commiseration which gives her license to turn her hatred and her hand against everyone, and she imposes her principle of judgement and conduct upon Tattycoram.

In short, it is part of the complexity of this novel which deals so bitterly with society that those of its characters who share its social bitterness are by that very fact condemned. And yet – so much further does the complexity extend – the subversive pathos of self-pity is by no means wholly dismissed, the devil has not wholly lied. No reader of *Little Dorrit* can possibly conclude that the rage of envy which Tattycoram feels is not justified in some degree, or that Miss Wade is wholly wrong in pointing out to her the insupportable ambiguity of her position as the daughter-servant of Mr and Mrs Meagles and the sister-servant of Pet Meagles. Nor is it possible to read Miss Wade's account of her life, 'The History of a Self Tormentor', without an understanding that amounts to sympathy. We feel this the more – Dickens meant us to feel it the more – because the two young women have been orphaned from infancy, and are illegitimate. Their bitterness is seen to be the perversion of the desire for love. The self-torture of Miss Wade – who becomes the more interesting if we think of her as the exact inversion of Esther Summerson of *Bleak House* – is the classic maneuver of the child who is unloved, or believes herself to be unloved; she refuses to be lovable, she elects to be hateful. In all of us the sense of injustice precedes the sense of justice by many years. It haunts our infancy, and even the most dearly loved of children may conceive themselves to be oppressed. Such is the nature of the human will, so perplexed is it by the disparity between what it desires and what it is allowed to have. With Dickens as with Blake, the perfect image of injustice is the unhappy child, and, like the historian Burck-hardt, he connects the fate of nations with the treatment of children. It is a commonplace of the biography and criticism of Dickens that this reflects his own sense of having been unjustly treated by his parents, specifically in ways which injured his own sense of social status, his own gentility; the general force of Dickens's social feelings derives from their being rooted in childhood experience, and some-thing of the special force of *Little Dorrit* derives from Dickens having discovered its matter in the depths of his own social will.

At this point we become aware of the remarkable number of false and inadequate parents in *Little Dorrit*. To what pains Dickens goes to represent delinquent parenthood, with what an elaboration of irony he sets it forth! 'The Father of the Marshalsea' – this is the title borne by Mr Dorrit, who, preoccupied by the gratification of being the First Gentleman of a prison, is unable to exercise the simplest paternal function; who corrupts two of his children by his dream of gentility; who will accept any sacrifice from his saintly daughter Amy, Little Dorrit, to whom he is the beloved child to be cherished and forgiven. 'The Patriarch' – this is the name bestowed upon Mr Casby, who stands as a parody of all Dickens's benevolent old gentlemen from Mr Pickwick through the Cheerybles to John Jarndyce, an astounding unreality of a man who, living only to grip and grind, has convinced the world by the iconography of his dress and mein that he is the repository of all benevolence. The primitive appropriateness of the strange – the un-English! – punishment which Mr Pancks metes out to this hollow paternity, the cutting off of his long hair and the broad brim of his hat, will be understood by any reader with the least tincture of psychoanalytical knowledge. Then the Meagles, however solicitous of their own daughter, are, as we have seen, but indifferent parents to Tattycoram. Mrs Gowan's rearing of her son is the root of his corruption. It is Fanny Dorrit's complaint of her enemy, Mrs Merdle, that she refuses to surrender the appearance of youth, as a mother should. And at the very centre of the novel is Mrs Clennam, a false mother in more ways than one; she does not deny love but she perverts and prevents it by denying all that love feeds on – liberty, demonstrative tenderness, joy and, what for Dickens is the guardian of love in society, art. It is her harsh rearing of her son that has given him cause to say in his fortieth year, 'I have no will.'

Some grace – it is, of course, the secret of his birth, of his being really a child of love and art – has kept Arthur Clennam from responding to the will of his mother with a bitter, clenched will of his own. The alternative he has chosen has not, contrary to his declaration, left him no will at all. He has by no means been robbed of his ethical will, he can exert energy to help others, and for the sake of Mr Dorrit or Daniel Doyce's invention he can haunt the Circumlocution Office with his mild, stubborn, 'I want to know. . .'. But the very accent of that phrase seems to forecast the terrible 'I prefer not to' of Bartleby the Scrivener in Melville's great story of the will in its ultimate fatigue.

It is impossible, I think, not to find in Arthur Clennam the evidence of Dickens's deep personal involvement in *Little Dorrit*. If we ask what Charles Dickens has to do with poor Clennam, what The Inimitable has to do with this sad depleted failure, the answer must be: nothing, save what is implied by Clennam's consciousness that he has passed the summit of life and that the path from now on leads downward, by his belief that the pleasures of love are not for him, by his 'I want to know . . .', by his wish to negate the will in death. Arthur Clennam is that mode of Dickens's existence at the time of *Little Dorrit* which makes it possible for him to write to his friend Macready, 'However strange it is never to be at rest, and never satisfied, and ever trying after something that is never reached, and to be always laden with plot and plan and care and worry, how clear it is that it must be, and that one is driven by an irresistible might until the journey is worked out.' And somewhat earlier and with a yet more poignant relevance: 'Why is it, that as with poor David, a sense always comes crushing upon me now, when I fall into low spirits, as of one happiness I have missed in life, and one friend and companion I have never made?'

If we become aware of an autobiographical element in *Little Dorrit* we must of course take notice of the fact that the novel was conceived after the famous incident of Maria Beadnell, who, poor woman, was the original of Arthur Clennam's Flora Finching. She was the first love of Dickens's proud, unfledged youth; she had married what Dickens has taught us to call Another, and now, after twenty years, she had chosen to come back into his life. Familiarity with the story cannot diminish our amazement at it – Dickens was a subtle and worldly man, but his sophistication was not proof against his passionate sentimentality, and he fully expected the past to come back to him, borne in the little hands of the adorable Maria. The actuality had a quite extreme effect upon him, and Flora, fat and foolish, is his monument to the discovered discontinuity between youth and middle age; she is the nonsensical spirit of the anticlimax of the years. And if she is in some degree forgiven, being represented as the kindest of foolish women, yet it is not without meaning that she is everywhere attended by Mr F.'s Aunt, one of Dickens's most astonishing ideas, the embodiment of senile rage and spite, flinging to the world the crusts of her buttered toast. 'He has a proud stomach, this chap,' she cries when poor Arthur hesitates over her dreadful gift. 'Give him a meal of chaff!' It is the voice of one of the Parcae.

It did not, of course, need the sad comedy of Maria Beadnell for Dickens to conceive that something in his life had come to an end. It did not even need his growing certainty that, after so many years and so many children, his relations with his wife were insupportable – this realization was as much a consequence as it was a cause of the sense of termination. He was forty-three years old and at the pinnacle of a success unique in the history of letters. The wildest ambitions of his youth could not have comprehended the actuality of his fame. But the last infirmity of noble mind may lead to the first infirmity of noble will. Dickens, to be sure, never lost his love of fame, or of whatever of life's goods his miraculous powers might bring him, but there came a moment when the old primitive motive could no longer serve, when the joy of impressing his powers on the world no longer seemed delightful in itself, and when the first, simple, honest, vulgar energy of desire no longer seemed appropriate to his idea of himself.

We may say of Dickens that at the time of *Little Dorrit* he was at a crisis of the will which is expressed in the characters and forces of the novel, in the extremity of its bitterness against the social will, in its vision of peace and selflessness. This moral crisis is most immediately represented by the condition of Arthur Clennam's will, by his sense of guilt, by his belief that he is unloved and unlovable, by his retirement to the Marshalsea as by an act of choice, by his sickness unto death. We have here the analogy to the familiar elements of a religious crisis. This is not the place to raise the question of Dickens's relation to the Christian religion, which was a complicated one. But we cannot speak of *Little Dorrit* without taking notice of its reference to Christian feeling, if only because this is of considerable importance in its effect upon the aesthetic of the novel.

It has been observed of *Little Dorrit* that certain of Dickens's characteristic delights are not present in their usual force. Something of his gusto is diminished in at least one of its aspects. We do not have the amazing thickness of fact and incident that marks, say, *Bleak House* or *Our Mutual Friend* – not that we do not have sufficient thickness, but we do not have what Dickens usually gives us. We do not have the great population of characters from whom shines the freshness of their autonomous life. Mr Pancks and Mrs Plornish and Flora Finching and Flintwinch are interesting and amusing, but they seem to be the fruit of conscious intention rather than of free creation. This is sometimes explained by saying that Dickens was fatigued. Perhaps so, but if we are aware that Dickens is here expending less of one kind of creative energy, we must at the same time be aware that he is expending more than ever before of another kind. The imagination of *Little Dorrit* is marked not so much by its powers of particularization as by its powers of generalization and abstraction. It is an imagination under the dominion of a great articulated idea, a moral idea which tends to find its full development in a religious experience. It is an imagination akin to that which created *Piers Plowman* and *Pilgrim's Progress*. And, indeed, it is akin to the imagination of *The Divine Comedy*. Never before has Dickens made so full, so Dantean, a claim for the virtue of the artist, and there is a Dantean pride and a Dantean reason in what he says of Daniel Doyce, who, although an engineer, stands for the creative mind in general and for its appropriate virtue: 'His dismissal of himself [was] remarkable. He never said, I discovered this adaptation or invented that combination; but showed the whole thing as if the Divine Artificer had made it, and he had happened to find it. So modest was he about it, such a pleasant touch of respect was mingled with his quiet admiration of it, and so calmly convinced was he that it was established on irrefragable laws.' Like much else that might be pointed to, this confirms us in the sense that the whole energy of the imagination of *Little Dorrit* is directed to the transcending of the personal will, to the search for the Will in which shall be our peace.

We must accept – and we easily do accept, if we do not permit critical cliché to interfere – the aesthetic of such an imagination, which

375 Dorothy Van Ghent

will inevitably tend toward a certain formality of pattern and towards the generalization and the abstraction we have remarked. In a novel in which a house falls physically to ruins from the moral collapse of its inhabitants, in which the heavens open over London to show a crown of thorns, in which the devil has something like an actual existence, we quite easily accept characters named nothing else than Bar, Bishop, Physician. And we do not reject, despite our inevitable first impulse to do so, the character of Little Dorrit herself. Her untinctured goodness does not appall us or make us misdoubt her, as we expected it to do. This novel at its best is only incidentally realistic; its finest power of imagination appears in the great general images whose abstractness is their actuality, like Mr Merdle's dinner parties, or the Circumlocution Office itself, and in such a context we understand Little Dorrit to be the Beatrice of the *Comedy*, the Paraclete in female form. Even the physical littleness of this grown woman, an attribute which is insisted on and which seems likely to repel us, does not do so, for we perceive it to be the sign that she is not only the Child of the Marshalsea, as she is called, but also the Child of the Parable, the negation of the social will.

(50–65)

Dorothy Van Ghent

from 'On *Great Expectations*', *The English Novel: Form and Function* 1953

Dickens lived in a time and an environment in which a full-scale demolition of traditional values was going on, correlatively with the uprooting and dehumanization of men, women and children by the millions – a process brought about by industrialization, colonial imperialism and the exploitation of the human being as a 'thing' or an engine or a part of an engine capable of being used for profit. This was the 'century of progress' which ornamented its steam engines with iron arabesques of foliage as elaborate as the antimacassars and aspidistras and crystal or cut-glass chandeliers and bead-and-feather portieres of its drawing rooms, while the human engines of its welfare groveled and bred in the foxholes described by Marx in his *Capital*. (Hauntingly we see this discordance in the scene in *Great Expectations* where Miss Havisham, sitting in her satin and floral decay in the house called Satis, points her finger at the child and outrageously tells him to 'play'. For though the scene is a potent symbol of childish experience of adult obtuseness and sadism, it has also another dimension as a social symbol of those economically determined situations in which the human soul is used as a means for satisfactions not its own, under the gross and transparent lie that its activity is its happiness, its welfare and fun and 'play' – a publicity instrument that is the favorite of manufacturers and insurance agencies, as well as of totalitarian strategists, with their common formula, 'We're just a happy family.') The heir of the 'century of progress' is the twentieth-century concentration camp, which makes no bones about people being 'things'.

Dickens's intuition alarmingly saw this process in motion, a process which abrogated the primary demands of human feeling and rationality, and he sought an extraordinary explanation for it. People were becoming things, and things (the things that money can buy or that are the means for making money or for exalting prestige in the abstract) were becoming more important than people. People were being de-animated, robbed of their souls, and things were usurping the prerogatives of animate creatures – governing the lives of their owners in the most literal sense. This picture, in which the qualities of things and people were reversed, was a picture of a demonically motivated world, a world in which 'dark' or occult forces or energies operate not only in people (as modern psychoanalytic psychology observes) but also in things: for if people turn themselves or are turned into things, metaphysical order can be established only if we think of things as turning themselves into people, acting under a 'dark' drive similar to that which motivates the human aberration.

There is an old belief that it takes a demon to recognize a demon, and the saying illustrates the malicious sensibility with which things, in Dickens, have felt out and imitated, in their relationship with each other and with people, the secret of the human arrangement. A four-poster bed in an inn, where Pip goes to spend the night is a despotic monster that straddles over the whole room,

putting one of his arbitrary legs into the fireplace, and
another into the doorway, and squeezing the wretched little
washing-stand in quite a Divinely Righteous manner.
(chapter 45)

Houses, looking down through the skylight of Jaggers's office in
London, twist themselves in order to spy on Pip like police agents
who presuppose guilt. Even a meek little muffin has to be 'confined
with the utmost precaution under a strong iron cover', and a hat, set
on a mantelpiece, demands constant attention and the greatest quick-
ness of eye and hand to catch it neatly as it tumbles off, but its ingenuity
is such that it finally manages to fall into the slop basin. The animation of inanimate objects suggests both the quaint gaiety of a forbidden life and an aggressiveness that has got out of control – an
aggressiveness that they have borrowed from the human economy
and an irresponsibility native to but glossed and disguised by that
economy.

Dickens's fairly constant use of the pathetic fallacy (the projection of
human impulses and feelings upon the nonhuman, as upon beds and
houses and muffins and hats) might be considered as incidental
stylistic embellishment if his description of people did not show a
reciprocal metaphor: people are described by nonhuman attributes,
or by such an exaggeration of or emphasis on one part of their
appearance that they seem to be reduced wholly to that part, with an
effect of having become 'thinged' into one of their own bodily
members or into an article of their clothing or into some inanimate
object of which they have made a fetish. Dickens's devices for producing this transposition of attributes are various. To his friend and
biographer, Forster, he said that he was always losing sight of a man
in his diversion by the mechanical play of some part of the man's
face, which 'would acquire a sudden ludicrous life of its own'.
Many of what we shall call the 'signatures' of Dickens's people – that
special exaggerated feature or gesture or mannerism which comes to
stand for the whole person – are such dissociated parts of the body,
like Jaggers's huge forefinger which he bites and then plunges mena-
cingly at the accused, or Wemmick's post-office mouth, or the clockwork apparatus in Magwitch's throat that clicks as if it were going to
strike. The device is not used arbitrarily or capriciously. In this book,

whose subject is the etiology of guilt and of atonement, Jaggers is the representative not only of civil law but of universal Law, which is profoundly mysterious in a world of dissociated and apparently lawless fragments; and his huge forefinger, into which he is virtually transformed and which seems to act like an 'it' in its own right rather than like a member of a man, is the Law's mystery in all its fearful impersonality. Wemmick's mouth is not a post-office when he is at home in his castle but only when he is at work in Jaggers's London office, where a mechanical appearance of smiling is required of him. And as Wemmick's job has mechanized him into a grinning slot, so oppression and fear have given the convict Magwitch a clockwork apparatus for vocal chords.

Or this general principle of reciprocal changes, by which things have become as it were demonically animated and people have been reduced to thing-like characteristics – as if, by a law of conservation of energy, the humanity of which people have become incapable had leaked out into the external environment – may work symbolically in the association of some object with a person so that the object assumes his essence and his 'meaning'. Mrs Joe wears a large apron, 'having a square impregnable bib in front, that was stuck full of pins and needles' – she has no reason to wear it, and she never takes it off a day in her life. Jaggers flourishes a large white handkerchief – a napkin that is the mysterious complement of his blood-smeared engagements. Estella – who is the star and jewel of Pip's great expectations – wears jewels in her hair and on her breast; 'I and the jewels', she says, as if they were interchangeable. This device of association is a familiar one in fiction; what distinguishes Dickens's use of it is that the associated object acts not merely to *illustrate* a person's qualities symbolically – as novelists usually use it – but that it has a necessary metaphysical function in Dickens's universe: in this universe objects actually usurp human essences; beginning as fetishes, they tend to – and sometimes quite literally do – devour and take over the powers of the fetish-worshipper.

The process of conversion of spirit into matter that operates in the Dickens world is shown working out with savage simplicity in the case of Miss Havisham. Miss Havisham has been guilty of aggression against life in using the two children, Pip and Estella, as inanimate instruments of revenge for her broken heart – using them, that is, as if they were not human but things – and she is being changed retributively into a fungus. The decayed cake on the banquet table acts, as it were, by homeopathic magic – like a burning effigy or a doll stuck with pins; its decay parallels the necrosis in the human agent. 'When the ruin is complete', Miss Havisham says, pointing to the cake but referring to herself, she will be laid out on the same table and her relatives will be invited to 'feast on' her corpse. But this is not the only conversion. The 'little quickened hearts' of the mice behind the panels have been quickened by what was Miss Havisham, carried off crumb by crumb.

The principle of reciprocal changes, between the human and the nonhuman, bears on the characteristic lack of complex 'inner life' on the part of Dickens's people – their lack of a personally complex psychology. It is inconceivable that the fungoid Miss Havisham should have a complex inner life, in the moral sense. But in the *art* of Dickens (distinguishing that moral dialectic that arises not solely from the 'characters' in a novel but from all the elements in the aesthetic structure) there is a great deal of 'inner life', transposed to other forms than that of human character: partially transposed in this scene, for instance, to the symbolic activity of the speckle-legged spiders with blotchy bodies and to the gropings and pausings of the black beetles on Miss Havisham's hearth. Without benefit of Freud or Jung, Dickens saw the human soul reduced literally to the images occupying its 'inner life'.

(128-31)

John Butt and Kathleen Tillotson

from 'Dickens as a Serial Novelist', *Dickens at Work* 1957

It is a commonplace in the criticism of early drama that the conditions in which a dramatist worked must be taken into account. He wrote for a theatre of a certain shape, with certain structural features, which permitted him to use certain dramatic effects. The analogy can be applied to the novelist who, though he has greater freedom than the dramatist, must also suit what he has to say to the current conventions of presentation. Just as Shakespeare thought in terms of a theatre without drop curtain, artificial lighting or scenery, and of a theatrical company of male actors only, so Dickens was accustomed to think in terms of publication peculiar to his time. Today novels are customarily published in single volumes. A hundred and fifty years ago this form of publication was unusual. In the eighteenth century, novels had appeared in five volumes, or even in as many as seven; but by the time of Scott and Jane Austen the usual number was three or four. The prices varied: it was not uncommon to charge as much as half a guinea a volume, which made novel-reading exceedingly expensive to those who did not belong to a circulating library. These were still the conditions ruling when Dickens began to write. His first novel, *Pickwick Papers*, shows him attempting to reach a larger number of readers by cutting the price to suit their pockets. The method chosen was to publish in 'what was then a very unusual form, at less than one-third of the price of the whole of an ordinary novel, and in shilling Monthly Parts'.[1]

After the first few numbers of *Pickwick*, each monthly 'part' or number consisted of three or four chapters, covering thirty-two pages of print, with two plates, and several pages of advertisements. It was issued in green paper covers and was published at a shilling, nominally on the first day, actually on the last day, of each month. This form of publication was chosen for *Pickwick* by Chapman and Hall, but Dickens found it so suitable that he adopted it for *Nicholas Nickleby*, *Martin Chuzzlewit*, *Dombey and Son*, *David Copperfield*, *Bleak House*, *Little Dorrit*, *Our Mutual Friend* and *Edwin Drood*. Each of these novels, except *Edwin Drood*, was planned for completion in nineteen monthly numbers, the last being a double number priced at two shillings, and containing, besides forty-eight pages of text and four plates, the title-page, frontispiece, preface, and other preliminaries. *Edwin Drood*, of which only six numbers were written, was planned for completion in eleven, the last to be a double number. Five of the other six novels were published in serial in weekly magazines and produced distinct problems of composition and form, which are touched upon in later chapters.

Although it might be supposed that Dickens would wish to complete a novel before permitting serial publication to begin, in fact he

1 Dickens's address announcing the 'cheap edition' of his works (1847). It is preserved in a scrap-book of cuttings in the British Museum (shelf mark K.T.C. 1.b. 5 (21)), and is reprinted in the 'National' edition, vol. 34, 1908, p. 433.

never wrote more than four or five numbers before the first was published, and by the middle of the novel he was rarely more than one number ahead of his readers. As might be expected, his practice differed at different stages of his career. Whereas *Little Dorrit* III was finished before the first number appeared and an even larger portion of *Our Mutual Friend* was ready before publication day, he had lightly embarked upon *Pickwick Papers* with nothing in hand;[1] and it seems that no more, or very little more, than the first numbers of *Nicholas Nickleby* and *Martin Chuzzlewit* were complete when publication began.[2] Furthermore, the writing of *Pickwick Papers* overlapped with *Oliver Twist*, and *Oliver Twist* with *Nicholas Nickleby*. In circumstances such as these, it is not surprising to learn that each number of *Nickleby* had been completed 'only ... a day or two before its publication';[3] and this in turn meant that when something compelled him to stop working for a prolonged period, a gap in the series supervened. Thus the death of Mary Hogarth, his sister-in-law, on 7 May 1837 moved him profoundly, and the effect upon his serial publication was immediate: there were no June numbers of *Pickwick Papers* and *Oliver Twist*. On the other hand, when he himself died on 9 June 1870 there was enough of *Edwin Drood* written to permit the publication of three more numbers, the third being only two pages short of the normal complement.

The disadvantages of this method seem obvious. As Trollope remarked, 'an artist should keep in his hand the power of fitting the beginning of his work to the end'.[4] And the difficulties seem equally great. Writing in serial involved maintaining two focuses. The design and purpose of the novel had to be kept constantly in view; but the writer had also to think in terms of the identity of the serial number, which would have to make its own impact and be judged as a unit. Incident and interest had therefore to be evenly spread, since 'the

1 See Forster, book 8, ch. 1; book 9, ch. 5; and John Butt and Kathleen Tillotson, *Dickens at Work*, 1957, p. 66.

2 'The first chapter [of *Nicholas Nickleby*] is ready ... so you can begin to print as soon as you like. The sooner you begin, the faster I shall get on' (*Letters*, vol.1, p. 161, 22 February 1838). The first number of *Martin Chuzzlewit* was 'nearly done' on 8 December 1842, with a little more than three weeks to go before publication day (*Letters*, W. Dexter (ed.), 1938, vol.1, p. 493).

3 *Letters*, vol. 1, p. 170.

4 *Autobiography* (World's Classics revised text), p. 127.

writer ... cannot afford to have many pages skipped out of the few which are to meet the reader's eye at the same time'.[1] Chapters must be balanced within a number in respect both of length and of effect. Each number must lead, if not to a climax, at least to a point of rest; and the rest between numbers is necessarily more extended than what the mere chapter divisions provide. The writer had also to bear in mind that his readers were constantly interrupted for prolonged periods, and that he must take this into account in his characterization and, to some extent, in his plotting. As early as the original preface to *Pickwick*, Dickens showed his recognition that not every story is suited to this type of publication.[2]

Great as these difficulties were, they were felt to be worth overcoming. To the reader the system meant not merely eager expectation of the day which brought a fresh batch of green covers to the bookstall, but also the impression that the story was in the making from month to month. Thus Lady Stanley is found addressing a friend in 1841 about the weekly progress of *The Old Curiosity Shop*:

How *can* you read Humphrey's last number and not *indulge*
me with an ejaculation or two about it? Are you satisfied with
the disposal of Quilp? My Lord is not, says it is too easy a
death and that he should have more time to *feel* his
punishment. Will Nelly die? I think she ought.'[3]

To the author it meant a larger public, but also a public more delicately responsive, who made their views known during the progress of a novel both by writing to him and by reducing or increasing their purchases. Through serial publication an author could recover something of the intimate relationship between story-teller and audience which existed in the ages of the sagas and of Chaucer; and for an author like Dickens, who was peculiarly susceptible to the influence of his readers, this intimate relationship outweighed the inherent disadvantages of the system.[4]

Yet the disadvantages were none the less apparent, and they could be mastered only by more systematic planning than this impulsive man

1 ibid., p. 132.
2 See J. Butt and K. Tillotson, op. cit., p. 65.
3 *The Ladies of Alderley*, N. Mitford (ed.), 1938, p. 2.
4 On serial publication see Kathleen Tillotson, *Novels of the Eighteen-Forties*, Oxford University Press, 1954, pp. 21–47.

has been credited with. Publication day was the last day of each month, known in the trade as 'magazine day'.[1] By that date Dickens had to plan and write the equivalent of thirty-two printed pages and to give his illustrator instructions for two engravings. The manuscript had to be sent to the printer in London, perhaps from Broadstairs or the Isle of Wight, or even from as far off as Lausanne.[2] Proofs were to be corrected and sent to press, and copies were to be sewn and distributed to booksellers. The publishers' agreement for *Nicholas Nickleby* specified that the manuscript should be delivered on the fifteenth day of each month.[3] During the progress of this novel it seems to have been recognized that the twenty-fourth would serve as the last date for a number,[4] but Dickens's subsequent practice was to aim at the twentieth. Frequently he had to go straight from one number to the next; but often he could allow himself a few days' respite at the end of the month before beginning the next month's instalment. Occasionally he resumed work as late as the seventh day.[5] Thus he had about a fortnight for writing his three or four chapters.

He did not always complete his number before sending it to the printer. Sometimes it was delivered in batches with instructions for a proof to be forwarded to the illustrator.[6] Hablôt Browne was accus-

---

1 For an account of the scene on 'magazine day' in Paternoster Row see Charles Manby Smith, *The Little World of London*, 1857, pp. 45–6. The arrangements were different for weekly serials. When W. H. Wills, the assistant editor of *All the Year Round*, was arranging for contemporaneous publication of a German version of *Great Expectations*, he told the German publishers that the translated portion was not to anticipate the original: 'we publish on the Wednesdays before the date upon our numbers, which is that of each Saturday. Therefore you can bring out each weekly portion every Wednesday after Wednesday the 28th Instant; when (and not before) you may issue the first portion.' (copy, dated 15 November 1860, in the *All the Year Round* letter-book, Henry E. Huntington Library.)

2 Part of *Copperfield* was written at Broadstairs, part in the Isle of Wight; part of *Dombey* was written at Lausanne, part in Paris.

3 Forster, book 2, ch. 2.

4 *Letters*, vol. 1, 177.

5 Occasionally even later. On 9 March 1847 he told Miss Hogarth that he had 'not yet written a single slip' of *Dombey* VII (*Letters*, vol. 2, p. 17.)

6 Thus Dickens wrote to Evans from Broadstairs about *Copperfield* IV (10 July 1849): 'I send you, by this Post, 9 slips of copy, containing Mr Browne's second subject. Get it up *with all speed*, and send a proof to him . . .' (*Letters*, vol. 2, p. 160).

tomed to work to orders. At best he had a proof to go upon; at worst
his instructions were verbal.[1] Sometimes he had a letter such as this,
which embodies directions for the first illustration in *Dombey* VII:

. . . The first subject which I am now going to give is very
important to the book. *I should like to see your sketch of it, if
possible.*

I should premise that I want to make the Major, who is
the incarnation of selfishness and small revenge, a kind of
comic Mephistophilean power in the book; and the No. begins
with the departure of Mr Dombey and the Major on that
trip for change of air and scene which is prepared for in the
last Number. They go to Leamington, where you and I were
once. In the Library the Major introduces Mr Dombey to a
certain lady, whom, as I wish to foreshadow dimly, said
Dombey may come to marry in due season. She is about
thirty, not a day more – handsome, though *haughty* looking
– good figure. Well dressed – showy – and desirable. Quite
a lady in appearance, with something of a proud indifference
about her, suggestive of a spark of the Devil within. Was
married young. Husband dead. Goes about with an old
mother, who rouges, and who lives upon the reputation of a
diamond necklace and her family. Wants a husband. Flies at
none but high game, and couldn't marry anybody not rich.

1 'It is due to the gentleman, whose designs accompany the letterpress, to state
that the interval has been so short between the production of each number in
manuscript and its appearance in print, that the greater portion of the Illustrations have been executed by the artist from the author's mere verbal description
of what he intended.' Original preface to *Pickwick Papers*. David Croal Thomson,
Life and Labours of Hablôt Knight Browne 'Phiz', London, 1884, pp. 63ff., 73ff.,
prints instructions from *Dombey*, plate 7, and *Nickleby*, plate 33; manuscript
instructions for the plates 18, 37 and 38, frontispiece, and title-page vignette of
Martin Chuzzlewit are preserved in the Henry E. Huntington Library. On the
instructions for plate 18, *The thriving city of Eden as it appeared in fact*, Browne has
pencilled a mild protest: 'I can't get all this perspective in – unless you will
allow of a long subject – something less than a mile'. Nevertheless he produced
a sketch, on which Dickens commented 'The stump of the tree should be *in*
the ground in fact a tree cut off two feet up. Too wide – cannot it be compressed
by putting Martin's label on the other side of the door, and bringing Mark with
his tree forwarder. Qy is that a *hat* on his head?'

Mother affects cordiality and *heart*, and is the essence of sordid calculation. Mother usually shoved about in a Bath chair by a Page who has rather *outgrown and outshoved his strength* and who *butts at it* behind like a ram, while his mistress *steers herself languidly* by a handle in front. *Nothing the matter with her to prevent her walking*, only was once *sketched (when a Beauty) reclining in a Barouche*, and having *outlived the beauty and the barouche too*, still *holds on to the attitude* as becoming her uncommonly. Mother is in this machine in the sketch. Daughter has a *parasol*.

The Major presents them to Mr Dombey, gloating within himself over what may come of it, and over the discomfiture of Miss Tox. Mr Dombey (in deep mourning) *bows* solemnly. Daughter bends. The Native in attendance, *bearing a camp-stool and the Major's greatcoat*. Native evidently afraid of the Major and his thick cane.

If you like it better, the scene may be in the street or in a green lane. But a great deal will come of it: and I want the Major to express that, as much as possible in his apoplectic Mephistophilean observation of the scene, and in his share in it.

Lettering: *Major Bagstock is delighted to have that opportunity.*[1]

The letter is typical of the attention to detail which Dickens paid in all his undertakings. At a time when it might be expected that his energies would be fully expended upon writing his monthly instalment, he must turn aside to create a scene in Browne's imagination, letting him into secrets, appropriately enough, which less privileged readers were left to guess, and speaking out straight on matters which in the novel he is content to hint at, but embodying here and there with little verbal change significant details from the manuscript before him.[2] Browne responded rapidly. The directions were dated 10 March 1847; on the evening of 15 March Dickens was writing to express his delight at the sketch which Browne had furnished, and to ask him to re-dress the Native ('who is prodigiously good as he is') in

1 D. C. Thomson, op. cit., pp. 68–71; *Letters*, vol. 2, pp. 17–18.
2 We have italicized these passages in the second and third paragraphs.

European costume ('He may wear ear-rings and look outlandish, and be dark brown') and to make the Major older, and with a larger face.[1]

The last book which Browne illustrated was *A Tale of Two Cities*. For *Our Mutual Friend* – neither the weekly serial nor the first 'volume' edition of *Great Expectations* was illustrated – Dickens chose Marcus Stone, the son of an old friend. Though Stone was only twenty-five when he began work on *Our Mutual Friend*, Dickens seems to have given him a freer hand than he allowed Browne. Stone used to get proofs and select his own subjects, though Dickens reserved the right to criticize and to demand alterations, and was always 'ready to describe down to the minutest details the personal characteristics, and . . . life-history of the creations of his fancy'.[2] But though Stone was allowed to draw the cover of *Our Mutual Friend* without more than the first two monthly numbers to go upon, Dickens's son-in-law Charles Collins, who drew the cover of *Edwin Drood*, admitted that he did not in the least know the significance of the various groups in the design, which were drawn from instructions given him personally by Dickens.[3]

Much is known about Dickens's habits at the desk. In the middle of his career, it was his normal custom to work in the mornings only from nine o'clock till two; but he was no clockwork performer like Trollope. He described himself beginning *Little Dorrit*, in a letter to Mrs Watson (21 May 1855),

walking about the country by day – prowling about into the strangest places in London by night – sitting down to do an immensity – getting up after doing nothing – walking about my room on particular bits of all the flowers in the carpet – tearing my hair (which I can't afford to do) – and on the

1 D. C. Thomson, op. cit., p. 65; *Letters*, vol. 2, p. 19. Thomson, p. 234, also prints a table of work, without mentioning book or year, which shows that Browne received his instructions for the first plate on Friday, 11 January, posted his sketch to Dickens on Sunday, received it back on Monday evening with instructions for the second plate, forwarded his sketch for that on Tuesday, and received it on Wednesday. The first plate was finished on Tuesday, 22 January, and the second on Saturday, 26 January.

2 Notes of an interview with Stone, quoted in *The Dickensian*, August 1912, pp. 216–17.

3 Luke Fildes in *The Times*, 3 November 1905.

whole astonished at my own condition, though I am used to
it. . . .[1]

As a young man he had been a fluent writer, able to drive himself to
work all day; and the surviving sheets of manuscript of his earliest
novels suggest a hand racing to keep pace with the mind's conceptions. As Heminge and Condell said of Shakespeare, 'We have scarce
received from him a blot in his papers.' His letters to Forster written
at this time suggest that eleven or twelve of these sheets, or 'slips' as
he called them, could be written in a day, or, at a push, as many as
twenty.[2] But at the height of his powers, he found more difficulty in
satisfying himself, and from *Dombey and Son* onwards his manuscripts
are characterized by frequent erasures and interlineations. Of these
slips Georgina Hogarth is witness[3] that an average day's work was
two or two-and-a-half, and 'a very, *very* hard days work was four of
them'. The different shades of ink which he used from time to time
show that his habit was to correct as he wrote, sentence by sentence,
and that though he subsequently read through the whole of his
chapter, he rarely needed to make any later alteration.

The manuscripts he sent to press were these corrected first drafts. He
never dictated to an amanuensis, nor used a secretary to make a fair
copy, and only in a few instances can we be sure that he took the
trouble of rewriting a much-corrected slip.[4] Indeed there was no

1 *Dickensian*, June 1942, pp. 165–6.
2 Forster, book 2, chs. 1, 2, 3.
3 Letter to F. Harvey, 15 December 1880, accompanying the MS. of *The
Battle of Life* (Pierpont Morgan Library).
4 When sending Charles Edward Lester a sheet of the MS. of *Oliver Twist* on
19 July 1840, he remarked, 'I should tell you perhaps as a kind of certificate of
the Oliver scrap, that it is a portion of the original and only draught. – I never
copy' (letter in the New York Public Library, Berg Collection). But this does
not represent his invariable practice later in life. The sheet on which Stagg's
Gardens is described in *Dombey and Son*, ch. 6, is so clean and so conspicuously
different from its neighbours in that respect as to suggest that he had decided to
make a fair copy of a passage which had involved him in unusually heavy
corrections. On the same reasoning it seems likely that he rewrote the first
MS. slip of *Hunted Down* and of *A Holiday Romance* (both in the Pierpont
Morgan Library), and certain passages in *Barnaby Rudge* (see p. 81 n.). In the
MS. of *Little Dorrit* there are traces of rough draft on the versos of some sheets
of the first and last numbers; three leaves of the last number have been pasted
on to slips concealing an earlier version.

time for what a modern printer regards as normal courtesy from his author; and as for dictation, it would only have hindered him, for he relied upon the knowledge that he had to fill about thirty slips in his normal handwriting to complete a monthly number. Thus Bradbury and Evans, his printers, had to make do with 'copy' obscure enough to daunt the most experienced compositor. Not only was it written in a small hand with all too little space left between lines for the numerous interlineations, but the text was sprinkled with peculiar proper names – not Cox but Tox, not Tomlinson but Towlinson – and with phonetic spellings of standard English. The difficulties presented even to a compositor accustomed to Dickens's hand may be gauged from the printer's setting up 'Mr Dick was very partial to going abroad' for 'Mr Dick was very partial to ginger bread'. But the compositors were picked men,[1] clean, quick and accurate. To ensure rapid despatch they were accustomed to distribute copy amongst several hands by dividing each slip across the centre and endorsing the lower half with a starred numeral corresponding to the number of the original slip.[2] Their accuracy cannot be properly attested until the manuscripts have been carefully collated with the proofs by some future editor of a standard text of the novels; but it may be said that neither Dickens nor Forster, who also read the proofs, found much to need correction.

Surviving copies of proof sheets suggest that the printer was instructed to provide galley proof when time permitted. Thus corrected proofs of *Copperfield*[3] consist of two sets of galley proof of Number I, one set of page proof of Numbers II to XVIII, and two sets of page proof of Numbers XIX–XX. It seems unlikely that Numbers II to XIX–XX were first set up in galley, for time was short; and, as will be seen, the bulk of correction was necessarily done in page. We can be almost certain that Number II (chapters 4–6, published on 31 May 1849) was not set up in galley, for Dickens sent the end of the number to Evans on 5 May 1849 with the note, 'If it should make a little too much (as I think it may) let them begin Chapter 5 on page 46, where there is now a great blank.'[4] A reason-

---

1 Mamie Dickens, *My Father as I Recall Him*, 1897, p. 63.
2 See letter to Mrs Procter, 29 October 1865 (*Letters*, vol. 3, p. 442).
3 Victoria and Albert Museum Library, 48 B 16.
4 *Letters*, vol. 2, p. 152.

able inference is that he had already seen page proofs of at least chapter 4 and possibly of chapter 5 as well.

There was not infrequently 'a little too much', for though he used the numbering of his slips as a guide to quantity – 30 slips would yield about 32 pages of print – the reckoning was only approximate. In every number of *Copperfield* except V, X, XI, XIV, XVI, XVIII, and XIX–XX, the proofs show what was called 'over-matter' extending, in Number VI, to as much as 96 lines of print. Dickens was so well accustomed to this happening that he could write to a correspondent on 28 January 1848, when *Dombey and Son* was drawing to a close:

I never accept an engagement for about this day in the month: being always liable, if my *proofs are late, to have to revise them at the printers*, and if there is too much matter (as is the case this month) to take it out, and put them all to rights and leave them on the press.[1]

But the amount taken out rarely corresponded at all exactly with the amount of 'over-matter'. Thus in *Copperfield* VI Dickens saved little more than 50 of the 96 lines excess; and in Number IX, where there were 58 lines excess, he saved 40 but inserted the equivalent of 6 more, adding as a note to the printer, 'the over-matter must be got in somehow – by lengthening the page'. This expedient was needed only in extreme cases, a 51-line page then taking the place of a page of 50 lines of type. Where the over-matter was small, less drastic methods were employed. In *Copperfield* XIII, for example, where there were a mere 11 lines too many, the printer preferred to save the space by resetting a letter, quoted at the end of chapter 11, in smaller type; and on numerous occasions a small saving was readily made where the final words of a paragraph overlapped into a new line.

When forced to lop and crop, Dickens was accustomed to make his cuts at the expense of the comedy. In *Dombey and Son*, where passages of greater significance were also removed, Mrs Chick, Miss Tox and Major Bagstock originally had longer parts;[2] so had Skimpole in *Bleak House* II and Honeythunder in *Edwin Drood* V; and in *David Copperfield*, chapter 21, he had to remove a capital scene in which

1 *Letters*, vol. 2, p. 70.
2 See J. Butt and K. Tillotson, op. cit., pp. 97, 98.

Steerforth successfully exerted his charms upon the lugubrious Mrs Gummidge and entered into a league with her to be lone and lorn together.[1] The future editor of Dickens will have to consider restoring these passages to the text, since they were removed only because of the fortuitous demands of serial publication.

But too little copy was even more troublesome than too much. 'Fancy!' Dickens wrote to Forster[2] early in July 1865, while *Our Mutual Friend* was on the stocks, 'fancy my having under-written number sixteen by two and a half pages – a thing I have not done since *Pickwick*!' He had forgotten *Dombey and Son* VI and *Bleak House* XVI where in each instance he was two pages light, and numerous other numbers deficient by half a page or more, notably *Little Dorrit* X, which concludes the first book with the release of Old Dorrit from the Marshalsea Prison. On that occasion he was the best part of a page too short even after he had added in proof a long paragraph describing the friends who assembled at the prison gate to welcome Mr Dorrit on his discharge. He disliked giving his readers short measure. The text of a number must usually end well down on the thirty-second page. 'Couldn't the end of the *next* chapter, which is crowded, be brought over to the following page?' he asked on the proofs of *Copperfield* XV, 'then, the blanks at the end of the No. would be avoided'.

Proofs also provided opportunity for other types of alteration. Sir Leicester Dedlock's hair is turned from white to grey in *Bleak House* I, Richard Carstone's age is increased from seventeen to nineteen, and it is only at this stage that Skimpole's first name is changed from Leonard to Harold – one of a number of changes designed to weaken the resemblance to Leigh Hunt – that Jobling's assumed name is altered from 'Owen' to 'Weevle', that Matthew Bagnet's nickname is changed from 'Number Seventy-Four' to 'Lignum Vitae' and Minnie Meagles's from 'Baby' to 'Pet'. It is more surprising to discover that until proof Miss Flite had been 'Maggie' – a name to be used in *Little Dorrit* for another crazy woman[3] – and that even then Dickens had toyed with 'Flighty'.

1 First published in *Review of English Studies*, new series 1 (1950), p. 251. It is obvious, too, that space is most easily saved in dialogue, where short lines of print are frequent.
2 Forster, book 9, ch. 5.
3 Her surname also is changed in proof – from Flinx to Bangham.

Forster had also been accustomed to lend a hand ever since 1837.[1] He provided another pair of eyes for detecting errors of the press, and he was trusted as a judge of what the average reader would stand. Proofs show that he softened such expletives as Dickens himself had overlooked, and removed the description of Miss Tox ejecting the bugs from the wainscoting of her house by means of a brush dipped in paraffin. Furthermore, Forster was usually in London and could deal with last-minute adjustments sent from Broadstairs or further afield. Thus in July 1841 Dickens wrote from the Highlands – a 'place which no man ever spelt but which sounds like Ballyhoolish' – inquiring 'whether the blind man, in speaking to Barnaby about riches, tells him they are to be found in *crowds*. If I have not actually used that word, will you introduce it? A perusal of the proof of the following number (70) will show you how, and why.'[2] The addition was needed in chapter 47 in the next number. A few years later on, as the last number of *Dombey* was going to press, he recollected that in the final parade of his pantomime one character had been overlooked – the dog Diogenes; he therefore sent Forster alternative versions, leaving to his judgement which was to be inserted in proof. There is no evidence of his consulting anyone else at proof stage, except for a mystifying reference in a letter of 15 May 1861, where he tells Lytton that 'a woman' had frequently shown, when proofs were read to her, 'an intuitive sense and discretion that I have set great store by'.[3] (13–24)

J. Hillis Miller

from '*Martin Chuzzlewit*', *Charles Dickens: The World of his Novels* 1958

The aim of *Martin Chuzzlewit*, as Dickens himself said, is to show 'how selfishness propagates itself; and to what a grim giant it may grow, from small beginnings' (Preface to the first cheap edition, *Martin Chuzzlewit*, p. xi). But selfishness exists in the novel not only

1 Forster, book 2, ch. 1.
2 Forster, book 2, ch. 9.
3 *Letters*, vol. 3, p. 220. Could the unknown woman have been anyone but Georgina Hogarth?

as the ethical bent of the characters, but also as the state of isolation in which they live. The novel is full of people who are wholly enclosed in themselves, wholly secret, wholly intent on reflexive ends which are altogether mysterious to those around them. As Sairey Gamp says in what might serve as an epigraph for the entire novel: '. . . we never knows wot's hidden in each other's hearts; and if we had glass winders there, we'd need keep the shetters up, some on us, I do assure you!' (chapter 29). This self-enclosure is explicitly made the predominant trait of some of the characters of *Martin Chuzzlewit*: '. . . the whole object of [Nadgett's] life', says Dickens, 'appeared to be, to avoid notice, and preserve his own mystery' (chapter 38). The key term for Nadgett is 'secret'. He represents in a pure state what the characters of *Martin Chuzzlewit* look like not from within their own private worlds, as in the case of our vision of Mr Mould, but from the outside. Nadgett's behavior, his speech, his action and appearance can be seen and described, but they remain unintelligible, preserving untouched within the secret of what he is: '. . . he was born to be a secret. He was a short, dried-up, withered, old man, who seemed to have secreted his very blood; for nobody would have given him credit for the possession of six ounces of it in his whole body. How he lived was a secret; where he lived was a secret; and even what he was, was a secret' (chapter 27). Why does Nadgett remain an unfathomable secret? He is not hidden behind protective screens, like Mr Mould. He is out in the open where he can be inspected. Even the contents of his pocketbook are no secret. Nevertheless he cannot be known. *What* he is cannot be known, in spite of the evidence, because it is wholly impossible to find out *who* he is. There is no possible direct access to the inner life of Nadgett. What is missing here, and throughout *Martin Chuzzlewit* for the most part, is any inter-subjective world. There is no world of true language, gesture or expression which would allow the characters entrance to one another's hearts. And Dickens does not permit himself, except on a very few occasions, to employ the convention of the omniscient narrator, able to enter at will the inner consciousnesses of his characters. The world of *Martin Chuzzlewit* is a public world, a world in which what exists is only what could be seen by any detached observer. It is in this sense that it is a fundamentally comic world. For the essential requirement of comedy is an unbridgeable gap between narrator (and reader) and the characters. Far from identifying himself with the subjective experiences of the characters, and realizing them from the inside, the reader of *Martin Chuzzlewit*, like the narrator and the characters themselves, in their relations to one another, remains separated from the personages. He may attribute to the characters the subjective states appropriate to the speech, expression or gesture which he sees, but the characters actually exist as their appearance and their actions and only as these. They are simply visible, audible, tangible objects, animate, but apparently otherwise exactly like other objects in the world.

For some characters such as Mr Mould, this presents no problem. Mould exists only as undertaker and as pampered family man. He has no secret. But for certain people, like Nadgett, the manifest data do not hang together and one is forced to assume the existence of something hidden, something which is on principle utterly beyond the reach of mere detached observation. And yet Nadgett is not a special case. He is one example of a large group produced by the peculiar conditions of modern urban life: 'he belonged to a class; a race peculiar to the City; who are secrets as profound to one another, as they are to the rest of mankind' (chapter 27). The city has brought about this crisis in our knowledge of our neighbor by separating altogether public role and private self. Constant changes of employment, the lack of distinguishing outward characteristics to label members of each profession, the sheer size of the urban community, all these tend to make it more and more impossible to identify a person satisfactorily in terms of his occupation. There is no way to reach Nadgett's secret subjective self. But neither is there any way to define him certainly by his public roles, for he carries in his pocketbook 'contradictory cards', which label him as coal merchant, wine merchant, commission agent, collector and accountant (chapter 27). Such are the conditions of city life that it is impossible to know which of these professions he actually practices, if any.

In the end Nadgett exists not as a coherent and intelligible self, either private or public, but as a collection of eccentric and baffling appearances, wholly external appearances which are known to be no true index to that large proportion of his life which remains secret:

He was mildewed, threadbare, shabby; always had flue upon his legs and back; and kept his linen so secret by buttoning

up and wrapping over, that he might have had none –
perhaps he hadn't. He carried one stained beaver glove,
which he dangled before him by the forefinger as he walked
or sat; but even its fellow was a secret. . . .
(chapter 27)

The characters of *Martin Chuzzlewit* tend to exist, then, not through
the visible expression of a coherent inner life, but as fixed and innate
idiosyncrasies behind which one cannot go, because there is apparently nothing behind them. '. . . why does any man entertain his own
whimsical taste? Why does Mr Fips wear shorts and powder, and
Mr Fips's next-door neighbour boots and a wig?' (chapter 39). There
is no answer. For Dickens the idiosyncrasy of character is an absurd
and irreducible fact. Everyone in *Martin Chuzzlewit* resembles the
boarders at Todgers's each of whom has a 'turn' for something or
other, but no one of whom has an existence with any psychological
depth or integration: 'There was . . . a gentleman of a smoking turn,
and a gentleman of a convivial turn; some of the gentlemen had a
turn for whist, and a large proportion of the gentlemen had a strong
turn for billiards and betting' (chapter 9). When there is a party at
Todgers's, 'every man comes out freely in his own character' (chapter
9). There is nothing else he can do. The endless repetition by such a
character of an eccentricity which is superficial and meaningless and
yet is the only identity he possesses is as spontaneous and undeliberate,
and as little human, as the putting forth of maple leaves by a maple
tree. . . .

The characters of *Martin Chuzzlewit*, then, must leave their ambi-
ent milieux, the milieux that are so intimately fused with themselves,
and seek in the outer world, the world that is alien and unfamiliar,
some support for their own beings. Mr Mould must leave his own
'premises' and enter into the 'strife' of the city; Tom Pinch must lose
his innocent faith in Pecksniff and go down to London; and Martin
Chuzzlewit must leave England altogether and go to America.

This exit from himself plunges the individual immediately into a
labyrinth. In a moment he loses the way:

Todgers's was in a labyrinth, whereof the mystery was known
but to a chosen few.
(chapter 9)

[Tom Pinch] lost his way. He very soon did that; and in trying
to find it again, he lost it more and more. . . . So, on he
went, looking up all the streets he came near, and going up
half of them; and thus, by dint of not being true to Goswell
Street, and filing off into Aldermanbury, and bewildering
himself in Barbican, and being constant to the wrong point
of the compass in London Wall, and then getting himself
crosswise into Thames Street, by an instinct that would
have been marvellous if he had had the least desire or reason
to go there, he found himself, at last, hard by the Monument.
(chapter 37)

Mr Pecksniff, with one of the young ladies under each arm,
dived across the street, and then across other streets, and so
up the queerest courts, and down the strangest alleys and
under the blindest archways, in a kind of frenzy: now
skipping over a kennel, now running for his life from a
coach and horses; now thinking he had lost his way, now
thinking he had found it; now in a state of the highest
confidence, now despondent to the last degree, but always
in a great perspiration and flurry. . . .
(chapter 8)

But in losing his way, the protagonist loses himself. In *Oliver
Twist* the hero began lost, at the center of a labyrinth, seeking through
a maze of hostile ways his absent identity. But in *Martin Chuzzlewit*
the characters are initially 'found', or so they think, surrounded, like
Mr Mould, with a friendly and reassuring world which mirrors back
themselves. Their entrance into the labyrinth is the discovery of a
world which is not consubstantial with themselves. It is thus the exact
reverse of the labyrinth of *Oliver Twist*: a process of the unintentional
losing of oneself rather than a frantic attempt to become 'found'.

The state of mind of the person who has thus inadvertently entered
the maze is one of increasing bewilderment and anxiety. What had
begun as a deliberate and rational attempt to find his way to a certain
goal becomes 'frenzy', a perpetual state of 'great perspiration and
flurry'. At last he realizes the truth, that he is irrevocably off the track,
and an utter state of resignation and hopelessness ensues. He gives
himself up for lost:

You couldn't walk about in Todgers's neighborhood, as
you could in any other neighborhood. You groped your
way for an hour through lanes and by-ways, and
court-yards and passages; and you never once emerged upon
anything that might be reasonably called a street. A kind of
resigned distraction came over the stranger as he trod those
devious mazes, and, giving himself up for lost, went in and
out and round about and quietly turned back again when he
came to a dead wall or was stopped by an iron railing, and
felt that the means of escape might possibly present
themselves in their own good time, but that to anticipate
them was hopeless.
(chapter 9)

This 'resigned distraction' is something like the catatonic trance of
certain types of insanity. The 'stranger' is faced with a world which
refuses altogether to yield a sense, to relate itself to his mind. He is
both within and without at the same time, within the hostile maze
from which he wishes desperately to escape, and outside the hidden
meaning behind the 'dead walls'. In fact he is doubly shut out,
estranged now from the comfortable home he has so recently left, and
unable to understand the world he has so abruptly entered. Like Martin Chuzzlewit, cast out by his grandfather and alone in London, he
has 'a pretty strong sense of being shut out, alone, upon the dreary
world, without the key of it' (chapter 13).

At this halfway point, en route, there are, it seems, two choices.
The protagonist can go forward seeking a way out of the maze, or he
can run back into the safety of home – like the 'people who, being
asked to dine at Todgers's had travelled round and round for a weary
time, with its very chimney-pots in view; and finding it, at last, impossible of attainment, had gone home again with a gentle melancholy
on their spirits, tranquil and uncomplaining' (chapter 9). But it is in
taking the latter alternative that a person may make an astonishing
discovery. The milieu which had seemed so solid and enduring as
long as he dwelled monotonously within it has suddenly, through his
absence, itself entered the world of vertiginous change:

Change begets change: nothing propagates so fast. If a man
habituated to a narrow circle of cares and pleasures, out of

which he seldom travels, step beyond it, though for never so
brief a space, his departure from the monotonous scene on
which he has been an actor of importance, would seem to be
the signal for instant confusion. As if, in the gap he had left,
the wedge of change were driven to the head, rending what
was a solid mass to fragments, things cemented and held
together by the usages of years, burst asunder in as many
weeks. The mine which Time has slowly dug beneath
familiar objects, is sprung in an instant; and what was rock
before, becomes but sand and dust.
(chapter 18)

The discovery of sand and dust where there had been solid rock leads
inevitably to a shocking deduction: the world which had seemed so
perdurable while the individual was within it, such a substantial support for his selfhood, had actually not been constitutive of the self at
all. Rather it was the self which, by dwelling permanently at the
center of certain objects, had constituted them as an integrated whole.
Home is not really a protective cocoon. It is only the presence of the
inhabitant which makes it seem so and which makes it keep on seeming so. In actuality, each milieu is only a kind of insubstantial fabric, a
psychic rather than an objective phenomenon. The human presence
at the center is the creative idea which makes it and holds it together.
When that is removed by the inhabitant's own removal the whole
scene collapses into fragments and he discovers a world that is everywhere, from the center to the horizon, a mere agglomeration of disconnected things:

Tiers upon tiers of vessels, scores of masts, labyrinths of
tackle, idle sails, splashing oars, gliding row-boats,
lumbering barges, sunken piles, with ugly lodgings for the
water-rat within their mud-discoloured nooks; church
steeples, warehouses, house-roofs, arches, bridges, men and
women, children, casks, cranes, boxes, horses, coaches, idlers
and hard-labourers: there they were, all jumbled up together,
any summer morning, far beyond Tom's power of
separation.
(chapter 40)

At first this scene reveals itself as a group of independent objects, each
one of which, like the boarders at Todgers's, 'comes out strongly in
[its] own nature'. Each noun is matched by an adjective, or rather,
not by a mere adjective of static quality, but by a verbal adjective, a
participle. Each such form defines its object as existing in a ceaseless and
repetitive activity which is the very expression of its nature: 'splashing
oars, gliding row-boats, lumbering barges, sunken piles'. But each of
these activities, except for chance collisions, remains wholly isolated,
unrelated to the others, like the particles in a Brownian movement. It
is not possible to discover a hierarchy among these objects, or a causal
chain, or a central principle of organization. In the end the world no
longer even seems to be inhabited by active entities. It becomes
merely an indefinite number of self-enclosed objects, 'all jumbled up
together'. Men, horses, bridges, it is all the same: even the division
into kingdoms of animal, vegetable or mineral is lost. Finally, as the
list is extended, the items even cease to be things and become mere
names, names which, it is true, correspond to different parts of the
visual field, but labels which now seem to be increasingly superficial.
They identify only surface distinctions which cover without depth
an undifferentiated mass underneath, a mass which is beyond anyone's 'power of separation', and is the sheer pulp or stuff of
things.

We may find ourselves at last at the center of the world, at the
center of the maze. But what we discover there is that the world has
no center, but is an unimaginable number of plural and interchangeable objects, plural because each individual is only one among an unlimited supply of the type, and interchangeable because no individual
entity has any distinct quality or value of its own: 'Then there were
steeples, towers, belfries, shining vanes, and masts of ships: a very
forest' (chapter 9). In the end we face simply a forest, a wilderness,
wilderness upon wilderness, in which each separate entity is to be defined only by its hostility, by its implacable resistance to our attempts
to comprehend it, to find ourselves in it: 'Gables, housetops, garret-
windows, wilderness upon wilderness' (chapter 9).

In a world of this sort a person cannot pretend to have a precise
object in view. To attend to a certain object or to attend to another, it
is all the same, and in the end such a person reaches a complete state of
indifference, of ennui, of passive despair, in which he returns over and

over again to the same object because there is absolutely no difference now between one object and another:

In his first wanderings up and down the weary streets, he counterfeited the walk of one who had an object in his view; but, soon there came upon him the sauntering, slipshod gait of listless idleness and the lounging at street-corners, and plucking and biting of stray bits of straw, and strolling up and down the same place, and looking into the same shop-windows, with a miserable indifference, fifty times a day. . . .
(chapter 13)

A character like Tom, at this stage of his exploration of the external world, has reached a strange impasse. He can no longer rest assured that he is in effect the only person in the world, the only spiritual presence around which things organize themselves. He knows now that someone else exists, and he knows that he cannot remain safely in his self-enclosure. The very continuation of his existence depends on establishing some kind of satisfactory relation to what is outside himself. But this alien world and the people hidden behind its walls remain mysteries. The people especially exist as an inexplicable menace, something behind the door, in the other room, spying on him, hiding wherever he is not, never seen directly, and yet present and active everywhere in the world. How can he come face to face with this incomprehensible and ubiquitous threat, seize it, understand it and control it?

In *Martin Chuzzlewit*, the apogee of this relation to the world is a striking passage describing the view from the roof of Todgers's boardinghouse.[1] This is a text of capital importance for the entire work of Dickens, since Dickens here most explicitly expresses the dangerous end point to which his characters can be brought by the attitude of passive and detached observation:

After the first glance, there were slight features in the midst of this crowd of objects, which sprung out from the mass without any reason, as it were, and took hold of the

1 Dorothy Van Ghent, in an excellent article, 'The Dickens World: A View from Todgers's', *Sewanee Review*, vol. 58 (1950), no. 3, pp. 419–38, uses this passage as her center of focus. Her interpretation, however, differs from mine.

attention whether the spectator would or no. Thus, the
revolving chimney-pots on one great stack of buildings,
seemed to be turning gravely to each other every now and
then, and whispering the result of their separate observation
of what was going on below. Others, of a crook-backed
shape, appeared to be maliciously holding themselves
askew, that they might shut the prospect out and baffle
Todgers's. The man who was mending a pen at an upper
window over the way, became of paramount importance
in the scene, and made a blank in it, ridiculously
disproportionate in its extent, when he retired. The gambols
of a piece of cloth upon the dyer's pole had far more interest
for the moment than all the changing motion of the crowd.
(chapter 9)

The observer of this scene knows that there is a spiritual life other
than his own present somewhere, but he does not know exactly
where it is, and is forced to attribute life indiscriminately to everything he sees. As a result, the spectator perceives a nightmarish animation of what ought to be inanimate objects, from the revolving
chimney-pots which seem to whisper gravely to one another to the
piece of cloth which 'gambols' with an apparently intrinsic life of its
own. And this animation is deliberately and intensely inimical to man.
The chimney pots are gossipy spies, or are maliciously hiding the
view from the observer on Todgers's roof, or from Todgers's itself,
which is here conceived of as an animate being.

Before all this life the observer is absolutely passive. He is at the
mercy of these things and especially at the mercy of their motion.
There is no stability in the world he sees, but, more astonishingly, he
discovers that to this constant metamorphosis of things there corresponds a metamorphosis of himself. When something changes in the
scene outside himself, he too changes. The perpetual change in things
imposes itself on the spectator until, in the end, he exists as the same
person only in the infinitesimal moment of an enduring sensation.

But the spectator on Todgers's roof discovers something even more
disquieting. He discovers that the withdrawal of something from the
scene produces not simply a blank in his consciousness, a blank which
he can easily replace with his own interior life, but an unfillable gap.

The exterior and visible void is 'ridiculously disproportionate in its extent' because it proves to the observer his own interior nothingness. The removal of the man in the window is the removal of an irreplaceable part of himself, and the observer comes to make the discovery that he is, in one sense, nothing at all, since he is nothing in himself, and, in another sense, is everything, since he can become by turns everything he beholds.

The climax of this experience is a double disintegration of the self. On the one hand, the view from Todgers's brings the spectator a recognition of his aloneness and lack of a stable and substantial self. But, on the other hand, and in the same moment, this alien world, this collection of objects which has no relation to the observer, and no meaning for him, rushes into the inner emptiness, and swamps and obliterates his separate identity. Moreover, this movement of things into the self is matched by a corresponding plunge of the self into things. The ultimate danger is that the looker-on will fall headforemost into the hosts of things, and lose himself altogether:

Yet even while the looker-on felt angry with himself for
this, and wondered how it was, the tumult swelled into a
roar; the hosts of objects seemed to thicken and expand a
hundredfold; and after gazing round him, quite scared, he
turned into Todgers's again, much more rapidly than he
came out; and ten to one he told M. Todgers afterwards that
if he hadn't done so, he would certainly have come into the
street by the shortest cut: that is to say, head foremost.
(chapter 9)

Mere passive observation, it seems, will not do. Active steps must be taken to escape from the situation of vacillation and nonentity. If the external world merely encountered will yield neither a sense nor a support, the individual must take matters in hand, either build an impregnable defense against the outside world, or cleverly manipulate it, force it to recognize and sustain him.

There are some characters in *Martin Chuzzlewit* who are perfectly aware that there is an alien world outside themselves, but who are able to live by a continual manipulation of that world and of other people. Through this manipulation they transform what is alien into an instrument ministering to their own selfish needs. Sairey Gamp is the magnificent dramatization of this way of inhering in the world. It is a way very different from that of Mr Mould. Mould is present and visible in all that surrounds him as milieu, but what surrounds him is like himself, and therefore is a direct expression of his nature. But Sairey is present in things which are unlike herself and separate from her. She thus is at once present in and absent from her milieu. Presented wholly from the outside, from the point of view of the detached observer, she is Dickens's fullest expression of the paradoxical inherence in a body and in the objective world of a consciousness which always transcends its body and can never be identified with any object.

This presence-absence is strikingly apparent in the animation of objects in the neighborhood of Sairey. Her maltreatment of Tom Pinch is not, apparently, intentional, but is caused by the independent malice of her umbrella:

This tremendous instrument had a hooked handle; and its vicinity was first made known to him by a painful pressure on the windpipe, consequent upon its having caught him round the throat. Soon after disengaging himself with perfect good humour, he had a sensation of the ferrule in his back; immediately afterwards, of the hook entangling his ankles; then of the umbrella generally, wandering about his hat, and flapping at it like a great bird; and, lastly, of a poke or thrust below the ribs, which gave him ... exceeding anguish. ... (chapter 40)

Sairey's ignorance of the malign actions of her umbrella is akin to her complete insensitivity to her patients. '... may our next meetin',' she says to Mrs Prig, 'be at a large family's, where they all takes it reg'lar, one from another, turn and turn about, and has it businesslike' (chapter 29). All things, for Sairey Gamp, including her own body, and her clothes, are dissociated from her, and yet are related intimately to her. They are dissociated from her in so far as she takes no account of them as they are in themselves, the objects as mere objects, the people as other human beings with lives of their own. These 'realistic' and 'objective' elements in the world disappear altogether for Sairey. She is cut off from them, and has no idea, for example, of what her patients Lewsome and Chuffey are suffering or thinking.

What does connect her intimately to the world both of objects and people, so intimately that her mark is apparent everywhere around her, is the fact that everything is used by her to satisfy her own selfish desires. This dissociation produces the immense comic tension of her appearances. Everything but her own mind with its selfish intents is objectified, and so complete is the cleavage between Sairey and her own body that even her own actions seem to be performed not by human volition, but by inanimate objects horribly endowed with life. So it is not Sairey herself who insists that her luggage must be treated in a certain way, but the luggage itself which has certain human requirements: 'every package belonging to that lady had the inconvenient property of requiring to be put in a boot by itself, and to have no other luggage near it, on pain of actions at law for heavy damages against the proprietors of the coach' (chapter 29). It is not Mrs Gamp's stipulation, but an 'inconvenient property' of the luggage itself, and the language of the rest of the sentence suggests that not Mrs Gamp, but the luggage itself, will sue the coach company. In the next sentence the personification is explicit: 'The umbrella with the circular patch was particularly hard to be got rid of, and several times thrust out its battered brass nozzle from improper crevices and chinks, to the great terror of the other passengers' (chapter 29). There is a hidden human malignity here acting blindly through insentient objects. It is not simply the fact that objects appear to be unnaturally human; this fact itself is the unmistakable evidence that somewhere a human intelligence exists, a human intelligence which has somehow got itself magically entangled with inanimate objects and acts through them, but without full cognizance of what it is doing. The umbrella is not conscious. It is the sign of consciousness, an object magically endowed with life by the presence of consciousness. The fact of Sairey's intensely self-centred consciousness makes everything in her neighborhood orient itself around her like iron filings around a magnet. Thus everything in her proximity is evidence of her presence – the pattens, the umbrella, the rearrangement of her patients' rooms (and the patients) for her comfort, the famous bottle on the chimney piece – all testify to the existence of Sairey Gamp. But the fact that she transforms everything, including other people, into what they are not, does not give us direct access to her subjectivity. The evidence of her subjectivity is a masked evidence. We do not know it directly, but only through the transformation of things in her neighborhood, the animation of umbrella and luggage, and the change of people into something which approaches the status of pure instrumentality. Everywhere we see signs through which we can directly and intuitively understand Sairey, but we have no direct access to that toward which the signs point. Sairey herself remains alone, apart, above and beyond all her evident inherence in the world, and it is this ambiguous presence–absence which is the real source of the brilliant comedy of the scenes in which she appears.

But in the end Sairey fails, fails because she has never ceased to be alone, selfish. Her way is very firmly rejected by Dickens when he includes her among the villains exposed in the denouement, and has old Martin Chuzzlewit give her advice 'hinting at the expediency of a little less liquor, and a little more humanity, and a little less regard for herself, and a little more regard for her patients, and perhaps a trifle of additional honesty' (chapter 52). But more essentially, perhaps, Sairey fails because she can never bring together the two halves of her contradictory presence–absence in the world. On the one hand, she remains wholly alone, isolated in a private world of self-seeking which is so narrow that it uses even her own body as the instrument of its gluttonous pleasure. But, on the other hand, whatever outside herself she becomes related to is immediately transformed into an extension of herself. She never succeeds any more than did the spectator on the roof of Todgers's in establishing a relation to something which while remaining other than herself, is support for herself. . . .

Everywhere in *Martin Chuzzlewit*, then, we find in the characters a vacillation between the desire to be wholly autonomous, and the even more intense desire to discover something outside themselves which will recognize their being.

The dramatic action of *Martin Chuzzlewit* is disentangled through a human relationship which represents an escape from this vacillation, the only escape which Dickens can discover at this time. The escape is *love*, the joining together of heroes and heroines which ends the novel, and sends the protagonists off to live happily ever after. Love is for Dickens that human relationship in which each partner, by giving himself unselfishly to the other, becomes the foundation and justification of the other's selfhood. But at this stage of Dickens's career love is shown from the outside, as a mystery. It brings the story happily to

a close, but Dickens cannot really show how that happens. Love makes the Temple fountain sparkle and smile for John and Ruth, but not for Dickens. Nowhere is Dickens's self-betraying sentimentality more present here than in the treatment of the love affairs of his characters. All Dickens's attempts to get inside these relationships and show their reciprocity only move him (and the reader!) further and further away into the isolation of a self-generated emotion.
(104-40)

Raymond Williams

'The Industrial Novels: *Hard Times*', *Culture and Society 1780–1950*
1958

Ordinarily Dickens's criticisms of the world he lives in are casual and incidental – a matter of including among the ingredients of a book some indignant treatment of a particular abuse. But in *Hard Times* he is for once possessed by a comprehensive vision, one in which the inhumanities of Victorian civilization are seen as fostered and sanctioned by a hard philosophy, the aggressive formulation of an inhumane spirit.

This comment by F. R. Leavis on *Hard Times* serves to distinguish Dickens's intention from that of Mrs Gaskell in *Mary Barton*. *Hard Times* is less imaginative observation than an imaginative judgement. It is a judgement of social attitudes, but again it is something more than *North and South*. It is a thorough-going and creative examination of the dominant philosophy of industrialism – of the hardness that Mrs Gaskell saw as little more than a misunderstanding, which might be patiently broken down. That Dickens could achieve this more comprehensive understanding is greatly to the advantage of the novel. But against this we must set the fact that in terms of human understanding of the industrial working people Dickens is obviously less successful than Mrs Gaskell: his Stephen Blackpool, in relation to the people of Mary Barton, is little more than a diagrammatic figure. The gain in comprehension, that is to say, has been achieved by the rigours of generalization and abstraction; *Hard Times* is an analysis of Industrialism, rather than experience of it.

The most important point, in this context, that has to be made about *Hard Times* is a point about Thomas Gradgrind. Josiah Bounderby, the other villain of the piece, is a simple enough case. He is, with rough justice, the embodiment of the aggressive money-making and power-seeking ideal which was a driving force of the Industrial Revolution. That he is also a braggart, a liar and in general personally repellent is of course a comment on Dickens's method. The conjunction of these personal defects with the aggressive ideal is not (how much easier things would be if it were) a necessary conjunction. A large part of the Victorian reader's feelings against Bounderby (and perhaps a not inconsiderable part of the twentieth-century intellectual's) rests on the older and rather different feeling that trade, as such, is gross. The very name (and Dickens uses his names with conscious and obvious effect), incorporating *bounder*, incorporates this typical feeling. The social criticism represented by *bounder* is, after all, a rather different matter from the question of aggressive economic individualism. Dickens, with rough justice, fuses the separate reactions, and it is easy not to notice how one set of feelings is made to affect the other.

The difficulty about Thomas Gradgrind is different in character. It is that the case against him is so good, and his refutation by experience so masterly, that it is easy for the modern reader to forget exactly *what* Gradgrind is. It is surprising how common is the mistake of using the remembered name, Gradgrind, as a class-name for the hard Victorian employer. The valuation which Dickens actually asks us to make is more difficult. Gradgrind is a Utilitarian: seen by Dickens as one of the *feeloosofers* against whom Cobbett thundered, or as one of the *steam-engine intellects* described by Carlyle. This line is easy enough, but one could as easily draw another: say, Thomas Gradgrind, Edwin Chadwick, John Stuart Mill. Chadwick, we are told, was 'the most hated man in England', and he worked by methods, and was blamed for 'meddling', in terms that are hardly any distance from Dickens's Gradgrind. Mill is a more difficult instance (although the education of which he felt himself a victim will be related, by the modern reader, to the Gradgrind system). But it seems certain that Dickens has Mill's *Political Economy* (1849) very much in mind in his general indictment of the ideas which built and maintained Coketown. (Mill's reaction, it may be noted, was the expressive 'that creature Dickens'.) It is easy now to realize that Mill was something more than a Gradgrind. But we are missing Dickens's point if we fail to see that in condemning Thomas Gradgrind, the representative figure, we are invited also to condemn the kind of thinking and the methods of inquiry and legislation which in fact promoted a large measure of social and industrial reform. One wonders, for example, what a typical Fabian feels when he is invited to condemn Gradgrind, not as an individual but as a type. This may, indeed, have something to do with the common error of memory about Gradgrind to which I have referred. Public commissions, Blue Books, Parliamentary legislation – all these, in the world of *Hard Times* – are Gradgrindery.

For Dickens is not setting Reform against Exploitation. He sees what we normally understand by both as two sides of the same coin, Industrialism. His positives do not lie in social improvement, but rather in what he sees as the elements of human nature – personal kindness, sympathy and forbearance. It is not the model factory against the satanic mill, nor is it the humanitarian experiment against selfish exploitation. It is, rather, individual persons against the System. In so far as it is social at all, it is the Circus against Coketown. The schoolroom contrast of Sissy Jupe and Bitzer is a contrast between the education, practical but often inarticulate, which is gained by living and doing, and the education, highly articulated, which is gained by systemization and abstraction. It is a contrast of which Cobbett would have warmly approved; but in so far as we have all (and to some extent inevitably) been committed to a large measure of the latter, it is worth noting again what a large revaluation Dickens is asking us to make. The instinctive, unintellectual, unorganized life is the ground, here, of genuine feeling, and of all good relationships. The Circus is one of the very few ways in which Dickens could have dramatized this, but it is less the circus that matters than the experience described by Sleary:

that there ith a love in the world, not all Thelf-interetht after all, but thomething very different . . . it hath a way of ith own of calculating or not calculating, which thomehow or

another ith at leatht ath hard to give a name to, ath the wayth
of the dogth ith.
(book 3, chapter 8)

It is a characteristic conclusion, in a vitally important tradition which
based its values on such grounds. It is the major criticism of Industrialism as a whole way of life, and its grounds in experience have
been firm. What is essential is to recognize that Dickens saw no social
expression of it, or at least nothing that could be 'given a name to'.
The experience is that of individual persons. Almost the whole
organization of society, as Dickens judges, is against it. The Circus can
express it because it is not part of the industrial organization. The
Circus is an end in itself, a pleasurable end, which is instinctive and
(in certain respects) anarchic. It is significant that Dickens has thus to
go outside the industrial situation to find any expression of his values.
This going outside is similar to the Canada in which *Mary Barton*
ends, or the legacy of Margaret Hale. But it is also more than these,
in so far as it is not only an escape but a positive assertion of a certain
kind of experience, the denial of which was the real basis (as Dickens
saw it) of the hard times.

It was inevitable, given the kind of criticism that Dickens was
making, that his treatment of the industrial working people should
have been so unsatisfactory. He recognizes them as objects of pity, and
he recognizes the personal devotion in suffering of which they are
capable. But the only conclusion he can expect them to draw is
Stephen Blackpool's 'Aw a muddle!'

This is reasonable, but the hopelessness and passive suffering are set
against the attempts of the working people to better their conditions.
The trade unions are dismissed by a stock Victorian reaction, with the
agitator Slackbridge. Stephen Blackpool, like Job Legh, is shown to
advantage because he will not join them. The point can be gauged by
a comparison with Cobbett, whose criticism of the System is in many
ways very similar to that of Dickens, and rests on so many similar
valuations, yet who was not similarly deceived, even when the trade
unions came as a novelty to him. The point indicates a wider comment on Dickens's whole position.

The scathing analysis of Coketown and all its works, and of the
supporting political economy and aggressive utilitarianism is based

on Carlyle. So are the hostile reactions to Parliament and to ordinary ideas of reform. Dickens takes up the hostility, and it serves as a comprehensive vision, to which he gives all his marvellous energy. But his identification with Carlyle is really negative. There are no social alternatives to Bounderby and Gradgrind: not the time-serving aristocrat Harthouse; not the decayed gentlewoman Mrs Sparsit; nowhere, in fact, any active Hero. Many of Dickens's social attitudes cancel each other out, for he will use almost any reaction in order to undermine any normal representative position. *Hard Times*, in tone and structure, is the work of a man who has 'seen through' society, who has found them all out. The only reservation is for the passive and the suffering, for the meek who shall inherit the earth but not Coketown, not industrial society. This primitive feeling, when joined by the aggressive conviction of having found everyone else out, is the retained position of an adolescent. The innocence shames the adult world, but also essentially rejects it. As a whole response, *Hard Times* is more a symptom of the confusion of industrial society than an understanding of it, but it is a symptom that is significant and continuing.

(92–7)

Randolph Quirk

from 'Charles Dickens and Appropriate Language', a lecture given at Durham University 1959

The Royal Academician, W. P. Frith, tells us in his Reminiscences of an occasion when Dickens was a member of a dinner party at the modest establishment of another artist friend, Augustus Egg. Contentedly replete, Dickens proposed to thank the cook personally.

'Let us have her in, bless her! and I will address her in appropriate language.'

  'No doubt you would,' said Egg: 'but, like most good cooks, she has an uncertain temper, and I shouldn't advise you to try it – she wouldn't understand your "appropriate language" as meant seriously, and she might resent it in her own language, which, I believe, is sometimes described by her kitchen companions as "bad language"....'[1]

Certainly, there is little evidence that if Dickens himself had proceeded from his blacking warehouse to a university he would have shared the linguistic interests of Miss Blimber in *Dombey and Son*, who was 'dry and sandy with working in the graves of deceased languages. None of your live languages for Miss Blimber. They must be dead – stone dead – and then Miss Blimber dug them up like a Ghoul' (chapter 11). Rather, it would have been the sociological, communicative, and literary functions of the contemporary English language that he would have sought to explore: the ones, indeed, that he made his life-study, without benefit of university syllabus. That would have been his idea of 'appropriate language', and he proceeded to make himself master of a language that was sensitively appropriate and responsive to a thousand occasions, and proceeded to operate selectively a linguistic range that few users of our tongue can have exceeded.

And one may say that, at student age, he started on phonetics: not that Thomas Gurney's *Brachygraphy*, with the help of which he became a brilliant verbatim reporter, could give him the phonetic insight which the Pitman system – first published in 1837 – would have done, but it would be enough to develop in him that sophisticated awareness of the sound behind orthography which makes possible many of his most ambitious effects as well as his various kinds of word-play.

Much of the phonetic word-play is mere burlesque. The place appointed for 'The Great Winglebury Duel' is Stiffun's Acre (on learning which Mr Trot not unnaturally shuddered). In an early, imprudent version of another *Sketch*, an orator is called Mortimer O'Silly-one, after the actual Rev. Mortimer O'Sullivan,[2] and his fun with the Irish patronymic prefix is shown also in the title of his burlesque, *O'Thello*. But phonetic word-play had often a more structural role in his art. There is a pleasing use of phonetic similarity to match a dramatic equation when we are told that the worldly Mrs Merdle 'concurred with all her heart – or with all her art, which was

1 N. Wallis (ed.), *A Victorian Canvas*, Bles, 1957, pp. 61–2.
2 See J. Butt and K. Tillotson, *Dickens at Work*, Methuen, 1957, p. 47.

exactly the same thing' (*Little Dorrit*, chapter 51). The half-crazed grief of Old Chuffey is given an added ironical pathos:

'Oh! why – why – why – didn't he live to four times
ought's an ought, and four times two's eight – eighty?' ...
'Come, Mr Chuffey,' said Pecksniff, '... Summon up
your fortitude, Mr Chuffey'.
'Yes, I will,' returned the old clerk. 'Yes, I'll sum up my
forty – How many time's forty – Oh, Chuzzlewit and Son –
Your own son, Mr Chuzzlewit.'
(*Martin Chuzzlewit*, chapter 19)

There is even a kind of applied phonetics. Mrs General teaches that 'The word Papa ... gives a pretty form to the lips. Papa, potatoes, poultry, prunes and prism are all very good words for the lips. ... You will find it serviceable, in the formation of a demeanour, if you sometimes say to yourself in company. ... Papa, potatoes, prunes and prism, prunes and prism' (*Little Dorrit*, chapter 61).

It would be misleading, however, to expatiate on phonetics in isolation, since for Dickens – very rightly – mere sounds were not in general to be dissociated from total communicative activity. Dickens's abiding interest was in the act of expression, in whatever aspect and of whatever kind. When the once fact-obsessed Gradgrind softly moved Louisa's scattered hair, we are being shown a man who has never learnt the language for what he dimly now seeks to convey, and we are told that so expressive were such actions in him that Louisa 'received them as if they had been words of contrition' (*Hard Times*, chapter 29). Even the inorganic world communicates. The flakes of soot in *Bleak House* (chapter 1) are seen as 'full-grown snowflakes – gone into mourning ... for the death of the sun'. 'A bell with an old voice' in *Great Expectations* (chapter 33) is imagined as having 'often said to the house, Here is the green farthingale, Here is the diamond-hilted sword'. In a gloomy street, 'a wretched little bill, FOUND DROWNED, was weeping on the wet wall', expressing itself with two-fold aptness, while the fiery spurts from the street lamps as they are lit suggests that they are 'astonished at being suf-fered to introduce any show of brightness into such a dismal scene' (*Little Dorrit*, chapter 3). In some novels, the expressiveness of the inanimate works with a powerful choric effect through dominant recurrent symbols: the wind and the sea in *David Copperfield*, for example – the wind with its 'solemn sound ... a whispered wailing that was very mournful' (chapter 51), 'the great voice of the sea, with its eternal "Never more!"' (chapter 66).

If the urge of the inanimate to express itself could be so compelling, of how much greater moment was this urge in humanity. It is no passing obsession which makes Dickens pause in his travelogue *American Notes* to let us share for some fifteen pages (chapter 3) his excitement and wonder at the skill with which blind and deaf children in Boston were taught to associate objects with signs for objects and gradually acquire a substitute language by generalizing the use of these signs. His writings from the *Sketches* onwards bear constant testimony to an overt interest in language. The relation between standard grammar and substandard usage is noticed in 'The Boarding House', where Mrs Bloss (to be joined later by a whole gallery of colleagues) had 'a supreme contempt for the memory of Lindley Murray'.

Among the manifold references – mostly trivial – to the humdrum mechanics of language, the grammar of the verb is especially prominent as a minor theme. Miss Peecher in *Our Mutual Friend* (chapter 18) tries to expose the looseness of our indefinite 'they say' by making Mary Anne parse the expression. Tom Gradgrind, with some ironic relevance, runs through the present forms of the 'Verb neuter, not to care', in reply to Harthouse's inquiry about the present as distinct from the past feelings of Louisa (*Hard Times*, chapter 19). But an interest in tense, mood and verbal action goes much deeper than Lindley Murray reflexes of this kind. It has been noticed that verb usage contributes a remarkable effect at the opening of *Bleak House*.[1] For the first page and a half, what there is of action is expressed without finite verbs, as entirely verbless sentences like 'London', 'Implacable November weather' are placed in a network of sentences whose verbs are participles: 'Smoke lowering down ... Foot-passengers, jostling ... Fog creeping into the cabooses of collier brigs'. This gives the activity of the whole scene an oppressive simultaneity, a timeless continuum which prepares us for and at the same time is

1 See J. Hillis Miller, *Charles Dickens: The World of his Novels*, Harvard University Press, 1958, pp. 164 ff.

reinforced by both the present tense of the finite verbs when they come and also the endless, futureless present of the Chancery case of Jarndyce and Jarndyce, for which the verb usage turns out to be an accumulative symbol. 'Jarndyce and Jarndyce drones on', we are told, the tense of the verb now joined by a semantic symbolism whose end is the same; the case 'drags its weary length before the Court, perennially hopeless'.

David Copperfield gave Dickens admirable opportunity to indulge his interest in the verb, since the first-person narrative invited a Janus-eyed view of events. The narrator is a novelist, but the present record is his 'written memory', quite distinct from his fictions (chapter 68), a 'manuscript intended for no eyes but' his (chapter 62). No historical, step-by-step unfolding is forced on him, therefore: memory and imagination can slide back and forth over the events; he can muse on the later effects of actions without – in terms of the convention – 'spoiling the story'.[1] We have already noted that the sea reiterates the forward-looking theme, 'Never more.' The tenth number plan has as the second and final note on chapter 29, 'Never more to touch that passive hand', and so it happens that before we learn of Steerforth's treachery we are given the ejaculatory chapter-ending, 'Never more, oh, God forgive you, Steerforth! to touch that passive hand in love and friendship. Never, never, more'. It is noteworthy that the language is planned to be distanced from the chronicle by its elevated nature; however dangerously close to the rhetoric of melodrama, repetition and archaic usage are deliberate at such points, marking the movement away from narrative and at the same time giving the comment an added emotional force.[2]

No less than four of the chapters in *Copperfield* are called 'Retrospect', and in them the sudden switch to the present tense mirrors the halting of time's movement. The first achieves this halting symbolically by verbless sentences like those at the opening of *Bleak*

1 Even in novels which followed the historical mode, of course, Dickens reserved the right to stand back from the narrative on occasion and make choric comment; the ninth number plan of *Little Dorrit* provides for such a movement in chapter 32: 'Oh! If he had but known, if he had but known.'
2 cf. David's reflection on his last glimpse of Emily, emigrating with Mr Peggotty: 'Ay, Emily, beautiful and drooping, cling to him with the utmost trust of thy bruised heart: for he has clung to thee with all the might of his great love' (*David Copperfield*, chapter 57).

House: 'My school days! The silent gliding on of my existence – the unseen, unfelt progress of my life – from childhood up to youth!' In the sudden absence of the narrative verb, it is as though the onward driving engine of his narrative has fallen silent, and the imperative that then follows, calling for retrospection, may – not too fancifully, I think, in the context of water images – be apprehended as the backward drive of the paddles which brings us to a halt amid the present tenses of static description: 'Let me think, as I look back upon that flowing water . . . whether there are any marks along its course by which I can remember how it ran. A moment, and I occupy my place in the Cathedral' (chapter 18). This is not the first imperative to have pulled us up in the passage of time. The pattern of recurrent retrospects is earlier established in chapter 10, the number plan having the abruptly ejaculative note, ' "Behold me" &c'. As David, after his mother's death, is sent off to work in London, the language forces us to contemplate this moment of time in all its impact upon a child's imagination which obscurely apprehends it as a turning point: 'Behold me on the morrow . . . with my little worldly all before me in a small trunk. . . . See, how our house and church are lessening in the distance . . . how the spire points upwards from my old playground no more, and the sky is empty!' In his worldly all *before* him and the spire pointing upward *no more*, we have a double edge and also a reciprocity admirably indicating the past-future tension with which the novel is concerned and admirably endorsing the sudden emptiness of the sky over his world at this moment.

But the retrospections in the chapters so entitled do more than call a halt for contemplation, comment and evaluation. The present tenses that follow the call for a halt represent a halt for only a short space: they subtly change function to historic presents which allow the narrative to be in fact speeded up; thus the nine brief pages of chapter 18 cover several years and take us from David's childhood to his early manhood. But the speeding up is in a staccato series of stills, the cinematic term fitting the tenses used and the fiction mirrored thereby of the author 'standing aside', as he says (for instance in chapter 43), viewing himself at a distance. To these systematic waves of retrospective stills, he adroitly adapts in chapter 43 the old rhetorical device of *occupatio*, seeing some of these static fragments of time as parts (he says) of 'a more or less incoherent dream', only fragments of which therefore can be recalled: 'A dream of their coming in with Dora; of the pew-opener arranging us. . . .' And so follow a dozen paragraphs beginning with *Of* and a participle, the temporary absence of finite verbs matching the timelessness of dream-vision. The dream is of his marriage, and the dream language which represents it is, at one level, of a piece with the consistently insubstantial language in which is couched all his relations with Dora,[1] and, at another level, is a convenient form for representing events one remove further from narrative than the present-tense stills in which it is embedded. The dream ends, not with a return to historic narrative, but to the intermediate present tenses: 'We drive away together, and I awake from the dream'. The series of retrospects is now drawn to a close.

And I may bring to a close this discussion of time and tense in *Copperfield* by mentioning chapter 53, only six pages long, but prepared for in the number plan with a disproportionately large group of notes which begin: '*Three times* – White line before each[2] *Speaks of herself as past.*' Three significant moments of time are considered, but first we have the familiar devices of the retrospect chapters, with a slowing down of the language and an invocation to focus the normally ranging vision: 'Oh, my child-wife' – a frequently used term which itself symbolizes the two-way tension of time – 'Oh, my child-wife, there is a figure in the moving crowd before my memory, quiet and still, saying . . . Stop to think of me – turn to look upon the little blossom, as it flutters to the ground!' We then have the typographical device of white space to symbolize the distancing and discreteness. The narrative which follows is now, as we should expect, in the historic present: 'It is morning: and Dora . . . shows me . . . how long and bright (her hair) is. . . .' Another white space, and we have come to the second moment of time: 'It is evening; and I sit in the same chair. . . .' A third white space, and then 'It is night; and I am with her still. . . .' We need not dwell on the mutual congruence of the morning, evening, night, or the symbolic congruence of the third

1 'What an idle time! What an unsubstantial, happy, foolish time! Of all the times of mine that Time has in his grip, there is none that in one retrospection I can smile at half so much and think of half so tenderly' (chapter 33). This passage again, like so many which are of dramatic or structural importance, is drafted in the number plan.
2 The last two words are uncertain; cf. J. Butt and K. Tillotson, op. cit. p. 167.

with Dora's death: more noteworthy are the poignantly apt preterites of Dora's utterances, the more prominent and effective in the now established context of present tenses: ' "I was too young . . . I was not fit to be a wife . . . if I had been more fit to be married, I might have made you more so too . . . I was very happy, very." '

In the seventeenth number plan of *Copperfield*, Dickens reminds himself to use the item of information that fevers can cause one to forget a foreign language and revert to the mother tongue of one's chlidhood.[1] Language learning was no mere academic interest. Lamartine said that he rarely met a foreigner who spoke French as fluently as 'ce cher Boz',[2] and we read in Forster of Boz's claim to a fair degree of skill in Italian after even the first month.[3] *Little Dorrit* is one of several novels which reflect his interest in foreign languages. The care taken to provide linguistic local colour is shown in the number plans, which stress Baptist's omnibus word *altro* and twice cite in French the opening of the song 'Qui est-ce qui passe ici si tard?' which recurs in English on Rigaud's lips. Characters freely speak a transparent kind of French idiom: 'My faith!', 'How do they call him?', 'All the world knows it', 'Death of my life!', 'May one ask to be shown to bed, madame?' With a serious undercurrent of irony and awareness of linguistic problems, much fun is made of the Island Race, confronted with the phenomenon of the benighted foreigner to whom English is inexplicably unfamiliar. In 1844, a letter from Dickens described his servants in Genoa addressing the native inhabitants 'with great fluency in English (very loud: as if the others were only deaf, not Italian)'.[4] Just so, the people of Bleeding Heart Yard spoke to Baptist 'in very loud voices as if he were stone deaf. They constructed sentences, by way of teaching him the language in its purity, such as were addressed by the savages to Captain Cook, or by Friday to Robinson Crusoe. Mrs Plornish attained so much celebrity for saying "Me ope you leg well soon", that it was considered . . . but a short remove . . . from speaking Italian' (*Little Dorrit*, chapter 25).

1 In consequence, Mr Peggotty is twice made to bring this rather self-consciously into his account of Emily's ordeal (*David Copperfield*, chapter 51).
2 See U. Pope-Hennessy, *Charles Dickens: 1812-1870*, London, 1945, p. 330.
3 J. Forster, *The Life of Charles Dickens*, J. W. T. Ley (ed.), Palmer, 1928, p. 334.
4 J. Forster, op. cit., p. 330.

One can scarcely forbear from quoting in this connexion from the conversation at Podsnap's dinner party in *Our Mutual Friend*. Dickens indicates Podsnap's ponderous emphasis in addressing his French guest by giving many of his words an initial capital:

'How do You Like London? ... Londres, London? ... You find it Very Large ... And Very Rich?' The foreign gentleman found it, without doubt, *énormment riche*. 'Enormously Rich, We say ... Our English adverbs do Not terminate in Mong, and We pronounce the "ch" as if there were a "t" before it. We Say Ritch'. 'Reetch', remarked the foreign gentleman. 'And Do You Find, Sir', pursued Mr Podsnap, with dignity, 'Many Evidences that Strike You, of our British Constitution in the Streets Of The World's Metropolis, London, Londres, London?' The foreign gentleman ... did not altogether understand. 'The Constitution Britannique', Mr Podsnap explained ... 'We say British, But You Say Britannique, You Know' (forgivingly, as if that were not his fault). 'The Constitution, Sir!' The foreign gentleman said, 'Mais, yees; I know eem'. A youngish ... gentleman ... here caused a profound sensation by saying, in a raised voice, 'ESKER', and then stopping dead. 'Mais oui', said the foreign gentleman ... 'Est-ce que? Quoi donc?' But the gentleman ... spake for the time no more. 'I was Inquiring', said Mr Podsnap ... 'Whether You Have Observed in our Streets as We should say, Upon our Pavvy as You would say, any Tokens –' The foreign gentleman with patient courtesy entreated pardon; 'But what was tokenz?' 'Marks', said Mr Podsnap; 'Signs, you know, Appearances – Traces'. 'Ah, of a Orse?' inquired the foreign gentleman. 'We call it Horse' said Mr Podsnap, with forbearance. 'In England, Angleterre, England, We Aspirate the "H", and We say "Horse". Only our Lower Classes Say "Orse!"' 'Pardon', said the foreign gentleman: 'I am alwiz wrong!'
(*Our Mutual Friend*, chapter 11).

This passage does more than make its sharp criticism of linguistic pedantry and naïvety: it illustrates Dickens's never-ending struggle to

make full use of the conventions of written English for a precise indication of linguistic form. As one devoted to the stage, as a public
reader whose skill in representation moved audiences to laughter,
terror and tears, he knew the importance of 'rising and falling inflec-
tion, and a variety of emphatic tonal patterns',[1] of which orthography
gave no sign. His characters' speeches are therefore repeatedly
accompanied by instructions as to tempo, stress, pitch, ligature and
other prosodic features, rather like stage directions – which in the
Sketches, indeed, they often are. In 'Private Theatres', we are told
that *Richard III* is 'very easy to do – "Orf with his ed" (very quick and
loud; then slow and sneeringly) – "So much for Bu-u-u-ucking-
ham!" Lay the emphasis on the "uck".' In 'Mrs Joseph Porter', an
'old gentleman, who was a great critic', instructs his niece in playing
Desdemona: 'Make a pause here and there . . . "But that our loves
and comforts should increase" – emphasis on the last syllable,
"crease", loud "even", one, two, three, four; then loud again, "as
our days do grow"; emphasis on *days*'. Outside such theatrical situations, too, similar parenthetic notes appear from time to time, as in
the slipshod woman's harangue in 'The Pawnbroker's Shop': 'you
wagabond? (loud) . . . He's got a wife, ma'am, as . . . is as 'dustrious
and hard-working a young 'ooman as can be (very fast).' An example
with 'forgivingly' as a sarcastic note on tone appears in the Podsnap
passage just quoted.

Parentheses may also be used as a visual sign of lowered prominence: '"But Mr Copperfield was teaching me –" ("Much he knew
about it himself!") said Miss Betsey in parenthesis' (*David Copperfield*,
chapter 7). Such an indication of a second level of prominence is perhaps seen at its best in *Bleak House* when Conversation Kenge inter-
lards a general farewell message with individual farewells as he shakes
hands: 'Then it only remains . . . for me to express my lively satisfaction in (good day, Miss Clare!) the arrangement this day concluded, and my (*good*-bye to you, Miss Summerson) lively hope that
it will continue to the happiness, the (glad to have had the honour of
making your acquaintance, Mr Carstone!) welfare, the advantage in
all points of view, of all concerned!' (*Bleak House*, chapter 4). Nothing could have illustrated better than these concurrent utterances the

1 T. and R. Murphy, 'Charles Dickens as Professional Reader', *Quarterly
Journal of Speech*, vol. 33 (1947,) p. 305.

polished, conscious rotundity of Kenge's conversation, to which, as we have been earlier told, he himself listened 'with obvious satisfaction'.

For the most part, guides to expression are straightforwardly descriptive, a means difficult to avoid if the required nuance is to be conveyed. One may instance the alternation of tone as Little Dorrit tells Clennam about Maggy in her presence: '"So Maggy stopped there ..." said Dorrit, in her former tone of telling a child's story; the tone designed for Maggy's ear' (*Little Dorrit*, chapter 9). 'Mrs Micawber's conviction that her arguments were unanswerable gave a moral elevation to her tone' (*David Copperfield*, chapter 57). And we find descriptions at times far more detailed than these. Miss Knag in *Nicholas Nickleby* 'was accustomed, in the torrent of her discourse, to introduce a loud, shrill, clear "hem!" the import and meaning of which, was variously interpreted by her acquaintance; some holding that Miss Knag dealt in exaggeration, and introduced the monosyllable, when any fresh invention was in course of coinage in her brain; others, that when she wanted a word, she threw it in to gain time, and prevent anybody else from striking into the conversation' (*Nicholas Nickleby*, chapter 17).

For certain prosodic features, however, Dickens developed excellent typographical devices, involving slight departures from orthography but rarely indulging in forms which would puzzle or slow down the reader accustomed only to orthography. Hyphenating syllables enables him to express level stress, as when the footman announces the guests at the Veneering dinner party: 'Mis-ter and Missis Podsnap' (*Our Mutual Friend*, chapter 2), and the device is much used in *American Notes* and *Chuzzlewit* to indicate the stressing of American English: *cons-sider*, *lo-cation*, *pre-ju-dice*, *en-gine*, and the like,[1] sometimes in conjunction with vowel diacritics as well. Hyphens together with capital or italic letters, appear in Camilla's 'The i-de-a!' (*Great Expectations*, chapter 11), Joe Gargery's 'as-TON-ish-ing' (chapter 13), and his wife's 'a pr-r-recious pair you'd be' (chapter 2), and an example like the latter has been quoted above from the *Sketches*. Dashes in place of hyphens suggest both additional stress and syllabic stretch in Mrs Joe's 'Oh, Un—cle Pum—ble—chook!'

1 cf. L. Pound, 'The American Dialect of Charles Dickens', *American Speech*, vol. 22 (1947), especially p. 128.

(chapter 4). Dashes also indicate the 'gasping, puffing and sobbing' of Micawber in what are called the 'inarticulate sentences' of his vow to unmask Heep: 'No more to say—a—or listen to persuasion—go immediately—not capable—a—bear society' (*David Copperfield*, chapter 49), reminding us of Mr Jingle's habitual inarticulation: 'mother—tall lady, eating sandwiches—forgot the arch—crash— knock—children look round—mother's head off—sandwich in her hand—no mouth to put it in' (*Pickwick Papers*, chapter 2).[1] Yet this pointing device may have a sharply different function when used in conjunction with explicit description of speech; Ham 'was not crying when he made the pauses I shall express by lines. He was merely collecting himself to speak very plainly' (*David Copperfield*, chapter 51).

As David Copperfield's speech starts being affected by the wine on what is called his 'first dissipation' (chapter 24), Dickens notes first the slurred junctures and transitions that take place in these circumstances: 'and I said (in two words) "Steerforth, you'retheguidingstar-ofmyexistence', the absence of word-spacing as neatly symbolizing the slur as the recurrent dash the inarticulate jerkiness of Mr Jingle. But as David's tipsiness increases, so does the difficulty of indicating its effects, and we depart further from orthography in 'Neverberrer', 'Lorblessmer', and the crowning example (of which Dickens takes prior note in the number plan): 'Amigoarawaysoo?' for 'Am I going away soon?'

Dickens's willingness to indulge in such phonetic spellings scarcely calls for illustration: his extraordinary ability to create or re-create a wide variety of speech, and his ingenuity in expressing this variety by means of free spelling, the use of hyphens and other devices, are among the features which most immediately strike generations of readers. One thinks at once of Sam Weller, Mrs Gamp and half a dozen other comic figures, but we must not forget that Dickens can sustain with high seriousness a complicated linguistic system which is markedly non-standard in grammar, lexicon and above all in the visually represented sounds: the language of Stephen Blackpool in *Hard Times* is a notable example. These things I must pass, however, in order to draw attention to something not so frequently observed: the double

1 cf. Bulwer Lytton's illustration of colloquial speech, *England and the English*, London, 1833, vol. 1, p. 133.

thrust of his spelling devices for phonetic and also visual effect. This was important to Dickens because, while he knew that his works were read aloud in the family circle and must be effective as sound, it was through the page as *seen* that he must make his main impact.

It would in any case have been a hopeless task to attempt a complete phonetic portrayal: the public's associations of spelling symbols were much too constricting, and we see a constant tug-of-war (as in the representation of Mrs Gamp) between the desire to indicate imagined pronunciation and the need to cling to a basic fabric of orthography to keep the speech comprehensible to the reader. For the most part, he attempted only a guide to some outstanding features of a character's pronunciation, leaving the rest to be supplied by the reader according to his linguistic taste or skill. Dickens was probably not greatly surprised when George Dolby told him in Boston of a man who had just walked out in disgust from the author's own reading of Sam Weller, telling Dolby that he could not believe the reader was Dickens, because 'he knows no more about Sam Weller 'n a cow does of pleatin' a shirt, at all events that ain't *my* idea of Sam Weller'.[1]

In fact, the visual dimension gave his art considerably added scope, since it permitted a highly exploitable tension between sound as uttered and sound as interpreted in terms of orthographic and morphemic entities. This can be seen even in the *Sketches*: '"A shay?" suggested Mr Joseph Tuggs. "Chaise," whispered Mr Cymon. "I should think one would be enough," said Mr Joseph Tuggs ... "However, two shays if you like"' ('The Tuggs's at Ramsgate'). Polybius was 'pronounced Polly Beeious, and supposed by Mr Boffin to be a Roman virgin' (*Our Mutual Friend*, chapter 5).

Here is a device which may usefully display the impact of linguistic form on a child's mind. Among the treats that Peggotty promises young David at Yarmouth is that he will have 'Am to play with', *Am* representing at once Peggotty's pronunciation and David's morphemic association of it, as is made clear by the comment, 'Peggotty meant her nephew Ham ... but she spoke of him as a morsel of English Grammar' (*David Copperfield*, chapter 2). In Yarmouth itself, David segments the dialect forms he hears according to the grid which his imagination and limited experience can provide. He learns of the toll which the sea has taken on Mr Peggotty's family; dying and drowning are brought (importantly for the progress of the novel's symbols) to near identity in David's mind: '"Dead, Mr Peggotty?" I hinted after a respectful pause. "Drowndead", said Mr Peggotty' (chapter 3). The same analysis of *drownded* appears a few lines later, and although elsewhere in the novel it is spelt with the verbal ending *-ed*, in both these instances the ending is given a spelling phonetically similar enough but visually indicative of David's alternative and contextually significant interpretation.

When Joe Gargery says 'she Ram-paged out', the form suggesting that his wife 'paged out like a ram', it is not clear whether this analysis is his or Pip's (*Great Expectations*, chapter 2), but there are many cases where the interpretation is certainly meant to be regarded as the speaker's and not the hearer's. Mrs Gamp's version of the word *apparently* is spelt 'aperiently' (*Martin Chuzzlewit*, chapter 49), a slip which only this member of the medical profession could make. Sissy in *Hard Times* calls statistics 'stutterings', because the one word always reminds her of the other (chapter 9).

And one should not overlook a further way in which phonetic spellings may have an impact. The speech of uneducated characters often includes spellings like *ses* 'says', *p'raps, wos, wot*, and Sam Weller speaks of 'the English langwidge'. Dickens was well aware that such pronunciations were common to educated and uneducated alike: they are uneducated forms in spelling only, visually suggesting substandard usage in the context of a convention which represents standard usage by standard spelling.[1]

(3–18)

Harry Stone

from 'Dickens and Interior Monologue', *Philological Quarterly*, vol. 38 January 1959

When in 1926 Wyndham Lewis juxtaposed Bloom's thought-stream in *Ulysses* and Jingle's conversation in *Pickwick*, he made a comparison which was to be oddly significant and strangely recurrent. The

---

1 cf. Dickens's juxtaposition of 'ESKER' and 'Est-ce que' (p. 417 above), 'chaise' and 'shays' (p. 421 above).

authors of two recent books on the modern novel quote Lewis on Dickens and Joyce and then proceed to disallow the appropriateness of Lewis's comparison.[1] Doubtless these latterday critics were correct in refusing to accept Jingle's speech as an example of interior monologue, but the Jingle–Bloom comparison will be much more revealing, I think, if it is viewed as an early and inconsiderable item in a much larger context – an item in the hitherto unexplored context of Dickens's increasingly sophisticated attempts to examine and represent the mind's flow and to recreate the immediacy of experience.[2]

Lewis's juxtaposition of Bloom and Jingle was indeed ingenious, and the surface similarity of Bloom's thinking and Jingle's speaking may account for the recurrent citations of Lewis's comparison. Lewis placed the following passages from Joyce and Dickens side by side and sought to show thereby that both authors were doing something essentially similar. First he quoted Bloom:

Provost's house. The reverend Dr Salmon: tinned salmon.
Well tinned in there. Wouldn't live in it if they paid me.
Hope they have liver and bacon today. Nature abhors a
vacuum. There he is: the brother. Image of him. Haunting
face. Now that's a coincidence. Course hundreds of times
you think of a person: etc.

Feel better. Burgundy. Good pick-me-up. Who distilled
first. Some chap in the blues. Dutch courage. That
Kilkenny People in the national library now I must.

1 Lewis's comparison appears in 'Mr Jingle and Mr Bloom', *The Art of Being Ruled*, New York, 1926, pp. 413–16. The books referred to are Leon Edel, *The Psychological Novel 1900–1950*, New York, 1955, pp. 24–5, and Melvin Freidman, *Stream of Consciousness: A Study in Literary Method*, New Haven, 1955, pp. 31–2. The Bloom–Jingle reference appears in other places, in Herbert Gorman's 'Introduction' to *A Portrait of the Artist as a Young Man*, New York, 1928, p. viii, for example. Joyce himself was probably referring satirically to Lewis's comparison when he wrote, 'Could you wheedle a staveling encore out of your imitationer's jubalharp, hey, Mr Jinglejoys?' (*Finnegans Wake*, London, 1949, p. 466).
2 The term 'interior monologue' is vague and has been applied to a wide variety of phenomena. My own use of the term in this article is limited, and is meant to apply to literary attempts to render in written words that semi-structured and evanescent aspect of private consciousness which is composed of disorganized and yet meaningfully associated speech-thought.

And then Jingle:

Rather short in the waist, ain't it?—Like a general
postman's coat—queer coats those—made by contract—no
measuring—mysterious dispensations of Providence—all the
short men get the long coats—all the long men short ones.
　　Come—stopping at Crown—Crown at Muggleton—met a
party—flannel jackets—white trousers—anchovy sandwiches
—devilled kidneys—splendid fellows—glorious.[1]

Even a cursory examination of these passages shows that Jingle's
clipped speech is not the same as Bloom's wandering and private
thoughts. Jingle is consciously and effectively speaking, while Bloom
is engaged in an internal reverie which lacks the organization and self-
awareness of spoken language. Jingle's allusions are simple and can be
understood in their immediate context; Bloom's allusions are complex, and can be fully understood only in the context of the whole of
Ulysses. Furthermore, Jingle is conversing and his conversation is
entirely coherent; the links of association between his telegraphic
bursts of speech are perfectly rational and easily followed. Jingle's
speech is really a mannerism; it is Dickens's means of distinguishing
Jingle as a character in the same way that he delighted in differentiat-
ing other characters through pet phrases or bodily movements or
oddities of speech. His purpose, then, was not to reveal the inner
workings of Jingle's mind, but to present a strongly differentiated and
easily remembered character.
　　That Jingle's speech is a surface characteristic, a conventional device
rather than a means of psychological analysis or representation, becomes even more evident when one places Jingle in historical perspective. When Dickens created Jingle in 1836, he was creating him in a

1 Lewis, p. 415. The passages from Joyce and Dickens are quoted as they
appear in Lewis, but they appear there in highly inaccurate form. Not only
are there changes in punctuation and spelling in the Joyce passage, but a paragraph has been eliminated and two others fused together – all without textual
indication. Furthermore, the two 'paragraphs' in the quotation are drawn
from different portions of *Ulysses*. In a similar manner, the passage from *Pickwick* contains ellipsis (without indication), misspelling and inaccurate quotation. It too is a composite quotation made up of speeches taken from different
chapters of *Pickwick*.

well-known image. Long before Dickens's time, the Jingle-like character who spoke in explosive staccato bursts was a familiar figure in literature and on the stage. As a matter of fact, the young Dickens was intimately acquainted with at least one such character – Goldfinch in Thomas Holcroft's popular play *The Road to Ruin* (1792). Holcroft was a favorite author of the youthful Dickens. As a youth, Dickens had often seen *The Road to Ruin*; and in his earliest book, *Sketches by Boz*, he had referred with easy familiarity to Young Dornton, a character in Holcroft's play.[1] Consequently, it is not surprising to find that the similarities between Jingle and Goldfinch go beyond their manner of speech; those similarities include diction and content as well.[2] But this evidence merely emphasizes the fact that Dickens thought of Jingle as a type, a picturesque stock representation, not a unique and thinking human being. And, of course, such a conception reinforces the certainty that Jingle's speech was an external device, that Jingle himself was a humor, and that Dickens was not attempting to capture and depict the quality of consciousness.

However, in subsequent works Dickens gave increasing attention to the problem of depicting consciousness and experimented with techniques which would make such representations appear convincing. This growing concern with the ways of the mind and their representation is significant for a number of reasons. It demonstrates that

1 'Private Theatres', *Sketches by Boz, Scenes*, ch. 13.

2 For example, not only do Goldfinch and Jingle (both flashy rogues who calculatingly pursue wealthy women) speak in the same way, but they tell similar stories and sometimes use identical phraseology. Here is Goldfinch's description of a coach ride: '—Drive the Coventry stage twice a week all summer—Pay for an inside place—Mount the box—Tip the coachy a crown—Beat the mail—Come in full speed—Rattle down the gate-way!—Take care of your heads!—Never killed but one woman and a child in all my life—' (Act 2, Scene i). Compare this with Jingle's similar story and his identical warning, 'Take care of your heads': ' "Heads, heads—take care of your heads!" cried the loquacious stranger, as they came out under the low archway, which in those days formed the entrance to the coach-yard. "Terrible place—dangerous work—other day—five children—mother—tall lady, eating sandwiches—forgot the arch—crash—knock—children look round—mother's head off—sandwich in her hand—no mouth to put it in—head of a family off—shocking, shocking!" ' (vol. 3, p. 14). It is quite clear, then, that Dickens not only thought of Jingle as a conventionalized and familiar literary type but consciously or subconsciously thought of him in the particular image of Holcroft's Goldfinch.

the increasing psychological emphasis and subtlety of the evolving nineteenth-century novel is clearly reflected in Dickens's works. It helps to underline the fact that in many ways the great twentieth-century experimental novelists were merely extending, modifying and carrying forward older methods and traditions. And finally it emphasizes Dickens's growing artistic versatility, his increasing mastery of fresh and complicated techniques, and his constant and often startling experimentation.

Of course, Dickens did not move from the externals of Jingle's staccato to the meanderings of the inner mind in a single leap. But even the year or so which separated *Pickwick* (1836–7) and *Nicholas Nickleby* (1838–9) made a difference. Mrs Nickleby in the latter work is a clear advance over Jingle, both in the subtlety of the technique by which her speech is represented and in the mode by which her mind is displayed in its internal as well as its external workings. Here, for example, is Mrs Nickleby's disorganized and yet rationally associated ruminations on the subject of roast pig:

'Upon my word, my dear, I don't know,' replied Mrs
Nickleby. 'Roast pig; let me see. On the day five weeks
after you were christened, we had a roast – no that couldn't
have been a pig, either, because I recollect there were a pair
of them to carve, and your papa and I could never have
thought of sitting down to two pigs – they must have been
partridges. Roast pig! I hardly think we ever could have had
one, now I come to remember, for your papa could never
bear the sight of them in the shops, and used to say that they
always put him in mind of very little babies, only the pigs
had much fairer complexions; and he had a horror of little
babies, too, because he couldn't very well afford any increase
to his family, and had a natural dislike to the subject. It's very
odd now, what can have put that in my head!
(chapter 41)

Obviously this is not interior monologue. For Mrs Nickleby is quite self-consciously addressing her remarks to another person, her daughter. However, because of Mrs Nickleby's undisciplined mind and lack of self-criticism, her speech does approach interior monologue. She is so uncontrolled in her conscious speech that her soliloquy exhibits some of those qualities of private association and discontinuity that one finds in interior monologue. And Mrs Nickleby emerges from the pages of the novel as something more than a female Jingle, as something more than a silly woman with a highly differentiated pattern of speech. By means of her speech we become acquainted with her mode of thinking, her quality of mind, and her superficial and disorganized habits of association. Although striving primarily for humorous effects, and although still circumscribed by restricting conventions, Dickens was already grappling with the problem of representing private consciousness.

One is quickly impressed by the increasing complexity and sophistication of his similar later attempts at such representations if one turns to Flora Finching in *Little Dorrit* (1857-8) – Dickens's ultimate refinement in the scatter-brained character whose disorganized speech is a direct reflection of disorganized thought. Like Mrs Nickleby, Flora thinks aloud, and thus her speech is an exact image of that semi-organized verbalization which lies somewhere between normal organized speech and normal unspoken reverie. But although Mrs Nickleby and Flora are characters struck from the same mold, Flora is a more delicate and artful rendering of disorganized and yet meaningfully associated speech-thought. Dickens now has a much firmer and deeper understanding of his character and her complex pattern of associations, and he displays her consciousness through a more intricate web of interrelated thoughts:

'I declare,' she sobbed, 'I never was so cut up since your mama and my papa not Doyce and Clennam for this once but give the precious little thing a cup of tea and make her put it to her lips at least pray Arthur do, not even Mr F's last illness for that was of another kind and gout is not a child's affection though very painful for all parties and Mr F a martyr with his leg upon a rest and the wine trade in itself inflammatory for they will do it more or less among themselves and who can wonder, it seems like a dream I am sure to think of nothing at all this morning and now Mines of money is it really, but you must you know my darling love because you never will be strong enough to tell him all

about it upon teaspoons, mightn't it be even best to try the
directions of my own medical man for though the flavour is
anything but agreeable still I force myself to do it as a
prescription and find the benefit, you'd rather not why no
my dear I'd rather not but still I do it as a duty, everybody
will congratulate you some in earnest and some not and many
will congratulate you with all their hearts but none more so
I do assure you than from the bottom of my own I do
myself though sensible of blundering and being stupid, and
will be judged by Arthur not Doyce and Clennam for this
once so good-bye darling and God bless you.
(chapter 35)

This private but illuminating blending of associations renders consciousness and character more artfully than the somewhat arbitrary
and mechanical digressions of Mrs Nickleby. And, of course, Dickens
has now come an immense way from the conventionalized staccato
bursts of Mr Jingle. Nevertheless, he pushed his technique in this area
even farther, and in some of his lesser-known later pieces came even
closer to approximating interior monologue in its twentieth-century
refinement. In some of these later works he depicted rambling
thought and soliloquy with startling freedom and effectiveness. The
listener becomes more of a shadow, the discontinuity more calculated
and bold, and the associations more private and subtly revealing.
Perhaps the best and most sustained example of his use of this technique occurs in the Christmas story 'Mrs Lirriper's Lodgings' (1863).
The overwhelming bulk of this work is in the form of a monologue
by the widowed Mrs Lirriper, the keeper of a lodging house. The
story begins in the midst of Mrs Lirriper's stream of speech, and many
of her initial allusions and associations only become clear as one
enters the story through her peculiar consciousness. The convention of
a listener is still provided, but the listener is here so vague that he is
never heard, seen or even mentioned by name. To all intents and purposes Mrs Lirriper is ruminating to herself. Of course, this rumination
is still above the level of completely private reverie; Dickens was not
here willing to let the reader fend for himself. But even so his representation of consciousness has become increasingly complex, private,
and convincing. Here is Mrs Lirriper in a typical passage:

That's me my dear over the plate-warmer and considered
like in the times when you used to pay two guineas on ivory
and took your chance pretty much how you came out,
which made you very careful how you left it about afterwards
because people were turned so red and uncomfortable by
mostly guessing it was somebody else quite different, and there
was once a certain person that had put his money in a hop
business that came in one morning to pay his rent and his
respects being the second floor that would have taken it
down from its hook and put it in his breast-pocket – you
understand my dear – for the L, he says of the original – only
there was no mellowness in *his* voice and I wouldn't let him,
but his opinion of it you may gather from his saying to it
'Speak to me Emma!' which was far from a rational
observation no doubt but still a tribute to its being a likeness,
and I think myself it *was* like me when I was young and
wore that sort of stays.

(chapter 1)

Mrs Lirriper's associations are carefully calculated to reveal the texture and quality of her thoughts. Her free-flowing ramblings constantly turn to her daily preoccupations: her lodgers, her problems of
overseeing a rooming house, her distrust of men, her sense of the
proper. Dickens is now quite meticulous in maintaining the integrity
of Mrs Lirriper's mundane mind. He is no longer willing to introduce
fantastic associations for the sake of humor – a temptation which often
overwhelmed him when dealing with Mrs Nickleby and Flora
Finching. The humor, while still there, is now subordinated to the
more important conception of Mrs Lirriper's consciousness, and the
result is a character of greater depth and reality. Of course, such a
mode of presentation called for enormously increased labor and care.
But such care in no way destroyed the illusion of free, effortless,
wandering thought. Indeed, by means of highly contrived selection, he
at last produced a representation of consciousness which was at once
private and complex and at the same time convincing and illuminating. But he did not stop here. In the following year he refined his
technique even more. 'Mrs Lirriper's Legacy' (1864) contains passages which might be taken from a modern stream-of-consciousness

novel. The following intricate excerpt for instance, is startlingly free and allusive and yet rigidly disciplined so as to produce a preordained consistent illusion:

– if anything is where it used to be with these hotels calling
themselves Limited but called unlimited by Major Jackman
rising up everywhere and rising up into flagstaffs where they
can't go any higher, but my mind of those monsters is give me
a landlord's or landlady's wholesome face when I come off a
journey and not a brass plate with an electrified number
clicking out of it which it's not in nature can be glad to see
me and to which I don't want to be hoisted like molasses at
the Docks and left there telegraphing for help with the most
ingenious instruments but quite in vain – being here my dear
I have no call to mention that I am still in the Lodgings as a
business hoping to die in the same and if agreeable to the
clergy partly read over at Saint Clement's Danes and
concluded in Hatfield churchyard when lying once again by
my poor Lirriper ashes to ashes and dust to dust.
(chapter 1)

Such a rendering of individualized interior consciousness was sophisticated and daring. But Dickens portrayed consciousness in other ways than by recording the half-organized half-wandering monologues of garrulous women. He also attempted to depict the privacy of consciousness and the complexity of the associating mind by representations which were more flexible than overheard speech, however free in associations. For, in the time since he had created Jingle, he had grown immeasurably in his ability to understand and depict the intricate ways of the mind. In this respect, rather than follow Wyndham Lewis and compare Jingle to Bloom, it would be more instructive to juxtapose Jasper and Bloom. Indeed, the opening lines of Dickens's last novel, *Edwin Drood* (1870), underline the tremendous shift which had taken place in Dickens's methods and interests since the days of *Pickwick*. Significantly enough, *Drood* opens not with a Pickwickian description of a ludicrous club meeting or coach journey, but by plunging into Jasper's 'scattered consciousness' (the phrase is Dickens's) as he awakens from an opium dream. In the following opening sentences, and without warning or explanation, Dickens thrusts the reader into the private and unidentified mental imagery of the as yet unknown Jasper:

An ancient English Cathedral Tower? How can the ancient English Cathedral tower be here! The well-known massive grey square tower of its old Cathedral? How can that be here! There is no spike of rusty iron in the air, between the eye and it, from any point of the real prospect. What is the spike that intervenes, and who has set it up? Maybe it is set up by the Sultan's orders for the impaling of a horde of Turkish robbers, one by one. It is so, for cymbals clash, and the Sultan goes by to his palace in long procession. Ten thousand scimitars flash in the sunlight, and thrice ten thousand dancing-girls strew flowers. Then, follow white elephants caparisoned in countless gorgeous colours, and infinite in number and attendants. Still the Cathedral Tower rises in the background, where it cannot be, and still no writhing figure is on the grim spike.
(chapter 1)

Such an opening would have been inconceivable in 1836, and its complexity is a measure of the changes which occurred in both Dickens and the novel during the ensuing thirty-four years. Those changes are exemplified by the new seriousness with which Dickens approaches his opening, by the much larger demands which he makes upon the reader's attention, by the care and design with which he chooses his words, and most startlingly by the new emphasis on the individual mind and its labyrinthine ways. The opening is significant for other reasons. For the images in Jasper's consciousness as he awakes in the filthy London opium den are expressive of his origins, his mind, his abode and his murderous plans in ways which will be revealed only as the book unfolds – so that the opening continually modifies and illuminates the context and the context continually modifies and illuminates the opening. In this respect the opening is more nearly comparable to *Ulysses* than to *Pickwick*; but in other ways Dickens sacrificed psychological verisimilitude for comprehensibility. He was perfectly capable now (as his previous experiments demonstrate) of representing Jasper's dream-waking state with the more powerful and appropriate technique of interior monologue and its accompanying intricacies of association, discontinuity and privacy. Instead he chose to describe the images and thought processes of Jasper's scattered consciousness in clear and highly organized sentences. Technically, as a direct representation of the mind, this is a regression; but in terms of using the images and associations of a character's consciousness as an important means of unifying and illuminating a novel, *Drood* is a step forward. Apparently Dickens was afraid of perplexing and confounding his readers by superimposing upon the difficulties of interior monologue the additional complexities of unexplained (but crucially important) mental images and associations. He decided to sacrifice technique for the sake of intelligibility, verisimilitude for the sake of easing the reader's way. (52–65)

Georg Lukács

from *The Historical Novel* 1962 (translated by Hannah and Stanley Mitchell)

Even with a writer of Dickens's rank the weaknesses of his petty bourgeois humanism and idealism are more obvious and obtrusive in his historical novel on the French Revolution (*Tale of Two Cities*) than in his social novels. The between-the-classes position of the young Marquis Saint-Evremonde – his disgust with the cruel methods used for maintaining feudal exploitation and his solution of this conflict by escape into bourgeois private life – does not receive its due weight in the composition of the story. Dickens, by giving pre-eminence to the purely moral aspects of causes and effects, weakens the connexion between the problems of the characters' lives and the events of the French Revolution. The latter becomes a romantic background. The turbulence of the times is used as a pretext for revealing human-moral qualities. But neither the fate of Manette and his daughter, nor of Darnay-Evremonde, and least of all Sidney Carton, grows organically out of the age and its social events. Here again any social novel of Dickens, say *Little Dorrit* or *Dombey and Son*, will show how much more closely and organically these relations are portrayed than in *A Tale of Two Cities*.

Yet Dickens's historical novel is still grounded on classical traditions. *Barnaby Rudge*, where the historical events are more episodic, preserves entirely the concrete manner of portrayal of the contemporary novels. But the limitations of Dickens's social criticism, his sometimes abstract-moral attitude towards concrete social-moral phenomena inevitably come out much more strongly here. What otherwise was only an occasional blurring of line becomes here an essential defect in the entire composition. For in the historical novel this tendency of Dickens must necessarily take on the character of modern privateness in regard to history. The historical basis in *Barnaby Rudge* is much more of a background than in *A Tale of Two Cities*. It provides purely accidental circumstances for 'purely human' tragedies, and the discrepancy emphasizes what is otherwise only a slight and latent tendency in Dickens to separate the 'purely human' and 'purely moral' from their social basis and to make them, to a certain degree, autonomous. In Dickens's best novels on the present this tendency is corrected by reality itself, by its impact upon the writer's openness and receptivity. In the historical novel this kind of correction is inevitably weaker.

(243-4)

Angus Wilson

'The Heroes and Heroines of Dickens', in J. Gross and G. Pearson (eds.), *Dickens and the Twentieth Century* 1962

To examine the heroes and heroines of Dickens is to dwell on his weaknesses and failures. Only a strong conviction of Dickens's extraordinary greatness can make such an examination either worthwhile or decorous; since the literary critic, unlike the reviewer, can always choose his fields and should seek surely to appreciate rather than to disparage. Even in the weak field of his heroes and heroines, Dickens made remarkable advances, for though he matured – or, to use a less evaluating word, changed – late both as a man and as an artist, his immense energy drove him on through the vast field of his natural genius to attempt the conquest of the territory that lay beyond. The development of the heroes and heroines of his novels is indeed a reflection of this change or maturing, and a measure of his success in going beyond the great domain he had so easily mastered. Some of the dilemmas that lay at the root of his difficulties were personal to him; but others were historical, and some perhaps will never be solved by any novelist.

In general, the subject of Dickens's heroes has not received much attention from serious critics. Admirers have preferred to dwell on his excellencies; detractors had found more positive qualities to excite their antipathy. The child heroes and heroines brought tears to the eyes of contemporary readers, and have found equal portions of admiration and dislike in later times. There has been some general recognition that the now highly acclaimed late novels owe something of their declared superior merit to a greater depth in the portrayal of the heroes and the heroines.

I shall not here discuss the child heroes and heroines, except to suggest that as Dickens matured he found them inadequate centres for the complex social and moral structures he was trying to compose. The children too gained in realism by being removed from the centre. The peripheral Jo has a deeply moving realism that is not there in the necessarily falsely genteel Little Nell or Oliver. It is also perhaps worth noticing as a mark of Dickens's rich genius that he could be prodigal with his gifts, making masterly child portraits of Paul, David and Pip serve merely as fractions of a large structure. Most post-Jamesian novelists would have exhausted their total energies in such portrayals of the childhood vision.

It is, however, the adult heroes and heroines with whom I am concerned. Let me first suggest the limitations which I believe hampered Dickens in successfully creating central figures in his works and then, by analysis of the development of the heroes and heroines through his novels, throw some light perhaps upon how far he overcame or could overcome these limitations.

The historical limitations of the Victorian novelists are too well known to be worth more than a mention. The happy ending is an unfortunate distortion in Dickens's work as it is in that of the other great Victorians, but, despite the change made to *Great Expectations*, it goes deeper than a mere capitulation to the whims of readers. With Dickens as with Thackeray, though for different reasons, the contemporary idea of domestic happiness as the resolution of, or perhaps more fairly one should say, the counterpoise to social evil, was a strongly held personal conviction. Even more vital to Dickens was the idea of pure love as the means of redemption of flawed, weak or sinful men. Neither of these beliefs can properly take the weight that he imposed upon them; though the latter, at any rate, is not such a psychological falsity perhaps as many twentieth-century critics have thought. The main destructive effort of this exaggerated view of love as a moral solvent falls upon those characters in the novels who, under any view, could be regarded as heroes and heroines. Closely allied to the popular prejudice in favour of wedding bells and the patter of tiny feet is the contemporary absolute demand for sexual purity. There has been a recent tendency to play down the effects of this on the Victorian novel. True, these effects have so often been discussed as now to be trite, but that does not unfortunately diminish them. This censorship did, in fact, reduce the great Victorian novelists in the sexual sphere to a childish status beside their continental contemporaries. It is surprising how often they can get past the ban by suggestion; it is surprising how often the ban does not matter to an imaginative reader; again, our freedom is only relative and has its own danger of absurdity; all this is true – yet the fact remains that our great Victorian novelists were forced at times to devices that are false, ridiculous or blurred. And these faults occur too often at the moral heart of their work. In English fashion, and with reason, we may take pride in the degree to which our Victorian novelists achieved greatness in spite of this – but we can't efface it. No characters, of course, suffer so greatly as the heroes and heroines. Once again, however, I would suggest that Dickens had a special personal relationship to this sexual censorship – and that, while it sometimes led him into exceptionally absurd devices, it also produced a characteristically powerful effect. The sexual life of Charles Dickens, like that of most Victorians, has become a shop-soiled subject, but one may briefly say four things of it – he was a strongly sensual man, he had a deep social and emotional need for family life and love, he had a compensating claustrophobic dislike of the domestic scene, and he woke up to these contradictions in his sexual make-up very late. Surely the distressing feature about the famous letter to the press upon the break-up of his marriage is not so much the tasteless publicity, but the tasteless publicity sought by a man of Dickens's years and standing. He acted at best like a young man blinded by new fame. His emotional life, in fact, for all his many children, was by most standards immature. Thackeray, very percipient where his dislike of Dickens was concerned, hit the right note, when he said of Kate, 'the poor matron'. Dickens behaved not as a middle-aged man but as a young fool or as an old fool.

The contemporary censorship, in fact, went along with, rather than against, Dickens's natural inclinations. His submerged, but fierce, sensuality was to run some strange courses from the days of John Chester until it came to light in the diverging streams of Wrayburn and Headstone. Seduction withheld, deferred, foiled – at any rate never accomplished – produced many interesting and complex characters, who would not have been born in a fiction that reflected the real world where men are more resolute and women are weaker.

Perhaps even more important in its effect on his heroes and heroines than the imperfect view of love and the impossible view of sex that Dickens shared with his readers was the ambiguous view of Victorian society that he shared with so many of the artists and intellectuals of his age. Broadly speaking, one could say that the young Dickens aspired to a respectable middle-class radicalism attacking particular social evils, and ended as a middle-aged revolutionary with a peculiar hostility to the middle classes. Such an evolution in a man not given to intellectual self-analysis inevitably produced ambiguities in his portrayal of every social class at one time or another. And in no group of characters is this unconscious evolution with its accompanying contradictions more clearly displayed than in the young men who stand at the heroic centre of his books. This uneven course in his social opinions, now veering, now tacking, yet for all its changes moving in one final direction, affected his attitude to the future and to the past, to all classes, to education, to money, to ambition, to work, to play, to conformity, and to rebellion. This strange and complex pattern of life may be observed working out in various ways among his heroes and heroines.

Any account of Dickens must start with *Pickwick Papers*, the novel which announces an age of innocence before the course has begun. Perhaps Dickens never produced so satisfactory a hero as Mr Pickwick again – a man who, like his author, imperceptibly changes; but not from hope to despair, rather from nullity to positive goodness.

None of the problems of Dickens are met in this book: Mr Pickwick developed in the garden of Eden before the fall, the next step from him was to Oliver and Nell – children, at least, have their measure of original sin. Yet no article on Dickens's heroes should fail to salute the perfection of Mr Pickwick before it goes on to the real story.

Apart from the children, the first group of heroes may be seen leading up to the self-portrait of David Copperfield. Like Mr Pickwick, this 'walking gentleman', genteel hero group begins in near nullity: one cannot discuss Harry Maylie or Edward Chester, for they are not there. Nicholas and Martin advance us a few steps: they are haters of hypocrisy, cant and cruelty; sharp-tongued and humorous; hot-tempered; inclined to selfishness; a bit weak and spoilt; pale reflections, with their eye for the absurd, of the unintrospective young Dickens as he saw himself. Martin with Jonas and Chevy Slyme for his relations, can hardly claim gentility; but Nicholas is a born gentleman of a somewhat ill-defined kind, although his uncle is a money-lender. The young, socially unsure Dickens had need not only of false gentility and of hatred of the aristocracy, he needed also a suffused and vague love of the past – a mark of the genteel. So Nicholas's first act, when he became a rich and prosperous merchant, was to buy his father's 'old house ... none of the old rooms were ever pulled down, no old tree was ever rooted up, nothing with which there was any association of bygone times was ever removed or changed'.

It is something of the same undefined traditional gentility which so endears to David Copperfield Dr Strong's vaguely traditional old school and the aroma of scholarship given off by his improbable dictionary. David is the culmination, in fact, of these purely genteel heroes for whom Pip was later to atone. Of course, being a self-portrait, David has more life, but, after childhood, it is a feeble ray. To begin with, who can believe that he is a novelist? Indeed, although he is said to be a model of hard work, we never have any sense of it except in his learning shorthand. Dickens was far too extrovert in those days to analyse the qualities in himself that made for his genius. It is notable that David is no more than 'advanced in fame and fortune', where Dickens was advanced in literary skill and imaginative power. It is also notable that after childhood, nothing happened to David himself except the passion of his love for Dora and the shock of her death – and these, which should be poignant, are somehow made less so by being smiled back upon through the tears as part of youth's folly and life's pageant. *David Copperfield* is technically a very fine novel of the sentimental education genre, but the mood of mellow, wise reflection is surely too easily held; and, when we think of Dickens's age at the time of its writing, held all too prematurely. 'Advanced in fortune and fame', as a result, has inevitably a smug sound, and 'my domestic joy was perfect' seems to demand the Nemesis that was to come in real life.

Nor is this smug, genteel, conformist quality of David helped by Agnes. A successful novelist guided by her 'deep wisdom' would surely become a smug, insensitive, comfortable old best seller of the worst kind. Agnes, indeed, is the first of the group of heroines who mark the least pleasing, most frumpy and smug vision of ideal womanhood that he produced. Agnes, in fact, is betrayed by Esther Summerson, when Dickens in his next book so unwisely decided to speak through his heroine's voice. It is not surprising that this wise, womanly, housekeeping, moralizing, self-congratulating, busy little creature should have needed a good dose of childlikeness, a dose of Little Nell to keep her going when she reappears as Little Dorrit. If we cannot believe in the child-woman Little Dorrit, at least we are not worried as we are by Agnes or Esther Summerson about her complete lack of a physical body – a deficiency so great that Esther's smallpox-spoilt face jars us because she has no body upon which a head could rest.

But if nothing happens to David himself after Mr Murdstone goes off the scene, something does happen in the novel, about which David (Dickens) uses language that suggests that there lies the real drama – as well he may, for with Steerforth's seduction of Em'ly, and indeed with Steerforth himself, we are at the beginning of all those twists and turns by which Dickens eventually transforms a somewhat stagy villain into a new sort of full-sized hero. From Steerforth to Eugene Wrayburn is the road of self-discovery. Of all the would-be seducers in Dickens's novel, James Steerforth alone gets his prey; yet he is the only one, until Wrayburn, whom Dickens seems to have wished to redeem. If we look at the facts of Steerforth's character, it may be difficult to see why. From the moment that he so revoltingly gets Mr Mell dismissed at Creakle's school until his carefully planned seduction of Em'ly he *does* nothing to commend himself. Yet David (and surely Dickens) uses language that would save if it could – 'But he slept – let me think of him so again – as I had often seen him sleep at school; and thus, in this silent hour I left him. Never more, oh God forgive you, Steerforth, to touch that passive hand in love and friendship. Never, never more!' . . . 'Yes, Steerforth, long removed from the scenes of this poor history! My sorrow may bear involuntary witness against you at the Judgement Throne; but my angry thoughts or reproaches never will, I know.' And at the last – 'among the ruins of the home he had wronged, I saw him lying with his head upon his arm, as I had often seen him lie at school'. If Dickens could have redeemed Steerforth he surely would have done so. And, indeed, he did; for Eugene Wrayburn is as much a redemption of Steerforth as Pip is a scapegoat for the falsities in David. On the whole, as I suggest, redemption through Wrayburn is a somewhat arbitrary business; but before that redemption came about, the figure of Steerforth had suffered under many guises and, in the course of his translation to hero, had borne witness to many changes in Dickens's social and moral outlook, had even assisted in the birth of a heroine more adequate to Dickens's mature outlook than either Little Nell or Agnes, or indeed the strange hybrid figure of Little Dorrit.

To trace these changes we should perhaps go back before Steerforth to earlier seductions in the novels. At the start the seducer is a cynical rake or libertine – John Chester or Sir Mulberry Hawk. He stands full square for the aristocratic dandy whom the middle-class radical Dickens detests as the source of outdated arbitrary power. Yet we have only to look at Boz in his early pictures to see the beringed and ringleted dandy – or is it the 'gent'? Dick Swiveller is kindly treated. In his adolescence surely it was among the would-be swells of Dick Swiveller's world that Dickens moved – the direct butt, no doubt, of any real dandy's contempt and laughter. The seducer, then, up to *Dombey*, is a crude class symbol.

Dombey and Son brings us further forward. Carker has some genuine sensuality, of the cold, calculating, rather epicene imitation-Byron kind that the early nineteenth century must often have bred. True, he is vulgar, hypocritical and apparently subservient – but then, unlike Steerforth, he has to scheme and work for his living. Like Steerforth, his Byronic professional seducing spills over into other sorts of pleasure-loving – a somewhat ornately comfortable villa. There are four things in which Steerforth differs from him, apart from age: Steerforth despises the world, he puts other values above work, he sometimes wishes that he was not wasting his life, he has the vestige of a power to love or at any rate to want to be loved. It is not very much luggage, yet it proves enough to make the long journey to Eugene Wrayburn. Carker fails in his seduction, but then in Edith Dombey he has a much more difficult job than little Em'ly presents to Steerforth. There were two roads open for the Dickensian seducer – glamour (it was presumably this that Steerforth used, though little Em'ly's last note to Peggotty shows small evidence that she has felt it) or boredom. Boredom and self-distaste, these were the marks of the woman who had already sold herself into loveless marriage – Edith, Louisa Bounderby, Honoria Dedlock, if she had not already been seduced before the novel began. Pride saves Edith Dombey; pride would have saved Lady Dedlock; pride and an instinct of self-preservation saved Louisa. Yet it is hardly a fair contest – Mr Carker emits his faint ray of vulgar sensuality, James Harthouse his rather superior brand of Steerforth's worldly charm. But, if it only takes one to make a rape, it takes two to make a seduction; and there is nothing in Edith or Louisa to respond. They are looking for flight from a desperate situation and indeed they take it; but they are not looking for any species of sexual love. The female equivalent to the sort of professional minor Byronism that Steerforth and Harthouse and Gowan, no doubt, in his relations with Miss Wade, offer, is the minor, rather half-hearted coquetry that is touched on in Dolly Vardon, punished in Fanny Dorrit and Estella, and finally redeemed in Bella Wilfer. But Estella and Bella are more than coquettes, they are proud, frozen, unhappy women anxious to be free of desperate homes, they combine in fact the nearest approach that Dickens gets to a sensually alive woman with the proud cold beauties – Edith, Louisa and Honoria. *Our Mutual Friend*, in fact, contains the developed hero and the most developed heroine in Dickens's fiction. The one has come a long journey from the seducer-villain; and the other, almost as long a journey from the coquette and the runaway wife. Even so they remain separate, each is reclaimed by a nullity, John Harmon and Lizzie Hexam. Yet in them Dickens had admitted to the saved a degree of sexual reality that argues well for the future.

We may leave Bella on one side; she has brought some frailty, some liveliness and some sexual warmth to Dickens's heroines; but she plays little part in the evolution of Dickens's social or moral out-look – it was not a woman's role to do so.

Eugene Wrayburn is a far more interesting case. His salvation is really immensely arbitrary. Even after he has left Lizzie for the last time before Headstone's murderous attack, he has not given up his ideas of seduction entirely – his father's voice tells him, 'You wouldn't marry for some money and some station, because you were frightfully likely to become bored. Are you less frightfully likely to become bored marrying for no money and no station?' It is indeed his rival's blows that save him. Yet we have seen that Steerforth had certain pleas to offer; Wrayburn offers all the same pleas and by this time they have become more urgent to Dickens. First, contempt for the World and for success – this, once a hidden admiration, is now the centre of Dickens's moral values. Private income, public school and university education, all these may be forgiven if they produce a despiser of bourgeois society. Dandy insolence, once the mark of an arbitrary, outdated order, is now the badge of rejection of Podsnap. Other values above work and duty? This has been amply confirmed by a rather separate but very successful hero, the sad, Calvinist-destroyed Clennam. Then the vestige of regret for a wasted life has gone through many fires since Steerforth's day; it has been purified by Richard Carstone and above all by Sidney Carton, whom Shrewsbury, gentlemanly bohemianism and the Bar could not entirely destroy. Above all the need for love has also been through Carton's fire so that Lucie can say to Darnay, 'remember how strong we are in our happiness, and how weak he is in his misery'. Loneliness, failure, pride, bitter rejection of all that made up Victorian progress and Victorian morality, a considered rejection of duty and hard work as moral ends, Dickens comes through to acceptance of these in the per-son of Eugene Wrayburn. And sensuality? Does he also redeem his own strong sensuality? This, I think, is less certain. The thin, calculated sensuality that runs from the Byronic Steerforth to the Yellow Book Wrayburn is not surely of the obsessive, tortured kind that we suspect in Dickens. Does not this real sensuality peep through in more sinister places? In Pecksniff's scene with Mary Graham, in Jonas's wooing of Mercy, in Uriah's glances at Agnes – there is more real lust there than in all the wiles of Steerforth and Harthouse, in all the brutalities of Gowan. And now the lust comes up again on the wrong side, in slavery to the Victorian doctrines of hard work, of fact, of ambition and of self-betterment – all things that had played a large part in Dickens's own life and which he had now rejected. The obsessive lust of Bradley Headstone finds no redemption. Yet as he rolls on the ground, after Charlie Hexam has left him, I believe that Dickens feels as strong a pity for him as David had felt for Steerforth. Would Dickens perhaps have left from here on another long pilgrimage deep into the holy places of his own soul? Can Jasper be the next strange step in that new pilgrimage?

(3–11)

John Bayley

'*Oliver Twist*: "Things As They Really Are"', in J. Gross and G. Pearson (eds.), *Dickens and the Twentieth Century* 1962

Oliver Twist is a modern novel. It has the perennially modern pretension of rejecting the unreality of a previous mode, of setting out to show us 'things as they really are'. But its modernity is more radical and more unsettling than this pretension implies; it can still touch us – as few novels out of the past can – on a raw nerve; it can still upset and discountenance us. *Pickwick* is not modern. It is a brilliant and successful recreation of the English novel's atmospheres and personalities; but Dickens, like Kipling, had a bargain with his daemon not to repeat a success. It was not *Pickwick* that made Thackeray ruefully praise Dickens's perpetual modernity, or Chesterton announce that Dickens had remained modern while Thackeray had become a classic.

Oliver Twist lacks only one attribute of the modern novel – complete self-consciousness. No novelist has profited more richly than Dickens from not examining what went on in his own mind. His genius avoids itself like a sleep-walker avoiding an open window. Chesterton says what a good thing it is we are not shown Pecksniff's thoughts – they would be too horrible – but the point about Pecksniff is that he has no thoughts: he is as much of a sleep-walker as

Dickens: he is the perfect hypocrite because he does not know what he is like. Dickens recoiled from what he called 'dissective' art, and if he had been able and willing to analyse the relation between our inner and outer selves he could never have created the rhetoric that so marvellously ignores the distinction between them. Unlike us, he had no diagrammatic view of mind, no constricting terminology for the psyche. The being of Bumble, Pecksniff, Mrs Gamp is not compartmented: their inner being *is* their outer self. When Mrs Gamp says: 'We never know what's hidden in each other's hearts; and if we had glass windows there, we'd need to keep the shutters up, some of us, I do assure you' (Martin Chuzzlewit, chapter 29) – she is saying something that will be true of John Jasper and Bradley Headstone, but the great early characters are in fact windowed and shutterless. Noah Claypole carousing with Charlotte over the oysters, a *mass* of bread and butter in his hand; Bumble announcing the cause of Oliver's rebellion to Mrs Sowerberry – ' "It's not madness, Ma'am, it's meat", said the beadle after a few moments of deep meditation' – their monstrosity luxuriates without depth or concealment. When Proust sets out to 'overgo' the Dickensian monster with his Charlus and Françoise, the ebullience and energy are seen to proceed from a creative centre which is meticulous, reflective and the reverse of energetic: the peculiar Victorian harmony of created and creating energy is lost.

Their wholeness and harmony have a curious effect on the evil of Dickens's monsters: it sterilizes it in performance but increases it in idea. The energy of Fagin or Quilp seems neutral; there is not enough gap between calculation and action for it to proceed to convincingly evil works. By contrast, Iago and Verhovensky are monsters because they know what they are doing; their actions let us loathe them and recoil from them into freedom, but we cannot recoil from Dickens's villains: they are the more frightening and haunting because we cannot expel them for what they do; they have the unexpungable nature of our own nightmares and our own consciousness.

We cannot recoil – that is the point. For in spite of the apparent openness of its energy and indignation *Oliver Twist* is in fact the kind of novel in which we are continually oppressed by the disingenuousness of our own impulses and fantasies, the kind of novel in which the heroine, say, is immured in a brothel, and in which we, like her,

both shrink from the fate and desire it. *Clarissa* is in the background.
'Richardson', says Diderot in a famous passage, 'first carried the
lantern into the depths of that cavern . . . he breathes on the agreeable
form at the entrance and the hideous Moor behind it is revealed.'The
lantern has been carried pretty often into the cave since then, and the
hideous Moor has become a familiar enough figure: we are introduced
in many a modern fiction to our hypothetical sadomasochistic
interiors. But whereas a novel like *Death in Venice*, or *Les Caves du
Vatican*, divides one aspect of the self from another with all the
dramatic cunning and the nice impassivity of art – the author being
perfectly aware what he is up to – Dickens presents the nightmare of
what we are and what we want in its most elemental and undifferentiated form. All unknowing, he does not let us escape from the
ignominy of our fascinations, because he does not try to escape from
them himself.

   Oliver Twist is not a satisfying novel – it does not liberate us. In
achieving what might be called the honesty of the dream world it
has to stay in prison. The sense of complete reality in fiction can
perhaps only be achieved by the author's possessing, and persuading
his reader to share, a sense of different worlds, different and indeed
almost incompatible modes of feeling and being. The awareness of
difference is the awareness of freedom, and it is, moreover, the knowledge of reality we normally experience in life. But in *Oliver Twist*
there are no such contrasts, no such different worlds. Even the
apparent contrast between Fagin's world and that of Rose Maylie and
Mr Brownlow is not a real one, and this is not because the happy
Brownlow world is rendered sentimentally and unconvincingly by
Dickens, but because the two do in fact co-exist in consciousness: they
are twin sides of the same coin of fantasy, not two real places that
exist separately in life. And there is no true activity in the two worlds,
only the guilty or desperately innocent daydreams of our double
nature.

   The superior power and terror of the unreal is continually harped
on. Nancy tells Mr Brownlow that she can think of nothing but
coffins and had just seen one carried past her in the street.

'There is nothing unusual in that. They have passed me
often.'

'*Real ones*,' rejoined the girl. 'This was not.'
(chapter 46)

Where the reality of action is concerned, Fagin's world has the technical advantage over the Maylie one of *reporting* – as in the dialogue of the thieves' kitchen and the boys going out with Oliver to pick pockets – but it is significant that the long burglary sequence, when Sikes takes Oliver down to Chertsey to crack the Maylie house and the two worlds collide at last, is one of the most dreamlike in the novel. Dreamlike too is a later collision, the meeting of Nancy and Rose Maylie in the hotel bedroom: another novelist would make such a confrontation of worlds the most reality-enhancing note in his tale, but in *Oliver Twist* they only confirm the dream atmosphere. Even when he is firmly inside the Maylie world, Oliver can, so to speak, deprive another character of reality by compelling him to act out Oliver's fantasy of what life in such a world is like. Oliver goes out to gather flowers every morning, and when Henry Maylie returns home 'he was seized with such a passion for flowers, and displayed such a taste in their arrangement, as left his young companion far behind'.

As we shall see, Dickens frequently defends himself against the charge of using literary devices and conventions by pointing out their similarity to real life, and he seems to imply that he is using the dream atmosphere as a kind of convention in this spirit. He gives two accounts of the nature of waking dreams, the first at Fagin's, and the second when just after the flower episode Oliver sees Fagin and Monks at the window of the Maylie's parlour and their eyes meet. 'There is a kind of sleep that steals upon us sometimes which, while it holds the body prisoner, does not free the mind from a sense of things about it, and enable it to ramble at its pleasure' (chapter 34). So similar are the two accounts of this state that it seems likely Dickens repeated himself accidentally in the hurry of composition (for the second half of the novel was written under great pressure), but the effect is none the less potent for that. It is a dream from which Oliver awakes to find it true, even though no footprints of the pair can be found. It recalls the earlier waking dream, when he lay watching Fagin sorting his stolen goods, and we realize it is not physical distance that keeps him from Fagin's house, a house which had once belonged to respectable people like the Maylies, and in which the mirrors of the unused rooms where Fagin and Monks confer now only reflect the dusty floor and the slimy track of the snail.

That the two worlds are one in the mind appears even in Cruik-shank's drawings, where Oliver often has a distinct look of Fagin. Henry James remarked that as a child the pictures of the good places and people frightened him more than the bad! It is often said, and with some justice, that Dickens muddles the message of his novel by making Oliver immune to an environment which is denounced as necessarily corrupting. But Oliver is not psychologically immune, nor is Dickens, nor are we. It is true that Dickens cheerfully adopts a vaguely Rousseauesque notion of the innocent warped and made evil by institutions – ('what human nature may be made to be') and also seems to adopt with equal readiness the Tory doctrine that birth and breeding will win through in the end. But however muddled as propaganda – indeed perhaps because they are muddled – these con-tradictions are entirely resolved in the imaginative certainty of the novel. Dickens might well proclaim, as he did to critics who found Nancy's love for Sikes implausible – that IT IS TRUE! His imagina-tion makes nonsense, just as life does, of theories of how human beings will or will not behave in a given environment. Notwith-standing the claustrophobic nature of the book, and its heavy dream atmosphere, Dickens's triumph is to have made Oliver – and Charley Bates and Nancy too – free of all human possibility, free in spirit and impulse against all physical and factual likelihood. The world of the novel may be a prison but they are not finally enclosed in it. And he has made this ultimate freedom seem true.

Still, Fagin's wish to incriminate Oliver, and hence confine him for ever in the evil world, is an objective and social terror as well as a psychological one. There remains the plain and sickening fact that Fagin's school and all its stands for extinguishes the hope and chance of better things, though not necessarily the capacity for them: of his pupils, Oliver escapes by the needs of the plot, Charley Bates by the death of Sikes and Fagin, and Nancy not at all. Dickens himself had been at Fagin's school – the blacking factory – and the boy who chiefly befriended him there was actually called Fagin. No wonder Fagin the criminal is such an ambivalent figure when the real Fagin's kindness had, so to speak, threatened to inure Dickens to the hopeless routine of the wage-slave. So passionate was the young Dickens's desire for the station in life to which he felt entitled, and so terrifying his sense that it was being denied him, that he must have hated the real Fagin for the virtue which he could not bear to accept or recognize in that nightmare world, because it might help to subdue him into it. The real Fagin's kindness becomes the criminal Fagin's villainy.

Like Oliver reading the tales of crime in Fagin's den, Dickens 'prayed heaven to spare him from such deeds'. He came later, at the time of his readings from *Oliver Twist*, to have a clear and horrifying awareness of his split personality: he dreaded himself, and the possibility that he might be exiled by his own doing into the world of the murderer and the social outcast. The premise of *Oliver Twist* is the gnostic one of Melville's poem:

Indolence is heaven's ally here
And energy the child of hell. . . .

Dickens feared the surrender to the demon of energy which his nature continually imposed on him. One of the many biographical glosses on the novel is the idyll which in the summer of 1849 he claimed to be enjoying with his family in the Isle of Wight, an idyll rudely interrupted when Dickens could stand it no longer and hurried them all away again from the picnics, the charades and the flower gathering.

The power of *Oliver Twist* depends more than any other of Dickens's novels on his personality and background – that is why one has to insist on them so much. Everything in the novel means something else; it is shot through and through with involuntary symbolism, with that peculiar egocentric modernity which Edmund Wilson tells us to be fiction's discovery of its true self. Except possibly for Giles the butler, nobody and nothing exists merely in itself. Even the famous 'household' passages, like Oliver asking for more, do not have the legendary authority of an epic moment but make a piercing appeal to something private and vulnerable in the memory of the reader. 'Things as they really are' turn out to be things as the fantasy fears, and feared in childhood, that they may be. In *David*

Copperfield childhood fantasy is also dominant, but in the objective setting of true existences, David's mother, Peggotty, Betsy Trotwood and Barkis – there is the breadth and solidity of epic. In *Oliver Twist* the child is *right*: there is no suggestion that his vision of monsters is illusory or incomplete, and the social shock to us is that the child here is right to see things thus – the system is monstrous because he finds it to be so. His vision is the lens to focus Dickens's *saeva indignatio*. The grotesque conversation between Noah, Bumble and the gentleman in the white waistcoat, about what is to be done with Oliver, is true because it is just how Oliver would imagine it. But in *Copperfield* the child may be wrong; he only partially apprehends the existences around him, and Murdstone, for instance, is more arresting and intriguing than anyone in *Oliver Twist* because there is no assumption that David really knows what he is like.

Dickens's crusading purpose underwrites Oliver's view of things and creates a powerful satiric method at the cost of losing the actual child's involuntary existence. Indeed it is the loss of the mere condition of childishness, as an abused animal or bird loses its natural status, which is so heart-rending – Oliver is never allowed to *be* what he is, and when liberated he has to act the part, a fact unconsciously recognized by Cruikshank in drawings which have the look of a twenty-year-old actor playing a schoolboy. Oliver has been cheated of childhood like his friend Dick, whose limbs are 'like those of an old man'. Acting, indeed, as Dickens implies in his facetious but revealing preamble to chapter 17, is the clue to the mode by which we are to be moved by the persona and events of the story. We must put ourselves in their place and act as they are acting. We must be like the crazy old woman for whom her daughter's death was 'as good as a play'.

It is the custom on the stage, in all good murderous melodramas, to present the tragic and comic scenes in . . . regular alternation. . . . We behold, with throbbing bosoms, the heroine in the grasp of a proud and ruthless baron: her virtue and her life alike in danger, drawing forth her dagger to preserve the one at the cost of the other; and just as our expectations are wrought up to the highest pitch, a whistle is heard, and we are straightway transported to the great hall of

the castle: where a grey-headed seneschal sings a funny
chorus.

Such changes appear absurd: but they are not so unnatural
as they would seem at first sight. The transitions in real life
from well-spread boards to death-beds, and from mourning
weeds to holiday garments, are not a whit less startling; only,
there, we are busy actors, instead of passive lookers-on, which
makes a vast difference. The actors in the mimic life of the
theatre, are blind to violent transitions and abrupt impulses
of passion or feeling, which, presented before the eyes of mere
spectators, are at once condemned as outrageous and
preposterous.

It is a brilliant apologia for his whole creative method. He implies that
it is *because* Oliver is an actor that the spectator should not withhold
sympathy if the tale seems artificial and implausible, thus ingeniously
confounding the stage actor with the actor in real life and claiming
that in both cases the only true view is the participant's: we must
ourselves participate in order to feel the truth of the thing, and not
merely appraise it from outside.

In seeking to disarm criticism by drawing his readers into a hyp-
notic unity with the tale and the author, Dickens relies heavily on
convention to increase both the shared hypnosis and the emotion of
truth. As Forster tells us, he delighted in coincidence and in pointing
out how common it was in life. And in *Oliver Twist* he positively
takes refuge in melodramatic ceremonial: it would be a disaster if the
taste of the age had allowed him to describe what must have been the
continual and brutish sexual activity in Fagin's hole – (*Jonathan Wild*,
and *The Beggar's Opera*, which Dickens protests is unrealistic, are
much franker about this) – or to have rendered the actual oaths of
Sikes instead of giving him grotesquely and perhaps deliberately
exaggerated euphemisms like 'Wolves tear your throats!' ...
Though he may not have been conscious of it, Dickens knew that
such disguises and prevarications are indeed the truth of the fantasy.
And he enhances their effect by putting them beside facts of a
neutral and professional kind, like his catalogue of the districts –
Exmouth Street, Hockley in the Hole, Little Saffron Hill, etc. –
through which Oliver is led by the Artful Dodger, and through

which Sikes wanders after the murder. The setting in which Noah eavesdrops on the meeting between Nancy and the Maylies is detailed with the offhand expertise of Kipling:

These stairs are a part of the bridge; they consist of three flights. Just below the end of the second, going down, the stone wall on the left terminates in an ornamental pilaster facing towards the Thames. At this point the lower steps widen: so that a person turning that angle of the wall, is necessarily unseen by any others on the stairs who chance to be above him, if only a step.
(chapter 46)

The old device of the eavesdropper has never been more effectively localized. But reality depends on the convention. Dickens was the first to protest against the new French 'realism', because he felt it might discredit his mystery. He has often been blamed for giving the happy ending to *Great Expectations*, in deference to Bulwer Lytton, but he has there a sure sense, as in *Oliver Twist*, not of what the *donnée* demanded, but of upholding the kinds of agreement he had made with the reader. The artistic rigour of a Flaubert alienates, and Dickens is faithful only to what he and his audience can make of the thing together.

Yet in his last novels he is beginning to hold the reader off. It is extremely illuminating to compare *Oliver Twist* with *Edwin Drood*, because we are not required to participate in the exquisitely murderous atmosphere of the last novel. We can stand back, and watch the familiar two worlds – the world of goodness and innocence and the world of murder and hallucination – conjured into a real and objective existence. Canon Crisparkle and his mother, the Virginia creeper, and the home-made wines and jellies, are solid and reassuring presences: they have strength as well as gentleness. Rosa Budd and Helena Landless, 'a beautiful barbaric captive brought from some wild tropical dominion', are as meticulously alive as Jasper, raising his high voice in the shadowy choir and hating the role he has made for himself. Dickens has adopted the principle of depth; hypocrisy is real at last. Instead of the divided nature being flat and two-dimensional as a Rorschach ink-blot, spreading over the whole of life, it now exists in and perceives an upper and lower world. At the cost of transforming his social earnestness into an earnestness of craftsmanship Dickens keeps his imagination working at full pressure, but in a new sphere of complication and plurality. His vision proves to be as fecund as Shakespeare's, and to have the same power of continued transformation. It was transforming itself afresh when he died.

So far I have stressed the waking nightmare which is the imaginative principle of *Oliver Twist*, and the way it dispels any true distinction between the world of darkness which Oliver is in, and the world of light which he longs for. None the less the impressive power of the novel does depend upon a most effective distinction, of quite another kind, and of the force of which Dickens seems equally unaware. It is the distinction between crime and murder.

We are apt to forget how early-Victorian society, the society of *laissez-faire*, took for granted individual conditions of privacy and isolation. It was a society where each unit, each family and household, led their secret lives with an almost neurotic antipathy to external interference. It was the age of the private gentleman who wanted nothing but to be left alone. He could ignore politics, the Press, the beggar who happened to be dying of hunger in the coachhouse; he need feel no pressure of social or national existence. Noah Claypole provides an ironic gloss when he says about Oliver: 'let him alone! Why, everyone lets him pretty much alone!' And the poor had the same instincts as their betters. At the time of the Crimea, when a suggestion of conscription was raised, labourers and miners said they would take to the woods or go underground rather than be caught for it. There has probably never been a time when England was – in the sociological phrase – less integrated.

Dickens has a most disturbing feeling for this. Like most Victorians his sense of other things, other places and people, was founded on fear and distrust. The Boz of the Sketches seems to hate and fear almost everything, even though it fascinates him. For unlike other people he had no home to go to, no hole in which he could feel secure. Normal living and the life of crime are almost indistinguishable in *Oliver Twist*, for both are based on the burrow. Both Jacob's Island and the town where Oliver is born consist largely of derelict houses which are not owned or occupied in the normal way but taken possession of as burrows, or 'kens', with an 'aperture made into them wide enough for the passage of a human body'. Fagin, who when out of doors is compared to a reptile 'looking for a meal of some rich offal', has his den on Saffron Hill; when he first enters the district Oliver sees that from several of these holes 'great ill-looking fellows were cautiously emerging, bound, to all appearance, on no very well-disposed or harmless errands'. The stiltedness of the writing here somehow emphasizes the effect of evening beasts coming out on their normal business. Mr Brownlow (whose name oddly suggests a fox) and Mr Grimwig are holed up in Clerkenwell; Mrs Corney has her snug corner in the workhouse; the Maylies live behind the walls of their Chertsey house as if it were in the Congo. The house to which Oliver is taken before the abortive 'crack', and which he afterwards identifies, is found then to have some quite different tenant, an evil creature who is hastily left to his own devices. A man on the run makes the round of the kens and finds them already full, as if they were shells tenanted by crabs.

All these people have the same outlook and the same philosophy of life, a philosophy which that private gentleman, Fagin, sums up as 'looking after No. 1'. As one would expect, Dickens can see nothing in the idea of 'private vices, public virtues' except a degradingly mutual kind of blackmail. In presenting his characters as animals, purposeful, amoral and solitary in their separate colonies, with no true gregariousness or power of cohesion, he draws a terrifying imaginative indictment of what private life may be like in an open society, in his age or in our own.

Murder transforms all this. Like a magic wand it changes the animals back into men again: what we think of as 'human nature' returns with a rush. And it is an extraordinary and sinister irony that makes murder the only imaginative vindication in the book of human stature and human meaningfulness. Though Dickens may not have bargained for the effect it is the crowning stroke in the satirical violence of his novel. Just as murder, in the Victorian literary mythology, was cleaner than sex, so in Dickens's vision is it more human than crime and the inhumanity of social institutions, for crime is the most characteristic aspect of the social order. Bumble, Fagin and the rest are evil beings because they are not human beings; they are doing the best they can for themselves in their business, and Sikes was similarly an animal in the business – 'the mere hound of a day' as

Fagin says – until murder turns him into a kind of man. Thereupon, too, society develops the cohesion and point that it had lacked before – indeed this, like so much else in the book, is grotesquely though effectively overdone. Nancy's murder assumes the proportions of a national crisis, 'Spies', we hear, 'are hovering about in every direction'. Significantly, until the murder no one seems to take notice of Fagin – he is engrossed in his repellent business like any other citizen – but after it he is nearly lynched. Crime is like animal or mechanical society, cold, separated and professional, but murder is like the warmth and conviviality which Dickens always praises – a great uniter.

Undoubtedly Dickens is saying something here about society which has lost none of its potency. With a shudder we realize what we are still like. Of course, Dickens had a perfectly 'healthy' interest in murder and hanging, just as he took a normal English pleasure in illness, funerals and ballads like 'the blood-drinker's burial'; but murder in *Oliver Twist* has a more metaphysical status, is less literary and less purely morbid and professional, than any other in Dickens. His later murders, beautifully done as they are, have by comparison a dilettante flavour. In *Our Mutual Friend* and *Drood* other characters mime the murderous atmosphere in proleptic touches that are almost Shakespearian. Lammle wrenches the stopper off a siphon 'as if he wanted to pour its blood down his throat'. At the end of term celebrations in the dormitory of Miss Twinkleton's seminary, one of the young ladies 'gives a sprightly solo on the comb and curl-paper until suffocated in her own pillow by two flowing-haired executioners'. But murder in *Oliver Twist* is definitely not considered as one of the fine arts. It is not an aesthetic matter sealed off in its artifice and our satisfaction, but a moral act which for that reason penetrates not only the life of the novel but our own lives as well.

Dostoyevsky, a great admirer of *Oliver Twist*, also makes murder a kind of social revelation. Writers who learn from Dickens usually develop explicitly an effect which is implicit in their source, and Dostoyevsky makes Roskolnikov a rebel who murders the old money-lender out of frustration, as a kind of thwarted substitute for idealist terrorism. We know from his diary that Dostoyevsky was bothered by Roskolnikov's lack of an obvious motive – he realized that the significance with which the author endowed the crime was showing too clearly through the story. But Sikes's motive is brutally simple and straightforward. Nancy must be got rid of because she has betrayed the gang: the whole burrow principle of looking after No. 1 demands her instant elimination. None the less, it is a duty, and duty is a human and not an animal concept.

Without once turning his head to the right or left, or raising his eyes to the sky, or lowering them to the ground, but looking straight before him with savage resolution: his teeth so tightly compressed that the strained jaw seemed starting through his skin; the robber held on his headlong course, nor uttered a word, nor relaxed a muscle, until he reached his own door.
(chapter 47)

Like Macbeth, Sikes 'bends up each corporal agent to this terrible feat'. An animal kills naturally, like a cat killing a bird; and in Dickens's other murders the murderer's animality is increased by the deed. Jonas Chuzzlewit skulks like a beast out of the wood where his victim lies; Rogue Riderhood lives by furtive killing, and Dickens suggests his nature in two brilliant images – the fur cap, 'like some small drowned animal', which he always wears, and the shapeless holes he leaves in the snow, 'as if the very fashion of humanity had departed from his feet'. Headstone's course is the exact opposite of Sikes's: the lust to kill strips the veneer of decency and laboriously acquired culture from him, and turns him into the terrifying creature who grinds his fist against the church wall until the blood comes. Like Chuzzlewit he feels no remorse, only the murderer's *esprit de l'escalier* – he cannot stop thinking how much more ingeniously the deed might have been done. Reduced to the animal status of Riderhood, he loses even his own name, his last link with humanity, when at Riderhood's bidding he writes it on the school blackboard and then rubs it out.

But Sikes finds his name. It is on every tongue in the metropolis. Other murderers become conscienceless animals, but he acquires the form and conscience of a man, almost indeed of a spirit. 'Blanched face, sunken eyes, hollow cheeks . . . it was the very ghost of Sikes.' And as his killing of Nancy makes him a man, so her love for him transforms her into a woman. 'Pity us', she says to Rose Maylie, 'for setting our rotten hearts on a man. Pity us for having only one feeling of the woman left, and that turned into a new means of violence and suffering.' The act she puts on when she inquires for Oliver at the police station, and helps to recapture him in the street, is a nightmare parody of social pretences and what they conceal, a sort of analogue to the pomposities of Bumble and the realities of the workhouse. Her revulsion when Oliver is brought back to Fagin's den is one of the most moving things in the book, but its denizens suppose she is still keeping up the part ('You're acting beautiful,' says Fagin) and they eye her ensuing rage and despair with bestial incomprehension. 'Burn my body,' growls Sikes, 'do you know what you are?', and Fagin tells her 'It's your living.'

'Aye, it is!' returned the girl; not speaking, but pouring out the words in one continuous and vehement scream. 'It is my living and the cold wet dirty streets are my home; and you're the wretch that drove me to them long ago, and that'll keep me there, day and night, night and day, till I die!' (chapter 16)

Nancy's living is the living of England, a nightmare society in which drudgery is endless and stupefying, in which the natural affections are warped, and the dignity of man appears only in resolution and violence. It is a more disquieting picture than the carefully and methodically symbolized social panoramas of *Bleak House*, *Little Dorrit*, and *Our Mutual Friend*. It is as raw and extemporized as Nancy's outburst. *Oliver Twist* quite lacks the overbearing pretension of the later novels, a pretension which Edmund Wilson defers to rather too solemnly when he tells us that Dickens in *Our Mutual Friend* 'had come to despair utterly of the prospering middle class'. It is the same pretension which G. K. Chesterton notes apropos of Riah, the good Jewish money-lender introduced because of complaints from Jewish correspondents about Fagin: 'It pleased Dickens to be mistaken for a public arbiter: it pleased him to be asked (in a double sense) to judge Israel.'

Oliver is not in a position to despair of the middle class, or anything else, and the humility of this is communicated in some way to the author and moves us more than all his later stridency. Oliver is a true everyman: he does not, like David Copperfield or D. H. Lawrence, shriek at us incredulously – 'They did this to *me*!' It is logical that he has no character, because he has no physical individuality – he is the child element in a nightmare which is otherwise peopled by animals, and precariously by men. Child, beast and man indeed merge and change places phantasmagorically throughout the book. Oliver is sometimes adult, almost middle-aged, and sometimes like an animal himself, as when his eyes glisten at the sight of the scraps of meat in Mrs Sowerberry's kitchen – one of the few really physical intimations of him we have. After the murder the lesser criminals are as lost and bewildered as children, and the hardened Kags begs for a candle, saying 'Don't leave me in the dark.' Sikes and Nancy, as hero and heroine, have their transformation from beast to man: only Fagin remains a reptile throughout and to the end, losing at last even his human powers of speech and intellect and crouching in the dock like something snared, his glittering eyes 'looking on when an artist broke his pencil point and made another with his knife, as any idle spectator might have done'. He has the animal victim's unnerving air of detachment from his own predicament, and the butchery of one kind of beast by another is the final horror of his execution. 'Are you a man, Fagin?' asks the gaoler.

'I shan't be one long,' he replied, looking up with a face containing no human expression but rage and terror. 'Strike them all dead! What right have they to butcher me?' (chapter 52)

It is a horribly penetrating appeal, when we think of society as *Oliver Twist* presents it. And in contrast to the almost heroic death of Sikes, Fagin will lose even his animal identity at the very end, and revert to a dreadful human simulacrum, 'a dangling heap of clothes'.

'To be thoroughly earnest is everything, and to be anything short of it is nothing.' Dickens's credo about novel-writing is certainly true of *Oliver Twist*, but whereas in the later novels this seriousness extends to the technique which fashions symbols and symbolic atmospheres – the famous fogs, prison, dust, etc. – he does not insist on, or even seem aware of, the animal symbolism here: it hits the reader like a sleep-walker's blow, involuntarily administered. It seems a natural product of the imagination, like that of Shakespeare and Hardy; though Dickens's later symbolic technique is closer to Lawrence's, purposeful and claustrophobic, the meaning too unified to expand into an ordinary human range of possibility. Character remains imprisoned in the author's will and we are uneasily aware of the life that has been left out. The Dickens of *Hard Times*, whom Dr Leavis admires, manipulates symbolic meaning in a manner that reaches its apotheosis with Clifford Chatterley sitting in his motor-chair. Nor do his 'straight' characters always escape the same fate. It is with some complacency that he reports how his mother, his model for Mrs Nickleby, protested that there could not be such a woman. One sympathizes with her, and one is inclined to think she was right. Her son was rather too confident that his imagination could give another being its real life, and that what Mrs Nickleby (or Mrs Dickens) felt themselves to be was nothing in comparison with what Dickens saw them to be.

It is the more remarkable, therefore, that Sikes and Nancy have such a range. His intentions about them are overt enough. He says he is not going to abate one growl of Sikes or 'one scrap of curl-paper in Nancy's dishevelled hair'. This confidence of the realist is hardly very encouraging. The description of the Bow Street officers, based on a 'Wanted' notice, 'reveals them', says Dickens, 'for what they are'; and we are not allowed to forget Cratchit's shawl-pattern waistcoat or the humorous overcoat sported by the Dodger. Sikes himself

was a stoutly-built fellow of about five and thirty, in a
black velveteen coat, very soiled drab breeches, lace-up half
boots and grey cotton stockings, which enclosed a bulky
pair of legs, with large swelling calves – the kind of legs,
which in such costume, always look in an unfinished and
incomplete state without a set of fetters to garnish them.
(chapter 13)

The bit about fetters gives the game away, and shows that for all his protestations of realism Dickens is really drawing on Gay and Hogarth. But what brings Sikes and Nancy to life is the gap between what they look like and what they are like: between their appearance as Dickens insists we shall have it, and the speech and manner with which another convention requires him to endow them. They rise, as it were, between two stools; they achieve their real selves by being divided between two modes of artifice. Nancy looks like the slattern in curl-papers lifting the gin bottle and exclaiming 'Never say die'!

but inside there is the desperate being who confronts Fagin and bitterly describes herself to Rose Maylie. The Sikes in grey cotton stockings is the same man who goes to murder like Macbeth.

In asserting an apparent realism, Dickens actually achieves a striking balance – very rare in his characterization – between the outward and inward selves that make up a whole person. The nonsense talked by Bumble, Pecksniff or Squeers, their total lack of the responsibilities of intercourse, mark Dickens's most contemptuous, though most in-spired, refusal to recognize an inner self in such persons. But Sikes and Nancy have an eloquence, a brutal and urgent power of com-munication, that shows how seriously Dickens takes them, and how seriously they are compelled to take themselves. The dimension of these two is the triumph of the novel, and it closely corresponds to the main feat – surely unique in the history of the novel – which Dickens has achieved in combining the genre of Gothic nightmare with that of social denunciation, so that each enhances the other.

(49–64)

W. H. Auden

from 'Dingley Dell and the Fleet', *The Dyer's Hand*   1962

After Cervantes, as a writer who combines literary talent and a mythopoeic imagination, comes Dickens and, of his many mythical creations, Mr Pickwick is one of the most memorable. Though the appeal of mythical characters transcends all highbrow–lowbrow frontiers of taste, it is not unlimited; every such character is symbolic of some important and perpetual human concern, but a reader must have experienced this concern, even if he cannot define it to himself, before the character can appeal to him. Judging by my own experi-ence, I would say that *Pickwick Papers* is emphatically *not* a book for children and the reflections which follow are the result of my asking myself: 'Why is it that I now read with such delight a book which, when I was given it to read as a boy, I found so boring, although it apparently contains nothing which is too 'grown-up' for a twelve-year-old?' The conclusion I have come to is that the real theme of *Pickwick Papers* – I am not saying Dickens was consciously aware of it and, indeed, I am pretty certain he was not – is the Fall of Man. It is the story of a man who is innocent, that is to say, who has not eaten of the Tree of the Knowledge of Good and Evil and is, therefore, living in Eden. He then eats of the Tree, that is to say, he becomes conscious of the reality of Evil but, instead of falling from innocence into sin – this is what makes him a mythical character – he changes from an innocent child into an innocent adult who no longer lives in an imaginary Eden of his own but in the real and fallen world. . . .

When the novel opens, Mr Pickwick is middle-aged. In his farewell speech at the Adelphi, he says that nearly the whole of his previous life had been devoted to business and the pursuit of wealth, but we can no more imagine what he did during those years than we can imagine what Don Quixote did before he went mad or what Falstaff was like as a young man. In our minds Mr Pickwick is born in middle age with independent means; his mental and physical powers are those of a middle-aged man, his experience of the world that of a newborn child. The society into which he is born is a commercial puritanical society in which wealth is honoured, poverty despised, and any detected lapse from the strictest standards of propriety severely punished. In such a society, Mr Pickwick's circumstances and nature make him a fortunate individual. He is comfortably off and, aside from a tendency at times to over-indulge in food and drink, without vices. Sex, for example, is no temptation to him. One cannot conceive of him either imagining himself romantically in love with a girl of the lower orders, like Don Quixote, or consorting with whores, like Falstaff. So far as his experience goes, this world is an Eden without evil or suffering.

His sitting-room was the first floor front, his bedroom the second floor front; and thus, whether he was sitting at his desk in his parlour or standing before the dressing-glass in his dormitory, he had an equal opportunity of contemplating human nature in all the numerous phases it exhibits, in that not more populous than popular thoroughfare. His landlady, Mrs Bardell – the relict and sole executrix of a deceased custom-house officer – was a comely woman of bustling manners and agreeable appearance, with a natural genius for cooking, improved by study and long practice, into an

exquisite talent. There were no children, no servants, no
fowls – cleanliness and quiet reigned throughout the house;
and in it Mr Pickwick's will was law.
(chapter 12)

His three young friends, Tupman, Snodgrass and Winkle, are
equally innocent. Each has a ruling passion, Tupman for the fair sex,
Snodgrass for poetry and Winkle for sport, but their talents are not
very formidable. We are not given any specimen of Snodgrass's
poems, but we may presume that, at their best, they reach the poetic
level of Mrs Leo Hunter's 'Ode to an Expiring Frog'.

Say, have fiends in shape of boys
With wild halloo and brutal noise
Hunted thee from marshy joys
      With a dog,
      Expiring frog?

We are shown Winkle at a shoot and learn that the birds are in far less
danger than the bystanders. Tupman's age and girth are hardly good
qualifications for a Romeo or a Don Juan. Contact with the world
cures them of their illusions without embittering them, Eros teaches
the two young men that the favours of Apollo and Artemis are not
what they desire – Snodgrass marries Emily and becomes a gentleman
farmer. Winkle marries Arabella Allen and goes into his father's business – and Tupman comes to acquiesce cheerfully in the prospect of a
celibate old age.

The results of Mr Pickwick's scientific researches into the origin of
the Hampstead Ponds and the nature of Tittle bats were no more reliable, we may guess, than his archaeology but, as the book progresses,
we discover that, if his ability at inquiry is less than he imagines, his
capacity to learn is as great. What he learns is not what he set out to
learn but is forced upon him by fate and by his decision to go to
prison, but his curiosity about life is just as eager at the end of the book
as it was at the beginning; what he has been taught is the difference
between trivial and important truths.

From time to time, Dickens interrupts his narrative to let Mr Pickwick read or listen to a tale. Some, like the Bagman's story, the story
of the goblins who stole a sexton, the anecdote of the tenant and the

gloomy ghost, are tall tales about the supernatural, but a surprising number are melodramas about cases of extreme suffering and evil: a broken-down clown beats his devoted wife and dies of D.T.'s; the son of a wicked father breaks his mother's heart, is transported, returns after seventeen years and is only saved from parricide by his father dying before he can strike him; a madman raves sadistically; a man is sent to prison for debt by his father-in-law, his wife and child die, he comes out of prison and devotes the rest of his life to revenge, first refusing to save his enemy's son from drowning and then reducing him to absolute want.

Stories of this kind are not tall; they may be melodramatically written, but everybody knows that similar things happen in real life. Dickens's primary reason for introducing them was, no doubt, that of any writer of a serial – to introduce a novel entertainment for his readers at a point when he feels they would welcome an interruption in the main narrative – but, intentionally or unintentionally, they contribute to our understanding of Mr Pickwick.

Mr Pickwick is almost as fond of hearing horror tales and curious anecdotes as Don Quixote is of reading Courtly Romances, but the Englishman's illusion about the relationship of literature to life is the opposite of the Spaniard's.

To Don Quixote, literature and life are identical; he believes that, when his senses present him with facts which are incompatible with courtly romance, his senses must be deceiving him. To Mr Pickwick, on the other hand, literature and life are separate universes; evil and suffering do not exist in the world he perceives with his senses, only in the world of entertaining fiction.

Don Quixote sets out to be a Knight Errant, to win glory and the hand of his beloved by overthrowing the wicked and unjust and rescuing the innocent and afflicted. When Mr Pickwick and his friends set out for Rochester, they have no such noble ambitions; they are simply looking for the novel and unexpected. Their reason for going to Bath or to Ipswich is that of the tourist–they have never been there.

Don Quixote expects to suffer hardship, wounds and weariness in the good cause, and is inclined to suspect the pleasant, particularly if feminine, as either an illusion or a temptation to make him false to his vocation. The Pickwick Club expects to have nothing but a good time, seeing pretty towns and countrysides, staying in well-stocked inns and making pleasant new acquaintances like the Wardles. However, the first new acquaintance they make in their exploration of Eden is with the serpent, Jingle, of whose real nature they have not the slightest suspicion. When Jingle's elopement with Rachel Wardle opens his eyes, Mr Pickwick turns into a part-time Knight Errant: he assumes that Jingle, the base adventurer, is a unique case and, whenever he comes across his tracks, he conceives it his duty not to rest until he has frustrated his fell designs, but his main purpose in travel is still to tour Eden. Rescuing unsuspecting females from adventurers has not become his vocation.

During his first pursuit of Jingle, Mr Pickwick meets Sam Weller, decides to engage him as a personal servant, and in trying to inform Mrs Bardell of his decision creates the misunderstanding which is to have such unfortunate consequences. Sam Weller is no innocent; he has known what it is like to be destitute and homeless, sleeping under the arches of Waterloo Bridge, and he does not expect this world to be just or its inhabitants noble. He accepts Mr Pickwick's offer, not because he particularly likes him, but because the job promises to be a better one than that of the Boots at an inn.

'I wonder whether I'm meant to be a footman, or a groom,
or a gamekeeper or a seedsman? I looks like a sort of compo
of every one of 'em. Never mind; there's change of air,
plenty to see, and little to do; and all this suits my
complaint uncommon.'
(chapter 12)

But before the story ends, he is calling Mr Pickwick an angel, and his devotion to his master has grown so great that he insists upon being sent to prison in order to look after him. For Sam Weller had, after all, his own kind of innocence: about the evil in the world he had learned as much as anybody, but his experience had never led him to suspect that a person so innocent of evil as Mr Pickwick could inhabit it.

Mr Pickwick has hardly engaged Sam Weller when the letter arrives from Dodson and Fogg, announcing that Mrs Bardell is suing him for Breach of Promise, and his real education begins.

If, hitherto, he had ever thought about the Law at all, he had assumed that it was what the Law must always claim to be:

1. Just. Those acts which the Law prohibits and punishes are always unjust; no just or innocent act is ever prohibited or punished.
2. Efficient. There are no unjust acts or persons that the Law overlooks or allows to go unpunished.
3. Infallible. Those whom the Law finds guilty are always guilty; no innocent person is ever found guilty.

He has got to learn that none of these claims is fulfilled, and why, in this world, they cannot be fulfilled. . . .

Rightly or wrongly, it is believed in our culture that, in most criminal and civil trials, the best means of arriving at the ethical judgement guilty-or-not-guilty is through a kind of aesthetic verbal combat between a prosecuting and a defending counsel, to which the judge acts as a referee, and the verdict is given by a jury. To say that a lawyer is a good lawyer, therefore, is an aesthetic not an ethical description; a good lawyer is not one who causes justice to be done, but one who wins his cases, whether his client be innocent or guilty, in the right or in the wrong, and nothing will enhance his reputation for being a good lawyer so much as winning a case against apparently hopeless odds, a state of affairs which is more likely to arise if his client is really guilty than if he is really innocent. As men, Dodson and Fogg are scoundrels but, as lawyers, their decent colleague Mr Perkins has to admit that they are very good.

Mrs Bardell, supported by Mrs Chappins, was led in and placed in a drooping state at the other end of the seat on which Mr Pickwick sat. . . . Mrs Saunders then appeared, leading in Master Bardell. At sight of her child, Mrs Bardell started: suddenly recollecting herself, she kissed him in a frantic manner; then relapsing into a state of hysterical imbecility the good lady requested to be informed where she was. In reply to this, Mrs Chappins and Mrs Saunders turned their heads away and wept, while Messrs Dodson and Fogg intreated the plantiff to compose herself. . . . 'Very

good notion, that indeed,' whispered Perkins to Mr
Pickwick. 'Capital fellows those Dodson and Fogg;
excellent ideas of effect, my dear sir, excellent.'
(chapter 34)

Dodson and Fogg may be scoundrels but they are not wicked
men; though they cause undeserved suffering in others, they have no
malevolent intent – the suffering they cause gives them no pleasure.
To them, their clients are the pieces with which they play the legal
game, which they find as enjoyable as it is lucrative. So, too, when
Sergeant Buzfuz expresses his detestation of Mr Pickwick's character, or Mr Sumpkins bullies the unfortunate witness Winkle, what
their victims feel as real hostility is, in fact, the mock hostility of the
player: had they been engaged for the Defence, their abuse would
have been directed against Mrs Bardell and Mrs Chappins, and they
will have completely forgotten about the whole case by the next
morning. The Guild Hall which is a Purgatory to Mr Pickwick is to
them what Dingley Dell is to him, an Arcadia.

When he is found guilty, Mr Pickwick takes a vow that he will
never pay the damages. In so doing he takes his first step out of Eden
into the real world, for to take a vow is to commit one's future, and
Eden has no conception of the future for it exists in a timeless present.
In Eden, a man always does what he likes to do at the moment, but a
man who takes a vow commits himself to doing something in the
future which, when the time comes, he may dislike doing. The consequence of Mr Pickwick's vow is that he has to leave his Eden of clean
linen and polished silver for a Limbo of dirty crockery and rusty
broken toasting forks where, in the eyes of the Law, he is a guilty
man, a lawbreaker among other lawbreakers.

The particular class of lawbreakers among whom Mr Pickwick
finds himself in The Fleet are debtors. In selecting this class of offender
rather than another for him to encounter, one of Dickens's reasons
was, of course, that he considered the English laws of his day concerning debt to be monstrously unjust and sending his fictional hero
there gave him an opportunity for satirical exposure of a real social
abuse. But in a world where money is the universal medium of exchange, the notion of debt has a deep symbolic resonance. Hence the
clause in the Lord's Prayer as it appears in the Authorized Version of

St Matthew – 'Forgive us our debts as we forgive our debtors' – and the parable of the forgiving and unforgiving creditor.

To be in debt means to have taken more from someone than we have given whether the *more* refers to material or to spiritual goods. Since we are not autonomous beings who can create and sustain our lives by ourselves, every human being is in debt to God, to Nature, to parents and neighbours for his existence, and it is against this background of universal human debt that we view the special case of debt and credit between one individual and another. We are born unequal; even if all social inequalities were abolished, there would remain the natural inequalities of talent and inherited tendencies, and circumstances outside our control will always affect both our need to receive and our capacity to give. A rich man, in whatever sense he is rich, can give more than a poor man; a baby and a sick person need more from others than a healthy adult. Debt or credit cannot be measured in quantitative terms; a relation between two persons is just if both take no more than they need and give as much as they can, and unjust if either takes more or gives less than this.

In prison, Mr Pickwick meets three kinds of debtors. There are those like Smangle who are rather thieves than debtors for they have borrowed money with the conscious intent of not paying it back. There are the childish who believe in magic; they intended to return what they borrowed when their luck changed, but had no rational reason to suppose that it would. And there are those like the cobbler who have fallen into debt through circumstances which they could neither foresee nor control.

'An old gentleman that I worked for, down in the country,
and died well off, left five thousand pounds behind him, one
of which he left to me, 'cause I'd married a humble relation
of his. And being surrounded by a great number of nieces
and nephews, as well always quarrelling, and fighting among
themselves for the property, he makes me his executor to
divide the rest among 'em as the will provided, and I paid
all the legacies. I'd hardly done it when one nevy brings an
action to set the will aside. The case comes on, some months
afterwards, afore a deaf old gentleman in a back room
somewhere down by Paul's Churchyard . . . and arter four

counsels had taken a day a piece to bother him regularly, he
takes a week or two to consider and then gives his
judgement that the testator was not quite right in the head,
and I must pay all the money back again, and all the costs. I
appealed; the case comes on before three or four very
sleepy gentlemen, who had heard it all before in the other
court and they very dutifully confirmed the decision of the
old gentleman below. After that we went into Chancery,
where we are still. My lawyers have had all my thousand
pounds long ago; and what between the estate as they call
it and the costs, I'm here for ten thousand, and shall stop
here till I die, mending shoes,'
(chapter 44)

Yet, in the eyes of the Law, all three classes are equally guilty. This
does not mean, however, that all debtors receive the same treatment.

The three chums informed Mr Pickwick in a breath that
money was in The Fleet, just what money was out of it; that
it would instantly procure him almost anything he desired;
and that, supposing he had it, and had no objection to spend
it, if he only signified his wish to have a room to himself, he
might take possession of one, furnished and fitted to boot, in
half an hour's time.
(chapter 42)

The lot of the penniless debtor, like the Chancery Prisoner, was, in
Dickens's time, atrocious, far worse than that of the convicted criminal, for the convict was fed gratis by the State but the debtor was not,
so that, if penniless, he must subsist on the charity of his fellow
prisoners or die of starvation. On the other hand, for those with a
little money and no sense of shame, the Fleet Prison could seem a kind
of Eden.

There were many classes of people here, from the labouring
man in his fustian jacket, to the broken down spendthrift in
his shawl dressing-gown, most appropriately out at elbows;
but there was the same air about them all – a listless jail-bird
careless swagger, a vagabondish who's afraid sort of bearing
which is indescribable in words. . . . 'It strikes me, Sam,'

said Mr Pickwick, 'that imprisonment for debt is scarcely
any punishment at all.' 'Think not, sir?' inquired Mr
Weller, 'You see how these fellows drink and smoke and
roar,' replied Mr Pickwick, 'It's quite impossible that they can
mind it much.' 'Ah, that's just the very thing, sir,' rejoined
Sam, '*they* don't mind it; it's a regular holiday to them – all
porter and skittles. It is t'other wuns as gets down over,
with this sort of thing: them down-hearted fellers as can't swig
away at the beer, nor play at skittles neither: them as would
pay as they could, and get's low by being boxed up. I'll tell
you wot it is, sir; them as is always a idlin' in public houses
it don't damage at all, and them as is always a working wen
they can, it damages too much.
(chapter 41)

His encounter with the world of The Fleet is the end of Mr Pickwick's innocence. When he started out on his adventures, he believed
the world to be inhabited only by the well-meaning, the honest and
the entertaining; presently he discovered that it also contains malevolent, dishonest and boring inhabitants, but it is only after entering
The Fleet that he realizes it contains persons who suffer, and that the
division between those who are suffering and those who are not is
more significant than the division between the just and the unjust, the
innocent and the guilty. He himself, for instance, has been unjustly
convicted, but he is in prison by his own choice and, though he does
not enjoy The Fleet as much as Dingley Dell, by the standards of
comfort within the Fleet, he enjoys the advantages of a king, not because he is morally innocent while Jingle and Trotter are morally
guilty, but because he happens to be the richest inmate while they are
among the poorest. Then Mrs Bardell, who through stupidity rather
than malice is responsible for the injustice done to him, becomes a
fellow prisoner. Mr Pickwick is compelled to realize that he, too, is a
debtor, because he has been more fortunate than most people, and
that he must discharge his debt by forgiving his enemies and relieving
their suffering. In order to do his duty, he has to do in fact what he
had been falsely accused of doing, commit a breach of promise by
breaking his vow and putting money into the pockets of Dodson and
Fogg; for the sake of charity, he has to sacrifice his honour.

His loss of innocence through becoming conscious of the real world has the same consequences for Mr Pickwick as a fictional character as recovering his sanity has for Don Quixote; in becoming ethically serious, both cease to be aesthetically comic, that is to say, interesting to the reader, and they must pass away, Don Quixote by dying, Mr Pickwick by retiring from view.

Both novels are based upon the presupposition that there is a difference between the Law and Grace, the Righteous man and the Holy man: this can only be expressed indirectly by a comic contradiction in which the innocent hero comes into collision with the Law without appearing, in his own eyes, to suffer. The only way in which their authors can compel the reader to interpret this correctly – neither to ignore the sign nor to take it as a direct sign – is, in the end, to take off the comic mask and say: 'The Game, the make-believe is over: players and spectators alike must now return to reality. What you have heard was but a tall story.'

(408–28)

Philip Collins

from 'Dickens and his Age', *Dickens and Crime* 1962

'What he liked to talk about was the latest new piece at the theatres, the latest exciting trial or police case, the latest social craze or social swindle, and especially the latest murder and the newest thing in ghosts': thus George Augustus Sala described the conversation of his friend and master Charles Dickens. These are common tastes, and Dickens was, of all great writers, the closest in outlook to the common man of his day and of ours; he was not ashamed to avow these tastes, for he never assumed the airs of social or intellectual superiority. Not that these tastes were frowned upon at this time: even the *Annual Register* then devoted a generous amount of space to the year's most notable criminal trials. His interest in the more spectacular aspects of crime was, in the first place, that ordinary ghoulish delight which has made the fortunes, over the centuries, of the proprietors of *The Newgate Calendar*, *The Police Gazette*, broadsheet 'Last Confessions', *The News of the World*, and their like.

His concern with crime, was, however, more persistent and more serious than most men's. Extraordinary in character as well as in literary skill, he had strong and conflicting feelings about criminals. He readily identified himself, in imagination, with their aggressive activities, but would also strongly repudiate this sympathy by extolling their adversaries, the police, and by demanding severe punishment for offenders against the law. At one period he even contemplated becoming a paid Metropolitan Magistrate. This ambition came to nothing, for he lacked the necessary qualifications, but anyway he already had another kind of professional preoccupation with crime. The literary tradition in which he chose to write – the 'Sensation Novel', related both to Gothic fiction and stage melodrama – was rich in violence, villainy and mystery. Sinister strangers lurk in the background; there are secrets – long-lost wills or heirs, or undetected misdemeanours – which the wicked characters seek to maintain; crimes are committed, flights and pursuits ensue. Dickens's commercial interest in sensational excitement is seen at its simplest level in such a letter as this, to Wilkie Collins, who was collaborating with him on a story:

I have a general idea which I hope will supply the kind of interest we want. Let us arrange to culminate in a wintry flight and pursuit across the Alps, under lonely circumstances, and against warnings. Let us get into all the horrors and dangers of such an adventure under the most terrific circumstances, either escaping from or trying to overtake (the latter, the latter I think) someone, on escaping from or overtaking whom the love, prosperity and Nemesis of the story depend. There we can get Ghostly interest, picturesque interest, breathless interest of time and circumstance, and force the design up to any powerful climax we please. If you will keep this in your mind as I will in mine, urging the story towards it as we go along, we shall get a very Avalanche of power out of it, and thunder it down on the readers' heads.

(*Letters*, W. Dexter (ed.), 1938, vol. 3, p. 542)

Later he and Collins devised a suitable pursuer and pursued, and endowed the latter with an ample achievement in crime. For Dickens inclined more to the criminal regulars of sensational fiction – thieves, swindlers and murderers – than to such favourite civil offenders as heartless seducers, rapacious landlords and greedy money-lenders. Few of his novels are without one or two of the grosser offences against property or the person; few closing chapters lack the operation of justice, human or divine, against the offenders – prison, the gallows, disgrace, or providential sudden death.

There was a further reason why, inevitably, he gave so much attention to this topic. Crime, then as now, was not merely the morbid concern of the newspaper addict, and the great stand-by of popular story-tellers: it was an inescapable social problem, and Dickens is of course conspicuous among great novelists for his passion for dramatizing and commenting upon the outstanding topical issues of his day. Particularly in his earlier years, crime was formidably common and unchecked; pocket-picking, for instance, was then a highly-organized major industry. On this ground alone, the Gaol and the Gallows were found to occupy him, along with the School, the Workhouse, and other such central social institutions. This was the more likely, because his lifetime coincided with the greatest period of legal and penal reform in our history. . . .

Dickens's lifetime, then, spanned a period of remarkable developments in the criminal law and its administration, in the scale and spirit of punishment, in police organization and techniques, in the study of the causes of crime, and in attempts to remove or reduce these causes. Most of these developments occurred most strikingly, too, during his adult working life – from 1836, when his first books appeared, to 1870 when he died. A man so alert to the most dramatic social problems and changes of his day inevitably found occasion to dramatize these issues, and, as my reminder about the nature of his novel-tradition showed, his plots often provided opportunities for crime to occur in one form or another. . . .

In *Great Expectations* (1860–61) he describes Pip's visit to Newgate, supposedly about 1830. 'At that time,' he writes, 'gaols were much neglected, and the period of exaggerated reaction consequent on all public wrong-doing – and which is always its heaviest and longest punishment – was still far off. So, felons were not lodged and fed better than soldiers (to say nothing of paupers), and seldom set fire to their prisons with the excusable object of improving the flavour of their soup'. (chapter 32). It is sad to find Pip and Dickens speaking in the tone of the Mr Bounderby of *Hard Times* – who, it will be remembered, accused any of his employees who were not quite satisfied, of expecting 'to be set up in a coach and six, and to be fed on turtle soup and venison, with a gold spoon' (chapter 11). In the 1840s Dickens's opinions on prison-discipline had been, on the whole, enlightened; by the 50s and 60s he was running level with, or even behind, public opinion, let alone progressive opinion, in this field. In the 40s, too, he had advocated the abolition of capital punishment; by 1859, he was threatening to hang any Home Secretary who stepped in between one particular 'black scoundrel' and the gallows. 'I doubt the whipping panacea gravely,' he wrote in 1852 during a wave of brutal assaults; sixteen years later, during a similar outbreak, he writes of the street ruffian – 'I would have his back scarified often and deep.' These developments in his ideas about punishment must be traced in fuller detail, and related not only to other aspects of his life and works but also to changes in his society.

For there was a general reaction in public opinion on these issues, akin to that which Dickens displays. . . .

I am not arguing that Dickens, close though he generally was to public opinion, was merely its echo or reflector. He was not, I think, immune to the common tendency of mankind to be radical and reformist when young, and to become more conservative or reactionary in middle and later life. It is, of course, possible to be strongly radical in general outlook and at the same time reactionary on some particular social issue such as penology, but this capitulation to the retrograde popular, and official, ideas on prison discipline, together with the abandonment of his earlier opposition to flogging and hanging, consorts ill with the picture of the mature Dickens presented by Mr Wilson and Professor Johnson and so many other commentators – a Dickens increasingly clear-sighted in his radical opposition to the structure and ideology of his society. There is a further apparent paradox, which my book must attempt to explore. In these later years, when he displays in his comments on public affairs an increasing, and sometimes very distressing severity towards criminal offenders, he exhibits, in his novels, an ever-increasing intimacy with the criminal mind. His later criminals are more fully understood, and more fully and realistically presented, than his earlier ones, and they are closer to

Dickens himself in social position and in character. The early villains are, typically, outsiders – obviously professional criminals, grotesques and rogues, such as Sikes and Fagin, Quilp and Jonas Chuzzlewit. The murderers in his two final novels are middle-class – the painfully respectable schoolmaster Bradley Headstone, and the cathedral organist John Jasper. Evil is no longer associated with an immediately identifiable out-group of social enemies and misfits.
(1–22)

Louis James

from *Fiction for the Working Man 1830–1850* 1963

Dickens's *The Pickwick Papers* (1836–7) suffered more plagiarizing than any other book of its time. This novel started off with the poor circulation of only 400 copies; then, with the appearance of Sam Weller in the fifth number, caught the public imagination. By the fifteenth number it was selling 40,000 copies a month. One met *Pickwick* everywhere – one rode in 'Boz' cabs, wore Pickwick coats and hats and smoked Pickwick cigars.

> Even the common people, both in town and country, are
> equally intense in their admiration [wrote G. H. Lewes in *The
> National Magazine*]. Frequently, have we seen the
> butcher-boy, with his tray on his shoulder, reading with the
> greatest avidity the last 'Pickwick'; the footman (whose
> fopperies are so inimitably laid bare), the maidservant the
> chimney sweep, all classes, in fact, read 'Boz'.[1]

The Pickwick Papers, however, was something more to the lower-class mind than a particularly popular serial. The cultivated reader sees a character within the framework of a particular story, and is suspicious, generally rightly, of a further regeneration; the return of Pickwick and the Wellers in *Master Humphrey's Clock* was not successful. The popular imagination, however, is interested in character conceived on a simple, well-defined plane, which exists independent of a complex literary form. All the popular heroes have been sub-

1 December 1837, pp. 445 ff.; attributed to Lewes by Professor Kathleen Tillotson.

jects of prolonged story cycles, whether Odysseus, King Arthur, Sexton Blake or 'The Archers', the successful English radio serial. *The Pickwick Papers* created a set of characters that became common property.

Dickens's greatest characters can exist independently of the novels partly because of their pictorial conception in the tradition of portraying comic *types*. This tradition which arrived from the eighteenth century through the work of the Cruikshanks and Seymour's *Humorous Sketches* (1833–6) – the direct antecedent of *Pickwick* – has been defined by William West in his 'Rules for Drawing Caricaturas'.[1] He gives a gallery of 'normal' faces which are to be studied, then the artist is to portray a character by that which departs from the norm. James Cooke, who had himself used this technique in the series 'The World We Live in',[2] called Dickens 'an accurate copier of eccentric physiognomies'.[3] *The London and Westminster Review* noted he had 'delighted to employ these powers [of character drawing] mostly in describing and commenting on the comic peculiarities of the lower orders of Englishmen', and notes his ability to portray 'the striking outlines of character, – the peculiarities of manner'.[4] The early pages of *Pickwick* at once give a visual picture:

What a study for an artist did that exciting scene present!
The eloquent Pickwick, with one hand gracefully concealed
behind his coat tails, and the other waving in air, to assist
his glowing declamation; his elevated position revealing those
tights and gaiters. . . .

The tights, gaiters, round face and green spectacles are essential to the conception of Pickwick, and made plagiarization possible by writers incapable of seeing how, particularly through his relation to Sam Weller, Dickens raised him above mere comic peculiarity. 'I hope you aren't arter changing that broad-brimmed tile . . . celebrated black gaiters, or . . . them yaller tights', exclaims Weller in a plagiarism of 1840.[5]

1 In West's *Fifty Years' Recollections*, 1837.
2 *Odd Fellow*, vol. 1, 1839, pp. 93 et seq.
3 ibid., vol. 3, 1841, p. 107.
4 Vols. 5 and 27, 1837, pp. 196, 200.
5 'Noctes Pickwickianae', *Dickensian*, vol. 13, 1917, p. 187.

As *The Pickwick Papers* grew to a certain extent out of the traditions of pictorial comic types, the popular press brought it back into the world of illustration. J. Fairburn published a gallery of *Pickwick Characters* (*c.* 1837), and 'W.C.W.' made forty woodcuts of 'all the Pickwick characters' (of course by no means all: Dickens portrays some three hundred). These appeared in *Sam Weller's Scrap Sheet* (J. Cleave, *c.* 1837), and, selected, in *Portraits of the Pickwick Characters* (1837) and in *The Casket* (1837–8). This treatment was not confined to *Pickwick*. Cleave issued *The Twist and Nickleby Scrapsheet* (*c.* 1839), with twenty-four woodcuts, and the 'principal Characters' of Dickens's work appeared in *Sketches of Character, from Master Humphrey's Clock* (W. Brittain, 1840), by 'Brush'.

While the world of the Pickwickians was extended by woodcuts, it was also recreated in music hall and theatre. Dickens was soaked in the world of the theatre, and its influence is a major one on his writing, particularly up to and including *Nicholas Nickleby*. Sam Weller's cockney humour and bizarre comparisons were preceded, in a paler image in Captain Belfast's servant, Simon Spatterdash, of Sam Beazley Jr's popular farce *The Boarding House*. Jingle's staccato speech would have been familiar to those who had enjoyed Charles Mathew's entertainments 'At Home', or Goldfinch in T. Holcroft's *The Road to Ruin*: it is significant that when Pierce Egan Sr. introduces his Jingle-type character, Tim Bronze,[1] just *after* the publication of *Pickwick*, he says that his staccato sentences were given with 'the rapidity of a *Goldfinch*'. For what it is worth, I note that the 'Jingle' of both *Pickwick* and of *The Penny Pickwick* is a travelling player.

One could go on citing similar comparisons. The relevant point here, however, is that the dramatic element in Dickens's characters, as well as the pictorial, attracted the dramatists, who in any case preyed upon popular literary successes. William Leman Rede composed *The Peregrinations of Pickwick* after the appearance of the eighth number, and by October 1836 it was being played at the Adelphi theatre. It is hard to discover just how many other dramatic versions came out – at least three reached the permanence of print. These printed plays make very little attempt to follow Dickens's plot; their interest was almost entirely in the characters, and these characteriza-

1 *Pilgrims of the Thames*, 1838, p. 20.

tions became real to many who could not have appreciated the literary creations of Dickens. *Mr Pickwick's Collection of Songs* (*c.* 1838), for instance, has on the frontispiece a picture of Weller, not as portrayed by Hablôt K. Browne, but as impersonated by Edmund Yates.

As the above work would suggest, the Pickwickians invaded music hall and public house as well as the theatre. At 'Manders' (probably the Sun Tavern, a lower-class pub in Long Acre) members formed 'The Pickwick Club', where they could listen to songs such as 'Sam Weller's Adventures', sung by a Mr J. Thomas.[1] Here, however, names of the Pickwickians were used often merely as a selling tag. *The Pickwick Songster* (1839), or *Lloyd's Pickwickian Songster* (*c.* 1837), have little Dickensian in them other than the title. The name was used to denote something amusing, just as that of Joe Miller had been used previously – in fact, we find *The Pickwickian Treasury of Wit, or Joe Miller's Jest Book* (1846). This was especially true of Sam Weller, under whose name appear such works as *Sam Weller, a Journal of Wit and Humour* (1837) and *Sam Weller's Pickwick Jest Book* (1837).

From music hall and theatre it was not far to popular fiction. In April or early May of 1837, when the popularity of *The Pickwick Papers* was at its height, Edward Lloyd published the first number of *The Posthumorous Notes of the Pickwick Club*, 'edited by "Bos"'. The title on the yellow cover of the weekly parts was *The Penny Pickwick*, executed in a 'wood' motif similar to that used by Seymour in his design. In the preface it claimed a sale of 50,000 copies a week, which is quite possible: a much less noticed penny-issue plagiarism of *The Old Curiosity Shop* was said in court to have sold between 50,000 and 70,000.[2] Sala said of *The Penny Pickwick*, 'this disgraceful fabrication had an enormous sale'.[3] It ran for over two years, making two plump volumes of 112 numbers in all.

The identity of 'Bos' is not certain, but the evidence . . . points to Thomas Peckett Prest. The style is very like that of Prest in his comic recitations.[4]

'Bos' aimed directly at the lower classes.

1 *London Singer's Magazine*, vol. 2, *c.* 1839, pp. 9 ff.
2 E. T. Jacques, *Dickens in Chancery*, 1914, p. 71.
3 G. A. Sala, *Charles Dickens*, 1870, p. 74.
4 e.g. 'The Sensible Family', *London Singer's Magazine*, vol. 1, 1839, p. 97.

Upon the appearance of those Shilling Publications which
have been productive of so much mirth and amusement, it
occurred to us that while the wealthier classes had their
Momus, the poor man should not be debarred from possessing
to himself as lively a source of entertainment and at a price
consistent with his means. . . .

The story opens with the formation of the Pickwick Club, consisting of Christopher Pickwick, Percy Tupnall, Arthur Snodgreen,
Matthew Winkletop, Jeremiah Smuggins, and Captain Julius Caesar
[*sic*] Fitzflash. The following day they set out on their explorations,
not in a cab, but in a boat on the Thames in London. Pickwick falls
into the river, and is finally saved, when stuck in the mud, by one
Shirk (Jingle). Returning to the shore, they find themselves in the
middle of a working-class holiday celebration, in which they join.
Tupnall and Fitzflash climb a greasy pole along with a filthy sweep.
The next day Pickwick takes part in a donkey race. They leave London, and there is an episode in which Shirk goes to a dance in Snodgreen's clothes, leaving his own rags in their place. The episode of the
runaway coach is introduced, after which they all arrive at 'Mush-
room Hall, Violet Vale, near Uxbridge' (Dingley Dell). There Pickwick pursues a widow (Dupps), in competition with Tupnall.
Pickwick is successful, and the loving couple are surprised by the fat
boy and by a new figure, John White, a negro servant. They go to the
theatre, and recognize one of the actors as Shirk. Determined to recover Snodgreen's clothes, they bring the show to a close amid confusion. Pickwick pursues Shirk and the actors to a public house, but
he is no match for them. They all escape, leaving the publican to
understand that Pickwick will pay for their drinks. When Pickwick,
somewhat poorer, returns to the Hall, he finds his widow is missing –
she has eloped with Shirk. (This is a rehandling of the Rachel Wardle
incident.) Pickwick follows the pair – on the way he is robbed by
highwaymen – and eventually finds them at an inn. The popular
desire to see virtue triumphant did not allow 'Bos' to show Shirk
escaping; or perhaps 'Bos' did not feel capable of rewriting Dickens's
masterly picture of Jingle's insolence: in any case, Shirk is bundled off
to gaol for debt. At this point Samuel Weller appears for the first
time.

The long story continues with the same mixture of rearranged Dickens and crude innovation. Sam Weller reappears in response to Pickwick's advertisement for 'a companion of virtuous principles' – a reference similar to marital advertisements that can be found in lower-class papers. There is an election, not at 'Eatanswill' but at 'Guzzleton'. It is Pickwick who stands for Parliament, although he is defeated. The Reverend Smirkins makes love to Mrs Weller, and is well trounced by both Mr Weller and Sam.

The whole story is carefully adapted for the working-class reader. An example of this is seen in the way the archaeological discovery is made. The readers of 'Bos' would not have understood Dickens's satire on the newly formed British Association. Instead, 'Bos' inserts a comic episode in Dreary Castle, with Weller masquerading in armour as a ghost, and Pickwick attacked by rats. (This, incidentally, is the first time I have found a lower-class author laughing at gothic novels of the Minerva Press type.) In this castle a coin is found bearing the inscription:

GI

LE   SSNIP

EMA   NC

HEST

ER

The readers would have understood the joke of a Manchester-made antique. There must have been several Giles Snipes among their number.

The whole level of the comedy is altered. In the breach of promise case, all legal subtlety is removed, and Pickwick is tried for assault. For comic restraint physical slapstick is substituted wherever possible. Physical chastisement is inflicted on Shirk, and on Quizzgig and Fidge (Dodson and Fogg). Pickwick was seen as he would have actually appeared to a working-class person, not as a high-intentioned innocent, a Quixote to Weller's Sancho Panza, but as an odd, comically pompous old gentleman. He is treated as this audience would have treated him. In the course of the first volume alone, he is ducked eight times, generally in filthy water, and once, in a duel with Squib, the editor of the *Guzzelton Mercury*, he is shot in the buttocks.

As might be expected, Samuel Weller is the true hero. Dickens had balanced this character, so that while his native resourcefulness and wit endeared him to the lower-class reader, his devoted service to his master made him approved by those who had servants themselves. With 'Bos' this balance is lost. On one occasion, Pickwick finds Sam on the stage during a play and demands his immediate withdrawal; Sam insists on finishing his part – he is in command, and he must have his glory. The Society of Flunkeys, it is interesting to note, grows into a Trades Union, 'The Society of Grand United and Independent Flunkeys', which receives Sam as its respected leader. Weller had become the idol of the lower classes: one article in *Cleave's London Satirist* is called 'Sam Weller's Sentiments on the Poor Law'. (47–52)

Barbara Hardy

'Food and Ceremony in *Great Expectations*', *Essays in Criticism*, vol. 13   1963

We all know that food has a special place in the novels of Dickens. He loves feasts and scorns fasts. His celebration of the feast is not that of the glutton or the gourmet: eating and drinking are valued by him as proofs of sociability and gusto, but more important still, as ceremonies of love. The conversion of Scrooge is marked by his present of a goose to Bob Cratchit and his reunion at his nephew's table: both the giving and the participation show his newly found ability to love. The Christmas dinner and the geniality of the English pub are not sentimentalized as isolated institutions of goodwill, conveniently cut off from the poverty and hunger outside the window. Good housekeeping is proved by nourishing and well-ordered meals, and Mrs Jellyby cannot feed her family properly; but the same is true of the bleak housekeeping of England, which cannot feed Jo or the brickmakers. Chadband's superfluous feasts are put beside Jo's hunger and Guster's loving crust to qualify the approval of good appetite. The social emphasis in *Great Expectations* is rather different from that of *Bleak House*, but in both novels, and elsewhere, the same moral values are attached to meals – to the giving, receiving, eating and serving of food. These values might be summed up as good appetite without greed, hospitality without show, and ceremony without pride or condescension.

All these values are shown, positively and negatively, in the meals in *Great Expectations*. Food is used to define various aspects of love, pride, social ambition and gratitude, and the meals are often carefully placed in order to underline and explain motivation and development. Dickens's attitude to food has no doubt considerable biographical interest. Dickens – deprived child, food-lover, great talker, oral type – juxtaposes Mrs Joe's pincushion breast and her dispensation of bread, and this may well be his grimmest attack on the maternal image. But in spite of this grotesque instance, I believe that the generalized association of food and love in Dickens strikes us less by its neurotic fantasy than by its use of what we all feel to be the natural appropriateness of the metaphor 'hunger' when it is used of love. I do not call the meals in *Great Expectations* symbols: their affirmation of value seems to involve no conceptual transference and little heightening. It is our awareness of the Last Supper which often tempts us to describe this kind of significant meal as symbolic (the meal shared by Bartle Massey and Adam Bede in the upper room is a good example) but the Last Supper (like the Passover and other ritual feasts) became an effective symbol, in part at least, because it tapped the significance of ordinary communion – the eating, giving and receiving, in public, amongst friends and associates. The meals in Dickens convey no more, I suggest, than the elementary implications of natural domestic and social order, given particularity by the context of the novel. The generalizations which the meals in *Great Expectations* carry involve none of the transference associated with symbolism, nothing of the movement from a first term to a second which is involved in our reading of the symbol of the wild waves, the fog or the prison. There is certainly an accumulation of significance in *Great Expectations*, and we soon come to expect that when characters sit down to eat there will be more than a furtherance of action, local colour or comic play. We come to expect some extension or qualification of the moral significance already correlated with the meals. This is an extension of the particular definition of character, a way of emphasizing the connexions and distances between different characters or different events, showing the irony and necessity of the internal moral pattern. The meals themselves are charged with no more than the moral significances of everyday life, where good mothers feed their children lovingly; where meals are sociable occasions; where good manners are desirable but not all that important; where theft may be condoned if the thief is starving; where there is something distasteful about the host or mother or cook whose meals are merely boasts; where there is something meretricious in the splendid feast which is strikingly different from the routine meals of the same household; where abstinence may be either unhealthy or unselfish.

The first meal in *Great Expectations* is *demanded* in the first chapter. Magwitch in desperate hunger terrifies Pip into stealing food: 'You know what wittles is ... you get me wittles.' In the third chapter Pip brings the food, and Magwitch makes the first response of gratitude which begins the long chain of obligation, illusion, pride and love. It is important to see what moves his gratitude: it is not the mere provision of food, important though this is. Pip is doing more than satisfy the physical need, he is allowing nature more than nature needs. Magwitch is eating like a beast but Pip treats him as a guest and makes him respond as a guest:

He was already handing mincemeat down his throat in the
most curious manner – more like a man who was putting it
away somewhere in a violent hurry, than a man who was
eating it – but he left off to take some of the liquor. He
shivered all the while so violently, that it was quite as much
as he could do to keep the neck of the bottle between his
teeth, without biting it off. ...
He was gobbling mincemeat, meat bone, bread, cheese
and pork pie, all at once: staring distrustfully while he did
so at the mist all round us, and often stopping – even
stopping his jaws – to listen.

This is a grotesque table, spread in the wilderness of mist and marshes for a man who is wolfing down the food out of fear. Pip is no more in the conventional position of host than Magwitch is in the conventional position of guest, but the very lack of ceremony moves Pip to do more than steal and give in terror and in minimal satisfaction of need. Pity moves him to sauce the meat with ceremony and turn it into something more than Lady Macbeth's 'bare meeting'. Just as Lady Macbeth's rebuke has special point because it is made at a great feast to the host who is a guest-murderer, so Pip's ceremony has special point in this bare rough meeting where the guest is desperate and the host terrorized:

Pitying his desolation . . . I made bold to say, 'I am glad you enjoy it'.
   'Did you speak?'
   'I said, I am glad you enjoyed it.'
   'Thankee, my boy. I do.'

The child's civility and pity take no offence from his guest's table-manners. These are carefully observed, without revulsion:

I had often watched a large dog of ours eating his food; and now I noticed a decided similarity between the dog's way of eating, and the man's. The man took strong sharp sudden bites, just like the dog. He swallowed, or rather snapped up, every mouthful, too soon and too fast; and he looked sideways here and there while he ate, as if he thought there was danger in every direction of somebody's coming to take the pie away. He was altogether too unsettled in his mind over it, to appreciate it comfortably, I thought, or to have anybody to dine with him, without making a chop with his jaws at the visitor. In all of which particulars he was very like the dog.

The detached account makes the politeness more marked. It is apparent that Pip's naïve comparisons, to the dog and to more comfortable meals, imply no sense of social superiority, though the social implications are plain to the reader. Pip is not repelled by the resemblance to the dog, but is sorry for it, and instead of treating the man like a dog, gives with love. The 'I am glad you enjoy it' and the 'Thankee' turn the rudest meal in the novel into an introductory model of ceremony. What makes the ceremony is love, generosity and gratitude. I need not labour the attachment of this scene to the main themes of the novel.

This meal acts as a model of ceremony, and controls our response to the many related descriptions of meals which succeed it. The gratitude and compassionate love are both present in chapter 5, when Magwitch lies about stealing the food, to protect Pip, and is answered by Joe:

God knows you're welcome to it – so far as it was ever
mine.... We don't know what you have done, but we
wouldn't have you starved to death for it, poor miserable
fellow-creatur. – Would us, Pip?

This in its turn evokes another response of gratitude – an inarticulate working of the throat – from Magwitch. The first small links are forged in Pip's chain, 'of iron or gold, of thorns or flowers'.

It is not until much later, in chapter 38 that Pip sees that this is where his chain really begins, 'before I knew that the world held Estella'. The actual image is narrowed down, in the next chapter, to the 'wretched gold and silver chains' with which Magwitch has loaded him. When the image of the chain first appears (in the singular) it has no connexion with the convict for Pip sees its beginning in his encounter with Miss Havisham and Estella, in Satis House. The beginning of his illusory great expectations, like the beginning of the real ones, is marked by a significant meal. Estella is the hostess, Pip the guest. The meal is less grotesque than the meal with Magwitch but it too lacks the ceremonious cover of a roof, for Estella tells Pip to wait in the yard:

She came back, with some bread and meat and a little
mug of beer. She put the mug down on the stones of the
yard, and gave me the bread and meat without looking at
me, as insolently as if I were a dog in disgrace. I was so
humiliated, hurt, spurned, offended, angry, sorry – I cannot
hit upon the right name for the smart – God knows what
its name was – that tears started to my eyes.
(chapter 8)

The contrast is clinched by the comparison with the dog. Pip's full wants are not satisfied, even though this is the hospitality of Satis House, but in terms of physical need he is given enough. He is treated like a dog, given no more than nature needs, but he does not lose his appetite, any more than Magwitch, treated with courtesy, stops eating like a dog. Dickens makes this distinction unsentimentally and truthfully, merely allowing Pip to observe that 'the bread and food were acceptable, and the beer was warming and tingling, and I was soon in spirits to look about me'. Like Magwitch, and for similar reasons of protective love, Pip lies about this meal. His sense of humiliation and his desire to protect Estella from 'the contemplation of Mrs Joe' makes him elaborate the marvellous childish fantasy about the 'cake and wine on gold plates', which Pumblechook and Joe and Mrs Joe, in their social innocence, accept. Pip invents a meal appropriate to Satis House, and hides his shame, but he preserves both the hierarchy and the bizarre quality of his encounter by placing the meal in a coach, and saying that he 'got up behind the coach to eat mine, because she told me to'. Even the dog comes back, magnified into 'four immense dogs' who come off rather better than Pip did since they fight 'for veal-cutlets out of a silver-basket'. On his next visit to Satis House we return briefly to the dog. 'I was taken into the yard to be fed in the former dog-like manner.' The two meals respond in perfect anti-thesis.

The first ceremony of love finds another responsive scene when Magwitch discloses his responsibility and motivation to Pip. We are carefully reminded of the first meal on the marshes:

I drops my knife many a time in that hut when I was a
eating my dinner or my supper, and I says, 'Here's the boy
again, a looking at me whiles I eats and drinks!'
(chapter 39)

It is to this actual memory of the meal that he attaches his plan to 'make that boy a gentleman' but when the gentleman serves him with a meal he does not look at him as the boy did:

He ate in a ravenous manner that was very disagreeable, and
all his actions were uncouth, noisy and greedy. Some of his
teeth had failed him since I saw him eat on the marshes, and
as he turned his food in his mouth, and turned his head
sideways to bring his strongest fangs to bear upon it, he
looked terribly like a hungry old dog.
If I had begun with any appetite, he would have taken it
away, and I should have sat much as I did – repelled from
him by an insurmountable aversion, and gloomily looking
at the cloth.
(chapter 40)

The uncouth eating, the hunger, the sideways movement and the comparison with the dog are repetitions from the early scene which emphasize the distance between the child and the man. This time the observation is full of revulsion, the food is not sauced with ceremony. But if the host has changed, the guest has not, and he apologizes for his doglike eating with undoglike courtesy:

'I'm a heavy grubber, dear boy,' he said, as a polite kind of apology when he had made an end of his meal, 'but I always was. If it had been in my constitution to be a lighter grubber, I might ha' got into lighter trouble.'

The apology is made without shame or self-pity on the part of Magwitch, and provokes no sympathy on the part of Pip. In the early scene the child's pity was impulsive and provoked simply by the desperate eating and panic. In the later scenes, Pip is in a position to see the connexion between the heavy grubbing and the heavy trouble, but describes without pity the roughness and greed: 'there was Prisoner, Felon, Bondsman, plain as plain could be'.

The next meal is described without emphasis. We are told that Magwitch wipes his knife on his leg, but by now Pip is too concerned to hear the convict's history to have room for shame and revulsion. The very last meal described – supper on the night before the attempted escape – contains no comment on manners or response:

It was a dirty place enough . . . but there was a good fire in the kitchen, and there were eggs and bacon to eat, and various liquors to drink.
(chapter 54)

By now Pip's pride has been entirely subdued to the need for action. The quiet disappearance of comment testifies to the naturalness and literalness of the scenes of eating and drinking: a series of related scenes has been established, bringing out the moral significance of needs and hospitality and good manners, but it is brought to no formal climax. There is no explicit comment on the irrelevance of good manners in the crisis of need, no reminiscence of the fellowship of the first meal and the first occasion when Pip helped Magwitch to escape his pursuers, nothing of the climactic recognition of symbolism which we find in James's dove, or Lawrence's rainbow, or Dickens's own wild waves. The meals are only tapped for their moral significance on occasions when men need food desperately or when there is scope for hospitality: towards the end of the story the meals are inartificially subordinated to other features of the action. I do not make this distinction in order to decry the more contrived symbolism in other novels, but merely in order to bring out Dickens's unheightened and sober reliance on everyday moral and social facts. There is, I think, no question of an unconscious moral pattern, for the repetition of details makes the control quite plain, but Dickens is content to subdue this significant series of meals to the proportions and emphases of his story.

With the same almost unobtrusive reflection of ordinary moral fact, the meals with Estella are also described without schematic arrangement. They scarcely develop into a pattern, and Dickens can allow himself to describe a meal without relating it to earlier significances. When Estella and Pip have tea together in the hotel, or when Pip does eventually dine with some ceremony inside Satis House, no moral emphasis is present: on the first occasion Dickens is concerned to develop aspects of the relationship to which need and ceremony are irrelevant; on the second he is concerned with the tense understatement of Jaggers's observation of Estella. But although some of the meals in this novel make no moral definition, it is true that nearly all the characters and families are given, at some point, their significant ceremony of food. Magwitch tells Pip and Herbert how his heavy grubbing explains his troubled career and begins his life-story with the little boy who stole turnips and who was always driven by the need 'to put something into his stomach'. Pip as a child is not physically deprived in this way, but although he is given enough to eat, he is not given his food with love. In chapter 2, between Magwitch's demand for food and Pip's generous response, we are given a glimpse of Mrs Joe's 'bringing up by hand'. She is an unloving mother-surrogate who feeds her family unceremoniously:

My sister had a trenchant way of cutting our
bread-and-butter for us, that never varied. First, with her
left hand she jammed the loaf hard and fast against her bib –
where it sometimes got a pin into it, and sometimes a needle,
which we afterwards got into our mouths. Then she took
some butter (not too much) on a knife and spread it on the
loaf, in an apothecary kind of way, as if she were making a

plaister – using both sides of the knife with a slapping
dexterity, and trimming and moulding the butter off round
the crust. Then, she gave the knife a final smart wipe on the
edge of the plaister.

The pins and needles have already been mentioned as characteristic of
this unmotherly breast:

She was tall and bony, and almost always wore a coarse
apron, fastened over her figure behind with two loops, and
having a square impregnable bib in front, that was stuck
full of pins and needles.

Some of the implications of this juxtaposition are terrifying, but
the Gargery household is treated with comedy rather than with the
harsh violence which is the medium for the Murdstones. But both the
comic mode and the grim seem at times to draw freely on Dickens's
fantasy. The moral implications within the novel are plain: Mrs Joe
gives unlovingly, to put it mildly, taking most pleasure in the administration of Tar-Water and fasts, while Joe shares the wedges of
bread in love and play, and tries to make up for Pip's sufferings at the
Christmas dinner with spoonfuls of gravy.

The cold comfort of Mrs Joe's meals, like her uncomfortable
cleanliness, makes her an ancestress of Mrs Ogmore-Pritchard,
though Dickens inflicts a terrible revenge on her in the action. She
has the front-parlour mentality, and the only ceremony in the Gargery household apart from the rough meals shared by Pip and Joe, is
the false ceremony of hospitality. Her showing-off at the dinner-party
contrasts rudely with her earlier words to Joe and Pip: 'I ain't a going
to have no formal cramming and busting and washing-up now', and
they have their slices served out as if they 'were two thousand
troops on a forced march instead of a man and boy at home'. I need
not dwell on the Christmas dinner, with Mr Wopsle's theatrical
declamation of grace, with the adjurations to Pip to be grateful 'to
them which brought you up by hand', with Pumblechook's im-
modest generosity and gluttony and the comic nemesis when he
chokes on the Tar-Water. The contrast between the ceremony of
love and the false ceremony is there, together with the rebuke of
starvation. For Magwitch has eaten the pie and drunk the brandy.
This is underlined when Pip observes Pumblechook's possessive

appropriation of the wine he has given to Mrs Joe and his generous treating of the flattering sergeant. The false giving and receiving are put in the context of the first meal with Magwitch when Pip comments, 'I thought what terrible good sauce for a dinner my fugitive friend on the marshes was.'

Pip's humiliation by Estella is also put into a larger context when he explains that his susceptibility to injustice and shame was attributable to the unloving home. Joe makes even the hacked bread and superfluous gravy the food of love, but Estella sharpens the sense of false ceremony, in part by denying ceremony, and Pip becomes less conscious of love's seasoning than of good manners. He continues in fantasy, and eventually moves from the back of the coach. The actual social significance of eating habits becomes emphatic in a novel about snobbery and aspiration, and there are other meals which raise the question of love and ceremony. When Pip has his first meal with Herbert Pocket, a difficult social situation is eased by Herbert's friendly delicacy, and he gives both the strawberries and the lessons in etiquette with true ceremony. This is a scene which establishes both the importance of good manners and the importance of love. It contrasts strongly with the second meal with Magwitch, where Pip is the bad host, and is paralleled by the first, when Pip is the true host. It is closest of all to another scene, where Herbert and Pip are entertaining Joe to breakfast. Joe is 'stiff from head to foot', cannot say outright that he prefers tea to coffee, and is as selfconscious in his politeness as Magwitch is unselfconscious in his roughness:

Then he fell into such unaccountable fits of meditation, with his fork midway between his plate and his mouth; had his eyes attracted in such strange directions; was afflicted with such remarkable coughs; sat so far from the table, and dropped so much more than he ate, and pretended he hadn't dropped it; that I was heartily glad when Herbert left us for the city.
(chapter 27)

This failure in hospitality – 'I had neither the good sense nor the good feeling to know that this was all my fault' – prepares us for the greater failure, the greater social gulf and the greater shame, when Magwitch returns and Pip makes a first false, but healthy comparison between his shame for Joe and his shame before the convict, for whom he had deserted Joe.

There are other scenes, more or less emphatic, in which the social values of eating are defined. There is the false show, lightly touched on, in the last celebratory supper at the forge before Pip leaves home, when he sits ashamed in his splendour for their delight and they are all 'very low' despite roast fowl and flip. This contrasts with another kind of false show, in the same chapter, when Mr Pumblechook flatters and celebrates in a travesty of the love-feast. He toasts Pip in extravagant mock-abasement when he toasts Pip – 'May I? – *may* I?' – and elaborately deprecates the chicken and tongue – 'one or two little things had round from the Boar, that I hope you may not despise' – and apostrophizes the fowl – 'Ah! poultry, poultry! You little thought ... when you was a young fledgling, what was in store for you' (chapter 29). At the other social extreme from this exhibition of hospitable abasement, but close to it morally, is Pip's little fantasy, at the beginning of the same chapter, of feasting the villagers, 'bestowing a dinner of roast-beef and plum-pudding, a pint of ale, and a gallon of condescension'. There are many other meals too, which might be mentioned: the funeral repast after Mrs Joe's death, Jaggers's good food and ruthless hospitality, the geniality of the pub, Pip's susceptibility to wine on one or two occasions, the lavishness of his housekeeping with Herbert, and the ordered, warm and unpretentious hospitality of Wemmick.

Almost every character and family is given moral and social definition by their attitudes to food and hospitality. Old Barley keeps the provisions in his room, and provides Clara with bread and cheese while he has mutton-chops, potatoes and split peas stewed up in butter; he roars and bangs for his grog and growls in pain while trying to cut through a Double Gloucester with his gouty hand. The ill-fed children are the unloved children. The baby Pocket, like Pip, is endangered by being fed on pins, though in his case the inappropriate food is the result of neglect and disorder not of an aggressive display of good housekeeping. The disorder, bad economy and inadequate meals of the Pocket family are another version of the neglected Jellybys in *Bleak House*, and just as Mrs Jellyby is ironically exposed as a model of displaced charity, so Mrs Pocket is shown in her disorder as another qualification of class-distinction and great expectations.

Her delusions of grandeur lead to the disregard of proper ceremony. Although each bad mother is attached to the special theme of each novel, the basic moral failure is the same. It is a failure in love.

I have not yet mentioned one of the most prominent failures in love in *Great Expectations*. This is Miss Havisham's failure. Her love-feast is preserved in its decay to make the most conspicuous contribution to the themes of love and nature. Nothing remains of the expectations of Satis House but a gruesome parody of ceremony:

> The most prominent object was a long table with a
> tablecloth spread on it, as if a feast had been in preparation
> when the house and the clocks all stopped together. An
> épergne or centre-piece of some kind was in the middle of
> this cloth; it was so heavily overhung with cobwebs that its
> form was quite undistinguishable; and as I looked along the
> yellow expanse out of which I remember its seeming to
> grow, like a black fungus, I saw speckled-legged spiders
> with blotchy bodies running home to it. . . .
> (chapter 11)

Miss Havisham makes a symbolic correlation between the mouldering wedding-breakfast and her own life. She has been gnawed by pain as the food has been gnawed by mice, she was worn away with the meal, and when she is dead she too will be laid out on that table, where she has allocated the places for her predatory family to sit and 'feast upon' her. The betrayal of love and the hypocritical greedy show of love are both bracketed as false ceremony in this grisly image of transubstantiation. The ghastly conceit stands out from Dickens's other significant correlations of love and food as a product of a diseased fancy and an impossible attempt to pervert nature. Jaggers makes explicit the other implications of the stasis and decay which relate this meal to the pattern of normal routine and relationship:

> He asked me how often I had seen Miss Havisham eat and
> drink. . . .
> I considered, and said, 'Never'. 'And never will, Pip,'
> he retorted, with a frowning smile. 'She has never allowed
> herself to be seen doing either, since she lived this present life

of hers. She wanders about in the night, and then lays hands
on such food as she takes.'
(chapter 29)

Miss Havisham's rejection of ordinary public meals is like her
attempts to shut out the daylight. Food in *Great Expectations*, as in
Macbeth, is part of the public order, and the meals testify to human
need and dependence, and distinguish false ceremony from the ceremony of love. They are not symbols but natural demonstrations.
(351–63)

Steven Marcus

from 'The Myth of Nell', *Dickens: From Pickwick to Dombey* 1965

The raging contrarieties of Quilp's sadism and masochism are the
counterparts of the contradictory, sentimental emotions with which
Dickens invested Nell. Sentimentality cannot here be adequately
understood in its conventional definition: that it is an excessive and
self-indulging effusion of sentiment, a response grotesquely disproportionate to the reality of a situation. Such a formulation tells us very
little about the conditions which generate it. One of these conditions,
I suggest, is the presence, consciously or unconsciously, of a memory
around which a large reservoir of painful feelings has accrued, feelings
charged with the antipathies and suppressions of the experience from
which the memory grew. Whenever, therefore, its recollection takes
place, or whenever situations occur which call forth the memory for
whatever reason and in whatever form, the floodgates of all this
accumulation of feeling are forced open, and one might seem in
danger of being overwhelmed, were it not for that faculty of the
mind to repress and distort whatever meanings it finds too unpleasant
to know – though it cannot, in natures such as Dickens's, repress altogether the feelings themselves. The result of this process we call sentimentality when what we allow ourselves to *believe* we are feeling is
shaped somehow to what we want to feel, to what we ought to feel,
to what we think we deserve to feel – to a kind of self-deception.

This implies a separation of the energy of emotion from emotion
itself – that is, from the quality and content of emotion – which can

explain a good deal about the nature of sentimentality, and which I think is especially borne out in Dickens. For a large part of Dickens's sentimentality is not of the ordinary, maudlin quality we are most familiar with. Because his genius was fired by an especially abundant and intense energy, much of the sentimentality in his writings is of an unusually fierce order. We recognize a peculiar collapse and relaxation which always seem to characterize the ordinary forms of sentimentality, a certain foolishness, flabbiness and weakness. But with Dickens, all these components (none of which is lacking) frequently take on an intensity, a boldness, a sustained exertion of will which defy the kind of easy contempt we generally allow ourselves to feel towards the usual purveyor of sentimentality. Dickens was able to admit to sentimentality a greater quantity of the element of unpleasantness and pain than most who can be accused of this flaw. Here, indeed, is what makes Dickens's sentimentality often seem so extraordinary. Sentimentality, like self-pity, can be as amenable to the qualities of genius, both affective and intellectual, as any of our more primitive responses. Coleridge's poem *Dejection: An Ode* is, for example, a great poem of self-pity.

After the first shock of Mary Hogarth's death had worn off, Dickens wrote her mother that he intended never to behave as if her memory were to be avoided; he would never shrink from speaking of her; he was determined 'to take a melancholy pleasure in recalling the times when we were all so happy'.[1] A year and a half later, on the occasion of the death of the daughter of William Bradbury, Dickens wrote to Bradbury that he hoped the time was not far distant 'when you will be able to think of this dear child with a softened regret which will have nothing of bitterness in its composition – when it will be a melancholy but not a painful satisfaction to call up old looks and thoughts and terms of speech – and when you will be able to reflect with a grateful heart that those who yield most promise and are most

1 *Letters*, vol. 1, p. 133. One of Master Humphrey's last desires is 'that we would make him the frequent subject of our conversation . . . that we would never speak of him with an air of gloom or restraint, but frankly, and as one whom we still loved and hoped to meet again'. Another is 'his fancy that the apartment should not be inhabited; that it should be religiously preserved in this condition, and that the voice of his companion should be heard no more'. *Master Humphrey's Clock* (Conclusion). Again, the persistence with which Dickens identified himself with Mary is apparent.

richly endowed, commonly die young, as though from the first they were the objects of the Almighty's peculiar love and care'.[1] With its distinctions that do not quite distinguish, with its qualifications that slide into blurred incertitude, this passage reveals Dickens's senti-mentality as a condition of spirit in which doubt and pain and affirma-tion co-exist, and in which affirmation is commanded forcefully, wilfully, to prevail.[2]
(159–61)

Robert Garis

from 'Action and Structure in the Dickens Theatre', *The Dickens Theatre* 1965

The action of the early novels, when there is any at all, consists of manoeuvring performing theatrical characters into various arrange-ments, in order to provide new and different occasions for thrilling or affecting performances. It is theatrical action. And much of what goes on in the middle and late novels is also theatrical action.

Dickens's leading motive and consuming interest in the early period was in his own performances before his newly discovered public. The earliest newspaper and magazine sketches still sound, at their best, like auditions; at their worst they are depressingly eager merely to *exist* as professional writing, to be effective, to make an impression. Very soon after the beginning of *The Pickwick Papers* the wonderful sound of professional assurance is heard and the invention expands and flowers with self-delight under the warm sun of a known public's affection. What has been achieved is, in the flattest sense of the word, humorous writing, in the vein of exaggerated burlesque, but in this one style and tone the special Dickensian copiousness and freedom of invention is already fully operating. Now begins the professional business of ex-

1 *Letters*, W. Dexter (ed.), 1938, vol. 1, p. 203.
2 Earlier in this letter Dickens had characteristically asserted 'The certainty of a bright and happy world beyond the Grave which such young and untried creatures (half Angels here) *must* be called away by God to people.' *Letters*, vol. 1, p. 202.

panding the repertory, of deepening and broadening the humorous style already achieved and beloved, and of contriving new occasions for its use. In *Martin Chuzzlewit* and *Dombey and Son*, the experienced professional begins to take some interest in the large-scale organization of his material, by no means very successfully. Thematic consistency is attempted: *Martin Chuzzlewit* is organized on the theme of hypocrisy and greed, *Dombey and Son* on the theme of pride. Moreover, the action of both books depends upon a basic change of attitude on the part of a leading character: both young Martin and old Dombey are softened and made less selfish by painful experience and by love. Engineering these metamorphoses wastes a lot of energy and the resulting serious pages are laboriously tedious; but there is plenty of energy available, and the minor characters in both these books are brilliantly vivid.

From one point of view, this early career is a beautiful thing to contemplate. The basic operation is a pure projection of will, but this takes the form of doing, performing, acting – never of self-revelation or vanity. The great entertainer claims attention and love for what he does, not for what he is, with the result that wonderful work is done, immense quantities of energy are expended. (I am taking for granted the superlative quality of the talent.) And all this work has the self-delighting spontaneity of play. Dickens's ambition is to encompass the world through mimicry; not by dominating the world, owning it and depriving it of its free life, but by copying and thus experiencing its life in his own actions. The generosity and spontaneity of this spirit everyone has recognized. Dickens entirely lacked the impulse to 'do dirt on life', to destroy something because he wanted to see it dead (though he had, one grants, plenty of the 'impulse to kill'). Dickens *knows* the world through mimicking it, and to his youthful eyes the life in the world is as infinite as he feels his own vitality to be: he can mimic everything and there is everything to be mimicked. He can make contact only with what can be mimicked, but it is also true, and this is the most important point about his early career, that mimicry is *sufficient* contact with the world as he saw it. Communication is unnecessary.

From another point of view, however, this early career is not so completely attractive or successful. Since Dickens's impulse is completely outgoing, none of the advantages of self-criticism is available to him, and we encounter repeatedly a callow unawareness of his limitations. This leads on occasion to an undignified and nervous dependence on the goodwill of his public. More often it leads to deliberate and self-delighting ineptitudes, crudities, banalities, sheer vacuities such as are to be found in the work of no other great writer. Nevertheless these gross faults of taste are really negligible because the theatrical situation is always so clear: since we are so comfortably aware that we are being an audience for his performances, we are comfortably cheerful about rejecting his failures without irritation. And I think every admirer of Dickens is glad that he never acquired the sort of self-knowledge that turns so many of our present-day comedians into cautious entrepreneurs and their routines into a commodity instead of a gift. That Dickens retained his innocence throughout his entire career is registered in the fact that he perhaps actually killed himself by working too hard for applause.

When self-knowledge came to Dickens, it took a form which has little to do with what we ordinarily understand by the term. *David Copperfield* is generally agreed to mark the mid-point in Dickens's career, even though in its methods and substance it belongs decidedly to the early half. It is common knowledge that this novel uses as some of its material certain of Dickens's own experiences, and there is general agreement too that the differences in method and tone between the early novels and the later ones are in some way connected with Dickens's 'coming to terms with himself'. But we can discover the nature of this process only by examining the evidence in the novels themselves and making a speculative hypothesis about Dickens's own inner happenings, for even his 'revelations' to Forster were hopelessly reticent.

The fact that Dickens never really developed a fictional mode suitable for self-examination suggests that what took place within him was not really self-examination at all. My guess is that there had been taking place a gradual breakdown in the process of mimicry I have described above. Mimicking the performances going on in his world gradually began to produce a less and less vivid sense of living in Dickens himself and a less vivid sense of contact with the world outside – this may have been caused merely by growing older and by being successful. Gradually there developed a sense of discrepancy between Dickens's inner images of true vitality and true contact with other people and what the world seemed to offer in these respects. The writing of *David Copperfield*, which can be described as mimicry of his own experience, amounted then to a testing of that experience, with disappointing results. For although *David Copperfield* puts on stage some of Dickens's richest and most vivid performing characters (Uriah Heep's villainy is as inexhaustible and as irresistible as Pecksniff's), and although David is promised both life and love in his marriage with Agnes (though few readers have found this ending very interesting or more than perfunctorily convincing), although, in short, Dickens's former attitudes saw him through the actual composition of *David Copperfield*, everything that happened afterwards shows that an important change had taken place. And with *Bleak House* begins the great campaign of indignant criticism of the world for failing to embody his own images of living and loving. The theatrical method remains basic to the new art, which has changed its tone and its methods of organization but not its essential direction. The performance continues; mimicry is still the essential artistic and moral process; self-examination, and the imaginative understanding of the centre of self of others, to which self-examination is the only path, have never been discovered, much less practised. Instead, celebration has turned to accusation.

To this change in Dickens's view of the world, the moral and philosophic answer is easy enough to articulate. 'You are a mimic and you see in human behaviour only what can be mimicked: physical appearance (face, build, posture, clothes) and habitual physical and verbal movements. You see people this way because you, a professional mimic, are always interested in building effective routines. But people really are like this, and you observe accurately; people who say you exaggerate have simply, for one reason or another, good or bad, closed their eyes and ears to this part of the world which you see so clearly.

'You have discovered that these routines, the more you look at them and the more clearly you see them, are no longer as interesting as they once were. There are still plenty of them to be discovered – the number is infinite – but this has become less important than the fact that the routines themselves are beginning to seem mechanical, lifeless, determined, unfree. You *feel* alive, inside of you; you know exactly what being alive feels like. But it seems that no one else does.

Everywhere you see mechanical routines of behaviour instead of anything that matches the sense of life and freedom you have within you.
Everybody is dead: those recurrent twitches and speeches are a
parody of life, not the real thing. This is loathsome enough in itself.
But worse is the fact that the free inner life within you yearns for a
living contact with the free life of another person, whereas all you can
make contact with are mechanical routines. You have loved and
pitied and hated particular people before, particular routines, but that
has come to be not enough.

'You are experiencing a classic dilemma: you have, as it were,
made your kind of discovery of determinism and you cannot account
convincingly for your own sense of freedom. The traditional solution
to this dilemma is through introspection and self-criticism. It is unlikely that you are the only free person in the world, and therefore it
is likely that many people feel the way you do. You must put yourself in their place and realize that to other people you, too, seem nothing but a mechanical routine of habits, a performing fool or clown or
monster. Thus converted to a new perspective, you will begin to get a
vision of the free sense of life within other people, and you will then
perhaps be able to make contact with that life. Such contact will always be a limited and faltering thing in comparison with the fullness
and vividness of your actual sensuous vision and you will find that
your conscience, in this respect, needs continual recreating.'

I have phrased my answer to Dickens's dilemma in direct discourse
because one tends to feel a warm personal attachment to the manager
of the Dickens theatre. If this also makes my answer seem condescending, that too is not inadvertent – for it dramatizes what seems to me
an inevitable reaction to Dickens's solution. Indeed, a straightforward
statement of his solution may be found by some readers unworthy of
serious attention, yet the solution provides precisely that 'social
vision' which makes him a great and inspired social prophet.

The conversion never took place. Instead, Dickens developed a
view of the world as almost totally in the grip of a gigantic conspiracy
which takes myriad forms but of which the sole effect is to thwart and
stifle human freedom and the free contact between free spirits. This
view is saved from the charge of paranoia and lent a kind of generosity
and grandeur by Dickens's ambiguity as to whether it is a deliberate
and intentional conspiracy. Conspiracy seems the wrong word, in so

far as those in control of the conspiracy are often presented as having inherited their functions from the past, or as being decent people in private life, or underlings in a hierarchy of power, or inept or half-hearted in their role; and these people in control are always repre-sented as being themselves dehumanized and deprived of freedom by their functions. But they deserve to be called conspirators because for the most part they work hard and deliberately at their function, and regard themselves as worthy of respect and honour because of it. They all reap material advantages at the same time, and are insensitive to the suffering they cause.

Whether or not we use the word conspiracy to describe this im-mense blight which, in Dickens's view, has fallen over the world, it will be agreed that the blight involves three factors: first, a universal-ity of mechanical, systematized behaviour; second, a class of people who willingly give themselves over to this systematic behaviour, to the System, and therefore acquire power over the lives of others which they dignify with the name of duty or respectability or charity or law; and third, the unwilling victims of the System. The victims are driven into mechanical routines of behaviour, but are pitied be-cause their compulsive tics and obsessive eccentricities are unquestion-ably involuntary and are therefore evidence of the pressure of the System on their lives. Among the rulers of the System in these later books, to name only the most obvious, are the lawyers and the members of the 'fashionable' world in *Bleak House*, the utilitarian schoolmasters and the mill-owners in *Hard Times*, the Puritans, the jailers, Mrs General, and the members of the Circumlocution Office in *Little Dorrit*, Mrs Wilfer and Mr Podsnap in *Our Mutual Friend*. Typical victims are Miss Flite and Prince Turveydrop in *Bleak House*, Maggy and Affery in *Little Dorrit*, Mr Wilfer and the dolls' dress-maker in *Our Mutual Friend*.

Dickens quite frankly argues for the validity of his new view of the world in four of the novels which follow *David Copperfield*: *Bleak House*, *Hard Times*, *Little Dorrit* and *Our Mutual Friend*. He argues often with the greatest persuasiveness: what he thought he saw before him was really there. But it is also true that this insight was the result of his peculiar perspective, of his fundamental identity as a mimic, a theatrical performer of life. It is not then surprising that theatrical methods turn out to be exactly the right ones for demonstrating the validity of that view. Moreover, the most successful of the four novels are those in which the argumentative intention is most overt and the burden of the argument least complex. Dickens's purpose in *Bleak House* is to demonstrate that the whole world is penetrated, stifled and terrorized by a huge network of interconnecting systems: the structure of the novel embodies this vision by offering a satisfyingly large number of examples of systematized characters, and by contriving many and pointed interrelations between them. *Hard Times* is a logical refutation of the Utilitarian definition of human nature and of the Utilitarian mechanics for the production of human happiness: the structure of this novel is accordingly that of a 'moral fable' (to use Dr Leavis's term), a pointed cautionary tale. These two novels are triumphs of convincing theatrical rhetoric by virtue of the extraordinary energy of Dickens's richest invention and the brilliant simplicity of his themes, which is thoroughly in consonance with his odd perspective on life. In neither novel is the success of the whole structure damaged by the generally recognized failure of individual elements: an experienced habitué of the Dickens theatre can casually reject the sentimentalities connected with Esther Summerson and Stephen Blackpool without believing that this rejection in the least endangers the success of the books as wholes.

In *Little Dorrit* and *Our Mutual Friend*, an attack on System is again theatrically rendered, and often (in particular in *Little Dorrit*) with great success. But in these novels Dickens chose to combine loud and simple denunciations of System with an attempt to focus on and to render dramatically the spiritual progress by which certain individuals, who are deeply implicated in System, nevertheless emerge from its blight into some small kind of freedom and happiness. Arthur Clennam's sick will is healed by the love of Little Dorrit, and Bella Wilfer's hard-hearted pursuit of money is softened into love by Mr Boffin's monitory impersonation of money-madness. In these novels, then, Dickens honourably but unwisely attempted the drama of human choice and change. Unwisely, for even when Clennam's inner spiritual state is fairly convincingly described, there is a disturbing discordance between this element of the novel and the brilliant theatrical mimicries and denunciations which surround it. The process through which Clennam's sick will is healed is a theatrical manipulation tricked out to look like drama, and Bella Wilfer's change of heart is tediously conventional. One simply regrets that Dickens should have spent his waning energies in attempting a mode of art so alien to his genius. His rendering of the drama of the inner life suffers, even at its best, from inevitable comparison with the work of novelists to whom this mode of representing human beings came naturally. But the best is rare, and for the most part we are embarrassed by a disastrous mixture of modes: again and again Dickens seems simply unable to keep himself from working up lurid theatrical routines out of material which would seem to call for a more self-effacing method. *Our Mutual Friend*, furthermore, exhibits a decided loss of inventive energy.

Great Expectations stands apart from these four novels by virtue of Dickens's temporary loss of interest in his attack on System. This novel theatrically impersonates the voice of a man who has learned how to live in a systematized world, but who is not for the moment interested in mounting a rhetorical attack on it. But *Great Expectations* stands apart from the other late novels by virtue of another characteristic which makes it an altogether unique literary phenomenon. The life story of Pip is in perfect accordance with the traditional language of pride, love and duty by means of which it is explicitly moralized. But this story also speaks quite different meanings in and of itself, which are not the same as the explicit meanings and which were not, one imagines, available to the conscious part of Dickens's mind. This odd state of affairs produced, in *Great Expectations*, a beautiful and successful work of art.

(92–100)

W. J. Harvey

from 'Character and Narration', *Character and the Novel* 1965 (revised from 'Chance and Design in *Bleak House*', in J. Gross and G. Pearson (eds.), *Dickens and the Twentieth Century*, 1962)

Dickens has often been likened to a Jacobean dramatist both for his vivid, exuberant, 'poetic' use of language and for his methods of characterization. There is a third point of likeness. Critics frequently discuss Jacobean plays in terms of 'episodic intensification'. By this they mean the impulse to exploit to the full possibilities of any particular scene, situation or action without too much regard for the relevance of such local intensities to the total work of art. Clearly much of Dickens's fiction is of the same order. To admit this is to risk the displeasure of much modern criticism of fiction which, largely deriving from James, lays great stress on the organic unity of the novel and demands that no part shall be allowed autonomy if this threatens the integrity of the whole.

We can defend in four ways the novel of episodic intensification from such criticism. First, we may admit that in some cases the work may fail as a whole while succeeding in some part. The result may be a dead or crippled work which yet intermittently achieves the vigour of a masterpiece. We may admire what we can and regret the waste of so much else. This, I think, is true of *Barnaby Rudge*. Second, we may deny the fiat of organic unity and maintain that in some cases a novel achieves no more than episodic intensification and yet possesses so much vitality that we are content simply to accept its greatness. In James's terms there must be room in the house of fiction for such 'loose, baggy monsters'. With much less certainty I would place *Pickwick Papers* in this category. Third, we may accept the idea of organic unity and yet maintain that by its standards Dickens's novels are entirely successful. Sometimes he achieves an economy, firmness and clean-cut clarity of control that can only be called classical. This is surely true of *Great Expectations*. Finally, we may accept the idea of organic unity but argue that the criteria by which we judge its presence or absence have been too narrowly conceived and that there exist conventions and methods of organization which are non-Jamesian but still appropriate and effective. (James, unlike some more recent critics, admitted as much.) *Bleak House* is here a relevant example. Indeed, I would say that one of the reasons for its greatness is the extreme tension set up between the centrifugal vigour of its parts and the centripetal demands of the whole. It is a tension between the impulse to intensify each local detail or particular episode and the impulse to subordinate, arrange and discipline. The final impression is one of immense and potentially anarchic energy being brought – but only just – under control. The fact that the equipoise between part and whole is so precariously maintained is in itself a tribute to the energy here being harnessed.

How well does an examination of the novel's structure support this general view? *Bleak House* is for Dickens a unique and elaborate experiment in narration and plot composition. It is divided into two intermingled and roughly concurrent stories; Esther Summerson's first-person narrative and an omniscient narrative told consistently in the historic present. The latter takes up thirty-four chapters; Esther has one less. Her story, however, occupies a good deal more than half the novel. The reader who checks the distribution of these two narratives against the original part issues will hardly discern any significant pattern or correlation. Most parts contain a mixture of the two stories; one part is narrated entirely by Esther and five parts entirely by the omniscient author. Such a check does, however, support the view that Dickens did not, as is sometimes supposed, use serial publication in the interest of crude suspense. A sensational novelist, for example, might well have ended a part issue with chapter 31; Dickens subdues the drama by adding another chapter to the number. The obvious exception to this only proves the rule; in the final double number the suspense of Bucket's search for Lady Dedlock is heightened by cutting back to the omniscient narrative and the stricken Sir Leicester. In general, however, Dickens's control of the double narrative is far richer and subtler than this. Through this technique, as I shall try to show, he controls the immense, turbulent and potentially confusing material of his novel. Indeed, the narrative method seems to me to be part of the very substance of *Bleak House*, expressive of what, in the widest and deepest sense, the novel is about.

Let us first examine the structural functions of Esther Summerson and her narrative. Esther has generally been dismissed as insipid, one of Dickens's flat, non-comic good characters, innocent of imaginative life, more of a moral signpost than a person. Even if we accept this general judgement we may still find good reasons why Dickens had necessarily to sacrifice vitality or complexity here in order to elaborate or intensify other parts of his novel. If Dickens, far from failing to create a lively Esther, is deliberately suppressing his natural exuberance in order to create a flat Esther, then we may properly consider one of Esther's functions to be that of a brake, controlling the runaway tendency of Dickens's imagination – controlling, in other words, the impulse to episodic intensification.

Can we possibly accept this view? The contrasting styles of the two narratives, while they offer the reader relief and variety, also seem to me evidence of Dickens's control in making Esther what she is, even at the risk of insipidity and dullness. The omniscient style has all the liveliness, fantastication and poetic density of texture that we typically associate with Dickens. Esther's narrative is plain, matter-of-fact, conscientiously plodding. Only very rarely does her style slip and allow us to glimpse Dickens guiding her pen – as when, for instance, she observes 'Mr Kenge, standing with his back to the fire, and casting his eyes over the dusty hearthrug as if it were Mrs Jellyby's biography' (chapter 4), or when, as Turveydrop bows to her, she could 'almost believe I saw creases come into the white of his eyes' (chapter 14). Here one may glimpse Dickens chafing at his self-imposed discipline. Such moments apart, any stylistic vivacity or idiosyncrasy in Esther's prose comes from the oddities and foibles of other characters. Dickens imagines them; Esther merely reports them. Even when, at moments of emotional stress, her prose strays into the purple patch, one still feels that this is the rhetoric of an amateur, not to be compared, for instance, with the controlled crescendo of Jo's death. Similarly, whenever the straightforward flow of Esther's narratives falters – as in her over-casual mention of Allan Woodcourt at the end of chapter 14 – we prefer to see this as appropriate to her character rather than to spot Dickens signalling a new relationship to us behind her back. That, of course, is precisely what he is doing, but the disguise of style persuades us to focus on Esther and not on her creator. (There is, I think, a corresponding and quite remarkable impersonality about the omniscient narrative. The general impression is of a vast, collective choric voice brilliantly mimicking the varied life it describes, yet able to generalize and comment without lapsing into the idiom of one man, of Dickens himself. Obviously the style exploits and manipulates our sympathies; yet surprisingly rarely do we feel that Dickens is directly buttonholing us.)

As I have said, the two narratives are *roughly* concurrent. Deliberately so; Dickens juggles the two chronologies by keeping the details sufficiently vague. Only rarely do we feel any awkwardness in this temporal matching together and any obvious discontinuity generally has a specific narrative or dramatic point. Esther's tale, taken in isolation, plods forward in the simplest kind of sequence. Yet, being autobiographical, it is retrospective and was written, so we are told, at the very end, seven years after the main events. This simplicity is rarely disturbed; only occasionally does Esther sound the note of 'If I had known then what I know now'; only occasionally does she throw an anticipatory light forward into the shadowy future of her tale as, for example, she does at the end of chapter 37. The reason is that, despite the retrospective nature of her story, Esther must *seem* to be living in a dramatic present, ignorant of the plot's ramifications. Dickens is *really* omniscient in the other narrative; god-like he surveys time as though it were an eternal present and Esther must seem to belong to that present. It is a convention most readers readily accept.

In what ways does Esther's tale throw light on its teller? During his later period Dickens showed considerable interest in the possibilities of the first-person narrative. In some cases – *David Copperfield, Great Expectations* – the adult narrator judges, implicitly or explicitly, his growth towards maturity. Esther is clearly not in this category; she swiftly advances from child to woman and scarcely changes at all. We feel that she was 'born old' – a feeling reflected in the nicknames given her, though in fact she is little older than Ada Clare. On the other hand, she cannot be classed with Miss Wade, of *Little Dorrit*, whose story is taken by some critics as an early exercise in that kind of point-of-view technique which dramatizes a limited or crippled consciousness so that what is conveyed to the reader differs radically from the intention of the narrator. Clearly, we are meant to take Esther on trust. If what she tells us is wrong or limited this signifies no moral blindspot in her, no flaw in her sensibility but only her necessary innocence of the full ramifications of the plot. Dickens's treatment of Esther is devoid of irony. We have only to imagine what narrative would have resulted if the teller had been Skimpole – or even Richard Carstone – to see that Esther's responses, attitudes and actions are never qualified or criticized. She is, in short, thoroughly idealized.

One result of the idealizing process is the static nature of Esther's character, the essentials of which we quickly come to know. These never change; her story merely exhibits them in a variety of situations in which she is generally the patient rather than the agent. That is, Esther *does* very little in the sense of initiating a chain of actions by a deliberate choice. Things are done to her or because of her rather than by her. Devastating things happen to Esther from the moment of her birth, but she generally emerges with her usual placidity and acceptance of duty. Indeed, at times Dickens takes care to subdue the effect on the reader of these crises through which Esther as patient must pass. The chapter which deals, for example, with the recognition scene between Esther and her mother closes in fact with Esther's reunion with Ada. The curious thing is the feelings aroused by the Esther–Ada relationship seem more intense – and intensely rendered – than those aroused by the Esther–Lady Dedlock encounter.

Esther then is static, consistent, passive. She is also good. The difficulties of combining these qualities to produce a compelling character are so immense that we should wonder not that Dickens fails, but that his failure is so slight. Still, he does fail. The exigencies of the narrative force him to reveal Esther's goodness in a coy and repellent manner; she is, for instance, continually imputing to others qualities which the author transparently wishes us to transfer to her. Esther's goodness is most acceptable when she is least conscious of its effects radiating out to impinge on others. Similarly, her narrative is most acceptable when she is pushed from the centre of the stage by the typical inhabitants of the Dickens world. Happily, this is usually so. In other words, Dickens has to reconcile in Esther the demands of a narrator and a main character and he chooses to subdue Esther as a character in the interests of her narrative function. We do not, so to speak, look *at* Esther; we look *through* her at the teeming Dickensian world. This viewpoint is no Jamesian dramatization of a particular consciousness; Esther is as lucid and neutral as a clear window. We look through at a human landscape but we are not, as with James, constantly aware that the window is limited by its frame or that it has a scratch here and an opaque spot there. The penalty Dickens pays for this is the insipidity of Esther's character. But then, *Bleak House* is a thickly populated novel; each character claims his own share of attention and all are connected by a complicated series of interlocking actions. There is no single centre, no Jamesian *disponible*; rather we have a complex field of force, of interacting stresses and strains. Given this complication it would be too much to ask of the reader that he concentrate on the perceiver as well as the perceived. Were Esther to be complicated the novel would have to be correspondingly simplified and the Dickens world depopulated. Who would wish it so? If the real subject-matter of a novel is a subtly dramatized consciousness then the objects of that consciousness will tend to the sparse refinements of the closet drama. Dickens is the opposite of this; he is to Shakespeare as James is to Racine.

While this, I hope, explains the necessary limitations of Esther's character, it only pushes the real problem one stage further back. Why was it necessary to have a narrator of this kind at all? Any adequate answer must also take into account the omniscient narrative as well. The two narratives are the systole and diastole of the novel and between them they produce the distinctive effect of *Bleak House*; something that I can only call, in a crudely impressionistic manner, the effect of *pulsation*, of constant expansion and contraction, radiation and convergence.

The famous first chapter of *Bleak House* has had more than its fair share of critical attention; at the risk of tedium, therefore, I wish to isolate two striking features of Dickens's method. The omniscient eye which surveys the scene is like the lens of a film camera in its mobility. It may encompass a large panoramic view or, within a sentence, it may swoop down to a close scrutiny of some character or local detail. Closely related to this mobility is the constant expansion and contraction from the omniscient eye to Esther's single viewpoint. Closely related again is the constant expansion and contraction of the total narrative; now concentrating at great length on some episode, now hustling the plot along with a rapid parade of characters. Dickens's narrative skill is nowhere more evident that in his control of tempo.

All this I mean by *pulsation*. But chapter 1 displays yet another related effect. The scene contracts to the Court of Chancery at the heart of the fog, but suddenly this process is reversed; Chancery monstrously expands to encompass the whole country:

'This is the Court of Chancery; which has its decaying
houses and its blighted lands in every shire; which has its
worn-out lunatic in every madhouse, and its dead in every
churchyard. . . .'

The heart of Chancery in this respect is Tom All Alone's, the breeding-ground of disease (again the radiation of infection). The two are appropriately linked, for Chancery *is* a disease and is constantly described in these terms.

This theme is, of course, abundantly worked out in the novel – in Miss Flite, in Gridley and, above all, in Richard Carstone. The idea of corruption radiating out from a rotten centre (Chancery *and* Tom All Alone's) is reflected, in geographical terms, in the constant to-and-fro movement between London, Bleak House and Chesney Wold. But this idea is counterpointed, in plot terms, by the sense one has of convergence, especially the sense of something closing-in on Lady Dedlock. Geography and plot coalesce in the final constriction of the chase and the discovery of Lady Dedlock dead near her lover's tomb.

This pulsation, this interaction of radiation and convergence, is also temporal. The case of Jarndyce and Jarndyce does not merely fan out in the present to enmesh innocent and remote people; it also has a terrible history:

Innumerable children have been born into the cause;
innumerable young people have married into it; innumerable
old people have died out of it. Scores of persons have
deliriously found themselves made parties in Jarndyce and
Jarndyce, without knowing how or why; whole families
have inherited legendary hatreds with the suit.
(chapter 1)

Diverse pressures from the past converge to mould the present; Jarndyce and Jarndyce bears down on Richard Carstone; the past catches up with Esther and finally with her mother. This temporal convergence is reflected in the structure of the novel as a whole and locally, in its parts. Thus the first chapter given to Esther (chapter 3) quickly brings us from her childhood back to the dramatic present already described in the omniscient first chapter. Sometimes the dramatic present is illuminated by a shaft driven back into the past; thus both Boythorn and Miss Barbary are in some sense enlarged by the revelation of their abortive love long ago. Or again, the dramatic present will be left unexplained until time has passed and many pages have been turned; thus, on a small scale, the mystery of Jo's disappearance from Bleak House or, on a large scale, Bucket's uncovering of Tulkinghorn's murderess.

Granted the extremely complicated tangle of effects I have labelled *pulsation*, the desirability of a simple, lucid, straightforward narrative such as Esther's should be obvious. It offers us stability, a point of rest in a flickering and bewildering world, the promise of some guidance through the labyrinth. The usual novel may be compared to a pebble thrown into a pool; we watch the ripples spread. But in *Bleak House* Dickens has thrown in a whole handful of pebbles and what we have to discern is the immensely complicated tracery of half-a-dozen circles expanding, meeting, interacting. Esther – to change the metaphor – has the stability of a gyroscope; by her we chart our way.

She is, of course, much more than this. She is, as well, a moral touchstone; her judgements are rarely emphatic but we accept them. She can see Richard more clearly than Ada; through her Skimpole is revealed in his true colours and the Growlery becomes a sign of Jarndyce's obtuseness. She is also the known constant by which we judge all the other variables of character. Through her we can see the horrifyingly vivid notation of decay and infection that signals the slow process of Richard's destruction. (Among other things, the intertwining of the two narratives enables Dickens, drastically to foreshorten and mould the *apparent* time sequence here.) Again, by her consistency Esther contributes to the wonderfully skilful charcterization of Sir Leicester and Guppy, who change by fits and starts throughout the novel. Because these characters demand very different reactions from us at different times we impute complexity and development to them. In fact they are not so much complex as discontinuous. Dickens's art lies in masking this discontinuity and Esther in large part provides a convincing façade; because she is a simple unity we are conjured into believing that the heterogeneity of Guppy or Sir Leicester is a unified complexity.

Finally – and perhaps most important – by intertwining the two narratives Dickens compels us to a double vision of the teeming, fantastic world of *Bleak House*. We – and Esther – are within; we – and the omniscient author – are outside. This double perspective forces us as readers to make connexions which as I have said, because *we* make them have more validity than if Dickens had made them for us. The most crucial instance is Esther's ignorance of so much that surrounds her. What she sees she sees clearly; but she cannot see more than a fraction of the whole. In this she is not alone; one of the triumphs of the novel is the delicacy with which Dickens handles the knowledge, suspicions, guesses and mistakes of the various characters. Some of them are limited to one or other of the narrative streams; Esther is never seen by the omniscient eye, nor does Tulkinghorn ever appear personally in Esther's narrative. This corresponds to their limited knowledge; Tulkinghorn, for all his plotting, never knows of Esther's relation to Lady Dedlock while there is no substantial evidence that Esther knows anything of her father until after her mother's death.

Granted this, the opportunities for dramatic irony are clearly enormous and it is to Dickens's credit as an artist that with great tact he refuses many of the chances for irony offered by the interlocking narratives. How close – all unknowing – is Esther to meeting her father during her first visit to Krook's? Yet we scarcely perceive this, even on a re-reading of the novel. A lesser artist would have wrung dry the irony of such an incident, but Dickens is sound in his refusal to do so. For the novel, as it stands, is so taut, so potentially explosive, that to expatiate on, or to underline, its implications would make it quite intolerable. Of course the irony is there but it is kept latent and, so to speak, sub-critical; it does not explode in the reader's conscious attention. In this, of course, its effect is almost the opposite of that which I tried to analyse in *Death In Venice*. Mann's story depends largely on its insistently schematic nature, whereas Dickens's problem – like that of most novelists – is to avoid over-schematization, to control the complex and manifold life of the novel without drawing too much attention to the art involved. In this he is again helped by his chosen mode of narration. Through the double narrative Dickens refracts, reflects, varies, distorts, reiterates his major themes, and the disturbing resonance thus set up is expressive of his deepest sense of what life is like. *Bleak House* is so dense with examples of this process that I will quote only one, very minor example. In chapter 25, Mrs Snagsby is suspicious:

Mrs Snagsby screws a watchful glance on Jo, as he is brought into the little drawing-room by Guster. He looks at Mr Snagsby the moment he comes in. Aha! Why does he look at Mr Snagsby? Mr Snagsby looks at him. Why should he do that, but that Mrs Snagsby sees it all? Why else should that look pass between them; why else should Mr Snagsby be confused, and cough a signal cough behind his hand. It is as clear as crystal that Mr Snagsby is that boy's father.

Mrs Snagsby's magnificent illogicality is a comic analogue, a parody of the dominant atmosphere of the book, that of hints, guesses, suspicions, conspiracies. It is also a distorted echo of one of the novel's major themes, that of parents and children. Even here, in an insignificant corner of the book, its major concerns are repeated and echoed in a different key; this abundance of doubling, paralleling, contrasting, this constant modulation from sinister to pathetic or comic, serves to create a density of life providing a context for those vivid scenes of episodic intensification. We accept these, take them on trust as more than brilliant but isolated moments, because we know they mesh with that complicated web of human affairs which entangles all the characters, even the most trivial. We weave this web, this pattern, as the tale shuttles to and fro between its two tellers and, of course, it is a pattern which gradually and continuously develops and emerges.

(89–99)

Henry Gifford

'Dickens in Russia: The Initial Phase', *Forum for Modern Language Studies*, vol. 4, no. 1   January 1968

Dickens had in Russia nearly the same phenomenal success as at home or in the United States. We hear from Henry James how 'he entered into the blood and bone of our intelligence', how 'it had been laid upon young persons of our generation to feel Dickens, down to the soles of our shoes'. And so, with little difference, it was for the Russians. They might lack those delighted recognitions of the Dickensian scene, as when James noted 'the incomparable truth to type' of the waiter at the Adelphi Hotel in Liverpool, 'truth to history, to literature, to poetry, to Dickens, to Thackeray, positively to Smollett and to Hogarth'; or when Henry Adams found that 'Oliver Twist and Little Nell lurked in every churchyard shadow, not as shadow but alive'. Nevertheless they felt drawn to Dickens by the closest of ties. Shakespeare and Scott were, of course, already familiar. No doubt Dickens could hardly be expected to penetrate the Russian mind in the way that he did the American, thanks to a common language. Still, no foreign writer of that time (or since) ever became so thoroughly domiciled in the Russian imagination.

How and why it happened is made clear by an admirable account lately published in Moscow.[1] From this source I derive my main argument and many of my examples.

Dickens came on the scene with perfect timing. What was topical and imperative for England would appear to have been so, in essentials, for Russia. It is only natural that Mr Katarsky should dwell on the humane and democratic impulses of Dickens. Soviet criticism takes its lead from the radical spokesmen of last century, from Belinsky, Chernyshevsky, Dobrolyubov and others, who admired Dickens just for these qualities. To a large extent Belinsky and his successors formed and schooled public opinion, though it would be absurd to argue that everyone who enjoyed Dickens in Russia at that time was a radical. But the opposing camp was certainly not altogether at ease with him; and of course his writings had difficulties with the censor. Russian critics during the 1840s often mentioned him with George Sand – 'one of our saints', as Turgenev would describe her in retrospect. Belinsky cherished her work because it was concerned with current issues and problems. At first he tended to slight Dickens, seeing him as talented but too English, the apologist of bourgeois society. However, *Dombey and Son* (which he never lived to read through) revealed Dickens to him in a new, almost a blinding, light. After 1848 there followed seven years of extremely severe censorship in Russia, and it was then that Dickens really came into his own. The note of protest in his novels may have been muffled somewhat by translators and by the censor, but it was unmistakable. Dickens and Thackeray were for the Russian reader 'manna in the wilderness'. The democrats saw Dickens as a champion of the oppressed. And his attitudes were congenial. The Russian intelligentsia at this time held the same ethical ground as Dickens; broadly it was humanitarian, indifferent or hostile to organized religion, and with a confidence in the mass of mankind as naturally good.

The 'Gogol period of Russian literature', which saw Dickens emerge, made room for him as 'the younger brother of Gogol'. These two writers have indeed a strong family resemblance – in their

1 I. Katarsky, *Dikkens v Rossii: Seredina XIX veka* (Dickens in Russia: Middle of the Nineteenth Century), Izdatel'stvo 'Nauka', Moscow, 1966.

quick eye for the absurd and the pretentious, in their rich and often wild fantasy, and in their delighted exploitation of language. *Pickwick* was very soon compared with *Dead Souls*; the opening pages of Gogol's *Nevsky Prospect* anticipate many of the *Sketches by Boz*; the same grotesques, the same defenceless small people (clerks and the city poor), the same urban misery are prominent in the work of both. Their satirical understanding is much the same. Who are more eligible than the impostor of *Dead Souls*, Chichikov, for a seat on the board of Montague Tigg's Anglo-Bengalee Disinterested Loan and Life Assurance Company? Who would more have appreciated the handsome furniture of its board room, the sumptuous meals, the ceremonial, the high-sounding talk – and not least the 'light-hearted little fiction' that sustains all these? Chichikov with his delicate sense of what words can do would have applauded the butterfly emergence of Tigg Montague, Esquire, from Montague Tigg. And everywhere we find a similar verve, a similar apprehension. Sobakevich's room that reflects its owner in every item has the trick of a hundred Dickensian rooms; Korobochka's clock that assumes a peevish life of its own is a Dickensian clock; and even when they describe a journey by *britzka* or waggon (*Dead Souls*, chapter 11; *The Old Curiosity Shop*, chapter 46) with the fitful impressions between dozing, the momentary sights on the road that rise up and fall away, the same hand seems to be at work. They have a similar talent for lighting on grotesque names and exuberant catch-phrases; they are alike in their verbal gaiety.

And yet Gogol remains the more freakish, the more elusive and unsure of his stance. Gusto for him is curiously mingled with a sense of dreariness and nullity not characteristic of Dickens at any rate till *Our Mutual Friend*. Belinsky insisted on treating Gogol as a writer of social purpose, and was chagrined when Gogol at last produced a purpose not to his liking. Dickens could voice the determination 'to strike the heaviest blow in my power for these unfortunate creatures', and social protest, releasing as it does for him an energy of the imagination from deeper, personal sources, often helped to drive forward his work. But with Gogol the indictment lacks such a clear intention; his pain seems existential. The story of Captain Kopeykin in *Dead Souls*, a crippled veteran who cannot obtain recompense from the state, comes much nearer to Kafka than to Dickens. The magnate when Kopeykin will not be silent bestows on him a look which from such a quarter is like 'a firearm: your heart goes into your boots'. Gogol seems affronted by the disposition of some men to tyrannize and of others to cringe: perhaps it is the system he exposes, which later consigns Kopeykin to the outer darkness, but another name for the system, one fancies, is human life. Belinsky once acclaimed Gogol as 'the Columbus of naturalism', and Columbus, as Vassily Gippius pointed out, discovered a continent on which he had not reckoned. The social novelists of his 'school' made Gogol their anxious pupil (in the unfinished second part of *Dead Souls*).

It was no accident that Gogol and Dickens should have these affinities. Michael Futrell showed in *The Slavonic and East European Review* (June 1956), and Katarsky accepts his finding, that influence on either side can virtually be ruled out. They emerge, like Balzac a little before them, to interpret a new form of experience – life as it is known to the under-privileged of the anonymous modern city. Gogol wrote about this in the Petersburg tales; Dickens carried the exploration much farther.

Even without Gogol Dickens would have captivated Russian readers. Gogol, however, speeded the process, and once a translator had been found to exploit their affinity Dickens became a household presence. The translator was Irinarkh Vvedensky, and he made memorable if at times arbitrary versions of *Pickwick*, *Dombey* and *David Copperfield*. Korney Chukovsky bears witness to his ability to catch the tone, the rhythm, the gestures (though often not the literal meaning) of Dickens. And Vvedensky was the ideal interpreter for that time, brought up himself on Gogol, belonging to the radical intelligentsia, but gifted like few among them with an extreme sensitivity to words. Thus Dickens became more than a projectionist of scenes and images: he entered the language as a verbal phenomenon, a recognizable voice.

It was *Dombey and Son* (in Vvedensky's translation) that truly established Dickens for the Russian reader. Capitalism and the railway were just coming to Russia, and the emancipation of the serfs in 1861 would make the Dombey world a vision of the near future. For the first time readers – and novelists too – in Russia could see a Dickens novel in its true lineaments. Everyone knows that Tolstoy, Turgenev, Goncharov write a different novel from Dickens. His elaborate plots, with all their intrigue and suspense, are reflected by Dostoyevsky alone of the great Russian novelists. And yet Tolstoy, for one, may have learned a deeper principle of organization from works like *Dombey* and *David Copperfield*. It is suggested by Steven Marcus in *Dickens: From Pickwick to Dombey* that Forster's gift of a pocket Shakespeare which Dickens took with him to America in 1842 altered the character of his imagination. 'In any one of Dickens's mature novels', says Marcus, 'scarcely a page goes by which does not in some way further the central course of development.' The structure of *Anna Karenina*, with its many correspondences and overriding symbols, may be called, loosely, Shakespearian. But Tolstoy, as we know from the hostile essay on *King Lear*, found Shakespeare intolerable. Dickens, however, he knew and loved with an extravagant devotion.

Long after this period, in 1894, Tolstoy wrote that Maupassant for all his merits failed to show 'the correct, that is moral, attitude to the subject'. Tolstoy abhorred the indifferentism of Maupassant and modern French writers. He extolled the Christian feeling of Dickens, and was prepared to sift all the world's prose fiction down to *Copperfield*, and *Copperfield* itself down to the storm scene, in which Ham, the simple fisherman, dies to save the corrupt worldling Steerforth. It is the old, reformed Tolstoy who says this. What drew him to *David Copperfield* originally seems to have been the concern with childhood experience.

Tolstoy's trilogy *Childhood, Boyhood and Youth* could hardly have taken the form it did without the example of *Copperfield*. This he spoke of later as having made an 'enormous' impression on him. True, at the same time he was reading Rousseau and Sterne, but *Childhood* at least has almost wholly derived its tone and perspective from the first ten chapters of *Copperfield*. These form the prelude to Dickens's most intimate disclosure of his own early years – the blacking factory episode – which does not seem to have caught Tolstoy's interest. But he did learn from the Blunderstone chapters a new complex awareness – that of the adult mind recovering its childhood impressions and treating them with the tenderest irony. Those chapters told of a child-centred idyll broken by estrangement and loss. The mother is idealized; so is the little boy. Dickens found unspeakable charm in their relationship, in David's attitude to Peggotty, in the boy's first readings of experience. The mature David in fact sees himself through his mother's eyes. Childhood means for him adoring his mother and getting in return her undivided attention – until the intruder comes. David seeks to recover that earlier state. 'The mother who lay in the grave, was the mother of my infancy; the little creature in her arms, was myself, as I had once been, hushed for ever on her bosom.' There is the lost intimacy that Tolstoy imagines in chapter 15 of *Childhood* (a key chapter bearing the title of the book).

Tolstoy's narrative, like Dickens's, culminates in bereavement. (Murdstone does not appear until *Boyhood* as the tutor St Jérôme, and he assumes a much less significant role). Nikolenka's reaction to this bereavement is akin to David's, and yet a striking difference appears. Both boys naturally look inward: it is the final moment of individuation. David feels distinguished by his grief as he walks alone in the playground, and 'rather good in himself not to be proud' to any of the boys. There is an absurd pathos here, but Dickens implied no condemnation. Nikolenka strains to make his grief pure and exclusive: 'I felt a certain pleasure', he tells, 'in knowing that I was unhappy. I tried to arouse the sense of my unhappiness, and this egotistical feeling . . . smothered true grief in me.' Tolstoy, as Mr Katarsky notes, had been studying the complexity of feeling in Sterne. And even now he is the moral rigorist who cannot, in the way Dickens could, indulge egotism. Self knowledge came very late, if it ever did, to Dickens. It is the ground of all Tolstoy's success.

Many chapters in *Boyhood* and *Youth* have Dickensian headings. But Tolstoy eventually shows himself much sterner towards Nikolenka than Dickens could possibly be towards David. Nikolenka is arrogant and snobbish as a young man – closer to the Pip of *Great Expectations*. Only in the last phase, after he had parted from his wife in 1858, do we find Dickens making a more realistic appraisal of youthful selfishness. It was his way to show evil as a menace from outside: for example, the Murdstones, or more melodramatically Fagin and Monks. Later this would take the form of a system – Chancery or the Circumlocution Office. Evil is opposed to the domestic innocence it will martyrize. But already in Tolstoy's *Childhood* that innocence is found not to be perfect. The nurse Natalya Savishna fills the place here of Peggotty. When David asks Peggotty why she had never married, the author has in view the impending second marriage of Mrs Copperfield. Peggotty says nothing here about her own past. If she didn't marry it involved no renunciation, and when Murdstone dismisses her she is free to wed Barkis. The case of Natalya Savishna stands out in painful contrast. Natalya as a serf had to ask permission from Nikolenka's grandfather to marry the footman Foka. Her wish was treated as ingratitude; she was hustled away to a steppe village, and recalled only when found irreplaceable, upon which she begged to have her never-to-be-repeated 'folly' forgiven.

The later Tolstoy would seem to have prized in Dickens what we chiefly mistrust – the 'Christian' imagination that too readily creates an Agnes Wickfield or a Little Dorrit. There is a point at which naïve feeling, so often the warrant of integrity in a Russian novel, gets close to sentimentality. Yet on the whole Russian readers were more critical in their attitude to Dickens than was Tolstoy. The Cheerybles did not impose upon an audience made sceptical by knowledge of a social wrong like serfdom that paralysed goodwill. So too the conversion of Mr Dombey was thought preposterous. The almost unfailing realism that distinguishes many Russian novels may be owing to the brutalities and disappointments of Russian life. It may have as much to do with the 'creatural' sense, forfeited by Western Europe, that Auerbach still found Russian novelists to possess. The sentimentality of Dickens, at any rate where it concerns children like Oliver Twist or Little Nell, falsifies, as A. O. J. Cockshut has said in *The Imagination of Charles Dickens*, from 'an honest, because unconscious, evasion of some fact, desire or fear, which is too shocking to be faced'. And Steven Marcus has pointed out the vehemence of Dickens's writing when it turns sentimental. He was able to admit more 'unpleasantness and pain' into his sentimentality than is generally the case. It does not in any way diminish a sense of deep and disturbing realities, though he cannot properly confront them. The conception of Little Nell, so Marcus perceives, generated in Dickens's mind her opposite, and would-be violator, Quilp. They are, one might suppose, complementary in the same way as Myshkin and Rogozhin, though Dickens may scarcely have known this.

We have seen what he meant to Tolstoy. The revelation of the child's mind in David and, less satisfactorily, in Paul Dombey was followed by many such attempts in Russian literature. Turgenev's *Bezhin Meadow*, Goncharov's *Dream of Oblomov*, Aksakov's childhood recollections, and two stories by Dostoyevsky before his exile, *Netochka Nezvanova* and *The Little Hero*, all appear not before 1849.

The autobiographies that have derived from Tolstoy's *Childhood* and so indirectly from Dickens are beyond counting. Very near to it in feeling stand the opening chapters of Bunin's *Life of Arsenyev: Youth*; as much can be said for the early episodes of *Doctor Zhivago*. But Dostoyevsky takes small part in this tradition, unless the two stories mentioned above are to be given undue prominence. When his return from Siberia was pending he wrote two other works that bear some trace of Dickens. In *Uncle's Dream* a calculating mother tries to make a profitable marriage for her daughter as Mrs Skewton does for Edith in *Dombey*; and the daughter's cold pragmatism resembles the attitude of Edith. The benevolent landowner in *The Village of Stepanchikovo* (known to English readers as *A Friend of the Family*) is another Mr Wardle, though his Dingley Dell has an oppressor in Foma Opiskin, sometimes compared with Pecksniff and Uriah Heep, and by Mr Katarsky also with Chadband. But the Dostoyevsky who had yet to write *Crime and Punishment* would appear at this stage to be engaged more with *The Old Curiosity Shop* than any other novel by Dickens.

A sign of this interest had already been given in *White Nights* (published before his exile). *The Old Curiosity Shop* opens with a narrator who soon drops out, Master Humphrey. The 'dreamer' who tells of his encounter with Nastenka in *White Nights* shares Master Humphrey's taste for wandering round the streets after dark to observe their life. After his exile Dostoyevsky thought once more of *The Old Curiosity Shop*. It had been twice translated into Russian, but in such a watered down form that it became quite devoid of social significance. Belinsky indeed when reading the first version (1843) concluded that Dickens's 'immense talent' had gone into a decline. The image of Nell, however, prompted Dostoyevsky to create his own Nelly, and endow her with a grandfather named Smith (an unyielding old man) in *The Insulted and Injured* which marks his return to social themes. The child whom Master Humphrey meets and takes home to her grandfather has, appropriately, 'a little bed that a fairy might have slept in'. She belongs without question to the world of myth – perhaps the myth of Dickens's own childhood innocence, for she resembles him in being 'quick, eager, delicate and soon hurt, bodily or mentally'. The glances she turns on Humphrey are 'very sharp and keen', but without the suspicion that comes naturally to the Marchioness, the little servant who is a genuine city child. In contrast the glance of Nelly in

The Insulted and Injured betrays not only intelligence but 'a kind of inquisitorial distrust and even suspicion'. Like the Marchioness she is dirty and unkempt. In the epilogue she will inspire the same love and solicitude, on approaching her death, as Little Nell. She will be associated with a green garden and lilac, just as Nell's funeral coach is dressed with winter berries and green leaves. But Nelly Valkovsky has not the angelic forbearance of Little Nell. Shortly before dying she curses her father, as her mother had done. The experience of his cruelty has left an indelible mark.

Like Dickens, Dostoyevsky is fascinated by the image of the child forced to bear suffering beyond its years. He made Ivan Karamazov reject a theodicy in which the torment of children had any place. And he is much more brutal than Dickens in his imagination of outrage upon children. Nelly Valkovsky has acquired an habitual 'mistrust, spite and obstinacy', which she will only be able to shed in the kindness surrounding her last days. Some time later, in Jenny Wren, Dickens too would present a child whom circumstances have made cruel, even sadistic. But that was in the mid sixties, as Mr Katarsky reminds us – a period beyond the scope of his book and of this article[1] – when a more sombre realism, akin to the Dostoyevskian, began to invade Dickens's novels.

The Insulted and Injured, more than any novel by Dostoyevsky, may be termed Dickensian. (The old grandfather especially in his stubborn pride is an Englishman moulded on the pattern of Mr Dombey.) The democratic pathos of this narrative, expressed in its very title, aligns Dostoyevsky at this stage of his career with Dickens. *Crime and Punishment* belongs to a different era when both Tolstoy and Dostoyevsky, now that the worst rigours of censorship had abated, were able to write novels unequalled in depth, range and moral stamina. The modern reader of Dickens cannot help gauging his most impressive achievements – and particularly the work that appeals most to this age, the novels from *Dombey* onwards – by comparison with *Crime and Punishment* and its successors. In his book *Dostoyevsky and Romantic Realism* Donald Fanger has warned against the temptation of turning

[1] Dr Futrell, in 'Dostoyevsky and Dickens', *English Miscellany*, Rome, 1956, has set out for the English reader all the evidence for Dostoyevsky's concern with Dickens in this later period, and has some further points, not mentioned here, on the earlier.

Dickens into 'a kind of Dostoyevsky *manqué*'. He quotes Gissing who deplored 'the defects of education and the social prejudices' which thwarted the tragic impulse in Dickens, so making him inferior to Dostoyevsky. Dickens, indeed, as Fanger contends, had his own vision, and a very potent one. It may in part have imposed itself on Dostoyevsky: the sense of urban nightmare (though probably Balzac exerted a prior influence); the concern for deprived children; the obsession with crime and its punishment; the partiality for good-hearted innocents (a Mr Dick or Prince Myshkin). Dostoyevsky has treated all these things more profoundly than Dickens, and with a metaphysical passion not shared by him. No doubt even if he had not known Dickens, Dostoyevsky would have been compelled to take up such themes. He felt for Dickens a profound admiration, and in many ways they were akin. Not only do they belong to the same class of novelist – writing against the clock and with a penchant for popular modes like melodrama and farce – so that both seem appropriate to the modern city, its true poets. They also share certain qualities of mind and temperament. Marcus, for instance, has seen the movement of Dickens's mind as 'naturally dialectical', which is certainly true of Dostoyevsky's; and both men suffered from a neurotic disquiet, and an ineradicable sense of alienation (for Dickens the blacking factory, for Dostoyevsky the mock execution and subsequent exile were ordeals that set them apart). Gissing is not wide of the mark in his comments on Dickens's slight formal education and its result. One might claim that his essential education derived from Shakespeare; but Shakespeare had lived in a different epoch. Dostoyevsky was not only better educated in the sense that he knew Racine and Schiller, and something of Hegel: he grew up at a time when Pushkin had fully humanized Russian literature, and proved its capacity to touch on the greatest issues simply and boldly. In that famous panegyric of 1880 Dostoyevsky revealed an almost fatal misunderstanding of what Pushkin meant. And yet his foremost contemporaries among novelists – Tolstoy, Turgenev and Goncharov – still maintained a continuity with Pushkin. The imagination could work more freely in Russia, despite the censorship, because a great poet had so recently given his example. Dostoyevsky profited by this to learn a directness and an uncomfortable candour that are the foundations of his realism. Possibly Keats, if he had lived long enough, might have taught the same lesson to his countrymen. Yet Dickens – though limited in this way – never lost his appeal for the Russian reader. What allied him so closely with the genius of their own writers was a capacity to see the world with a child's unprotected vision. Both Tolstoy and Dostoyevsky meet him in this region of consciousness; and so intermittently do other Russians. It was the primitive, the poetic and myth-working element in his imagination that gained Dickens an entry to Russian literature as if by an underground passage, so that he occupied it from the inside.

(45–52)

Sylvère Monod

'Dickens's Language and Style in *David Copperfield*', *Dickens the Novelist* 1968 (a revised translation by the author of *Dickens Romancier*, 1953)

Dickens's most inspired and spontaneous, and his most careful and elaborate, novel is probably *David Copperfield*. It is, therefore, particularly well adapted to a study of the author's language and style. The pages, paragraphs, sentences and even words of that book illustrate how fifteen years of literary life and success have perfected the wonderful instrument which nature and the accidents of an eventful formative period had placed at the writer's disposal.

Dickens's use of language in *Copperfield* is characterized above all by the frequent recurrence of a number of words each of which corresponds to some aspect of his personality. In the first place, there are three adjectives whose significant repetition emphasizes the author's sentimentality: 'little', 'own' and 'old'. 'Little' is constantly used by Dickens where another author might have used 'small'. His preference for this word, which has, according to the *Oxford Dictionary*, 'emotional implications not given by small', reveals his personal emotional approach to situations in a way that makes 'little' the most characteristic word in the whole Dickensian vocabulary. In a series of fifteen chapters – chapters 9–23 – without taking into account the many occasions when Emily is called 'Little Emily', this favorite adjective occurs 186 times.[1] Its sentimental value is easily perceived. Within a single page of chapter 9, while David is in the shop of Mr Omer, the Yarmouth undertaker, shortly before Mrs Copperfield's burial, a moment when the atmosphere is supremely emotional, the word 'little' is used five times. David asks: 'Do you know how my little brother is, sir?' Then, on hearing that the child is in his mother's arms, in other words, dead, he exclaims: 'Oh, poor little fellow!' All so far is quite normal and in strict accordance with the traditional distinction between 'little' and 'small'. Yet emotion soon extends from persons to things and David speaks of the 'little room' in which he finds himself, of the 'little trip' which Minnie plans to take with her young man on the occasion of the funeral, and even of the 'little nails' – they are coffin nails, of course – which the workman keeps in his mouth.

The frequent recurrence of 'own' has a slightly different connotation. It is particularly striking in the Murdstone and Grinby episode, a passage of intense self-pity. In the same group of fourteen chapters as above there are eighty-five 'owns'. Most of them are applied by David to himself, often quite appropriately, but sometimes unnecessarily. Let us look at three examples from one page of chapter 10: 'A solitary condition . . . apart from the society of all other boys of my own age, apart from all companionship but my own spiritless thoughts', and 'A little small light-haired wife, whom I can just remember connecting in my own thoughts with a pale tortoise-shell cat.' The first two are legitimate, as their function is clearly to oppose David's solitude to the normal outside world, but the third could have been dispensed with. There is even something morbid in David's way of emphasizing the privacy of his thinking.

'Own' is occasionally employed by other characters, such as Mr Murdstone, who is of course not sentimental, but who is intensely proud, with similar results: 'I have my own opinion . . . founded . . . in part on my knowledge of my own means and resources. . . . I place this boy under the eye of a friend of my own, in a respectable business', he tells Miss Betsey, who then retorts: 'About the respectable business . . . if he had been your own boy, you would have put him to it, just the same, I suppose!' And Miss Murdstone cuts in with: 'If he

1 Most of the figures mentioned in the following paragraphs concern that section of the novel.

had been my brother's own boy ... his character, I trust, would have been altogether different' (chapter 14).

A complete examination of Dickens's sentimental vocabulary in *Copperfield* ought to deal with the emotional use of 'poor' and 'miserable', but they are not of comparable importance to the third favorite – 'old'. In chapters 11–21, 'old' occurs ninety-seven times. Dickens's liking for that adjective is striking and he almost invariably uses it in the emotional sense of 'familiar' rather than in the primary sense of 'not young'. This is not surprising in a novel written under the influence of sincere and vivid emotion and in which sentimental complacency in the contemplation of the past imparts to whatever belongs to former days – to the time 'of old' – an irresistible charm. There are numerous examples of this attitude in *Copperfield*. Speaking to David of his young, dead mother, Peggotty says: 'The last time that I saw her like her own old self was the night when you came home, my dear ...' (chapter 9). Here the combination of the two keywords 'own' and 'old' is the sure sign of an emotional crisis, like the combination of 'old' and 'little' in a tender description of Little Emily. 'She sat, at this time, and all the evening, on the old locker, in her old little corner by the fire' (chapter 21). At the end of the novel, when David, now a widower, sees Agnes again in her home after three years' separation, she tells him: 'Here are the old books, Trotwood, and the old music' to which he replies: 'Even the old flowers are here ... or the old kinds' (chapter 60). Dickens's fondness for the word is such that even when he uses it in its primary sense, he cannot help presenting it in an amiable light. David, for instance, is immediately under the spell of Mr Wickfield's home, where everything is old: 'the quaint little panes of glass and quainter little windows ... as old as the hills'; 'the tall old chimney-piece'; 'a wonderful old staircase'; 'old oak seats'; 'all old nooks and corners'; 'a glorious old room' (chapter 15).

Besides his sentimental tendency, many other aspects of Dickens's character are illuminated by the study of his vocabulary. His natural intensity is clearly revealed by words like 'quite', 'great', 'indeed', by the phrase 'a good' – or 'a great' – 'deal', and by the presence of numerous superlatives and other forms of reinforcement. 'Quite' appears eighty-nine times in chapters 9–21, and that adverb is called upon to intensify a wide variety of adjectives throughout the narrative. Its frequency is strikingly great in the Yarmouth scenes, which shows its implicit connexion with his sentimental vocabulary. It is first found in chapter 3 – 'I Have a Change' on David's first visit to Mr Peggotty's – and in that single chapter occur the following expressions: 'I was quite tired'; 'the counterpane made my eyes quite ache'; 'you're quite a sailor'; 'I felt it difficult to picture him quite at his ease'; 'I hardly know enough of the race ... to be quite certain'; 'I am sure I loved that baby quite as truly, quite as tenderly'; 'I did not quite understand'; '"Peggotty!" said I, quite frightened'; 'I knew quite well that he was looking at us both.' Within eight chapters – 14–22 – are to be found thirty uses of 'indeed', most frequently in the characters' speeches. Uriah Heep, in his constant fawning and in his desire to be persuasive is a great wielder of 'indeed'. The slightly childish 'a good deal' and 'a good many' for 'much' or 'many' also crop up often. Finally, in the intensifying vocabulary, the first place is occupied by 'great', which appears as the counterpart of 'little'. The difference between 'great' and 'big' or 'large' is said, by the *Oxford Dictionary* again, to be that 'great' is employed 'usually with implied surprise, contempt, indignation, etc.' so that Dickens's preference once more goes to the more sentimental English word. In chapters 11–21, 'great' occurs eighty-five times.

Intensity is expressed in other ways also. The superlative recurs so often in *David Copperfield* that there can hardly be a single emotion not experienced by the hero in its supreme degree, or a single kind of sight not seen by him in its most representative form. In the quotations that follow, it will often be observed that the superlative is itself reinforced and intensified by 'ever' or 'never'. Of the old clothes dealer in Chatham, David says: 'There never was such another drunken madman in this line of business' (chapter 13), and to him the laid up Barkis 'looked the queerest object I ever beheld' (chapter 21); yet when Miss Mowcher appeared, 'I never did in my days behold anything like Miss Mowcher' (chapter 22). 'In my days' does not add perceptibly to the meaning and is only a way of reinforcing and intensifying the expression. David meets with a fierce-looking milkman 'As to his dealing in the mild article of milk ... there never was a greater anomaly' (chapter 27). Of Mrs Crupp he tell us: 'I never was so much afraid of anyone' (chapter 28). Miss Dartle's song is 'the most unearthly I have ever heard in my life, or can imagine' (chapter 29), in which 'in my life' – like 'in my days' of the previous quotation

– and perhaps 'or can imagine' add very little to the sense of an expression which really means: Miss Dartle's song was very unearthly. Of Miss Betsey, her nephew writes, 'I believe there never was anybody with such an imperturbable countenance when she chose' (chapter 35); of Mr Micawber: 'I never saw a man so thoroughly enjoy himself . . . as Mr Micawber did that afternoon' (chapter 28); and of Mr Micawber's culinary masterpiece, one page later, 'There never was a greater success.' When Agnes and Dora become acquainted: 'I never was so happy. I never was so pleased as when I saw those two sit down together' (chapter 42). Within a single page of the melodramatic scene on the bank of the Thames with Martha Endell occur two superlative notes: 'I have never known what despair was, except in the tone of those words. . . . I never saw, in any painting or reality, horror and compassion so impressively blended' (chapter 47), and again after the departure of the emigrants' ship: 'A sight at once so beautiful, so mournful and so hopeful . . . I never saw' (chapter 57). David makes the acquaintance of young Mrs Traddles and concludes: 'A more cheerful, amiable, honest, happy, bright-looking bride, I believe . . . the world never saw' (chapter 59).

When they are thus accumulated, such vigorous expressions destroy one another's effect. When the characters' whole emotional life goes on in the superlative degree, there occurs a downward leveling of all emotion. The author's fondness for strong expressions is shown explicitly in a fragment of conversation between the hero and Littimer, who says:

'Mr Steerforth will be glad to hear how you have rested, sir.'
'Thank you,' said I, 'very well indeed. Is Mr Steerforth
quite well?' 'Thank you, sir, Mr Steerforth is tolerably well.'
Another of his characteristics. No use of superlatives. A cool
calm medium always.
(chapter 21)

It will be observed that the contrast between David/Dickens's warm words ('very well indeed', 'quite well') and the servant's prudent coolness ('tolerably well') does not seem sufficiently clear to the author. He must emphasize the point: 'No use of superlatives.' Mildness of speech is a serious, unforgivable offense. It is hardly an exaggeration to say that the absence of superlatives, the cold, calculating reticence, and the lack of impulse and passion already betray the criminal in Littimer and foreshadow his later imprisonment. Dickens will not have 'a cool calm medium', or certainly not 'always'.

Now and then, however, Dickens would realize the potential danger in his excessive fondness for intense and energetic expressions and use such terms as 'almost', 'nearly' and 'hardly ever', (instead of 'never') in order to tone down the effect of being too categorical in his assertions. The use of extenuating phrases even becomes a secondary, though perceptible, characteristic of his style. Within a few pages, in chapters 10 and 11, an imposing series can be found: 'so squeezed that I could hardly bear it'; 'until the breath was nearly wedged out of me'; 'he ... almost choked her'; '[Steerforth] will give you almost as many men as you like at draughts, and beat you easily'; 'I have almost lost the capacity of being much surprised by anything'; 'I hardly ever ... saw both the twins detached from Mrs Micawber at the same time.'

Still, Dickens's tendency to use and even abuse reinforcing adverbs is very pronounced – they will often miss their aim when they are applied to terms intrinsically energetic. The tendency is perceptible in Dickens's letters, always written in a highly tense style, and also in *Copperfield*, especially, it would seem, when his self-control is relaxed and he lapses into his most spontaneous, least elaborate modes of expression. Words like 'heart-broken', 'dejected', 'angelic', 'luxurious', 'wretched and miserable', 'atrocious', 'worn out', 'dreadful', 'assuredly', 'terror', 'elated', 'amazing' and 'appalling', are undoubtedly among the most energetic in the English language. For this reason, any attempt at further intensifying them can only detract from their vigor, since it amounts to treating them like ordinary adjectives and disguising their distinctive force. Yet that is just what Dickens does when he writes: 'quite heart-broken', 'greatly dejected'; 'perfectly angelic'; 'a very luxurious state of mind'; 'a very wretched and miserable condition'; 'a most atrocious criminal'; 'quite worn out'; 'the most dreadful manner'; 'perfectly miserable'; 'most assuredly'; 'infinite terror'; 'greatly elated'; 'most amazing'; 'most appalling.'[1]

1 Chapters 2, 3, 4, 5, 10, 14, 22, 55. In *Sketches by Boz* were already to be found the forms 'the most hopeless extreme' ('Scenes', chapter 11); 'perfectly astonishing' ('Scenes', chapter 9); 'most striking' ('Scenes', chapter 7); 'a

Another kind of leveling can be achieved through a less close juxta-position. For instance, when the adverbs 'exquisitely', 'utterly' and 'perfectly' are all three used in one and the same paragraph (chapter 11), or within a few lines of each other, one finds the following ex-pressions: 'in a most distrustful manner'; 'such extreme joy', 'a very unmelodious laugh'; and 'a most delicious meal' (chapter 5), an impression of uniformity is created, instead of the impression of high relief that Dickens was aiming at in each case.

The remarkable and sustained vigor of expression in Dickens's style is accompanied by a curious hesitancy which nothing in his character seems to suggest, but which is revealed by the recurrence of the phrases 'a kind of' or 'a sort of'. Dickens's thinking and creative vision were vague or blurred very little, yet the text of Copperfield leaves no doubt about the existence of the opposite tendency. In chap-ters 9–21, the two phrases are employed no fewer than seventy-seven times. This may result from an attempt at compensating for the exces-sive trenchancy to be found more often. Or it may be due to the author's desire to produce, by dint of apparent scrupulousness, a greater sense of truth, again in connexion with the autobiographical character of the work. But, as the frequency of such forms is hardly less in Dickens's other novels, it is more probable that the main cause for this phenomenon lies in Dickens's liking for approximate illustra-tion and simile. Dickens was aware that the proliferation of 'a sort of' or 'a kind of' was mainly characteristic of unintellectual and unculti-vated persons. His awareness is shown by the implicit criticism con-tained in the awkward speech of men like Mr Omer – 'By that sort of thing we very often lose a little mint of money' (chapter 9) – or the coachman who takes David from Canterbury to London. Yet David's own frequent use of these phrases is not of decidedly higher quality. Almost invariably, 'sort of' or 'kind of' could be cancelled without suppressing anything except an element of unprofitable in-accuracy: 'it made no sort of difference in her'; 'he carried a jaunty sort of a stick'; 'he was a sort of town traveller'; 'a sort of grass-grown battery'; 'in a sort of tune'; 'with every sort of expression but

perfectly wild state' ('Tales', book 1, chapter 2); 'most inimitably ('Tales', chapter 11); and, as in the famous letter about Oliver Twist, 'indispensably necessary' ('Tales', chapter 12).

wonder'; 'with a strange kind of watery brightness' (chapters 10, 11, 13).

To bring to a close the list of the external, though significant aspects of Dickens's language in *Copperfield*, a word should be said of the stage directions with which the speeches of the characters are interspersed. It will be observed that he usually designates the author of each speech with great care. It is very seldom that a phrase, however brief, and even when it occurs unequivocally in dialogue, is mentioned without some specific reference to its origin. Almost invariably, there is at least a 'said he' after the speech. Nor is there much variety in that respect. Sometimes, in the longer speeches, a second 'said he' or an 'added he' is inserted at or near the end, but the predominance of 'said' over all the other verbs that can be similarly used is overwhelming. In chapters 16–18, for instance, are to be found the following verbs: 'asked' ten times and 'inquired' twice, but 'said' is often used after an interrogation in the sense of 'asked'; 'returned' twenty-four times; 'answered' four times; 'replied' six times; 'retorted' three times; 'exclaimed' three times; 'observed' twice; 'interposed' once; 'pursued' and 'repeated' three times each; 'continued' and 'hinted' once each; while 'said' occurs ninety-three times. Only nineteen speeches are given without any verb. These rarely exceed a word or two – 'Shall I?' 'Certainly,' 'Yes, sir' – and when they occur in rapid conversation, they can be completed by a genuine stage direction without a verb, for instance, 'with astonishment'. Finally, within speeches already introduced by 'he said' are to be found one 'he added' and eleven repetitions of 'he said'.

The clear predominance of 'said' shows that Dickens does not take much interest in this particular aspect of the presentation of dialogue. He is often bordering on theatrical writing, in which information of this kind has no place, while the suggestion of gestures and emotions plays a great part. This is precisely what happens in *Copperfield*. One can take a conversation from that novel almost at random, and the results will always be the same. For example in the case of the brief interview between David and Steerforth in a London hotel (chapter 19), there are many stage directions:

I looked at him . . . but I saw no recognition in his face. . . .
I grasped him by both hands, and could not let them go. . . .

shaking my hands heartily. . . . I brushed away the tears. . . . I made a clumsy laugh of it, and we sat down together, side by side. . . . clapping me on the shoulder. . . . He laughed as he ran his hand through the clustering curls of his hair, and said gaily. . . . Steerforth laughed heartily . . . clapping me on the shoulder again . . . 'Holloa, you, sir!' this was addressed to the waiter who had been very attentive to our recognition at a distance, and now came forward deferentially. . . . the waiter with an apologetic air. . . . the waiter, still apologetically.

Every detail is described and the reader can visualize the scene as though he were seeing it performed in a theatre. The amount of attention bestowed by Dickens on gestures and attitudes is almost greater than his interest in the words spoken by the characters. His passionate attraction to the stage and the influence it had on his fictional art are made perceptible in such passages, which also confirm the somewhat visual and external rather than analytical nature of his approach to psychology and characterization.

Dickens's style in the days of *Copperfield* is much more distinctly his own than it had been at the time of *Sketches by Boz*. The words, phrases and devices studied in the foregoing paragraphs ought to make a page by Dickens easily identifiable. And the habits concerned are, by the time of *Copperfield*, so ingrained that, with minor variations, they endure to the end of his career.

'(335-43)

Appendix

The Number Divisions of Dickens's Novels

This table shows the distribution of chapters in each of Dickens's novels into the monthly or weekly parts of Dickens's serials. These details have largely been taken from K. J. Fielding, 'The Monthly Serialization of Dickens's Novels' and 'The Weekly Serialization of Dickens's Novels', both in the *Dickensian*, vol. 54, 1958. Under the heading 'part', roman numerals refer to the book and arabic to the magazine.

Pickwick Papers

	1836		1837	
	Part	Chapter	Part	Chapter
January	—	—	X	27–28
February	—	—	XI	29–31
March	—	—	XII	32–33
April	I	1–2	XIII	34–36
May	II	3–5	XIV	37–39
June	III	6–8	—	—
July	IV	9–11	XV	40–42
August	V	12–14	XVI	43–45
September	VI	15–17	XVII	46–48
October	VII	18–20	XVIII	49–51
November	VIII	21–23	XIX/XX	52–56
December	IX	24–26	—	—

There were two chapters 28, an error entailing fresh numeration in later editions. There was no publication in June 1837, owing to the death of Mary Hogarth.

Oliver Twist

	1837		1838		1839	
	Book	Chapter	Book	Chapter	Book	Chapter
January	—	—	1	20–21	3	11: resumed at: 'Your tale is longest.' Then follow two chapters 12.
February	1	1–2	2	1–3		No chapter number. Resumes at 'Yes,' said Monks, scowling.'
March		3–4		4–5		14–15
April		5–6		6–7		
May		7–8		8–9		
June	—	—		10–11		
July		9–11		12–14		
August		12–13	3	1–2		
September		14–15		3–4		
October	—	—		5–6		
November		16–17		7–8		
December		18–19		9–11		

Published in monthly instalments of about sixteen pages in *Bentley's Miscellany*. No instalment appeared in June 1837 owing to the death of Mary Hogarth; nor in October for the same year.

It was completed under different circumstances from the other monthly serials, since Dickens raced ahead and finished the whole work in time for publication in three volumes in November 1838, before it had finished appearing in the *Miscellany*.

The chapter-division is extremely confusing. There were fifty-four chapters as it appeared in serial form. In the three-volume edition of 1838, these were reduced to fifty-one, by re-numbering, and the division into books was dropped. All editions after 1847, however, have only fifty-three chapters, much as above except that chapters 30 and 31, and chapters 44 and 45, have been combined.

Nicholas Nickleby

	1838		1839	
	Part	Chapter	Part	Chapter
January	—	—	X	30–33
February	—	—	XI	34–36
March	—	—	XII	37–39
April	I	1–4	XIII	40–42
May	II	5–7	XIV	43–45
June	III	8–10	XV	46–48
July	IV	11–14	XVI	49–51
August	V	15–17	XVII	52–54
September	VI	18–20	XVIII	55–58
October	VII	21–23	XIX/XX	59–65
November	VIII	24–26		
December	IX	27–29		

The Old Curiosity Shop

In *Master Humphrey's Clock* from 25 April 1840 to 6 February 1841.

Part	Chapter	Part	Chapter	Part	Chapter
4	1	19	23–24	32	48–49
7	2	20	25–26	33	50–51
8	3–4	21	27–28	34	52–53
9	5	22	29–30	35	54–55
10	6–7	23	31–32	36	56–57
11	8	24	33–34	37	58–59
12	9–10	25	35–36	38	60–61
13	11–12	26	37	39	62–63
14	13–14	27	38–39	40	64–65
15	15–16	28	40–41	41	66
16	17–18	29	42–43	42	67–68
17	19–20	30	44–45	43	69–70
18	21–22	31	46–47	44	71–72
				45	73

Barnaby Rudge

In *Master Humphrey's Clock* from 13 February 1841 to 27 November 1841, on which date parts *LXXXVI* and *LXXXVII* appeared together.

Part	Chapter	Part	Chapter	Part	Chapter
46	1	60	27–28	74	54–56
47	2–3	61	29–30	75	57–58
48	4–5	62	31–32	76	59–60
49	6–7	63	33–34	77	61–62
50	8–9	64	35–36	78	63–64
51	10–11	65	37–38	79	65–66
52	12	66	39–40	80	67–68
53	13–14	67	41–42	81	69–70
54	15–16	68	43–44	82	71–72
55	17–18	69	45–46	83	73–74
56	19–20	70	47–48	84	75–76
57	21–22	71	49–50	85	77–78
58	23–24	72	51–52	86	79–80
59	25–26	73	53–54	87	81–82

Martin Chuzzlewit

	1843		1844	
	Part	Chapter	Part	Chapter
January	I	1–3	XIII	33–35
February	II	4–5	XIV	36–38
March	III	6–8	XV	39–41
April	IV	9–10	XVI	42–44
May	V	11–12	XVII	45–47
June	VI	13–15	XVIII	48–50
July	VII	16–17	XIX/XX	51–54
August	VIII	18–20		
September	IX	21–23		
October	X	24–26		
November	XI	27–29		
December	XII	30–32		

Dombey and Son

	1846		1847		1848	
	Part	Chapter	Part	Chapter	Part	Chapter
January	—	—	IV	11–13	XVI	49–51
February	—	—	V	14–16	XVII	52–54
March	—	—	VI	17–19	XVIII	55–57
April	—	—	VII	20–22	XIX/XX	58–62
May	—	—	VIII	23–25		
June	—	—	IX	26–28		
July	—	—	X	29–31		
August	—	—	XI	32–34		
September	—	—	XII	35–38		
October	I	1–4	XIII	39–41		
November	II	5–7	XIV	42–45		
December	III	8–10	XV	46–48		

David Copperfield

	1849		1850	
	Part	Chapter	Part	Chapter
January	—	—	IX	25–27
February	—	—	X	28–31
March	—	—	XI	32–34
April	—	—	XII	35–37
May	I	1–3	XIII	38–40
June	II	4–6	XIV	41–43
July	III	7–9	XV	44–46
August	IV	10–12	XVI	47–50
September	V	13–15	XVII	51–53
October	VI	16–18	XVIII	54–57
November	VII	19–21	XIX/XX	58–64
December	VIII	22–24	—	—

Bleak House

	1852		1853	
	Part	*Chapter*	*Part*	*Chapter*
January	—	—	XI	33–35
February	—	—	XII	36–38
March	I	1–3	XIII	39–42
April	II	5–7	XIV	43–46
May	III	8–10	XV	47–49
June	IV	11–13	XVI	50–53
July	V	14–16	XVII	54–56
August	VI	17–19	XVIII	57–59
September	VII	20–22	XIX/XX	60–67
October	VIII	23–25		
November	IX	26–29		
December	X	30–32		

Hard Times

In *Household Words*, vol. 9, 1854

	Chapter		*Chapter*		*Chapter*
April 1	1–3	May 20	15–16	July 8	25–26
April 8	4–5	May 27	17	July 15	27–28
April 15	6	June 3	18–19	July 22	29–30
April 22	7–8	June 10	20–21	July 29	31–32
April 29	9–10	June 17	22	August 5	33–34
May 6	11–12	June 24	23	August 12	35–36
May 13	13–14	July 1	24		

On first publication in volume form, the work was divided into three books, and the chapters were re-numbered: *Book the First*, 'Sowing', chapters 1–16; *Book the Second*, 'Reaping', chapters 17–28; and *Book the Third*, 'Garnering', chapters 29–37.

Little Dorrit

	1855		1856		1857	
	Part	Chapter	Part	Chapter	Part	Chapter
January	—	—	II	5–8	XIV	12–14
February	—	—	III	9–11	XV	15–18
March	—	—	IV	12–14	XVI	19–22
April	—	—	V	15–18	XVII	23–26
May	—	—	VI	19–22	XVIII	27–29
June	—	—	VII	23–25	XIX/XX	30–34
July	—	—	VIII	26–29		
August	—	—	IX	30–32		
September	—	—	X	33–36		
October	—	—	XI (11)	1–4		
November	—	—	XII	5–7		
December	I (1)	1–4	XIII	8–11		

A Tale of Two Cities

In *All the Year Round*, from no. 1, vol. I, 1859. It was designed to be in three books, as shown, from the beginning: *Book the First*, 'Restored to Life'; *Book the Second*, 'The Golden Thread'; and *Book the Third*, 'The Track of a Storm'.

Book One	Chapter			Book Three	Chapter
30 April	1–3	2 July	9	17 September	1
7 May	4	9 July	10–11	24 September	2–3
14 May	5	16 July	12–13	1 October	4–5
21 May	6	23 July	14	8 October	6–7
		30 July	15	15 October	8
Book Two		6 August	16	22 October	9
28 May	1–2	13 August	17–18	29 October	10
4 June	3	20 August	19–20	5 November	11–12
11 June	4–5	27 August	21	12 November	13
18 June	6	3 September	22–23	19 November	14
25 June	7–8	10 September	24	26 November	15

Great Expectations

In *All the Year Round*, IV–V, 1859–60. Pip's Expectations were divided into three 'Stages' from the beginning. They corresponded with the three volumes in which the book was published when the serialization came to an end.

First Stage		Second Stage		Third Stage	
	Chapter		Chapter		Chapter
1 December	1–2	23 February	20–21	18 May	40
8 December	3–4	2 March	22	25 May	41–42
15 December	5	9 March	23–24	1 June	43–44
22 December	6–7	16 March	25–26	8 June	45–46
29 December	8	23 March	27–28	15 June	47–48
5 January	9–10	30 March	29	22 June	49–50
12 January	11	6 April	30–31	29 June	51–52
19 January	12–13	13 April	32–33	6 July	53
26 January	14–15	20 April	34–35	13 July	54
2 February	16–17	27 April	36–37	20 July	55–56
9 February	18	4 May	38	27 July	57
16 February	19	11 May	39	3 August	58–59

Our Mutual Friend

	1864			1865		
	Book	Part	Chapter	Book	Part	Chapter
January	—	—	—	2	IX	11–13
February	—	—	—		X	14–16
March	—	—	—	3	XI	1–4
April	—	—	—		XII	5–7
May	1	I	1–4		XIII	8–10
June		II	5–7		XIV	11–14
July		III	8–10		XV	15–17
August		IV	11–13	4	XVI	1–4
September		V	14–17		XVII	5–7
October	2	VI	1–3		XVIII	8–11
November		VII	4–6		XIX/XX	12–17
December		VIII	7–10	—	—	—

The Mystery of Edwin Drood

1870

	Part	Chapter		Part	Chapter
April	I	1–5	July	IV	13–16
May	II	6–9	August	V	17–20
June	III	10–12	September	VI	21–23

Edwin Drood was published in monthly parts of the same length as before, but it was intended that there should be only a dozen of them counting the final, double-number as two.

Acknowledgements

For permission to use copyright material acknowledgement is made to the following:

For the extract from *Le Roman Social en Angleterre* by Louis Cazamian translated by Stephen Wall to La Librairie Didier; for the extracts from *Charles Dickens* by G. K. Chesterton to Miss D. Collins; for the extracts from the *Diaries* of Franz Kafka translated by Max Brod to Martin Secker & Warburg Ltd and Schocken Books Inc.; for the extract from 'Dickens' by George Saintsbury from *The Cambridge History of English Literature* to the Cambridge University Press; for the extract from 'Dickens' by George Santayana to Daniel Cory; for the extract from *The Craft of Fiction* by Percy Lubbock to the Executors of the Estate of Percy Lubbock, Jonathan Cape Ltd and the Viking Press Inc.; for the extract from *Dostoyevsky* by André Gide to Martin Secker & Warburg Ltd and Alfred Knopf Inc.; for the article 'David Copperfield' from *Collected Essays* by Virginia Woolf to Quentin Bell, Angelica Garnett, The Hogarth Press Ltd and Harcourt, Brace & World Inc.; for the extract from *Aspects of the Novel* by E. M. Forster to Edward Arnold (Publishers) Ltd; for the extract from 'Wilkie Collins and Dickens' from *Selected Essays* by T. S. Eliot to *The Times Literary Supplement*, Faber & Faber Ltd and Harcourt, Brace & World Inc.; for the extract from 'Vulgarity in Literature' from *Collected Essays* by Aldous Huxley to Mrs Laura Huxley, Chatto & Windus Ltd and Harper & Row Inc.; for the extract from *Victorian England: Portrait of an Age* by G. M. Young to the Oxford University Press; for the extract from the Foreword by George Bernard Shaw to *Great Expectations* to The Society of Authors for the Bernard Shaw Estate; for the extract from 'Charles Dickens' from *Inside the Whale* by George Orwell to Miss Sonia Brownell, Martin Secker & Warburg Ltd and Harcourt, Brace & World Inc.; for the extract from *The Dickens World* by Humphry House to the Oxford University Press; for the extract from *The Living Novel* by V. S. Pritchett to Chatto & Windus Ltd and Random House Inc.; for the extract from *A Treatise on the Novel* by Robert Liddell to Jonathan Cape Ltd and Dufour Editions Inc.; for the extract from 'The Macabre Dickens' from *All in Due Time* by Humphry House to Rupert Hart-Davis Ltd; for the extract from *An Introduction to the English Novel* by Arnold Kettle to the Hutchinson Publishing Group Ltd; for the extract from 'The Young Dickens' from *The Lost Childhood and Other*

Essays by Graham Greene to The Bodley Head Ltd and the Viking Press Inc.; for the extract from the Introduction by Lionel Trilling to *The New Oxford Illustrated Dickens: Little Dorrit* to the Oxford University Press; for the extract from *The English Novel: Form and Function* by Dorothy Van Ghent to Holt, Rinehart & Winston Inc.; for the extract from *Dickens at Work* by John Butt and Kathleen Tillotson to Methuen & Co. Ltd; for the extract from *Charles Dickens: The World of His Novels* by J. Hillis Miller to the Harvard University Press; for the extract from *Culture and Society 1780–1950* by Raymond Williams to Chatto & Windus Ltd and the Columbia University Press; for the extract from 'Charles Dickens and Appropriate Language' by Randolph Quirk to the author and the University of Durham; for the extract from 'Dickens and Interior Monologue' by Harry Stone to the *Philological Quarterly*, University of Iowa; for the extract from *The Historical Novel* by Georg Lukács translated by Hannah and Stanley Mitchell to the Merlin Press Ltd; for the extract from 'The Heroes and Heroines of Dickens' by Angus Wilson and for the extract from 'Oliver Twist: Things as They Really Are' by John Bayley from *Dickens and the Twentieth Century* edited by John Gross and Gabriel Pearson to Routledge & Kegan Paul Ltd and the University of Toronto Press; for the extract from 'Dingley Dell and the Fleet' from *The Dyer's Hand* by W. H. Auden to Faber & Faber Ltd and Random House Inc.; for the extract from *Dickens and Crime* by Philip Collins to Macmillan & Co. Ltd and St Martin's Press Inc.; for the extract from *Fiction for the Working Man 1830–1850* by Louis James to the Oxford University Press; for the article 'Food and Ceremony in *Great Expectations*' by Barbara Hardy to the editors of *Essays in Criticism*; for the extract from *Dickens: From Pickwick to Dombey* by Steven Marcus to Chatto & Windus Ltd and Basic Books Inc.; for the extract from *The Dickens Theatre* by Robert Garis to the Clarendon Press; for the extract from *Character and the Novel* by W. J. Harvey to Mrs M. A. Harvey, Chatto & Windus Ltd and the Cornell University Press; for the extract from 'Dickens in Russia: The Initial Phase' by Henry Gifford to the author and the editors of *Forum for Modern Language Studies*; for the extract from *Dickens the Novelist* by Sylvère Monod to the University of Oklahoma Press.

Select Bibliography

Editions

The *New Oxford Illustrated Dickens* (21 vols., Oxford University Press, 1947–59) is the best currently available complete edition of the novels. It is not textually satisfactory, and will be superseded by the *The Clarendon Dickens*, of which *Oliver Twist*, edited by Katheleen Tillotson, was the first volume to appear, in 1966.

The *Nonesuch Dickens*, edited by A. Waugh, W. Dexter, T. Hatton and H. Walpole, is chiefly of value because it includes three volumes of letters. Published in 1937–8 in twenty-three volumes in a limited edition only, it is now difficult to obtain.

The definitive edition of Dickens's letters will be the *Pilgrim Edition* (Clarendon Press): *The Letters of Charles Dickens*, vol. 1, *1820–1839*, edited by M. House and G. Storey, appeared in 1965; vol. 2, *1840–1841*, in 1969.

The Speeches of Charles Dickens have been authoritatively edited by K. J. Fielding, Clarendon Press, 1960.

Biography and Criticism

John Forster, *The Life of Charles Dickens*, 3 vols., 1872–4; revised edition, 2 vols., 1876; edited by J. W. T. Ley, Palmer, 1928, in one volume, and by A. J. Hoppé, Dent, 1966, in two volumes, both with additional material.

George Gissing, *Charles Dickens: A Critical Study*, 1898.

G. K. Chesterton, *Charles Dickens*, Methuen, 1906.

George Orwell, 'Charles Dickens', in *Inside the Whale*, Secker & Warburg, 1940; most recently reprinted in *Decline of the English Murder and Other Essays*, Penguin Books, 1965.

Edmund Wilson, 'Dickens: the Two Scrooges', in *The Wound and the Bow*, W. H. Allen, 1941.

Humphry House, *The Dickens World*, Oxford University Press, 1941.

F. R. Leavis, *The Great Tradition*, Chatto & Windus, 1950. Includes '*Hard Times*: An Analytical Note'.

E. Johnson, *Charles Dickens: His Tragedy and Triumph*, Little Brown, 1952; Gollancz, 1953. The standard modern biography.

Sylvère Monod, *Dickens Romancier*, Hachette, 1953; translated and revised as *Dickens the Novelist*, Oklahoma University Press, 1968.

Kathleen Tillotson, *Novels of the Eighteen-Forties*, Clarendon Press, 1954. Includes a chapter on *Dombey and Son*.

G. H. Ford, *Dickens and his Readers: Aspects of Novel Criticism since 1836*, Princeton University Press, 1955.

K. J. Fielding, *Charles Dickens: A Critical Introduction*, Longmans, 1957; enlarged edition, 1964.

John Butt and Kathleen Tillotson, *Dickens at Work*, Methuen, 1957.

J. H. Miller, *Charles Dickens: The World of his Novels*, Harvard University Press, 1958.

A. O. J. Cockshut, *The Imagination of Charles Dickens*, Methuen, 1961.

J. Gross and G. Pearson (eds.), *Dickens and the Twentieth Century*, Routledge & Kegan Paul, 1962. A symposium including essays on each novel by various writers.

P. A. W. Collins, *Dickens and Crime*, Macmillan, 1962.

P. A. W. Collins, *Dickens and Education*, Macmillan, 1963.

R. Garis, *The Dickens Theatre: A Reassessment of the Novels*, Clarendon Press, 1965.

Steven Marcus, *Dickens: From Pickwick to Dombey*, Chatto & Windus, 1965.

Bibliography

A. Nisbet, 'Dickens', in L. Stevenson (ed.), *Victorian Fiction: A Guide to Research*, Harvard University Press, 1963. Should be supplemented by the annual bibliography in *Victorian Studies*.

Index

Extracts included in this anthology are indicated by bold page references.